FEB 18 2000

273.6   Gregory, Brad S.
G   (Brad Stephan),
           1963-

         Salvation at stake.

$49.95

DATE			

BAKER & TAYLOR

Harvard Historical Studies · 134

Published under the auspices
of the Department of History
from the income of the
Paul Revere Frothingham Bequest
Robert Louis Stroock Fund
Henry Warren Torrey Fund

Thomas J. Wilson Prize

The Board of Syndics of Harvard University Press
has awarded this book the twenty-eighth annual
Thomas J. Wilson Prize, honoring the late director of the Press.
The prize is awarded to the book chosen by the
Syndics as the best first book accepted
by the Press during the calendar year.

Salvation at Stake

Christian Martyrdom in Early Modern Europe

BRAD S. GREGORY

HARVARD UNIVERSITY PRESS

Cambridge, Massachusetts, and London, England   1999

Library of Congress Cataloging-in-Publication Data

Gregory, Brad S. (Brad Stephan), 1963–
　　Salvation at stake : Christian martyrdom in early modern Europe /
Brad S. Gregory.
　　　　p. cm. — (Harvard historical studies ; 134)
　　Includes bibliographical references and index.
　　ISBN 0-674-78551-7 (hardcover : alk. paper)
　　1. Christian martyrs—Europe—History—16th century.
　　2. Martyrdom (Christianity)—History of doctrines—16th century.
　　3. Reformation.　I. Title.　II. Series: Harvard historical studies ; v. 134.
　　BR307.G74　　1999
　　273.6—dc21　　　　　　　　　　　　　　　　　　　99-29379

To Kerrie and Sean

Acknowledgments

It is a pleasure to thank the institutions that have made this book possible, and even more the many people who have made it better than it otherwise would have been.

I am most grateful to Anthony Grafton and Theodore Rabb, under whose guidance the thesis behind the book took shape at Princeton University. In addition—and heroically—Tony offered his typically meticulous scrutiny of every sentence and footnote in the book manuscript. For his willingness to pore over certain passages in half a dozen versions, I am deeply indebted to him. I thank Peter Brown, ever an inspiration and supporter; an offhand comment of his about Ramon Lull sparked the idea for this project in the spring of 1991. I extend my thanks to others from my time at Princeton, many of them now elsewhere, who offered advice and criticism: Alastair Bellany, Hilary Bernstein, Betsy Brown, Cynthia Cupples, Peter Lake, Louis Miller, April Shelford, Ben Weiss, and John Wilson. Robert Kingdon graciously served as the outside reader of the dissertation. As a Junior Fellow in the Harvard Society of Fellows, I received further input in various ways from Daniel Aron, Bernard Bailyn, Herbert Bloch, Géraldine Johnson, Robert Kendrick, Sarah McNamer, Robert Nozick, and Christine Thomas. Steve Ozment welcomed me to Cambridge and read the thesis for the press, offering astute suggestions, as did William Monter, the other reader for the press. My gratitude to both of them. I thank as well Caroline Walker Bynum, John O'Malley, and Arnold Snyder, who carefully read chapters and shared knowledge of their respective specialties while offering bibliographic leads. Since arriving at Stanford, I have been blessed with wonderful colleagues, faculty and graduate students alike, who have also offered suggestions: I am indebted to Paula Findlen, Laurie Koloski, Steve Schloesser, Brent Sockness, and Steve Zipperstein. Jim Sheehan deserves particular thanks for reading the full thesis plus parts of the book, and for his unfailingly good advice. Philippe Buc scrutinized the entire book manuscript with extraordinary care and offered many valuable suggestions. My gratitude as well to Tom Brady for his detailed comments on the introduction.

In the United States, the following institutions and organizations have facilitated my research, for which I render thanks: the University Center for Human Values at Princeton; the staffs of Firestone and Marquand Libraries, Princeton; Speer Library, Princeton Theological Seminary; Widener and Houghton Libraries, Harvard; Green Library, Stanford; and the Mennonite Historical Library, Goshen College, Indiana, where John Roth, Joe Springer, and Janet Shoemaker were all extremely helpful. From 1994 to 1996, the Harvard Society of Fellows provided a working environment that was a young scholar's dream come true. I would also like to thank the Board of Syndics of the Harvard University Press for awarding this book its annual Thomas J. Wilson Prize, and Donna Bouvier, also of the press, for her meticulous copyediting.

I appreciate the financial support provided by the Joint Committee on Western Europe of the American Council of Learned Societies and the Social Science Research Council with the aid of the Ford and Mellon Foundations. The SSRC made possible a year of research in England, Belgium, and the Netherlands in 1992–1993. The generosity of David and Karen Kratter to the Stanford history department funded another research trip in 1997. I am grateful to the staffs of the following libraries and archives for their assistance during my research abroad, particularly to the individuals mentioned by name: the British Library, London; Ian Dickie of the Archive of the Archbishops of Westminster, London; D. J. Wright of the Library of the Huguenot Society, University College, London; the Universiteitsbibliotheek, Amsterdam; Koninklijke Bibliotheek and Algemeen Rijksarchief, The Hague; Bibliotheek der Rijksuniversiteit, Leiden; Bibliotheek der Rijksuniversiteit, Utrecht; Stadsarchief, Antwerp; Koninklijke Bibliotheek and Algemeen Rijksarchief, Brussels; Rijksarchief and Stadsarchief, Bruges; Rijksarchief, Stadsarchief, and Bibliotheek van de Universiteit, Ghent, including Albert Derolez, Theo Van Poucke, and Roland De Groote. To Piet Visser of the University of Amsterdam I express particular gratitude for his hospitality. I also thank Paul Valkema Blouw for sharing his unparalleled knowledge of sixteenth-century Dutch printing.

Among those who have contributed most to my intellectual formation, I owe an enormous debt to Heiko Oberman, who has unstintingly supported my work ever since I had the privilege of participating in his graduate seminar for two years. Without his insistence that one distinguish understanding from evaluation in doing history, my approach to early modern Christianity would never have taken shape. Thanks also to my close friend John Steffen, a philosopher whose analytical brilliance enabled him to see more clearly than I the full implications of my approach to the history of religion. His penetrating attention to both the thesis and the book manuscript is deeply appreciated.

To my undergraduate mentor, Len Rosenband, I owe more than can be appropriately expressed here. His passion for the past—wedded to deep learning and shared in the classroom—inspired me to become a historian. Whatever skill I have as a writer stems from his influence. Far transcending what any student could ever expect or dare hope for, he has offered constant support, advice, and intellectual companionship over more than a decade.

To my family I am most indebted. My parents, Eugene and Mary Lou Schaefer, have constantly backed me in everything I have ever done—never imagining, I am sure, that the son to whom they gave the middle name "Stephan" would one day write about Christian martyrdom. Likewise, no one could hope for better parents-in-law than mine: Ken and Linda McCaw, and Frederick and Barbara Hecht, tireless in their support and love. The two people to whom I owe the most are my wife, Kerrie McCaw, and our son, Sean McCaw-Gregory. Infinitely patient, always understanding, repeatedly making sacrifices for me, they have made this book possible, enduring all along my obsessive single-mindedness. Better than anyone else, they understand my calling. Fittingly, this book is dedicated to them.

Contents

Figures

Where two principles that cannot be reconciled with one another really do meet, then each man declares the other a fool and a heretic.

—LUDWIG WITTGENSTEIN, *ON CERTAINTY*

A Note on Translations and Orthography

Except where otherwise indicated, all translations are my own. I have striven for translations that remain close to the sense of the original; in the case of poetry and song lyrics, this has meant sacrificing their rhythms and rhymes for the sake of preserving a more literal meaning. Biblical quotations are taken from the New Revised Standard Version (NRSV), occasionally amended in favor of another translation. For direct biblical quotations within early modern sources, I have translated the original rather than lifting the equivalent verse(s) directly from the NRSV and interjecting them into early modern sources.

In the text, the spelling and punctuation in late medieval and early modern quotations have been modernized. In the notes, I have retained the original orthography of publication titles and quotations from languages other than English; quotations from English in the notes have been modernized, as in the text. The only exception is that the German umlaut has been used consistently, rather than reproducing the variety of ways in which it was indicated in early modern sources. Where line numbers are indicated, a slash (/) separates them from page numbers.

CHAPTER ONE

A Complex of Martyrs

After this I looked, and there was a great multitude that no one could count, from every nation, from all tribes and peoples and languages, standing before the throne and before the Lamb, robed in white, with palm branches in their hands . . . Then one of the elders . . . said to me, "These are they who have come out of the great ordeal; they have washed their robes and made them white in the blood of the lamb."

    —REVELATION 7:9, 13–14

God the Almighty grants to all magistrates and judges the grace to pass judgment on the wicked and to protect the devout. But how does one recognize the devout? They are those who hear God's word and believe it with their whole hearts, as Christ taught us. Who are the wicked? Those who despise God's commandment, to which they give public witness before the whole world with their sinful actions.

    —JAKOB DACHSER, *A GODLY AND FUNDAMENTAL*
    REVELATION (1527)

Modern Western Christianity was forged in a crucible of conflicting convictions and dramatic deaths. In the sixteenth century thousands of men and women with divergent beliefs were executed for refusing to renounce them. This book explores the meaning and significance of Christian martyrdom in the Reformation era among Protestants, Anabaptists, and Roman Catholics. Beginning in July 1523 with the burning of two Augustinian monks in Brussels, the executions continued—with shifting rhythms, with varying intensities, in different towns and countries across Western Europe—into the seventeenth century. Hundreds, sometimes thousands of contemporaries gathered to witness public spectacles of burning, beheading, drowning, or hanging, drawing, and quartering. Sympathizers published pamphlets, wrote poetry, sent letters, sang songs, commissioned paintings, printed prison missives, and compiled collections narrating the martyrs' words and deeds. In combination with the ubiquitous oral communication in a largely preliterate society, these channels of expression meant that the large majority of Western Europeans, from the most to the least educated, must have known about the executions for heterodox Christian views.

    I have sought the measure of martyrdom not from a fascination with tales of tortured and dying bodies, but from a desire to plumb the living souls of

1

those who prayed and prepared in prison before stepping to the stake or scaffold. Martyrdom forces us to confront fundamental religious sensibilities, convictions, and practices of committed Christians. We meet not just their beliefs, but their beliefs boldly enacted; not only their differences across and within traditions, but also their striking similarities; not merely scattered, circumspect comments, but explicit, nuanced voices in hundreds of highly interpretive sources, remarkable in their variety. Martyrdom's multiple facets pose challenges to much recent research on the Reformation and Counter-Reformation. With this book I intend to make not only a historical contribution to our understanding of early modern Christianity, but also a methodological contribution to how historians approach it.

Geographically, this study concentrates on areas where the intense prosecution of heterodoxy bore down on vibrant religious minority movements or remnants: England, France, and the Low Countries. Switzerland and the Germanic lands of the Holy Roman Empire also receive attention. Italy and Spain are largely excluded, not because Catholic prosecutorial machinery was idle, but because the lack of sustained Protestant or Anabaptist communities yielded fewer executions than north of the Alps and Pyrenees. Early modern executions engendered not three (or in some respects, four)[1] independent martyrological traditions, but interrelated, competing interpretations about what the deaths meant. Protestants, Catholics, and Anabaptists all esteemed martyrdom and memorialized their respective heroes. All were well aware of their religious rivals' contrary beliefs and divergent martyr claims. Christian martyrdom in early modern Europe demands analysis as a cross-confessional whole. What has been researched as three traditions is better seen as one comprehensive story. It begins in the late Middle Ages and runs into the seventeenth century, linked by shared values as well as violent conflict.

Numerous scholars have recognized that Catholics, Anabaptists, and Protestants had their respective martyrs.[2] None, however, has made a sustained effort to understand them together, comparatively, and thus to assess their significance for communities of believers, confessional formation, and doctrinal controversy in a divided Christendom. Despite gestures in this direction,[3] the situation remains largely where Jean-François Gilmont left it in 1968, when he wrote that "it seems to us necessary to consider Catholic martyrologies at the same time as the Protestant collections in order to have a precise view of the phenomenon."[4] In 1984 Alan Kreider suggested that comparing Thieleman Jans van Braght, the seventeenth-century Dutch Mennonite martyrologist, with his Protestant predecessors "could be most instructive."[5] Gilmont devotes less than one page each to Catholic and Anabaptist martyrologies in his latest article on the subject, and is similarly laconic in his entry "Books of Martyrs" in the recent *Oxford Encyclopedia of the Refor-*

mation.[6] Remarkably, this comprehensive reference work treats neither martyrs nor martyrdom per se. Henri Meylan has briefly discussed "false martyrs" or "martyrs of the devil" in the period, but without seeing their integral relationship to the celebration of martyrs.[7] Scholars have skirted the cross-confessional study of martyrdom without seizing upon it. The previous lack of such a study becomes comprehensible, however, when one considers the legacy of confessionalized Reformation research and the quantity of relevant source material.

Confessional church history framed scholarship on Reformation-era martyrs until well into this century. This traditional, confession-specific investigation of the martyrs is readily intelligible, given their abiding importance to nineteenth- and twentieth-century Mennonites, Catholics, and Protestants, respectively.[8] In general, the traditional significance of the martyrs has waned along with confessional history in recent decades. Yet echoes of earlier research have guided even postconfessional scholarship in the tracks of a confessionalized historiographical past. Recent scholars of early modern martyrdom have generally restricted their work to one tradition or a single martyrologist.[9] The lack of comparative perspective has sometimes led to dubious claims and even outright error.[10] More fundamentally, it has severed the connections among traditions and obscured their collective dynamic. Taken together, however, the research on these three traditions suggests a second reason for the previous lack of a cross-confessional history of early modern Christian martyrdom: the profusion of source material.

Early modern awareness of martyrs cannot be inferred directly from publication statistics, but neither is it unrelated to them. From the start, pamphlets about evangelical martyrs poured from German presses. Multiple editions were common: the first publication about the Augustinians burned in Brussels in 1523 saw sixteen editions by year's end, produced by at least eight separate printers working in seven different German cities. A pamphlet about Casper Tauber went through seven editions in 1524, while in 1527 two *Flugschriften*, one each about Leonhard Keyser and Johannes Heuglin, were published at least nine and five times, respectively.[11] If we conservatively estimate 500 to 1,000 copies per average print run[12] and allow for copies damaged and confiscated, there must still have been thousands of martyr pamphlets in circulation by 1530, a full generation before the first major Protestant martyrologies appeared.

These later collections proved their popularity at once. John Foxe's *Acts and Monuments*, first printed in 1563 (following his two Latin contributions to the genre), went through nine folio editions by 1684, including six by 1610.[13] Jean Crespin's martyrology was published in some form at least thirty-seven times, beginning with thirteen installments and editions in

French between 1554 and 1563. These were expanded into the first French folio edition of 1564. There followed six French folio editions from 1565 through 1619, three Latin editions between 1556 and 1560 (with a fourth in 1627), and ten editions of an abridged German translation plus three more of a different, complete German translation between 1590 and 1682.[14] Adriaen van Haemstede's *History and Death of the Devout Martyrs* was published in Dutch twenty-three times from 1559 through 1671, with fifteen editions by 1616.[15] Less imposing martyrological publications continued to appear in the tradition of the early pamphlets. Multiple sermons and treatises urged the faithful to stand fast unto death, while songs rhymed the trials and triumphs of the persecuted.

Catholic Europe, too, was awash in martyrological literature. Between 1566 and 1640 more than fifty different publications were devoted wholly or in part to the persecution or martyrdom of English Catholics, including 163 editions from 1580 through 1619—and these were works in languages other than English.[16] In Latin, French, Spanish, Italian, German, and Dutch, news of the martyrs streamed across the Continent during the reigns of Elizabeth and James I. At least twenty different works in English on the same subjects were published between 1564 and 1630. Meanwhile the *Roman Martyrology,* the Church's revised liturgical collection of saints' lives, appeared in at least nineteen Latin editions between 1584 and 1613, not to mention translations into every major European vernacular.[17] Counter-Reformation patrons commissioned hundreds of martyr paintings and engravings, while both clergy and laity invoked martyr-saints as intercessors and eagerly sought their relics.

Among Anabaptists, only the comparatively literate Dutch Mennonites printed sources as plentifully as their Protestant and Catholic contemporaries. Their martyrological collection, *The Sacrifice unto the Lord,* was published eleven times between 1562–1563 and 1599, alongside dozens of pamphlets containing martyrs' letters, songs, and confessions of faith, some of them assembled into do-it-yourself martyrologies.[18] The Anabaptist martyrs' greatest legacy consists of the hundreds of Dutch and German songs written by and about them. Often from prison, martyrs set their stories to familiar tunes, admonishing perseverance despite the danger of death, voicing sorrow as well as the experience of God's consolation. Postmortem musical narratives of their suffering preserved their memory and celebrated their witness. Besides their prose publications, Dutch Anabaptists produced song collections by the dozens.[19] The Swiss Brethren printed martyr songs as broadsheets by the late 1520s and published their first hymnal in 1564. Hutterites assembled manuscripts of their histories and songs into codices that remained unpublished until this century.[20] To grasp the importance of martyrdom for sixteenth-century Anabaptists, we must analyze their songs, as scholars have long been aware.[21]

Counting editions cannot tell us how or even whether people actually read these sources, nor reveal how the illiterate or semiliterate might have encountered them. Still, this cursory overview strongly suggests a widespread celebration of Christian martyrs. In addition, martyrdom and related themes regularly surfaced in correspondence, theological treatises, political writings, devotional tracts, poetry, biblical commentaries, and memoirs. An extensive literature of exhortation and consolation, spanning confessional divides, prescribed comportment for persecuted Christians. In short, this surfeit of sources helps to explain the previous lack of a cross-confessional history of early modern Christian martyrdom.

All historical scholarship requires choices and trade-offs. I have not exhausted the available sources on Christian martyrs. Important domains for future research include the specific alterations in the successive editions of the major Protestant martyrologies (Crespin, van Haemstede, and Foxe) and in the Dutch Mennonite tradition from *The Sacrifice unto the Lord* through the second edition of van Braght (1685). Close textual comparisons should reveal how martyrologists, sometimes in combination with other interested parties, carefully shaped their collections over time as circumstances changed.[22] Nor does this book even touch upon the importance of martyrdom for medieval and early modern Jews.[23] My primary concern has been to read widely and deeply enough to understand the nature, implications, and chronology of Christian martyrdom in its cross-confessional context.

The massive range of sources reflects the deaths of thousands of people. Yet determining the number of martyrs entails more than simply counting judicial executions for religion. "Martyr" was an essentially interpretive category, inextricable from one's religious commitment. Used collectively in this study, the term "martyr" designates generically those recognized as such by *some* group. Within a given tradition, some would-be martyrs evoked divergent opinion: Crespin and van Haemstede, for example, excluded executed iconoclasts from their collections lest their inclusion validate Catholic accusations of Calvinist subversion, while Foxe, writing under a Protestant regime, could afford to be less scrupulous. Moreover, contemporary Christians also considered martyrs to be those who died while imprisoned for religion or who perished in collective violence. Thus Simon Goulart, Crespin's continuator, memorialized the victims of the St. Bartholomew's Day massacres.[24] In this sense, then, there were more martyrs than there were people executed for religion. In another sense, however, there were fewer, since compilers were often poorly informed, cut off from information by political unrest and dependent upon mobile informants and the smuggling of manuscripts. Indeed, both Crespin and van Haemstede admitted their ignorance and solicited sources from readers about neglected martyrs for future editions.[25] A. L. E. Verheyden's extensive archival research in Belgium shows how underin-

formed they and van Braght were. The three martyrologists together recorded an average of only 30 percent of the deaths, never more than 48
percent from a single town, and just 12 of Valencienne's 173 executions (6.9
percent).[26] For all these reasons, we need to distinguish those executed for
religion from those understood as martyrs. The categories are not coextensive
and should not be conflated.

Let us ask, then, how many people were judicially executed for religion
and might have been understood as martyrs by some group, according to
contemporary criteria. Like so many sixteenth-century statistics, our figures
should be regarded as rough indications. William Monter has recently combined earlier research with his own work on France, concluding that approximately 3,000 Protestants and Anabaptists were executed for heresy in Europe
between 1523 and about 1565, with 1,100 more executions in the Low
Countries between 1567 and 1574, and perhaps another 280 throughout
Europe in the final third of the century.[27] To this rough figure of some 4,400
should be added at least 300 English Catholics, executed as political traitors
between 1535 and 1680, but understood and honored as religious martyrs.[28]
Most of the approximately 130 Dutch Catholic priests killed between 1567
and 1591 could be classified as casualties of war, yet their deaths often capped
a quasi-judicial ritual during which they could have renounced their Catholicism and saved themselves.[29] Beyond the scope of this study lie the thousands
of Catholic missionaries and converts killed in Asia and the Americas. In
Western Europe, we are talking about perhaps 5,000 people altogether. Subject to multiple influences, executions varied considerably in number and
intensity over time; nowhere did they occur constantly throughout the sixteenth century. The martyrologists' primary raw material were not isolated
occurrences, but they pale in comparison to the genocidal slaughters of the
twentieth century. The Nazis on average killed more Jews *each day* in 1941
and 1942 than there were Christians executed for heterodoxy in the entire
sixteenth and seventeenth centuries.[30]

The collective dynamic of martyrdom helped shape the character of early
modern Christianity. Martyrs are not simply another axis for comparing Catholics, Protestants, and Anabaptists, the way one might compare their sacraments, liturgies, or ecclesiologies. Rather, martyrs intensified every other disagreement. Theologians disputing before civic magistrates or controversialists
fighting pamphlet wars did not endure bloody, visible death for matters of
religion. Bound to the stake or standing at the scaffold, martyrs were the
living embodiment of what they believed and practiced as members of religious communities. In dying they left fellow believers behind, people who had
known, cared about, worshiped with, and prayed for them. Martyrdom cau-
tions us against focusing on "a body of believers rather than the more modern

definition of a body of beliefs" or emphasizing "the social rather than the theological" in approaching early modern Christianity.[31] It is hard to see how believers without beliefs makes any sense, regardless of the period in question or the nature of the beliefs. If we want to understand martyrs and their communities of faith, a social history of religion that neglects belief, theology, and spirituality is as deficient as an intellectual history of doctrines that bypasses flesh-and-blood believers in social relationships.

By dying for doctrines about which Christians disagreed, martyrs infused religious dispute with human urgency. Any compromise could unfold only "over their dead bodies" and the memory of their refusal to submit. Compromise would have meant negotiating with murderous authorities, or at least those who identified with them. It would have dishonored the martyrs' deaths with the implicit retrospective judgment that they too, instead of persevering, should have saved themselves by dissembling. Ultimately, it would have denied that the teachings for which they had died were worth dying for.

No compromise came. Contested teachings such as papal primacy, believers' baptism, and justification by faith alone already separated Christians from one another. Martyrs demonstrated their willingness to die for these beliefs, proclaiming that commitment to the truth outweighed the prolongation of their lives. Doctrines were tightly linked to deaths. Catholics, Anabaptists, and Protestants celebrated their respective heroes, creating mutually exclusive martyrological traditions that became woven into their collective identities. Memorializing different martyrs amplified preexisting dissonance over Christian truth; martyrs' willingness to die for specific doctrines fostered confessionalization and fueled antagonism. Even where Christians of different creeds coexisted in relative tranquility, martyrdom helped insure that they would do so as members of distinct communities, whose broad outlines have persisted down to the present. Even in the absence of socially and politically overt intolerance, separate traditions clung to divergent commitments that martyrdom, through the shedding of blood, had helped to set in stone.

Yet as the impact of martyrdom helped solidify group identities, it also altered the beliefs of certain individual Christians. Public executions became a powerful arena for evangelization. From the perspective of civil and ecclesiastical authorities, the condemned ought to have begged for forgiveness and reconciliation. To onlookers, the sight of men and women going to their deaths willingly, and bearing extreme pain with extraordinary patience, could spark interest and even conversion. Hostile controversialists admitted as much and lamented the fact. Over the long term, mutually exclusive martyrological traditions helped cement religious divisions; yet individual reactions to executions made this a fluid process. Among witnesses to Anabaptists' deaths in Antwerp in the 1550s, who would detest them and who would be moved to join them? Who would revile the Catholic priests executed in London in the 1580s, and who would be led to Rome by their steadfastness? The spectacle of executions deterred some and inspired others, but fore-knowledge of individual responses remained elusive.[32]

Others resemble religious martyrs in their willingness to die for a cause, whether soldiers who risk their lives in war, political activists who resist an oppressive regime, or social crusaders who flirt with assassination by provok-ing hostility. All these, including martyrs, are committed to values more important than prolonging their own lives. In this sense, religious martyrs are not sui generis. At the same time, the character of religion distinguishes martyrdom in important ways from other sorts of willingness to die for a cause (which can, of course, themselves be investigated). The content, ori-gins, and implications of the cause make for different sensibilities, experi-ences, and behaviors. Christian martyrs in early modern Europe will remain opaque to the extent that their religiosity—with all that that entails—remains alien, obscured by modern and/or postmodern assumptions.

Martyrs are not statistically representative of sixteenth-century Christians. They tell us not about rank-and-file believers and the clergy who struggled to inculcate minimal religious comprehension and observance, but rather about what such a process ideally produced: men and women self-consciously steeped in their faith, willing to make it their overriding priority. There was nothing esoteric about the martyrs—their beliefs and worldview are stated or implied in the period's most elementary catechisms. Accordingly, the extrem-ism of martyrdom should be understood not as a fanaticism of the fringe, but as exemplary action. Martyrs were exceptional in their behavior, but not in their beliefs or values. Were this not the case, friends and family members would not have urged them to persevere; attitudes linked to martyrdom, such as the importance of setting aside temporal concerns in the hope of eternal reward, would not have found such widespread expression; and fellow believ-ers would not have championed so enthusiastically their martyrs as examples for others to follow. Once we understand central aspects of sixteenth-century Christian faith, martyrdom is intelligible precisely as their enactment in spe-cific circumstances. If martyrdom seems bizarre or incomprehensible, we should suspect that we have insufficiently grasped the religious convictions at its heart.

On Understanding Early Modern Christianity

Religion is expressed and transmitted through cultural forms.[33] Certain as-pects of it are appropriately studied by anthropology, sociology, psychology, and other disciplines. At the same time, the content, purported origins, and implications of religion distinguish it in important ways from other sorts of beliefs and practices. Courtship customs or epistolary conventions, for example, do not generate notions like revelation, faith, sin, redemption, God's will and judgment, eternal salvation and damnation. Societal norms of dress or marketplace mores do not prescribe prayer, worship, or charitable works. Gift giving or managerial practices have no bearing on divine providence, belief in which can structure a worldview that encompasses human values, behavior, and destiny.

The distinctiveness of religion demands methodological astuteness if we want to understand its practitioners, lest we misconstrue them from the outset. In seeking to explain religion, many scholars have employed cultural theories or social science approaches in ways that preclude its being understood. Instead of reconstructing religious beliefs and experiences, they reduce them to something else based on their own, usually implicit, modern or postmodern beliefs.

Much recent poststructuralist theory alleges a radical disjunction between representations and realities, rendering truth claims unverifiable. No adjudication between incommensurable representations is possible, because no shared standard exists that permits their evaluation. Those alleging truth are therefore effectively asserting the impossible: that their words, their representations, might *really* be describing the world. Applying this notion to early modern Christianity would have far-reaching implications, for members of sixteenth-century groups not only claimed truth for their views, but killed and died for them. One might then conclude that through ignorance of the nature of their cultural constructions, they wrongly took their representations for truth, reprehensibly inflicting and enduring violence for them. Misunderstanding the subjective nature of all readings, they mistook their necessarily tentative character.

Such a position assumes the very correspondence theory of truth it repudiates: "*it is true* that no truth claims are verifiable." And it is, presumably, as subjective as the positions it criticizes—on what grounds could one allege its objectivity, having claimed that objectivity is a chimera? But let us bracket these (considerable) problems, which the poststructuralist position shares with traditional epistemological skepticism. More fundamentally for our present purposes, it cannot help us understand sixteenth-century religious practitioners. Presumably no one would argue that sixteenth-century Christians endured enormous hardships, including exile, imprisonment, torture, and execution, for self-consciously held subjective constructions. Clearly, those who sacrificed for their convictions did not regard them as mere constructions or provisional readings. The implicit argument, therefore, must be that although *they* believed they were correct, in fact they were mistaken. This claim, however, reflects a present judgment about their views, itself based on contentious convictions. Committed Christians believed that their "constructions," while formulated in human language, articulated truths revealed by God with direct bearing on their eternal salvation and damnation. As diversely understood and experienced, faith was the foundation that assured and reassured men and women that their words fit the world. If our objective is to understand these people rather than to judge them, to fathom what Patrick Collinson once called "the living content of belief,"[34] then we ought to declare a postmortem for poststructuralism and avoid its dead end. Not to take such people on their own terms fails utterly to comprehend them, the character of their actions, and the basis of their lives.

So too, if we want to understand early modern Christians, we ought to eschew any anthropological or psychological theory whose analytical horizon stops at the level of symbols as such. Early modern Christians had their own views of religious symbols, none of which terminated in a "symbolic order" or a "system of symbols." To the martyrs above all, God, Satan, sin, grace, heaven, hell, and the like were by no means part of a merely "symbolic" realm—as opposed to the domain of the "real" or "material." They were divinely revealed realities, and as such *more* real than the fleeting, temporal aspects of their lives. To call the spiritual the "symbolic," and then to contrast it to the "real" or the "material," far from helping us understand the martyrs, not only distorts but essentially inverts their whole way of seeing things. To claim that their beliefs in these realities were really the effects of a "symbolic order" on their experience, or something similar, cannot help us *understand* them, however much it might *explain* them to the satisfaction of those who share the metaphysical assumptions embedded in such a claim. In the end, the cultural anthropologist or psychologist who reduces beliefs in spiritual realities to the effects of (mere) symbols does the same thing as the poststructuralist who reduces beliefs in absolute truths to (mistaken) cultural constructions. In fact, all reductionist theories evince an impoverished historical imagination, one insufficient to understand the lived realities of the past.

What people believed in the past is logically distinct from our opinions about them. Understanding others on their terms is a completely different intellectual endeavor than explaining them in modern or postmodern categories. What we (diversely) believe is one thing; what they (diversely) believed is another; and what relationships might exist between our varied beliefs and theirs is a third. The three should not be confused. I fail to follow the logic of a leading literary scholar who recently implied, during a session at the American Historical Association convention, that because he "cannot believe in belief," the religion of sixteenth- and seventeenth-century people is not to be taken seriously on its own terms.[35] Strictly speaking, this is an autobiographical comment that reveals literally nothing about early modern people. One might as well say, "I cannot believe in unbelief; therefore, alleged post-Enlightenment atheism should not be taken seriously on its own terms."

Could bedfellows be any stranger? Reductionist explanations of religion share the epistemological structure of traditional confessional history. Just as confessional historians explore and evaluate based on their religious convictions, reductionist historians of religion explain and judge based on their unbelief. Both assume present-day convictions, whether theistic or atheistic, as their starting point. The corrective to traditional confessional history is not atheistic history of religion, which substitutes one bias for another. What is needed is an approach that does justice to any and all evidence we might encounter, without distorting the convictions of any of its protagonists. This I have sought to provide. It is precisely a cross-confessional study of martyrdom that forces the issue: "martyrdom" because it resists reductionist theories but is intelligible on the martyrs' own terms, and "cross-confessional" because it compels the attempt to understand people willing to die for divergent beliefs.

My depiction of sixteenth-century Christians is intended to be one in which they would have recognized themselves, not puzzled over modern or postmodern reconfigurations of who they were. I have sought to reconstruct, not deconstruct, their commitments and experiences as far as the evidence permits. This holds not only for the martyrs, but also for fellow believers who encouraged them, authorities who tried to dissuade them, and those who responded to their deaths both positively and negatively. Several objectives can be achieved by telling a story of embattled convictions in action not from an external perspective based on explanatory theory, but rather through an exploration of the relevant traditions in turn, one that is sensitive to their emphases, nuances, and changes over time.

We can meet early modern Christians in their communities without subverting their own, rival claims to objective truth. When the Anabaptist leader Menno Simons, the Protestant martyrologist Jean Crespin, and the Catholic cleric William Allen asserted that their respective martyrs were in heaven, blessed by God, that is literally what they meant. Our accounts should reflect this. By no means should we "dismiss the hagiographic fiction that sanctity is 'discovered,'" or concur that "People are not saints unless others consider them saints. Sanctity is in the eye of the beholder."[36] The period's ubiquitous wrangling about true and false martyrs does not imply that sanctity is a "fiction," but only that people disagreed about its recognition and application. This holds for conflicts within as well as across traditions. Likewise, contemporary disputes over the status of Martin Luther King, Jr., as a "moral hero" do not make moral heroism a fiction. Early modern Christians believed that recognized and unrecognized forms of holiness were equally real, because sanctity was neither created by nor contingent on its acknowledgment by others. Disagreement over who was holy leaves untouched the nature of their respective contentions. If we subjectivize their competing claims to "Truth with a capital T," we drastically distort the lived meaning of their beliefs and behaviors. The alternative to misrepresenting all their convictions is to explore each one in turn.

In this way we can encounter religious people with their antagonistic, absolutist convictions at full strength. Nothing is diluted. Miri Rubin claims that we must relativize orthodox medieval Christian faith if we are to understand the Jewish and heretical martyrs of the later Middle Ages.[37] On the contrary, we must simply endeavor to understand them with the same care that we direct toward orthodox Christians. This requires only the self-conscious neutrality necessary for anyone who wants to grasp more than one perspective, insofar as it is possible to do so. The point is precisely *not* to relativize competing faith claims themselves, but to let each resonate fully, creating a formal relativism of competing absolutisms. Otherwise the variegated topography of religious belief and practice is leveled to a homogeneous plane of cultural constructions. Believers become intelligible only through theories that explain religion by explaining it away.

This study is not "merely" an exercise in retracing people's past beliefs and actions. To seek to understand multiple, opposed views in context is more than committed early modern Christians did, wanted to do, and were perhaps able to do. What they understood, respectively, as true Christianity we ought to regard as interpretations that indeed they believed were true, but whose truth we need not accept for the purposes of understanding. This move makes possible a neutrality that shields us from "taking sides" or twisting the nature of their convictions. We can discover the character of the various contentions in turn. We can discern interpretive watersheds beyond which discussion could not flow because common ground for debate was lacking. And we can see how divergent readings of the Bible were linked to distinct modes of worship, disciplinary practices, and ecclesiologies—indeed, to different experiences of being Christian.

Early modern charges of constructivism and subjectivism belong in the story. Protestant and Anabaptist writers commonly accused medieval Catholic prelates of inventing rituals and doctrines without scriptural foundation and therefore without authority. Catholic apologists asserted that heretics' doctrinal divergences disclosed their subjective origins and revealed the de facto disaster of "scripture alone" as a foundational principle. These voices should resound—it is gravely misguided to consign the era's writings of religious controversy to the dustbin of "polemics." There is a tendency to condemn the virulence of the period's doctrinal disputes as disproportionate to the issues involved. According to whom? The voluminous rancor of sixteenth-century controversialists is *evidence to be understood*. Issues bitterly contested for decades, even centuries, cannot fairly be dismissed as "dogmatic minutiae." With its often strident tone and fierce language, controversy reveals key points of disagreement and constantly reminds us what mattered to its protagonists. Again modern convictions intrude, here often borne by liberal theological trends and ecumenical yearnings that diminish and even trivialize bygone battles. It is entirely misleading to put terms like "heresy" and "superstition" in quotation marks when paraphrasing controversialists' views, as though their contentiousness compels subjectivization—implying that Protestants were not *really* heretics, Catholics were not *really* superstitious. The point is to capture the contemporary character of the denunciations, to see what they meant in context.

Sixteenth-century souls were often devout, but they were never disembodied—as the martyrs knew with painful clarity. Contextual understanding compels us to relate religion to other aspects of life—social, political, economic, cultural—while resisting absorption by any of them. To treat early modern Christians on their own terms is not to study their religiosity in splendid isolation. Indeed, to do so would misrepresent them badly: if they did not separate religion from their political engagements, familial relationships, attitudes toward education, and conceptions of order, then neither should historians who want to understand them. Preserving the distinctiveness of religion does not mean carving out for it an anachronistic insularity. Its character is inseparable from its rootedness in the social relationships, institutions, and cultural expectations of real life.

In such a broad, programmatic discussion, general categories such as "religious traditions" and "the Christian worldview" are inevitable. In practice, however, understanding early modern Christians demands that we see them as individuals within communities, and recognize change over time as well as diversity within traditions. Not all Anabaptists, Calvinists, or Catholics thought or acted alike, and their respective versions of Christianity were always in motion. Blanket claims about the unchanging coherence of religious traditions are unjustified, but so is an excessive nominalism that would speak only of "Catholicisms" or "Calvinisms" regardless of context. Whether our analysis leans more toward essentialism or nominalism depends on the issue in question.

Some might find this approach to religion naïve in its willingness to take at face value the self-understandings and self-presentations of the past. Certainly people often act for covert interests and resort to self-justificatory rationalizations for their actions. To adopt a "hermeneutics of suspicion" as our guiding interpretive assumption, however, is highly problematic.[38] Duplicity and dissembling should be demonstrated one case at a time, not assumed as a global principle for analyzing human behavior. In particular, neither unsettling historical difference nor present-day disagreement with past values warrants a hermeneutics of suspicion as a modus operandi. This pertains especially to historians for at least two related reasons.

First, using a hermeneutics of suspicion to "unmask ideologies" destroys the very possibility of understanding historical difference. With arbitrary condescension, it pigeonholes the past according to contemporary values and assumptions, separating the "ideological" from the "authentic," the "reactionary" from the "progressive." Functioning as a presentist mirror, it predictably yields a history reflecting the interpreter's commitments.

To take a simple example from the sixteenth century: construing the threat of eternal damnation as an ideological "strategy of domination" reflects modern, secular conceptions of liberation from sociopolitical oppression and individual rights to freedom of thought and behavior. Yet it misses or dismisses the very different understanding of liberation of early modern reformers (who incidentally demanded even more of themselves than of those whom they allegedly oppressed). For them hell was no "ideological construct," but a terrifying prospect for souls stained by sin, a danger magnified by thoughtless indifference. Quite correctly, they knew that if hell is real, then trying to disbelieve it away is folly. "Liberation" meant not securing political rights or escaping from cyclical poverty, but turning to God for forgiveness to address the sin that otherwise threatened *eternal* oppression. A relaxed attitude toward behavior would have been unconscionably negligent, "humane" moderation a monstrous inhumanity.[39] We are left with starkly different interpretations of the reformers. Fundamentally, were they social control ideologues who imposed their constructions on an oppressed populace, or conscientious pastors who strove to rattle the complacent out of their deadly spiritual stupor?[40]

Besides nullifying historical difference, a hermeneutics of suspicion often implicitly undermines the sincerity and integrity of people whose actions fall beyond the boundaries of behavior enacted "in good faith." In order to explore the "compelling contemporary logic of precisely those viewpoints that may now seem distasteful or even repugnant,"[41] these limits must be drawn very widely indeed. Otherwise, present values—regardless of their content—inevitably construe the past in their own image: the "progressive" anticipation of modern tolerance and relativism, for example, is judged with favor, whereas intransigence and intolerance are condemned. The self-professed reasons why people did what they did are suspect in proportion to the moral offense they give to modern or postmodern sensibilities. The problem here is not *which* sensibilities pass judgment, but that *any* do.

Martyrdom scrambles the picture once more. Actions speak louder than words. And few actions speak more dramatically than a willingness to die for one's beliefs, or more clearly when combined with martyrs' prison writings as they anticipated death. Disputing their sincerity or integrity makes no sense. What Christian leaders articulated meshed with what martyrs showed themselves willing to die for—indeed, leaders themselves were often executed for their views. Moreover, the attitudes and practices cultivated by committed Catholics, Protestants, and Anabaptists dovetailed with the respective spiritualities of their martyrs. This does not imply that no early modern Christians used religion in deliberately manipulative ways. Doubtless some did, perhaps quite a few. But this is a matter for empirical demonstration, not methodological assumption. A social-control hermeneutics of suspicion seems plausible when analyzing confessional state-building and acculturation; it founders when facing people who willingly were burned alive or drawn and quartered. By contrast, with a general presumption of sincerity all around and a deliberate avoidance of any modern or postmodern judgmentalism, we can account for killers and killed in terms that both would have recognized.

Fundamentally, my approach seeks simply to answer the question "What did it mean to them?"—shifting as necessary depending on who "they" are and on what "it" is. To what end? This is a question about the purpose of history. The payoff is evocation and presentation of the world of past people, of their experience, and consequently a better understanding of the character of early modern Christianity. If one considers this a wrongheaded goal—if one believes that explaining, not understanding, past people is the point of doing history—then my approach must necessarily appear misguided. "Understanding" does not mean "perfect reconstruction"—but the impossibility of the latter neither justifies a general skepticism nor warrants the adoption of reductionist theories. Only historians have the time and training to pursue past experience as it was lived and construed. Without the effort, past worlds will be utterly lost, not only because human experience is fleeting, but because even the ideal of reconstructing it will have passed as so much grist through the mill of the theories and commitments of the moment. The aim of this book is to analyze early modern martyrdom without recasting or judging the convictions, attitudes, or actions of the protagonists through any theories or values that distort them. The first prerequisite is one of the most difficult: to set aside what we think in order to listen to what they said. Only then can we even attempt to comprehend why people would die and kill for their understandings of the Lord's Supper, rather than reassure ourselves by dismissing their "fanaticism." In doing so, we might even gain insight into some of the differences that divide our own world.

The Nature of the Martyrological Sources

It might seem that this ambitious objective is built on intellectual sand. Using early modern martyrdom as a historical wedge assumes an accurate depiction of martyrs' beliefs and behaviors, but such accuracy is exactly the issue in question. The linguistic turn in historical research has shown how all writers fashion narratives according to divergent agendas and view events through distinctive interpretive lenses. Martyrological literature would seem doubly suspect: in some ways it resembles later medieval hagiography, a genre notorious for its imaginative flights of fancy. Moreover, sixteenth-century martyrological writers were overt propagandists. They wrote with the aim, often made explicit, of commemorating their heroes, edifying fellow believers, denouncing religious opponents, and convincing readers that they were chronicling stories of the *real* witnesses of Christian truth.[42] Their writings are worlds away from detached reporting. How can we penetrate their partisan depictions of the executions they claim to portray?

Let us begin by ignoring them. Let us pretend that not a shred of early modern martyrological literature exists, and that we must turn elsewhere to learn something about martyrs' deaths. Indeed, let us look in the very place least likely to show martyrs in a flattering light: sources written by antagonists, often expressly intended to condemn false martyrs and to justify their execution. Given the period's fiery confessional strife, hostile writers were far from disposed to say anything about false martyrs that could be construed in a positive light.

What we find is quite remarkable. Listen to Catholic and Protestant writers on German-speaking Anabaptists. A Catholic chronicler in the small Bavarian town of Kaufbeuren reported that five executed in May 1528 were "completely cheerful" [*ganz frölich*] and that one kissed the executioner and praised God.[43] One of Luther's companions asked him in 1532 about the many Anabaptists whom Ferdinand had put to death, "and how constantly and joyfully [*beständig und freudig*] they had died."[44] In 1550 Johannes Fabri von Heilbronn detailed Anabaptist martyrs' behavior:

> They dance and jump in the fire, view the glistening sword with fearless hearts, speak and preach to the people with smiles on their faces; they sing psalms and other songs until their souls have departed, they die with joy, as if they were in happy company, they remain strong, assured, and steadfast [*starck, getröst, vnnd standthafftig*] to the point of death. And if with all possible diligence the Catholics dare and endeavor to make them turn away from their errors with the plain holy scriptures, telling them that those who recant their errors will have mercy shown them and not

be executed, also following after them right to the gallows, admonishing them, calling to them without fail, begging and desiring that they acknowledge their errors and recant, all this warning, begging, and imploring they regard as a fairy tale, laughing and ridiculing, and sooner than recant one article they would suffer another hundred deaths, [and] thus they remain so obstinate in their resolve that they also defy all pain and torment [*pein vnd marter*].[45]

This portrait in determined constancy comes from a Dominican controversialist attacking Anabaptism. In 1565 an anonymous Protestant author, concerned about the impact of Dutch Anabaptist martyrs in the southern Netherlands, sounded much the same. They were "suffering persecution under the most beautiful appearance of sanctity," he wrote, and they "laugh right into the act of dying [*tot in het midden des doots lachen*], indeed die with great boldness."[46] There is no conceivable reason why *hostile* writers would have invented such depictions. If Anabaptists had typically, or even with some regularity, died with less than impressive resolve, Catholic and Protestant denouncers would have said so.

Similarly, Catholic apologists were far from disposed to represent Protestant martyrs in a favorable manner. Johannes Eck published an attack on a pamphlet about the evangelical martyr Leonhard Keyser. In his riposte, Eck reprinted a letter by the local judge in Schärding, Christoph Frenckinger, which confirmed a sympathetic account of Keyser's death: just before being burned, he asked the people to sing "Come, Holy Ghost," which they did, and then from the fire, "he called out 'Jesus' three or four times."[47] Antoine Du Val, another theologian, wrote against the Huguenot martyrs from Paris in 1559 partly because he saw "many simple-minded men and women being deceived and seduced, astounded at the ability to suffer and the steadfastness [*la patience et constance*] of some of them when they are executed and burned," saying things like "Do we not see that they are so steadfast and sure in their opinion when they are burned? How do they do that? It must be that they have the spirit of God."[48] Marian Protestants in England likewise annoyed Reginald Pole. Young people especially, he said, resisted a return to Roman Catholicism when they witnessed "the constancy of those that willingly offer themselves to death for the defense of their opinion."[49] Florimond de Raemond, a Catholic apologist and royal *conseiller* in the Parlement of Bordeaux, commented frankly on the Huguenot martyrs' manner of dying. Perturbed about the effect of their executions, Raemond said that people

see the simple-minded little women seek out tortures as a way of proving their faith, and going to death they cry out only "Christ," "Savior," singing some psalm, the young virgins walking more cheerfully to their place of execution than they would have done on the way to the marriage bed. The men rejoice seeing the terrible and frightening preparations and instruments of death that have been readied for them, and half-burned and roasted, they regard from above the executioners the cuts received by the pincers with an unconquered courage [*d'vn courage inuaincu*], bearing a joyous appearance and comportment among the hooks of the executioners, as though they were rocks standing against waves of sadness.[50]

This sounds like Fabri von Heilbronn again, half a century later, describing French Calvinists instead of Austrian Anabaptists.

None of these writers supports a recent assertion that "the Protestant depiction of unwavering faith, a mixture of joyful resignation and defiance, leaving many spectators impressed and edified, may be matched by the contradictory version by Catholic writers of the same event, describing recantation and recognition of the evils of Protestantism."[51] We might reasonably have expected this pattern, but in fact hostile writers repeatedly described the deaths of false martyrs in terms recognizably like those of sympathetic martyrologists. The few cases in which martyrs' behavior is described contradictorily, such as that of Thomas Bilney, executed in Norwich on August 16, 1531, are the exception.[52] No sustained literature casts doubt on their comportment in general. Even if our evidence of martyrs' behavior relied exclusively on hostile sources, we would have to conclude that they usually died with a joyful resolve that often impressed onlookers.

To understand why denunciations confirmed martyrs' dying behavior, we must grasp the relationship between public executions for heterodoxy and controversialists' intentions in a world divided by religious disagreement. One risked harming one's cause by alleging dutiful recantations or cowardly deaths when nothing of the sort had occurred. Too many people knew better, having witnessed it themselves. In 1527, an anonymous pamphlet about the Bavarian Anabaptist Jörgen Wagner noted his unperturbed appearance and "happy heart" as he was put in the fire, "as everyone indeed saw" [*wie yederman wol sahe*].[53] Having orchestrated public spectacles that they might deter others, authorities—and their apologists—could not reinvent resolve as recantation, nor construct constancy as cowardice.

Returning to our problematic martyrological sources, we can see that sympathetic writers faced the same intersubjective constraints. Without inviting opprobrium and thus damaging their wider cause, they could no more allege joyful deaths where there were none than hostile writers could claim abjurations where martyrs had died steadfastly. It mattered that these were executions for religious nonconformity in religiously divided contexts, rather than, say, executions for murder, the pamphlet literature for which J. A. Sharpe has discussed for Stuart England.[54] In contrast to communities of Marian Protestants or Elizabethan Catholics, no "pro-murderer party" existed that would have cared if the narratives about these criminals' contrite deaths had been wholly invented. Potential critics of the narrated events were lacking because both the stories and the executions themselves affirmed virtually unanimous values. Executions for religion differed dramatically: fellow believers attended to observe the dying words and deeds of people understood not as social and political subversives, but rather as witnesses to Christian truth. It was not only difficult, but ultimately self-defeating, to perpetrate pious frauds about carefully staged events seen by hundreds or thousands of people. Regardless of their views, partisan writers were pressured not to contradict what had happened. What occurred was interpreted and presented in radically different ways, but the behavior of the condemned was not disputed.

This is clear in comparing two pamphlets about the execution of the Elizabethan Catholics Edmund Campion, Ralph Sherwin, and Alexander Briant on December 1, 1581, one critical and the other sympathetic. Both Anthony Munday's *Discovery of Edmund Campion* and Thomas Alfield's *True Report* were published within three months of the executions.[55] An apologist for the regime, Munday recounted Campion's comportment less elaborately than did the Catholic priest Alfield, as we would expect, yet he confirmed many of its details. Comparing the two accounts of Campion's *observable behavior*, as opposed to his *internal disposition*, reveals their striking congruity.

Listen to each writer recounting Campion's first words to the crowd (Alfield's text is on the left, Munday's on the right):[56]

after some small pause in the cart, with grave countenance and sweet voice [he] stoutly spake as followeth. *Spectaculum facti sumus Deo, Angeli et hominibus* saying, These are the words of St. Paul, Englished thus: We are made a spectacle, or a sight unto God, unto his Angels, and unto men: verified this day in me, who am here a spectacle unto my Lord God, a spectacle unto his angels, and unto you men.	Edmund Campion was first brought up into the cart, where, after the great rumor of so many people somewhat appeased, he began to proceed in his confession. First he began with a phrase or two in Latin, when soon after he fell into English as thus. I am here brought as a spectacle, before the face of God, of Angels and of men, satisfying myself to die, as becometh a true Christian and Catholic man.

Both writers said that from the cart he paraphrased 1 Cor. 4:9, beginning in Latin, then switching to English. Munday then stopped describing Campion's behavior and began interpreting his interiority. He thought that a pause bespoke "the great temerity and unstable opinion of his conscience" that blocked him from confessing his treason: "fear had caught hold on this brave boaster, and terror entered his thoughts."[57] Then Munday resurfaced, as it were, and noted "that the outward protestations of this man, urged some there present to tears, not entering into conceit of his inward hypocrisy." In other words, their interpretation and reaction to Campion's actions differed from his. Munday then used Campion's Oxford career, his gifts, and his ostensible misuse of his talents as "proof" of his fear and deception in the face of death—all without a word about his behavior at that moment. Returning to Campion's actions, Munday reported that he *again* denied any treason after all, a point confirmed by Alfield.[58]

After Munday's elaborate digression, the two narratives again run closely parallel:[59]

In fine, preparing himself to drink his last draught of Christ his cup, was interrupted in his prayer by a minister, willing him to say, Christ have mercy upon me, or such like prayer with him: unto whom he looking back with mild countenance, humbly said: You and I are not one in religion, wherefore I pray you content yourself, I bar none of prayer, only I desire them of the household of faith to pray with me, and in mine agony to say one *Credo*. Some also called upon him to pray in English: to whom he answered, that he would pray in a language that he well understood . . . And so he meekly and sweetly yielded his soul unto his Savior, protesting that he died a perfect Catholic.

Pray with them in English, as he was desired, he would not, but said his *Pater noster* in Latin, and desired all those of the household of faith, to say one *Credo* for him. Many indirect answers he made, as when he was moved to ask the Queen forgiveness, and when the preacher requested him to shew some sign of a penitent sinner, when shortly he replied: You and I, we are not of one religion. After a few silent prayers to himself, the cart was drawn away, and he committed to the mercy of God. There he hanged till he was dead, when being cut down, he was boweled and quartered, according as it was appointed by justice.

The chronology differs: Alfield wrote that Campion rebuked the minister's request and then the plea to pray in English, whereas Munday put these in reverse order. Yet the two concur on what he said, his interaction with the crowd, and his overall comportment, down to a virtually verbatim agreement about his utterance, "You and I, we are not of one religion" ("You and I are not one in religion"). Munday even included details not in Alfield that would have enhanced a Catholic rendition—it is he, not the priest, who wrote that the Jesuit moved some spectators to tears. The close resemblance between these two ideologically opposed accounts implies a common fidelity to what actually happened.

Unfortunately, a lack of sources prevents such detailed comparisons for most executions. Many more examples could be given,[60] but the wider point is clear and very significant: even where specific corroboration is impossible, we can use the sympathetic descriptions of martyrs' public words and actions with a high degree of confidence. This restricted conclusion serves a narrow purpose. It does not, of course, justify generalizing about the reliability of everything in the vast and varied corpus of martyrological sources. Still, neither these sources in general, nor their depictions of martyrs' public behavior, are inherently suspect due to their authors' ideological commitments. Indeed, something quite the opposite is very likely true: precisely *because* these writers wanted to promote their respective causes, they strove to make their interpretations, however highly charged, however shaped by literary conventions, fit the best available information about executions. Facts, not fabrication, best served propaganda. This would explain why martyrologists admitted ignorance and requested materials from readers. It also accounts for why entries on martyrs in the major collections vary in quantity and detail from single sentences up through dozens of folio pages.[61] There is no reason in general to doubt that martyrs really sang psalms en route to their deaths, joyfully ascended the gallows, quoted scripture to the crowd, repeated Christ's dying words, or stood unflinching in fires that were burning them alive. Unless there is cause to question a particular account, we have good reason to trust reports of such behavior, extraordinary as it is. The underlying problem is less early modern invention and credulity than modern or postmodern skepticism and cynicism. During the Vietnam War, too, Western television viewers were shocked by Buddhist monks' eerie immobility in the flames that consumed them, their self-immolation a protest against the ravages of war in southeast Asia.

Martyrs' actions at their deaths were intimately connected to the convictions that led them there. Yet observable, public behavior is one thing, the religious sensibilities of people dead more than four centuries quite another. How can we reconstruct the latter? Besides recounting martyrs' executions, many writers printed their prison letters, songs, and confessions of faith, following in the footsteps of ancient Christian historians such as Eusebius of Caesarea (ca. 260–339). For most of the martyrs, to be sure, we have no such sources at all. Yet by comparing the relatively few surviving holographs and manuscript copies with published versions, we can discern the editorial hand of the martyrologists—and simultaneously gauge the reliability of the extant printed sources.

The Calvinist Godefroy de Hamaelle was executed in Tournai on June 22, 1552. Shortly thereafter, a pamphlet appeared with several of his writings, including three prison letters. The first letter also exists in a mid-sixteenth-century manuscript copy preserved in the Leiden University Library.[62] Comparing de Hamaelle's epistle in these two versions plus that in the 1570 edition of Crespin's martyrology shows their extremely close correspondence to one another, as well as their mutual fidelity to a now-lost original (the Leiden manuscript version is on the left, the pamphlet in the middle, and Crespin on the right):[63]

je scay que pour icelle croyance et vrays articles de foy ne seray juge a la mort: mais seullement pour non adherer et vouloir croyre aux comandemens dhommes. Or bien le Seigneur face de moy sa volonte: Je suis a luy et a la vye, et a la mort. Je vous escriptz cecy seullement (au moins sil fault que je seuffre) que ne me jugez pour hereticque, car je ne suis ignorant de la croyance et articles des Chrestiens. Mais les croy toutz simplement selon la petite capacite de foy que le Seigneur ma distribué de grace, comme vous oyrez.	ie scay que pour tele croyence & uray article de foy, ie ne seray iuge a la mart mais seulement pour non adherer & uouloyr croyre aux comendementz des hommes or bien le Seigneur face de moy sa uolente, ie suis a luy & a la uie & a la mort ie uous escris ceci seulement aumoyns sil faut que ie soufre que ne me iuges pour heretique. Car ie ne suis ignorent de la croyence & articles des chrestiens mais les croy toutes simplement selon la petite capacite de foy que le Seigneur ma distribue de grace commes uous oyres.	ie say que pour telle croyance & vrais articles de foy, ie ne seray iugé à la mort: mais seulement pour non adherer & vouloir croire aux commandemens des hommes. Or bien, le Seigneur face de moy sa volonté: ie suis à luy & à la vie & à la mort. Ie vous escri ceci seulement, au moins s'il faut que ie soufre, que ne me iugiez pour hereticque. Car ie ne suis ignorant de la croyance & articles des Chrestiens: mais les croy tous simplement, selon la petite capacité de foy que le Seigneur m'a distribué de sa grace, comme vous orrez.

This excerpt does not prove the accuracy of all the letters that Crespin reprints. The lack of similar manuscripts makes analogous comparisons impossible. Nonetheless, this example is direct evidence against the allegations by Arthur Piaget and Gabrielle Berthoud, who claimed that Crespin, perhaps with the help of Genevan theologians, had significantly altered or even substantially written the martyrs' letters in his collection.[64]

Maeyken Wens, a Dutch Mennonite, was burned along with three other Mennonite women in Antwerp on October 6, 1573.[65] The day before her execution she wrote to her son, Adrien, the only surviving holograph letter by an Anabaptist martyr, now in the Doopsgezinde Bibliotheek of the Amsterdam University Library.[66] This letter was first published in the 1615 Dutch Mennonite martyrology compiled under Hans de Ries in Haarlem, then reprinted in subsequent collections in 1617, 1626, and 1631–1632, and finally included in the 1660 and 1685 editions of van Braght's *Martyrs' Mirror*.[67] The appendix sets the original text beside the version from the second edition of van Braght, as it came from her hand and as it appeared more than a century later, after multiple reprintings. The slight variations derive mostly from changes in the Dutch language during this interval, and from the simple correction of several grammatical and compositional errors in Wens's original.[68] As with Crespin's treatment of Godefroy de Hamaelle's letter, there are no substantive interpolations. We cannot therefore conclude with certainty that every letter in van Braght is equally faithful to its original. We are, however, justifiably disposed toward confidence rather than suspicion in using his Anabaptist letters for which we cannot compare printed and manuscript versions.

Further, van Braght admitted that some martyrs' writings, which he might convincingly have forged, had been lost. Speaking of Joost Joosten, for example, executed in Zeeland in 1560, van Braght noted that besides a song, "he had written a confession of faith on five pieces of paper but it has been lost through the long passage of time."[69] If van Braght had announced the discovery of this missing testimony, then fabricated it himself, who would have known? People were aware that this Dordrecht minister tracked down everything he could about the martyrs. He knew exactly what such sources should sound like. The doctrinal divisions among Dutch Mennonites make van Braght's integrity even more noteworthy: he could have patterned a forgery to fit a lost original, but he did not. This reinforces the supposition that he did not significantly alter the martyrs' writings he reproduced.[70]

Surviving manuscripts of the Marian Protestant martyrs are much more abundant. Susan Wabuda has compared those in Emmanuel College, Cambridge, used by John Foxe, his collaborator Henry Bull, and Miles Coverdale, with the printed versions in both the *Acts and Monuments* and Coverdale's 1564 edition of the Marian martyrs' letters. She has concluded that Bull, the main editor, made two principal kinds of alterations, which my own research has confirmed. He frequently cut concluding, personal information from letters, perhaps wanting to spare the survivors of persecution from publicity. Second, Bull deleted passages that compromised the martyrs' doctrinal unity, such as references revealing that some were involved in the free will controversy.[71] Foxe likewise suppressed certain embarrassing, radical Protestant views held by some of his martyrs.[72]

We must reflect carefully on the specificity of this editorial work. Wabuda suggests that "Bull's editing enhanced the scriptural style of the letters, and their universal application, by removing personal or mundane details which otherwise might have distracted the readers."[73] A desire to protect those involved from publicity, however, sufficiently explains these excisions. Contemporary readers would not have assumed that the letters' "enhanced scriptural style" signified an asocial otherworldliness, nor thought that the universality of their values would remain veiled unless the personal and the particular were pruned away. Readers knew that in the previous decade, the martyrs had readied themselves for death as links in chains of human relationships. Knowing about the editors' activity permits us to anchor the letters in the social circles in which they were written, copied, circulated, read, and eventually printed, a rootedness that Wabuda shows so well elsewhere in her article.[74] Significantly, the editors neither inserted nor substantially altered the letters' copious quotations from and paraphrases of scripture. Their presence reflects the martyrs' own activity.

In interpreting the suppression of beliefs and activities deemed unfit for true martyrs, we must distinguish carefully between martyrs and martyrologists. These deletions are crucial for grasping Bull's or Foxe's criteria for inclusion in their martyrological community, but they do not impinge on our understanding of martyrs' willingness to die for their religious views. The edited, printed sources remain saturated with traces of the convictions that supported the willingness to die.

Protestant, Catholic, and Anabaptist martyrs alike produced documents steeped in scripture. It is dangerous to posit generally, on the basis of their educational backgrounds or prison experiences, the extent to which sixteenth-century Christians memorized biblical passages. Piaget and Berthoud claimed that many of Crespin's martyrs could not have known scripture as well as the printed letters imply. As examples they mention the Calvinist clothworker François Varlut and sockmaker Alexandre Dayke, who allegedly wrote some long, detailed letters, thick with biblical verses.[75] Independent sources, however, corroborate the factual aspects of their letters, and even their interrogators and judges noted their extraordinary facility with scripture in disputation. Moreover, Crespin apparently got their epistles from a pamphlet, now lost, that imperial officials confiscated from day laborers near Tournai in 1563 or 1564.[76] The letters in the Dutch Mennonite collection *The Sacrifice unto the Lord* are laden with biblical verses. They vary in length, tone, and emphasis. As Samuel Cramer noted long ago, the editors frequently explained in the margins ambiguous expressions that simple editorial alterations would have made unnecessary, implying a scrupulous fidelity to manuscript originals or copies.[77] As with the Marian Protestants, the scripture came from the martyrs, not the martyrologists.

The Bible was, after all, God's word. Its exclusivity as the normative source of Christian truth was the raison d'être for Protestant and Anabaptist Christianity as movements opposed to Roman Catholicism. In our own time, street preachers and televangelists display a remarkable ability to memorize and recall scripture. It makes perfect sense that people willing to die for biblically based views would have known the Bible extremely well. It also makes sense that given the opportunity, they would sometimes have written at length, considering that this activity could help them sustain their ordeals.

Other evidence, too, is consistent with the martyrs' writings and helps situate them in concrete milieux of origin and reception. Most medieval martyr-saints' lives were crafted centuries after the events they allegedly portray. By contrast, early modern martyrs were often memorialized shortly after their deaths, following prosecution as heretics or religious traitors. The surviving legal records of their interrogations and trials corroborate several aspects of the martyrological sources.[78] That martyrs were repeatedly coaxed to abjure but resisted, for example, suggests a commitment wholly in keeping with what they wrote. Martyrs' public behavior is likewise consonant with the content of their writings. People who sang psalms, quoted the Bible, proclaimed their willingness to die, and endured burning or disemboweling were likely to have internalized scriptural passages and, if they were literate and given the chance, to have expressed intense religious sensibilities in letters, songs, and confessions of faith.

Martyrs often sent their writings through porous prison walls to family members and friends from their communities of faith. Just as fellow believers attended executions to record dying words and gestures for posterity, the recipients of martyrs' writings kept and frequently copied them as profoundly precious documents. Desire alone did not insure preservation, however, as the son of the Dutch Mennonite Adriaen Willems explained:

> As for the accounts of the discussions with the papists and monks, as well as his confession of faith and other letters that were written in prison and that we received—they lay, or rather I stuck them with the others, behind the cupboard underneath the roof because of the great uneasiness due to the persecution and the great tyranny that was active at the time. Thus it happened that the water from the *Diefdijk* came so deep or strong in February of 1571 that many houses were carried away and some walls knocked down and the letters got into the water and were lost. This made me very sad, because our children should have been able to have seen or read about how pious and well-disposed [*vroom en welgemoed*] their grandfather was to profess the Gospel and to die for it, and how joyful he was when people visited him in prison, for I myself was there even though the danger was great.[79]

A flood had foiled the son's plans to save his father's prison writings as a family heirloom. Having seen Adriaen in prison, he thought his father's correspondence would have revealed to the grandchildren his disposition before death, even though his experiences were long gone. The son knew that the letters conveyed something vital about Adriaen's beliefs and behavior. The present excursus on the nature of the martyrological sources has given us reason to agree. Their value for probing the religiosity of the martyrs is far greater than many scholars have claimed or assumed.

This does not, of course, imply that we should relinquish our critical guard. Every account remains subject to scrutiny, and it would be rash to speculate beyond them. We should not, for example, assume particulars about the beliefs of Protestant or Anabaptist martyrs whom we know as little more than names. Similarly, the specific sensibilities of many individual martyrs remain unrecoverable. The present discussion serves the restricted purpose of assessing the reliability of martyrs' writings and depictions of their public behavior in the martyrological sources. It is not a defense of the sources' trustworthiness in toto. Yet the sources are not inherently untrustworthy because they were fashioned by ideologically committed authors about people who allegedly did extraordinary things. Given even the limited evidence marshaled here, to assume an intrinsic unreliability would suggest that the historian's properly critical attitude has metastasized into an ideological bias of its own.

Based on the evidence, I have assumed that particular accounts of public executions may be accepted as substantially accurate, and the texts of martyrs' writings received as fundamentally sound, unless there are reasons to think otherwise in individual cases. This still leaves us less than fully confident about individual accounts that cannot be corroborated. We simply might lack evidence that casts doubt on certain writings that were nevertheless, for some reason, substantially invented or based on misinformation or rumor. Accordingly, all of my main arguments rest on multiple examples, themselves chosen from a much broader base of research. In the unlikely event that even a fair number of the specific accounts and writings turned out to be untrustworthy, the remaining evidence would still sustain a deep, detailed understanding of the martyrs and their milieux—because the present discussion has shown that we cannot dispute the reliability of the martyrological sources as a whole. For those who seek to understand martyrdom, the road to reconstruction is open.

The Course of Exposition

To travel this road, we can and indeed must reject reductionist theories, but we cannot dispense with organization, a necessity for intellectual coherence and therefore for doing history at all. Without certain formal, conceptual prerequisites, religious martyrdom cannot be significant in any age or culture. First, the notion of martyrdom must exist and be available to contemporaries. Second, there must be people willing to punish the heterodox with death.

Third, there must be people willing to die for their religious convictions. Finally, there must be survivors who view those executed for their religious convictions as martyrs. These conceptual requirements structure this study. Without them martyrdom either does not exist, does not occur, or is not understood as such. Approaching martyrdom in this minimalist manner permits us to meet the martyrs and their contemporaries on their own terms. Together with the evidence, this framework encompasses multiple perspectives (authorities willing to kill, martyrs willing to die, and contemporaries as interpreters) as well as multiple traditions (Protestant, Anabaptist, and Roman Catholic) across England, France, the Low Countries, and German-speaking lands.

There are no martyrs without the notion of martyrdom. By the late Middle Ages, opportunities for Catholic martyrdom had virtually vanished in Western Europe. Nevertheless, I argue in Chapter 2 that late medieval Christianity was permeated with attitudes and actions closely related to it. Monks had transmuted martyrdom into ascetic practices, which in the fourteenth and fifteenth centuries were embraced by committed laity as well. The ubiquity of the saints, many of whom were ancient martyr-saints, insured an abiding awareness of martyrdom in the decades prior to the Reformation. The *ars moriendi* (art of dying) focused attention on the moment of death, instructed Christians how to die properly, and shaped expectations about what a good death looked like. Meanwhile devotion to Christ's passion flourished, encouraging affective identification with a uniquely important martyrdom. Finally, the execution of unrepentant Lollards, Hussites, and Waldensians prefigured the explosion of martyrdom in the sixteenth century.

There are no martyrs without someone willing to kill people for religious heterodoxy. In Chapter 3 I examine common arguments about Christian rulers' responsibility to uphold orthodoxy, as well as the contingencies affecting the enactment of legislation against religious nonconformity. With few exceptions Catholic and Protestant religious and political authorities sought not to slaughter the deviant, but to correct them. Even when laws prescribed a mandatory death penalty, civil authorities and inquisitors were often willing to spare those who recanted their errors. A last resort for those who repeatedly refused, execution marked a defeat rather than a triumph for the regime in question. Seeing heresy as a grave danger to souls, paternalistic authorities used executions for "damage control," a public health initiative in the spiritual domain, lest heretics endanger others by spreading their views. Personal initiative and concrete circumstances affected the ways in which these convictions were carried out.

There are no martyrs if people are unwilling to die for their religious convictions. In Chapter 4 I endeavor to reconstruct the martyrs' religiosity.

Martyrs were willing to die because they believed with a singular intensity the biblical admonitions about the blessedness of those who suffer for Christ's sake. Such people would receive eternal life in heaven, whereas those who abjured risked eternal damnation. The form and content of this aspect of Christianity were shared by Roman Catholics, Protestants, and Anabaptists alike. In all three traditions martyrs were encouraged to persevere unto death via personal contact and correspondence with fellow believers. They all understood themselves to be participants in a historical community of the unjustly persecuted, rooted in scripture and exemplified in their savior's crucifixion. And they all practiced their beliefs and reinforced them in prison through prayer, writing, and reflection on biblical promises.

Martyrdom can become culturally significant only if some people understand the executions of religious dissidents as martyrdoms. In Chapters 5 through 7 I examine in detail the ways in which fellow believers interpreted, memorialized, and publicized Protestant, Anabaptist, and Catholic martyrs. One chapter is devoted to each tradition; each traces chronological developments and compares the traditions' similarities and differences. Here, attention shifts from the martyrs themselves to the martyrologists and to wider communities of belief. In these three chapters I examine the interaction between martyrology and common religious sensibilities against a backdrop of broader developments during the sixteenth and seventeenth centuries, drawing on a wide range of sources. Close attention is paid to the ways in which news and views about martyrs were disseminated—orally, visually, by letters, songs, and the printed word. It becomes clear that martyrologists shared the same basic commitments, values, and interpretive frameworks as the martyrs whom they celebrated.

In Chapter 8 I analyze the period's persistent controversy about true and false martyrs, which began in the 1520s. In all three traditions, being a genuine martyr meant dying for true doctrines. Yet because dispute over God's truth already separated Christian groups from each other, each recognized only its own martyrs as authentic. As far as controversialists were concerned, to perish for wayward teachings necessarily made one a false martyr, no matter how horrifically one suffered or how heroically one died. Publicly observable behavior could be interpreted negatively ("obstinacy," "stubbornness") and ascribed to Satan's power, or positively ("steadfastness," "constancy") and attributed to God's grace. This standoff could not be resolved given the interpretive categories shared across confessional divides. Only doctrinal agreement could have ended this conflict of interpretations, but compromise would have dishonored the martyrs' memory and diluted the value of the rival doctrines for which they had died.

This study embodies an approach to early modern Christianity that is comparative and cross-confessional in essence, with religious controversy at its heart. We should constantly be aware of the rejection that greeted every assertion, and the ramifications of this dissonance. Otherwise we risk minimizing what is perhaps Christianity's central feature in the period: disagreement itself, with its enormous significance for the subsequent development of Western thought, society, and political institutions. The discord reconstructed here should resonate today in a world riven with divisions that rupture its ideals of "diversity."

CHAPTER TWO

The Late Medieval Inheritance

> Do not fear those who kill the body but cannot kill the soul; rather fear him who can destroy both body and soul in hell . . . Everyone therefore who acknowledges me before others, I also will acknowledge before my Father in heaven; but whoever denies me before others, I also will deny before my Father in heaven.
>
> —MATTHEW 10:28, 32–33

> Now you have the argument of that great saint from the word of Christ: "Do not fear those who kill the body"; that everyone, whether priest or layman, who knows the truth, ought to defend it to death; otherwise he is a traitor of the truth and thus of Christ as well.
>
> —JOHN HUS, LETTER TO THE PEOPLE OF PILSEN, CA. OCTOBER 1411

In the early fifteenth century Margery Kempe fantasized about being a martyr for Christ: "She imagined in herself what death she might die for Christ's sake. [She] thought she would a be slain for God's love, but dread for the point of death, and therefore she imagined herself the most soft death, as [she] thought, for dread of impatience, that was to be bound, her head and her feet to a stock, and her head to be smet [struck] off with a sharp axe for God's love."[1] More than fear inhibited her prospects. Traversing England during a period of anti-Wycliffite sentiment, this devout pilgrim was herself more than once suspected of Lollardy. Kempe wanted to die for Christ within his Church, however, not to burn for heresy. This presented a problem: where was she to turn in a Christian society to become a Christian martyr?[2]

At first sight the contrast between Christian martyrdom in the late Middle Ages and in the sixteenth century appears stark, a simple opposition of absence to presence. Between the fourth and the eleventh centuries, the Church transformed Western European society (except for Jewish and Islamic minorities) into a community of the baptized as it appropriated, transmuted, or destroyed cultural practices in accordance with its aims. As non-Christian enemies disappeared so did opportunities for Christian martyrdom. Dying for the faith became a frontier phenomenon in the West, a real possibility only for Crusaders or, from the thirteenth century, for mendicant missionaries in the Middle East, Asia, or northern Africa. Between 1254 and 1481, popes canonized not a single person who had died a violent death.[3] By the fourteenth century, as Richard Kieckhefer has said, "the quest for martyrdom was essentially a pious dream."[4] Margery Kempe dreamed it nonetheless.

Yet just as the Reformation did not emerge ex nihilo with Luther, the sixteenth-century renaissance of Christian martyrdom did not come from nowhere. Ordinarily it was indeed a "pious dream" to die for Christian orthodoxy in Western Europe, when institutions were interwoven with Christian beliefs and committed to defending the Church against its enemies. The few medieval martyrs who were canonized in the twelfth and thirteenth centuries—such as Thomas Becket (d. 1170) and Peter Martyr (d. 1252)—reveal the special circumstances required to die for Roman Catholicism. The struggle between ecclesiastical and monarchical powers that peaked between the late twelfth and the early fourteenth centuries produced a number of martyr-bishops like Becket.[5] Active opposition to the Cathars yielded a martyr-inquisitor in the second-generation Dominican Peter Martyr. Despite the slim opportunities and the papal reluctance to canonize those who endured violent deaths, however, martyrs and values linked to martyrdom were deeply embedded in Christianity in the decades prior to the Reformation.

The Absence and Presence of Martyrs in the Late Middle Ages

On the feast of the translation of St. Martin's relics, July 4, 1458, Janneken Pinnocx, a twenty-one-year-old nun from St. Elizabeth's cloister in Brussels, finished copying a manuscript of the life, death, and miracles of St. Barbara.[6] Such a confluence of saints—Martin's day, Elizabeth's cloister, a text about Barbara, plus Janneken's own name, a variation on St. Anne—is wholly typical of Western Europe in the fifteenth century.

The saints were everywhere. Time was reckoned in their honor: the days bore their names, memorializing their deaths or the translations of their relics in an annual liturgical cycle rooted in "the calendar of heaven" itself, "which with the turning about showeth the days of the saints what time they shall solemnize their feasts."[7] Places—not only churches and monasteries, but also often streets and towns themselves—were designated after holy men and women, such as Ghent's Sint Margrietstraat and Sint Veerleplein. Parents named their infants after the saints, co-opting for them important, lifelong patrons and guardians. Just like great cathedrals, humble parish churches were packed with painted and carved saints' images, male and female. Their woodcut likenesses graced collections of saints' vitae and were stamped on single-sheet depictions so popular in Germany, such as Hans Schäufelein's rendering of Saints Roche and Sebastian (Figure 1), or the anonymous metal-cut of St. Barbara from Cologne (Figure 2). Hundreds of such images were churned out in the fifteenth century, sometimes accompanied by prayers to be said to the saint(s) represented.

Figure 1. Hans Schäufelein, *Saints Roche and Sebastian,* woodcut, 1510. Reproduced with permission from Max Geisberg, *The German Single-Leaf Woodcut: 1500–1550* (New York: Hacker, 1974).

Figure 2. *St. Barbara,* anonymous metalcut, Cologne, 1480 or later. Rosenwald Collection, photograph © Board of Trustees, National Gallery of Art, Washington.

Many of these saints, such as St. Barbara, were also (or were believed to have been) martyrs. Real or legendary, most of them predated Constantine's conversion to Christianity in the early fourth century. More than a millennium later their holy deaths were important not as models for imitation, but as the wellspring of their particular favor with God. Near the end of her carefully copied book, Janneken Pinnocx addressed a short prayer in verse to St. Barbara:

> O Barbara, virgin of youthful age
> who earned the wearing of the crown
> above all ordinary maidens,
> help us on the last day
> that we might please God
> with confession and with pure hearts
> and bring our souls to the heavenly fields.[8]

Although she narrated Barbara's martyrdom and repeatedly referred to her as a *martelares* (female martyr) in her book, and although she may well have identified with the young virgin martyr, Pinnocx's relationship with her was fundamentally that of supplicant to intercessor. It was primarily this tie that bound late medieval Christians to the saints in general. Martyr-saints were important less because of their heroic deaths per se than because martyrdom was the source of sanctity that made them God's powerful friends. They in turn could do favors for their friends—the laity and clergy devoted to them.

The martyr-saints' extreme suffering for love of Christ made them compassionate toward the hardships of ordinary Christians. They were eager to help their devotees, with whom they shared a common humanity. As the early fifteenth-century English priest John Mirk put it in his sermon for the Feast of All Saints: "The holy saints the which been in heaven were sometime as we be now, both in flesh, blood, body, and bone and were our elder fathers, and they be full glad and make much joy when that they may get any prayers or almsdeeds of us, with the which they may present our savior and our blessed lady praying for us."[9] Hearers of such sermons did not need martyrs as models of literal self-sacrifice. Imitating their deaths lacked relevance in the absence of active enemies of the Christian faith. But in a world burdened with bodily and spiritual afflictions, Christians direly needed the powers that God had granted his heavenly friends. Thus Mirk hoped his sermons for the principal feast days would inspire people to "come unto the church to serve God and pray his holy saints of their help."[10]

Preindustrial Europe was a world in pain, a world filled with bodily suffering: high infant mortality, waves of plague and other infectious diseases from the mid-fourteenth century on, little remedy for physical discomfort, death in childbirth. Unexpected death loomed as a pressing spiritual concern, since it precluded final confession of sins and a last chance to receive the Eucharist, thus sharpening anxiety about one's ultimate destiny. Death could strike without warning in many ways: "How many have been deceived thinking to live long and suddenly have deceased. How oftimes hast thou heard of those that be departed: how some have been slain with sword; some drowned; some falling from high place have broken their neck; some eating have been strangled; some with fire; some with iron; some with thieves have been destroyed and so the end of every man in this world is death; and the life of man in this world as a shadow vanish away."[11] The *danse macabre* likewise reminded late medieval Christians of the certainty of death, regardless of their social status.[12] Mercifully, God loved human beings so much that he had assumed human flesh, shared their tribulations, and suffered death on a cross. Having befriended the saints, he would insure their attentiveness to the full range of human needs, specific problems as well as broad aspirations.

The intercessory role of martyr-saints is clear in the cult of the "Fourteen Holy Helpers" or "Auxiliary Saints," the *Nothelfer*, which flourished on the Continent in the fifteenth century and throughout the early modern period, particularly in Germanic lands (Figure 3).[13] With the exception of St. Giles, all fourteen of these saints were martyrs. Their importance, however, lay in the problem-specific aptitudes for which they were invoked: St. Blaise, for example, fought diseases of the throat, St. Barbara protected against sudden death and fire, St. Erasmus assisted people with intestinal problems, while St. Margaret watched over women in childbirth. Christians were to pray to specific saints for help as needed. Many entries in the English vernacular version of the *Golden Legend* conclude with exhortations to pray to the saints, some aimed at particular or general problems, others simply for help in reaching heaven.[14] Similar prayers in vernacular verse, addressed to particular saints, were legion in both manuscript and printed prayer books in fifteenth- and early sixteenth-century France.[15] "O martyr, Saint Sebastian," one begins,

> I am your lowly servant
> may you not forget me
> but I pray you with all my heart
> that you might pray to God for me
> that I can be untied
> from the wicked bond of sadness
> and at the end cry gratitude
> to God my father [and] creator.[16]

Even when St. Sebastian was depicted bristling with the arrows that made him the obvious patron saint for civic archers across Europe, he remained a media-

Figure 3. *The Fourteen Auxiliary Saints (Nothelfer),* anonymous woodcut, Swabian, ca. 1500. From left to right, top to bottom, the fourteen are Acacius, Blaise, (Christ), Christopher, Denis; Giles, Erasmus, Eustace, George, Cyriac; Pantaleon, Vitus [Guy], Barbara, Catherine, and Margaret. Rosenwald Collection, photograph © Board of Trustees, National Gallery of Art, Washington.

tor rather than a model to be imitated. A prayer accompanying Thomas Anshelm's German woodcut from 1501 (Figure 4) linked the valiant martyr's death to his specific, protective action. Because St. Sebastian had endured "such horrible, unsettling pain and martyrdom," he had become a conduit for God's grace and had "protected and delivered many people on earth from the horrible, fearsome disease of the plague."

Martyrdom flowed into a wider sea of sanctity. Hence martyrs were seamlessly integrated into one of the core components of Books of Hours, the litany of saints. "Book of Hours" often evokes images of museum-piece manuscripts with exquisite miniatures and illuminations commissioned by the royalty and nobility that could afford to pay for their production. More important historically was the flood of inexpensive editions published from the 1470s. These prayer books were printed in greater numbers than any other work in the half century prior to the Reformation, just as they had been among the first manuscript books to be produced in quantity.[17]

The litanies of the saints in these Books of Hours presented the male martyrs after the apostles and before the confessors of the faith, each category of saint reflecting its place in the heavenly hierarchy. After the confessors came monks and hermits, followed by female saints of all sorts, including martyrs. Thus female martyrs (usually early Christian, virgin martyrs) were not singled out within the hierarchy of saints as were male martyrs, who received an independent enumeration.[18] Each of the saints was evoked in minimalist fashion in the Latin litany, his or her name followed by the phrase "ora pro nobis." To "pray for us" was the essence of the saint's activity, whether apostle, martyr, confessor, or virgin—this was what laity and clergy sought from their protectors. It was why Erhard Schoen could join the image of the *Anna Selbdritt* (the combination of St. Anne, the Virgin, and the infant Jesus), so popular in the Rhineland, in an early sixteenth-century prayer sheet with frames depicting the third-century martyr St. Sebastian and the fourteenth-century pilgrim St. Roche, the latter two being antiplague specialists (Figure 5).[19] This devotional aid was neither age- nor gender-specific: at the left a man and boy kneel in prayer, mirrored at the right by a woman and girl. Another prayer invoked a similar amalgam of heavenly advocates: "O Virgin glorious hope, certain refuge of sinners, and you my good angel, and you blessed Saint Peter and the glorious ten thousand martyrs of great merit that suffered such martyrdom as Jesu Christ wherefore ye be glorious in paradise, be then unto me help, be ye there for to comfort me."[20]

French vernacular litanies of the saints often rendered supplications more expressively, in verse. A litany extant in four fifteenth-century manuscripts from eastern France devoted one verse to each saint invoked, including the first Christian martyr, St. Stephen, whose death is recounted in Acts 7:54–60:

Figure 4. Thomas Anshelm, *Martyrdom of St. Sebastian*, woodcut, 1501. Reproduced with permission from Max Geisberg, *The German Single-Leaf Woodcut: 1500–1550* (New York: Hacker, 1974).

Saint Stephen, most true friend
who prayed for your enemies
when they stoned you long ago,
pray to God that he will grant me paradise.

The same prayer petitioned the female virgin martyr St. Margaret for the aid she offered women, but without mentioning her martyrdom:

Most holy virgin Margaret
who by your merit are able
to help women in time of need,
pray to God that he will have pity on me.[21]

A compressed litany in French verse from a printed book of prayers to Christ, Mary, and the saints recalled the succinctness of the Latin *(Omnes sancti martyres Dei, orate pro nobis)* in its supplication to the martyrs. Yet it combined the appeal with remembrance of their violent deaths:

All martyrs in general
who have in many ways
endured pains and torment,
render prayers for us to God.[22]

Figure 5. Erhard Schoen, prayer sheet with *Anna Selbdritt,* St. Sebastian, and St. Roche, woodcut, ca. 1515. Reproduced with permission from Max Geisberg, *The German Single-Leaf Woodcut: 1500–1550* (New York: Hacker, 1974).

As the martyrs assumed their intercessory role with the other saints in heaven, their brutal deaths were not forgotten, but they had receded.

A martyr's "martyrhood" was therefore less important than his or her sainthood. Martyrs could simply be called "saints" and invoked as such without diminishing their stature or influence with God. This is clear from the appellations of martyr-saints in manuscripts and early printed editions of the *Golden Legend*. The Dominican Jacques de Voragine (ca. 1230–1298) had written the *Golden Legend* in Latin in the 1260s. It was subsequently expanded and translated into numerous Western vernaculars, becoming one of the most widely read works of the late Middle Ages.[23] Although the *Golden Legend* frequently recounts the grisly tortures purportedly endured by the early martyrs, medieval editors and copyists did not consistently refer to them as martyrs in their rubrics and indexes. They called them "saints" more often than "martyrs," with no discernible pattern in the respective designations.[24] French vernacular prayers to martyr-saints sometimes call them martyrs or allude to their passions, but not always.[25] The same impression emerges if one looks at the designations of a specific martyr-saint, such as St. George, across different manuscripts and printed collections.[26]

These pervasive irregularities imply that the martyrhood of the martyrs was not integral to their saintly status, that they were not automatically identified as martyrs. This suggests an additional dimension to Vauchez's observation that "at the end of the Middle Ages, the identification of sanctity with martyrdom is no more than a memory."[27] Not only were popes reluctant to acknowledge as martyrs those who had died violent deaths for the faith from the mid-thirteenth century on, but ancient martyrs who *were* part of the Church's cult were not always conceived as such. It is also apparent in the depiction of the fourteen *Nothelfer* in Figure 3: only three of the thirteen martyrs in the group (Sts. Cyriac, Pantaleon, and Vitus) display the visual equivalent of the title "martyr," the palm branch (derived from Rev. 7:9) symbolizing their particular status.

Martyrhood and sainthood were separable because praying to martyr-saints did not depend on recalling their martyrdom. Somewhat paradoxically, however, even if their deaths had receded, they were not forgotten. More precisely, perhaps, given the intervening centuries and the unconcern with critical verification of the stories told, many ancient martyrdoms were vividly imagined and elaborated in both image and text. Except for the St. Sebastian woodcut, the images reproduced thus far depict martyr-saints "iconically," the triumphant saints usually standing, posed much as they were sculpted in French churches or painted on English rood screens. Yet "action" or "narrative" depictions of the martyrs were also common in the decades prior to the Reformation. Here martyrs are portrayed just before, during, or immediately after their tortures or deaths. The anonymous Master of the Figdor Deposition painted his *Martyrdom of St. Lucy* (ca. 1500), for example, with the young virgin calmly enduring the executioner's sword being driven through her neck (Figure 6). Fingertips delicately poised in prayer, she seems oblivious to the flames swelling around her feet, an imperviousness to pain common in late medieval depictions of martyrdom. Such images expressed visually the theological view that the martyrs had withstood their torments through a terrestrial foretaste of the beatific vision.[28] The martyrs in the *Golden Legend* bear the most horrific tortures without any indication of pain, indeed sometimes expressing delight.[29] The same seems evident in a Parisian woodcut of the martyrdom of St. Erasmus, who appears comfortable as his intestines are wound on a windlass (Figure 7), and in Hans Baldung Grien's woodcut of the martyrdom of St. Lawrence on his gridiron (Figure 8).[30] Narrative depictions were not limited to the ancient martyrs. In Giovanni Bellini's *Assassination of St. Peter Martyr* (Figure 9), the Dominican suffers a knife plunged into his breast with a resignation that is gesturally reminiscent of St. Francis's stigmatization. Woodcutters parallel the act in the background, their axes slashing at the trees.[31]

What was true of images was true of texts. Even if martyr-saints were not instinctively addressed or regarded as martyrs, graphic stories of their agonies patiently borne "because of the love of God" were prominent in saints' lives: the principal saints in two-thirds of the chapters in the *Golden Legend* are martyrs.[32] Their horrific tortures and dramatic dying moments fascinated late medieval Christians. When St. Felician refused to sacrifice to Roman idols, nails were driven into his feet and hands, while the man overseeing St. Victor's torture "commanded that all the sinews of his body should be all drawn out, and after put him in boiling oil, and after did so hang him by chains and set unto his sides pots brenning."[33] Similar descriptions abound in Richard Whitford's vernacular martyrology published in 1526, which is essentially a hybrid of a legendary (collection of saints' lives) and the more strictly liturgical and monastic martyrologies of the medieval Church.[34] St. Apollonia's persecutors, for example, "first knocked out her teeth, and after because she would not worship their idols, she was burned," the first part of which torment was also shown in a small woodcut from Basel or Upper Germany from the mid-fifteenth century (Figure 10).[35] The vernacular collection of vitae known as *The South English Legendary,* which originated in southwestern England in the late thirteenth century, contains depictions even more graphic than the *Golden Legend*. They abound, too, in the *Legends of Holy Women,* written by the Augustinian Osbern Bokenham in the 1440s.[36]

Although their reception by readers, listeners, and beholders undoubtedly varied, it seems clear that such accounts were primarily intended not to titil-

Figure 6. Master of the Figdor Deposition, *Martyrdom of St. Lucy,* ca. 1500. Reproduced with permission of the Rijksmuseum, Amsterdam.

Figure 7. *The Martrdom of St. Erasmus,* anonymous woodcut, Paris, 1480–1490. Rosenwald Collection, photograph © Board of Trustees, National Gallery of Art, Washington.

Figure 8. Hans Baldung Grien, *Martyrdom of St. Lawerence,* woodcut, ca. 1505. Reproduced with permission from Max Geisberg, *The German Single-Leaf Woodcut: 1500–1550* (New York: Hacker, 1974).

late people with details of torture and dismemberment, but to indicate God's power at work in the martyrs—with whom, as Jesus had said to his followers, "all things are possible" (Matt. 19:26). Divine favor had enabled them to endure unspeakable torments, then extended beyond death to heaven and the saints' intercessory powers. Graphic gore served to inspire greater admiration and thus love for martyr-saints. John Mirk related what St. Stephen had "suffered for Christ's sake" in order "to stir [listeners'] devotion the more to this holy martyr."[37]

Martyr-saints' relationship to their martyrdom was thus somewhat Janus-faced. Their intercessory powers depended not on their being martyrs per se, but rather saints, along with apostles, confessors, hermits, and virgins. At the same time, their astounding heroism and holy death, itself the reason why God had made them intercessors, assured that their martyrdom was not forgotten. This contrast between present role and past origin underpinned supplications to martyr-saints and their "iconic" images on the one hand, and the vivid descriptions and narrative representations of their deaths on the other. The combination is assumed in two series of woodcuts of the apostles by Lucas Cranach the Elder from about 1512: one is a narrative cycle of their martyrdom, the other an iconic series of them as saints. In the respective

Figure 9. Giovanni Bellini, *Assassination of St. Peter Martyr,* ca. 1507. © National Gallery, London.

pictures of St. Bartholomew, for example, the martyr-apostle is being flayed alive on a cross, while in the iconic portrait he stands in triumphant tranquility as a glorified saint, his earthly carcass draped over his arm (Figures 11 and 12). The suffrages in Books of Hours (prayers to saints arranged according to the hierarchy of heaven, as in the litany) include both iconic and action

Figure 10. *St. Apollonia,* anonymous woodcut, Basel or Upper Germany, ca. 1450. Rosenwald Collection, photograph © Board of Trustees, National Gallery of Art, Washington.

representations of martyr-saints as well.[38] Although Christianization had reduced the possibilities for martyrdom, both martyrs and the stories of their deaths continued to occupy an important place within the late medieval cult of the saints.

Their importance probably nurtured the readiness to venerate as martyrs those who had not been formally canonized or celebrated as saints. Late medieval Christians continued a centuries-old tradition of local, popular veneration of holy men and women typical long before popes monopolized canonization.[39] By the later thirteenth century the extremes were the views of the parsimonious papacy, which would canonize no one as a martyr for well over two centuries, and the attitudes behind cases like St. Guinefort, the "holy greyhound" venerated north of Lyons after his master mistakenly killed him.[40] These extremes were related: the papal control of canonization from the mid-thirteenth century sought to steer popular piety toward saints distinguished for their charismatic service, their doctrinal orthodoxy, and often their learning. So reluctant were popes to recognize martyrs that with the exception of Peter Martyr, no Franciscan or Dominican friars killed during their missionary and inquisitorial work were canonized until 1481, when the five Franciscan protomartyrs executed at Marrakesh in 1220 were named saints.[41] Popes suspected that the laity were too willing to consider a "martyr" anyone who died an unjust death—such as Panacea, a young woman killed by her mother-in-law in northern Italy in 1383—whether or not they had perished for their faith. Papal reluctance to canonize more friars was possibly strengthened by the disturbing way in which Spiritual Franciscans and their sympathizers venerated as martyrs those among their number who were burned as heretics.[42]

A bipolar model of "official" or "central" as opposed to "popular" or "local" religion does not do justice to the keen sensitivity to martyrdom in late medieval Christianity. Despite the lack of papal recognition, Dominicans and Franciscans honored as martyrs their brothers who died in the mission field.[43] A dualistic view of medieval society and culture cannot account for the local lay and clerical veneration of the Benedictine Thomas Hales, killed in a French military raid on Dover in 1295, nor bridge the gap between this popular veneration and the fact that his canonization proceedings opened in Rome in 1380.[44] Two tiers are not enough to account for the flourishing cult of Archbishop Richard Scrope of York after his execution in 1405, nor the even greater success of the devout Lancastrian king, Henry VI, whose martyr's cult in England was thriving more than Thomas Becket's in the late fifteenth century.[45] Most fundamentally, these examples and even that of St. Guinefort reveal how deeply martyrs and martyrdom stamped religious awareness, from the humblest laypeople through parish priests and friars to

Figure 11. Lucas Cranach the Elder, *Martyrdom of St. Bartholomew,* woodcut, ca. 1512. Reproduced with permission from Max Geisberg, *The German Single-Leaf Woodcut: 1500–1550* (New York: Hacker, 1974).

Figure 12. Lucas Cranach the Elder, *St. Bartholomew,* woodcut, 1512. Reproduced with permission from Max Geisberg, *The German Single-Leaf Woodcut: 1500–1550* (New York: Hacker, 1974).

influential clergymen. People continued to look for martyrs. The success of Christianization had not diminished the power of martyrdom.

Meanwhile, would-be saints like Margery Kempe still dreamed about the real thing, about dying for love of Christ at the hands of enemies of the Christian faith. Other late medieval men and women fantasized about martyrdom, like John of Alverna, who on the vigil of St. Lawrence's feast day had visions of the martyr bearing the gridiron on which he had suffered. St. Lawrence did not ask John to imitate him directly, but rather to sublimate martyrdom into the tranquil acceptance of adversity: "No torment should be too grave for a Christian. If you wish for glory and sweetness, bear the harshness of this world patiently."[46] Similarly, after her musings Kempe was told by Christ that what mattered was not actual martyrdom, but the equally meritorious desire for it.[47] It must have been consoling for the Lord to esteem one's willingness to die when circumstances had all but eliminated chances to fulfill the desire.

Suffering Patiently, Dying Well, and the Passion of Christ

John of Alverna and Margery Kempe were participating in a sublimation of martyrdom that stretched back a millennium. As the model of Christian perfection shifted to monasticism in the centuries after Constantine's conversion, martyrdom was transformed rather than abandoned.[48] Prior to this, Western church leaders such as Cyprian had already broached the subject of Christian suffering in the absence of active persecution.[49] In the later fourth and early fifth centuries Jerome and Augustine had written of "spiritual" or "white" martyrdom, which linked Christian self-renunciation, endurance of suffering, and ascetic practices to the martyrs' deaths. Gregory the Great reinforced spiritual martyrdom in the late sixth century and passed on views like these: "Even though we do not bend our bodily neck to the sword, nevertheless with the spiritual sword we slay in our soul carnal desires," and "if, with the help of the Lord, we strive to observe the virtue of patience, even though we live in the peace of the Church, nevertheless we bear the palm of martyrdom."[50] Such notions would thrive within Christian spirituality for over a thousand years.[51]

From one perspective martyrdom was the limiting case of the patient endurance of suffering. Its essence might be seen less as death for Christ—which, depending on circumstances, might not be possible—than as willing perseverance in whatever adversities one faced. In this light, martyrdom was simply the most radical display of the virtue of patience open to all Christians. In the early fifteenth century, when Christ assured Margery Kempe about her meritorious desire for martyrdom, John Mirk explained in his sermon for

St. Stephen's feast day that one could "be a martyr though he shed not his blood: that is when he suffereth great wrong of cursed people and thank God thereof, and took it with a good will and prayed for his enemies devoutly in clean charity."[52] With twenty-three printed editions from 1483 to 1532, Mirk's collection was popular right into the period of early English Protestantism.[53] Likewise, the thirteenth-century *Golden Legend* saw over two hundred printed editions across Europe in the half-century before the Reformation. In its entry for All Saints we immediately find, with reference to Gregory the Great, a threefold description of spiritual martyrdom as patience in adversity, compassion toward the needy, and endurance of injustice combined with love of one's enemy. A person who enacts these virtues is a martyr "without iron," "he beareth the cross in his thought," he "is a martyr secretly in his mind."[54]

The Christian virtue of patient suffering was central to the *devotio moderna*, the movement that blossomed in the Low Countries and the Rhineland in the late fourteenth and fifteenth centuries. Near the end of his life the movement's founder, Geert Grote (1340–1384), wrote a consolatory letter to an unknown monk, into whose monastery Grote had failed to block the entrance of an unworthy man. Grote turned to scripture for relevant passages that "might offer some solace," just as sixteenth-century Christians would comfort imprisoned fellow believers. "Is not trouble a sign from the Lord of his love and keeping, because those whom he loves he chastises and those whom he receives he punishes (cf Heb 12:6)? 'Blessed is the man, it was said to Job, who is corrected by the Lord. Do not despise his discipline, because he wounds and will bind up, he strikes and his hands will heal' (Jb 5:17–18)."[55] Dirk of Herxen (1381–1457), probably the most important figure in the movement's second generation, held the same views. Rector of the community in Zwolle from 1410 to 1457, he urged Christians to trust in God amid difficulties: "In time of evil and misfortune, give thanks to God, saying: 'May it so please you, Lord God,' or 'My sins require this, Lord God,' or 'This is necessary for my salvation,' or 'Dear Lord God, give me patience to discern what I should be doing,' or 'Beloved, give me three loaves of bread, that I might understand, might love, and might always do your will,' or 'Teach me goodness and discipline and learning,' or 'Teach me to do your will because you are my God.'"[56] A deep penetration of the virtue fostered subtle variations suited to different persons and occasions.

The same spiritual mastery permeates the *Imitation of Christ*, the most influential text associated with the *devotio moderna*. Likely written by Thomas à Kempis (ca. 1379–1471), it survives in more than 800 manuscripts and was printed in more than 120 editions in seven languages between 1470 and 1520.[57] The *Imitation* extolled the patient perseverance of affliction as a paradigm established by Christ himself. The martyrs had followed the Lord in bearing the cross, and all Christians were obliged to do likewise:

> How shouldest thou sinful creature think that thou shouldest go to heaven by any other way than by the plain, right and high king's way, that is to say the way of the cross . . . Now since the leader of life with all his martyrs have passed by the way of tribulation and the cross, who so ever intend to come to heaven without the way of tribulation and the cross they err from the right way, for all the way of this mortal life is full of miseries and crosses of tribulation.[58]

As so often, the truth was counterintuitive: to shirk adversity was a mistake. As disciples followed their master, Christians emulated their savior's passion: the more the soul sustained pain and affliction "for his love, the more acceptable it shall be in his sight," for "by adversity thou art made conformable unto Christ and all his saints."[59] This view, fundamental to late medieval Christian devotion, was grounded in the Gospels: "Blessed are you when people revile you and persecute you and utter all kinds of evil against you falsely on my account" (Matt. 5:11). Or again: "If any want to become my followers, let them deny themselves and take up their cross and follow me" (Matt. 10:24). To deny the value of patient suffering was to contradict the Lord. Christians demonstrated discipleship by bearing the affliction that made them spiritual martyrs.

In the *Imitation* Thomas à Kempis addressed preparation for death, another central aspect of late medieval spirituality. After the Council of Constance (1414–1417), the two texts collectively known as the *Ars moriendi* instructed Christians in the "art of dying." Extensively disseminated, they are extant in more than three hundred manuscripts, were printed at least seventy times between 1470 and 1500, and survive in greater numbers than any other fifteenth-century xylographic book.[60] The *Ars* was widely adapted and expanded: single-sheet broadsides of the dying man tempted by five demons and consoled by five angels, for example, were popular in late-fifteenth-century German-speaking lands.[61] Many less-than-literate laity were almost certainly acquainted with the themes and images of the *Ars moriendi,* which "circulated throughout the western world, constituting an exceptionally stable group of commonly held notions centering on the death agony."[62]

These notions included the idea that one ought to prepare for death before it arrived. Christian views about the afterlife eased the prospect of dying: hopes of heavenly reward helped tame death's terror and undo its seeming finality. Properly understood, bodily death was simply the "discharging of a right grievous burden" and the "end of all maladies and sicknesses" because it was "entry into joy and glory." To die well was to die gladly, properly disposed, so that when death arrived one would "receive it without any contradiction but also joyously, as he should abide the coming of his good friend."[63] Thomas à Kempis gave the same advice in his *Imitation of Christ*. Those persons were blessed

> that continually have the hour of death before their sight, and that every day dispose themselves to die. Reduce to thy remembrance some person that thou hast seen depart and think that likewise thou must needs depart. When thou risest in the morning doubt whether thou shalt continue in bodily health unto night. And therefore ever dispose thyself to be ready that death never may find thee unready [nor] a sleeper . . . How gracious and happy is that soul that now in his life laboreth to be in that state that it desireth to be found in his death.[64]

This advice was self-conscious, pragmatic, and starkly unromantic. Death was a sure thing. Its undeniable certainty plus life's manifest uncertainty unmasked the unprepared as foolish, negligent, or both.

The *Ars moriendi* depicted the hour of death as a singularly dangerous ordeal. The devil would try his utmost to drag the dying Christian down to damnation. The second section of the longer (CP) *Ars* text warned of Satan's deathbed temptations, which also comprised most of the shorter (QS) text and its woodcuts.[65] The five temptations were falling into error or heresy against faith, despairing of hope in God, becoming impatient with affliction, being spiritually complacent out of pride, and growing preoccupied with worldly things, including one's family.[66] One's precarious final hours were pitched between God and the devil on the edge of eternity. Failure to navigate temptation could mean the shipwreck of the soul, a sinking to the hideous, congested floor of a Hieronymus Bosch hellscape.

Naturally, one would yearn to bemoan one's pain and plight. Complaint, however, implied a deficient love of God that ultimately challenged his providence: "For we suffer by good right all the evils that come to us, and yet be not the passions of this world condign nor worthy to the glory to come . . . For like as the soul is possessed in patience, and by murmur the soul is lost and damned."[67] The discomfort of dying demanded steadfast equanimity, the *Ars moriendi* applying to the deathbed the broader virtue of patience. The martyrs, paragons of patient suffering, mingled with family and friends as accessible partners in perseverance. There stood Stephen cradling his rocks, Catherine with her wheel, Barbara holding her tower, and Lawrence displaying his gridiron along with Christ, all helping the expiring Christian (Figure 13). Perseverance would reassure those present that the Christian had died at peace with God, humbly hopeful of eternal salvation via purgatory. Beyond the interpretation of verbal and bodily signs, knowledge about the actual fate

Figure 13. Exhortation to patience from the *Ars moriendi,* woodcut, Paris, 1492. Reproduced with permission from *Ars Moriendi (1492) ou L'art de bien mourir* (Paris: Editions Dervy, 1986).

of the deceased would remain hidden, vouchsafed perhaps to a few in visions or dreams.

The values and practices of the *Ars moriendi* were directly relevant to martyrdom. Whatever the setting, Satan would foment despair of God's grace, seek to pry men and women from their faith, and prompt them to lament their predicament. Would-be martyrs, too, faced temptations to recant—the executions for heterodoxy that accompanied the growing crisis of the 1520s made a public spectacle of the struggle for steadfastness. When crowds gathered to witness the execution of religious criminals, town squares displaced the domestic intimacy of the deathbed. Spectators scrutinized the condemned, looking for behavior to which the *Ars moriendi* had sensitized them for more than a century.

The normative example of patient suffering and perfect death was Christ himself. The central events in human history were his passion, crucifixion, and resurrection, which redeemed humanity and made salvation possible. The Lord and savior was not often called a martyr, perhaps because he so obviously was one, yet the explicit identification was not unknown.[68] His endurance of calumny, pain, and violent death gave late medieval Christians a martyr-savior who, having known and overcome afflictions, could offer comfort: "Because he himself was tested by what he suffered, he is able to help those who are being tested" (Heb. 2:18). Thomas à Kempis wrote that "if there had been any more expedient mean to the health of man, than to suffer pain and tribulation, our Lord Christ would have showed it by words and examples. But he exorted his disciples and all other[s] that would follow him to heaven to take the cross as the most mediate mean to follow him."[69] A world in pain had a guide—and a God—who had been there before.

The primary image in late medieval Christianity depicted a martyr: the crucifix, central to the space of collective worship from the smallest chapel to the grandest cathedral. This was not the triumphant Christ of earlier centuries who seemed to float in timeless glory, but a broken, bleeding man hammered to a wooden cross, thrust before the beholder. Accented, even exaggerated, realism was common in late medieval paintings, sculptures, manuscript illuminations, and woodcuts of the crucifixion.[70] These visual depictions fed the devotion to Christ's passion that was fundamental to late medieval spirituality, successively reshaped by major figures such as Anselm of Canterbury, Bernard of Clairvaux, and Francis of Assisi as it gained momentum from the eleventh century on.[71] By the fourteenth and fifteenth centuries, as Eamon Duffy has said, this "tradition of affective meditation on the passion . . . had become without any rival the central devotional activity of all seriously minded Christians."[72]

Devotion to Christ's passion was elaborated in so many forms that by the fifteenth century, in Huizinga's phrase, "consciousness was entirely permeated and saturated with Christ and the Cross."[73] Throughout Western Europe the events prior to the crucifixion were reenacted in civic passion plays during Holy Week celebrations. Beginning in the late fourteenth century, Christians in Germanic areas symbolically repeated Christ's walk to Calvary by processing to different churches, accompanied by preachers who evoked the Lord's travails and urged the faithful to identify with him.[74] Some towns fixed routes self-consciously modeled on Jerusalem's *via dolorosa,* which were traced by inhabitants each year on Good Friday. The best known was Louvain's, initiated in 1505 by Pieter Sterckx after he returned from a pilgrimage to the Holy Land.[75] The practice might be turned inward as well: the *Devout Meditation upon the Passion,* a contemporary Flemish pamphlet, assured readers that to trace Christ's walk devoutly in their own minds was "as efficacious [*volcomelijc*] as if they were within the city of Jerusalem and there sought out all the holy sites in the flesh."[76] Events from the passion plays were parceled out in discrete segments for prayerful meditation. Beginning principally in the southern Netherlands, linked to a cycle of prayers and indulgences, these narrative depictions were eventually moved inside churches and became standardized as the fourteen stations of the cross.[77]

Scenes from the martyr-savior's sacrificial suffering seemed to be everywhere. They were wedded to the traditional times for daily, monastic prayer in the Hours of the Cross, a standard component of Books of Hours.[78] Paintings and sculptures portrayed them for the liturgy, while woodcuts, such as Hans Schäufelein's rendering of the flagellation (Figure 14) or Christ bearing his cross by a follower of Dürer (Figure 15), catered to individual users. The passion episodes were also prominent in lives of Christ, the most important being the pseudo-Bonaventuran *Meditations on the Life of Christ* composed in the middle third of the fourteenth century, and its expansion in Ludolph of Saxony's *Mirror of the Life of Christ.*[79] The Yorkshire Carthusian Nicholas Love translated the *Meditations* into English at the beginning of the fifteenth century. His adaptation retained the original division according to the days of the week, each day elaborating scenes from Christ's life: the events leading to and culminating in the passion were appropriately placed on Friday.[80]

Related images and corresponding devotions flourished. One of the most widespread was Jesus as the Man of Sorrows, the beaten and crucified Christ displaying his wounds, which abounded in Germanic churches and woodcuts. In a broadsheet image from the Low Countries, a lacerated Christ says, "O man, take heed of my bitter suffering if you want to rejoice at the hour of death" (Figure 16).[81] The instruments of the scourging and crucifixion were honored for their role in the Lord's salvific act. Christ's five wounds (both hands, both feet, and side) were venerated apparently as early as the eleventh

Figure 14. Hans Schäufelein, *Flagellation of Christ,* woodcut. Reproduced with permission from Max Geisberg, *The German Single-Leaf Woodcut: 1500–1550* (New York: Hacker, 1974).

Figure 15. School of Dürer, Christ carrying the cross, from the "Albertina Passion," woodcut, ca. 1500. Reproduced with permission from Max Geisberg, *The German Single-Leaf Woodcut: 1500–1550* (New York: Hacker, 1974).

Figure 16. *Christ as the Man of Sorrows,* anonymous woodcut, Netherlandish, ca. 1500. Rosenwald Collection, photograph © Board of Trustees, National Gallery of Art, Washington.

century, a practice that proliferated after the stigmatization of St. Francis.[82] In late medieval England devotion to the wounds was expressed in prayers, plays, woodcuts, and sermons, while their likenesses were carved on bench ends and tombstones. Masses in their honor were endowed in wills, and King Henry VI insisted that they be represented at every royal meal.[83] Prayers to the wounded Christ were often intensely evocative. One from the Flemish *Devout Meditation* greeted "all the holy, bloody fountains of your deep wounds that you have received for my sake in your holy body, all of which flowed with your dear blood. My Lord, my God, what more could you have suffered for my sins than you have done?"[84] Throughout the period Mary as the anguished *mater dolorosa* provided the model of compassion—literally, co-suffering—for Christ, inviting beholders emotionally to engage with and respond to her son's suffering and death.[85]

On the eve of the Reformation, piety was suffused with the awareness of Christ's suffering and death. In plays, prayers, poems, and pamphlets, in hymns, woodcuts, sculptures, and paintings, in churches, at roadside shrines, and in their homes, Christians saw, heard, read about, and sang of the harsh yet perfect martyr's death, endured to redeem sinful humanity. The devout understood. Words and images reinforced each other and nourished experience, as we can sense by reading John Fisher, the English bishop of Rochester, as we study an anonymous Netherlandish painting of the Man of Sorrows from the early sixteenth century (Figure 17). As he delivered this Good Friday sermon Fisher was likely gesturing to such a painting or to a vivid crucifix, as preachers often did for their congregations:

> behold and view every part of this blessed body, what pain it endured for thy sake? Seest thou not his eyes, how they be filled with blood and bitter tears? Seest thou not his ears, how they be filled with blasphemous rebukes, and opprobrious words? His cheek and neck with buffets, his shoulders with the burden of the cross? Seest thou not his mouth, how in his dryness they would have filled it with eisel [vinegar] and gall? . . . Seest thou not his sides, how they were scourged with sharp whips? Seest thou not his arms, how they were strained by the violence of the ropes? Seest thou not his hands, how they be nailed just unto the cross?[86]

Thomas More, too, pored over Christ's shattered body like some time-traveling cinematographer. Beginning with "the many sore bloody strokes" on "every part of his holy tender body, the scornful crown of sharp thorns beaten down upon his holy head," he moved downward and out to "his lovely limbs drawn and stretched out upon the cross to the intolerable pain of his forebeaten and sorebeaten veins and sinews," eventually reaching "the great long nails cruelly driven with hammers through his holy hands and feet."[87]

Was all this a twisted obsession with death and suffering per se? Not according to late medieval practitioners; for them it signified infinite love that sought love in response. Here is Fisher again: "O most unkind sinner, all this he suffered for thy sake. No greater kindness ever was, or could be showed to thee by any creature, than this which sweet Jesus did show for thee and for thy sake, and where is now thy kindness again?"[88] Parallel to the graphic descriptions of martyrs' torments, the intense corporeality of the crucifixion was not primarily about morbidity, Christ's sexuality, or even his humanity as such. The cross had unmasked the fragile humanity of Jesus, to be sure—but being who he was, *God* had bled and died as well.[89] Paul had called it "a scandal to the Jews and folly to the Greeks" (1 Cor. 1:23), and so it was. For devout late medieval Christians, however, it was a foundational truth that surpassed human comprehension: the creator and sustainer of the universe had willingly embraced human weakness, dreadful pain, and humiliating death to save sinful humanity. In its dumbfounding immensity and sheer daring, this

Figure 17. Style of Dirk Bouts, *Christ as the Man of Sorrows,* early sixteenth century. © National Gallery, London.

love—depicted, grasped, felt—dwarfed everything else, indeed crushed it. The only excess and obsession here lay not in late medieval devotion, *pace* Huizinga and company, but in God's love: all the visual and verbal depictions of the sweat of Gethsemane, the blood of Golgotha, the wounds of Christ's lacerated body and its surges of pain put together could never adequately express the infinite reality they proclaimed. Grünewald's *Isenheim Altarpiece?* It was a pitiful cartoon next to God's redemptive madness. If reflection on all this could not "inflame our key-cold hearts, and set them on fire in his love," then nothing could.[90]

In 1535 Fisher and More readied themselves for execution from the Tower of London, steeped in religious sensibilities they had known for decades.[91] In both men, late medieval devotion to Christ's passion met and meshed with sixteenth-century martyrs' willingness to die. Radically changed circumstances fanned the heat of committed religiosity into the flames of active martyrdom. More's chapter title in his *Dialogue of Comfort* was frank: "The consideration of the painful death of Christ is sufficient to make us content to suffer painful death for his sake."[92] Over a century earlier, Thomas à Kempis had told readers to "desire to suffer death for [Christ's] love" at about the same time that Margery Kempe had imagined her own martyrdom.[93] For Fisher, More, and many others in the sixteenth century, it was no longer merely a dream.

Suffering patiently, dying well, and nurturing a devotion to Christ's passion were tightly interwoven in late medieval piety. Although actual martyrdom remained remote on the eve of the Reformation, it circumscribed all three as a limit. The most dramatic examples of patient suffering were the martyrs whom Christians invoked as intercessors, male and female saints who had themselves imitated Christ's passion. Seeking to die not merely well, but best, the devout yearned to bypass purgatory by shedding their blood for Christ. And the ultimate imitation of Christ would be to emulate the passion of Christ out of reverent love, even though ersatz martyrdom in the form of ascetic practices usually had to suffice. As the 1510s became the 1520s, however, the remoteness of martyrdom ended and its renaissance began.

Christian Martyrs outside the Church in the Late Middle Ages

According to some, by the early sixteenth century a new period of Christian martyrdom was already well under way. In 1401 William Sawtry was burned for Lollardy just before the promulgation of the English statute *De haeretico comburendo*, which provided for the execution of heretics. When William Emayn was questioned for heresy in Bristol in March 1429, he named Sawtry among those who were "holy men . . . worshiped in heaven as holy martyrs."[94] In July 1412 three young men, inspired by the preaching of John Hus (ca. 1370–1415) and Jerome of Prague, were beheaded for agitating against papal indulgences in the churches of the Bohemian capital. Their corpses were borne through Prague's streets to Hus's preaching headquarters, the Bethlehem Chapel, with a placard declaring, "These men are martyrs" [*Ita sunt martyres*]. The next day Hus honored them with a mass for martyrs, not simply an ordinary mass for the dead, then interred their bodies in the chapel.[95] Apparently, German Waldensians had preceded them: in 1409 Jerome of Prague said that heretics had been burned in the same city within living memory.[96]

The Lollards, Hussites, and Waldensians did not produce martyrs in sixteenth-century numbers. Nevertheless, they honored as martyrs their fellow believers executed as heretics. Members of these three groups were at least as sensitized to martyrdom as their contemporaries within the Roman church. As such, they too reveal the martyr-related continuities between late medieval and early modern Christianity.

In 1410–1411 two future martyrs exchanged letters. The Lollard priest Richard Wyche, who would be burned thirty years later, wrote from London to Hus and his followers in Prague. Bohemia's religious climate had proven receptive to the writings of the condemned Oxford theologian John Wyclif (d. 1384). Matthias of Janov (d. 1394) and others had urged reform of abuses and spiritual renewal in Prague for decades prior to Hus's appointment as rector of the city's Bethlehem Chapel in 1402, one year after Jerome of Prague had carried copies of Wyclif's works back from Oxford.[97] Marking Lollard-Hussite interaction despite the distances involved, Wyche wrote in his September 1410 letter that he "rejoiced when my dearest friends came and brought me testimony of your truth, how you also walk in the truth."[98] Although the Antichrist—that is, the Roman church—was afflicting the Hussites, Wyche encouraged them to trust in the Lord's goodness:

> let no tribulation or anguish for Christ cast us down, knowing for certain that whomever the Lord deigns to receive as His sons, He scourges. For the merciful Father wills, that we be tried in this miserable life by persecution or persecutions, so that afterward He may spare us. For the gold which the supreme Artificer has here chosen, He purges and probes by fire, so that afterward He may lay it in His purest treasury. We see, that the time during which we abide here is short and transitory, while the life we hope for is blessed and eternal.[99]

Reflecting the Wycliffite emphasis on the New Testament, Wyche applied 1 Pet. 1:7 and Heb. 12:6 to a Bohemian situation analogous to that faced by the English Lollards. In the sixteenth century as well, such biblical passages would be fundamental to the martyrs and their fellow believers. Wyche concurred with others among the devout that suffering was the high road to salvation—Geert Grote had quoted the same verse, Heb. 12:6, to comfort his Dutch monastic friend.

The Epistle to the Hebrews also provided Wyche with models for the Praguers: "Let us consider the companionship of the fathers who preceded us and the saints of both testaments. Have they not passed through this sea of tribulation and persecution? Have not 'some of them been cut to pieces, others have been stoned, and slain with the sword? Some of them wandered about in sheepskins and goatskins', as the apostle to the Hebrews witnesses" [Heb. 11:37]. Wyche recalled what Christ had suffered at sinners' hands so "that we would not be wearied" and rejoiced "that in our kingdom and elsewhere God has so greatly strengthened the hearts of some people, that they gladly endure imprisonment, exile, and even death for the Word of God."[100] Happily, the English "known men" were not alone in challenging the Roman church. Because persecution signified divine favor, it was cause for celebration, shaping an expectation that true Christians would always provoke opposition from the Antichrist.[101]

Fifteenth-century travel and transport being what they were, Wyche's letter did not reach Prague until six months later. Hus's reaction showed that it struck a common chord: he told a huge congregation about the letter from "our dearest brother Richard, a fellow-worker of Master John Wyclif in the labours of the gospel." They clamored for a translation and Hus obliged. In writing back, Hus fused gratitude with extravagant praise of Wyche's letter: "It contains so much sweetness, efficacy, strengthening, and consolation, that if all other writings were swallowed up by the Antichrist's gullet, it alone would suffice to the Christ's faithful for salvation."[102] The English epistle showed Hus that others outside his immediate circle had seized the marrow of God's word and applied it to real life. Such recognition was a measure of how far this passionate preacher had come from his peasant origins in southwestern Bohemia. After early academic distinction as a careerist cleric in Prague and a profound conversion in the late 1390s, his charismatic sermons captivated crowds and impressed Queen Sophia herself with a blend of reforming exhortation and anti-German, Czech nationalism. Like Wyche, in his correspondence Hus would repeatedly adapt scripture to the tribulations facing himself and his followers, right up to his execution in Constance in the summer of 1415.

Hus's surviving letters superbly illustrate martyrological sensibility in late medieval Christianity. About ninety date from his final five years, and over thirty were written from the Franciscan monastery in Constance within a month of his death. They reflect in detail Hus's convictions and fears as his execution approached. They resonate with emphases on suffering patiently, dying well, and revering Christ's passion, deepened by years of scriptural immersion. Exiled from Prague before journeying to Constance, where eventually he would be betrayed, imprisoned, condemned, and burned as a heretic, Hus dwelt on these themes with mounting urgency.

Hus was ruminating about martyrdom long before Constance or even his exile from Prague. Sensing where the hostility provoked by his reforming efforts might lead, on numerous occasions he expressed his willingness to die for the truth.[103] Stating the same idea as Thomas à Kempis in a different context, he asked an anonymous nobleman in 1410, "Am I greater than Christ and His apostles, that I suffer not for the gospel? Be it far from me! For our Saviour says: 'The servant is not greater than the lord, nor a disciple than his master' [John 15:20, Matt. 10:24]. 'If, then, they call the head of the household Beelzebub, how much more shall they call those of his household?' [Matt. 10:26] 'If they persecuted me, they will also persecute you' [John 15:20]."[104] Already Christ's passion began to intimate actual imitation, suggesting more than ascetic practices or patience in adversity. "If here we suffer something for Christ, there we shall be blessed," he wrote. "For He tests us by the cross and suffering, as gold is tested by fire by the Creator, Who out of nothing created the whole world. Blessed then shall we be if we persevere in the good to the end."[105]

In July 1412 Hus was excommunicated, technically for sending representatives instead of showing up in person to respond to heresy accusations before the curia in Rome. When Prague was threatened with an interdict, he embraced exile, protected by sympathetic nobles in southern Bohemia for more than two years. During this period he replied to detractors with *On the Church,* his best-known theological work, which drew a fundamental distinction between the true church of the predestinate and the visible church militant.[106] Throughout his exile he maintained epistolary contact with his supporters.

Hus seems at first to have been somewhat anxious about accepting exile rather than remaining in Prague and perhaps risking his life. But by the end of 1412 he apparently had grown content to live or die as dictated by events, which he understood as the unfolding of God's will.[107] He regularly quoted biblical passages about the endurance of persecution, urging his followers not to bend. Since Christ was reviled, afflicted, and killed, he wrote, and they were following Christ, they should expect nothing less from "the present-day messengers of Antichrist," experiencing the fulfillment of Paul's prophecy (2 Tim. 3:12) that "all who wish to live a godly life in Christ will suffer persecution."[108] As Hus refracted late medieval spirituality through scripture, the imitation of Christ mingled with devotion to the passion: "He left us his example [1 Pet. 2:21] that we likewise suffer according to His will," he told the Praguers late in 1412. More than once he pushed the imitation of Christ to its logical extreme, mulling over his own martyrdom.[109] The promise of heaven sustained his readiness to die, just as the *Ars moriendi* would prescribe. Indeed, martyrdom epitomized "dying well" as it most nearly conformed to the imitation of Christ: "What shall we lose if for His sake we surrender wealth, friends, honour, the miserable world, and this poor life? Surely we shall be freed from this misery, and will receive wealth [a] hundredfold more splendid, friends far more dear, and joy more perfect. Death will not separate us from these things. For whoever dies for Christ, conquers, escapes all misery and enjoys eternal bliss."[110]

In the autumn of 1414 Hus journeyed to Constance, where an ecumenical council was assembling. The prelates wanted to end the schism that had saddled Western Christianity with competing popes for nearly forty years and to address the religious ferment in Bohemia. They knew that Hus was central to the Bohemian movement, some of whose members, such as Nicholas of Dresden, were clearly heretical according to contemporary Roman orthodoxy. Hus's status was more ambiguous: he repeatedly denied holding any heresy and appropriated Wycliffite ideas selectively. Although certain of his views, such as the Church's being able to continue indefinitely without a pope, might justifiably have been judged heretical, council members twisted many of his theological propositions in order to accuse him of heresy.[111] Hus was therefore pressured to abjure views he had never held, something he had condemned at least as early as 1412, and which he reiterated from prison.[112] Despite King Sigismund's assurance of safe conduct to the council, he was taken into custody and imprisoned a few weeks after his arrival in Constance in early November 1414, where he remained until he was burned on July 6, 1415.

Hus knew that refusal to recant made his execution likely. His last months in prison were an ordeal in every respect: he vomited blood and suffered from headaches, toothaches, fever, and kidney stones. On June 9, a month before his death, he told the Czech supporters who had accompanied him to Constance that he "had the greatest temptations both in body and mind" and "felt the greatest fear lest I transgress the commandments of the Lord Jesus Christ."[113] If the contours of martyrdom's path were growing sharper, they exposed more clearly its forbidding narrowness and formidable snares, pitfalls that had seduced St. Peter himself as though Jesus had meant nothing to him.[114] Here were the temptations from the *Ars moriendi,* face to face. Hus would resist them. In March he wrote, "Only now [*Primo nunc*] am I learning to understand the Psalter, to pray as I ought, to ponder the abuse of

Christ and the sufferings of the martyrs."[115] How could a devout man intimately familiar with God's word, a man who had preached some three thousand sermons in Prague, say this? Change was afoot. Prison experience was transforming Hus with its own hermeneutic, exposing relevant passages and dictating their sense. Martyr-saints transcended their roles as intercessors and again appeared as models for mimesis. Hus balanced them against the Old Testament examples of Jonah, Daniel, the three youths in the fiery furnace, and Susanna, whom God had liberated from seemingly certain death.[116]

While believing that God might yet save his life, Hus readied himself for the execution he expected. The martyrs and their deaths recurred to him, their gender seeming not to matter: he noted Eleazar and the seven young men from 2 Macc. 7 in two letters written around June 20, St. Catherine on June 26, and the martyrdoms of Peter and Paul on June 29.[117] Just over a week before his death, Hus told his Bohemian friends why the executions were being postponed: the Lord was giving him and Jerome more time to recollect and regret their sins, granting them "time to remember our King, the merciful Lord God Jesus' terrible disgrace, and to meditate on His cruel death and, for that reason, to suffer more gladly." Finally, their deaths were being delayed

> that we may remember that the saints entered the heavenly kingdom through many sufferings; for some were cut up piece by piece, others impaled, others boiled, others roasted, others flayed alive, buried alive, stoned, crucified, crushed between millstones, dragged, drowned, burned, hanged, torn to pieces, having first been vilified, imprisoned, beaten and chained. Who can describe all the tortures by which the saints of the New and the Old Testaments suffered for God's truth, particularly those who rebuked the priestly wickedness and preached against it!
>
> It would be strange if now one would not suffer on account of a brave stand against wickedness, especially that of the priests, which does not allow itself to be touched![118]

Not all of these torments, however, are biblical—the "saints of the New and the Old Testaments" had not displaced those from the *Golden Legend*. They had reinforced each other, helping to sustain Hus to the end: their past experience confirmed his present hermeneutic. Scripture and prayer through several years of tribulation, exile, and imprisonment had fused patient suffering, proper death, and devotion to Christ's passion into the common terminus of martyrdom.

On July 6, 1415, Hus refused for a final time to abjure the propositions read to him by the prelates at Constance, denying that they had been fairly drawn from his writings. The proceedings against him, his ritual degradation (an additional step in clerical executions), the procession to the meadow between the gates and moats of Constance, and his eventual burning were narrated in detail by Peter of Mladoňovice. A Catholic chronicler, Ulrich von Richental, wrote a much sparser account that contradicted Peter's story, claiming that Hus was not singing and praying as the flames engulfed him, but rather "raised his voice with terrible screaming and was soon burned." For several reasons Peter's account seems more reliable;[119] but whatever the truth about Hus's dying comportment, his death marked a watershed in the Hussite movement. The day before he died he implored his followers to "preserve the letters carefully," along with his memory.[120] They heeded his plea: Hus's celebration as a martyr went hand in hand with the movement's increased politicization. He was venerated in Bohemia and Moravia in the fifteenth century and beyond. His potent fusion of Czech nationalism and Hussite Christianity embodied and extended themes from his sermons long beyond the Middle Ages. From the early 1520s on he was for Protestant leaders the exemplary proto-Reformation martyr, a pathbreaking hero who had presaged the Gospel's full restoration and stood up to Rome.[121]

Hus was not alone in his witness. Just days before his death, on June 29, 1415, two lay preachers were burned by German townsmen in Olomouc, far from Prague in eastern Moravia. One had been a student at the University of Prague, whose Hussite masters thus appealed on his behalf to Lord Lacek of Kravaře, the royal captain of Moravia. This episode reinforced the opposition between German Catholic townsmen and Czech Hussite nobles.[122] In September 1415 a petition with over 450 signatures from the Hussite nobility was presented to the Council of Constance protesting Hus's execution, while the Hussite leaders at the University of Prague declared their support for him and Jerome.[123] More fuel was added to the fire—in grimly literal fashion—when, after nearly a year in prison, Jerome was burned in Constance on May 30, 1416. Late that year Sigismund heard outraged complaints from council members: followers of Hus and Jerome were calling them blessed, setting them beside the saints in sermons, and commemorating them in prayers and masses for martyrs.[124] The local canons in Olomouc registered similar displeasure about Hussites who administered the Eucharist as both wine and bread, criticized the Church's doctrines and leaders, abused the sacraments, and venerated Hus and Jerome, singing songs in their honor "as though for martyrs, comparing them in merits and sufferings to Saint Lawrence the martyr, and preferring them to Saint Peter and other saints."[125] The Hussite reaction in southern Bohemia was much the same, specifically in Kozí Hradek and Písek, where Hus and Jerome were also esteemed as saints.[126]

Hussite leaders drew on the martyrs in exhorting their followers to resist Catholic pressure. In 1417 Hus's colleague, Jakoubek of Střibo, preached a sermon on them in the Bethlehem Chapel based on Matt. 5:10: "Blessed are those who are persecuted for righteousness' sake, for theirs is the kingdom of heaven."[127] On July 30, 1419, the radical preacher Jan Želivský led the demonstration that issued in the defenestration of Prague and the Hussite takeover of the city. A week earlier, he had blasted the authorities responsible for executing the martyrs: "To kill out of malice is murder," he said. "This is what took place in Constance, hence everyone is a murderer who consented to the death of Master John Hus and Jerome, as well as to the death of the laymen who were beheaded in the Old City in Prague and those who were burned in Olomouc."[128] In March 1420, during the early Catholic reaction to the Hussite coup, the Prague merchant John Krása was burned in Wrocław after making known his Hussite views. Among other offenses, he refused to consent that the condemnation of Hus and Jerome had been just and holy.[129]

Veneration of the Hussite martyrs continued throughout the fifteenth century. Even when the Hussites were reincorporated into the Roman church between the 1436 Jihlava accord and its repudiation in 1462, the legacy of Hus and Jerome remained contentious. When Rome failed to endorse Jan Rokycana as Archbishop of Prague, he reinstated July 6 as their feast day.[130] A Latin Hussite liturgical book dating probably from the early 1450s incorporated Hus and Jerome into chants for mass and included a clever word play on "constancia"—specifying both where they had died and their quality in dying.[131] Beginning in the late 1450s a Hussite outgrowth, the Unity of the Czech Brethren *(Unitas Fratrum)*, also sustained ideas about persecution and Christian suffering, reinforced by their own vulnerability in the later fifteenth and sixteenth centuries. The man who inspired them, Peter Chelčický, championed passive nonresistance as the only acceptable Christian response to persecution and viewed Christian life as one of victory through suffering.[132] In 1495 Jan Kamp printed a Czech edition of the *Golden Legend* with protest documents by the Hussite nobility, four letters from Hus's imprisonment in Constance, Poggio Bracciolini's letter about Jerome of Prague's death, and part of Peter of Mladoňovice's account of Hus's trial and execution. Poggio's letter gained currency in humanist circles as well, having been published several times in Latin by the early sixteenth century.[133] The martyrs were also honored in Germany, presaging their appropriation in the early Reformation: when Matthau Hagen was burned at Stettin in 1458, for example, he was charged with claiming Wyclif, Hus, and Jerome as saints.[134] By the eve of the Reformation active Hussite martyrdom had long cooled, but the memory of the martyrs still simmered. John Hus and Jerome of Prague were brilliantly suited to evangelical reformers seeking heroic precursors, as these two had defied the same institution that the reformers reckoned tyrannical and corrupt.

Between the late fourteenth century and the arrival of Lutheran ideas in

England, the Lollards lacked a leader of Hus's stature, a moment as significant and potentially unifying as his death, or enough support from the political nation to pose a threat to the country. (The closest they came was John Oldcastle's rebellion in 1414, which was quickly crushed.) Although he was esteemed by fifteenth-century Lollards, Wyclif was less central to Lollardy than Hus was to Hussitism. Despite the royal protection he enjoyed, Wyclif was primarily a university theologian rather than a preacher leading a broad-based movement. There is some basis for speaking of an academic Lollardy in the years following his death, but after 1414 Lollard teachers simplified and adapted his ideas as they dispersed them.[135] In 1415 the two movements were headed in opposite directions: whereas the Hussites would soon pose the toughest late medieval challenge to the Church, Oldcastle's failure sent the Lollards into low-profile incubation. In pockets across southern England, they read and copied the vernacular Bible, especially the Gospels and Epistles. When tried for heresy they overwhelmingly abjured rather than suffer death.[136] Their willingness to recant, plus the ordinarily lenient treatment by churchmen who wanted first-time offenders to return to the Church,[137] kept the number of executed Lollards relatively small.

Yet their fellow Lollards honored as martyrs those who were put to death. *De haeretico comburendo* stipulated burning for convicted, heretical recidivists. One such was Richard Wyche, executed as a relapsed heretic in London, thirty years after he had written to Hus and company in Prague. He had sympathizers: a royal writ of July 15, 1440, prohibited pilgrimages to his burial site, noted claims that he had died a holy man, and denied popular allegations that he had worked miracles. Some of his followers made a pile of stones on his execution site, but authorities destroyed it, heaped a dunghill in its place, and policed the location for six weeks.[138] When Walter Comber of Bristol abjured his views in April 1457, among them was the opinion that William Smith, previously burned in the same city, "died a martyr afore God."[139] Writing about the same time, the bishop of Chichester, Reginald Pecock, argued against the "full many undiscreet and unwise persons" who thought that people who died at odds with the Church could be holy, noting those who "holdest the now late brenned men in England to be martyrs."[140] According to the *Great Chronicle of London,* on the night after the octogenarian Lollard Joan Boughton was burned at Smithfield on April 28, 1494, "the more part of the ashes of that fire that she was brent in were had away, and kept for a precious relic in an earthen pot."[141] Her daughter, Lady Yonge, widow of former London mayor Sir John Yonge, apparently was also burned for heresy; Joan Baker claimed before Bishop Fitzjames in 1510 or 1511 that she had died a martyr.[142]

Like the Waldensians,[143] the Lollards emphasized avoidance of detection and, following Christ's directive in Matt. 10:23, flight in the face of persecu-tion. They also seem to have cultivated the giving of deliberately evasive and ambiguous answers to questions by ecclesiastical authorities.[144] At the same time, Lollards were not to deny their faith when made to answer for it. The great, late fourteenth-century liturgical cycle of Lollard sermons included one noting that Christ taught both to flee and to "stand and suffer." Flight was only to be employed for clandestine escape, for to "flee our enemies right when they follow us, and see us in men's presence . . . were evil cowardice, to fear men that saw this flight."[145] In keeping with devotion to the passion, more than one sermon calls Christ the "head of martyrs." Consistent with ideas in the *Imitation of Christ* as well as Hus's letters, another sermon told hearers to "lose this life here for God, in the time that is now present, and thou shalt trust to find thy life afterward in bliss of heaven."[146] According to Anne Hudson, the main objective of the Lambeth–Royal Psalms commen-tary, a Lollard work, was "to console and encourage the committed during persecution." The commentary noted the many verses from the Psalms that comfort the afflicted. It warned, too, against spiritual appeasement, urging fellow Lollards "to stand by the truth unmovably . . . And most glad we should be for to have a true cause and to suffer therefore martyrdom . . . And who that for any love of worldly thing or for dread of any bodily discase [discomfort] forsaken this heavenly grace when it is proffered, that is ever when it may be had, they leesen [forfeit] herefore all heavenly love."[147]

Passages about persevering through persecution must have reinforced Lol-lards' sense of themselves as God's chosen remnant in a world corrupted by the Antichrist. They could reasonably assume that priests had forbidden them the vernacular Bible lest it fortify their anticlericalism.[148] In the sermon cycle this anticlerical thrust was developed more than any direct, consistent call to remain steadfast unto death, even in conjunction with Gospel passages about sustaining persecution. When the subject of martyrdom was broached it often became a stepping-stone to criticism of the Catholic clergy, whose hypocrisy and cowardice, Lollards contended, inhibited their proclamation of the Gos-pel. Doing so would have provoked the persecution they were too timid to abide.[149]

The importance of biblical passages about affliction and suffering to both Hussites and Lollards can hardly be overstated. What late medieval Christians within the Church directed toward daily struggles with pain or sin, they applied to their predicaments as persecuted minorities within Christian soci-ety. In so doing, Lollards and Hussites themselves stood in an older medieval tradition. The last section of the late thirteenth-century *Book of the Two Prin-ciples,* the most sophisticated Cathar treatise, is entitled "On Persecutions." In large measure, it simply catalogues New Testament passages about persecution and suffering, intending to show that as the prophets, Christ, and his apostles endured affliction and death, so "in the last days Christ's followers must endure many offenses, tribulations, sufferings, sorrows, and even death from the false Christians and false prophets and from wicked men and seducers."[150] Save for its Latinity, the text might have been written by a sixteenth-century Anabaptist. This similarity across disparate communities, contexts, and centuries signals the persistence and power of a fundamental mode of Christian perception. Moreover, it underscores the sine qua non of late medieval dissent as well as of sixteenth-century Protestantism and Anabaptism: the Bible as the touchstone for conceptions of true Christianity and the fulcrum for criticism of Rome. Hussites, Lollards, and Waldensians used scripture to model their purer, primitive churches and attacked Roman Catholicism for not measuring up.[151] The Bible, too, guided their views about fulfilling the prophecies of coming persecutions. Whatever else might be said about the complex relationship of late medieval heretics to sixteenth-century Protestants and Anabaptists, in this sense they were indeed "forerunners of the Reformation."

Coupled with their celebration of slain fellow believers, late medieval heretics repudiated the Church's latter-day martyrs. In this respect they point to the bitter disputes over true martyrs in the early modern period. The two most important canonized martyrs of the preceding centuries, Peter Martyr and Thomas Becket, did not fare well. In 1397 an inquisitor mentioned a Piedmontese Waldensian who reversed the Catholic position, saying "of the glorious, blessed Peter Martyr that he was evil and a sinner and not holy, and is damned in hell, because he persecuted Christ's servants, implying that the heretics and Waldensians, by whom the said Saint Peter was killed, are the servants of Christ, and that the death of brother Jacobo Bechi was more precious in God's sight than the death of blessed Peter Martyr."[152] When Margery Baxter, a Lollard active in Martham, East Anglia, was tried for heresy in April 1427, she unloaded on Thomas Becket. He was a false traitor, she said, damned in hell, and had been killed while trying to flee rather than standing patiently at the altar. By contrast, the recently burned Lollard leader William White was a great saint in heaven to whom she would pray daily for intercession before God.[153] To recognize as martyrs the fellow believers who had opposed the Church meant repudiating the Church's own fallen defenders. This stark, concretely divisive logic would mark early modern Christian communities as well, with their entanglement of competing doctrines and contested deaths.

Considering the sparse opportunities to die for Christ in the late medieval Church, martyrdom seems anachronistic, rendered superfluous by Christianization. In multiple ways, however, martyrs and martyrdom coursed through the veins and strengthened the sinews of late medieval Christianity. Attitudes and practices that coalesced in martyrdom—suffering patiently, dying well, and cultivating a devotion to Christ's passion—were shared by holy men and women who substituted asceticism for frustrated dreams of martyrdom, and by committed heterodox Christians who risked death for their beliefs and practices. The same piety nurtured both. When late medieval dissenters turned to scripture, God's word plainly reinforced the same sensibilities. Yet familiar surroundings were drastically remade for those who spurned the Church: a world that had seemed without room for latter-day Christian martyrs now loomed as an ecclesio-political monster designed to create them. The Reformation would arrive in a Christendom not devoid of martyrdom, but replete with its possibility.

CHAPTER THREE

The Willingness to Kill

If anyone secretly entices you—even if it is your brother, your father's son or your mother's son, or your own son or daughter, or the wife you embrace, or your most intimate friend—saying, "Let us go worship other gods," whom neither you nor your ancestors have known, any of the gods of the peoples that are around you, whether near you or far away from you, from one end of the earth to the other, you must not yield to or heed any such persons. Show them no pity or compassion and do not shield them. But you shall surely kill them; your own hand shall be first against them to execute them, and afterwards the hand of all the people. Stone them to death for trying to turn you away from the Lord your God, who brought you out of the land of Egypt, out of the house of slavery. Then all Israel shall hear and be afraid, and never again do any such wickedness.

—DEUTERONOMY 13:6–11

. . . nevertheless, it very often happens that two good men, both of whom have good intentions, carry out great persecutions against and contradict each other as a result of their different opinions.

—FRANÇOIS DE SALES, *INTRODUCTION TO THE DEVOUT LIFE* (1609)

When sixteenth-century Christians were executed for their religious convictions, were they persecuted or prosecuted? Those who suffered at the stake or scaffold, like the Lollards and Hussites before them, denounced such treatment as tyrannical cruelty. Many Roman Catholic and Protestant authorities, however, both ecclesiastical and secular, considered persistent Christian heterodoxy the gravest of offenses. Men and women deserved severe punishment if they resisted every effort made to correct their errors. Such action did not persecute innocent Christians—it prosecuted religious criminals.

Referring to authorities' willingness to kill, one scholar has recently written that "to the modern mind it is unthinkable that a man should burn for his religious beliefs alone."[1] What to the "modern mind" seems "unthinkable" is for the modern historian a challenge. Sixteenth-century authorities not only entertained this thought—they acted on it several thousand times. It is somewhat misleading, however, to say that people were executed for their "religious beliefs alone." Entirely private, personal heterodoxy would have been undetectable. "If heresy remains secretly in people's hearts," Urbanus Rhegius noted in 1536, "then it is judged by God alone."[2] Yet in the admonitions of religious leaders and of Jesus himself—"Why do you call me 'Lord, Lord,' and not do what I tell you?" (Luke 6:46)—beliefs almost always entailed visible behavior. Grasping the truth of the Gospel meant not hiding it "under a bushel basket" (Matt. 5:15), but rather living it with others, whether in conventicles, via printed literature, or through clandestine worship. Spurning the Mass as idolatrous implied that one ought not to attend it, rejecting infant baptism that one ought not to practice it. Heterodox Christians were prosecuted not "for [their] religious beliefs alone," but for what they did or failed to do on the basis of their convictions.

Prosecuting Religious Criminals

By the early sixteenth century judicial mechanisms for the prosecution of heresy were well established. Theologically, the most important influence on the Middle Ages was Augustine, whose attitudes on religious coercion were integrally related to his views of scripture, authority, and providence.[3] In the early Middle Ages, the legal precedent set by the Justinian Code had been idle. Still, the concern of churchmen about heresy persisted even when heresy seems to have been absent, as in the tenth century. A 1022 burning in Orléans was the first recorded execution for heresy in Latin Christendom in over six hundred years.[4] Ecclesiastical involvement began to change in the mid-twelfth century, when a relatively lenient, piecemeal approach by individual bishops yielded to a stricter, more centralized, papally driven strategy, marked by greater cooperation with secular authorities. In 1148 the Council of Rheims handed over heretics to secular authorities for burning. Thereafter, through the Fourth Lateran Council (1215) and the commissioning of papal inquisitors under Pope Gregory IX in the 1230s, measures against heretics were stiffened to counter burgeoning Cathar influence in southern France.[5] From the mid-thirteenth century on, with varying degrees of commitment and success, ecclesiastical and secular authorities across diverse regions combined to seek out, question, and punish heretics. Inquisitors imposed a wide range of penalties within a flexible system of punishments, depending on the nature of the offense and the response of the suspect.[6] Only those who refused clerical pressure to recant and be reconciled to the Church, or who relapsed after a previous abjuration, faced execution. Secular magistrates then enacted the capital punishment, most commonly by burning.

In the sixteenth century this system led to several thousand deaths. Sympathizers understood them as martyrdoms. Had there been no judicial executions, some Christians—those killed in popular violence, for example, or those who perished in prison—would probably have been recognized as martyrs, but no full-blown renaissance of martyrdom would have occurred. The perception of persecution and the widespread celebration of martyrs presupposed the pattern of prosecution and its underlying willingness to kill. Without the latter, martyrdom would have remained the fantasy it had been for Margery Kempe, or the sixteenth-century fancy of the young Teresa of Avila and her brother in Catholic Spain, who imagined a speedy route to heaven at Moslem hands.[7]

Judicial executions for heterodoxy are not coextensive with the broader category of religious violence, a subject explored by Natalie Zemon Davis and Denis Crouzet for the French Wars of Religion.[8] Early modern religious riots and religious wars fall outside the present discussion. Nevertheless, executions coupled with general repression of Protestants helped spark war in France in 1562, just as they spurred iconoclastic revolt in the Netherlands four years later. Protestant martyrologists distinguished judicial from extrajudicial violence as well, yet they perceived an underlying continuity between them.

By design, executions for heresy almost never turned on ambiguity or doctrinal manipulation, as they had to some extent in the case of John Hus. Authorities asked specific, litmus-test questions about religious teachings and practices. If one willfully denied an article of Christian faith in response, heresy was manifest. In this sense, men and women executed for their persistence were not "made" into heretics. If Anabaptists denied the validity of infant baptism, for example, they were patently heretical according to both Catholics and Protestants. Quite different were cases in which denunciations were wielded *within* traditions against those who understood themselves as obediently orthodox, as when the faculty of theology of the University of Paris condemned the Jesuits in December 1554.[9] Certain interests within the sprawl of Roman Catholicism—including other religious orders—were almost sure to resent the innovative style and rapid success of the Society of Jesus. Yet an order that self-conciously vowed special obedience to the pope could not and did not self-consciously reject the teachings of Roman Catholicism. Executed Protestants and Anabaptists, by contrast, condemned the pope as the Antichrist.

In the twelfth century Gratian had codified Augustine's notion that the subjective aspect of heresy entailed *deliberate* persistence in false doctrine.[10] Accordingly, inquisitorial proceedings were designed to sift defiant heterodoxy, which was heresy, from mere ignorance or confusion, which was not. Thomas More, a relentless opponent of heresy, counseled gentle treatment for the inculpably wayward: "I would not they were overhastily handled, but little rigor and much mercy showed where simpleness appeared, and not high heart or malice."[11] John Calvin's distinction among three levels of error echoed this point: fraternal correction and encouragement were the antidote to mild superstition or ignorance.[12]

Heresy was both a serious and an unusual crime. Viewed as a deliberate error, it was judged amenable to correction. In contrast to crimes such as murder, theft, or arson, the offense could be undone. First-time culprits courted execution only if they were unwilling to recant. On the eve of the Reformation, suspects could admit and renounce their errors, accept penitential punishment, and return to the Church, albeit often with a stigma that could be socially damaging.[13] As the sixteenth century unfolded, secular authorities in England, France, and the Netherlands assumed greater control of prosecution. At times they made laws mandating automatic execution for various heretical activities. In practice, however, there persisted a willingness to release penitent heretics.

In trials for witchcraft and other crimes on the Continent, judicial torture was often necessary to secure the confessions required for "full proof."[14] Heresy suspects, by contrast, were rarely tortured to make them confess their errors. In Bordeaux, Languedoc, and Paris between 1540 and 1560, only between 2 and 10 percent of those examined for heresy were tortured at all. In Paris during 1535–1536 and 1545–1546, torture was used in 21 percent of homicide cases, 23 percent of robberies, and 30 percent of forgeries, but only 7 percent of heresy cases.[15] These figures are consistent with contemporary convictions about the nature of heresy. Torturing people to make them confess their beliefs would have undercut the idea that heresy reflected a willful choice. Furthermore, defiant persistence in heterodoxy rendered torture superfluous: suspects openly admitted what their examiners sought. When torture was employed, authorities wanted heretics to name names, to identify fellow believers, not to make their own confessions. People were killed not because they were bullied into acknowledging fictitious heresies, but because they confessed proscribed beliefs, though admittedly from a vulnerable judicial position.[16] Specific scriptural and social influences fostered forthright confession by the accused. Overall, however, there is little question that many more people dissembled or abjured than stood firm.[17]

Sixteenth-century penal codes were harsh by modern Western standards. Besides lesser punishments such as pillorying, whipping, branding, severing limbs, and confining aboard galleys, capital punishment was used against thieves, arsonists, counterfeiters, murderers, traitors, and abductors of women.[18] In this light Raymond Mentzer has written that "the use of the death sentence for heresy was neither singular nor extreme when compared to its application for other felonies."[19] The willingness to kill the heterodox can be abstracted only arbitrarily from this wider context, which is integral to the understanding of heresy prosecution. Those convicted of all capital offenses were typically put to death in public, ritualized executions meant to deter would-be criminals and to reinforce the existing authority.[20] In a world without professional police forces, the preservation of public order depended partly on the effectiveness of such executions. To a large extent, stability required the widespread acceptance of legal norms and cultural values, plus more or less cooperative central and local authorities.

Except in Hussite Bohemia, repression had worked. Late medieval sects and their heretical beliefs were by no means eliminated, but they were contained and controlled. The Lollard underground endured into the sixteenth century, but without seriously challenging either the Church's power or its place in the lives of the vast majority of English men and women. Waldensian communities did likewise in Provence and the Piedmont. After three centuries of largely effective containment, the willingness to kill was firmly situated in authorities' assumptions about the exercise of power. Their pervasive social and political conservatism prompted no fundamental innovations. Why fix what was not broken? On the eve of the Reformation, nothing hinted that judicial suppression would be any less effective in the future than it had been in the past.

The Duty of Intolerance

Justifications for the execution of heretics seem clearly to manifest ideology in the service of self-interest. Crushing dissent by killing dissenters is a less than subtle way to buttress a dominant order. Examples abound in the twentieth century. In an earlier era of expanding state power, influential men stood to consolidate their control by eliminating resistance. Conform or be killed: executions seem to express the brutal extreme of ambitions to impose social discipline and to insure obedience. Some princes and prelates perhaps opposed heresy mostly to maintain their power and prestige. Nonetheless, there are good reasons not to assume that opposition to religious heterodoxy in general was primarily the ideological glove on the fist of political self-interest.

The first contrary argument is the simplest: it is far from clear that the violent punishment of heterodoxy in the sixteenth century always served the sovereign's perceived political interests. Both Mary Tudor and Philip II, for example, kept executing heretics despite their awareness of the political cost. Had they mitigated their heresy policies, they probably would have strengthened their respective regimes. Thomas More and John Fisher tirelessly countered heresy in England in the 1520s and early 1530s. Yet in the light of their own deaths in 1535, they cannot be seen as Henry VIII's self-serving political agents. Had self-seeking ambition driven them, both would have assumed exalted positions in the king's new regime. More broadly, it is scarcely imaginable that when conscientious, implicated Catholics—including the writers who justified the executions, the rulers who made the laws, and the local magistrates who carried them out—made their sacramental confessions, they all sought forgiveness for complicity in the mortal sin of murdering heretics. It is much more plausible to take them and their Protestant counterparts at their word: executions were not only legitimate, but obligatory. Even contemporary antagonists conceded the sincerity of mistaken authorities. When the Protestant Anthony Gilby attacked Stephen Gardiner, the Henrician bishop of Winchester, in 1548, he acknowledged the good intentions of those responsible for the execution of Protestants, but denied the rightness of their actions.[21]

As the examples of More, Fisher, and others show, the willingness to die for one's beliefs was not necessarily the simple opposite of the willingness to kill for them.[22] Both dispositions embraced central Christian notions about truth, faith, the afterlife, answerability to God, and responsibility to others. Political vulnerability dictated an openness to martyrdom, political responsibility a willingness to punish those who disparaged God's truth. Just as men and women interrogated about their faith were answerable to God, so were rulers responsible to God (and their subjects) for maintaining true religion. The issue was not suffering as opposed to meting out punishment, but rather what commitment to the truth called for in divergent circumstances.

In contrast to twentieth-century dictators, early modern princes and prelates cannot be seen as tyrannical exterminators. The gratuitous cruelty of certain officials, such as the Elizabethan Richard Topcliffe, should not be conflated with authorities' general willingness to kill unrepentant heretics. "Well may it be," wrote Thomas More in 1531, "that as we be all men and not angels, some of them may have sometime either over fervent mind or undiscreet zeal, or percase an angry and a cruel heart, by which they may offend God in the self same deed, whereof they should else greatly merit."[23] John Tedeschi's intensive research has revealed the Roman Inquisition's procedural scrupulosity and prosecutorial restraint.[24] With rare exceptions, neither ecclesiastical nor secular authorities wanted to slaughter religious deviants. They sought rather to reclaim the wayward for Catholicism, Reformed Protestantism, or Lutheranism by securing formal recantations. Had this not been so, Charles V, for example, would not have given heretics a grace period before implementing the imperial placards of 1529 and 1530. He was "not seeking," he stated, "the death of our subjects . . . nor their goods, but only the maintenance of the faith and of the statutes, ordinances, and constitutions of the holy Church and of our ordinances, and the suppression and reformation of errors, abuses, and endeavors to the contrary."[25]

Was this a rhetorical show, the language carefully calibrated merely to avoid the appearance of ruthlessness? Authorities' willingness to release penitent heretics suggests otherwise. In December 1521 the prior of Antwerp's Observant Augustinians, Jakob Probst, was imprisoned in Brussels on suspicion of heresy. When pressured he publicly recanted, then was permitted to go free.[26] The unyielding Anabaptists imprisoned with Michael Sattler were executed, whereas the recanting majority were exiled, made to wear grey smocks with symbols of the sacraments they had impugned: a chalice and host on one side, a baptismal font on the other.[27] Even in Catholic Bavaria, where apparently between seventy and one hundred Anabaptists were executed between 1527 and 1530, "the persecution of Anabaptists did not simply consist in savage killing," although an April 1530 mandate technically subjected them all to capital punishment.[28]

Where heresy was linked to overt sedition—for example, in the German Habsburg lands after the Peasants' War, in Amsterdam following the Anabaptist militancy of 1535, and in the Low Countries after the Iconoclastic Fury of 1566—retaliation was usually severe. Otherwise authorities were not especially bent on executing heresy suspects. Only 62 (5.8 percent) of the 1,074 persons accused in Languedoc between 1511 and 1562 were killed; the Parlement of Bordeaux executed just 18 (3.8 percent) of the 477 suspects it pursued from 1541 through 1559; and even the notorious *chambre ardente* of Paris put to death only 58 (10.4 percent) of at least 557 suspects between May 1547 and March 1550.[29] In Cologne in June 1565, 57 Anabaptists were arrested. Of the 37 who had been (re)baptised, 34 refused to recant, but only their teacher, Michael Servaes, seems to have been executed.[30] Over his twenty-year career the zealous inquisitor Pieter Titelmans handled at least 1,120, and perhaps as many as 1,600, heresy cases. Just 127 (7.9 percent to 11.3 percent) ended in execution.[31] *Contravening* the mandatory death sentence then prescribed by imperial law, Titelmans and members of the Council of Flanders released penitent Anabaptists in the 1550s. Titelmans personally interceded with secular authorities on behalf of others.[32]

Far from yearning to kill heretics, members of the clergy frequently strained to save them. Often joined by civic officials or friends of the accused, they pleaded with the heterodox to abandon their beliefs and thus avoid death. The bishop of Vienna, along with other theologians, secular authorities, and even a choirmaster, repeatedly urged Caspar Tauber to recant in 1524, to no avail.[33] Wendelmoet Claes was questioned by The Hague's city council in November 1527. In prison over the next two days, "monks, priests, and women" as well as a cousin implored her to capitulate, again in vain.[34] Aided by his assistants, the Marian bishop of London, Edmund Bonner, tried fifteen times to make John Philpot see his errors, six times with Richard Woodman, and nine with Elizabeth Young.[35] In Ghent, twelve attempts were made with the Anabaptist Soetken van den Houte and her three female companions. From late July through their eventual execution on November 20, 1560, inquisitors, members of Ghent's four male religious orders, civic authorities, and secular clergymen all tried and failed to make them renounce their be-liefs.[36] What more could have been done? Should twenty attempts have been made, or a hundred? Heinrich Bullinger derided the idea that authorities should forestall indefinitely the execution of obstinate heretics in the hopes that they might eventually come round. This would imply, he argued, that no murderers, thieves, rebels, or other malefactors ought to be put to death either, giving them time to acknowledge their wrongdoing and become devout.[37]

Ecclesiastical and secular authorities wanted to correct the heterodox, not kill them. True, their efforts are consistent with interpretations that stress self-interest, since every repentant heretic reinforced the prevailing order. Their attempts also support readings that emphasize apologists' self-professed religious motives, such as concern for heretics' and others' souls. However, their actions undermine the view that early modern states were bent on simply annihilating any and all resistance they encountered. With respect to examinations and executions for heresy, Lionello Puppi's sweeping, Foucauldian claim of a medieval and early modern "absolute order of Power" engaged in a "constant acting out of a vendetta on innumerable nameless victims; an unbroken, interminable slaughter," is nonsense.[38] Both David Nicholls for Henry II's France and Susan Brigden for Marian England have recently confirmed officials' care to correct the religiously wayward. Every unrepentant, executed heretic marked a political defeat, not a victory.[39]

Puppi invokes—and dismisses—an incident that epitomizes the issue at hand: Pope Sixtus V was moved to tears by paintings of Catholic martyrs in Rome's San Stefano Rotondo, yet he authorized for criminals and heretics some of the same punishments depicted.[40] The pope's actions are not only intelligible, but fully consistent with the conviction that uniquely important events for all humanity had occurred in Christ's incarnation, life, death, and resurrection; that the saving truth therein revealed and apprehended by faith could be distinguished from damning error; that the Roman Catholic Church was the custodian of this truth; and that Christian magistrates were obliged to defend it for God's honor, others' well-being, and the common good. The heart of this position was based on the Gospels: Christ had said no one came to the Father apart from him (John 14:6), that he would build his church on Peter, against which hell's gates would not prevail (Matt. 16:18), and that he would remain always with his disciples (Matt. 28:20). As elaborated in the sixteenth century, this position intertwined biblical exegesis with arguments based on logical principles, historical precedent, pastoral concern, the threat of social disorder, and the obligations of Christian magistrates. These in turn meshed with commonplace commitments about the priority of the corporate over the individual, the soul over the body, and eternal life over earthly existence. When Anabaptists were drowned in Zwinglian Zurich or beheaded in Lutheran Saxony, when Michael Servetus was burned in Calvin's Geneva, the arguments, mutatis mutandis, remained fundamentally the same,[41] even though the precise hermeneutical bases differed. Protestant magistrates were obliged to defend the Gospel's restored, salvific truth, rescued from its medieval Catholic perversions.

The Trajectory of Argumentation

Johannes Eck first published his *Handbook of Commonplaces* in 1525. One of the leading Catholic controversialists of the early Reformation period, he intended it to offset Philipp Melanchthon's *Commonplaces* (1521), a concise presentation of Luther's teachings organized around biblically based, soteriological themes. Eck compiled scriptural, patristic, and other authoritative sources by topic, giving Catholic clergy a defensive tool to meet evangelical challenges. Many thousands of priests and doubtless some literate laity must have acquired it, since over one hundred editions, including vernacular translations, were published by 1576.[42] Eck articulated traditional arguments for execution in Chapter 27, entitled "On the Burning of Heretics."

Whether they were trained scholastically or humanistically, Eck and other proponents of execution leaned on scripture to support their arguments. The Pentateuch prescribed the killing of those among God's chosen people who blasphemed, prophesied falsely, disobeyed God's ministers, or enticed others to worship different gods. Given certain assumptions about the Old Testament in a Christian hermeneutic, the same sanctions were adapted easily enough to a Christian context.[43] Well versed in biblical proof texts and Augustinian commonplaces, Eck quoted from Deuteronomy in his *Handbook:*

> If prophets or those who divine by dreams appear among you and promise you omens or portents, and the omens or the portents declared by them take place, and they say, "Let us follow other gods" (whom you have not known) "and let us serve them," you must not heed the words of those prophets or those who divine by dreams; for the Lord your God is testing you, to know whether you indeed love the Lord your God with all your heart and soul . . . But those prophets or those who divine by dreams shall be put to death for having spoken treason against the Lord your God . . . (Deut. 13:1–3, 5).[44]

When Calvin justified the execution of Servetus in 1554, he employed the verses immediately following—which are also the epigraph to this chapter—to make clear the duty of magistrates and to demonstrate the precedence of

God's honor over even the closest of human relationships.[45] Eck quoted Deut. 17:12, Deut. 18:20, and Lev. 24:14 as well. These verses condemn, respectively, those disobedient to appointed priests, those prophesying in the name of other gods, and blasphemers. Eck asked simply, "Why not heretics too?" and cited further the case of Elijah slaying the false prophets of Baal (1 Kings 18:40).[46] At a Worms colloquy in 1557, Lutheran theologians applied to Anabaptists the capital mandate against blasphemers. They claimed that it bound "not only Israel," but was "rather a natural law which binds all authorities in their rule, whether king, princes, judges, etc. For civil government should not only preserve the bodies of subjects as a shepherd preserves cattle or sheep, but should also uphold outward discipline and regulate government to God's honor, should remove and punish public idolatry and blasphemy."[47]

Others argued, however, against the weight of Augustine's influence, that Christ's coming had supplanted the Mosaic mandates. The parable of the wheat and the tares (Matt. 13:24–30), it was claimed, sanctioned the coexistence of the good and the wicked until Christ's second coming, lest "grain" be mistakenly uprooted with "weeds." The Old Testament laws applied to the ancient Israelites and perhaps still to latter-day Jews, but not to sixteenth-century Christians.[48] At least as early as Balthasar Hubmaier's *On Heretics and Those Who Burn Them* (1524), this parable figured importantly in arguments against the execution of heretics.[49] In contrast to the Pentateuch, the New Testament nowhere explicitly commends putting blasphemers or false believers to death. Besides the parable of the wheat and the tares, other passages seem to counsel less extreme action. Paul's letter to Titus, for example, states, "After a first and second admonition, have nothing more to do with anyone who causes divisions, since you know that such a person is perverted and sinful, being self-condemned" (Tit. 3:10–11). Presumably, ignoring such a person would preclude putting him or her to death. In the sixteenth century, such verses grounded the disciplinary practices of banning and shunning among certain Anabaptist groups. These passages had led medieval churchmen to go no further than excommunication in punishing heretics. Execution remained the preserve of secular authorities.

Medieval and early modern magistrates, however, were "secular" only in the legal and institutional sense of being nonecclesiastical. Christian teachers, pastors, and advisors helped shaped their sense of duty. When political manuals and treatises addressed the responsibilities of magistrates, they quoted not the Pentateuch, but Paul:

Let every person be subject to the governing authorities; for there is no authority except from God, and those authorities that exist have been instituted by God. Therefore whoever resists authority resists what God has appointed, and those who resist will incur judgment . . . if you do what is wrong, you should be afraid, for the authority does not bear the sword in vain! It is the servant of God to execute wrath on the wrong-doer (Rom. 13:1–2, 4).

Rhegius cited this passage five times in his brief justification for the execution of Anabaptists.[50] He added two additional Pauline excerpts on law and just punishment:

> Now we know that the law is good, if one uses it legitimately. This means understanding that the law is laid down not for the innocent but for the lawless and disobedient, for the godless and sinful, for the unholy and profane, for those who kill their father or mother, for murderers, fornica-tors, sodomites, slave traders, liars, perjurers, and *whatever else is contrary to the sound teaching that conforms to the glorious gospel of the blessed God,* which he entrusted to me (1 Tim. 1:8–11). (My emphasis.)

> For the Lord's sake accept the authority of every human institution, whether of the emperor as supreme, or of governors, as sent by him to punish those who do wrong and to praise those who do right (1 Pet. 2:13–14).

These passages cleared the way for a fortiori arguments about the execution of heretics. What the Old Testament might not provide directly, the New Testament seemed to demand for the sake of judicial consistency. Heresy was a crime committed not against mere masters or even rulers, but against God.[51] In his imperial legal digest that was published over thirty times, Bruges jurist Josse Damhouder argued that the worst crimes were those that offended the divine majesty.[52] Unrepentant heretics therefore merited pun-ishment no less severe than that applied to lesser criminals. Antoine Du Val stated the point clearly in light of the soul's priority over the body: "If it is right that thieves, murderers, and robbers are punished, is it not with greater reason that one ought to punish heretics, who steal [*desrobent*] the soul and the understanding from those whom they deceive? Is it not with good reason that a poisoner and corrupter of bodily health is punished? Then why would it not be more reasonable to punish one who deprives the soul of its well-being [*qui oste la bonne santé de l'ame*], as our Calvinists do?"[53] Despite their differ-ent targets, Eck, Rhegius, Calvin, Bullinger, and the lay Catholic controver-sialist Miles Huggarde all made the same argument.[54] In the early seventeenth century Benedikt Carpzov, a Lutheran jurist of Saxony, echoed this view as well—quoting (though not acknowledging) Pope Innocent III in support.[55]

As heresy affronted God's majesty, it twisted the truth that alone could lead one "to the Father" (John 14:6), thereby threatening others' eternal salvation. Murderers killed bodies, but heretics killed souls. On February 26, 1526, John Fisher preached a sermon at St. Paul's in London, in conjunction with Robert Barnes's recantation and a public burning of heterodox books. He meant exactly what he said: "heresy is a perilous weed, it is the seed of the devil, the inspiration of the wicked spirits, the corruption of our hearts, the blinding of our sight, the quenching of our faith, the destruction of all good fruit, and finally the murder of our souls."[56] In his Good Friday sermon quoted in Chapter 2, Fisher urged the devotion to Christ's passion that nourished every human sense and faculty; here he warned against adulterating them all through the heresy that repudiated Christ. Thomas More, too, should be taken at his word when he wrote that heretical books, "when they be drunken down infect the reader and corrupt the soul unto everlasting death."[57] Sixteenth-century beliefs about spiritual realities should not be distorted through twentieth-century lenses. Eternal damnation was no mere symbol: it was *literally* what happened to heretics who died at odds with Christ and his mystical body, the one Church. Nor were common images like slaying the wolf for the sake of the flock, or cutting away the putrid flesh to save the body, mere metaphors. As employed by both Protestant and Catholic writers,[58] these images witnessed to the weakness of language as believers grasped for graphic, material analogies to express convictions about spiritual realities. Protestant preacher Hugh Latimer likened false doctrine to a consuming fire: just as "the nature of fire is to burn and consume all that which is laid in the fire," so too "the nature of false doctrine is to condemn, to bring to everlasting damnation; that is the nature of false doctrine."[59] Embedded in a diligent paternalism, sharpened by a sense of accountability, and strengthened by assumptions about the common good, such beliefs fostered urgent, practical concern. "My duty is to endeavor me after my poor power, to resist these heretics, the which cease not to subvert the church of Christ," Fisher told those gathered at St. Paul's. "If we shall sit still and let them in every place sow their ungracious heresies, and everywhere destroy souls, which were so dearly bought with that most precious blood of our saviour Christ Jesu, how terribly shall he lay this until our charge, when we shall be called until a reckoning for this matter!"[60]

Mary Tudor's chaplain and confessor, John Christoferson, wrote that Protestant preachers had "killed more souls upon one day, than all the naughty physicians in England had killed bodies in twenty years."[61] Because heresy was worse than murder, theft, or rape, its eradication was imperative—"such a good and holy work," according to a French ordinance from 1549.[62] If concerted persuasion and pressure failed to produce recantation, then conscientiousness pointed to execution as a final recourse. By foisting deadly criminals on others, banishment, although sometimes employed, was the epitome of antifraternalism. What was worse, as an imperial edict lamented in 1540, exile emboldened heretics and failed to stop the spread of heretical "errors and false doctrines . . . to the great danger, scandal, and destruction" of the sovereign's own lands and subjects.[63] A lack of appropriate facilities meant that long-term imprisonment was rarely a viable option. The procession to the scaffold or sight of the stake might trigger a last-minute recantation, allowing authorities to save lives. Even if the execution were still enacted, the condemned, by recanting, would avoid otherwise certain damnation. In the end and as a last resort, the public execution of criminals eliminated wrong-doers with an admonitory didacticism.

Coddling heretics expressed a misplaced mercy that placed others at risk. Against his detractors, Calvin argued that it was "more than cruel" to "spare the wolves" and expose the sheep to possible soul-murder through the "poisoning of [heretics'] false doctrines."[64] As Mary Tudor's bishop of London, Edmund Bonner presided over many heresy trials, more than one hundred of which ended in excommunication.[65] It was not contrary to but part of charity, Bonner asserted, for secular authorities to punish heretics, based on Rom. 13:3–4: "rulers are not a terror to good conduct, but to bad . . . It is the servant of God to execute wrath on the wrongdoer." The charity of sovereigns included praise and reward for the good, rebuke and punishment for the wicked. If attempted correction failed, execution was the proper course of action:

> As one thief may both rob many men, and also make many thieves, and one seditious person may allure many, and annoy a whole town or country. And such evil persons, that be so great offenders of God, and the commonwealth, charity requireth to be cut off, from the body of the commonweal, lest they corrupt other good, and honest persons: like as a good surgeon cutteth away a putrified, and festered member, for the love he hath to the whole body, lest it infect other members, adjoining to it.[66]

Eck, Du Val, and Reginald Pole agreed: others paid the price if heretics were shown (false) clemency.[67] The spreading of heresy was religious reckless endangerment by spiritual serial killers. Indeed, heretics were worse than multiple murderers, because their victims lived on to harm others in turn. Small wonder, then, that Elizabethan apologist John Jewel seemed genuinely proud that Protestant rather than Catholic authorities had detected, condemned, and executed Michael Servetus and other heretics.[68] The danger of heresy was mitigated, however, because the heterodox were not compelled to cling to their errors—hence the strenuous efforts made to reclaim them for orthodoxy.

Every soul that Satan seduced was one lost to the hope of salvation. Heresy called for neither negotiation nor toleration, but rather swift and severe retaliation, lest even greater damage ensue. There were contemporary success stories: Bavarian Anabaptism was all but eliminated through a concerted campaign between 1527 and 1530.[69] Thomas More wrote in 1531, "As for heretics rising among our self, and springing of our self, [they] be in no wise to be suffered, but to be oppressed and overwhelmed in the beginning. For by any covenant with them, Christendom can nothing win. For as many as we suffer to fall to them we lose from Christ."[70] Eck quoted Jerome, reminding readers how the early Church's failure to suppress Arius at once had led to a massive expansion of his heresy. Du Val ruefully applied this lesson to Luther and Calvin.[71] Even if some began to regret missed opportunities, the growth of heresy did not necessarily disrupt the logic of aggressive suppression. If somewhere heretics were twice as numerous as before, this might simply call for redoubled efforts to stem still greater proliferation—to oppose heresy with "all diligence possible," as the French Edict of Châteaubriand put it in 1551, "day by day, and hour by hour."[72] Repressive efforts were undermined only when effective prosecution proved politically and practically impossible. Between the spring of 1560 and the last-ditch Edict of Saint-Germain in January 1562, this occurred in France. So too, in April 1566, a hard-pressed Margaret of Parma agreed to moderate the treatment of heretics in the Netherlands.[73]

Repeatedly, the willingness to kill was not defended on the basis of authorities' abstract right to maintain established religion; it was not justified as the expression of political power per se. Only *true* religion was legitimately defensible. Indeed, without this qualification, complaints about persecution would have been groundless. Just as Augustine's dictum "not the punishment, but the cause, makes a martyr" separated true from false martyrs on the basis of doctrine across confessional divides, its mirror image distinguished lawful prosecution from unjust persecution: not the punishment, but the cause, makes a persecutor. Hence Calvin condemned the papacy's murderous tyranny as he defended the rightful punishment of Servetus and his ilk. "We have to judge the zeal one has to maintain religion as we judge the religion itself," he wrote, separating legitimate suppression grounded in the "pure Word of God" from the "frantic and unlearned" oppression of the papists.[74] On the Catholic side, Stanislaus Hosius, a Polish prelate and legate to the Council of Trent, sounded no different than Calvin. Of persecution, he stated that "sometime he that doth suffer it is unrighteous, and he which doth practice it is righteous . . . without doubt, the evil men have always persecuted the good, and the good have persecuted [that is, prosecuted] the evil men . . . They outrageously, these discretely: they giving place to their malicious affection, these applying themselves wholly to charity."[75]

In 1579 Thomas Hide, an expatriate Catholic priest, published at Louvain his *Consolatory Epistle to the Afflicted Catholics* of England. Like Hosius, he distinguished persecution from prosecution in a discussion of true and false martyrs. Drawing on the book of Exodus, Hide noted that the Egyptian Pharaoh afflicted God's people as "a wicked persecutor, but Moses afflicted the same people for disobedience to himself and God as a good man . . . The one afflicted with tyrannical affection to oppress them, the other punished with charitable zeal, to amend them."[76] "Certain it is," Hide continued,

> that both good and evil do sometime afflict, use the like punishments, and pretend the same cause, even the cause of religion. The difference is, both do it not in like order, with one mind, nor to one end. In the cause of religion, the good afflict the evil by censures and Church law to repress division, to eschew error, and to save verity. The evil afflict the good against law and order, to serve their intended purpose, to prefer their faction, and to maintain heresy. In the cause of religion the good afflict the evil, for disobedience and breach of justice; the evil afflict the good for keeping obedience and holding with justice. *And here in the name of justice is implied truth of doctrine, which standeth in inward belief, and outward profession.*[77]

Whereas Calvin had emphasized Catholic cruelty, Hide stressed Protestant subjectivism and sedition. True doctrine legitimated prosecution, indeed *made* it prosecution rather than persecution. Doctrinal dispute therefore subverted any consensus about the prosecution of heterodoxy. Yet disagreement in no way altered authorities' respective obligations to defend the truth as they saw it.

Heresy imperiled souls. Its frequent links to sedition made its suppression even more urgent. Thomas More claimed that throughout the Church's history, the prosecution of heretics had always been a response to their initial rebelliousness and violence.[78] This was surely overstated, yet associating heresy with the Peasants' Revolt of 1524–1525 was no polemicist's fancy. Nor was it far-fetched to link Luther to the fissiparous spread of the early evangelical movement, despite the Wittenberger's contempt for many of the movement's strands. In 1534–1535 the Anabaptist Kingdom of Münster evoked near-universal horror and cemented the association of heresy with sedition. To rulers preoccupied with stability and acutely aware of its fragility, heterodoxy signified political unrest and war. Fundamentally, the Peace of Augsburg (1555) institutionalized the view that intraterritorial religious pluralism was unworkable. The Holy Roman Empire's political diversity and "dispersed governance" made religious allegiance as prescribed by individual rulers feasible for a time.[79] France and England's stronger monarchies, however, precluded analogous solutions. In 1543, the Edict of Paris described heretics as "seditious and disturbers of the peace and tranquility of our republic and subjects, and secret conspirators against the prosperity of our state, which depends chiefly and in large measure on the preservation of the integrity of the Catholic faith in our kingdom."[80] The Lutheran Justus Menius, writing in 1538, and the Catholic Antoine Du Val, writing in 1559, argued that combining different religious communities was a sure recipe for violence.[81]

Concerned about the salvation of souls and the threat of sedition, writers found indirect support for a willingness to kill in the New Testament. They leaned on Augustine's long-dominant interpretation of the parable of the wheat and the tares, which had displaced earlier Christian readings. Miles Huggarde was among the many who repeated Augustine's providential perspective in the sixteenth century. In the Church's infancy the difficulty of telling the wheat from the tares, and the absence of Christian magistrates, had rendered the lenient treatment of heretics appropriate. Yet thereafter the Church had grown so strong "that hell gates shall not prevail against it. That is to say: neither the persecution of tyrants, nor the perversity of heretics, can overthrow it. The church, I say, now being in this state, and that heretics may easily be discerned, as cockle is in harvest . . . doth by excommunication cut them off, as scripture commandeth."[82] Calvin invoked the same parable, noting that to refrain from punishing heretics would imply that other criminals should be left unpunished as well.[83] Eck, Calvin, and Bullinger noted the case of Ananias and Sapphira (Acts 5:1–11), both of whom died when Peter rebuked them. Because Jesus had driven mere moneylenders from the temple (John 2:14–16), Eck argued, he would have done far worse to heretics.[84] Christian *caritas* implied neither tolerance of nor infinite patience toward obstinate heretics, but a responsible, early modern tough love, enacted for the sake of others and the common good.

At the root of the willingness to kill were fiercely held convictions about Christian faith. Thomas More allowed for "variety, mutation, and change" in the Church over time. Yet to accuse the one, Catholic Church of wayward doctrines in any "substantial point of the faith," he wrote, was to label Christ a liar, for the Lord had promised to send both the Holy Spirit and himself "unto the end of the world to persevere and abide in his Church."[85] Christian doctrinal pluralism was not merely implausible, but contradictory: it effectively asserted that truth was both A and not-A. In a related key, Calvin ridiculed those who would permit people to read and understand the Bible as they pleased. He had only contempt for claims, like Sebastian Castellio's,[86] that scripture was often enigmatic "and that the truth is as though hidden in obscure clouds." Such views made of God a soteriological sadist who deliberately kept men and women unsure of the truths necessary for salvation.[87] The problem was not the obscurity of truth, but rather the obstinacy of those who spurned its challenging clarity. As with More, there was simply no room for doctrinal divergence within Christianity. The very notion of tolerating deliberate heterodoxy was abhorrent. It was tantamount to letting dangerous people seduce others to damnation, sully God's honor, and subvert the social fabric—surely no victimless crime. Ultimately, the certainty of faith plus a paternalism both pastoral and political separated dutiful executions from the sin of murder.

Laws, Institutions, and the Contingencies of Practice

Rigorous theological arguments, no matter how compelling, of themselves put no one to death. In order to pass from prescription to practice, the willingness to kill required determination, resources, and means. It was put into practice through formal institutions, by men observing established laws. Yet there was no direct link between laws and actual prosecution. Not only did early modern authorities vary in their individual conviction and temperament, but they also juggled diverse and frequently divergent priorities. Repression depended in part on states' judicial resources, rulers' own commitments, other political issues, military involvements, fiscal pressures, the perceived threat of heterodoxy, and the ever-present, overriding concern to maintain order. Charles V governed an empire that stretched from Portugal to Poland; in the early 1520s, he could not have tabled everything else to deal with the evangelical movement in Germany. Nor, once heresy had spread beyond a certain point, could the means available to any early modern regime contain it. Prosecution depended, too, on the sometimes strained cooperation between central and local authorities, the former craving greater control, the latter always keen to protect their privileges. From the 1520s, in France, the Low Countries, and England, authorities addressed multiple concerns within a framework of active lawmaking and shifting institutional relationships. The interaction of these variables shaped the basic course of the prosecution of heresy and religious treason during the era.[88]

In France, the sovereign's attitude toward heresy coupled with the relationship among the crown, the Parlement of Paris, and the faculty of theology of the University of Paris, was crucial.[89] In October 1534, Protestants papered several cities, including the capital, with broadsheets denouncing the Mass in the Affair of the Placards. Francis I's careful categories crumbled: he was much less willing to shield the reform-minded at court, or to distinguish their erudite Erasmianism from seditious heterodoxy. Afterward he still sought a political alliance with Protestant princes against Charles V, but the 1538 Truce of Nice he struck with the emperor rendered any such overtures irrelevant. Now fundamentally aligned with the Parlement and the Paris faculty of theology, the king turned vigorously against heresy, with concrete results. Henry II's *chambre ardente* (1547–1550) and Edict of Châteaubriand (1551) did not spring from a vacuum—they extended the tough legislation and the sharp increase in executions of his father's final years.[90] Henry kept the pressure on until his early death in 1559, but Huguenot numbers and influence surged nonetheless. By the spring of 1560, fearing civil war, Catherine de Medici led a moderate court party that favored conciliation with the Calvinists as the lesser of two evils. Repeated attempts at compromise, however, failed to satisfy the intransigent on both sides. Between the Parisian Affair of the Rue Saint-Jacques in September 1557 and the Massacre of Vassy in March 1562, judicial proceedings against heterodoxy gave way to open warfare via mutual hostility and popular violence.

In the Low Countries, neither Charles V nor his son, Philip II, needed a watershed experience like the Affair of the Placards to persuade them of heresy's dangers.[91] Their committed opposition to heterodoxy seems never to have wavered. Yet for decades they faced on-and-off friction from provincial councillors and civic magistrates across the particularist provinces of the Netherlands. Beginning in the 1520s a steady stream of placards, like France's repeated censorship laws, both testified to the insufficiency of repression and dictated more stringent measures. When the political threat of heresy was manifest, as in the later 1530s after Anabaptist militancy at Münster, local authorities acted swiftly and with severity, in concert with the emperor's wishes. But when they judged that prosecution was likely to spur, not squelch, further disorder and dissent, they frequently relaxed their efforts, leaving him frustrated. Charles turned to the inquisition, which he reorganized in 1546, as a means to enforce his will in towns from Holland to Hainaut. This initiative fed tensions between inquisitors and magistrates, not softened by the spread of Reformed Protestantism and the so-called Bloody Placard of 1550. Philip II's implacable opposition to doctrinal deviance— he preferred to lose "all my states and even a hundred lives, if I had them," rather than to become the "sovereign of heretics"—would eventually cost him the northern provinces.[92] Like Catherine de Medici, the regent Margaret of Parma faced a volatile situation of her own by the mid-1560s: an absentee king unwilling to compromise, persistent inquisitorial efforts, swelling numbers of aggressive heretics, and frequently uncooperative local authorities. This constellation could not last. In April 1566 a pressured Margaret told magistrates to moderate their treatment of heretics. Emboldened heretical preachers attracted thousands to open-air sermons, and by August their fervor incited a widespread burst of anti-Catholic image-smashing in the Iconoclastic Fury. This destruction would call forth the Duke of Alva and a justice far less forgiving than that of the inquisitor Pieter Titelmans.

England's prosecution of religious nonconformity followed a different pattern, one that paralleled the country's dramatic ecclesio-political swings between 1530 and 1560.[93] There, evangelical ideas reached a country in which anti-Lollard heresy laws had been operative for over a century. In 1521 Henry VIII put his name to a theological treatise defending the Church's seven sacraments against Luther. Yet the king's "Great Matter"—his desire to divorce Katherine of Aragon and to marry Anne Boleyn—precipitated the undoing of English obedience to the Roman Catholic Church by 1534. Fidelity to the pope was recast in purely political terms and defined as treason. With the lone exception of the Observant Franciscan John Forest, who was burned in 1538, the Roman Catholics executed in the British Isles under Henry VIII, Elizabeth I, and in smaller numbers in the seventeenth century perished as traitors, not heretics.[94] Save for a window of relative leniency between 1535 and 1538, however, Henry remained staunchly opposed to Protestants too, a number of whom were executed after the break with Rome. The pendulum swung dramatically in the Protestants' favor under the boy-king Edward VI (1547–1553), then no less sharply back under the Roman Catholic Mary Tudor (1553–1558), with antiheresy legislation repealed and reinstated accordingly. About three hundred heretics were burned in Mary's reign from 1555 to 1558. With Elizabeth (1558–1603), everything changed once more, as a Protestant polity was established and, by dint of longevity, gradually took hold. After 1580, amidst international tensions, it was especially Catholic missionary priests and their supporters who were executed as religious traitors. From 1585, to be a Catholic priest in England was ipso facto treason. Executions waned after the 1590s, but not until 1681, with Oliver Plunkett, was the last Catholic clergyman hanged, drawn, and quartered.

Laws remain dead letters unless acted upon, as Charles V and others knew only too well. Although monarchs might order the scrupulous observation of antiheresy laws from on high, local magistrates might not heed them. A number of variables affected actual prosecution and the enactment of punishments.[95] Even in countries and territories theoretically absolute in their opposition to heterodoxy, dissenters' prospects of dying for their convictions—and thus of being recognized by their fellow believers as martyrs—were far from certain.

Within a given regime, some magistrates zealously enforced the law, others did so leniently, and still others not at all. Such differences comprised perhaps the most fundamental variable in the prosecution of nonconformity. They are readily observable in both England and on the Continent in the 1550s, for example. Of the Marian heretics condemned in London's diocesan courts, at least sixty came from Essex, as opposed to only thirty from London, one from Middlesex, and one from Hertfordshire. This is scarcely attributable to Essex having twice as many dissenters as London, or sixty times as many as Middle-sex. Rather, it reflects above all the diligent pursuit of prosecution by certain justices of the peace in Essex.[96] By contrast, late in her reign Mary wrote to Richard Pexsall, sheriff of Hampshire, noting how "very strange" it was that a condemned heretic named Bembrigge had not yet been executed. She ordered him to get on with it.[97]

Magistrates could and did understand their responsibilities in specific cases differently, while sharing the same general framework of beliefs. Calvin sent his published justification of the execution of Servetus to Nicholas Zerkinden, Chancellor of Berne. Zerkinden told Calvin that only extreme mockers of religion should be punished harshly, not simple misbelievers. He noted the strong impression that the execution of an eighty-year-old Anabaptist woman and her daughter had made on him.[98] Apparently some French magistrates exhibited similar tendencies. The 1557 Edict of Compiègne remarked that "very often it has happened that our judges are moved out of pity by the 'holy' and malicious words of the defendants in these crimes [against religion]."[99] Willem Bardes, Amsterdam's bailiff, obstructed other Catholics on the town council from prosecuting Anabaptists with severity in the years after 1552. One of his daughters and a daughter-in-law were in touch with and eventually joined the *doopsgezinden,* which must in part have contributed to Bardes's actions.[100] By the later sixteenth century a wide gulf existed in German Lutheran territories between theological prescriptions and judicial practices: the theologians' exhortation to execute Anabaptists, issued at Worms in 1557, seems to have had no impact on magistrates who were unwilling to carry it out.[101]

Raymond Mentzer provides an excellent example of magistrates' disagreement about whether and how the heterodox ought to be punished.[102] The panel of presidial court judges in Nîmes sentenced Etienne Geynet in October 1553. Following the Edict of Châteaubriand, Jehan Robert, the *lieutenant criminel,* called for strangulation, burning, and confiscation of Geynet's possessions for the crown. Jehan du Port, an official of the diocese of Arles, concurred with the verdict but strongly objected to the death sentence. Jehan Albenas, another official, wanted an inquiry into Geynet's objections about witnesses. Yet another member of the court, Jehan Rochemaure, urged that final sentencing be stayed until through torture Geynet might reveal the names of other heretics. Instead of execution, one Richier called for an *amende honorable,* a beating, tongue piercing, perpetual banishment from the seneschalsy, and confiscation of goods and property save one-third for Geynet's children. Another official named Brueis recommended only an *amende honorable* and a fine of twenty-five livres. In the end, Geynet was sentenced to Richier's recommended punishments except for the tongue piercing. Clearly, this was not a unanimous judicial body slavishly following the letter of the law.

In Geynet's case, authorities' disagreement and compromise had saved his life. On other occasions jurisdictional disputes meant the difference between life and death. In 1538, for example, officials in Amiens and members of the Parlement of Paris disagreed about who should try Jean de Rez. He exploited their disagreement, avoided prosecution, and charged his accusers with false testimony.[103]

Even when French edicts or imperial placards mandated automatic capital punishment, a door to survival remained open. Between the execution of six Anabaptists in April 1551 and seven more in July, Ghent's magistrates released three young Anabaptists. The three had at first remained steadfast but then abjured, promising to commit themselves to a Catholic life and to an examination after two years.[104] Even Philip II was willing to bestow royal mercy on repentant heretics, at least occasionally: on his way to England in 1557, for example, he pardoned five Anabaptists in Ghent. At about the same time, responding to requests from the Secret Council and the Council of Flanders, he sanctioned the pardon of penitent heretics, provided they were not allowed to return to (presumably heretical) family and friends.[105]

Authorities' willingness to spare the lives of most repentant heretics is crucial for understanding the dynamic of prosecution. It let those arrested know that they might still be released, with lesser punishments, if they showed remorse and abjured. Meanwhile inquisitors and magistrates knew that leaving a door open might save some lives—they might entice some recantations from people who otherwise would have been put to death as a matter of course.

Geopolitical factors also influenced executions for heterodoxy. John Oyer provides an example from the adjoining territories of Hesse and Electoral Saxony in central Germany.[106] Philipp of Hesse's men arrested the Anabaptist leader Melchior Rink along with eleven other Anabaptists in the border village of Vacha on November 11, 1531. An official in the Saxon district of Eisenach wrote to Philipp, urging him to execute Rink for his revolutionary views and blasphemy. This official also advised Johann of Saxony to pressure Philipp for Rink's death, which Johann did, telling Philipp to follow the imperial mandate of April 1529. But since Philipp, unlike some other Lutheran princes, regarded blasphemy—the public teaching of erroneous doctrine—as insufficient grounds for the execution of Anabaptists, he instead sentenced Rink to life imprisonment. Had Rink been taken by the Elector's officials, he almost certainly would have been executed. Just as disagreement among the presidial court officials in Nîmes had made Etienne Geynet a banished Protestant instead of a likely Protestant martyr, Melchior Rink's apprehension by Hessian rather than Saxon officials led to prison rather than to probable recognition as an Anabaptist martyr.

National vicissitudes in religious polity directly and dramatically affected England's prosecution of heterodoxy. Similar shifts are discernible elsewhere on a smaller scale. For example, Duke Ulrich of Württemberg was exiled from his territory between 1528 and 1534. During these years the region came under Austrian control, and correspondingly more Anabaptists were put to death. When Ulrich returned, the executions subsided and were replaced by imprisonment or exile.[107] In 1529 the Protestant estates endorsed the imperial decrees against Anabaptists, reversing the previous year's fairly widespread, evangelical consensus against executing them. By 1531 Luther and Melanchthon had come to favor capital punishment for Anabaptist preachers and their unrepentant followers.[108] In England, a considerable de facto latitude for Protestants changed radically with the Act of the Six Articles in 1539. In late 1584, Elizabeth banished over twenty imprisoned missionary priests who might otherwise have been executed.[109] Clearly, being put to death for nonconformity depended greatly on where one happened to be at a given time.

To some extent it also turned on whether one was a man or a woman. Conspicuously fewer women than men are celebrated in the Christian martyrological sources of the early modern period.[110] This stems partly from the tendency of authorities to treat female dissidents less severely than men. Not only were the Elizabethan laws, for example, directed above all at missionary priests, who of course were exclusively male, but women who were guilty of capital infractions were treated more leniently by Elizabethan officials. At Winchester in 1591, eight or nine young women pleaded "with open outcries and exclamations" that they merited execution alongside Catholic priest Roger Dicconson and layman Ralph Milner. Like the two men, they had heard Mass, supported a priest, and confessed their sins after the Catholic rites. The women, however, were condemned but not sentenced, whereas the men were put to death.[111] In tending to hold husbands responsible for their wives suspected of heterodoxy, officials apparently embraced the common assumption that women were in general less than fully accountable for their actions.[112] In 1551 the Council of Flanders wrote to the magistrates of Ghent urging clemency for an Anabaptist woman with three children who had forsworn her views, saying that she had been pressured into heresy by her husband.[113]

Social status, too, frequently influenced prosecution and punishment. In the 1520s, Francis I protected court-connected, evangelical sympathizers, but not the heterodox from humbler social and educational backgrounds. In Marian England, John Boswell, an assistant to Bonner in London, complained that heretics of humbler origin were prosecuted while "arch-here-tics"—presumably of higher social status—were left alone.[114] Magistrates in Dutch towns were less willing to carry out sentences against their social equals than against their social inferiors.[115] Local authorities, after all, had to keep the peace despite the religious divisions that threatened stability. Popular disruptions at public executions—which in Holland occurred in Amsterdam in 1546, Enkhuizen and Haarlem in 1557, and Rotterdam in 1558[116]—forced them to reevaluate the balance between the defense of orthodoxy and political obedience on the one hand and the maintenance of order on the other.

The greater the disturbances, the less likely authorities were to prosecute heretics fully. Unrest pushed them to favor secret executions over the public spectacles whose purpose the demonstrations had subverted. The growth of heretical communities made it ever more difficult to pursue policies of concerted repression. In the 1550s and 1560s, increasingly severe directives in France and the Low Countries became harder to enact: prescription grated against practice, monarchs conflicted with magistrates, and orthodox officials clashed openly with heretical communities.[117] At a certain point, even authorities who detested heresy with every fiber of their being could not root it out. Resistance and riots had unmasked the rulers' absolutist pretensions in the judicial sphere. Yet the limits of state power had not been reached: in France and the Netherlands, war would broaden the means of suppression.

The contingencies of practice do not alter the fact that thousands of men and women found themselves in mortal danger for their religious convictions. Once suspects were on trial, the possible outcomes narrowed if repeated efforts to dissuade them proved fruitless. Politically sensitive magistrates and pastorally concerned clergy were far less indulgent toward defiant than deferential suspects. Principled persistence invited death. It was precisely this steadfastness that characterized the martyrs and their willingness to die.

CHAPTER FOUR

The Willingness to Die

For as the rain and snow come down from heaven, and do not return there until they have watered the earth, making it bring forth and sprout, giving seed to the sower and bread to the eater, so shall my word be that goes out from my mouth; it shall not return to me empty, but it shall accomplish that which I purpose, and succeed in the thing for which I sent it.

—ISAIAH 55:10–11

For now it pleases God to accomplish in me that which I have many times desired, as you well know: namely, that he grant me the grace to die for his Gospel, to the edification of his people. This he will do in the near future, delivering me from all evils and setting me in his kingdom.

—FROM PIERRE BRULLY'S FINAL LETTER TO HIS WIFE,
FEBRUARY 18, 1546

Early modern Christian martyrs endured horrifying deaths rather than renounce their religious convictions. They had their reasons. To comprehend their sensibilities and motivations calls for a careful analysis of both their words and their deeds. The fusion of their religious beliefs and their behavior shaped paths that led to their execution. The surviving evidence for hundreds of Protestant, Anabaptist, and Roman Catholic martyrs makes this clear. Let us meet one, chosen somewhat at random from among martyrs about whom we are neither especially well nor poorly informed. Joyce Lewis was a well-to-do, married woman from Lichfield, England. Unlike some of the martyrs, she was neither highly educated nor illiterate. During Mary Tudor's reign she became an ardent Protestant and was burned on September 10, 1557. John Foxe tells her story in four folio columns of his *Acts and Monuments*.[1]

At first Joyce Lewis conformed to the Marian restoration of Roman Catholicism in England. Then she learned that Laurence Saunders, an erudite Protestant theologian, had been burned as a heretic for opposing the Mass. She sought out John Glover, a committed "man of God" who was her neighbor. Glover, "perceiving both her unquiet mind, and also the desire she had to know the truth, did most diligently instruct her in the ways of the Lord." Soon "she began to wax weary of the world thoroughly sorrowful for her sins, being inflamed with the love of God, desirous to serve him according to his word, purposing also to fly from those things the which did displease the Lord her God." Having learned that the Mass was "evil and abominable, she began to hate it." Compelled by her husband, Thomas Lewis, to attend Mass at some point in 1556, she turned her back during the sprinkling of holy water. This earned her a trip before the bishop of Coventry and Lichfield, Ralph Baynes, a master of Greek and the author of a Hebrew grammar. Her husband was furious when the summoner delivered the episcopal citation: he ordered him to return it, and when the summoner refused, Thomas forced him at knifepoint to eat the document. Nonetheless, the bishop questioned Joyce, who offended him with her replies. Yet in part "because she was a gentle woman," Baynes treated her leniently: he ordered Thomas to bring her back after a month to be questioned again. Failure to do so would cost the husband a hundred pounds.

During this month, Joyce "gave herself to most diligent prayer and invocating of the name of God, resorting continually to the above named man of God master John Glover, who did most diligently instruct her with God's word." After the month was up, Baynes found her "more stout than she was before." The bishop then had her sent to prison, where she remained for over a year. Despite being "oftentimes examined" by authorities seeking to secure her recantation, she refused to relinquish her Protestant views. Eventually she was sentenced to be burned as an obstinate heretic.

As her execution drew near, like-minded friends helped her prepare for the ordeal:

> She desired certain of her friends to come unto her, with whom (when they came) she consulted how she might behave herself, that her death might be most glorious to the name of God, comfortable to his people, and also most discomfortable unto the enemies of God. "As for the fear of death, I do not greatly pass when I behold," said she, "the amiable countenance of Christ my dear savior, the ugsome face of death doth not greatly trouble me." In the which time also she reasoned most comfortably out of God's word of God's election and reprobation.

Lewis passed the final evening of her life, September 9, 1557, "wonderfully cheerful and merry with a certain gravity." She was not afraid of her impending death and spent the time "in prayer, reading, and talking with them that were purposely come unto her for to comfort her with the word of God." Yet about three in the morning that same night, Foxe tells us, Satan—"who never sleepeth, especially when death is at hand"—troubled her tranquility. He asked "how she could tell that she was chosen to eternal life, and that Christ died for her." This skeptical challenge unsettled Lewis, but by recalling Gal. 2:20—that Christ "loved me and gave himself for me"—she sensed "that her vocation and calling to the knowledge of God's word, was a manifest token of God's love towards her." As a result, "specially by the comfortable promises of Christ, brought out of the scripture, Satan was put to flight, and she comforted in Christ."

About eight o'clock on the morning of September 10, the sheriff said she had but one hour to live. She was "somewhat abashed" at these words, but a friend reminded her of her "great cause to praise God, who will vouchsafe so speedily to take you out of this world, and make you worthy to be a witness to his truth, and to bear record unto Christ that he is the only savior." After this encouragement, Lewis told the sheriff, "Your message is welcome to me, and I thank my God that he will make me worthy to adventure my life in his quarrel." Two friends were permitted to accompany her to the stake; "a great multitude of people" were present along the way. Unaccustomed to the fresh air after her long confinement, she requested and received some beer. After praying that the Mass would be abolished, she drank, "the most part of the people cried 'Amen,'" and "a great number, especially the women of the town, did drink with her," though others jeered at her. Lewis sustained her death with joyful equanimity:

> When she was tied to the stake with the chain, she showed such a cheerfulness that it passed man's reason, being so well colored in her face, and so patient, that the most part of them that had honest hearts did lament, and even with tears bewail the tyranny of the papists. When the fire was set upon her, she neither struggled nor stirred, but lifted up her hands towards God, being dead very speedily, the under-sheriff being favorable, who at the request of her friends did provide such stuff by the which she was suddenly dispatched out of this miserable world.[2]

Joyce Lewis rejected a gentlewoman's comfortable existence in order to embrace illegal convictions that led to the stake. She had defied her husband, Bishop Baynes, and the others who tried to dissuade her as she spent more than a year in prison. She knew just where her actions would lead and carefully planned the performance of her public *ars moriendi*. At every step along the way, from her initial disquiet to her steadfast death, Lewis's faith and friends had brought her consolation and courage.

The Poverty of Theory

It is unsurprising that few scholars have sought to understand the experience of people like Joyce Lewis. The postconfessional history of early modern Christianity has been dominated by reductionist social, political, anthropological, and cultural-theoretical explanations of religious belief and behavior. Yet the demographic diversity of the martyrs across confessional divides and over long stretches of time frustrates explanation by any of these means. Any prospective theory or combination of theories must account for men and women, clergy and laity, teenagers through septagenarians, erudite theologians through the moderately literate to the wholly unlettered, the privileged and powerful as well as middling sorts and the most humble folk, across national, linguistic, and confessional boundaries. Equally important, any theory would have to explain why particular individuals, but not others, in a given group were willing to die for their religious convictions. Social-historical explanations of religion, for example, cannot even explain why a particular artisan became Protestant instead of remaining Catholic, so it is inconceivable that they might explicate why specific martyrs across the social spectrum were willing to die. Nobody was willing to die *because* he was an artisan, a gentleman, or even a priest, not to mention a female servant, a gentlewoman, or a cloistered nun. It would be overreaching to assert, a priori, that no theory or theoretical hybrid *could* explain the willingness to die of all these different people. But it is fair to say, I think, that no available theory or theories even comes close.

Having to account for individual differences suggests that modern psychological explanations may be useful. Yet the problem remains of explaining the actions of men and women with such disparate backgrounds and experiences. Circular arguments—for example, that the willingness to die was a function of neuroses that expressed themselves in the martyrs' willingness to die—explain nothing. Seymour Byman's dubious application of psychoanalytic theory to the Marian martyrs assumes this form. According to Byman, the martyr is "the most fervent and enigmatic of all religious types" whose manner of death "was pathological, both in its sources and in its pattern": "The compulsive neurotic constructs a ritualistic pattern manifested by repetitive, orderly, and, at times, seemingly senseless behavior that he must perform slavishly to escape from anxiety."[3] Byman claims that these supposedly pathological rituals included the martyrs' praying repetitively, following ascetic routines, kissing or embracing the stake, and enduring death by fire without flinching. (He makes no reference to martyrs quoting scripture, even though the letters and stories of martyrs to whom he refers, such as John Bradford and John Philpot, are dense with biblical references.) By implying that modern values such as originality and self-sufficient individuality provide a transhistorical standard with which to assess their purported pathologies, Byman seems oblivious to the most basic values of early modern Europeans.[4]

Behind modern psychological theories like Byman's lie assumptions that regard self-preservation and the prolongation of one's life as the greatest of all values. These views seem to underlie Richard Marius's incomprehension of Thomas More's willingness to die as a Roman Catholic martyr:

> Still, we are left with the most puzzling question of all: what kind of man chooses to die for his faith. Martyrdom is an exceptional talent; that is

why we make so much of it. And people like Thomas More, refusing to save his life by speaking a few words, remain as mysterious to us as suicides are to those who love life and hate the thought of giving it up. It is all well and good to spell out, as I have done, the intellectual reasons behind More's supreme act, but somehow they do not get to the heart . . . Confronted by such mysteries, social historians quote statistics, historians of theology cite doctrines, and biographers recoil before the task of sorting out the conflicting strands in the weave of character that add up to such an end.[5]

This assessment suffers from a biographer's myopia: More's prison experience and execution, dramatic and well-documented though they are, do not make him terribly unusual. Several thousand Christians were executed for "refusing to save [their lives] by speaking a few words," not just an "exceptionally talented" handful. Like Byman, Marius implies that martyrs comprise a "type." He suggests that there is a "kind of man" (and woman?) willing to die a martyr's death, and that this in turn should prompt a search for "the conflicting strands in the weave of character that add up to such an end." The fact, however, is that the intensity and the uncompromising nature of their religious commitment are the only common (and the most important) strands in the "weave of character" among early modern Christian martyrs. Once the nature of this commitment is understood, martyrdom appears as its consistent enactment. If we do not "get" martyrdom, it is because we do not "get" the martyrs' religiosity. By collapsing More's belief into a *desire* to believe, Marius seems to evince just this bewilderment: "As with all martyrs who are not insane, it may be argued that he died not for what he believed but for what he wanted to believe."[6]

What about insanity? Or fanaticism? One can maintain as an axiom that a willingness to die for religious views is insane. This is not an explanation, however, but rather simply the expression of (secular) values and beliefs different from those of the martyrs. Almost no evidence could be employed to argue that early modern martyrs were insane, if by this is meant some sort of mental disorder or delusional madness. The martyrs and their fellow believers regarded their actions as laudable, not pathological or imbalanced. By contrast, the renunciation of one's beliefs was foolish and dangerous. Many martyrs expressed with precision and elegance the reasons for their willingness to die. They were not raving lunatics, but men and women who articulated and enacted values held in common with fellow believers in their respective communities of faith.

To accuse the martyrs of fanaticism is simply a tacit admission that no acceptable explanation for their actions can be found. Calling behavior "fanatical" merely dismisses its intelligibility. In addition, as a category "fanaticism" entirely lacks analytical rigor, since its criteria change depending upon who defines it. What many people today would doubtless consider fanatical behavior—such as engaging in ascetic practices, praying for hours on end, remaining always aware of God's Last Judgment, memorizing scripture, and refusing to attend disapproved church services—was considered exemplary and widely praised by early modern Christians. Nor were martyrs fanatics in the sense of being oblivious to their situation or confused about what they were dying for. Those who seem to take satisfaction in finding bygone people riddled with conflicting commitments are indeed likely to be baffled by early modern martyrs. Inquisitors asked specific questions to determine whether suspected heretics were in error; Elizabethan authorities sought to ascertain precisely what Roman Catholics thought about papal and royal authority. If anything, martyrs were often extraordinarily self-concious about what they were doing. Their purposeful clarity and articulate resolve often startles modern readers.

Consider the case of John Frith, burned in England in 1533. He was willing to die not because he was convinced he had understood the Lord's Supper accurately, but because he was not certain that transubstantiation was a necessary article of faith. "The cause of my death is this," he wrote: "because I cannot in conscience abjure and swear, that our prelates' opinion of the sacrament (that is that the substance of bread and wine is verily changed into the flesh and blood of our savior Jesus Christ) is an undoubted article of the faith, necessary to be believed under pain of damnation."[7] Frith was willing to die for his uncertainty about Catholic orthodoxy. This was not an unthinking man seizing on a doctrinal whim, but a Cambridge-trained theologian, meticulously introspective about what he believed and why.

Penny Roberts has recently implied that the willingness to die was born of the inevitability of execution. The martyrs' resolve stemmed from their inability to escape automatic death sentences for nonconformity: "embracing death for one's faith is the prerequisite of those who are on their way to the stake or the scaffold, or in prison without hope of release . . . Once captured, then was the time for commitment to the cause, unless another opportunity presented itself for evasion. This more practical side certainly provides for most of us a more empathetic view of the path of martyrdom."[8] Roberts rightly mentions examples of Huguenots who disguised themselves and seized opportunities to escape from prison. Catholic missionaries in Elizabethan England also employed disguises and false identities. It cannot be argued, however, that in general the inevitability of death engendered the willingness to die. Such a contention overlooks several important points.

First, laws prescribing the execution of heretics, even those ordering automatic execution, were frequently not carried out. Since inquisitors and local magistrates were often willing to release penitent heretics, imprisoned suspects knew they might avoid death by abjuration. Second, Roberts's view underestimates the level of commitment required simply to be a Protestant and remain in France, for example, during the 1550s. The prospect of apprehension and death hovered constantly over Huguenot existence; it was not enkindled only by imprisonment, or when execution was unavoidable. Third, if imprisoned Christians seized the opportunity to escape from prison, we cannot assume that they lacked the willingness to die. John Calvin, Pierre Viret, and others said that exile and martyrdom were both acceptable responses to persecution. Christians who fled prison might well have been exercising the scripturally based option recommended by their leaders (see Matt. 10:23).[9] Indeed, it was risky to presume that God was still calling one to martyrdom despite mercifully providing for one's escape. The early Swiss Anabaptist Karli Brennwald combined the willingness to die with the fact of later flight: from prison he said on March 5, 1526, that he would seal his views "with his blood"—but he escaped along with Conrad Grebel and other co-believers on March 21.[10] Finally, Roberts overlooks the extent to which perseverance amid persecution strengthened Christian commitment in the first place. This widespread attitude fostered a willingness and even desire to die as a martyr that far transcended the specific prison experiences of those who were actually executed. Roberts's interpretation may indeed provide "for most of us a more empathetic view of the path of martyrdom"—but this is beside the point. It does not account for the martyrs' path of martyrdom.

Contrary to Roberts's view, we might ask whether martyrs had a "death wish": that is, whether execution was what they wanted all along, as a result of which they placed themselves in situations where in effect they were committing suicide. Marius associates martyrdom with suicide in discussing More, suggesting that both are equally baffling "to those who love life and hate the thought of giving it up." But this gratuitously assumes that because martyrs were willing to die for their religious views, they must not have loved life—as if anything less than maximizing one's temporal existence were akin to suicide. The martyrs considered the prolongation of their lives as one, less than absolute, good among others.

Nevertheless, the evidence demands that we take seriously the notion of the martyrs having a "death wish." Some men and women imprisoned for their convictions, held under often appalling conditions, expecting execution, sometimes having been tortured, wanted deliverance through death. Before her execution in 1564, for example, Mayken Boosers wrote to fellow Anabaptists, "I hope that shortly it will be done with me, for I want nothing more than to please the Lord and to die a holy death."[11] Similarly, when missionary priest Ralph Sherwin wrote to friends before he was drawn and quartered in 1581, he lamented that "delay of our death doth somewhat dull me, it was not without cause that our Master himself said, *Quod facis fac cito*" [what you do, do quickly].[12] Such sentiments, however, were not unique to martyrs. They were not fundamentally different from the desires of people who, suffering from a fatal illness or a mortal injury on their deathbeds, longed for death to release them from suffering.

Certain devout Christians, particularly within post-Tridentine Catholicism, actively yearned for martyrdom. Cornelius Musius, a learned Dutch priest, nurtured "an ardent desire for martyrdom." Once active conflict with the Calvinists began in the Netherlands, "he showed himself still more fervent and desirous to suffer martyrdom," talking about it frequently with friends and attentively reading exhortations to martyrdom.[13] The Jesuit rector of the English College in Rome wrote to William Allen in June 1579, just before the English mission began in earnest, telling Allen that "within the college, so great is the enthusiasm of all the students as they prepare themselves for that combat in England, and so daily pant for tortures and death [*anhelant quotidie ad tormenta et mortem*] for the Catholic faith, that it would seem to be impossible that God would not powerfully assist such a devout and such a holy desire."[14] The same sensibility was expressed more than half a century later. Marie Guyart Martin, a French widow turned Ursuline nun and missionary to Canada, wrote to her son, a Benedictine monk in France, thanking him for "the good hope that you expressed for me (martyrdom)," adding that "if someone came to me and said, 'Your son has been martyred,' I think that I would die of joy."[15]

Protestants sometimes held similar views, as can be seen from Pierre Brully's remark to his wife in the epigraph to this chapter. In the 1520s Luther himself seems to have struggled with the fact that other evangelicals were being martyred instead of him.[16] Jan van Woerden baited his inquisitors in The Hague in 1525: responding to their threats of execution should he fail to abjure, he told them to "go away, and bring on that fire," asked them if it was not yet made, and said, "I see that the wood for the fire hasn't been brought yet—where is it?"[17] Venetian ambassador Giovanni Michiel, in a letter of May 19, 1556, reported that during the previous week Marian authorities had continued "to burn male and also female heretics, all of whom, so far from evincing fear of the flames, seek them voluntarily, accusing themselves, and going to make their depositions in person."[18] Similarly, Boutzon le Heu was frequently heard to say, "O, how happy I would be were the Lord to call me as a witness to his truth—what greater honor could come my way from God?"[19]

The ideal of martyrdom was held in high esteem by Protestants, Anabaptists, and Catholics. Even when devout Christians earnestly desired martyrdom, however, they and their contemporaries drew a sharp distinction between people killed for actions consistent with religious commitment—which might involve considerable danger or even deliberate provocation—and people who took their own lives.[20] The former were martyrs, heroic witnesses rewarded by God with eternal joy; the latter were suicides, certain to be damned for rejecting God's gift of life. The traditional Christian condemnation of suicide survived the Reformation: actively taking one's own life ruled one out as a martyr in all three traditions. Even among those most desirous to die, I know of no one who was regarded as a martyr in the Reformation period after committing a "holy suicide," as some early Christian virgins allegedly did to avoid idolatry or intercourse with non-Christian men.[21] For this reason, the phrase "to martyr oneself" is an oxymoron when applied to the early modern period; to be reckoned a martyr, one had "to be martyred." People could, however, enter or remain in situations overshadowed by the threat of death. Frequently this was highly praised, as with missionaries or itinerant preachers, who, if they were killed, were recognized as martyrs. Such missionaries did not value the prolongation of their lives above everything else. Rather, they were willing to risk a shorter life that might end in a brutal death in order to help guide other souls to eternal salvation. Even hostile controversialists typically understood false martyrs to be obstinate, not suicidal. They had stubbornly clung to their wicked views, not wantonly thrown away their lives.

To become a missionary, or to refrain from voluntary exile under repressive conditions, derived from the same attitudes that made people cleave to their convictions rather than recant them. *Wanting* to die for Christ was continuous with the *willingness* to die for him. Some martyrs indeed had a death wish—they literally wished to die—yet they wished to die *as martyrs*, not simply to end their lives. When asked by an interrogator whether his seeming desire to die meant that he no longer wanted to live, Jan van Woerden explained himself by paraphrasing Matt. 16:25–26: "life is not annoying to my flesh, but Christ teaches me that I must lose my life here in order to find it in eternal life; that it profits a man nothing to win the whole world, and harm and lose his soul."[22] In short, the martyrs' willingness to die should be neither conflated nor confused with suicidal impulses. The issue was rather whether certain commitments were worth dying for, and if so, which ones. The challenge of comprehending deep religious commitment looms once more. The poverty of theory compels us to attempt to understand why and how these martyrs came to their resolve.

Foundations: Faith and Scripture

Martyrdom possesses an arresting logic and lucidity if approached on the martyrs' own terms. Put simply, martyrs were willing to die for their religious views because they believed them to be true, because revealed by God. The eternal ramifications of Christian truth led them radically to relativize temporal concerns, including death. Among Protestants, Anabaptists, and Roman Catholics, faith, with its relationship to scripture, was absolutely central to their willingness to die.

This was written in 1534 or 1535:

> Since all our principal comfort must come of God, we must first presuppose in him to whom we shall with any ghostly counsel give any effectual comfort, one ground to begin withall: *whereupon, all that we shall build must be supported and stand, that is to wit, the ground and foundation of faith, without which had ready before, all the spiritual comfort that any man may speak of, can never avail a fly.* For likewise as it were utterly vain to lay natural reasons of comfort, to him that hath no wit, so were it undoubtedly frustrate to lay spiritual causes of comfort, to him that hath no faith. *For except a man first believe, that holy scripture is the word of God, and that the word of God is true, how can a man take any comfort of that, that the scripture telleth him therein?* Needs must the man take little fruit of the scripture, if he either believe not that it were the word of God, or else wene [suppose] that though it were, it might yet be for all that untrue. *This faith as it is more faint or more strong, so shall the comfortable words of holy scripture stand the man in more stead or less.*[23]

Despite its emphasis on the irreplaceable foundation of faith and scripture, this passage comes not from an early English Protestant, but from one of their staunchest opponents. Thomas More wrote it as he ruminated about his own faith and possible martyrdom from the Tower of London. In the sixteenth and seventeenth centuries, the most basic Christian convictions were shared among Roman Catholics, Anabaptists, and Protestants. Scripture and faith were less exclusively important in early modern Catholicism than they were for other Christians, but the rejection of *sola fide* and *sola scriptura* in no way repudiated faith or scripture. The delegates to the Council of Trent, for example, declared in 1546 that the Gospel had been promised through the prophets, then promulgated by the mouth of the Son of God, whence Christ "ordered that it be preached to all creatures by his apostles as the source of both all saving truth and precepts of conduct."[24] Catholics as well as varieties of Protestants and Anabaptists concurred that scripture was the word of God, that it was true, that it was every bit as relevant in the sixteenth century as it had been in ancient times, and that correct faith was necessary for eternal salvation. The embrace of these fundamental convictions grounded the martyrs' experience in all three traditions.

So axiomatic are these contentions in early modern Christianity that their massive presence in the sources usually remains implicit. Anabaptists, for example, rarely referred to any sources other than the Bible, and their quotations, paraphrases, and allusions often occur with extraordinary frequency.[25] Marginal scriptural citations frame the pages of thousands of sixteenth-century printed works in a wide variety of genres. When used as expository building blocks, they functioned like the right-hand column in a geometry proof: the point being made was indubitable because it was supported by scripture, the expression of God's will. By extension, whoever invoked a passage in this manner implied that he or she had understood it correctly—and such claims of exegetical rectitude were seldom uncontroversial.

Though it was rarely necessary to lay them out as More did, the most basic assumptions of Christian faith were sometimes made explicit. Scripture was God's word, the very record of his communication with humanity. Its truth was foundational. Unless a person believed this, as More made clear, offering spiritual counsel was like talking to a stone. When Heinrich Bullinger exhorted the English Protestants in Zurich to show hospitality to their fellow exiles, he reminded them that "all the words of God are true, steadfast, and undoubted. For heaven and earth shall pass away, but the eternal word of God shall never perish, nor shall one jot or tittle fall from it."[26] Before their translation of the Gospels, the Marian exiles who compiled the Geneva Bible (1560) stated that there is "no joy nor consolation, no peace nor quietness, no felicity nor salvation, but in Jesus Christ, who is the very substance of this Gospel."[27] They sounded much like Jacques Lefèvre d'Etaples, the reform-minded humanist who had translated the New Testament into French almost forty years earlier. *"Let us know that human beings and their doctrines are nothing, except to the extent that they are corroborated and confirmed by the word of God,"* he wrote. "But Jesus Christ is everything; he is fully human and fully divine; and each person is nothing, except in him; and each human word is nothing, except in his word."[28] Life without faith, without Christ, who was the very incarnation of God's word, was a desert of self-deception. Without the orientation that faith provided, one could only starve, fruitlessly seeking sustenance among endless human fictions and their flickering mirages.

What was true when God revealed it through the Holy Spirit was still true in the sixteenth century. Every application of scripture to contemporary issues implied this virtually universal conviction. William Tyndale told the Old Testament story of what God had done for Moses and the Israelites. "This is written for our learning," he stated. "For verily he is a true God, and is our God as well as theirs, and his promises are with us as well as with them, and he present with us as well as he was with them."[29] In More's *Dialogue of Comfort,* Vincent asks his uncle Antony whether one might outwardly conform to

Islam—a thinly veiled reference to the Henrician religious settlement—but still remain loyal to Christ. The uncle replies that because Christ, "while he was living here fifteen hundred years ago . . . foresaw this mind of yours that you have now . . . he telleth you plain fifteen hundred years ago [with] his own mouth, that he will no such service of you, saying, *Non potestis servire Deo et mammone,* you can not serve both God and your riches together."[30] Henrick Alewijns, a Dutch Mennonite, wrote to his children in the name of "your father's God, the God of all believers from the beginning of the world, the God of Abel, the God of Noah, the God of Abraham, Isaac, Jacob, Israel, the God of Jesus Christ and of all the saints."[31] God's biblical dealings with humanity mirrored his sixteenth-century dealings with men and women, whether in London, Leiden, or Lyons.

God's revelation was as essential to salvation in the present as it had been in the past and would be in the future. And as John Hus and other late medieval Christians had known so well, scripture had plenty to say about the human predicaments of suffering, persecution, and the danger of death for the truth. Like symphonic variations on a theme, related passages on the subject fill martyrs' letters, exhortations to steadfastness, and martyrological interpretations. They shaped the outlook of beleaguered Christians across confessional divides.

Scripture's truth for all times meant that this Old Testament verse applied to the latter-day experience of persecuted Christians: "Precious in the sight of the Lord is the death of his faithful ones" (Ps. 116:15). Jesus himself had said, during his Sermon on the Mount, "Blessed are those who are persecuted for righteousness' sake, for theirs is the kingdom of heaven" (Matt. 5:10). Even more explicitly, he told his disciples, "Do not fear those who kill the body but cannot kill the soul; rather fear him who can destroy both soul and body in hell"; and "everyone therefore who acknowledges me before others, I also will acknowledge before my Father in heaven; but whoever denies me before others, I also will deny before my Father in heaven" (Matt. 10:28, 32–33). The savior had warned his apostles that "they will hand you over to be tortured and will put you to death, and you will be hated by all nations because of my name . . . But the one who endures to the end will be saved" (Matt. 24:9,13). He had told his followers to expect affliction: "If the world hates you, be aware that it hated me before it hated you . . . Remember the word that I said to you, 'Servants are not greater than their master.' If they persecuted me, they will persecute you" (John 15:18, 20).

The Acts of the Apostles records numerous instances in which Christ's early followers were persecuted for their faith. When the early Christian representatives departed from the Council of Jerusalem, for example, "they rejoiced that they were considered worthy to suffer dishonor for the sake of the name [of Jesus]" (Acts 5:41). Paul straightforwardly affirmed that to suffer for Christ was an honor: God "has graciously granted you the privilege not only of believing in Christ, but of suffering for him as well" (Phil. 1:29). James made the same point, saying that "whenever you face trials of any kind, consider it nothing but joy, because you know that the testing of your faith produces endurance" (James 1:2–3). Peter reinforced the idea that God favors those who suffer for what is right, saying that "if you endure when you do right and suffer for it, you have God's approval. For to this you have been called, because Christ also suffered for you, leaving you an example, so that you should follow in his steps" (1 Pet. 2:20–21; cf. Ps. 116:15 and Matt. 5:10 above). And Revelation flatly stated: "Do not fear what you are about to suffer. Beware, the devil is about to throw some of you into prison so that you may be tested, and for ten days you will have affliction. Be faithful until death, and I will give you the crown of life" (Rev. 2:10).

A list like this might be thought tedious, but it is only the tip of a much larger iceberg.[32] By themselves, these excerpts lack context. Yet the convictions expressed in such verses, taken together and understood by persecuted Christians in early modern Europe, comprised a biblical blueprint for martyrdom.

Late medieval Christians had applied such verses to the ordinary hardships of life or in the pursuit of ascetic practices. In the sixteenth century they appeared in a new light, with a dramatic applicability. God had not revealed himself for nothing; he had not created and redeemed humanity without providing for sustenance in adversity: "For whatever was written in former days was written for our instruction, so that by the encouragement of the scriptures we might have hope" (Rom. 15:4).[33] These sayings were neither abstract nor merely theoretical. They were both an authoritative exhortation and a definitive hermeneutic—God's own admonition that both explained the meaning of persecution and enjoined the proper response to it.

Unlike prolonging one's life, fidelity to God was an absolute value. Otherwise scripture would not so often and so clearly have extolled it as the basis for a willingness to endure deprivation and even death. It was an undeniably pervasive theme in the Bible, not an idiosyncratic reading dependent on an ambiguous verse or two. The God who was himself perfect love would not require such absolute trust without fulfilling his promises to those who remained steadfast. Despite his own son's humiliating death, he had not failed to raise him to eternal glory.

Biblical martyrs reinforced this picture. Eleazar, an elderly scribe, was beaten to death for his refusal to eat pork in violation of Mosaic law (2 Macc. 6:18–31), seven brothers and their mother were killed for the same reason (2 Macc. 7), and Stephen was stoned in Jerusalem as the first Christian martyr for verbally denouncing the Jews (Acts 7). Jesus's crucifixion was more than the inspiration for elaborate devotional practices: it was the paradigm for what his closest followers could expect. The savior was himself a martyr who had suffered a violent death by execution. "Take up your cross and follow me" (Matt. 16:24, Luke 9:23)—were these just words? If Christians took seriously this command, they too might meet with tribulation and death.

Martyrs endured persecution, torture, and death because they believed that scriptural injunctions and promises, plus the underlying view of reality that they implied and presupposed, were true. The *way* that they believed—the *character* of their faith—was crucial. Thousands of people endured death for their religious beliefs, but many more dissembled their convictions, and literally millions of Europeans, it would seem, more or less conformed to religious changes without significant incident. Thomas More's statement about faith and the word of God helps us understand the difference between run-of-the-mill conformists and candidates for martyrdom: "This faith as it is more faint or more strong, so shall the comfortable words of holy scripture stand the man in more stead or less."[34] *The efficacy of scripture was proportional to the strength of faith.* The stronger one's faith, the greater the Bible's consolation for those who reflected on, prayed over, and sang songs about persecution and suffering. Just as scripture was dead to those who were largely indifferent to it, so it could displace and overwhelm the competing concerns of those who believed that "all that we shall build must be supported and stand" by it.

Taken seriously, Christian faith made one a candidate for martyrdom, but it did not guarantee steadfastness. The willingness to die internalized by devout Christians was not coextensive with actual perseverance through execution. Rather, faith and fear—religious conviction and the natural aversion to painful suffering and death—comprised a tense dialectic in the lives of many martyrs. Other things being equal, sixteenth-century Christians wanted to live. It was not easy to resist against sin "to the point of shedding your blood" (Heb. 12:4). Imprisoned Christians often bemoaned their "weakness of the flesh," which made them balk at the prospect of torture and execution. A Huguenot song from the 1550s captures the tension well:

> This wicked body asks for healing,
> my dear brother, and the spirit on the contrary
> wants to leave it like a filthy prison.
> One tends toward the world, the other's distracted by it;
> It's pitiful to hear them bray:
> "Whoa!" says the body, "must we die like this?"
> "Go," says the spirit, "must we languish here?"
> "Whoa!" says the body, "better than for you, I hope."

"Go," says the spirit, "you must and me too;
Let the will of the Lord God be done."[35]

The willingness to die was not deducible from faith, nor was perseverance unto death taken for granted by even the deeply committed. Peter's repudiation of Christ (Matt. 26:31–35, 69–75) was a sobering reminder of how easily the chief among Christ's own apostles had succumbed to the temptation to deny him altogether. For this reason, sixteenth-century Christians were generally wary of ostentatious bravado in the face of death. The martyrs often expressed trust, consolation, and joy, but within a broader context that acknowledged weakness and dependence on God. Even strong faith frequently provided but a fragile hold on fear—one that torture, for example, could sometimes crush.

Many people believed deeply, moved in the same circles as martyrs, and professed their complete steadfastness, yet recanted rather than face torture or death. Their capitulations baffled and dismayed fellow believers. Early in Mary Tudor's reign, before the burnings had begun, Protestant reformer Peter Martyr Vermigli wrote to Heinrich Bullinger about events in England. He told Bullinger, "it is indeed a distressing and most remarkable fact, that we perceive those very persons in that kingdom, whom you would have considered the most resolute, now wavering, and even yielding."[36] Even sensitive sixteenth-century observers could not straightforwardly predict martyrdom—that is, make a direct correlation among the strength of faith, the willingness to die, and actual perseverance through execution. Richard Barret, the Catholic prefect of studies in the English College at Rheims, said that there had been more initially fearful than eager seminarians who had persevered through martyrdom in England.[37]

Profound religious faith therefore accounts for martyrdom, but it is not retrospectively predictive of actual martyrs. Similarly, so-called belief systems do not permit differentiation between the merely conformist and the devout. Recourse to a period *mentalité* tells us nothing about why, among people from similar backgrounds and subject to similar influences, some but not others were zealous, why some but not others embraced new creeds. Early modern Christianity comprises a spectrum of religiosity, from ignorance or indifference to passionate commitment. Sensitive reconstruction of their beliefs and behaviors is the best means to try to understand the diverse experiences of the individual men and women, in their respective communities of faith, across this spectrum. By exploring the ways that faith and the willingness to die were woven into the martyrs' lives, we can penetrate the character of their convictions and experiences. We must historicize—that is, contextualize and understand concretely—the stark logic of Christian faith implied in the biblical passages about the endurance of persecution and suffering.

Contemporary Communities: Social Support and Sustenance

Even when martyrs went to their deaths by themselves, they did not go alone. Their lives were intertwined with those of like-minded Christians. The antithesis of Durkheim's isolated candidates for suicide, they were not marginal figures from the social fringe. Friends and family members supported them, urging them not to compromise the truth in order to prolong their lives, lest they jeopardize their eternal salvation. From prison, future martyrs sent letters to and received them from fellow believers still at liberty. Sometimes visiting servants or friends facilitated this exchange; sometimes prison guards helped them, motivated by sympathy or bribery. Future martyrs consoled each other in prison as well. Even before their imprisonment, they had heard earnest exhortations to steadfastness, warnings not to dissemble faith, and admonitions not to capitulate to pseudo-Christian persecutors. These specific human interactions made up the social context for the willingness to die among persecuted Protestants, Anabaptists, and Roman Catholics.

Protestants

Wherever we look in the Protestant sources, we find the martyrs encouraged and comforted by others. Joyce Lewis did not come to her beliefs in a vacuum, but through the instruction and continued tutelage of an already committed Protestant, John Glover. Her friends reassured her in prison and accompanied her to the stake. Just before her death she drank beer with open sympathizers in the crowd.[38] From the early years of the Reformation there were many more like her.

Supporters encouraged martyrs by correspondence. Martin Luther himself, for example, wrote from Wittenberg to the imprisoned Leonhard Keyser before the latter's execution in 1527. Conveying a promise from Psalm 91, Luther exhorted him to "be strong and steadfastly overcome or indeed, patiently bear, the weakness of the flesh through the power of Christ, who is with you and in the prison and will also be by you in every difficulty."[39] In the same manner, over a period of more than a year in 1552–1553, John Calvin and Pierre Viret dispatched a series of letters to several students imprisoned in Lyons. They repeatedly urged them to cleave to Christ for the sake of his glory, even if it meant their deaths.[40] Sometimes one future martyr exhorted another, as when William Tyndale wrote to John Frith in the Tower of London before the latter's execution in 1533. Tyndale told him not to confide in men, but rather to "trust him that is true of promise, and able to make his word good. Your cause is Christ's Gospel, a light that must be fed with the blood of faith." Tyndale reminded Frith of others executed in Antwerp, Brussels, and Paris, setting him in an international context of those specially favored by God: "*See ye are not alone:* Be cheerful and remember that among the hard-hearted in England, there is a number reserved by grace. For whose sakes if need be, ye must be ready to suffer."[41] More than just epistolary contact between two friends, Tyndale's letter embraced a much broader community that included all those suffering for the cause of the Gospel.

Face-to-face contact helped Protestant martyrs prepare for their deaths. In Brussels on the night before tailor Joost Jusbergh was to be executed in 1544, other prisoners sought him out to say their last farewells. Jusbergh considered it a great blessing from Christ to seal heavenly doctrine with his blood, and so to receive "for a light and short-lived agony, the crown of glory offered to me in heaven."[42] Then Gilles Tielemans, the deacon of Brussels' first evangelical church, who himself would be killed less than three weeks later, entreated Jusbergh to persevere. He led all the prisoners in prayer:

> My brothers, I ask that getting down on our knees, we commend to God the soul of our brother, Joost. Living and eternal God . . . Father of our Savior, Jesus Christ, who sees our hearts, governs our actions, and grants the prayers of his own: we are here gathered before you in your name and are assured by our mediator, Jesus Christ, that you want to hear our requests and grant us all that we ask of you. Thus we pray to you right now, that it might be your good pleasure to strengthen this servant of yours, Joost, up to his final breath; and when this last hour will have come, in which he must give glory to you by the sacrifice of his body, that you will receive it pure and unblemished into eternal joy.

After this, Jusbergh said that he felt "a great light, which delights me with a joy that I don't know how to express, and now desire nothing else than to die and to be with Christ." The other prisoners spent the better part of the night with him before he was beheaded the next day.[43]

Whether in England, France, or the Low Countries, whether during the 1520s or the 1550s, persecuted Protestants helped sustain one another. Joan Ward was a young woman brought before Bishop Bonner of London during Mary's reign for tending to her imprisoned mother and stepfather, Elizabeth Ward and Robert Lashford. Robert went to the stake in May 1555, Elizabeth in July or August, and Joan herself was one of the seven martyrs burned at Smithfield on January 27, 1556.[44] Henrick Snoelacke and Adriaen Coreman shared a final meal with other members of the Calvinist community in Antwerp on January 18, 1559, the night before both were executed. Van Haemstede related how "the brothers of the Christian community went to these God-fearing men in the castle prison, and ate a farewell dinner with them, and consoled them with the loving and comforting promises of God, and so with friendly embraces and kisses commended them to the Lord."[45] Like Joyce Lewis, Marguerite le Riche defied her husband to turn Protestant. Through a small hole in her cell, she encouraged Anne Du Bourg, a member of the Parlement of Paris likewise imprisoned for his Calvinism, to hold firm. Du Bourg later credited her with helping him persevere.[46] Such social support was reinforced beginning in the 1520s by printed exhortations to steadfastness. By the 1540s and 1550s these directives had grown into a virtual torrent of Protestant literature that coupled admonition with consolation.

Anabaptists

Protestants were not alone in their use of scripture, or the faith that made it efficacious, or the fellow believers who heartened the martyrs. From their earliest days, the Swiss Brethren found contact among members to be vital. Johannes Brötli, for example, sent a letter from prison in Hallau to Fridli Schumacher and other Anabaptists sometime after February 19, 1525. He asked how his brethren fared and whether or not rumors that some had "flown from the cross" were true.[47] Two years later, Michael Sattler wrote from Binsdorf, where he was imprisoned, to the Anabaptist congregation at Horb. "Let no one displace your objective," he wrote, "as has previously happened to some, but rather proceed ahead, firm and unwavering, in all patience, not abolishing or putting aside the cross that God has applied to you against God's honor and praise, as well as with the breaking and dissolution of his eternal, truthful, righteous, and vivifying [*lebendig machende*] commandments."[48]

In 1534 Jakob Huter, the founder of Hutterite Anabaptism, wrote from Auspitz in Moravia to Anabaptists imprisoned in Hohenwart, in Lower Austria.[49] They should feel no shame in suffering afflictions for Christ, Huter told them, "but rather be glad about them with all your hearts [*freuet euch dessen von ganzem Herzen*], for you know that nothing else is pledged or promised to you here on this earth than suffering and death, sadness, anxiety, distress, as well as great persecution, pain, martyrdom, humiliation, and abuse from all godless people. That is the true sign and seal of all the devout children of God."[50] Huter offered them a virtual catalogue of New Testament passages about the blessedness of those who endure persecution for Christ.[51] The Lord had not promised his followers an exemption from suffering, nor did Huter pretend that he had. The issue was neither the pleasure nor the preference of Christians, but rather what God, who knew better, had both foretold and given them the means to overcome.

Dutch Anabaptists wrote to their imprisoned spouses, invoking the same scriptural verses.[52] Coppersmith Jeronimus Segers and his wife, Lijsken Aerts, wrote at least nine letters to each other in 1551, when both were incarcerated in Antwerp. Aerts rejoiced, she told her husband, when people reviled her for Christ's sake, because her reward would be great in heaven (Matt. 5:12), and she recalled Paul's assurance that the Lord would not let them be tested beyond their strength (1 Cor. 10:13).[53] In January 1572 Jan van Dort wrote from Rotterdam to his "dear wife, Ariaenken Jansdochter, out of love, in order to strengthen your spirit." Van Dort strung together and gave his wife biblical passages like pearls on a necklace, concluding with Matt. 5:10, "Blessed are those who are persecuted for righteousness' sake, for theirs is the kingdom of heaven."[54] Maeyken Wens's husband was willing to surrender his wife to her new "bridegroom," Christ, in 1573. Holding up Job as a model, he wrote, "my dear wife, do not be frightened, the Lord will help you in your distress, when you shall be delivered from all human beings."[55] Precisely because their spouses were so dear, Anabaptists reminded them that God's truth, the love of Christ, and the promise of salvation transcended their own human relationships.

The recipients were grateful. Letters reassured prisoners that they were not forgotten. Soetken van den Houte thanked both her sister and her daughter for their correspondence. Several times Christian Rijcen expressed gratitude to his wife.[56] "I thank you deeply from the heart for the comforting treasures that you sent me," he wrote. "You should know how very joyful they made me, when I heard your feelings [*ghemoet*] and that you still strengthen me in the truth, to remain devout in the Lord unto death."[57] Far from being taken as unwelcome marital pressure or coercion, such exhortations were tender lifelines of love and concern. When epistolary ties seemed tenuous, prisoners clamored for word from their spouses: "Write to me right away, tell me how things are with you, so that I will be better comforted."[58]

Besides letters, the singing of songs strengthened Anabaptists. Valerius Schoolmeester was a Dutch Anabaptist preacher active in Zeeland. "There are also many songs," he stated in 1568, "written by exceptional people, full of hope, through which in time much is eased if they are sung by people without hope, who give scarcely any thought to the Lord."[59] Singing the right song with the right attitude could help diminish despair, much like faith could conquer fear. Valerius noted just two examples in a huge corpus of Anabaptist songs about suffering, all of which were set to well-known tunes. Although written by individuals, these songs imply activity that was social by its very nature. Sung in clandestine meetings in homes, fields, or forests, their texts reflect shared Anabaptist experience under persecution.[60]

The first song mentioned by Valerius—"An Eternal Joy Not Forgotten Comes Always before Me"—was written by Peter van Olmen, who was killed in Ghent on July 27, 1552. It appeared in several song collections.[61] The third stanza is constructed entirely out of scriptural verses:

> Rightly indeed has the Lord said
> I shall not leave you as orphans   (John 14:18)
> I am preparing a place for them   (John 14:2)
> who do not forsake me here   (Luke 12:8)
> But those who confess me here
> I shall at all times
> confess them all together
> before my Heavenly Father
> Don't be afraid, little flock   (Luke 12:32)
> I alone am your unburdener.[62]   (Matt. 11:28)

Each time Anabaptists sang this song at a gathering, they reapplied Christ's dicta to each other. Considering that Anabaptism was a capital crime, none of them would have missed the relevance of the lyrics.

Valerius's second song was first printed in 1569, though it must have been current earlier. Its back-and-forth stanzas create a dialogue between Christ and one who longs to be with him. In the second stanza Christ paraphrases Luke 12:32 and John 14:18, verses that Peter van Olmen had also employed:

> You little gathering, have no fear
> whoever conquers shall receive the crown
> I am coming to you, I will not leave you as orphans
> O my chosen ones, I will not let you be defeated.[63]

Adapted from the Gospel, such lyrics came from Christ to afflicted brothers and sisters in Bruges and Brussels, in Antwerp and Amsterdam. Shared in song, Christ's promises had power because Anabaptists had faith. Trust overcame tribulation.

Roman Catholics

Though viewed by fellow believers as exceptionally favored by God, Roman Catholic martyrs lived as members of broader communities of belief. The English missionary priests provide perhaps the clearest example, with their common education, spiritual formation, and sense of specific purpose. A half-century earlier, Thomas More knew the importance of friends when he sat alone in the Tower of London. He exchanged letters with John Fisher, the bishop of Rochester, who occupied a different cell during 1534 and 1535.[64] As he pondered the trust necessary to sustain pain and death for the truth, More considered friends to be instruments of divine grace—consistent with

Christ's promise in Matt. 18:20. Reason grounded upon the foundation of faith is "helped also forward with the aid of God's grace, as it ever is undoubtedly, when folk for a good mind in God's name come together thereon, our savior saying him self, *Ubi sunt duo vel tres congregati in nomine meo ibi et ego sum in medio eorum,* where there are two or three gathered together in my name, there am I also even in the very midst of them."[65] In prison, this passage of More's might have reflected the desire more than the experience of comforting sociability. Unlike Anabaptist spouses, More's family members, including his beloved daughter Meg, repeatedly urged him to consent to Henry VIII's oath of supremacy.

When the Dutch clergy faced violence by the Calvinist Sea Beggars in the early 1570s, they drew on scripture for sustenance. Aert Swaens van Goerle, a deacon in St. Geertruidenberg, recounted the hanging of Willem vander Gouwe in the town in early September 1573. He added "a short lesson based on this martyrdom," which prevailed upon all Dutch Catholics to maintain their faith, and included twenty-two scriptural citations in the margins of three pages of text.[66] The Bible was no less God's word for Catholics than it was for Protestants or Anabaptists. Franciscan Rutger Hessels van Est wrote a song about the Gorcum martyrs of 1572 that was published three years later in Amsterdam. After portraying their heroism through arrest and martyrdom, the song's thirtieth stanza versified Matt. 10:28:

> Do not fear the man
> who can kill the body alone
> but fear the praised Lord
> who can permit life and soul
> together, eternally
> in the terrifying fire of hell
> where there will be weeping eyes
> and gnashing of teeth.[67]

Had Catholics ignored Christ's warning, they would have been self-destructively negligent, courting a final resting place of horrific unrest.

Elizabethan Catholics commonly supported each other through correspondence. William Weston, for example, a Jesuit, was imprisoned between September 1586 and January 1588. During this period, he later wrote, he received "letters encouraging me to martyrdom from the same Father Robert [Southwell] and from Father John Cornelius, both of them now martyrs of the Society [of Jesus]."[68] Before his own execution in 1594, missionary priest John Ingram penned at least two letters to fellow Catholic prisoners. From prison he reminded them of "the golden sentences which issued out of the mouth of all verity, 'He that hateth his life in this world keepeth it for life everlasting' [Matt. 16:25] and 'He that confesseth me before men I will confess him before my father which is in heaven' [Matt. 10:32]." Expecting his imminent death, Ingram asked the others to "pray for me earnestly."[69]

Face-to-face contact was also part of Catholic martyrs' experience. Willem vander Gouwe and another priest, Jan Vogelsanck, were constrained for the three days before vander Gouwe's death. They discussed how God's saints had confessed the faith and how the martyrs had sealed it with their blood, and "they comforted one another with the holy scripture, which teaches that those who suffer for righteousness will be saved, that after suffering they will rejoice with Christ and receive the eternal crown."[70] English laity and missionary clergy likewise consoled one another during the second half of Elizabeth's reign. Three priests, Edmund Geninges, Eustace White, and Polidore Plasden, along with four laypeople who had attended a Mass in Swithun Wells's London home, were arrested in November 1591 and tried on December 5 at Westminster. After enduring denunciations and insults before a jury,

> the glorious Confessors all embraced one the other, and mutually encouraged themselves to sustain the future assault, as they had done the combat already past, to the great edification of many standers by. But Mr. Geninges especially persuaded them all with a pleasant sweet speech (in the hearing of many Catholics) not to yield one iota to any of their enemies' allurements, animating them with the saying of St. James, *Appropinquate Deo, et appropinquabit vobis:* Approach to God, and he will approach to you [James 4:8]. And so they passed all the time of the counsel's dinner within the bar in prayer and exhortation to perseverance.[71]

There was solidarity in their suffering. They trusted in scripture as God's word and will, as his Church had preserved and promulgated it. They applied it directly to their concrete predicament, which helped them overcome fears of pain and death. Human contact was vital, as More knew in talking fondly of friends assembled in Christ's name. Richard Bristow, the prefect of studies at the English College in Douai, was right: "word of mouth hath incomparably more force than the dead pen, whether it be to edify or to destroy."[72]

When they urged their persecuted fellow believers to persevere, Protestants, Anabaptists, and Catholics differed only over the invocation of extrabiblical authorities. Protestant and especially Catholic authors regularly quoted patristic writers such as Augustine and Cyprian, whereas Anabaptists referred almost exclusively to the Bible. The underlying difference was not the content of the injunctions (when the Church fathers or medieval theologians were quoted, it was to reinforce the same biblical directives) but rather the status of ecclesiastical tradition and whether extrabiblical "authorities" were in fact authorities.

Early modern Christians would have puzzled over an analytical distinction between "the social" and "the religious." Had not Christ promised to be present wherever two or three were gathered in his name (Matt. 18:20)? They expected that being Christian meant being Christian *together,* whether they were facing martyrdom, attending church services, or rearing children in ordinary households. To abstract social relations from religious life, or to reduce the religious to the social in Durkheimian terms, is to commit an anachronistic blunder foreign to these people's experience. Dutch Anabaptist Wouter van Stoelwijck might have been speaking for them all when he said, "the Lord God usually consoles people through other people [*door anderen menscen*], because all the saints and Christians on earth have community with each other . . . for when one suffers pain and distress, he does not suffer that alone, but Christ and all Christians suffer the same with him."[73]

Historical Communities: Pedigrees of the Persecuted

Just as martyrs were not isolated mavericks, neither were they adventurous novelty-seekers. Martyrdom was not a journey into the unknown. It meant conformity to an ancient course of action, grounded in scripture and epitomized in the crucifixion of Christ himself. In Donald Kelley's apt phrase, it was "a form of mimesis—*imitatio Christi* with a vengeance."[74] The emulative sacrifice of the early Christian martyrs extended an Old Testament tradition that included Abel, the prophets, and the Maccabees. God was no mere theorist: in demanding the willingness to die for him, he had given men and women concrete models. New Testament texts such as Heb. 11:37 and Heb. 12:1–2 had already appropriated the Old Testament witnesses and applied the moral for first-century Christians: "They were stoned to death, they were sawn in two, they were killed by the sword . . . Therefore, since we are surrounded by so great a cloud of witnesses, let us also lay aside every weight and the sin that clings so closely, and let us run with perseverance the race that is set before us, looking to Jesus the pioneer and perfecter of our faith, who for the sake of the joy that was set before him endured the cross, disregarding its shame, and has taken his seat at the right hand of the throne of God." Protestant, Anabaptist, and Catholic martyrs were all keenly aware of standing in this tradition. Their respective accents varied within the framework of a common language. The ongoing story of the unjustly persecuted included both an ancient foundation and a modern reenactment.

The Inspiration of the Ancients

Protestants who remained "under the cross," proscribed and punished in Catholic countries, knew what biblical witnesses had faced. If the Gospel's original proclamation had provoked resistance and persecution, why should its reproclamation have been any different? Before he was burned on June 10, 1555, English Protestant Thomas Haukes was consoled in the knowledge of his illustrious predecessors. He told the "Congregation" by letter that although "the world rage, and blaspheme the elect people of God, ye know that it did so unto Christ, his Apostles, and to all that were in the primitive church, and shall be to the world's end."[75] The following year, in Lille, Jeanne Baudichon saw God's favor in the affliction that she and fellow Calvinists endured: "it is obvious," she said, "that we are on the right path by the things that we suffer." Further, she asked, "are we thus heretics for believing nothing except what the holy prophets and apostles taught? That's not possible."[76]

Men like Thomas Haukes and women like Jeanne Baudichon were heeding the words of Protestant writers who counseled identification with the suffering of Christ and the ancient martyrs. Consider the following excerpt from a work translated (and perhaps written) by Richard Tracy, *Of the Preparation to the Cross, and to Death* (1540):

> We have not only Christ for our example, but also the godly, both prophets and apostles, which in like wise be tempted, persecuted, stoned, killed, and crucified, as Paul of himself witnesseth. It is a great comfort to the godly, when for the name of Christ and his holy Gospel, they suffer persecution, imprisonment, and at the last death, in which troubles yet joy and affliction have place and be mixed together. If they be punished, it is joy and comfort to them, to have Christ and all good and holy men and fellows with them in their afflictions, as Paul sayeth.[77]

Three years later John Calvin wrote his *Brief Treatise* against those who dissembled their faith to avoid persecution. The reality of past martyrdom helped to rebut those French detractors who ascribed Calvin's rigor to the luxury of Genevan tranquility, whereas they, in France, were daily exposed to death. Calvin wrote:

> *I require nothing of them except to follow as much as what a thousand martyrs before us have done, men and women, rich and poor, humble and powerful.* Therefore this doctrine is not a speculation that I have concocted from my position of security, but it is the one that the martyrs of Jesus Christ have pondered in the middle of all the torments that they had to endure. And through this reflection, they were strengthened for conquering the horror and the fear of prisons, furnaces, fire, the gallows, the sword, and every other kind of death. *If they had not had this thought imprinted in their hearts—it would be preferable to die a hundred times than to do anything contravening the honor of God—they never would have*

had the courage to expose themselves to death for the sake of confessing their Christian faith; but they would rather have let themselves be persuaded to honor idols. *Yet their steadfastness is not recited for us so that we merely praise it, but so that it will be an example for us, and so that we will not renounce the truth which they so powerfully maintained;* that we will not deny and will not corrupt the glory of God, which they so esteemed that they shed their blood to seal and confirm it.[78]

The ancient martyrs had not dissembled their faith, but rather confessed it at the expense of their lives. John Scory, an exiled English bishop, wrote to Protestants at home in 1555, after the Marian executions had begun. He told those facing death to identify with specific biblical martyrs for a whole range of methods of execution—including Jonah for drowning, Stephen for stoning, John the Baptist for beheading. If threatened with burning, they should look to the three youths cast into the "fiery furnace" from Dan. 3.[79] Many other Protestant leaders added to this admonitory chorus. Those who persevered were measuring up to a widely touted ideal.

Anabaptists stressed even more exclusively the scriptural legacy of persecution. Occasionally they offered nonbiblical amplifications. The third song in the *Ausbund,* the hymnal of the Swiss Brethren, included both early Christian and biblical martyrs, complete with marginal references to Eusebius. Menno Simons also referred in passing to Eusebius in his *Comforting Admonition*— but before doing so, he discussed persecuted biblical figures for over forty pages.[80] His admonitions, plus those by so many other Anabaptist leaders, directly parallel the promptings of Protestant writers.[81] Anabaptist martyrs, too, sought to conform to the prescriptions that predecessors had enacted.

Here is how Anneken Jans, who was probably a follower of the Dutch Anabaptist leader David Joris,[82] opened her *Testament* to her infant boy Isaiah in 1539: "Listen, my son, to the instruction of your mother, open your ears to hear the words from my mouth; see, I am now going the way of the prophets, apostles, and martyrs, and drinking from the cup from which they all have drunk."[83] Jeronimus Segers, the coppersmith husband of Lijsken Aerts, told her to "be patient amid oppression, for it is the right path that leads to eternal life, which all God's saints, prophets, and apostles, indeed, Christ himself, have gone through."[84] Ariaenken Jans wrote to her husband, "we bear all things and are patient according to the example of Job, the prophets, the apostles, and the end of our Lord and other martyrs after them; now we go firmly forward in order to complete our struggle through the Lord's help with trusting hearts, unto death, for we know and believe that the crown of eternal life is prepared for us."[85] Concrete models plus the hope of salvation helped them to forge ahead.

When Roman Catholics faced genuine prospects of death for their convictions, they patterned themselves on previous martyr-saints. An emphasis on tradition and continuity meant that the early Christian martyrs had a greater presence in Catholicism than in Protestantism, and a much greater presence than in Anabaptism. Still, Catholic writers were not about to relinquish earlier biblical martyrs, just as they had not yielded the Bible to heretics despite the latter's misguided insistence on *sola scriptura*.

John Fisher wrote to his half-sister Elizabeth during his imprisonment. Whereas Calvin had stressed the martyrs' unwillingness to taint God's glory, Fisher highlighted their fervent love for Christ, very much in line with late medieval devotion to the passion. "Martyrs innumerable, both men and women," he wrote, "have shed their blood, and have endured every kind of martyrdom were it never so cruel, were it never so terrible. No pain, no tormentry, might compel them to forsake his love: so desirous were they of his love, that rather than they would forgo it, they gave no force of the loss of all this world beside, and their own life also."[86] Like his heretical contemporaries, Thomas More was aware that Christians ought to expect persecution, since the servant was not greater than his master (John 15:20). As though glossing Thomas à Kempis, whose *Imitation* he knew so well, More wrote: "Our head is Christ, and therefore to him must we be joined, and as members of his must we follow him, if we will come thither . . . Who can for very shame desire to enter into the kingdom of Christ with ease, when him self entered not into his own without pain[?]"[87] Those baffled by More's willingness to die should listen to what he said. "The consideration of [Christ's] incomparable kindness" in dying for our sake "could not fail in such wise to inflame our key-cold hearts, and set them on fire in his love, that we should find our self not only content, but also glad and desirous to suffer death for his sake." To die for love of Christ was a supremely difficult demand, but hardly novel or impossible, "when we see so many a thousand holy martyrs by his holy help, suffered as much before, as any man shall be put to now."[88]

The Elizabethan martyrs would have understood perfectly. A friend advised imprisoned missionary priest John Nelson "for his greater comfort and the more to animate him against the terrors of death . . . to read and meditate upon the lives and deaths of martyrs, as they are set down in the service according to the use of Rome." Nelson was already familiar with their example from the Church's liturgical martyrology: "And being put in mind by the same friend, with what alacrity and joy of mind many thousand martyrs had suffered exquisite torments for Christ's sake, and that they never complained or shrunk thereat, he answered, that that cogitation came oft to his mind, and that he took such comfort thereof, that he doubted nothing but that he should find and feel the grace of God's consolation in the midst of his agony."[89] The day before Ralph Sherwin's execution in 1581, he wrote to his uncle, John Woodward, a priest who was living in Rouen. The turn of the Catholic liturgical calendar, plus the ancient witness of St. Andrew, prompted Sherwin's specific aspiration: "This very morning, which is the festival day of St. Andrew, I was advertised by superior authority, that tomorrow I was to end the course of this life, God grant I may do it, to the imitation of this noble Apostle and servant of God, and that with joy I may say rising of the hurdle: *Salve sancta crux etc.*"[90]

Catholic martyrs, too, followed admonitions like those of Protestants and Anabaptists. In 1579 Thomas Hide, a priest writing in exile from Louvain, exhorted English Catholics to obey God when his law contradicted the sovereign's commands. They should act "as the children of Israel did, as Daniel did, as Mattathias did, as the Apostles did, as St. Polycarp did," for although the ruler "threateneth prison, God threateneth hell." Like Calvin, Hide asserted that it was unswerving obedience to God that had motivated ancient martyrs such as Athanasius, Gordius, and Julitta.[91] Writing in 1581, William Allen linked male and female martyrs to latter-day English men and women, "to whom God giveth even now the spirit of constancy, by the example of St. Sebastian, St. Vincent, St. Maurice with the whole legion of Thebes . . . to say nothing of them, nor of St. Catherine, St. Margaret, St. Agnes, St. Lucy, and the like mirrors for our devout maidens and widows to behold."[92] We have met these martyr-saints before, as intercessors for late medieval Christians. Now their "martyrhood" resurfaced from its submersion in the wider sea of Catholic sanctity.

All three traditions fostered participation in a historical community of men and women who were unjustly persecuted although they were "precious in the sight of the Lord" (Ps. 116:15). Despite their different emphases, they all looked to follow paths well worn by paradigmatic predecessors. The fourth song in the Swiss Anabaptist *Ausbund* tells the story of the seven brothers in 2 Macc. 7. Calvin invoked them in his *Brief Treatise,* stressing their willingness to die for the avoidance of idolatry. And William Allen referred to the seven priests executed in London during May 1582 as "these seven Maccabees."[93]

The ancient martyrs had not compromised their fidelity to God in order to prolong their lives. Early modern martyrs measured temporal pain against eternal gain and drew the logical conclusion. Torture and death were surely horrific—but incomparably less so than eternal suffering. Because scripture spoke plainly of eternal punishment, those with *sanitas* would "fear him who can destroy both soul and body in hell" (Matt. 10:28), and who promised heaven for perseverance. According to More, for example, "reason plainly telleth us, that we should rather suffer and endure the less and shorter here, than in hell the sorer and so far the longer too." And as George Joye, an English Protestant, put it, "surely all the afflictions, heavinesses, and persecutions here, are very light and little to us, if we well ponder our felicity and blessed joyous state shortly to come." For Dutch Mennonite Jan Wouters van Cuyck, "this suffering that men can inflict upon us is short and light and brings to us an eternal and immeasurable glory."[94] To prefer the short-lived agony that led to eternal joy over the repudiation of Christ that portended eternal damnation was not insanity; it was simply clear thinking. Only unreflective, dimwitted, or doctrinally uncertain people would jeopardize their souls through a principled rejection of this line of thought.

The Reenactment of the Moderns

Early modern martyrs considered their precursors relevant to latter-day circumstances just as they thought the Bible, a set of ancient texts, essential to their own quest for salvation. It was not only, as Tertullian had remarked in the late second century, that "the blood of Christians is seed"—it was specifically the seed for more martyrs. As Calvin stated with characteristic force, the early witnesses were not mere props for purposes of style and edification; they were models to which to conform. The historical community of the unjustly killed was alive, reborn and thriving with the modern witness of fellow believers.

The renaissance of Christian martyrdom added a new dimension to mimesis. Those whose constancy wavered, who feared the flames or the sword or the gibbet, saw before themselves the reality of persistence. Whether the ancient martyrs had died just as described in the *Golden Legend* receded in importance: men and women were proving, *in the present,* that such deaths were possible. The historical community was as far from being simply "symbolic" or "imagined" as shattered corpses were from their mere representation. In dying for their religious convictions, the new martyrs proclaimed the transcendent importance of their beliefs. Accordingly, besides receiving courage by example, would-be martyrs faced greater pressure to follow their lead and not to recant the views ratified by the blood of their fellow believers. Besides identifying with the ancient martyrs, Christians in all three traditions read what recent martyrs had written and looked to them as models.

In 1555, when Lutheran brothers Nicolaes and Frans Thijs went to the stake in Mechelen, Nicolaes recalled the burning of a man named Johannes seventeen years earlier.[95] Writing the same year from the Continent after the Marian burnings had begun, John Scory said that

if any of you shall after the example of the late blessed Martyrs (for which of all the shameless Papists, and most filthy Sodomites, could or can justly convince the glorious Martyrs of Christ, Ferrar, Hooper, Taylor, Rogers, Saunders, Bradford, Glover, Cardmaker, or any of them, whom they have most willfully and maliciously murdered, of any notable crime) if, I say, any of you shall after their example, suffer as a Christian man: let him not be ashamed, but let him glorify God on this behalf, and commit his soul unto him with well-doing, as unto a faithful creator.[96]

In Antwerp, Cornelis Halewijn and Herman Janssens witnessed the execution of fellow Calvinists Adriaen Coreman and Henrick Snoelaecke in January 1559. As a result they were strengthened to face their own executions the following month.[97]

Jacques de Lo was burned in Lille on February 15, 1561. From prison he had written to members of his Calvinist community. With specific reference to the "cloud of witnesses" from Heb. 12:1, de Lo told them to "remember the words of our brother who went before me to martyrdom, who often said that it was not time to sleep and relax, considering that we who are your members are in agonies and pains."[98] Crespin identified this "brother" as Martin Oguier, a man killed in Lille several years earlier. De Lo had paraphrased a passage from one of Oguier's letters, to which Crespin directed the reader. The martyrologist wrote, "thus we see how the writings of the martyrs function for those who soon after them follow in the same battle."[99]

Dutch Anabaptist martyrs drew inspiration from their recent witnesses. Valerius Schoolmeester imperfectly recalled a line from *The Sacrifice unto the Lord* written by Hans van Overdam, who had been executed in Ghent almost twenty years earlier: "'The Spirit testifies to this [*Dit getuycht de Geest*],' said Hans van Overdam. Ah Hans, Hans, dear, faithful Hans, from God you understood better what was to come than many of us understand about what is present."[100] Similarly, in 1588 Christiaen Rijcen paraphrased a passage from a letter by the Flemish Anabaptist leader Jacob de Roore, who was burned in Bruges on June 8, 1569.[101] And Soetken van den Houte linked her husband's martyrdom to that of the prophets, apostles, and Christ, coupling the whole with an exhortation to her children. People alleged that her husband, Gilein de Meuleneere, had held deviant doctrines. "Don't believe it," she told them, "for in all that he was able to understand he confessed the truth about baptism and the incarnation of Christ and devoutly witnessed to righteousness, and left his life as an example to you, his being the same way in which the prophets, the apostles, and Christ himself had gone. He had to battle through for Christ's sake with much tribulation and suffering, leaving his children behind; therefore do likewise, for there is no other way" [*gheenen anderen wech*].[102]

Roman Catholic martyrs evinced similar attitudes. Besides longing for martyrdom, erudite Dutch priest Cornelius Musius celebrated the anniversaries of recent martyrs, including More and Fisher, whose painted pictures he carried with him.[103] Missionary priest William Hart wrote to his mother shortly before his death at York in 1583. "Neither am I alone in this kind of suffering," he said, "for there have of late suffered twenty, or two and twenty . . . just, virtuous, and learned men for the self same cause for the which I now do suffer. You see Mr. James Fen and John Bodye are imprisoned for religion, and I dare say they are desirous to die the same death which I shall die."[104]

Sometimes the authoritative witness of previous martyrs itself influenced the willingness to die. A Protestant pamphlet from 1588 justified the executions of three Catholics for treason. One of the three, a schoolteacher named Robert Sutton, claimed that Elizabeth was not supreme governor over all matters in England, "and yet [had] nothing to defend his assertion, but a forward will, and a sentence of a father alleged (as he sayeth) by Campion, which he did not well remember."[105] John Frith had been burned in 1533 because he carefully and self-consciously doubted transubstantiation. Sutton, by contrast, was apparently willing to die not because he could articulate his Catholic beliefs, but because he sensed that his particular lack of learning did not impinge on their truth. The theologically sophisticated Edmund Campion, however, had been martyred for the same cause seven years earlier.

Knowing that co-believers had persevered through pain and death did not guarantee that faith would conquer fear, but it made victory more likely. God through the scriptures and fellow believers in their letters and songs were dictating the difficult, not the impossible. Would-be martyrs knew it, based on what they had seen, read, and heard for themselves. Still, the willingness to die required a profound internalization and prioritization of religious convictions above every competing concern. Without this, future martyrs would have written prison letters saying "Leave me alone" or "Get me out of here." Grisly executions would not have incited them to martyrdom, but deterred them from it. To persevere in the willingness to die, they had to practice their beliefs under the most difficult of circumstances.

Prison Activities: Practicing the Beliefs

Early modern martyrs placed absolute trust in God as the guarantor of biblical promises. The sources bear traces of the experience through which they reached their resolve. Sixteenth-century Christians anticipating death were exemplars of contemporary modes of spirituality. They manifest the era's religiosity in action, displaying with a distilled intensity many of the same practices and sensibilities much more widely shared among the devout. The prospect of beheading or burning made prison no place for extraneous activity, for More's "fancies of the world." Christ had pledged that God would give if they asked, would open doors if they knocked (Matt. 7:7–11). By writing letters, praying, and rehearsing memorized biblical passages, they tested that promise—and testified by their subsequent actions to God's response. Their descriptive language about faith reflects the processes by which trust was deepened. Word choice and metaphor point to ways in which the character of their faith distinguished the martyrs from most of their contemporaries.

In the spiritual meditation that John Fisher wrote to his half-sister from the Tower of London, he told her to do three things to derive profit from his treatise. First, "devise in your mind" the specific conditions of a person about to die, without a chance to avoid death. Second, "never read this meditation but alone by your self in secret manner, where you may be most attentive thereunto." And third, as preparation, "you must afore lift up your mind to almighty God, and beseech him that by the help and succor of his grace the reading thereof may fruitfully work in your soul a good and virtuous life."[106] The text would not mechanically generate its intended effect. The goal was not to seek an "objective" reading, but the right one. Such demanded that one have the proper attitude, which involved foreshortening the temporal distance to death, focusing attentively without distractions, and actively calling on God for help. Without these, the text was a dead letter. Similar attitudinal prerequisites obtained for the reading of the Bible and early modern devotional literature in general, as Thomas More implied in linking the efficacy of God's word to the strength of faith.

Christian fortitude was not magic. It worked only if one had the faith on the basis of which God could make one strong. Otherwise the Bible was just another book of ancient texts. Unless one thought that *God* spoke through scripture, one could as well expect to find the strength to sustain death in the Bible as in Aesop's fables. Fisher prescribed not a critical exercise in detached reading, but an urgent engagement that impinged upon eternal salvation. The issues involved were literally more than a matter of life and death. For the martyrs, the power of the process turned decisively on one foundational trust: that whatever they might suffer, God would make good on his promises, just as he had raised Christ to glory despite his crucifixion.

In prison, martyrs who could write commonly put quill to paper. As a practice, the writing of letters, songs, or confessions of faith helped imprisoned Christians maintain their focus as they retraced the links in the case for their willingness to die, almost as a lawyer would compile evidence. This is especially clear with those who wrote extensively in prison, such as More (who of course *was* a lawyer). Biblical passages particularly important to him recur in the *Dialogue of Comfort,* such as Matt. 10:32–33, or the synoptic parallel in Luke 12:8–9: "Everyone therefore who acknowledges me before others, I also will acknowledge before my Father in heaven; but whoever denies me before others, I also will deny before my Father in heaven."[107] More wrote frequent letters, as did other martyrs. Van Haemstede reported that Cornelis Halewijn "wrote daily to the brothers" from prison in Antwerp, while in Lille, Jacques de Lo sent six letters between February 3 and February 8, 1561.[108]

Another prolific letter writer was the Dutch Anabaptist Jan Wouters van Cuyck. Of his eleven epistles printed in 1579, eight are dated, all between March 1 and March 6, 1572. He was writing letters every day for at least a couple of hours, considering their length. Certain scriptural passages surfaced repeatedly: the parallel verses of Matt. 10:24 and John 13:16 about the servant not being greater than the master; Heb. 12, the oppressed "cloud of witnesses" and the directive to resist sin "to the point of shedding [one's] blood"; and the parallel passage in 2 Esd. 7:7, Matt. 7:13, and Luke 13:24 about entering through the narrow gate that leads to life.[109] Writing occupied the hours and allowed prisoners to reach out to relatives and fellow believers, channel their thoughts into a concrete activity, and rehearse biblical passages directly relevant to their ordeal.

Jacques de Lo was imprisoned in Lille on January 29 or 30, 1561, and was executed about two weeks later, on February 15. Shortly after his imprisonment began, he wrote a letter to his "beloved brothers and sisters in Christ," noting how several days in prison had affected his understanding of key scriptural verses:

> "It is given to us by Christ not only to believe in him, but also to suffer and endure for him" [Phil. 1:29]. I am now experiencing the whole, for the four or five days that I am in this prison . . . from day to day and from hour to hour I wait to be stretched on the rack like a parchment; I expect in the end a harsh and rigorous sentence, to be burned alive. These are frightful things to the flesh, and nevertheless my God has made it so that there is only jubilation and joy in me; when I think on the promises of Christ, when I meditate on this excellent saying of St. Peter [1 Pet. 4:13–14], who said that in speaking about the afflictions of Christ, we must rejoice and are blessed, for the spirit of God rests on us—I have a consolation that outstrips all anxieties.[110]

De Lo did not claim to be without tribulations *(ennuis);* rather, meditation on Christ's promises had helped him to transcend and rejoice in them. More than thirty years earlier a Dutch pamphlet, *A Comforting Letter for All Who are Persecuted for the Truth and for Christ's Name,* had asserted that genuine understanding of scripture was forged in the adversity of prison, not grasped through dispassionate scholarship in university classrooms. "My chosen brothers," the anonymous author wrote, "this is the lesson that we must learn in the school of persecutors and in the prisons and dungeons of tyrants, where God's children learn more and make more progress than do the philosophers and the sophists' followers in their schools." Only through suffering, the writer claimed, do we "come to a genuine knowledge and understanding [*waerachtighe kennisse ende verstant*] of the things that we read."[111]

Three days after Jacques de Lo wrote his letter, he said that in being chosen by God to witness to his truth, "I am beginning to experience in my person the truth of what St. Paul said [1 Cor. 10:13], that 'God is faithful, and will not allow you to be tempted beyond what you can bear' . . . So then, my brothers, having heard such promises from God, what remains except to take courage and not to fear falling into the hands of men? For I well assure you that there is nothing but jubilation and consolation here; here God is understood to be true to what he promises."[112] This new experience of scripture is reminiscent of John Hus's prison comment, written despite his years of previous intimacy with the Bible: "Only now am I learning to understand the Psalter, to pray as I ought, to ponder the abuse of Christ and the sufferings of the martyrs."[113] When pushed to the edge, devout Christians could see more clearly the staggering power of God's word: a practical hermeneutics of the prison fused the relevant biblical passages into the only sensible framework within which to understand their experience. No matter how excruciating the temporal pain of torture and execution, God's promise of eternal joy had relativized it absolutely.

The martyrs exercised their beliefs, like athletes committed to staying in top competitive form. In so doing they tailored widespread devotional attitudes, common across confessional divides, to meet their specific demands. More's *Dialogue of Comfort* buzzes with the language of repetition and internalization. Commenting on passages such as Matt. 10:32–33 and Luke 12:8–9, he noted that "Christ spoke so often and so plain of the matter, that every man should upon pain of damnation, openly confess his faith." Despite death and the fear it inspired, it was

necessary for every man and woman, *to be always of this mind,* and *often to think thereupon,* and where they find in the thinking thereon, their hearts agrice, and shrink in the remembrance of the pain that their imagination representeth to the mind, then must they *call to mind and remember,* the great pain and torment that Christ suffered for them, and *heartily pray for grace,* that if the case should so fall, God should give them strength to stand. And thus *with exercise of such meditation,* though men should never stand full out of fear of falling, yet must they persevere in good hope, and in full purpose of standing.[114]

Here, as surely as in More's prison prayer-book marginalia,[115] is the trace of faith overcoming fear. For those who found the promise of heavenly joy less than powerful, More wrote, "let us . . . have often in our eyes by reading, often in our ears by hearing, often in our mouths by rehearsing, often in our hearts by meditation and thinking, those joyful words of holy scripture, by which we learn now wonderful, huge, and great those spiritual heavenly joys are."[116] Then might the promises be experienced aright, properly anesthetizing suffering and death.

As Heinrich Bullinger put it in a sermon against dissembling one's faith in 1555, "we must never let slip out of our minds those most holy, most true, and healthful words of our Lord Christ, which I see need oftentimes to be repeated and inculcated: Every one that shall knowledge me before men, him will I knowledge also before my father which is in heaven. But whosoever shall deny me before men, him will I also deny before my father which is in heaven."[117] Without a firm grasp of such verses, the pressure to dissemble would prove too much to resist. Anneken Jans told her infant son to make God's words a very part of his being: "remember all his words so that you do them, write them on the tablets of your heart, bind them on your forehead [*Bintse voer v voerhoefft*], speak of his laws day and night."[118] John Ingram told fellow prisoners in July 1594 that "I have long since (I confide in God) imprinted in my heart constant and immutable not to fear 'those that kill the body but the soul they cannot destroy.'"[119]

The use of evocative metaphor and the language of interiorization was not unique to the martyrs. A 1528 pamphlet entitled *On the Genuine Cross of Christ* stated that the Lord's help would come by grasping the "staff" [*stab*] of God's word "in the heart with a solid faith."[120] Calvin declared that Abraham's absolute trust in God, when commanded to sacrifice his son, "ought to be written [*escrite*] in our hearts."[121] In 1544 George Joye wrote that when "the image of terrible death is present" and "the flesh trembleth and quaketh," one must turn to the scriptures, which "confirming our hearts so, that evermore we may endure constant in faith, firm in hope, glued unto the Gospel, to persevere in this strong, jeopardous battle against Satan, the world, and against our own selves."[122] Standing in wider currents of spirituality, this is exactly what the martyrs were doing.

Of their prison activities, martyrs mentioned prayer most often. Its efficacy also presupposed the proper attitude. Prayer was an earnest supplication to God, in whom one placed all trust and from whom one looked for consolation in keeping with his promises. Thus English Protestant Thomas Haukes exhorted his wife "in the bowels of Christ, that you will exercise and be steadfast in prayer: for prayer is the only means to pierce the heavens, to obtain at the hand of God, whatsoever we desire."[123] John Bradford, another Marian martyr, in a sort of Protestant transmutation of medieval monastic routine, prescribed prayer to accompany every activity from before dawn until after dusk. When one dressed in the morning, for example, one should recall how Christ "doth clothe us" with his protection; returning home at day's end prefigured one's final entry into heaven.[124] Dutch Anabaptist Wouter van Stoelwijck took his cue from Christ: because the Lord had spent whole nights in prayer, his followers should do likewise, "especially in [their] distress."[125] He sounds like Thomas More, who wrote, "Christ tells us to stay awake, but not for cards or dice, not for rowdy parties and drunken brawls, not for wine and women, but for prayer. He tells us to pray not occasionally, but constantly. 'Pray,' he says, 'unceasingly.' He tells us to pray not only during the day (for it is hardly necessary to command anyone to stay awake during the day) but rather He exhorts us to devote to intense prayer a large part of that very time which most of us usually devote entirely to sleep."[126] Jesuit missionary John Gerard—who was not executed but was repeatedly tortured—recalled his prison experience of 1597 a dozen years after the fact. He described his time spent in the Tower of London: "Left to myself in my cell I spent most of my time in prayer. Now, as in the first days of my imprisonment, I made the Spiritual Exercises [of Ignatius Loyola]. Each day I spent four or sometimes five hours in meditation; and so for a whole month. I also had my breviary with me; and every day, too, I rehearsed the actions of Mass, as students do when they are preparing for ordination . . . This practice brought me much consolation in my sufferings."[127]

Martyrs prayed prior to torture or interrogation. The night before Protestant Arnout Diericks was to face inquisitorial monks in Bruges, "he passionately called on God, that in accord with his promises he would give him his Holy Spirit, which might speak through him in order to witness to the evangelical truth."[128] Before missionary priest Alexander Briant was tortured in 1581, he gave his "mind to prayer, and commending my self and all mine to our Lord, I was replenished, and filled up with a kind of supernatural sweetness of Spirit. And even while I was calling upon the most holy name of Jesus, and upon the blessed virgin Mary (for I was in saying the rosary), my mind was cheerfully disposed, well comforted, and readily prepared and bent, to suffer and endure those torments which even then I most certainly looked for."[129]

Paul's dictum in 1 Cor. 10:13, that God would not let one be tempted beyond one's strength, was perfectly suited to the forbearance of torture.[130] Adriaen Jans described the effect of this verse on him: "Men hung me up by my hands so that I couldn't touch the ground. Yes, my dear, beloved wife, I was very afraid, so that I could hardly stand it, when they made demands of me for the third time, *and so I thought of the words of the Apostle* when he says 'The Lord will not let you be tempted above your ability,' *and they supported me.*"[131] Far from bursting with bravado, Jans was "very afraid" [*seer banghe*]—yet still God provided through his word. John Gerard was suspended in manacles for hours, hands above his head, without informing against other Catholics. He credited his endurance to the Lord, who "saw my weakness with the eyes of His mercy, and did not permit me to be tempted beyond my strength. With the temptation He sent me relief."[132] The same promise that preserved the Dutch Anabaptist worked for the missionary priest, because both trusted absolutely that God would sustain them.

This sort of trust produced sharp focus and purposefulness. It was supposed to: would God have misled the beloved men and women from whom he demanded so much? According to Menno Simons, God was the one and "only" [*allenich*] place to seek refuge in affliction, "just as all devout cross-bearers have done from the beginning."[133] For Calvin, pastoral concern dictated that one inculcate proper fear of the Lord as the organizing principle of Christian life: "The fear of God must therefore possess and occupy our heart in such a way that we condemn the whole world and all creatures in order to obey him and follow his will."[134] Thomas More implied that a single biblical verse, properly grasped, would permit the endurance of every torment plus death for the sake of God's truth. The verse was Rom. 8:18: "I consider that the sufferings of this present time are not worth comparing with the glory about to be revealed in us." More wrote that "we should not . . . need much more in all this whole matter, than that one text of Saint Paul, if we would consider it well."[135] Martyrs might express their singular faith with minimalist austerity. After writing a confession of faith and a song in 1529, Willem van Zwolle stated simply, "All my hope and trust in God." Following a song they wrote in 1562, François Varlut and Alexandre Dayke said, "Jesus Christ is my all."[136]

Christ had not abandoned the martyrs, but drawn close to them in their suffering—indeed, his strength displaced their weakness. He grew more powerful in them as they relied less on themselves. They experienced the truth of Paul's words: "It is no longer I who live, but Christ who lives in me. And the life I now live in the flesh I live by faith in the Son of God, who loved me and gave himself for me" (Gal. 2:20). This was no theological abstraction: conviction of its truth, individually internalized, enabled the martyrs to greet suffering and death with joy. Luther stressed that the power of Gal. 2:20 stemmed from the outrageous truth that Christ really had died *"for me"* [*pro me*].[137] Speaking of Christ's passion, John Fisher said, "Believe this for a very truth, good sister, that for your sake he suffered all, *as if there had been no more in all the world but only yourself.*"[138]

The voluntary nature of martyrdom was profoundly paradoxical: the martyrs' agency depended upon relinquishing control, their strength upon a naked admission of their utter impotence and total dependence on God.

Thomas More thought it crucial not to place any "foolish trust in our own strength"; when facing tribulation we ought to "prepare our self with prayer, with our whole trust in his help, *without any trust in our strength.*"[139] Marian Protestant John Philpot played off John Careless's name, telling him to "*cast all your care on him:* set the Lord before your eyes always, for he is on your right side that you shall not be moved."[140] According to Christiaen Rijcen, Christ had sent him the experience of terror in prison, "so that I would not boast of myself, but *that I would rely on the Lord alone and not on my strength* [*alleene op den Heere verlaten, ende niet op mijn sterckheyt*], as I indeed hope to do."[141]

The prospect of perseverance came not from gearing up, but rather from emptying out, being acutely aware that only total reliance on God could sustain the horror of being burned alive, or being hanged, drawn, and quartered. There is nothing esoteric or mysterious about this. Such a disposition simply pushed to its limit the blatant relevance of Jesus' admonition: "If any want to become my followers, let them deny themselves and take up their cross and follow me. For those who want to save their life will lose it, and those who lose their life for my sake will find it" (Luke 9:23). The martyrs' paradoxical, voluntary self-denial means that the assertion by Donald Weinstein and Rudolph Bell, if taken at face value, is deeply misleading: "This motif of human agency, in which the Christian decides upon a spiritual course and follows it to an ultimate conclusion despite all worldly considerations, is the essence of the martyr's story . . . the martyr is a hero honored as a supreme example of how men and women *by the exercise of their own will* can further God's work."[142] On the contrary, such determined self-reliance would have been to Satan like raw meat dangled before a hungry lion.

Similarly, the martyrs' own words and actions show that whatever utility the postmodern, New Historicist notion of Renaissance self-fashioning might have, it is inapplicable to them. Prison experience entailed not calculating agency and self-interest, but passivity in a double sense—both suffering and "being done unto." Behind stone walls there were no courtly patrons from whom to curry favor, no theatrical poses to strike; the Lord saw behind every mask, including dissimulation of his truth. The only sensible course of action lay not in "constructing" a self, but in stripping away every pretense to acknowledge the self one was: a weak, enfleshed soul, created by and radically dependent on God. Elizabethan priest Ralph Sherwin understood this: "My sins are great, I confess, but I flee to God's mercy; my negligences are without number, I grant, but I appeal to my redeemer's clemency. I have no boldness but in his blood, his bitter passion is my only consolation."[143]

Let us conclude with a letter written in 1591 by Swithun Wells to his brother-in-law, Gregory Martin. The discovery of a secret Mass in Wells's

London home had led to his imprisonment, and would soon result in his execution plus that of three other laymen and three priests.[144] Faith and scripture made Wells's prison experience an occasion for gratitude: "The comforts which captivity bringeth, are so manifold, that I have rather cause to thank God for his fatherly correction, than to complain of any worldly misery whatsoever: *Dominus de caelo in terram aspexit, ut audiret gemitus compeditorum* [Ps. 102:19–20]. *Exaudivit pauperes, et vinctos suos non despexit* [Ps. 69:33]. *Introeat in conspectu tuo gemitus compeditorum* [cf. Ps. 38:10]. *Potiùs mihi habetur affici pro Christo, quàm honorari à Christo.*" Understood and internalized properly, heavy with the hope of eternal reward, God's word and gift of faith shaped Wells's experience in profoundly counterintuitive ways: "These and the like cannot but comfort a good Christian, and cause him to esteem his captivity to be a principal freedom, his prison a heavenly harbor, and his irons an ornament, and comely badge of Christ himself. These will plead for him, and the prison will protect him . . . I have been long time in durance, and endured much pain, but the many future rewards in the heavenly payment make all pains seem to me a pleasure." Conscious of fellow believers outside his cell, Wells asked God for their help: "God send me withall the prayers of all good folks to obtain some end of all miseries, such as to his holy will and pleasure shall be most agreeable." At the same time, despite solitary confinement, he felt that he was never less alone, for Christ was ever with him:

> And truly custom hath caused, that it is now no grief to me at all to be barred from company, desiring nothing more than solitariness; but rather I rejoice that thereby I have the better occasion with prayer to prepare my self to that happy end, for which I was created, and placed here by God, assuring my self always of this one thing, that how few soever I see, yet am I not alone: *Solus non est, cui Christus comes est.* When I pray I talk with, when I read he talketh to me, so that I am never alone. He is my chiefest companion, and only comfort: *Cum ipso sum in tribulatione.*

Shortly after he wrote this, Swithin Wells was hanged, drawn, and quartered in London on December 10, 1591.

The Art of Dying Well

As mentioned earlier, even antagonistic writers repeatedly described martyrs' dying behavior in terms similar to those of sympathetic martyrologists. We can now understand even better that accounts of the martyrs' deaths are more than mere literary tropes. Joyce Lewis, hoping to subvert Catholic designs to cast her as a criminal, consulted with friends about how to die best before the crowd. Public execution was the martyrs' climactic moment, after weeks or months of anticipation in prison. Here selfless dependence on God was both most visible and most important. The spectacle of the martyrs' deaths could frame a final act of evangelization more powerful than a thousand sermons. And the martyrs had every reason to believe that death was also the high road to eternal joy with God. Small wonder that so many of them seemed so content.

In the early 1550s brothers Frans and Nicolaes Thijs left their native Mechelen in Brabant and went to Germany, where they became staunch Lutherans. Upon returning to Mechelen the young men were imprisoned, examined, and, after repeatedly refusing to recant their views, sentenced to be burned. Throughout their ordeal they helped sustain each other. On the morning of their execution, when they were led out of the prison,

> they comforted each other like this: "Dear brother, be of good cheer, we have a faithful shepherd, Jesus Christ, who has given his life for us that we might be saved; let us not budge from this shepherd lest the wolf tear us in pieces and throw us in the eternal pit. Though our bodies are already taken from us, yet our souls cannot be taken. Today we shall instead confess our faith with the apostle Paul before the authorities." And with many more words besides they consoled one another; many people who were nearby wept and had great sympathy for them.

The articles of faith for which they had been sentenced were read publicly as part of the execution ritual, while "in the meantime the two brothers spoke to each other out of the scriptures." Their mutual support continued as they were led away from the area before the city hall. As they were taken to the stake, Nicolaes said to Frans, "'Let us fight like knights [*Ritterlich*] a little bit in the Lord Jesus Christ, for today we shall be with him in his Father's kingdom.' They began to sing 'We All Believe in One God,' etc."[145] The song's opening lines reflected the traditional Credo and reinforced a sense of God's care for his children:

> We all believe in one God
> creator of heaven and earth
> who gave himself as Father
> that we might be his children.
> He will support us always
> and also preserve body and soul
> He will defend from every misfortune,

> no harm shall befall us
> He cares for us, protects and keeps watch
> Everything lies in his power.[146]

The two brothers endured the stake through their shared sense of God's overriding concern, confident that in losing their lives for Christ's sake, the Lord was claiming them for himself forever.

French Huguenots also sang songs, often psalms, on the way to their executions.[147] This makes perfect sense considering the psalms' frequent message of divine solace: they expressed perfectly the trust in God demanded by the moment. When Rogier Du Mont went to his death on December 2, 1563, in Tournai, he sang the first couplet of Psalm 16, followed by Psalm 6:[148]

> Protect me, O God, for in you I take refuge. I say to the Lord, "You are my Lord; I have no good apart from you" (Ps. 16:1–2). O Lord, do not rebuke me in your anger, or discipline me in your wrath. Be gracious to me, O Lord, for I am languishing; O Lord, heal me, for my bones are shaking with terror. My soul also is struck with terror, while you, O Lord—how long? Turn, O Lord, save my life; deliver me for the sake of your steadfast love (Ps. 6:1–4).

What could have been more fitting? Judging from the verses he chose, du Mont was still wrestling with fear ("my bones are shaking with terror"), but he was not overcome by it. Hundreds of passages in the Psalms speak of God as a refuge for the afflicted. For persecuted Christians, these were indeed ancient songs for modern times.

Just prior to their executions, martyr after martyr exemplified different aspects of the willingness to die. When officials made a final effort to get Caspar Tauber to renounce his evangelical views in Vienna in 1524, he refused: "Even if your theologians numbered eighty thousand," he said, "they would neither be able nor permitted to get anything from me, so long as the word of God stood on my side." Just before the executioner struck off his head, he looked heavenward and thanked Christ "that you have chosen me unworthily and made me worthy to die for the sake of the divine word."[149] Group solidarity ran deep when Margriete van den Berghe was burned in Ghent along with three other Anabaptists in 1551. She told the magistrates to spare three stakes and burn them all at one, "for spiritually we are all of one mind."[150] The Gorcum martyrs killed in 1572 entrusted their ordeal to God and urged one another to persevere to the end. As they were waiting to suffer "death for the defense of the Catholic faith, by mutual supplications and prayers they commended their last struggle to God. There each one depicted to one another before the eyes of the understanding the hope of the celestial kingdom, and the eternal reward which was close, exhorting one another out of mutual duty [*office*] to suffer with constancy the agony of death."[151] Decades earlier the first two martyrs of the Reformation period, Hendrik Vos and Johann van den Esschen, had done likewise. When told they must recant their views or be burned, they said that "they were glad that God had given them the grace to die for the Christian faith."[152] Another account stated that "they repeatedly bore witness that they wanted to die as Christians" and exhibited such composure and joy that "they seemed to many to look cheerful" [*multis ridere viderentur*], singing the hymn *Te deum laudamus* back and forth to each other as the flames rose up around them.[153] Protestant, Anabaptist, and Roman Catholic martyrs died similarly, just as they had prepared for death similarly.

Martyrdom looks radically different when understood from the inside rather than explained from the outside. It appears "crazy" only if one considers Christian conviction and devotion crazy; on the martyrs' own terms, its meaning and logic are crystal clear. The Christian willingness to die in the sixteenth century was shared, in both form and content, by Protestant, Anabaptist, and Roman Catholic martyrs. Faith and scripture grounded Christian life in all three traditions. The centrality of trust in God and his word in the martyrs' lives, their rigorous commitment to the ramifications of Christian belief, and the consequent power of faith to displace competing concerns and to relativize even horrific death distinguished the martyrs' faith from that of ordinary Christians. The *content* of their faith was shared with less devout fellow believers—but taking it with uncompromising seriousness greatly transformed its *character*. Above all, the martyrs believed that, in scripture, God was speaking to them. Biblical verses about enduring persecution and transcending fear by faith were meant for them as they suffered in the sixteenth century. God's word accomplished its purpose, and Christ sustained them.

In these respects early modern Christian martyrs were much alike. But their respective communities of faith were also deeply divided. The martyrs died for their fidelity to Christ, but they disagreed about what it meant to be Christian. They died for God's truth, but they disputed what his truth was. Their disagreements proved central to the formation of the three principal, mutually exclusive martyrological traditions.

The following three chapters explore the distinctiveness of these traditions over time. They examine the ways in which fellow believers understood their martyrs, and how news and views about them were disseminated after the executions had taken place. In all three traditions, martyrology was interwoven with broader religious sensibilities and figured importantly in the formation of confessional identities. Taking each tradition on its own terms, being sensitive to the respective emphases of each, is essential if we are to avoid reductionist distortion as well as modern or postmodern value judgments, whether confessional or atheistic. By examining the three traditions in this way, we can understand the dispute over true and false martyrs and appreciate fully the nature and long-term consequences of religious disagreement in the Reformation era.

CHAPTER FIVE

Witnesses for the Gospel:
Protestants and Martyrdom

Therefore, since we are justified by faith, we have peace with God through our Lord Jesus Christ, through whom we have obtained access to this grace in which we stand; and we boast in our hope of sharing the glory of God. And not only that, but we also boast in our sufferings, knowing that suffering produces endurance, and endurance produces character, and character produces hope, and hope does not disappoint us, because God's love has been poured into our hearts through the Holy Spirit that has been given to us.

> —ROMANS 5:1–5

When those things which the prophets and apostles and other martyrs endured to uphold God's truth are set before us, we are that much more strengthened to cling to the faith that we hold, which they sealed with their blood.

> —JOHN CALVIN, *BRIEF INSTRUCTION AGAINST THE ANABAPTISTS*
> (1544)

Augustianian monks Hendrik Vos and Johann van den Esschen went to the stake in Brussels on July 1, 1523. Sympathetic to Luther, they were immediately hailed as the first martyrs for purified Christian truth. Over the next forty years, hundreds more men and women, chiefly in France, England, and the Low Countries, were executed for their Protestant convictions. This chapter explores how Protestant writers appropriated the values associated with martyrdom and celebrated their slain witnesses for the restored Gospel.

The most important themes of the famous Protestant martyrologists—John Foxe, Jean Crespin, and Adriaen Cornelis van Haemstede—were already in place by the 1520s or early 1530s. In the generation that followed, the growth of Calvinism plus stiffer resistance to heresy broadened the scope and steeled the character of Protestant martyrdom. The historical vision of the midcentury martyrologists stressed the relationship between faith and suffering, a link graphically embodied in the surge of executions during the period. In the later sixteenth and the seventeenth centuries, the relationship of the martyrologies to Protestant communities of faith was heavily influenced by very different national contexts.

Countervailing concerns tugged at Protestant writers as they identified and promoted their martyrs. On the one hand, the principle of *sola scriptura* reaffirmed the esteem for patience, preparation for death, and devotion to Christ's passion. Biblical verses prescribed behavior, while scriptural martyrs such as John the Baptist, Stephen, and Jesus himself inspired imitation. Protestant leaders, along with the martyrs, repeatedly invoked these passages and patterns. In the early Reformation, for example, Luther preached on Christ's passion and on preparation for death, exhorted persecuted Christians to perseverance, and wrote pamphlets about several of the evangelical martyrs.[1] Protestant writers invoked scripture as the authoritative basis for this cluster of activities and values. Because the analogous late medieval positions ultimately derived from the same source, the continuity of Protestantism with the past is more striking than any rupture.

At the same time, however, Protestants repudiated the saints' traditional intercessory role for the living and the dead. They rejected it as unbiblical and hence as unjustified, a scandalous infringement on Christ's uniqueness as humanity's sole redeemer. The importance of ancient and recent martyrs lay not in their bodily remains, purported vessels of divine power that allegedly empowered them to work miracles. As Christians were to pray directly to Christ, Protestants evinced a narrower, more etymological understanding of martyrs as witnesses (derived from the Greek term *martus*, "witness"). By God's grace the martyrs had witnessed to scripture's saving truth, freshly rediscovered after centuries of clutter and distortion. The essence of this truth was the experience of justification by faith alone in the crucified and risen Christ: the conviction that salvation was something utterly and freely given by God through his son, to which men and women, regardless of their exertions, could contribute nothing. Martyrdom proclaimed that the integrity of God's truth and the reality of saving faith were values greater than the prolongation of human life. Indeed, Christian faith gave life its meaning.

The martyr-saints of Christian hagiography bequeathed an ambiguous legacy. Protestants had to distance themselves from customs that compromised the relationship between Christians and their savior without diminishing the importance of those who had died for that relationship and everything for which it stood.[2] They had to peel away the witness to the truth from the wonder-working intercessor. The martyrs witnessed to Christ's uniqueness, but could not impinge on it. They were models in times of persecution, but not objects for veneration or patrons who desired supplication.

Protestant martyrologists faced further ambiguities. Celebrating heroic witnesses was an organic process of identity formation and preservation, which necessarily excluded certain people while it included others. In principle, Augustine's dictum ("not the punishment, but the cause, makes a martyr") provided fenceposts for the barrier between true martyrs and false. It supported the lattice of Protestant doctrine that corralled genuine witnesses to nourish the community and barred radicals and Roman Catholics lest they compromise it. Yet what of disagreements and divisions among Protestants themselves? As the solidarity of international survival in the 1550s gave way to the later vicissitudes of Protestantism in divergent national settings, the legacy of the martyrs changed as well.

The Early Evangelical Martyrs and Emergent Protestant Identity

Early evangelicals were late medieval Christians, so martyrdom was in the air before a single execution had occurred. During his trip to the Low Countries in May 1521, Albrecht Dürer heard rumors of Luther's murder and lamented his demise. He compared him to Christ and hoped that Erasmus might "attain the martyr's crown."[3] In the same year, Poggio Bracciolini's account of Jerome of Prague appeared at least three times in German translation. Considering the Edict of Worms and the papal condemnation of Luther, Germany was potentially the new Bohemia. Early evangelicals saw their own movement prefigured in Jerome and John Hus, a perception they expressed in pamphlets and woodcuts.[4] Poggio stopped short of calling Jerome a martyr, yet his sympathy for the Hussite preacher and his eloquence is evident.[5]

Luther was not dead in the spring of 1521, but rather hidden away in the Wartburg castle, translating the New Testament into German. There, in the late winter of 1522, he wrote a consolatory letter to those who suffered persecution for the sake of God's word. It is laced with his theology of the cross—"the nature of the divine word is that it is received by a few with profound sincerity and horribly persecuted by the many"—and expressly linked the papacy's Hussite victims to forebodings that he might be next.[6] Precedents reinforced Luther's view that proclaimers of the Gospel attracted persecution. He gauged his enemies' intentions accordingly.

The earliest executions fit into an interpretive framework that was already firmly in place. The reformers did not scrap the late medieval inheritance; rather, their emphasis on scripture focused it more sharply. Dürer's lament, Poggio's German publication, the Hussite martyrs' significance, and Luther's remarks all exemplify a vigorous martyrological sensibility. This explains why the earliest evangelicals who were put to death were instantly celebrated as martyrs. In pamphlets and songs, in correspondence and treatises, in sermons and visual sources, the same themes that were present in the 1520s would preoccupy the midcentury martyrologists. German and Swiss towns, the engines of the early evangelical movement, seem to have been especially sensitized to notions related to martyrdom. Two scholars have recently discussed the early martyr pamphlets, particularly for Germany.[7] The presence of a more widespread martyrological sensibility in the early Reformation, however, remains underappreciated.

Specific doctrines and articles of faith are central to early evangelical sources about martyrs—which makes perfect sense, since they were the reason for the martyrs' deaths. In the martyrs' encounter with authorities, doctrines assumed a human concreteness unmatched by scholarly debate or literary polemic. Martyrdom was a deeply polarizing phenomenon: at a time when the boundaries between confessional communities often remained unclear, executions distilled the grey of the reform-minded into the white of witnesses for the truth and the black of their bloodthirsty persecutors.[8] Martyrs' trials and public deaths sharply accented the confrontational character of apprehension, interrogation, and execution for religion; "us" and "them" could scarcely have been clearer. The contrast between persecutor and martyr was reinforced by habitual modes of understanding and countless biblical texts. Apocalyptic expectations heightened interpretive sensitivity: "latter days" was a phrase teeming with anticipation of the Last Judgment and a yearning for final liberation. Martyrs were a sign of the end times. They would complete the number of persecuted victims under the altar (Rev. 6:9–11) before God would finally silence the raging of the Roman Antichrist.

Reformation publicists recognized the powerful combination of evangelical doctrines and martyrs' deaths. In a still fluid religious context, they associated martyrs with the specific articles of faith for which they had been killed. This link helped both to constitute and to confirm a new Christian tradition clearly separate from Rome. This identity remained broadly evangelical, although some martyrs were more clearly Lutheran (in the sense of adhering specifically to Luther's views) than others. Martyrs did not always express their convictions with catechetical clarity. At times publicists must have wished for greater precision and congruity with official teachings. Some doctrinal differences could be overlooked. Executed Anabaptists did not belong among the new witnesses, but martyrs' variant views on the Eucharist could be absorbed, despite Luther's refusal to shake Zwingli's hand at Marburg in 1529 over just this issue. As evangelicals distinguished between essential and nonessential martyrs' beliefs, they were becoming aware of something "Protestant" about themselves, an aspect of religious identity that intra-Protestant disputes over liturgy, ministry, or the sacraments fail to reveal.

Publications and Communication

Many of the early evangelical martyrs were clergy; and, except for Wendelmoet Claes, who was executed in The Hague in 1527, all were men.[9] By contrast, the second generation of Protestant martyrs included proportionally more women and laypeople. The clerical background of many of the early martyrs probably facilitated a grasp of the relevant theological issues and a comprehension of the teachings they refused to abjure. It reflects, too, the traditional propensity of Catholic authorities to direct repressive efforts against heretical leaders rather than ordinary followers. In contrast to the geographical concentration of many executions in the 1540s and 1550s, the early martyrs were put to death at sites scattered from St. Andrews to Vienna.

Although relatively small in number, many of the early martyrs were widely publicized. The flood of *Flugschriften* in the early German Reformation included numerous martyr pamphlets, published shortly after their deaths, several in multiple editions. Indeed, the first publication, a brief story of Vos and van den Esschen's execution in Brussels, saw sixteen editions in 1523, published in no fewer than seven different German towns by at least eight different printers.[10] The anonymous *True History* about Caspar Tauber, a well-to-do Viennese layman killed on September 17, 1524, was published at least seven times, six of these editions in Nuremberg, Strasbourg, or Augsburg.[11] In 1527 nine editions of the anonymous *History or True Story of the Suffering and Death of Blessed Leonhard Keyser* appeared, and the same year a pamphlet about another pastor-martyr, Johann Heuglin, was published four times.[12] These works lacked dedicatory prefaces to patrons, which implies that they were not subsidized. Printers had to make money to stay in business, which in the absence of financial support required that they sell their products. Other things being equal, it would seem that reprints reflected demand, and that martyr pamphlets were popular and sold well.

Other publications were devoted to Hendrik van Zutphen (like Vos and van den Esschen, a former member of the Augustinian house in Antwerp), who was burned at Heide, in Holstein, on December 12, 1524;[13] Wolfgang Schuch, the Lutheran pastor of the village of Saint-Hippolyte, executed at Nancy during the Peasants' War on June 21, 1525;[14] Jan van Woerden, a married priest burned in The Hague on September 15, 1525;[15] Georg Winkler, a preacher from Halle murdered on the road on April 23, 1527;[16] learned layman Adolf Clarenbach and Peter Fliesteden, burned in Cologne on September 28, 1529;[17] Willem van Zwolle, a member of the court of King Christian II of Denmark, executed in Mechelen on October 20, 1529;[18] and John Frith, who wrote a treatise from prison shortly before his execution in London on July 4, 1533.[19] Despite the copies that were undoubtedly lost, damaged, or confiscated, tens of thousands of copies of martyr pamphlets must have been circulating by the late 1520s. Other martyrs were mentioned in different types of sources. François Lambert, for example, noted Jean Chastellain (executed in Vic, Lorraine, January 12, 1525) and Jean le Clerc (Metz, July 22, 1525) in the prefaces to Latin biblical commentaries, while

Erasmus wrote about Louis de Berquin (Paris, April 17, 1529) in a famous letter to Charles Utenhove.[20]

Judging from the extant sources, however, not all the evangelicals executed in the 1520s and early 1530s received published recognition.[21] Nevertheless, their public executions exposed large numbers of witnesses to the spectacle of their witness. Even more important, people talked about the events they had seen, spreading the news in a predominantly preliterate world.[22] "Listen, I want to sing for you," begins a song about Caspar Tauber, hinting at the publicly performed news songs that comprised one part of Germany's oral culture.[23] In all likelihood, surviving sources are only a weak echo of the actual lines of communication that hummed with word of the martyrs.

Nevertheless, surviving traces point to the ways in which news of the martyrs spread. Just three weeks after they were burned in Brussels, Luther had word of the two Augustinians, by what means he did not say. Two months later he generically credited "written and oral sources."[24] An anonymous Parisian diarist apparently learned of them independently of the pamphlets. In October 1523 he wrote a journal entry about the dissolution of the Antwerp Augustinian monastery, among whose members "two were burned alive in a fire, and while they were being put in it, they joyfully sang *Te Deum laudamus*."[25] In Wittenberg, Luther's very first German hymn took Vos and van den Esschen as its subject, and soon thereafter provided the model for an anonymous 1525 Dutch song about Jan van Woerden's martyrdom. Luther's hymn had jumped political and linguistic boundaries.[26]

Reformers corresponded with one another about the martyrs. From Basel in early 1525, Pierre Toussain wrote to Guillaume Farel in Montbéliard. He had seen Farel's letters to Oecolampadius that mentioned Jean Chastellain's January 12 execution, though he and the local curé had already heard about this "poor Augustinian."[27] Martyr news crossed the English channel as well. Thomas Hitton was executed at Maidstone in England on February 23, 1530; by the early summer, George Joye knew about it in Antwerp.[28] News of Hitton probably crossed to the Continent aboard one of the many merchant ships that sailed from London to the Netherlands' leading commercial city.

The spread of news about Hendrik van Zutphen's execution reveals the interplay of oral, written, and published sources. In his pamphlet about the martyrdom, Johannes Lange noted that "an upright, learned professor wrote to me and to my close brother, Peter Meyling, what happened to this devout Hendrik, as follows below. You should be aware that it is hence trustworthy as reported. The said professor heard it from someone who truthfully told him this entire story, but whose name I have not told or sent, not without reason."[29] In Erfurt, Lange wrote his pamphlet based on this report. After publication, Jakob Probst read it in Antwerp. Probst had been a member of the Antwerp Augustinian monastery with Hendrik. He was deeply saddened by his friend's demise ("my soul is sorrowful to the point of death") and regretted that his recantation in 1522 had cost him his own chance at martyrdom: "Ah, if I had had only a single droplet [*tröpflin*] of such grace and constancy, I would now be free of all cares, at rest in the Lord." He composed his own pamphlet based on Lange's and asked Luther to write a consolatory letter about Hendrik's death.[30] Like a conscientious pastor, Luther took the plea to heart in Wittenberg: drawing on additional material, he wrote a fuller version of Hendrik's martyrdom that was published seven times.[31]

Doctrines and Deaths

Whether by pamphlet, song, correspondence, or word of mouth, stories about the martyrs spread—and with them, the link between doctrines and deaths. These witnesses took Reformation teachings beyond publications and pulpits into the domain of dramatic public action. Even the earliest martyrological pamphlet of the Reformation, by no means a highly interpretive account, made the connection in general terms. Written in German, it stated that Vos and van den Esschen's "evangelical articles" included a denial of the pope's power to forgive and to bind and loose Christians from their sins, for the pope was a sinful man, equal in authority to any other priest. The two Augustinians preferred to die for "Christian faith" than to deny God's word.[32] Another anonymous pamphlet, this one in fine humanist Latin, included a list of sixty-two specific articles that the monks refused to recant, which were perhaps obtained after an official was bribed.[33] The Augustinians rejected the laws that prohibited the reading of Luther's works; affirmed that all human beings *(homines)* are priests before God; denied that confirmation, holy orders, matrimony, or extreme unction confer grace; asserted that all good works are performed by Christ, thereby denying any active human contribution to them; and stated that the pope is only the chief minister of the Church, not Christ's vicar.[34] Later the same year, an evangelical writer named Martin Reckenhofer defended these sixty-two articles at length, with copious and careful reference to scripture. The upshot was clear: having died for Christian truth, the two Augustinians should be celebrated as "righteous martyrs, burned at Brussels in Brabant for the sake of the Gospel."[35]

A pamphlet about Willem van Zwolle's martyrdom elaborated on the articles about which theologians in Louvain had questioned him. There are only eight articles, but they are presented three times: in their "raw" form as articulated by his inquisitors, then with Willem's commentary and response, and finally with a detailed defense by Lutheran theologian Johannes Bugenhagen.[36] What Reckenhofer had done for the two Augustinians, Bugenhagen did for this Dutch martyr seven years later. Willem held that all bishops and priests were equal in authority to the pope; that Masses were useless to the dead; that Christ was Christians' sole intercessor; and that monasteries and convents were unbiblical creations that anyone could leave at will.[37] His persistent refusal to abjure these convictions led to the stake.

Numerous other sources link doctrines and martyrs' deaths.[38] Although the articles differ in number and formulation due to the variations of inquisitorial procedure, their fundamentally evangelical character is evident. Among other convictions, Casper Tauber denied transubstantiation and the sacrament of penance, criticized purgatory, and repudiated the intercession of Mary and the other saints.[39] Jan van Woerden defended clerical marriage and admitted to secretly marrying while a priest, according to the report by a fellow prisoner in The Hague, Willem Voldersgraft. Set in dialogue form, Voldersgraft's account portrayed many central evangelical ideas in action, including the insistence that scripture was a self-sufficient basis to reject the prescriptions of the Roman church.[40] Writing a treatise from the Tower of London, John Frith connected specific doctrines about purgatory and especially the Eucharist to his own impending death.[41] Whoever read these pamphlets, or listened to them read aloud, would have known that these martyrs were neither Anabaptists nor other separatists. Nor, obviously, would they have been confused with the Roman Catholic authorities whose teachings they had rejected and who had put them to death.

Exalted Past, Embattled Present, Apocalyptic Future

Contemporaries knew that these witnesses had antecedents. Early publicists were primed to see the parallels because of the evangelical emphasis on scripture, the ubiquity of the ancient martyr-saints, and the publicists' knowledge of church history. In his *Letter to the Christians of the Low Countries,* Luther likened Vos and van den Esschen's oppressors to Christ's persecutors, while in his song about them, the two Augustinians were Abel to the Louvain theologians' Cain.[42] In 1525 François Lambert compared the Cardinal de Lorraine's decree against heresy to one by Nero or Diocletian. He analogized Jean le Clerc's tortures to those endured by the early Christian martyrs Lawrence or Vincent, le Clerc's persecutors to those who condemned Christ.[43] Such parallels only hint at the providential paths that Foxe, Crespin, and van Haemstede would later trace from the ancient to the recent martyrs. Still, they reveal the same historical sense.

Writers readily applied the terms "saint" and "martyr" to the recent witnesses, despite contemporary attacks on the notion of the saints as intercessors. The early publicists lacked the reticence of the Genevan city council in

1554, when its members approved the publication of Crespin's martyrology provided he avoided the two terms.[44] The acceptance of the terms in the early Reformation makes sense if evangelicals sought to distinguish witnesses for the truth, who were killed for testifying to God's word, from bogus saints and their pseudo-miracles. After the death of Vos and van den Esschen, Luther praised God "that we have lived to see and hear about genuine saints [*rechte heyligen*] and true martyrs [*warhafftige merterer*]; to this point we have exalted and prayed to so many sham saints" [*falscher heyligen*].[45] In the same vein, an anonymous author was inspired by Leonhard Keyser's martyrdom to proclaim, "praise, honor, and laud be to God in his saints."[46] Just as Catholics were not about to relinquish scripture to heretics, Protestants were not going to yield the notion of *genuine* saints to papists. Shunning the terms altogether threatened to marginalize their heroic sacrifice. The very celebration of true witnesses for the Gospel might well have been seen as a means to help displace legendary saints and their superstitious relics, as Luther seems to have wished.

Those who saw only the title page of Reckenhofer's treatise about Vos and van den Esschen, however, might have been somewhat confused. Both Augustinians are shrouded with halos, hands calmly clasped as they prepare to meet Christ, who from heaven opens his arms to receive them (Figure 18). Moreover, they are identified as "S. Heynricus" and "S. Johannes," which together with the traditional iconography might well have led viewers to regard them as new heavenly patrons. Similarly, people might easily have misconstrued the meaning behind Caspar Tauber's name, "with red letters in a calendar, as if he were holy," or Thomas Hitton as a "martyr" in the calendar in George Joye's *Ortulus anime* (1530).[47] The same anonymous author who wrote about Keyser reported—with no hint of unease—that after his execution, "some took the burned parts and the ashes and carried them away with them."[48] How exactly was God to be praised "in his saints"? Whether bits of Keyser's burned body were scuttled away or not, this sympathetic author calmly narrated actions in line with traditional views about saints' relics. François Lambert brilliantly captured the tension between exalting the new martyrs without attributing to them intercessory powers: *if* it were permissible to call upon saints *(si liceret Sanctos inuocare)*, he wrote, people would have no less reason to invoke Jean Chastellain than Peter, Paul, and the other apostles.[49]

Even as they evoked parallels with the apostles and Christ himself, the new martyrs were important figures in the embattled present. Their deaths represented not defeat but victory, a dramatic means by which God triumphed over Antichrist's tyranny. Opposition by Catholic authorities confirmed the conviction that persecution bespoke divine favor. Early evangelicals adopted and transformed late medieval attitudes about Christian suffering through a

Figure 18. Title-page woodcut of Hendrik Vos and Johann van den Esschen, from Reckenhofer, *Dye histori, so zwen Augustiner Ordens gemartert seyn tzü Bruxel . . .* [Erfurt: Wolfgang Stürmer, 1523]. Reproduced with permission of Ghent University Library.

direct emphasis on scripture, very much as Hus had a century before. In the 1520s, however, these sensibilities, the martyrs, and the doctrines for which they had died were promulgated in print and intertwined with a movement that was spreading throughout Europe.

Luther published his *Letter to the Christians of the Low Countries* within weeks of the execution of Vos and van den Esschen. He was brimming with enthusiasm about what God had wrought in them: "Praise and thanks be to the Father of all mercy," he began, expressing his joy that the Gospel had produced two men who had not only endured "disgrace and harm, anxiety and distress" for Christ's sake, but had also shed their blood for him.[50] Two years later, he saw Hendrik van Zutphen's burning as part of the reborn "form of a proper Christian life," in which "suffering and persecution" were horrible before the world but "precious in the eyes of God" (Ps. 116:15).[51] He also wrote that the assassination of Georg Winkler in 1527 ought to evoke comfort and rejoicing "that Christ made him worthy to suffer death for the sake of his word and truth."[52] Luther and his contemporaries were living in remarkable times. Because Christ had told his followers to expect persecution for his sake (Matt. 24:9, Luke 21:12, John 15:18–20), and because this was the experience of Paul, Stephen, and other apostolic Christians, persecution and martyrdom confirmed Luther's view that he had dared to proclaim the Gospel aright.[53]

This was anything but a quirk of Luther's theology of the cross. The inevitable persecution of the just is a prevalent theme in scripture. To question it would have been to dispute a central motif in God's word—hardly likely for people committed to the autonomy of the Bible as the basis for Christian life. Others chimed in with Luther. "Honor, thanks, and praise be to God," Johannes Lange wrote about Hendrik van Zutphen's death, "who also in our own times has confirmed his Gospel with the death of his chosen ones."[54] Martyrs provided a clear sign that the evangelical cause was just and right. Unable to bear the truth, the world persecuted its adherents. William Tyndale generalized this principle in his *Obedience of a Christian Man*. With abundant references to the New Testament, he claimed that God's word could not exist without persecution, "no more than the sun can be without his light."[55] The Gospel's recent blood witnesses embodied this truth, including Thomas Hitton in England and the "many that suffered in Brabant, Holland, and at Cologne and in all quarters of Deutschland and do daily."[56]

God's ways were frequently counterintuitive. "For as the heavens are higher than the earth, so are my ways higher than your ways, and my thoughts than your thoughts" (Isa. 55:9). "For God's foolishness is wiser than human wisdom, and God's weakness is stronger than human strength" (1 Cor. 2:25). Often he worked by manifesting unexpected power in apparent weakness. Thus evangelicals hoped that the new martyrs would advance their cause in the future, just as the ancient martyrs had helped establish Christianity in the Roman Empire. Preaching in London on Trinity Sunday in 1527, Thomas Arthur said that thousands would take his place were he to suffer persecution for proclaiming God's word.[57] Lange told Hendrik van Zutphen's persecutors that "with this blood God has fertilized [*gethunget*] the land of Dittmars so that it will bear many Christians."[58] And the author who celebrated Heuglin's martyrdom wrote that "the good seed which God, the Lord, has sown in some human hearts through the great patience and martyrdom of this man and the unjust actions of the papists will undoubtedly, with help, sprout and bring forth fruit."[59] Clearly these writers thought that Tertullian's famous remark—"the blood of Christians is seed"—applied to the present evangelical martyrs. Wolfgang Capito put the idea broadly to Marguerite de Navarre in 1528: "experience reveals that the harshest persecutions are for the weakest Christians the gentlest consolations."[60]

Anti-Nicodemism is associated above all with John Calvin. The term stems from the story of the Pharisee Nicodemus in John's Gospel, who at first visited Jesus by night rather than openly associating with him (John 3:1–2). In the sixteenth century, anti-Nicodemism specifically condemned those who, in order to avoid persecution, engaged in Catholic practices despite harboring Protestant sympathies. Conceived more broadly, in terms of what persecuted Christians were told to do and not do, the term discloses the continuity between early evangelical directives and the Protestant anti-Nicodemism of the 1540s and 1550s. Additionally, a wider perspective reveals parallel exhortations among oppressed Anabaptists and Roman Catholics. Like the link between martyrs and the doctrines for which they died, martyrdom and anti-Nicodemism would be paired for decades to come.

In fact, martyrdom, doctrines, and anti-Nicodemism were combined as early as the 1523 *History of the Two Augustinians*. Besides enumerating the sixty-two articles that Vos and van den Esschen refused to recant, this work contained a carefully crafted exhortation not to forsake Christian faith, entitled "A devout and Christian demand for when one who had professed the truth, was nevertheless pressured to deny it by the tyranny of the impious and the horror of death." Building on Augustine, the author wrote that consent to blasphemy might temporarily prevent danger to one's body, but it invited the destruction of the soul. Thus the Lord comforted his apostles by telling them not to fear those who kill the body (Matt. 10:28), since it profits a man nothing to gain the whole world and lose his soul (Matt. 16:26). Later in the treatise the author assumed a pastoral mode, reassuring readers of Christ's presence and reminding them that even if they had denied him, like Peter they could return and he would provide strength.[61] Readers of the *Trustwor-*

thy History about Caspar Tauber were urged to constancy like his: "Dear brothers, take to heart the faith and steadfastness of this devout Tauber." Even though God's word always cast the cross as its shadow, "be strong and comforted, Christ has overcome the world, and as long as we who believe in him are his body and he is our head, we have already with and in him overcome sin, death, the devil, and hell."[62] Luther begged Christ for strength like Leonhard Keyser's: "O dear Lord Jesus Christ, help us through your spirit likewise to confess you and your word according to such an example in the face of this blind, wicked world."[63]

Regardless of national context, similar views abound outside of explicitly martyrological sources. The Dutch *Comforting Letter for All Who Are Persecuted for the Truth and for Christ's Name* (1530) is a good example. Since "we are members of Christ's body," the author wrote, following Paul, it ought not be surprising "if we partake in his suffering and cross, for if we want to rejoice with him, then we must suffer with him."[64] A 1528 German pamphlet by the pseudonymous "Nicodemus Martyr," *On the True Cross of Christ,* castigated people for their self-imposed penitential practices, urging them to receive joyfully the true cross of affliction in their lives.[65] In 1531 Englishmen James Bainham and John Tewkesbury admitted during their heresy trials that they had possessed or read Tyndale's *Obedience of a Christian Man.* Its opening pages treat extensively the willingness to endure hardship and death for Christian truth.[66] In July 1532, when evangelicals in Geneva were just beginning to gain ground, they received at least two letters imploring them not to renounce the Gospel. Supporters in Payerne entreated them not to fear the "large number and power of your enemies, but be prepared not only to forsake your possessions, privileges, and families for Jesus Christ, but to renounce yourselves, proclaiming with good St. Paul that neither sword nor tribulation, neither things present nor those to come, neither death nor life, will separate us from the Gospel of salvation."[67] As the early evangelical martyrs were going to the stake, like-minded writers told others to hold firm even at the same cost. The supranational character of such Protestant exhortation continued in subsequent decades, despite redoubled Catholic efforts to eliminate heresy.

The restoration of God's word incited Antichrist's rage, which in turn signaled an imminent apocalypse. The Gospel was flowering one final time, epitomized in the martyrs, who were among the clearest heralds of Christ's second coming. In the summer of 1523 Anémond de Coct viewed the martyrdom of the Augustinians in Brussels as part "of these very last times." They were the successors to Hus and Jerome of Prague during an age in which Christ's mystical body lay festering, the Gospel was sullied, and the Church was oppressed by the "pernicious laws" of the papists.[68] That God permitted his preacher, Georg Winkler, to be murdered and other Christians killed, was for Luther a "certain sign" [*gewis zeichen*] that a "great catastrophe is at hand for Germany," from which God wanted to spare these elect in advance.[69] The annunciatory role of persecution and martyrdom in the "last days" would continue as a leitmotif in the midcentury martyrologies.[70]

Those who praised these martyrs had little affection for Antichrist's apocalyptic violence. Its perpetrators were not always simply despised: in a 1524 letter of consolation, for example, Luther called for pity for persecutors, considering their unwitting complicity with Satan. In 1527 he even said that Winkler's murderers should be praised—not for their wickedness and the devil's ill will per se, but insofar as God could turn even these evils to the salvation of his elect.[71] Nonetheless, the structure of heresy executions dovetailed with the dichotomies so common in the woodcuts of early evangelical *Flugschriften*.[72] If the martyrs were God's witnesses, then the ecclesiastical authorities who dispatched them to secular magistrates could only be the hatchet men of Satan himself.

These contraries were compounded by the conviction that prelates had for centuries withheld vital truths and spiritual sustenance from Christians. Only months after writing that Winkler's murderers should be forgiven, Luther called the authorities who had killed Keyser "tyrants" and "raging papists."[73] Reckenhofer condemned Catholic clergy as "Antichrist's priests" who bore the signs of the Beast from the book of Revelation, while another author decried the "blindness of the sophists and false learned men of Vienna" who sentenced Caspar Tauber.[74] Those who condemned the defenders of God's word demonstrated their hatred of the Gospel. When Jan van Woerden was questioned in The Hague, he called his interrogators "wolves," said they were ruled by the power of darkness, likened them to Judas and the Jews who condemned Christ, and implied that the Roman church was Babylon, calling it a "church of the wicked" and the Petrine see a "chair of pestilence."[75] Such attacks flowed into an already surging stream of early evangelical anticlericalism: besides their avarice, abuse of privilege, and sexual depravity, Catholic clergy were cruel persecutors.[76] The vituperation of persecutors would persist in subsequent decades.

Martyrdom had lain just beneath the surface of the late medieval Christianity in which it was so deeply rooted. In the 1520s it sprouted anew, needing not a moment's incubation, nourished by the repressive efforts of Catholic authorities. The execution of unrepentant evangelicals played directly into the hands of sympathetic interpreters. As German and Swiss towns opted for the Reformation, as the first converts were made in England, France, and the Netherlands, the martyrs' heroic deaths proclaimed God's power. Persecution bespoke divine favor: the devil opposed the Gospel because he could not bear its truth.

The divisiveness of martyrdom helped people attracted to the Reformation better understand what was at stake. The martyrs already knew. Together with the authorities who condemned them, they forced the issue for a wider public. Immediately before their execution, Vos and van den Esschen reportedly said to their would-be confessors, "we believe in God and in one Christian Church. *But we do not believe your church*" [*Aber euwer kirchen glauben wir nit*].[77] This is a remarkable expression for 1523. The early 1520s are often noted for their ambiguous theological positions and a lack of clear distinctions among evangelicals, humanists, and the reform-minded.[78] Yet after months in prison and just minutes before the flames were lit, the Augustinians' verdict was virtually inescapable.

The articles for which the martyrs died reinforced the content of emergent Protestant identity and diminished the prospects for compromise. In 1530 Justas Jonas represented the evangelicals in negotiations with Catholic authorities at the Diet of Augsburg. He had written to Luther about the demand that they make concessions to imperial Catholicism. In his response Luther mentioned Leonhard Keyser, nearly three years after his martyrdom. The recent executions rankled the reformer, inflaming other grievances. Let them insist on what they will, Luther said, yet "we and ours will insist that they bring back Leonhard Keyser and the many other people whom they have so unjustly killed, bring back so many souls lost through impious doctrine, bring back so many human resources wasted away by the fallacies of indulgences and other deceits, bring back the glory of God violated by so many blasphemies, bring back ecclesiastical purity in persons and practices that have been so disgracefully defiled. Who could give the whole list?"[79] Unlike Jesus, who had called forth Lazarus from the tomb, Luther could not resuscitate the martyrs from their ashes and bones. The martyrs' heavenly repose neither erased nor excused papist brutality. Such cruelty would not be forgotten.

Avoiding Idolatry, Following Christ: Convictions to Die For

The emergence of Reformed Protestantism changed the tone of Protestant martyrological sensibility. Between the mid-1530s and the mid-1550s, as its adherents multiplied in France, the Low Countries, and England, so too did the resolve of governmental and ecclesiastical authorities to suppress heresy. The clash of these forces set the stage for a harder-edged anti-Nicodemism. The offering of encouragements yielded to the making of demands: the willingness to die was not merely an extraordinary grace that God bestowed on a few, but a duty incumbent on all Christians. In addition, the continuing executions prompted calls for a more systematic compilation of latter-day accounts of the martyrs. A recognition of these developments is essential for understanding the genesis of the massive martyrologies in the 1550s.

Anti-Nicodemism without Compromise

Denunciations of dissembling and idolatry were repeated endlessly beginning in the early 1540s. Never did persecuted Protestants accept, en masse, their leaders' strict anti-Nicodemite views. Many complained about the stringent demands, which is partly why Calvin kept writing anti-Nicodemite works, from 1537, the year after his *Institutes* first appeared, until 1562, two years before his death.[80] When pressured, most men and women abjured. Others, to avoid persecution, engaged in Catholic practices despite their Protestant sympathies. Their numbers will always remain unknown because such activity rarely left traces. The link between anti-Nicodemism and martyrdom was never part of a collective Protestant *mentalité*. Instead, the response to persecution became a vexed issue: leaders insisted that idolatry be shunned no matter what, while most persecuted believers probably looked for pastoral consolation and ways to be Protestant without either embracing exile or risking martyrdom.[81]

The demanding ultimatum, exile or martyrdom, was not the sole Protestant position taken by major reformers during the 1540s and 1550s. Just before the Regensburg Colloquy of 1541, for example, Strasbourg reformers Wolfgang Capito and Martin Bucer maintained a more lenient view. Compared to anti-Nicodemite writers, they were less horrified by Catholic practices and more optimistic about reconciliation with Rome.[82] While he was living in Strasbourg, even Calvin seems to have been slightly less inflexible around 1540 than he had become by 1543.[83] By 1545, however, Bucer had endorsed Calvin's rigorous position, a support he reaffirmed in 1549–1550[84] after the first sessions of the Council of Trent and Charles V's reimposition of Catholicism in Germany.

Anti-Nicodemism was neither a behavioral status quo nor the only possible pastoral response to persecution. Often historians have identified with the majoritarian, lay Protestant reaction and have judged anti-Nicodemite demands to be unrealistic. When viewed in relation to martyrdom, however, a different picture emerges. Although many shrank from the uncompromising logic of anti-Nicodemite arguments, the martyrs did not. There is an unmistakable connection between the swell of sermons and treatises urging perseverance and condemning idolatry on the one hand, and the martyrs' words and actions on the other.

Between the late 1530s and the late 1550s, John Calvin and Pierre Viret were the most prolific anti-Nicodemite writers. Their works circulated both in manuscript and in print.[85] Calvin's treatises and sermons on the subject appeared in French and Latin, as well as in German, Dutch, Italian, English, and Czech.[86] In addition, writers such as Richard Tracy, George Joye, Wolfgang Musculus, Giulio della Rovere, John Hooper, Thomas Becon, John Bradford, Heinrich Bullinger, Peter Martyr Vermigli, and John Scory published works between 1540 and 1555 exhorting Protestant Christians to steadfastness and condemning capitulation to Catholic authorities.[87] Anti-Nicodemism transcended national and linguistic boundaries, finding application wherever Protestants were suppressed. George Joye closely based his *Present Consolation for the Sufferers of Persecution for Righteousness* (1544) on Urbanus Rhegius's *Consolatory Letter to All the Christians of Hildesheim* (1531), an example of the genre's international character and its continuity from the first to the second generation of the Reformation.[88]

This anti-Nicodemite barrage preceded and overlapped the first major Protestant martyrologies in 1552 (Rabus) and 1554 (Crespin, Foxe). Meanwhile, the widely publicized case of Francesco Spiera, an Italian layman who died in despair in 1548 after recanting his Protestant views, perfectly demonstrated the danger of sidestepping martyrdom.[89] Having failed to console Spiera in his anguish, Italian reformer Pier Paolo Vergerio broke decisively with Rome.[90] Anti-Nicodemite themes recur in Huguenot songs,[91] the correspondence of French and Swiss reformers,[92] and both controversial and catechetical works.[93] In years when persecuted exiles crisscrossed Europe and exchanged letters, anti-Nicodemite arguments would have been known to every threatened Protestant.

Whether Protestants might take part in Catholic practices was a specific issue embedded in a broader concern. What were those who had accepted the restored Gospel to do when pressured to renounce or compromise their faith? Numerous Reformed Protestant writers insisted that God's express commandment provided a clear answer: it was a duty never to compromise truth, even at the risk of one's life.

Interior commitment was not enough. Human beings were created by God and redeemed by Christ body and soul. Scripture spelled out the consequences of failure to bear witness to one's faith. Calvin said that Christ "proclaims to everyone this lesson upon the first entry to his school, that if we are ashamed of him before other people, he likewise will be ashamed of us when he appears in his majesty with the angels of God (Luke 9:26). It is therefore clear that our Lord is not satisfied if we acknowledge him in secret and within our hearts; he explicitly requires that we declare before other people, by exterior profession, that we are his."[94] Like Calvin, Viret quoted Rom. 10:10: "one believes with the heart and so is justified, and one confesses with the mouth and so is saved." He concluded that Paul "joins together oral profession with the faith of the heart because they are inseparable things, like the soul and the body, fire and its brightness, the sun and its light, the body and its shadow."[95] Combined with Old Testament prohibitions and Pauline warnings about idolatry (1 Cor. 8, 10), the upshot was clear: God commanded exterior profession of faith and true worship. He condemned idolatry as ipso facto worship of demons or false gods—which for these writers included Roman Catholic ceremonies and practices. Venturing voluntary exile or risking martyrdom were the only acceptable Christian responses to persecution. A Huguenot song from around 1550 was blunt: "Either flee, maintain, or die / That's what Christ teaches you, Christians."[96]

Christ's demands were nonnegotiable. For people in Calvinist conventicles in France and the Netherlands, or committed to Protestantism in the latter years of Henry VIII's reign in England, following them might mean death. Both Calvin and Viret were sensitive to the predicament of afflicted Protestants, but they refused to cut corners that contravened the clarity of scripture.[97] The difficulty and genuine danger of following Christ in no way altered the absoluteness of his commands. "I am not then going to say that white is black in order to satisfy them," Calvin responded to critics in 1544.[98] Why indulge dissimulation against God's commandments, if people still had to answer to him?[99] Far from expressing a loving sensitivity, to wink at idolatry signaled a complete abdication of pastoral responsibility. Those who cited fear of death to justify idolatry were effectively telling Christ to retract his words, that whoever holds his soul dear in this life will lose it.[100]

According to Eugénie Droz, Calvin's anti-Nicodemite views lacked doctrinal or theological bases, revealing a man "who has lost contact with reality."[101] On the contrary: they were based directly on specific biblical passages. Moreover, should everyone resolve to serve God in purity, Calvin wrote, the result would likely be many persecutions, with some Christians constrained to flee, others imprisoned, still others exiled, and some put to death.[102] Considering the plight of beleaguered Protestants in the mid-1540s, such expectations reflect the sober realism of a man with his eyes wide open.

Viret granted a bit more leeway in his 1543 *Letter Sent to the Faithful*. Yet he too held that God's express word ended any deliberation or dispute, "for it is no longer within our power, nor a matter of our judgment."[103] Bullinger thought the "sentence of our Lord and savior Jesus Christ" in passages like Matt. 10:29–33 (on acknowledging Christ before others) and Mark 8:35–38 (about losing one's life to save it) was "neither dark nor doubtful."[104] The pastor's role was not to wring from scripture a palatable reading to satisfy reluctant believers. His first duty was to God's word, the touchstone of the Reformation, which was to be used to admonish and encourage understandably timid Christians. Besides, others had demonstrated that God's commandments were not impossible to fulfill, even if they entailed painful death. The martyrs bridged difficult demand and concrete example in anti-Nicodemite arguments.

Calvin repeatedly turned to biblical and early Christian martyrs as models for the sixteenth century; in the *Brief Treatise,* for example, he invoked them four separate times. Cyprian, Daniel's companions, Eleazar and the Maccabees, and a host of early Christians suffered torture and martyrdom rather than commit idolatry—the same demand being made of latter-day Christians.[105] "If the faithful in the primitive Church" had thought idolatry justified by the threat of persecution, Calvin asked in the *Excuse,* "what would have become of Christianity? Would it not have perished and been abolished before it had ever come to be?"[106] His most explicit anti-Nicodemite work, the second of the interrelated *Four Sermons* (1552), included two lengthy passages about the martyrs and their example. Additionally, Calvin referred to "a young man who lived here with us" (in Geneva) before his martyrdom in Tournai. This was Michel Destoubequin, executed on October 26, 1549.[107] (By drawing on a recent martyr, Calvin foreshadowed the project that a repatriated printer would soon undertake in Geneva: Crespin published the first edition of his martyrology in 1554.) With obedience to God that preserved the integrity of faith, the men and women whom Calvin cited had not shrunk from martyrdom—and neither should modern persecuted Christians. This argument was hardly unique to Calvin, as the same use of martyrs by Viret, Hugh Latimer, and Bullinger makes clear.[108]

Scripture taught that idolatry must be avoided and faith preserved inviolate. Previous martyrs showed that this demand could be and had been followed. As such, the martyrs concretely rebutted the critics of anti-Nicodemism. Faith—a total trust in God and his providential dispensation—animated their witness. "The entire theology of the ancient martyrs," Calvin wrote, "was the knowledge that there is only one God whom one must adore, and that in him alone one must completely place all one's trust."[109] Without the certainty of faith, Calvin wrote, the endurance of persecution was senseless.[110] The Christian's model should be Abraham's willingness to sacrifice his son, Isaac, for "above all things God loves this confidence, that in observing his commandments we leave the outcome to his providence, and in this our spirit finds rest."[111] In no uncertain terms, obedience to God was more important than preserving one's life.[112]

According to Viret, Christian faith should generate a holy indifference about one's future. It might bring the martyrdom of a Stephen or James, or the deliverance of a Peter (Acts 12). In any event, "if we are imitators of the true servants of God, let us be certain that the Lord will not show his power and goodness less toward us than he did then. If he wills that we suffer, he will strengthen and give us steadfastness in order to persevere in the confession of his holy name. If he wills that we continue to serve, he will find some means agreeable to him to deliver us and draw us back from the hand of our enemies."[113] Providence meant that God guided the unfolding of events, often despite appearances. The seemingly trivial was no exception: "even the hairs of your head are all counted" (Matt. 10:30, Luke 12:7).[114]

This singular trust enabled martyrs to relativize suffering and death in light of God's promise of eternal life, and so "they went ahead with a cheerful heart to the fire or to another torture of death; even the women carried their children there."[115] Conversely, a lack of faith bred fear. Under peaceful conditions, the Protestant rejection of works righteousness challenged the natural human tendency to rely on oneself in seeking salvation. This propensity to self-regard was tested at its limit in facing martyrdom: would one trust God absolutely, or fall back on oneself? For the martyrs, ancient and modern, faith was all that separated the courageous acquiescence in death from a paralyzing self-absorption.

This is precisely what Christ had experienced, first wrestling with fear in Gethsemane, then submitting to his Father's will. The savior's final hours offered the perfect paradigm for the self-denial and trust to which Protestants were urging their fellow believers. To follow Christ meant to expect the sort of treatment that he had received. Scripture explained the persecution provoked by faith.

Early in English Queen Mary's reign, before he was himself burned, John Bradford told readers "to consider, that affliction, persecution, and trouble is no strange thing to God's children; and therefore it should not dismay, discourage, or discomfort us, being none other thing than all God's dear friends have tasted in their journey heavenward."[116] Like early evangelicals, Bradford and other second-generation Protestants saw an inherent connection between following Christ and persecution. Viret sounded as though he might have plagiarized Thomas à Kempis when he wrote,

> My dear brothers, since we are members of Jesus, it must be neither remarkable nor astonishing if we are participants in his cross and sufferings. For if we want to reign with him, we must suffer together with him. Since he is our head [*chef*], we are his members; the head cannot proceed by one path and the members by another, but rather the entire body and

the members follow the head who guides and governs them. If therefore our head was crowned with thorns, we cannot be part of the body without feeling their sting and without grief piercing our heart. If our king and sovereign master has been hoisted and hung on wood completely naked, completely bloodied, completely burdened with reproaches, insults, and blasphemies, it cannot be that we wait in this world to sleep always at our leisure, to be exalted with honors and dignities, being dressed in purple, velour, and silk like the rich evildoer, having all our pleasures and sensual delights on this lowly earth.[117]

Joye's language was even more graphic. Afflicted Christians were to commit themselves gratefully to God's pleasure, "giving ourselves over into his hands to fashion us by his cross, to exercise, whet, hew, square, and polish us at his benign will, to make us like his son our savior."[118] The rejection of works righteousness was not only compatible with the imitation of Christ; faith entailed an *imperative* to imitate the Lord. Richard Tracy called Christ "our captain, whom we ought to follow in suffering." Calvin stated that the willingness to die was no perverse hankering for affliction and death, but rather part of following Christ, "who walks before us as our captain."[119]

Protestant exhortations to martyrdom began and ended with God's word in a dialectic with lived experience. The unique authority of scripture was fundamental. Typically, Calvin made it plain: "if we, such as we are, would ponder well that it is God who speaks to us [in holy scripture], it is undoubtedly certain that we would be more attentive to listen to him, and with much greater reverence."[120] It is difficult to dispute this logic. Anti-Nicodemite writers drew out its implications. That the Bible alone expressed God's will was a conviction that could transform individual lives, just as it had powered Reformation criticisms of the Roman church.

The deepening of devotion did not arise spontaneously from reading the Bible. If it had, Calvin would not have written that people who regarded idolatry lightly had never "tasted" [*gousté*] God's word in Isa. 42:8 and 48:11, which make clear that God's glory is untransferable.[121] Viret used the same verb to distinguish an empty, scholarly comprehension of scripture from a practical, "true understanding and experience of the things we read." The latter entailed "tasting what the goodness, help, aid, and favor of God is."[122] Cyprian's unswerving resolve to follow God's commandments "ought to be well imprinted [*imprimée*] in our memory," Calvin stated, as a bulwark against the temptation to self-servingly twist God's word. Abraham's response when commanded by God to sacrifice Isaac—"The Lord will provide"—should be "inscribed [*escrite*] in our hearts," ready for immediate retrieval when necessary.[123] Members of Nicholas Shaxton's congregation in

Suffolk wrote to him after he abjured his Protestant views in 1546. Among other verses, they quoted 2 Tim. 3:12—all who want to live godly in Christ will be persecuted. Even as "God's truth" was "grafted in our hearts," they said, Shaxton should recover his former faith and "let these sayings of Christ pierce into thy conscience."[124]

Joye's language crackles with still greater intensity. Acutely aware of idolatry even as he textualized images of the crucified Christ, he told afflicted readers to "set the example of Christ before our eyes (I mean not our bodily eyes fastened upon any image forbidden of God) but before the eyes of our faith, seeing his passion painted and engraven in his holy word." When tempted to doubt Christ's promises, the remedy was not simply to read, but "to run to the scriptures which shall comfort us marvelous"; readers should "hold fast in mind" Christ's promise never to fail his followers; they were to be "rooted and framed" upon Christ, "persevering in faith, constantly cleaving to him, committing ourselves whole unto his goodness and mercy." Of the promise of salvation through Christ, Joye wrote, "receive it thankfully with all thy heart, embrace it with both thine arms"; "neither let us cease at any time to hear and read the scriptures, and the sweet promises let us engrave into our breasts and cleave to them constantly."[125]

Tasting, imprinting, grafting, piercing, engraving, running, holding, rooting, cleaving, embracing—these terms do not reflect dispassionate encounter with a text. Continuing a medieval monastic vocabulary as they probed the boundaries of sixteenth-century language, such metaphors resonate with purposeful commitment. They reflect the experience of people who not only read scripture, but made it part of their being.

The strength and urgency of such metaphors exemplify the uncompromising rigor of anti-Nicodemism. Had not Christ told his followers to "fear him who can destroy both soul and body in hell" (Matt. 10:28)? Consistent with scripture, then, Calvin wrote that warnings of the impossibility of eating at the tables of both the Lord and devils (1 Cor. 10:21–22) were "words to make us tremble," and that Christ's warning to forsake those who forsook him "should indeed make the hair on our heads stand on end."[126] Such Protestant writers maintained that a prayerful reading of the Bible that was open to radical transformation as a real possibility would lead to a recognition, then an internalization, of God's word.

Chapter 4 situated the martyrs' writings within the broader exhortations and social support of their communities of faith. Here we have moved in the reverse direction, reaching the writings of the martyrs via the warnings of anti-Nicodemism. Anne Askewe was burned in London in the summer of 1546 for denying transubstantiation. Before her execution she wrote a song that typifies the embrace of anti-Nicodemite attitudes:[127]

Like as the armed knight
Appointed to the field
With this world will I fight
And faith shall be my shield.

Faith is that weapon strong
Which will not fail at need
My foes therefore among
Therewith will I proceed.

As it is had in strength
And force of Christ's way
It will prevail at length
Though all the devils say nay.

Faith in the fathers old
Obtained righteousness
Which make me very bold,
To fear no world's distress.[128]

Faith was Askewe's foundation—exactly as anti-Nicodemite writers insisted it should be. She employed Paul's martial metaphors of the Christian's armor, likening herself to a male warrior bearing "the shield of faith" (Eph. 6:10–17), which was simultaneously a defensive tool and a "weapon strong." Despite any and all resistance, her faith would sustain her—"It will prevail at length / Though all the devils say nay." Askewe linked her faith to that of her predecessors—"Faith in the fathers old / Obtained righteousness"—and expressed precisely the sort of radical trust urged by Calvin, Viret, and others: she would "fear no world's distress," including even martyrdom.

Pierre Brully sounded much the same, not long after he had journeyed from Strasbourg to minister to Reformed Protestant communities in Wallonia in 1544. Writing from prison to men and women in Tournai, Valenciennes, Lille, Arras, and Douai, he cited several New Testament passages. Brully wrote that suffering for Christ was a gift and a privilege: "now we no longer fear prisons, floggings, condemnations, assaults, the fire, iron chains, insults, and mockery—in short, all the machinations, assaults, and other manners of the devil's or the world's work—as things cursed by God, but endure them as signs and testimonies of the mercy of God towards us."[129] Faith relativized physical threats (prisons, floggings, fire, iron chains) as well as verbal abuse (condemnations, insults, mockery). Christ's pain, death, and resurrection gave Christian suffering its meaning: "his captivities sanctify ours, his flagellation ours, his condemnation ours, his chains ours, his abuses and mockeries sanctify ours, and in general everything we endure is sanctified by Jesus

Christ, because we endure it for the love of him."[130] Brully's words echoed Paul's: "I am content with weaknesses, insults, hardships, persecutions, and calamities for the sake of Christ; for whenever I am weak, then I am strong" (2 Cor. 12:10).

For Reformed Protestants, perseverance might have harbored a special comfort, which bore on the issue of predestination. Perseverance in the face of death seems to have been promoted and sometimes understood as a sign of election, despite the unverifiability of predestination to eternal life. Calvin insisted that no external signs could corroborate the fact of election. Someone might seem to be among God's chosen, such as Judas, and yet fall away.[131] Thus only the certainty of faith combined with perseverance through death provided confidence of genuine election.[132] In his "Second sermon," Calvin stated that "persecution is indeed a true touchstone by which God discovers who are his own," and in his letters to the Lausanne students imprisoned in Lyons he hinted that perseverance in their plight conveyed *assurance* of their eternal reward.[133] George Joye wrote that "if we suffer with Christ for his name's glory: sure and certain be we that God loveth us and hath chosen us to be his sons and heirs of the celestial kingdom."[134] John Careless linked John Bradford's expected execution with his elect status in a 1555 letter: "when the fire doth his appointed office, thou shalt be received, as a sweet, burnt sacrifice, into heaven where thou shalt joyfully remain in God's presence forever, as the true inheritor of his everlasting kingdom, unto the which thou was undoubtedly predestinate and ordained by the Lord's infallible purpose and decree, before the foundation of the world was laid."[135] If perseverance in faith was secure only as one was dying, then staring down the stake might calm anxiety about predestination. Martyrdom was the final, and absolute, test of fidelity.

The Imperative of Memorialization

Protestant writers hoped that their martyrs would favorably influence the Reformed cause in at least two ways. First, as he had done in the early Church, God would use the martyrs' courageous deaths as a means to spread the Gospel. Their witness proclaimed the power of restored Christian faith. Joye made the point with Tertullianesque concreteness:

> Let us therefore, Christian brethren, be constant in obeying God rather then men, although they slay us for the verity. For our innocent blood shed for the Gospel, shall preach it with more fruit (as did Abel's, Stephen's, etc.) than ever did our mouths and pens. Consider the beginning of the Christian religion, and the first fruits of the primitive

Church, and we shall see innumerable innocents slain, as it hath been these twenty years past, for the preaching and bringing in again of the Gospel . . . Let us therefore rejoice and thank God that it would please him to use our bodies and blood unto his glory and promoting of his word and edifying of his Church. For the Lord's field when it waxeth dry, lean, and barren, it must be watered, made fat, dunged, and composed with the innocent blood and bodies of his faithful.[136]

The martyrs were holy fertilizer for Christian truth. John Bale wrote that the deaths of Anne Askewe, John Lassells, and their two companions exemplified martyrdom's power as a tool of conversion: "Full many a Christian heart have risen and will rise from the pope to Christ through the occasion of their consuming in the fire. As the saying is, of their ashes will more of the same opinion arise."[137] Glossing a common analogy, Henri Estienne claimed that the martyrs were more remarkable than the mythological phoenix, for they produced not merely one more like themselves, but "an infinite number" of other martyrs.[138] Despite divergent contexts, Protestant writers in the 1540s and 1550s concurred with early evangelicals about the accuracy of Tertullian's dictum.

Additionally, Protestant leaders hoped that the martyrs would have a political effect, turning persecutors into champions of the Gospel. Through their exposure to the *ars moriendi* tradition, princes knew as well as anyone what a good death looked like. In 1540 Viret asserted that "there is nothing that breaks the violence of tyrants like the patience of the saints."[139] By 1543 Francis I had frustrated Calvin for more than a decade. Yet Calvin still maintained that a large-scale willingness to suffer persecution would lead authorities to oppose idolatry or at least to soften their treatment of Protestants.[140] Richard Crowley reprimanded Nicholas Shaxton for his recantation: had he accepted martyrdom patiently, "your Prince [Henry VIII] might through your constancy have been moved to search the scriptures for the truth of your opinions."[141] Besides bearing on the fate of an individual's soul, behavior at the stake might affect rulers and communities for the good of the Gospel. Martyrdom harbored public potential for proselytization and political influence.

For this to happen, however, what God had wrought through the martyrs had to become widely known. Accordingly, the martyrs of these years were publicized internationally, across political and linguistic boundaries. Robert Barnes was burned in London on July 30, 1540, after which both manuscript and printed accounts of his execution circulated in England. Luther, who had befriended Barnes during his stay in Wittenberg years earlier, translated his *Confession of Faith* into German.[142] In 1546 Calvin, Philipp Melanchthon, and Francisco de Enzinas (with Martin Bucer) published accounts of the murder of Juan Diaz. By the end of the year, printed versions of his demise existed in French, German, and Latin.[143] John Bale saw to the publication in 1546 and 1547 of Anne Askewe's examinations, a decade after English readers had access to François Lambert's account in the vernacular of Jean Chastellain's martyrdom.[144] There was abiding international interest in the early evangelical martyrs. In 1546 Wendelin Rihel, a Strasbourg printer, republished Voldersgraft's treatise on the Dutch martyr Jan van Woerden in a Latin translation, together with van Woerden's defense of clerical marriage.[145]

Yet considering the circumstances of burgeoning persecution, these few publications were a meager showing. Even earlier—for example, after the retribution of 1534–1535 that followed the Affair of the Placards in France—the stories of the martyrs had been neglected. Charles V and Francis I negotiated the Peace of Crépy in 1544, which freed both rulers to concentrate on domestic heresy. The emperor reorganized the Inquisition (1546) and promulgated the "Bloody Placard" (1550) in the Low Countries, while Francis I pursued heterodoxy with unprecedented vigor, an initiative continued under Henry II and the *chambre ardente* (1547). The number of martyrs exploded. From 1536 through 1543, the Paris Parlement delivered just 17 death sentences for heresy; from 1544 through 1549, it issued 115.[146] The patchy publicization of the martyrs occurred in scattered pamphlets and treatises, or in brief collections like the one containing Godefroy de Hamaelle's letters, songs, and prayers (ca. 1552).[147]

To committed Protestants, such neglect was shameful. Fellow believers showed less initiative in memorializing the martyrs than papists exhibited in murdering them. Flames burned martyrs alive, yet failed to kindle cool Protestant hearts. This had to change. In 1546, Calvin wrote in his pamphlet on Juan Diaz that

> it is a profitable thing in the Christian Church to commit faithfully to writing the death of those who endure martyrdom for the word of God. In this matter we can see a major vice of our age, that we are so lukewarm in this regard. For we have seen many martyrs who have been cruelly killed for confessing the Gospel; nevertheless, no one has taken pen in hand to bear witness for the future, and consequently everything remains buried. It will be very difficult to have a basis to speak about this fifty years hence. Yet the main fruit that ought to come from this is to warn the faithful how God's Church is subject to many persecutions, so that they prepare themselves to bear their part, when it is their turn; and to represent to them, as in a mirror, the constancy and firmness which they ought to have, so that this serves as an exhortation, to give them courage.[148]

Just months later, John Bale urged the publication of martyrs' stories to disclose both God's glory and persecutors' cruelty: "the glory and the great power of the Lord, so manifestly apearing in his elect vessels, may not now perish at all hands, and be unthankfully neglected, but be spread the world over, as well in Latin as English, to the perpetual infamy of so cruel and spiteful tyrants."[149] In 1554, while discussing persecution in the Christian church in a catechetical treatise, Jan Gerrits Verstege (Veluanus) decried the "many thousands of Christians" who had been killed throughout Europe. "I hope that the story of these martyrs will shortly be written by someone," he added.[150] He and the others were not to be disappointed.

The Midcentury Martyrologies

Between 1552 and 1559 four major martyrologies appeared in a milieu of threatened international Protestantism. These works synthesized existing perceptions of persecution and martyrdom. Additionally, they helped shape the identity of Protestants in France, England, and the Low Countries in subsequent decades and indeed subsequent centuries. The four author-editors of these martyrologies—Ludwig Rabus, Jean Crespin, Adriaen Cornelis van Haemstede, and John Foxe—were born within a decade of one another, shared similar educational and intellectual backgrounds, and were themselves persecuted for their Protestant convictions.[151] Knowing something about their lives helps contextualize the genesis and significance of their martyrologies.

The Martyrologists and Their Friends

Born in Memmingen in 1524, the year the town accepted Luther's teachings, Ludwig Rabus was the only one of the four martyrologists born into a Protestant setting. Crespin (b. 1520) came from a prosperous family in French-speaking Arras in the southern Netherlands, while van Haemstede apparently came from the Dutch minor nobility, and was probably born in the Zeeland village of Zierikzee around 1525. These two men grew up within Charles V's territories in the Low Countries. John Foxe was the oldest of the four, born in Boston, Lincolnshire, in 1517. English evangelicals made their first inroads during his youth, and in his teens he witnessed the changes of the Henrician Reformation.[152]

All four martyrologists held university degrees, which placed them among the intellectual elite. Rabus was educated for the Lutheran ministry, Crespin and van Haemstede to become jurists, and Foxe for a career as a scholar and academic. Before he was twenty years old, Rabus was exposed to the humanistic currents at the University of Tübingen for four years, then studied further with Luther and Melanchthon in Wittenberg. Both Crespin and van Haemstede studied canon law at Louvain, the premier university in the Netherlands, a center for humanistic studies and a bastion of Catholic orthodoxy. Crespin was in Louvain from 1533 to 1541, first as an arts student. Van Haemstede's canon law studies began in 1547 and lasted into the early 1550s. Foxe's early scholastic promise and the patronage of John Hawarden, rector of Coningsby, near Boston, enabled him to enroll at Brasenose College, Oxford, beginning probably in 1534. Afterward he was named a fellow of Magdalen College, his home from 1538 until 1545. He learned Latin, Greek, and Hebrew, read patristic authors and medieval theologians, and became familiar with ecclesiastical decrees and canon law.[153]

These well-educated men were keenly aware of the religious turmoil within Western Christianity. In one form or another, each suffered for his religious convictions. Rabus came to Strasbourg in 1544 and lodged for over a year with the cathedral's chief pastor, Matthias Zell. He was assisting in the city's ministerial life, along with Martin Bucer, Paul Fagius, and Peter Martyr Vermigli, when Charles V's forces defeated the Protestant Schmalkaldic League. Soon Rabus felt for himself the pinch of the Interim. Scarcely had he settled in as Zell's successor when in 1549, as part of the negotiated settlement, he lost his position to the Roman Catholic clergy, who reoccupied several of the city's churches.[154] The papal Antichrist had violated his calling and was threatening the Gospel in Germany. Forced into semiretirement, Rabus seems to have begun compiling ancient and recent martyrs' stories soon after 1549. Between 1552 and 1558, Samuel Emmel published them in Strasbourg in eight volumes as *The History of God's Chosen Witnesses, Confessors, and Martyrs*.[155]

Crespin, too, suffered for his Protestant views. After his student days in Louvain, he was briefly apprenticed in Paris to Charles Du Moulin, a prominent jurist sympathetic to the Reformation. Crespin withdrew from Paris to his native Arras to practice law, where he joined a circle of jurists drawn to Reformed ideas. In late 1544, after Pierre Brully's arrest for heresy, Crespin and others were accused of the same crime. In the spring of 1545, his young wife pregnant, the twenty-five-year-old Crespin was banished from Arras, his possessions confiscated. More than three unsettled years as a refugee followed. He attempted to secure some of his estate in order to relocate in Geneva, a city he had visited in 1545. Friendships with men of similar background and religious commitment helped to sustain him: he remained in epistolary contact with Calvin and got to know Theodore Beza, François Hotman, and the Spanish Enzinas brothers. By the time his Genevan print shop was up and running in 1550, Crespin had endured considerable hardship for his Protestant beliefs.[156] The 1553 burning of the Lausanne students in Lyons sparked the first edition of his martyrology, which he published himself in 1554.[157]

As a preacher and minister for Antwerp's Flemish Calvinist congregation in the late 1550s, Adriaen van Haemstede confronted even tougher problems. After he arrived in early 1556, the proper exercise of his ministry became a matter of controversy. In 1558 his open preaching in the city helped provoke a severe retaliation. Fellow Protestant acquaintances—Gillis and Anthonius Verdickt, Boutzon le Heu, Cornelis Halewijn, and Herman Janssens—were executed as heretics in Antwerp and Brussels in late 1558 and early 1559. Van Haemstede might well have been present at some of their executions. In late January 1559 he fled Antwerp for the small Calvinist community in Aachen, to the east.[158] In this context of persecution van Haemstede composed his *History and Deaths of the Devout Martyrs.* Gilles van der Erve published it in Emden in 1559, probably just after the middle of March.[159]

John Foxe knew adversity for the Protestant views that he apparently embraced while a fellow at Magdalen College. In September 1538 he witnessed the burning of William Cowbridge in Oxford, much as Crespin had seen Claude le Painctre executed in Paris in 1541, and van Haemstede perhaps some of his colleagues in Antwerp and Brussels. His religious convictions deepened in the years after Henry VIII's anti-Protestant Act of the Six Articles (1539). In 1544 Foxe complained to Magdalen's president about the mistreatment he and others encountered for their Bible reading and prayer. Between the summers of 1545 and 1546, he resigned his position at Magdalen, unwilling to accept the celibacy required of college masters. During the next two years, while Crespin the refugee was trying to reintegrate his life, Foxe weathered a lean existence as a newlywed, unemployed scholar, moving to London in 1547. His situation improved when the Protestant Duchess of Richmond hired him to tutor her children, a position he held throughout Edward VI's reign. Mary's accession, however, was a disaster for the Protestants. Refusing to comply with restored Roman Catholicism, Foxe joined about eight hundred others in voluntary exile on the Continent. After brief stays in Strasbourg and Frankfurt, he struggled to make ends meet in Basel as the head of a refugee family, editing copy for Johannes Froben and Johannes Oporinus. But his problems paled beside the reports that began arriving from England after February 4, 1555, when John Rogers was burned, the first victim in a new wave of executions. These developments turned Foxe away from a two-part history of the Lollard and Henrician martyrs to a more ambitious work with the Marian martyrs as the focus.[160]

As members of the same generation shaped by similar experiences, Rabus, Crespin, and Foxe had numerous friends in common, though there seems to be no hard evidence that the martyrologists themselves were personally acquainted. They belonged to an international community of committed, educated Protestants[161] and shared convictions about the Christian past, the plight of present Protestants, and the hope for the future of the Gospel that reached far beyond martyrology per se. The beliefs that bound them together were not derived from leisured reflection on the abstract features of Christian life, but were hammered out on an anvil of Protestantism under pressure.

Rabus was in Strasbourg together with the reformers Martin Bucer, Paul Fagius, and Peter Martyr Vermigli, before these three departed for England during Edward VI's reign. He was friends with German Lutheran historian Johannes Sleidan, from whose *Commentaries on the State of Religion and the Republic Under the Emperor Charles V* (1555) he borrowed some martyr accounts. The French translation of this work was published in Geneva by none other than Crespin, who was himself in contact with Sleidan.[162] In April 1554 Sleidan sent a letter to Calvin, to whom he had first written fifteen years earlier. He asked about the first edition of Crespin's martyrology, which he had heard was being published in Geneva.[163] Crespin was in Arras when authorities arrested Pierre Brully in nearby Tournai in 1544. He knew the Spanish Enzinas brothers as well as Juan Diaz before the latter's assassination in 1546.[164] As a printer, Crespin published writings by Viret and Bullinger, plus many works by his fellow Genevan citizens Calvin and Beza, the latter of whom was a close friend.[165] Valérand Poullain, another member of this international circle, had sent copies of Calvin's *Brief Treatise* to the southern Netherlands in 1543 and was instrumental in the genesis of Brully's mission to Tournai. He went to England as a refugee during Edward's reign and spent time in Frankfurt as an exile during Foxe's stint in the city.[166]

Foxe knew Sleidan from his stay in Strasbourg in the summer of 1554. He remained in touch with the city through fellow exile Edmund Grindal during his subsequent period in Basel. Foxe dedicated his 1554 martyrology to Duke Christoph of Württemberg, to whom Rabus had dedicated the first volume of his martyrology two years earlier.[167] Basel was concurrently home to Foxe, John Bale, and Matthias Flacius Illyricus, a second-generation Lutheran writer whose *Catalogue of Witnesses to the Truth* (1556) was published by Oporinus, Foxe's employer and the publisher of his 1559 Latin martyrology. Along with Nicolas Brilinger, Oporinus also published Heinrich Pantaleon's *History of the Martyrs* (1563), a Latin collection devoted to the continental martyrs, complementing Foxe's, which concentrated on the English. Pantaleon was another of Foxe's friends.[168]

In 1563 John Daye published Foxe's *Acts and Monuments* in London. He had been imprisoned for his religious views and for secretly printing Protestant literature during Mary's reign. During Edward's reign he had published sermons by Hugh Latimer and treatises by Thomas Becon (both of which addressed anti-Nicodemite themes) as well as Robert Crowley's attack on Nicholas Shaxton's recantation.[169] Both Crowley and Foxe had been Protestant fellows at Magdalen College in the early 1540s before resigning their positions for religious reasons at about the same time.[170] Foxe knew several of the most prominent Marian martyrs, including Hugh Latimer, John Hooper, Nicholas Ridley, and John Rogers. More than two decades earlier Rogers had been the chaplain of the English House, a residence for English merchants in Antwerp, where he had known and supported William Tyndale before the latter's execution in 1536. Later he saw Tyndale's biblical translations through the press under the name of Thomas Matthew.[171] These overlapping social ties bound together members of a maturing movement who were themselves persecuted and had broken bread with the martyrs. The hardship of Protestant leaders was mitigated by solidarity.

The relationships within this community were critical to the formation of the martyrologies. In compiling their massive collections, Crespin, Foxe, van Haemstede, and Rabus all made direct or indirect use of scripture, ancient church histories, fifteenth-century chronicles, and the pamphlets of previous decades. In addition, links to eyewitnesses of recent executions and to people with letters written by and to the martyrs, were invaluable for Foxe and Crespin in particular. Foxe remained on the Continent throughout the Marian executions, while Crespin worked from his Genevan refuge. Unlike van Haemstede, neither man lived among the persecutions he narrated, yet this did not inhibit the creation of their collections.

After settling in Basel, Foxe remained in close contact with Edmund Grindal in Strasbourg. The two shared documents pertaining to the martyrs and planned that Grindal would publish their stories in English, Foxe in Latin.[172] In 1559 Foxe repeatedly solicited information about continental martyrs from Bullinger in Zurich.[173] The great watershed for Foxe as working martyrologist came in late 1559, when he returned to England a year after Mary's death. This allowed him to gather written documents and to hear oral recollections about events in the Marian period. Together with collaborators such as Miles Coverdale and Henry Bull (another old colleague from Magdalen), he collected martyrs' correspondence and consulted episcopal registers in London, Canterbury, Norwich, and Lichfield.[174] One William Wyntropp, for example, wrote to Foxe in November 1560 with the names of several steadfast witnesses "which have not bowed their knees to Baal."[175]

In Geneva, Crespin also made use of official documents, copies of which arrived courtesy of French Calvinist jurists.[176] He depended on informants such as Guy de Brès in Tournai, a Reformed minister to whom he wrote in 1559 for information about those worthy of the title "martyr." The first edition of Crespin's martyrology (1554) suggests the piecemeal manner in which he garnered contemporary sources.[177] Van Haemstede, too, used official documents, in both Antwerp and Brussels, and relied on oral accounts and sources written by the martyrs themselves.[178] By admitting the incompleteness of their information and soliciting material from their readers, van Haemstede and Crespin essentially invited them to collaborate as adjunct reporters and archivists.[179] The compilation of the martyrologies was grounded in human relationships that crossed political and linguistic boundaries, making the publications the collective products of an imperiled international community.

The four major collections were far from the only martyrological works published between the mid-1550s and the mid-1560s. Compensating for the lukewarm neglect decried by Calvin, cooperation among believers, writers, and printers yielded a host of more modest publications. The martyrologists incorporated many of them, just as they drew on the early *Flugschriften* and other appropriate documents. In 1556, for example, Crespin included an anonymous pamphlet about the December 1555 martyrdom of Frans and Nicolaes Thijs in Mechelen. Rabus reprinted it the following year with an afterword by Philipp Melanchthon, whence van Haemstede took it as well, in 1559.[180] Huguenot songs about martyrdom and perseverance were published throughout the 1550s and into the period of the French Wars of Religion, while several pamphlets about Anne du Bourg, a member of the Paris Parlement, appeared just before and after his execution in December 1559.[181] Antoine de la Roche Chandieu's extensive *History of the Persecutions and Martyrs of the Church of Paris* (1563) detailed the ordeal of Parisian Calvinists between 1557 and 1560, based on Chandieu's experience as a minister in the city. Crespin incorporated the work in his first folio edition the following year.[182] A substantial Dutch account of the imprisonment and martyrdom of Christopher Fabri appeared in 1565, which Guy de Brès translated into French.[183]

Three years before he printed van Haemstede's martyrology in Emden, Gillis van der Erve published Marten Microen's *Trustworthy History of Hoste (called Joris) vander Katelyne, Burned in Ghent* (1556).[184] Van der Erve was well connected to the English Protestant community, which included important Marian martyrs and exiles. He was himself a refugee from Flanders who, like fellow printer Steven Mierdman, had fled to England during Edward's reign, where he became a prominent member of London's Dutch refugee church. After departing for Emden early in Mary's reign, van der Erve established himself as a printer there together with Nicolaes van den Berghe.[185] Between 1554 and 1557 he published numerous works addressing the predicament of English and Scottish Protestants.[186] In this three-year period, van der Erve printed works dealing with martyrs or the persecution of Protestants in at least three (and perhaps four) languages. At the same time, Foxe and Grindal gathered sources on the Marian martyrs, while Rabus and Crespin published installments of their martyrologies. The massive collections joined the tradition of lesser martyrological works that had begun in 1523.

Synthetic Power and Contemporary Relevance

The international community behind all these works, the similar backgrounds of the four chief martyrologists, and the interdependent nature of their enterprises should not obscure the differences among the martyrologies. Although closely related, to read one is not to have read them all: they are not the same basic work in four different languages.

In the first edition of his *History,* Rabus arranged the ancient martyrs alphabetically rather than chronologically, a feature unique to his martyrology.[187] Moreover, Rabus's work is fundamentally a compilation of confessors, all of whom were "witnesses," but only some of whom had shed their blood.[188] By and large, Crespin and van Haemstede were preoccupied with martyrs in the narrower sense of those executed for their faith. Foxe, by contrast, was first and foremost an ecclesiastical historian who included much material not directly related to martyrs or persecution.[189] Finally, outside of his prefaces Rabus is much less authorially present than is Foxe, for example, in the *Acts and Monuments.*

The historical compass of the martyrologies varies as well. Crespin opened his 1554 edition with Wyclif and Foxe commenced his 1554 Latin collection with Hus, whereas Rabus and van Haemstede started with biblical times. Only in later editions did Crespin and Foxe extend their scope substantively to embrace ancient martyrs. Among contemporary witnesses, pre-1530 martyrs from German-speaking lands received the most attention from Rabus, whereas Crespin and van Haemstede focused on post-1550 French and Dutch martyrs.[190] Whereas Foxe and Crespin expanded their works during the 1550s, van Haemstede deliberately created a sort of martyrological digest, trimming the materials from Rabus and Crespin on which he drew heavily.

In the end, however, the affinities among these works run deeper than their differences. To analyze them and their many editions in comprehensive detail would require a lifetime of scholarship. Here the limited aim is to explore how their writers pursued important objectives through martyrology as a form of historical writing. This reveals much about how they understood martyrs and martyrdom.

All four writers made martyrs the backbone of a Protestant interpretation of Christian history, which they viewed as a universal, fundamental struggle between good and evil. Their basic framework is traditional and essentially Augustinian. As van Haemstede put it, "from the beginning of the world it has always been the case, and will always be so until the end, that the dark, blind, and ignorant world has persecuted the faithful children of light and will persecute Christ and all the members of Christ."[191] Rabus argued that just as the ancient Church was assailed by external enemies and deceived by false sects, so now it faced "the persecution of the abominable Antichrist," the combined fury of both sorts of oppression amid apocalyptic expectations.[192] Crespin commenced his martyrological enterprise similarly: "Among the marks of the true Church of God, this is among the principal ones, namely, that it has at all times sustained the attacks of persecutions."[193] Even before the Marian burnings had begun, Foxe's first collection sought to show the steadfastness of those afflicted by the wicked for the sake of God's truth. In 1563, with Mary's reign of terror past, Foxe elaborately likened Elizabeth to Constantine and himself to Eusebius: support had followed suffering in both early Christianity and in latter-day England.[194]

The martyrologies expressed a conviction that had been swirling for decades: preaching God's word and following Christ provoked persecution, but the power of faith and the grace of God sustained the oppressed and bestowed ultimate victory. The experience of thousands of Protestants confirmed this conviction in the 1550s and early 1560s, as they endured present suffering and prayed for future alleviation.[195] One sixteenth-century reader, perhaps a Marian exile, condensed this tried yet hopeful trust in a single line on the title page of a 1555 copy of Crespin: "cast thy care upon the Lord and he shall nourish thee and will in no wise suffer the righteous to be in perpetual trouble."[196] The martyrologist's duty was to document the ways in which God's providence had always guided his Church, despite Satan's tireless efforts to destroy it.

The midcentury martyrologists created neither a Protestant martyrological sensibility nor the idea of memorializing witnesses for the Gospel. Rather they offered comprehensive, detailed histories of Christianity that stressed existing Protestant ideas about persecution and martyrdom. Their distinctiveness and the force of their influence lay more in their scope and timing than in any conceptual originality. They expounded the history of Christian martyrdom in a compelling, compendious manner as Catholic authorities were squeezing heretics in England, France, and the Low Countries and as the German Lutheran Church was struggling to survive. Tertullian's dictum looked irrefutable: persecution had intensified, martyrs now numbered in the hundreds rather than the dozens, and yet Protestantism, especially Calvinism, was growing. Growth despite persecution was evidence that God was using martyrdom to draw people to his truth, as he had done in the early Church.

The martyrologists synthesized an enormous amount of material within an Augustinian conception of reality that spoke powerfully to oppressed Protestants. They punctuated their historical narratives with primary documents, in good humanist imitation of ancient church historians such as Eusebius. Medieval martyrologists, by contrast, had arranged their works calendrically for the liturgy.[197] Martyrs concretized the story in flesh and blood. In them the ongoing and inevitable attack of darkness against light, falsehood against truth, Satan against the Gospel, was both manifest and overcome, the steadying hand of divine providence perceived anew.

Concentrating on martyrs enabled Foxe, Crespin, Rabus, and van Haemstede to address several aims and multiple audiences.[198] Some of their chief objectives can be arranged according to the groups for which they seem to have been primarily intended. These potential readers included fellow believers, whether immediately facing persecution or not; people somewhere in the middle, perhaps sympathetic to or attracted by Protestant views but not committed to them; and Roman Catholics, especially civil and ecclesiastical persecutors. Protestant martyrology sought to provide different things for different readers.

FELLOW BELIEVERS   The martyrologists forcefully legitimated anti-Nicodemite arguments. They detailed the ordeals and constancy of hundreds of contemporaries who had met demands some derided as unrealistic. Regardless of how many abjured or what percentage capitulated (a matter whose publicization was not, of course, foremost among the martyrologists' aims), blood witnesses demonstrated that difficult did not mean impossible. In short, martyrs were the poster children for anti-Nicodemism.

The writers seized on the martyrs' heroic actions to inspire fellow believers. Aware that a long Elizabethan reign was far from guaranteed, Foxe told readers in 1563 not to "shrink or make much ado, if the case require martyrdom, or loss of our lives, but according to their example let us yield up the same in the defense of the Lord's flock."[199] Crespin wrote that "it is above all necessary that the faithful, to remedy their frailties, commit to memory and depict before their eyes the examples of those who have maintained the truth of the doctrine of the Son of God, and who have steadfastly endured death for confessing it." This was the best way to "make us proceed with a cheerful heart [*coeur allegre*] according to the teaching of our head and captain at times when adversity and confusion surround us."[200] Implying the universality of this directive, both Crespin and Rabus offered role models for all ages and both sexes.[201] Sounding as uncompromising as Calvin or Bullinger (and also citing Rom. 10:10), Lutheran pastor Rabus stated that "every Christian" was required to proclaim Christ "with the mouth" and not only in the heart.

The martyrs' example helped weak and naturally fearful, persecuted Christians to fulfill this obligation.[202] On one level the martyrologies functioned like anti-Nicodemite exhortations—but they married prescription with the power of the martyrs' practice.

The goal was to console, not to intimidate. Steadfastness and absolute trust in God were repeatedly realized facts, not reformers' ridiculous fantasies. Protestants facing martyrdom could take comfort in knowing that others had been there before and had triumphed with God's help. Rabus made this point more than once. He offered a pastoral exegesis of 1 Pet. 4:12–19, for example, which focused on rejoicing in persecution for Christ's sake and glorifying God for suffering as a Christian.[203] According to Foxe, martyrs' examples "confirm the faith, increase godliness, abate pride in prosperity, and in adversity do open an hope of heavenly comfort . . . they declare to the world what true fortitude is, and a way to conquer, which standeth not in the power of man, but in hope of the resurrection."[204] Crespin wrote that "if ever there was a time to set forth [the martyrs'] example, if ever the faithful had need to be strengthened in the middle of such afflictions, one can indeed think that this age, replete with calamities, requires it today."[205] The relevance of the martyrologies for oppressed Protestants was impossible to miss. The hope of eternal gain really could and had indeed overcome the fears of temporal pain. Rightly understood, persecution really was an arduous yet assured path to salvation. The prison writings and courageous deaths of martyr after martyr offered definitive testimony.

The martyrologists looked to the past with an eye toward the future. They sought to preserve the martyrs' heroic words and deeds as a Protestant patrimony. Crespin was explicit on this point. Like Calvin, he chided others' "lukewarmness" [nonchalance] in failing to conserve the martyrs' stories. He admonished "all believers" of their duty not to neglect "the great graces God daily renders his Church." The faithful were not to forget "the happy and precious deaths of his children, but to commit faithfully to memory everything that they have been able to hear and that they will be able to collect: not their bones or ashes, in the manner of this basilica [of Rome], forger of idols and new monsters, but concerning their constancy, their sayings and writings, their replies, the confession of their faith, their last words and exhortations, in order to bring everything into the bosom of the Church, so that the fruit of it comes down to posterity."[206]

Since ancient pagans had diligently recorded their peoples' deeds, Crespin and Foxe wrote, Christians ought to be even more fervent in doing likewise.[207] Foxe commented on the first edition of his Acts and Monuments as a material object. He hoped that people delighted with heroic stories of kings and princes "would carry about with them such monuments of martyrs as this is, and lay them always in sight, not only to read, but to follow, and would paint them upon their walls, cups, rings, and gates."[208] This remark encouraged a Protestant use of visual images.[209] Foxe did not want celebration to slide into idolatry, however, and so distinguished between the two. He acknowledged "the zeal of ancient Christians" who "flocked together with fervent desire unto the ashes of the martyrs, and kissed even the very chains wherewith they were tied," while "the sword wherewith they were beheaded, was laid up as a precious jewel, or relic." Yet he disallowed "the superstition that did after degenerate from sincere religion."[210] Foxe toned down this passage in 1570, perhaps prompted by others' objections. The original formulation, it would seem, had conceded too much to Catholic claims about the ancient origins of such practices.[211]

Foxe flirted with forms of memorialization that probably rankled Reformed purists. Yet his was not the sole instance of Protestants honoring their martyrs in ways that transcended the textual. Foxe's and Rabus's martyrologies were liberally dosed with woodcuts, and even Crespin's folio editions included two engravings.[212] Moreover, "relic behavior" of one sort or another, akin to the "incombustible Luther" memorably analyzed by Robert Scribner,[213] continued within Reformed Protestant communities despite official condemnation.

We have seen the traditional iconography of "Saints Henricus and Johannes" in 1523 and noted the report about the removal of Leonhard Keyser's remains in 1527. Magistrates in Brussels guarded Gilles Tielemans's ashes in 1544, Crespin wrote, until they could be dispersed—apparently fearing that sympathizers would steal them away.[214] Marian Catholic controversialist Miles Huggarde stated that Protestants would "gather together the burnt bones of these stinking martyrs, intending thereby (by like) to shrine the same, or to preserve them for relics, that at such a time as when an heretic is burnt, ye shall see a route enclosing the fire, for that purpose. And when the fire is done, they lie wallowing like pigs in a sty to scrape in that heretical dunghill for the said bones."[215] Huggarde's inflammatory language suggests a polemicist's slur. Yet many other sources, both Catholic and Protestant, report similar actions. In May 1555, for example, Mary's Privy Council lamented that two men, "carrying the bones of one Pygott, that was burned, about them, do show the same to the people as relics and persuade them to stand in their error."[216] According to Foxe, John Hullier's heart and bones were collected and distributed following his Cambridge execution in April 1556. And even John Knox wrote that after Walter Miln became Scotland's final Protestant martyr in St. Andrews in April 1558, "the people . . . in testification that they would his death should abide in recent memory, there was cast together a great heap of stones in the place where he was brent."[217] Anthonius Verdikt was executed in Brussels in January 1559, less than three weeks after his brother Gillis. Van Haemstede reported that he was not burned to ashes because "it is said among the common people that Gillis's ashes 'flew' to people's bosoms" [*in der menschen boesem geulogen was*], an apparent reference to onlookers who smuggled them away.[218] Such incidents continued in the seventeenth century.[219] Although Protestants jettisoned the saints as intercessors, such actions do not imply indifference, still less disdain, toward the bodily remains of their martyrs. It seems that these Christians of the Word frequently were not content to remember their martyrs through texts alone.[220]

Still, the martyrologies remained the primary means of memorialization. The dramas they portrayed benefited from the confrontation inherent in the apprehension, imprisonment, questioning, sentencing, and execution of Protestants by Catholic authorities. The showdown between martyrs and their persecutors put a human face on doctrinal controversy, rendering theological debates anything but abstract. Crespin, van Haemstede, and Foxe perhaps above all grasped the power of martyrdom and exploited its potential. In accord with their beliefs, they deftly transformed events into prose, very much in the tradition of ancient Christian historians. Their editorial sense in blending narratives with original documents is particularly impressive, considering the scope of their projects, the obstacles they faced in collecting and verifying sources, and the speed at which they worked. Turning earlier techniques of humanist historical writing to new ends, they combined letters to and by the martyrs, judicial condemnations, accounts of interrogations, oral reports, prison confessions of faith, poems, and songs. They crafted stories of relevant religious models who bolstered a sense of collective identity. More dramatically than sermons, catechisms, or common worship, martyrdom trumpeted what was at stake in disputes over the content and practice of true Christianity.

PEOPLE IN THE MIDDLE   One of the martyrologists' clearest purposes was propaganda in the etymological sense: they publicized the martyrs to proselytize for Protestant Christianity. What edified believers might make open supporters of the sympathetic or the curious, just as martyrs' dying behavior sometimes converted spectators. Only God's grace, the martyrologists claimed, could account for the martyrs' comportment: "in these men we have an assured and plain witness of God," Foxe wrote, "in whose life appeared a certain force of divine nature, and in their death a far greater signification, while in such sharpness of torments we beheld in them a strength so constant above man's reach."[221] The martyrs' witness would stun scoffers into silence and turn skeptics into believers. Or so the martyrologists hoped.

They appealed to potential converts by elaborating a Protestant historical vision and by interpreting, in a manner consistent with their convictions, the relationship between the martyrs and their persecutors.

These two endeavors were intertwined: the martyrologists' historical vision was built on the belief that the Gospel was inevitably persecuted, yet ultimately triumphant, whether in ancient times or in the sixteenth century. Catholic controversialists routinely charged Protestants with innovation and novelty in an age deeply committed to authoritative origins and established custom. By making martyrs the center of their histories, the martyrologists killed two birds with one stone: they provided a legitimizing pedigree of sympathy-evoking witnesses who at the same time indicted the Roman church as a persecuting institution.

As learned Protestants, the martyrologists emphasized scripture and a pristine Christian tradition. They sought to convince people that Protestant victims were the genuine descendants of the biblical and early Christian martyrs. In formal terms, this was simple: ancient martyrs had died for God's truth; recent martyrs had died for the same truth restored; therefore the recent martyrs were heirs to the ancient. Anti-Nicodemite writers praised the refusal of the Maccabees and other past martyrs to commit idolatry. Were not men and women who denied transubstantiation and refused to light candles before saints' images doing likewise? Rabus devoted considerable attention to ancient martyrs and confessors, beginning with Abel. He sketched the major persecutions of the early Church, drawn primarily from Eusebius.[222] Van Haemstede commenced the body of his collection with Christ and devoted nearly thirty pages to the Christian martyrs through the fourth century. In an introductory section, he surveyed persecuted Old Testament men and women from Abel through the Maccabees.[223] Sixteenth-century Europe was the latest—and likely the last—act in a perennial play prophesied by Christ himself: "Thus must it happen to Christians as it happened with Christ, the apostles, and the prophets. Should the disciples be better than the master? That cannot be."[224]

When Foxe likened himself to Eusebius and Elizabeth to Constantine, he fired off a series of questions linking the recent martyrs to their ancient predecessors. If the actions of "Christ's faithful servants" in the distant past had been diligently set forth, he argued, "why should they now be more neglected of us in the latter Church, such as give their blood in the same cause and like quarrel? For what should we say? Is not the name of Christ as precious now, as then? Were not the torments as great? Is not the cause all one?"[225] Near the end of the *Acts and Monuments*, he used the telling adjective "Stephenlike" to describe recent martyrs who "suffered for Christ and his truth."[226] After 1563, Foxe devoted more attention to the persecutions in the early Church, which resulted in the much expanded treatment of ancient and medieval Christianity in the second edition of 1570.

Crespin's martyrology developed similarly through successive editions. From the start Crespin implied that God had always displayed his strength in the martyrs. In 1564 he stated that the recent martyrs were not inferior to the ancient in number or in their "torments or afflictions." Yet only in 1570 did Crespin include a prefatory section "showing a conformity of persecutions and martyrs from these last times with those of the early Church."[227] He treated John the Baptist, Christ, the apostles in general, Stephen, and Paul, with passing mention of the postapostolic persecutions. These forebears, he argued, held the same doctrines as the recent Protestant martyrs, and they too were unjustly accused, judged, and condemned.[228] Nevertheless, this remained a cursory overview. For all practical purposes, Crespin still began his 1570 edition, the last one before his death, with Wyclif. In 1582 his continuator, Simon Goulart, added a first book about the afflictions of ancient Christians by the Romans, plus the medieval persecutions by Moslems and the papacy.[229]

The martyrologists turned the Catholic accusation of novelty on its head. It was not Protestants who had fabricated teachings beginning with Luther. Rather, Roman Catholic popes and prelates had been inventing self-serving, unbiblical doctrines and practices for centuries. The Reformation was essentially a rescue mission before the Apocalypse. Received in its original purity, the Gospel had remained fundamentally intact during the patristic centuries. Then the papacy's pretensions began to corrupt Christian doctrine and worship, a degeneration that accelerated between the Gregorian reforms and the decadence of the fourteenth-century Avignonese papacy. Tyrannical popes wielded scholastic theology, canon law, the Inquisition, and the mendicant orders against the Gospel. Antichrist was storming. Yet Christ's church—an invisible reality, not coextensive with the visible church—was never wholly extinguished, despite the ferocity of Rome's persecution. In the late Middle Ages God began to reawaken the desire for truth that culminated with the Protestant reformers. Because the Gospel provoked hostility, its proponents were persecuted in the late Middle Ages, just as they were in the pre-Constantinian Church and the sixteenth century. Hence executed Hussites, Waldensians, and Lollards were rightly understood as proto-Protestant martyrs.

From the early Reformation on, martyrological writers distinguished true from false martyrs on the basis of doctrine. At the same time, Crespin and Foxe knew that not all the beliefs of their late medieval martyrs coincided with contemporary Protestant beliefs. The martyrologists could accommodate this apparent contradiction because they understood God's role in restoring the Gospel as an incremental process. According to Crespin, the examples of Wyclif, Hus, Jerome of Prague, and others "show how the light of the Gospel, emerging from deep shadows of the night, bit by bit [*peu à peu*] bestowed its rays through tiny windows and holes, despite Satan and all his minions opposing this light with all the powers of this world."[230] Crespin included in his work Catherine Saube, burned in Montpellier in 1417, despite her erroneous views: "For although she did not have such a complete knowledge of all the points of Christian doctrine as do many in the period which came after, nevertheless she retained to the end the true foundation of Jesus Christ."[231] At times Foxe argued similarly. Fifteenth-century Lollards from the diocese of Norwich, for example, had "defended the same cause of doctrine, which now is received by us in the Church," even though "then they were not so strongly armed in their cause and quarrel, as of late years they have been, yet were they warriors in Christ's Church."[232]

In discussing Peter Valdes and the Waldensians, however, Foxe maintained a stronger position. He implied that the Waldensians, Wyclif, and Hus had held the same views as sixteenth-century Protestants. Catholic falsifications accounted for the errors attributed to them in medieval sources.[233] Ecclesiastical authorities willing to deliver exemplary Christians for execution would not hesitate to smear them along the way. This assumption might account for Foxe's omission of certain embarrassing Lollard practices and beliefs, which he encountered in the records of their heresy trials.[234] It was enough to situate the martyrs on the right side in the story of the Gospel's gradual reemergence or, as Euan Cameron has put it, to show "that they were better Christians than those who persecuted and punished them, and that their persecutors had acted with barbarous and antichristian cruelty."[235] In an Augustinian conception of history, what mattered was whether they were children of light or darkness.

As the second part of their propagandistic goal, the martyrologists denounced Catholic authorities as tyrannical persecutors. Filling in the scant outlines sketched by early evangelicals, the martyrologists peopled a vast historical canvas with hundreds of witnesses and persecutors. Besides smothering the Gospel with superstitions, Catholic authorities had ruthlessly punished any who dared call them on it. "Who then are the heretics?" van Haemstede asked in 1559, "those who follow the Lord's word, or those who rise up against it and oppress it?"[236] Foxe attacked the persecutors' "furious cruelty, in spilling the blood of such an innumerable sort of Christ's holy saints and servants." He was disgusted by the bodies they had "slain, racked, and tormented," the corpses they had cast on dunghills for birds and dogs, "without mercy, without measure, without all sense of humanity."[237] Leaving no room for ambiguity, Crespin juxtaposed two sonnets, one on "the steadfastness of the faithful martyrs of our Lord Jesus Christ mentioned in this book," and the other addressed "to the enemy." The latter opened with interrogatory condemnation:

> Why are you so hideously consumed by jealousy,
> blind, ignorant, senseless papist,
> against this book? Are you offended by it,
> and by the vermin like yourself?[238]

Throughout their works, the martyrologists hoped to make people see devout Christians in place of heretics, minions of the devil in place of defenders of the faith.

CATHOLIC PERSECUTORS   The martyrologists had a message for Catholic civil and ecclesiastical authorities. Both van Haemstede and Foxe warned them of God's wrath. They implored them to desist from persecution, repent their sins, and correct their errors. By calling authorities on their atrocities, they urged Catholics to heed their conscience (which they assumed to be in profound turmoil), to acknowledge their grievous wickedness, and to beg for God's mercy.

Van Haemstede admonished the secular authorities of the Low Countries at the outset of his martyrology. He began his appeal in a traditional manner, reminding them, with plentiful reference to scripture, of rulers' duty to protect the good and punish the wicked. This responsibility included the suppression of idolatry, a task to which the Lord "had awakened the devout King of England, Edward VI, and some of the German princes." In the Low Countries, by contrast, Bible reading was forbidden, and ignorance led to the persecution and killing of blameless Christians. Appealing to secular officials over the heads of the clerical "scribes and Pharisees," van Haemstede threatened magistrates who had irenic tendencies or Protestant sympathies. Their compliant timidity rendered their hands "entirely bloody with the innocent blood that is shed." They would face the same divine wrath that had punished persecutors "from Cain's death up to our own day," for "God's hand has not been shortened when it comes to punishing the cruelty of tyrants and avenging the blood of his martyrs." Still, the ironic horror of killing the very people who offered them, through faith, the gift of eternal life, did not preclude forgiveness and reconciliation: "convert, and give up shedding innocent blood, and the Lord who is rich in mercy shall take pity on you and receive you with open arms." Should authorities do this, their righteousness would shine forth, and they would live joyfully and govern peacefully over people imbued with the law of the Lord and the fear of God.[239]

Foxe's plea, "to the persecutors of God's truth, commonly called papists," was written in 1563 in a different context. Although directed at recently ousted English Catholic authorities now subject to a Protestant queen, it too both admonished and implored. After accusing Marian authorities of the grisly murders of people "whose wounds yet bleeding before the face of God, cry vengeance," Foxe reminded them of their inescapable accountability. He asked, "Think you blood will not require blood again? . . . If Christ in his Gospel, which cannot lie, doth threaten a millstone to such as do but hurt the least of his believers, in what a dangerous case stand you, which have smoked and fired so many [of] his worthy preachers and learned ministers?" He urged the persecutors to repent and embrace "the cause of Christ's Gospel": "I exhort you to turn to that which only may and will serve, that is to the blood of the lamb of God, which taketh away the sins of the world. Wash your bloody hands with the tears of plentiful repentance." Even though "you cannot call back again the lives of them whom you have slain: yet call your-selves back again from the way of iniquity, and from the path of destruction, which you were going to." Despite Foxe's anger and sense of divine justice, however, and despite his decade-long absorption in martyrology, he could still entreat persecutors to "bewail your iniquities, which though they be great, and greater than you are aware: yet they are not so great, but Christ is greater, if ye repent betime."[240] There was still hope of forgiveness, even for the Edmund Bonners and Nicholas Harpsfields of the world.

The martyrologists supported their claims that God's wrath threatened unrepentant persecutors. They told stories about defiant oppressors who had suffered horrible deaths, or about natural disasters that had befallen tyrannical countries. Such accounts probably edified fellow believers. They were also concrete warnings to persecutors: "lest you repent, this is you." Van Haemstede solicited such stories from readers "as an example to all others who continue to follow in such people's footsteps." He mentioned an Ant-werp magistrate who drowned after a strong wind pitched him into one of the city's canals. Similarly, a monk in Ghent was preaching against "the right-eous" [gherechtighen] when he "was struck by the hand of the Lord in the pulpit."[241]

Foxe laced his work with similar stories. After the section on Mary's reign, he juxtaposed a "chapter of such, as by the providence of God miraculously have been preserved from danger in the time of persecution" and a "chapter or treatise of tyrants and persecutors, and concerning God's scourge and punishment exercised upon the same."[242] The latter included the story of a priest who fell down some stairs and broke his neck while joking about Robert Ferrar's execution, and a report of the betrayer of George Eagles committing suicide. Crespin incorporated "obvious witnesses of the afflic-tions and furor of God on those who have condemned [the martyrs]." Such were the sudden deaths of clergy involved in Wolfgang Schuch's death in

1525, or the serious fire suffered by the Franciscan monastery in Antwerp during Lent in 1567.[243]

J. F. Mozley criticized Foxe's "credulity" in accepting such "judgment stories," calling them "the weakest part of his book." More recently, David Nicholls has spoken of "a 'Golden Legend' of Protestantism, in which persecutors invariably died horrible deaths, and which at times came perilously close to traditional miracle-tales."[244] Sometimes the eagerness to accept such stories led to outright error. Foxe, for example, reported that during Henry VII's reign, a bull gored the chancellor of the diocese of Worcester after he had procured a woman's execution, whereas in fact the man lived on for years.[245] The martyrologists' alleged credulity, however, warrants further analysis. The issue is not what actually happened, nor whether factual errors were sometimes made, but rather how the events they recounted were understood.

There is nothing inherently miraculous about a man drowning during a storm, the sudden death of priests, a fire in a monastery, or plague and famine afflicting France after Louis de Berquin's execution in 1529 (Nicholls's example). All of these might well have occurred; and, in some cases, independent sources might offer corroboration. But what did they mean? Within the Protestant providential worldview, all such happenings were consistently ascribed to God's judgment. If God had orchestrated the restoration of the Gospel and wanted it to prosper, then at least sometimes, it stood to reason, he would punish its adversaries, just as he strengthened its supporters through persecution. Since this worldview was comprehensive, in principle all events *had* to fit somewhere, even if their meaning was not always transparent. To have thought that particularly pro-Protestant occurrences favored Rome, however, or to have left them in interpretive limbo, would have been contradictory or at least excessively cautious. On this issue the martyrologists were neither credulous nor biased—they were simply Protestant.

Other claims in the martyrologies do clearly echo late medieval miracle tales. For example, Foxe alleged that Zwingli's fireproof heart, like Thomas Cranmer's, was "found in the midst of the fire whole, without any blemish."[246] By contrast, stories of divine retribution point above all to an interpretive framework highly sensitized to the perception of biblical patterns. Extraordinary escapes recalled Peter's delivery from prison (Acts 12); the travails of persecutors echoed God's plagues on Pharaoh and the drowning of the Egyptians in the Red Sea (Exod. 7–12, 14:26–31). The vast majority of execution accounts did not include retribution stories. Rather, the martyrologists commented on the martyrs' repose and/or persecutors' cruelty in detail that varied drastically from one execution to the next. They followed narrow formulas neither in describing executions nor in reporting retribution. It did

not invariably happen that persecutors met horrible deaths, and the martyrologists knew it—Pieter Titelmans, for example, kept going strong in Flanders for nearly twenty years. Indeed, Foxe explicitly admitted that "some
[persecutors] there be which escaped, and are alive, for what purpose suffered
of the Lord, whether for a further trial of God's people, or for space to repent,
the Lord knoweth."[247] The ultimate retribution would come only after death,
when God would judge all. Until then much of the mystery of his ways,
as always, would remain hidden. Meanwhile, given divine providence, the
proper attitude was one of trust in the Lord.

Confessional Differences: The Martyrologist as Editor

The martyrologists believed that God's incremental restoration of his Gospel
had culminated with the reformers. This grated against their commitment to
doctrine as the criterion that determined true martyrs. If God had grounded
the restored Gospel on the bedrock of *sola fide* and *sola scriptura,* why did
Protestants disagree among themselves about God's teachings? Why, as a
result, had their martyrs sometimes died for incompatible articles of faith?
Reading Crespin, one would never know that as he was publishing his martyrology in the 1550s, Calvin was engaged in a bitter dispute with Lutheran
theologian Joachim Westphal over the Lord's Supper.[248] Rabus says nothing
of the sharp split within Lutheranism that followed the Augsburg Interim,
even though the Interim's effects had prompted Rabus to compile his *History*
in the first place. True, we would not expect an account of such conflicts in
the martyrologies. Yet they point to historical realities that illuminate the
martyrologists' priorities and the wider settings in which they worked.

All four martyrologies delineated a community of Protestant martyrs
broader than the martyrs' respective confessional groups. Yet the martyrologists were not simply "Protestants." They belonged to different confessions
and held divergent beliefs: Rabus was a Gnesio-Lutheran pastor, Crespin a
strict Genevan Calvinist, van Haemstede a less doctrinaire Calvinist, and Foxe
a somewhat more theologically eclectic Reformed Protestant.[249] Like other
educated Protestants, they were only too well aware of divisive differences,
particularly regarding the Lord's Supper. Thomas Cranmer, while still the
Archbishop of Canterbury, wrote letters to Melanchthon, Bullinger, and
Calvin in March 1552, proposing a Protestant synod to counter the recon-
vened Council of Trent. "It cannot escape your notice," he wrote to Melanchthon, "how greatly religious dissensions, especially in the matter of the
Lord's supper, have rent the churches asunder . . . And it is truly grievous that
the sacrament of unity is made by the malice of the devil food for disagreement, and (as it were) the apple of contention."[250] Protestant disagreements

certainly did not escape the notice of Catholic controversialists. From the 1520s on, they needled Protestant adversaries about their internal disputes, so obviously contrary to the unity characteristic of truth.

Compiling a martyrology was unavoidably a decision-making process. The Protestant martyrologists had to select whom to include in their works, and how exactly to present them. In so doing, they had to choose between preserving their overarching vision—in the process dealing with doctrinal differences as best they could—and adopting confessional doctrinal criteria that would have produced exclusive martyrologies for divergent Protestant churches. Like the early evangelical writers, not wanting to construe their communities of witnesses too narrowly, they opted for the former. Rabus's work is not a "Lutheran" martyrology in the sense of embracing only Lutheran martyrs, nor is Crespin's a "Calvinist" martyrology with only Calvinist martyrs. As in the 1520s, however, there were limits: no contemporary Roman Catholic appeared as a martyr in any of their works, and Anabaptists were present only when ambiguities led to mistakes.[251] Nor did the martyrologists label their martyrs in denominational terms. Rather, they used generic phrases such as "martyr of God," "devout martyr and witness of Christ," "dear man and confessor of evangelical truth," and "true martyrs of the Lord."[252] Like "the American people" beloved by political leaders in the United States today, such phrases overlooked differences to imply a unity that Protestants themselves knew did not exist. The martyrologists circled the wagons against the persecuting wolves, but not so tightly that Calvinists would shut out Lutherans and vice versa. Challenged by learned Catholic controversialists, they needed a legitimizing historical interpretation of their past. The last thing they wanted was a self-imposed reminder that the recipients of God's restored truth could not agree on its content, present application, or embodiment.

The martyrologists identified a Protestant community more extensive than any single denomination. They were not so much constructing an artificial community as articulating their religious identity in a different register. Crespin was a Calvinist when he worshiped together with fellow Genevans; he was a Protestant when he excluded sectarians and papists from his martyrology. Nevertheless, the tension in identifying Protestant witnesses remained. We can discern traces of the martyrologists' editorial hands as they addressed the problem.

Consider the case of Jörgen Wagner, an Anabaptist burned in Munich in 1527. The martyrologists' direct or indirect source was an anonymous German pamphlet published shortly after his death. It gives four articles that Wagner publicly refused to abjure: a priest did not have the power to forgive sins; a man could not bring God down from heaven (a popular misunderstanding, it would seem, of transubstantiation); God was not present in the consecrated bread on the altar; and finally, "he also does not believe that baptism by water saves anyone" [*glaub er auch nit, das der Tauff des wassers yemandt selig macht*].²⁵³ The first three articles meshed well enough with Reformed Protestant views. The last, however, taken strictly as it stands, might have cast doubt on the sacramental efficacy of baptism by water.

The ambiguity was not lost on Crespin and Foxe when they claimed Wagner as a Protestant martyr. Crespin made him sound less Anabaptist than he had seemed in the pamphlet: "he does not believe that baptism by water *in itself* [*de soy-mesme*] makes a man blessed." According to Crespin, Wagner was really implying the Protestant necessity of God's grace and justification by faith.²⁵⁴ Foxe probably got his account from Crespin, as he did for many of his continental martyrs. He qualified Wagner's view even more: "he doth not believe, that the *very element* of the water *itself* in baptism doth not give grace."²⁵⁵ Both writers made Wagner fall within acceptable boundaries by altering his views about baptism. An Anabaptist song written about the same time as the original pamphlet, and very likely based on it, is revealing by contrast: it pushed Wagner's remark about baptism in a more explicitly Anabaptist direction.²⁵⁶

In a more striking fashion, Crespin altered the sixty-two articles that Hendrik Vos and Johann van den Esschen refused to recant in 1523.²⁵⁷ Rabus, the Lutheran, presented all the monks' articles, essentially identical with Luther's own teachings.²⁵⁸ To Crespin, however, several of them were insufficiently derogatory of Catholic errors for a 1560s Calvinist. Others were too patently Lutheran, considering Calvinist-Lutheran contentions over the sacrament. Without a word, therefore, Crespin simply omitted some articles—for example, "he does not know whether purgatory exists or not." He cut another that had the Augustinians merely "unwilling" [*nolle*] to pronounce on the adoration of the saints, and several dealing with the sacrament and the Mass—in all, a total of ten articles.²⁵⁹ Crespin thus made Vos and van den Esschen sound less distinctly Lutheran and more homogeneously Protestant than they really were. He did not want the restored Gospel's first two martyrs to seem so obviously sub-Calvinist.

Several scholars have noted Rabus's fidelity to his sources. He retained even Wendelmoet Claes's and Willem van Zwolle's sacramentarian-sounding remarks on the Lord's Supper.²⁶⁰ Although Rabus customarily acknowledged his sources, however, he took numerous martyr accounts from Crespin without citing him. Apparently, with Melanchthon and his ilk cozying up to Calvin, the Gnesio-Lutheran did not want to mention Crespin for confessional reasons.²⁶¹

Although Foxe did not acknowledge it, a fair number of his Marian martyrs either belonged or had belonged to sectarian groups outside of Edwardian Protestantism.[262] Elsewhere Foxe's qualifications suggest anxiety about martyrs' views of the sacrament. For example, in August 1555 Richard Coliar of Ashford said that "he did not believe, that after the consecration, there is the real and substantial body of Christ, but only bread and wine." While properly rejecting transubstantiation, Coliar's "only" smacked of a crude sacramentarianism, so Foxe clarified the matter: "Only in the substance he meaneth."[263] Both radicals and Reformed Protestants shared Marian authorities' touchstone heresy, namely denial of transubstantiation. This could make assessment tricky for someone sifting true from false martyrs on the basis of interrogation records.

In fact, Foxe said almost nothing about the specifics of many of his martyrs' beliefs. Nicholas Haule, for example, suffered martyrdom "for the same cause of his religion and profession," while John Aleworth perished in prison in Reading, "being there in bonds for the cause and testimony of the truth of the Lord's Gospel."[264] Readers were to fill in the silences with assumptions of doctrinal rectitude. In some instances, Foxe omitted compromising views and associations; in others, he could provide only a name, place, and the fact of suffering for views that were not distinctive of Edwardian Protestants, but rather shared with radicals. Obscure martyrs were anchored by affiliation with more heavily documented ones. The latter were the foundation of the Marian martyrs, their explicit convictions beyond reproach: Ridley, Latimer, Cranmer, Saunders, Philpot, Bradford, Hooper, Rogers, Taylor.[265]

Evaluating van Haemstede's 1559 edition—the only one he himself produced—is more problematic, because he compiled it "in brief" [op het kortste]. Some excisions might have been made for doctrinal reasons, others purely for purposes of compression. In general, however, his redactions do not seem calculated to disguise snags.[266] He meticulously excluded executed Anabaptists, whom he did not "reinvent" as Protestants. Between August 1555 and late January 1559 (when van Haemstede fled for Aachen), fifty-three people were executed for religion-related crimes in Antwerp. Van Haemstede included only five of them, each a nondisruptive Protestant. The forty-four Anabaptists were rejected, as were a few others—Frans Fraet, for example, decapitated for printing seditious books, and Karel Goris, a button-maker who had derided rulers. Van Haemstede's decisions reflect his criteria: Anabaptists and anyone who might confirm accusations of Calvinist subversiveness did not belong to the community of true martyrs.[267]

Just as doctrinal disputes strained Protestant unity, so the single international community was embodied in divergent national contexts. During the formative years of the Protestant martyrologies, Rabus (1552), Foxe (1554, 1559), Crespin (1556, 1560), and Pantaleon (1563) had all published in

Latin. In subsequent decades, the vernacular dominated. Accessibility demanded as much. Just after the *Acts and Monuments* was first published, Foxe sent a copy to his former Oxford college. He told the members of Magdalen, "I am only grieved that the book is not written in Latin, and so more pleasant to your reading: but the needs of the common people of our land drove me to the vernacular."[268] The international community of the 1550s would not hold together. Nor would the role of the martyrologies and the meaning of the martyrs in distinct national contexts.

The Protestant Martyrologies in National Contexts

In the 1560s and 1570s Protestantism took widely disparate turns in England, France, the Low Countries, and Germany. Its varied trajectories continued into the seventeenth century, intertwined with national and international politics. Foxe's *Acts and Monuments* largely dovetailed with the Elizabethan regime, despite friction within the English church and continuing fears of Catholic invasion and subversion. In France, an embattled Huguenot minority, at war with French Catholics, embraced Crespin's martyrology and clung to a tenuous toleration after the Edict of Nantes. Following the Iconoclastic Fury, Spanish retaliation, and the declaration of Dutch independence, a Calvinist minority appropriated van Haemstede's *History*. Lutherans seem never to have taken eagerly to Rabus's work, yet German Calvinists welcomed Crespin and made the Protestant martyrological community a battleground in central Europe.

By 1570, England was under Protestant rule, the provisions of the Treaty of Augsburg (1555) were in place, and war almost entirely displaced heresy executions in France and the Low Countries. After the mid-1560s, Protestant martyrdom—Lutheran and Reformed Christians judicially tried and executed as heretics by Catholic authorities—became virtually dormant. The martyrologies celebrated heroes from an increasingly distinct "Reformation" period.

After its first edition (1552–1558), Rabus's martyrology was published only once more, as a two-volume folio in 1571–1572.[269] Robert Kolb has noted several reasons why German Lutherans seem not to have seized upon martyrs and Rabus's work. Northern and eastern Germans may have been less attached to saints prior to the Reformation. German territories produced comparatively few Protestant martyrs, and the region's relative stability after 1555 diminished their relevance. Finally, Rabus failed to integrate his materials in a genuine historical narrative.[270]

Germany lacked the institutions and the political structures that would have enabled Catholic governments to bear down on Protestants in a sustained, widespread manner. The de facto independence of so many territories and cities in the early Reformation, coupled with inquisitors' idleness in Germany,[271] made it impossible to enforce the Edict of Worms. The Empire's dispersed governance militated against martyrdom: exile was easier for Lutherans, who could flee to a nearby town with the same language and similar customs, than it was for Marian Protestants, for example, who often lacked the means to cross the channel and live on the Continent. Finally, the small number of Lutheran martyrs might stem in part from Luther's sensitivity to the "tender conscience" and his acute awareness of human weakness. As a result, his exhortations to persecuted Christians lacked the edge of Reformed Protestant anti-Nicodemism. Luther seems to have viewed martyrs' steadfastness somewhat as he viewed celibacy—an extraordinary grace, not a standard requirement of all sinners who professed Christ.[272]

There is little 1550s material in Rabus's martyrology and no addenda for the years between the two editions (1558–1571). His work represents the end of a story, one that closes with Lutherans Frans and Nicolaes Thijs in December 1555. In his second edition Rabus said nothing about the hundreds of English, French, and Dutch Protestant martyrs of the later 1550s and 1560s. He could have drawn them from Crespin's 1560 Latin edition or from van Haemstede. Apparently Rabus was not concerned to keep his martyrology up to date, international, or multiconfessional.

He may have had his reasons. A decade before Rabus's second edition appeared, the Elector Palatine had shed Lutheranism for Calvinism. The first German prince to do so, he started a trend that continued into the seventeenth century.[273] Exacerbated by the crypto-Calvinizing tendencies of Philippist Lutherans, tension mounted between the two confessions as they competed for princely support. Their discord erupted in open dispute about who belonged to the Protestant community of martyrs. In 1590, Christoph Rab, a Herborn printer, observed that Lutheran preachers (*Euangelischen Predigern*) sided more nearly with the papists than with "confessors of evangelical truth"—that is, Calvinist martyrs. Distressed, Rab remarked that "they openly dare to proclaim from the pulpit and to write publicly in their books that the martyrs who heretofore have been martyred and executed in France, England, the Netherlands, and Spain are not God's, but rather the devil's, martyrs. Is this not regrettable, that the teaching of the Gospel [*lehr des Euangelij*] that they sealed with their blood is labeled a teaching of the devil [*lehr des Teuffels*]?"[274] Lutheran clergy were smashing the inclusive Protestant community of martyrs on the rocks of doctrinal difference. Rab sought to preserve solidarity under the inclusive rubric "the teaching of the Gospel." The most pressing concern for German Lutherans, however, was no longer concord with Calvinists against a common Catholic threat, but rather continued support from princes against Calvinist encroachment. Accordingly, they repudiated Reformed Protestant martyrs. For their part, German Calvinists took to martyrs in ways that Lutherans never did. Although Calvinists remained a small minority in early modern Germany, Rab's abridgment of Crespin appeared in seven further editions between 1591 and 1617. In addition, Paul Crocius translated the entire 1597 edition of Crespin into German; his translation went through three printings.[275]

Van Haemstede died probably in late 1562, and so never got to see his martyrology reprinted. Appropriated by the Calvinist minority in the northern Netherlands, it saw twenty-two further editions from 1565 through 1671, every one after 1566 by a printer from the northern provinces.[276] Van Haemstede's *History* remained a living book after his death; martyrology persisted as a collective enterprise. Despite receiving materials about recent witnesses, the anonymous editor of the 1566 edition admitted that many martyrs remained unknown. He advised readers to copy relevant, official legal documents and pass them along. He told them to consult the martyrs' friends, some of whom possessed their testimonies, "written with their own hands and sent to their fellow believers" [*medebroeders*]. Finally, they were to consult the journals of "certain earnest people" who had recorded the martyrs' stories.[277]

Significant additions to the *History* appeared in 1566, 1579, 1593, 1612, and 1633.[278] In June 1578 the National Reformed Protestant Synod of Dordrecht sanctioned Antwerp minister Johann Cubus to enlarge van Haemstede's martyrology and to oversee a new edition.[279] Cubus, assisted by two others, was to undertake the task, "because he has some authentic documents [*memorien*] pertaining to the martyrs in his possession." Ministers who had "any documents from genuine [*oprechte*] martyrs" were requested to send them to Cubus.[280] Still close to the experience of persecution, the martyrology's seven editions from 1579 through 1604 all bear on their title pages two biblical verses central to Protestant perceptions of martyrdom: "Everyone therefore who acknowledges me before others, I also will acknowledge before my Father in heaven" (Matt. 10:32) and "These are they who have come out of the great ordeal; they have washed their robes and made them white in the blood of the lamb" (Rev. 7:14).[281] Beginning in 1608, however, Matt. 10:32 appeared only intermittently, and Rev. 7:14 disappeared altogether.[282] Anti-Nicodemism and apocalypticism waned along with the threat of Spanish occupation.

Van Haemstede's name disappeared from his work beginning in 1566. He would remain unacknowledged as its author for nearly a century. The stricter Dutch Calvinists who appropriated the martyrology apparently viewed his orthodoxy with suspicion.[283] They also insured the collection's more rigorously Calvinist character. In 1566 a passage about van Haemstede's friend Anthonius Verdickt, who had voiced tolerance of adult baptism, was expunged. Van Haemstede had written that Verdickt was "strongly against" obligatory "human laws or commandments about the necessity to baptize when they are young, or when they are old." Although Verdickt esteemed infant baptism, Rom. 14 led him to "compel no one to do it against his conscience, for Paul calls that a sin."[284]

Deleting this passage served at least two purposes. First, in the year of the Iconoclastic Fury, it made Verdickt appear a stricter Calvinist than he really was, a move analogous to those sometimes made by Crespin and Foxe. Second, it squelched Verdickt's tolerance of adult baptism in years when Dutch Mennonites were celebrating their own martyrs in song and prose. From the early 1570s Dutch Catholics also had new, local martyrs to venerate. Throughout the Eighty Years' War, Calvinists lived among Mennonites, Catholics, and smaller Christian groups in the Netherlands. Van Haemstede's martyrology supported Calvinist identity—the martyrs' doctrines reinforced boundaries for believers. The work offered Calvinist readers the heroic stories of their forebears and warned them that Roman Catholicism meant foreign political subjugation and religious tyranny.

Suppression and tyranny were matters that French Huguenots could hardly forget. After 1562 they were combatants in a series of civil wars, and in the seventeenth century members of a beseiged minority. Like the anchor that Crespin chose as his printer's mark, his martyrology helped French Calvinists steady themselves. This was so regardless of their stance on internally divisive issues, such as the correct form of ecclesiastical polity prior to 1572.[285] The severity of Catholic opposition precluded the luxury of disputes about martyrs.

Crespin's work circulated widely and was held in high esteem. In Wallonia in January 1564, a book peddlar on the road between Tournai and Valenciennes was caught with eleven heretical books, eight of them copies of Crespin. Huguenots read aloud from the martyrology during collective worship in Normandy.[286] Other major Calvinist writers drew heavily on the work, including Beza in his *Ecclesiastical History* and Agrippa d'Aubigné in his epic poem *Les tragiques*. In 1622 the Catholic controversialist Jacques Sévert deplored its influence on readers: "it profoundly delights people's intellects, imperceptibly deceives and carries off their wills, offends the memory, and traitorously captures hearts," more than any Calvinist sermon.[287] In the Protestant households of mid-seventeenth-century Metz, Crespin's work was the most widely owned book after the Bible and the Psalter, with a distribution equal to that of Calvin's *Institutes*.[288] The last edition was published in 1619; ownership decades later implies that people held on to the book and passed it along to younger generations.

After Crespin's death from the plague in 1572, Genevan minister Simon Goulart (1543–1628) supervised subsequent editions.[289] By the time he edited the 1582 version, Goulart had published the *Memoirs of the Nation of France under Charles IX,* a huge work including many pamphlets, letters, and manuscripts about the St. Bartholomew's Day massacres. He added a final book to Crespin, in large part a town-by-town overview of the French massacres in August and September 1572.[290] Assassination victims had been viewed as martyrs when their religious views had prompted their murders, as with Georg Winkler (d. 1527) and Juan Diaz (d. 1546). Similarly, Protestants who perished in prison were understood as martyrs if religion was the reason for their imprisonment—an *Acts and Monuments* woodcut depicted their burial.[291] Finally, Crespin and other martyrologists included in their works massacre victims, people who were not judicially tried and executed. The most sensational episode prior to 1572 was the slaughter of the Provençal Waldensians in 1545.[292]

Did the victims of violence merit the same status as martyrs who had been executed after interrogations and refusals to recant? Goulart seems to have answered yes and no. The 1582 index noted the specific names of people "who by *arrêts* and judges' sentences have been condemned and executed," while known massacre victims fell "under the names of the persecutions during which each of them suffered martyrdom."[293] Some of the latter, he admitted, were less firmly grounded "in the knowledge of God" than others. They belonged in the martyrology with judicially executed martyrs, however, since "we did not want to divorce those whom [the Lord] had united."[294] The two groups were of a piece because Satan's warfare and massacres deployed via Catholic authorities were merely the judicial execution of heretics by other means:

> It is true that during the beginning of the Time of Troubles up to the present, the means by which the adversaries of the Gospel have been helped in wiping out the churches of the Lord have been and are somewhat different from those which they employed at the beginning; but in fact they proceed from one and the same source, namely from the hatred which these insane people bear towards the progress of the reign of our Lord Jesus Christ, against which they swarm so furiously. This was thus a strange trick of the devil, that unable to extinguish this great light which appeared in the steadfastness of the martyrs executed by the sentences of judges, he has endeavored to obscure it, wrecking them by the furious arms of war and by a mutinous populace (supported by those who ought to suppress it), all under the pretext of conspiracy, rebellion, sedition, and other such crimes of which the faithful have been and are still falsely accused . . . If we call "martyrs" those who have been executed one by

one according to legal procedures, should this not also be the term for so many thousands of excellent people who have been martyred all in one blow, when in place of one executioner there were an infinite number, and the swords of private individuals have been used against the Church?[295]

What the devil could not achieve by piecemeal executions, he pursued through war and slaughter. The scale and the means had changed, but the results were the same. Both tactics produced martyrs, even if the witnesses stood in something of a hierarchical relationship to one another.

When the threat of persecution was real, the relevance of martyrs as models persisted. Let us jump ahead a century, shortly before the revocation of the Edict of Nantes. In 1684 the Calvinist pastor of the Wallonian refugee church in The Hague, Daniel DesMarest, abridged Crespin's martyrology and had it published in Amsterdam.[296] His text included an anti-Nicodemite sermon, originally delivered in 1680, that urged men and women to imitate the martyrs.[297] The pastor wanted to "encourage the faithful currently suffering such a horrible persecution to the constancy and firmness which the cause that they are upholding deserves." Like his sixteenth-century predecessors, DesMarest coupled martyrology and anti-Nicodemism. His "history of our martyrs" was combined with "the reasons which indispensably oblige those who want to achieve their salvation [*faire leur salut*] to suffer all things and to give even their lives, when they are called to this and when the glory of God demands it."[298] The Reformation martyrs were to DesMarest what the biblical and early Christian martyrs had been to the sixteenth-century martyrologists: heroic exemplars from a past age who provided present paradigms. When Louis XIV revived policies that recalled those of Francis I and Henry II, DesMarest saw the obvious relevance of the biblical messages about suffering and the abiding significance of the martyrs' oblation.

Yet much had changed in the world of French-speaking Calvinism since 1619, when the *History of the Martyrs* had last been published. DesMarest's work reflects these transformations. Above all, he included only French martyrs, in a collection much smaller than Crespin's. As DesMarest explained, "although the others suffered for the same cause, it seems that the example of [the French martyrs] concerns us more directly, that it ought to affect us more, that we are able to regard their blood more specifically as the seed from which we have gone forth, and that we find in them persons born and raised in the same air that we breathe, who ought to have more nearly the same inclinations as us, and the same weaknesses on the side of nature as we have the same help on the side of grace."[299] This passage suggests a sense of national confessional identity and exclusivity absent in Crespin, and even—

notwithstanding his emphasis on England—in Foxe. Something similar, perhaps, is seen in the Netherlands after the Peace of Münster, when Jan van Woerden was touted as "the first Dutch [*Hollandsche*] martyr."[300] Such a sensibility reflects the maturation of nation-states and is foreign to the major Protestant martyrologies, with their stories about the persecuted Gospel throughout Europe.

In sharp contrast to Crespin among the Huguenots, the *Acts and Monuments* by 1563 was a work aligned with a new Protestant regime. It celebrated deliverance from oppression rather than supporting those who were still oppressed. Numerous authors have noted the influence of Foxe's work on English Protestants in the later sixteenth and seventeenth centuries, when the *Acts and Monuments* was published eight more times, three before Foxe's death in 1587.[301] Demand was heavy from the start: in the summer of 1568, as he was readying the second edition, Foxe wrote to William Cecil asking special permission that more than four printers be allowed to print it.[302] Archbishop Matthew Parker sanctioned it as an official, public book in a synod of April 1571. Bishops, deacons, and archdeacons were directed to place the work in cathedral churches along with the Bible. Many parish churches followed suit.[303]

Attempts to maximize the work's exposure took different forms. Thinner, cheaper paper and smaller typefaces reduced the 1576 edition to one volume from the two of 1570, and presumably lowered its price. Shortly after Foxe's death in 1587, Timothy Bright produced an abridged version, "by reason of the largeness of the volume, and great price," so that "both those that are busied in affairs, or not able to reach to the price of so great a book, might also have use of the history."[304] Bright's abridgment, still a weighty eight hundred pages, was followed by several others in the seventeenth century.[305]

Much as Jacques Sévert implied the influence of Crespin's martyrology, so the tireless Jesuit, Robert Parsons, did the same for Foxe's work in 1604. Parsons lamented that "by judgment of many men," Foxe's collection "hath done more hurt alone to simple souls in our country, by infecting and poisoning them unawares, under the bait of pleasant histories, fair pictures, and painted pageants, then many other [of] the most pestilent books together." Among the keys to its appeal was the complementarity of text and image: "the variety of the history itself, draweth many to read it; then the foresaid spectacle and representation of martyrdoms (as they are called) delighteth many to gaze on, who cannot read."[306] Later in the century, Thomas Fuller, a moderate preacher and divine, recalled the woodcuts' effect on him as a child. His remarks show vividly the fusion of the sixteenth-century English martyrs with the three youths from Dan. 3 and a hint of Matt. 10:30: "When a child, I loved to look on the pictures in the Book of Martyrs. I thought that there the martyrs at the stake seemed like the three children in the fiery furnace, ever since I had known them there, not one hair more of their head was burnt, nor any smell of the fire singeing of their clothes."[307]

London turner Nehemiah Wallington was only five years old when his mother died, yet he recollected that she had memorized "the stories of the martyrs." Godly Protestants made the *Acts and Monuments* one of the works most frequently excerpted in their seventeenth-century commonplace books.[308] It inspired other genres as well, including at least a dozen plays published between 1573 and 1631. Broadside ballads about the martyrs were peddled in the 1620s, about the time that the work's foldout woodcut of the ten persecutions of the primitive Church was first sold separately.[309] A 1666 catalogue described the image of these ancient persecutions as "a convenient table for ornament of every good Christian house, to stir them up to stand to the faith."[310]

Similar to van Haemstede's work in the Netherlands, Foxe's martyrology helped to create and sustain antipopery during Elizabeth's reign and throughout the seventeenth century. Edward Bulkeley composed an addendum to the 1610 edition. It described more "outrageous cruelties, committed in France" by Catholics, and briefly described "that savage, barbarous, and monstrous powder treason" of 1605. In writing, Bulkeley sought "that we may thereby be the more moved to hate and abhor that bloody Babylon of Rome, and to take the better heed, that by our sins and contempt of God's holy word, by his great mercy committed unto us, we do not again fall into the cruel claws thereof, and into the bloody hands of her followers."[311] The early Stuart godly were not to relive the sinful ingratitude of their Edwardian predecessors, which had called down God's wrath via Mary Tudor.

We might even call this printing of the *Acts and Monuments* the "Deliverance from Gunpowder Plot" edition. The attempt five years earlier to destroy the parliament house in London "was by God's great mercy discovered and defeated, to the just destruction of those detestable traitors." By telling this story, Bulkeley extended Foxe's massive account of God's providential care for his English children.[312] The timing of the other three seventeenth-century editions was not coincidental. All reflected English Protestant concerns about Catholicism or the crown's apparent movement towards it: the "Look Out for Laud" edition of 1632, a year before Charles I appointed William Laud the Archbishop of Canterbury; the "Puritans Ascendant" edition of 1641; and the "No Popish Princes!" edition of 1684, following the failure to exclude the Catholic convert James II from the throne, a year before he became king.

While the *Acts and Monuments* provided a bulwark against Catholicism, it became a source of contention among English Protestants. Disputes among

Protestants made Foxe's work a battleground in ways that chagrined its author. As early as 1570 he had disdained "our disputing and contending one against another." He asked the Lord "to still these winds and surging seas of discord and contention amongst us." In the early 1570s, John Whitgift and Thomas Cartwright both claimed that Foxe's work supported their opposed views on the nature of ministry in the church.[313] By 1583, the controversies among conformists, presbyterians, and nonpresbyterian Puritans incited Foxe to address a new preface to the various factions, in which he deplored their divisions and urged reconciliation.[314]

Moderate Puritanism—a zeal for further reformation combined with allegiance to the institutional church—could be difficult to sustain. It was even more difficult when the powerful legacy of uncompromising martyrs was at stake. Their singular commitment and heroism proved an irresistible inspiration to godly Protestants. They served, too, as justification for criticizing contemporaries who accepted papist remnants in liturgical dress and ecclesiastical organization. When under Laud in the 1630s crypto-Catholic aspects of church decorum and worship were actively promoted, a new generation of Puritans spoke out—and proved their willingness to suffer for their views. Refugees to Holland and New England followed the paths of the Marian exiles. In June 1637, William Prynne, Henry Burton, and John Bastwick were not executed for their open criticism of the Laudian church; they lost their ears and were sentenced to life imprisonment. Nonetheless, they understood themselves to be heirs to the Marian martyrs, suffering for Protestant truth, when they took their punishment before a large London crowd.[315]

Foxe's legacy is apparent among Protestant dissenters who repudiated the English church. John Knott has discussed the martyrological sensibility of separatist leaders Henry Barrow and John Greenwood, who were both hanged as traitors at Tyburn in June 1593. Their views regarding persecution and suffering resemble those of seventeenth-century nonconformists such as John Milton, George Fox and the Quakers, and John Bunyan.[316] The very success of the *Acts and Monuments,* and the broad swath of its influence deep into the seventeenth century, facilitated such appropriation by dissenters. Such a development surely would have distressed Foxe himself. Like a figure in fractal geometry, English Protestantism replicated in miniature Western Christendom's conflict over martyrs. English men and women with mutually incompatible beliefs were willing to suffer and die for them. All believed themselves to be the true heirs to the tradition of Christian martyrdom.

Protestant martyrs remained important long after Catholic authorities stopped executing heretics. Their heritage continued into the nineteenth and twentieth centuries. It is evident in the Oxford monument to Cranmer,

Ridley, and Latimer that offered a retort to the Oxford Movement; in the several thousand people who in Brussels celebrated the four hundredth anniversary of Vos and van den Esschen's deaths in 1923; and in the memorials and churches in Germany dedicated to Cologne's evangelical martyrs of 1529, Adolf Clarenbach and Peter Fliesteden.[317]

Martyrdom and related sensibilities stood close to the heart of the Reformation and its concerns. The willingness to witness unto death embodied the utter rejection of soteriological self-reliance. Nothing expressed more emphatically than martyrdom an absolute trust in God's providence. Fellow believers trumpeted the martyrs' significance from the very beginning of the Reformation. They celebrated their heroes with gusto and publicized them widely, despite ambiguities and tensions. To early evangelical leaders, anti-Nicodemite writers, and martyrologists alike, the martyrs' words and deeds were brilliant flashes of triumph in the flesh-and-blood spiritual battle that God and Satan waged in every age, and in every human being. The martyrological writers would not look past their sacrifice or the doctrinal issues involved, a disposition so alien to the ecumenical mood that prevails in many Christian circles today. In the sixteenth century the blood of Protestant martyrs acted as a solvent at once creative and destructive. It cemented persecuted Protestants more closely together even as it corroded the connections between Catholic and Protestant communities, poisoning prospects for their reconciliation.

CHAPTER SIX

Nachfolge Christi:
Anabaptists and Martyrdom

If the world hates you, be aware that it hated me before it hated you. If
you belonged to the world, the world would love you as its own. Because
you do not belong to the world, but I have chosen you out of the world—
therefore the world hates you. Remember the word that I said to you,
"Servants are not greater than their master." If they persecuted me, they
will persecute you . . . Indeed, an hour is coming when those who kill you
will think that by doing so they are offering worship to God.

—JOHN 15:18–20, 16:2

O God, preserve my heart and mouth!
Lord, watch over me in every hour,
Let me not be separated from you,
Though there be sadness, anxiety, and distress,
Maintain me pure in joy!

—URSULA HELRIGLIN, FROM A SONG WRITTEN IN PRISON, CA. 1540

Like early evangelicals, the first Anabaptists were late medieval Christians. As
such, they too were exposed to widespread attitudes about patience, suffering, and the following of Christ. With the evangelical reformers, they accepted the Bible as the sole source of Christian truth, and their understanding
of persecution was informed accordingly. Yet they read scripture differently
than did Protestants, and so drew disparate implications for Christian life. As
a result, their experience diverged drastically from that of Protestants over the
course of the sixteenth century. This chapter explores the central importance
of martyrdom for several of the most significant Anabaptist groups, particularly those from the Netherlands.[1]

Anabaptists held their martyrs in the highest regard. Singing more and
publishing less than Protestants, they celebrated their memory in distinctive
ways, consistent with their ecclesiological views and generally less educated
following. Their typical lack of formal theological training, however, did not
compromise the Anabaptist vision of Christianity. The New Testament did
not imply that faith's saving truth depended on linguistic sophistication or
university education in any substantive way. Nor was it obvious how the
practice of infant baptism followed from justification by faith alone. Doubt-

less *sola scriptura* Protestants found it a bitter pill to swallow, but no explicit sanction for infant baptism could be squeezed from scripture, regardless of the text or translation. Jesus had said, however, that the one "who believes and is baptized will be saved" (Mark 16:16). The Lord had taught and ministered to adults who committed themselves to follow him. On the basis of "scripture alone" and "faith alone," then, Anabaptists rejected infant baptism. Here a number of Anabaptist leaders seem to have radicalized Erasmus's views on Christ's "Great Commission" to his apostles in Matt. 28:18–20.[2] Infant baptism did not prefigure justification by faith alone. Rather, it was the flawed cornerstone supporting an edifice of ecclesiastical abuse, sinful behavior, and dubious religiosity.[3]

The relationship between Christian faith and life had to be rebuilt on solid foundations. Above all, self-conscious human beings had to know what a Christian really was in order to become one. Was it any wonder that with everyone "baptized" at birth into a "Christian society," pastors spent their lives begging people to repent, to learn the basics of their "faith," and to avoid sin? The cart had been set before the horse. Only consenting adults could understand faith, reform their lives, and truly follow Christ. Only they, like the savior's earliest disciples, would receive the external sign of baptism to mark their interior commitment. Christ's church embraced only the community of the faithful who had resolved to follow him, and together they embodied a *real* reformation. If comparatively few became Christian as a result, this only revealed how pervasively a fusion with the social, cultural, and political status quo had perverted Christian teaching and practice.

Discipleship was no halfway house. *Nachfolge Christi* implied an openness to rejection, oppression, and violent death for maintaining the truth for which Christ himself had been killed. Anabaptists' self-selecting radicalism, plus their experience of severe persecution, marked them more deeply than their Protestant or Catholic contemporaries with a martyrological mentality. As Cornelius Dyck has written, "the possibility of martyrdom had a radical impact on all who joined the group—on their priorities, status and self-consciousness."[4] Except for the Moravian Hutterite communities in the later sixteenth century, Anabaptists found few stable political havens. (The common Anabaptist view that "Christian government" was an oxymoron hardly helped matters.) Their martyrs far outnumbered their Protestant or Catholic counterparts. Anabaptist martyrologists and songwriters, many of whom remain anonymous, were often as vulnerable as those whose writings they collected and whose ordeals they versified. (By contrast, consider Jean Crespin writing from Geneva, or William Allen from Rheims.) Even to ponder becoming an Anabaptist was ipso facto to think about martyrdom.

Modern scholarship on Anabaptist martyrs and martyrology has a long pedigree.[5] One cluster of research has focused on the hundreds of songs related to martyrdom, analyzing their structure, themes, and tunes.[6] Other recent studies have addressed martyrdom and sensibilities integral to it, for the most part based almost entirely on Thieleman Jans van Braght's famous *Martyrs' Mirror.*[7] Both bodies of scholarship are important but can be better integrated. The songs should be combined with other relevant sources and, as far as possible, situated in the contexts in which they were written and sung. And although van Braght's fundamental reliability was established a century ago,[8] using the 1660 *Martyrs' Mirror* as a source for the sixteenth century conceals much about the formation and transformation of the Anabaptist martyrological tradition. Van Braght wanted readers to picture a pan-European movement of Anabaptists suffering here in the Low Countries, there in Switzerland, there again in Austria. In fact the stories from these different Anabaptist groups were combined for specific, controversial reasons in the early seventeenth century. Scholarship on Anabaptist martyrdom must heed the divergent character of distinct Anabaptist groups.[9] The geographical chronology of martyrdom varied drastically. Hundreds of Anabaptists had been executed in southern Germany, Austria, and Switzerland, for example, before Melchior Hoffman even set foot in the Low Countries in 1530.

The *Martyrs' Mirror* conceals much about how Anabaptists shared and expressed martyrological sensibility a century earlier. For example, we would never learn from van Braght's imposing tome that its sixteenth-century predecessor, *The Sacrifice unto the Lord,* was a tiny volume whose second half consisted entirely of songs. Neither would we guess that it included just one Anabaptist martyr from outside the Netherlands, nor that it lacked almost entirely the interpretive commentary integral to the *Martyrs' Mirror.* Much in the manner of Foxe and Crespin, van Braght compiled a huge number of Dutch Mennonite sources. Yet more than fifty martyrs' letters, printed in pamphlets between 1572 and 1592, were not incorporated into the Dutch Mennonite martyrological tradition, including the *Martyrs' Mirror.*[10] Like *The Sacrifice unto the Lord,* these pamphlets, many of which also included songs, were accessible to late sixteenth-century Mennonites. The *Martyrs' Mirror* was not. Accordingly, even for sources that van Braght incorporated, I have used the sixteenth-century editions.

Martyrdom and the memorialization of martyrs developed differently across Anabaptist groups. In the decade after the Peasants' War of 1524–1525, the Swiss Brethren, the south German and Austrian Anabaptists, and the Moravian Hutterite communities were stamped with a deep martyrological sensibility that persisted long thereafter. Dutch Anabaptists coped with persecution in the decades after the Kingdom of Münster. Between the late sixteenth and the mid-seventeenth centuries, Dutch Mennonites ceased to be a despised sect and found a place at the table of the Dutch Golden Age. As their position in Dutch society shifted, so too did the meaning of Anabaptist martyrs.

Müntzer to Münster: Forging an Anabaptist Martyrological Mentality

Early modern critics of the Anabaptists delighted in the alliterative similarity of "Müntzer" and "Münster." Protestant and Catholic controversialists alleged that the close likeness reflected a substantive affinity between the subversive apocalypticism of the Saxon reformer and the Anabaptist regime touted as the New Jerusalem. Modern scholars, however, have long severed the link. Müntzer himself was not, properly speaking, an Anabaptist. The Peasants' War and the Reformation in Münster were different and distinct phenomena. And the radicalization of Melchiorite Anabaptism in Münster and the northern Netherlands after 1533 owed little directly to German and Swiss events in the previous decade. Yet the pairing is not without scholarly, organizational utility. During the period from Müntzer's peak influence to the destruction of the Münster regime (1524–1535), the major German-speaking Anabaptist groups—most importantly, the Swiss Brethren and the Hutterites—were constituted with profound martyrological sensibilities. Moreover, both Thomas Müntzer and the Kingdom of Münster influenced Anabaptist views about martyrdom. Müntzer's legacy persisted among the South German and Austrian Anabaptists who would eventually people the Hutterite communities further east. Münster provided a model of negative self-definition for Dutch Anabaptists in subsequent decades—most importantly, in the long run, for the followers of Menno Simons.

Like their evangelical counterparts in Germany and Switzerland, certain Anabaptist leaders were keen to implement reform in the mid-1520s. They wanted communities, however, whose members had embraced believers' baptism. Many of the earliest Anabaptists proper, in and around Zurich, shared the aspirations of and themselves were involved in the rebellion of the "common man" in 1524–1525.[11] In Zurich itself, only the crumbling of the consensus between Conrad Grebel and Huldrich Zwingli led Grebel to jettison city reformation for believers' baptism.[12] Another of Zwingli's colleagues, Balthasar Hubmaier, introduced a civic Anabaptism to Waldshut, northwest of Zurich, between April and December 1525, as the small town sided with regional peasants in their revolt.[13] Zurich missionaries Wilhelm Reublin and Johannes Brötli directed similar efforts in nearby Hallau, a community that also supported the uprising.[14] Civic Anabaptism in Switzerland collapsed by December 1525 with the defeat of the Klettgau peasants. Hubmaier tried again elsewhere, pursuing civic reformation in Nikolsburg, just over the Austrian border in Moravia, between the summers of 1526 and 1527.

None of these reformers sought to exterminate the godless. Yet like Thomas Müntzer and the peasants, they desired to remake society along more socially egalitarian lines, the impetus for which they discerned in scripture. They all wanted communities of committed Christians, regenerated by God, to displace a hierarchy of clerical oppression.

Despite these initial aspirations, within five years the most important Anabaptist groups had become nonresistant separatists permeated by martyrological self-awareness. Intense persecution, far worse than anything faced by the early evangelicals, catalyzed their transformation. Both the peasants and the early Anabaptist reform efforts were crushed, leaving separatist withdrawal as the only way to preserve fundamental commitments about Christian truth. Adherence to adult baptism, without political protection, set Anabaptists apart from the larger society—and exposed them to Catholic and Protestant authorities, shaken by the Peasants' War, with a hair-trigger sensitivity to radicalism of any kind. Of the 845 known or "probable" executions of Anabaptists in Switzerland, south and central Germany, Austria, Bohemia, and Moravia between 1525 and 1618, 488 (57.6 percent) occurred between 1527 and 1530.[15] This represents about 10 percent of all the Christians judicially executed for heterodoxy or religious treason over the entire sixteenth and seventeenth centuries. As dreams of civic reformation gave way to the reality of separatist sects, late medieval views about suffering were reconfigured as the anticipation of martyrdom. Experience molded general cultural values into central structures of understanding. For early evangelicals, executions in the 1520s and early 1530s were sporadic events, albeit well-suited to promoting the Gospel. For Anabaptists, executions were part of life—and confirmation of the very meaning of being Christian.

Early Leaders Set the Tone

Regardless of their other disagreements, early radical reformers were nearly unanimous in their views about Christian suffering. Leaders told their male and female followers to persevere through the persecution that Christ's followers ought to expect. This was anti-Nicodemism in an Anabaptist key. Its relationship to martyrdom is as clear as the relationship of Calvin's anti-Nicodemism to Reformed Protestant martyrdom.[16]

Conrad Grebel, an educated patrician's son in his mid-twenties, baptized the first adults in Zurich in January 1525. Four months earlier he had written to Thomas Müntzer with both enthusiasm and concern. Pleased by Müntzer's attack on the evangelical preachers, Grebel was alarmed to hear that

Müntzer sanctioned armed defense of the Gospel. By contrast, Grebel championed the patient endurance of persecution: "Genuine, believing Christians are sheep in the midst of wolves, sheep for the slaughter," he wrote. They "must be baptized in anxiety and distress, sadness, persecution, suffering, and death, tried in the fire, and must obtain the fatherland of eternal rest not by strangling the bodily, but rather the spiritual."[17] Not a single Anabaptist had yet been baptized, let alone killed. Zurich's city council would make rebaptism a capital crime only in March 1526; as among early evangelicals, the executions did not create the sensibility. Yet Grebel saw that his commitments portended a radical vulnerability. Nevertheless, when God's word was at stake, he told Müntzer, "if you therefore have to suffer for it, you know well that it cannot be otherwise. Christ must suffer still more in his members. But he will strengthen them and keep them firm to the end."[18] As it turned out, despite inklings of his own martyrdom,[19] Grebel endured several months of imprisonment but not death. In March 1526 he escaped from Zurich's New Tower along with other Anabaptists and died from the plague that August. By then his premonition had been realized: Bolt Eberli and an unnamed priest were executed in Lachen (Schwyz) in May 1525, Hans Krüsi in Lucerne two months later.[20]

Imprisoned with Grebel was another early Anabaptist leader, Jörg Blaurock. He delivered written testimony to the Zurich authorities who had interrogated him. Adapting the Johannine Christ to his own situation, Blaurock wrote that like Jesus the good shepherd (John 10:11), "I too, I too offer my body and life and my soul for my sheep, my body in the tower, my life in the sword or fire, or in the winepress squeeze my blood from my flesh [*in der trotten uß trucken min blüt vom fleisch*] like Christ on the cross."[21] Direct pastoral identification with Christ's sacrifice supported his own anticipation of martyrdom. He escaped with the others in March 1526, but was rearrested in December. A noncitizen, Blaurock was publicly beaten and banished. Zuricher Felix Mantz, however, a close friend of Grebel's, became the city's first Anabaptist martyr. He was sentenced to be drowned on January 5, 1527. Blaurock proselytized further in Austria, carrying Swiss Anabaptism to the South Tirol on at least two separate occasions. The second time he was captured and burned, near Innsbruck, on September 6, 1529.[22]

The gathering at Schleitheim in late February 1527, under the apparent leadership of Michael Sattler, is widely recognized as a watershed in the development of Swiss Anabaptism.[23] Shortly thereafter Sattler, a former Benedictine monk, was arrested and imprisoned. In the spring of 1527 he wrote a consolatory letter to fellow Anabaptist prisoners at Horb. The smashing of the peasants and of Anabaptist efforts at civic reformation had had an effect. Sattler viewed his fellow prisoners as believers set apart, "who are separated from and should be separated from the world in everything that they do and allow," as the Schleitheim Articles put it. They were obliged to endure all persecution, he wrote in his letter, to "walk surely and cautiously against those who are on the outside as unbelievers," maintaining Christ's commands and their love for one another.[24] "If you do this," he continued, "you will soon see where God's sheep live among the wolves and will see a short and quick separation of those who do not want to walk the sure-footed [*füszrichtige*] and living way of Christ, namely through the cross, distress, imprisonment, self-renunciation, and in the end through death."[25]

A song attributed to Sattler, printed in 1531, succinctly combined separatism with suffering in its opening stanza:

> When Christ with his true teaching
> gathered together a little band
> he said that everyone with patience
> must follow him daily, carrying the cross.

Christ simultaneously set his followers apart and told them what to expect. The song elaborated with a rendering of Matt. 5:11–12: "When you are slandered and abused now, / persecuted and beaten for my sake, / be joyful, for see, your reward / is prepared for you on heaven's throne."[26] The basic separatist and suffering mold of the Swiss Brethren had been cast. It was hardened by the martyrdom of Mantz, Sattler, and at least fifty-eight more Anabaptists in Swiss towns and villages between 1525 and 1538.[27]

South German and Austrian Anabaptism was largely a transitional movement between the Peasants' War and the formation of Moravian Anabaptist communities. Swiss leaders such as Bläurock and Wilhelm Reublin had contact with south German and Austrian Anabaptists in the late 1520s. Additionally, Werner Packull has argued for the influence of late medieval "cross mysticism" on the movement. Thomas Müntzer bequeathed this sensibility to his principal heirs, Hans Hut and Hans Denck. A sensibility of suffering was reinforced as well by martyr-leaders such as Hans Schlaffer and Leonhard Schiemer.[28]

Although not himself an Anabaptist, Thomas Müntzer influenced South German and Austrian Anabaptism in important ways. His pamphlets, sermons, and correspondence between 1523 and 1525 are laced with views about Christian suffering—including the notion that godly rulers should expect to suffer in suppressing the godless. In July 1524, Müntzer delivered his "Sermon to the Princes" to Duke John of Saxony and his son, John Frederick. Müntzer saw himself as a latter-day Daniel, the princes as Nebuchadnezzar, and Luther and his followers as the Old Testament king's incompetent interpreters (Dan. 2). He urged the princes to lead a *real* reformation despite the costs:

> [God] will make it easy for your hand to strike and will also preserve you. But in the meantime you must suffer a great cross and tribulation [*anfechtung*], so that the fear of God may be made clear to you. That cannot happen without suffering, but it will not cost you more than the dangers risked for God's sake and adversaries' useless chit-chat [*unnütz geplauder der widdersacher*] . . . Therefore, dear fathers of Saxony, you must risk it for the sake of the Gospel, but God will chastise you in a friendly way as his beloved sons (Deut. 1[:31]), when he is ardent in his short-lived wrath. Blessed are all who rely upon God then. Just say openly with the spirit of Christ: "I will not fear even if a hundred thousand have encircled me" [Ps. 3:6].[29]

This was no call to endure oppression, but an exhortation to stir up resistance.

Müntzer wrote letters in the same month that he delivered this sermon. Depending on the addressees, he varied his accent on the theme of Christian suffering. He urged the Christians of Sangerhausen, who had recently been prohibited from worshipping in Allstedt, to follow God's will despite any worldly concern; to trust God enough to risk their lives for him; to model themselves on Job and the other martyrs in time of trial; and, when threatened, not to fear those who can kill the body, but the one who can cast body and soul into hell (Matt. 10:28).[30] Müntzer reminded the intendant of Allstedt, Hans Zeiss, that "we have made a covenant in baptism; a Christian should and must suffer." One had to learn what baptism was, had to ask whether one had God's testimony and could remain firm.[31] Müntzer was not talking about a transmutation of late medieval patience into the meek acceptance of persecution.[32] He meant the suffering inherent in the painful process of becoming a real Christian, as one passed from the conformist passivity of outer faith to the externalized zeal of inner faith.

Fighting for the Gospel inevitably provoked hostility. In the spring of 1525, with the peasant rebellion at its height, Müntzer pleaded with the Allstedters for immediate action. He assured several thousand peasants marching under his covenantal rainbow banner that God would vanquish the enemy. Yet when the slaughter of his peasants at Frankenhausen began on May 14, 1525, he seems to have fled quickly. Authorities found him hiding in a bed in the city. By the end of the month they had executed him.[33] In subsequent years, central German Anabaptists held him in high regard.[34]

Hans Hut was with Müntzer at Frankenhausen, but escaped. He shared Müntzer's intense apocalyptic sensibilities and concern for the religious transformation of the social order. Yet Hut recalculated the end as mid-1528 rather than 1525 and saw God's elect not in the revolutionary peasants but rather in Anabaptists, purified by separatist discipline. He made converts through his preaching, instruction, and baptizing in southern Germany, Moravia (where he clashed with Hubmaier in Nikolsburg), and Austria.[35] Before the Lord returned to claim his own, Christians would suffer, a necessary part of the redemptive purification that God worked through his "Gospel of all creatures." In his published treatise on the understanding of scripture (1527), Hut claimed that to experience Christ as the living son of God required following in his footsteps and bearing his cross.[36] Similarly, in his manuscript, "On the Mystery of Baptism," he called "the suffering or the cross of Christ, indeed the crucified Christ" the "means of justification." Everything suffered by a real friend of God, he asserted, "is called the suffering of Christ and not ours, since with Christ they are one body in many members, unified and bound through the bond of love [Rom. 12:4–5, Eph. 4:15–16]. Therefore Christ tends to such people as his own body, to which he testifies and says, 'Who touches you touches the apple of my eye' [Zech. 2:8], and further, 'what you do to the least of my followers you have done to me' [Matt. 25:40]."[37] Solidarity in suffering united the group through their love of the afflicted Lord, soon to be the apocalyptic Christ of glory. A fire took Hut's life in December 1527 as he awaited execution in an Augsburg prison. He died without seeing his apocalyptic predictions fail—yet his views about suffering lived on.

One who perpetuated them was Leonhard Schiemer, a former Franciscan who became Hut's follower. Before his apprehension in November 1527, he exercised a short-lived but energetic ministry in southern Germany and the Tirol. Schiemer's prison writings, produced during the seven weeks before his execution on January 14, 1528, disclose a strong apocalypticism and sense of suffering discipleship. He told fellow believers that once they endeavored to live as Christians, they would face the same conflicts as the Lord, for the disciple is not greater than the master: "Christ suffered in the flesh, so prepare yourselves also with the same thoughts."[38] Prescription and self-understanding fused, as they did so often for imprisoned Christians. A song attributed to Schiemer evoked the experience of the "little flock" [*heuflein klein*] in Austria under Ferdinand I:

> We slink around in the woods,
> men search for us with dogs
> and lead us like the silent lamb,
> imprisoned and bound.
> We are denounced before everyone
> as though we were rebels,
> we are outlawed

> like sheep for the slaughter
> as heretics and seducers.

Some Anabaptists had perished in prison, while others, "through the rigor of martyrdom / have been killed and died." This was par for the course: "Such is the patience / of the saints on earth; / hence all of us must be tested / through many afflictions."[39] Just like Protestant writers, Schiemer used Matt. 10:32–33 along with Rom. 10:10 and Acts 5:29 in good anti-Nicodemite fashion: Christ threatened to deny those who denied him, Paul said Christians must confess faith with the mouth, and the earliest Christians in Jerusalem said one must obey God rather than man, even if it meant witnessing with one's blood.[40] Had they not detested Anabaptists, Calvin and Viret would have applauded.

Those baptized by Hut, Schiemer, and other leaders, such as Hans Schlaffer, fed the stream of Anabaptist refugees to Moravia. After Hubmaier's arrest in the summer of 1527, a dispute in Nikolsburg provided the immediate catalyst for the formation of the first two Moravian communities. The *Schwertler* (sword-bearers), headed by Hans Spittelmaier, defended Hubmaier's view that Christian magistrates might employ force to maintain order. The *Stäbler* (staff-bearers), led by Jacob Wiedemann, seem to have advocated nonresistant separatism, much like the Swiss Brethren. In 1528 Wiedemann left Nikolsburg with a group of followers and established a community at Austerlitz, east of the Morava river.

The following year a Tirolean Anabaptist leader, Jakob Huter, began organizing refugee treks between the mountains of Austria and the Moravian communities. The latter practiced communal ownership of goods, blending emergency measures with inspiration from the Acts of the Apostles (Acts 2:44–45, 4:32–37).[41] Huter's extant letters from 1534 and 1535 are brilliant examples of anti-Nicodemite exhortation, swarming with scriptural quotations.[42] The separatism and suffering enunciated by Sattler is evident again and again. For example, consider Huter's greetings to imprisoned fellow believers at Hohenwart in Lower Austria: "Blessed be God the Father through Jesus Christ, our dear Lord, who has made us worthy to suffer for the sake of his most holy and almighty name, and has called us from the terrible darkness of this wicked and wretched world, and has accepted us into community with the chosen saints, into heavenly citizenship and the assembly of many thousands of angels."[43] In a letter to persecuted Moravian Anabaptists, Huter integrated apocalyptic language with praise for the recent martyrs' patience and the effect of their inspiring witness. He yearned to follow their example.[44] His desire would not go unrequited: in 1536 he was executed, as were so many other early Anabaptist leaders.

Balthasar Hubmaier was put to death in Vienna in March 1528. Because he defended the Christian magistrate's right and duty to wield the sword, however, his status as a martyr proved ambiguous in the legacy of nonresistant Anabaptism.[45] Hubmaier nonetheless held strong views about the suffering characteristic of Christian life. Moreover, he was the most widely published and probably the most learned of the early Anabaptist leaders, having earned a doctorate in theology under Johannes Eck.

While still in Waldshut in 1525, Hubmaier sounded like Luther or Tyndale on the inevitable resistance provoked by the Gospel. As soon as one received the healing power of Christ, he wrote, "there follows persecution, the cross, and every misery for the sake of the Gospel in the world, which hates the light and life and loves the darkness."[46] Celebrating the Lord's Supper implied a willingness to shed one's blood for one's neighbor, just as Christ had done for his followers.[47] Later, from prison in Zurich, he prayed to God for the strength to maintain his faith "through tyranny, torture, sword, fire, or water." In his Nikolsburg period, Hubmaier wrote that the surest way to eternal life was "through anxiety, distress, suffering, misery, persecution, and death for the sake of the name of Jesus Christ, who himself had to suffer in order to enter into his glory (Luke 24[:26]). Holy Paul says it too: 'All who want to live godly in Christ will suffer persecution' (2 Tim. 3[:12])."[48]

Anabaptism was imprinted with a martyrological mentality between 1525 and 1530. Anabaptist leaders, despite other disputes among themselves, insisted that Christian discipleship implied the willingness to follow Christ in suffering and death. Hubmaier and Hut, Grebel and Müntzer, for all their disagreements, voiced variations on this theme from Strasbourg to Moravia. Meanwhile authorities were putting Anabaptists to death by the hundreds—graphic evidence that persecution and martyrdom were indeed the cost of discipleship. Within the Radical Reformation, these Anabaptist leaders differed markedly from Sebastian Franck, Caspar Schwenckfeld, and other spiritualists. The latter, by downplaying the importance of exterior religious expression, simultaneously undercut the imperative to persevere no matter what the cost. Dissembling was acceptable because the completely inward character of faith rendered trivial its outward manifestations. The severe suppression of the later 1520s produced a major watershed within the early Radical Reformation, setting spiritualists and Anabaptists on fundamentally different trajectories.

Penetration among Ordinary Anabaptists

Leaders' exhortations are one thing, followers' actions another. To what extent did ordinary Anabaptists, the majority of whom were illiterate and of humble social origin, internalize these austere admonitions? Because we lack prison writings from the unlettered, attempting to answer this question demands that we piece together judicial records, the songs Anabaptists wrote and presumably sang, and reports of their words and behavior. Archival sources show that hundreds of Anabaptists abjured their views when they were interrogated. In so doing, they did not follow the directives of their leaders. Yet in itself, this is not evidence against the spread of *attitudes* related to martyrdom. Recantations point rather to the difficulty of *enactment.* Anabaptists who professed their willingness to die, but later recanted, show the penetration of views about martyrdom even as they reveal that fear often got the upper hand on faith. Anabaptist men and women were devout human beings, not automatons marching en masse to their death.[49]

Those who followed through seem to have been clear about their course of action. An anonymous pamphlet recounted the execution of Jörgen Wagner, a cartwright for the Cistercian monastery at Fürstenfeld who was burned in Munich in 1527. Repeated efforts failed to convince him to renounce his views. Wagner instead glossed the Lord's Prayer to imply his imminent salvation through martyrdom. When attempted persuasion yielded to public prayer by a "Master Conrad" just before his execution, the exchange reportedly went like this:

> Master Conrad prayed, "Our Father who is in heaven."
> Wagner answered, "Namely, you are our Father in heaven, today I will be with you . . ."
> Conrad: "Your kingdom come."
> Wagner: "Today your kingdom will come to me, and I will enter into your kingdom."
> Conrad: "Your will be done on earth as in heaven."
> Wagner: "Therefore I am here, Father, that your will be done and not mine."[50]

When asked whether he really believed as strongly as his confession of faith suggested, Wagner quoted Matt. 6:21—"Where your treasure is, there your heart will be also." He explained that "it would be a difficult thing for me to suffer death for the sake of something which I confessed with the mouth and did not believe joyfully [*festigklich*] in my heart."[51] Despite leaving a wife and children behind him, Wagner appears to have known exactly what he was doing.

Shortly after Michael Sattler's death, Wilhelm Reublin, the Anabaptist leader active with him north of Zurich, wrote letters about recent martyrdoms to fellow believers in several Swiss towns. Four men, Reublin reported, were offered reprieve if they would renounce their views. They replied that "God's grace was to them more precious than man's grace, 'and neither our lives nor any of the world's goods should hinder us in it.'" With "willing hearts" [*freilichem hertzen*] three of them knelt down and were beheaded. The fourth, a furrier from St. Gall named Matthias Hiller, given the same choice with his companions' fresh corpses at his feet, declined recantation. "'God would not go for that [*das wel got niemer mer*]. If I had seven heads, I would offer them all for the name of Christ.' He knelt down, commended his soul into God's hands. Thus their lives ended."[52]

The Anabaptists in Grüningen, southeast of Zurich, were sent Reublin's account of the recent Swiss martyrdoms. Several of them were apprehended and questioned by authorities in the summer of 1528. Among other views, Jacob Falks considered [adult] baptism proper (*recht*) and infant baptism improper, and "would persist therein and for that reason suffer death."[53] Several others expressed the same view, as did a baker's apprentice in Strasbourg, Hans Mether of Rottweil, in April 1534, even though he had not yet committed to baptism.[54] In 1527 Hans Ritter, a tailor baptized by Hans Hut, was questioned along with several others in Erlangen. He explained how he was baptized in running water "and thereby bound to God, to suffer and to have patience if that suffering transpired, and to take up and bear his cross and to follow the Lord up to death."[55] Interrogated about the sacrament of the altar, Ritter and several other Bavarian Anabaptists said that the chalice signified suffering and the willingness to suffer with Christ.[56]

Not only does such evidence help us understand the early Anabaptists and their attitudes toward suffering; it also is directly relevant to the issue of the Christianization of ordinary, lay Western Europeans in the sixteenth century. Evidence from the interrogation of Anabaptists renders untenable any claim that men or women with little or no formal education were somehow incapable of serious, scripturally based religious understanding or commitment. Gerald Strauss's findings about widespread catechetical failure in Lutheran Germany, for example, might mean that many people did not like Lutheranism. This failure might mean, too, as Strauss himself argues, that Lutheran pastors chose ineffective methods of indoctrination. But the findings cannot mean that the teaching and learning of religion based on the Bible were beyond the capacities of uneducated men and women.[57] Thousands of such people became Anabaptists. Many of them demonstrated an ability to memorize scripture and to articulate nuanced theological positions. The fact that humble Anabaptists even existed undercuts the view that the mass of common people were separated from the literate elite by a cultural chasm.

We still know too little about the settings in which early Anabaptists sang their songs.[58] No doubt this derives, at least in part, from the clandestine character of Anabaptist communities. Anabaptists sought to conceal their gatherings from would-be informers and captors. There was, however, a strong tradition of late medieval popular singing in German-speaking lands.

There is evidence from the 1520s of Anabaptists singing. And memorization of the songs' rhyming lyrics would have been facilitated by being set to familiar tunes, even—and perhaps especially—among the illiterate.[59] It is reasonable to assume that Anabaptists' songs, the content of which was directly relevant to their situation, were shared at meetings that usually remained hidden. Even considering only those songs known to have appeared in the early years (apart from later attributions by compilers of the *Ausbund* or Hutterite codices) permits us to move from texts to collective religious experience expressed in song.

Suffering and persecution are ubiquitous themes in Anabaptist hymns. For example, one verse in a song by Leonhard Schiemer combined Ps. 116:15 with the comfort of singular trust in God:

> How precious is the death of the saints
> in your sight!
> For this reason we have in all distress
> a consoling confidence
> in you alone.
> Otherwise there is nowhere
> any comfort, peace, or rest on earth;
> Whoever places hope in you
> becomes forever
> free from being harmed.[60]

Most of the song attributed to Sattler actually put biblical verses into Christ's mouth. Directly addressing Anabaptists, the Lord told them that in heaven, "your misery, fear, anxiety, distress, and pain / will there be tremendous joy for you / and this disgrace indeed a praise and glory / before the entire host of heaven."[61] Ludwig Hätzer, who spent some time with Sattler in Strasbourg, wrote a song published as a broadsheet in 1529. It specifically rejected the "world's" view that Christ's passion had rendered further suffering superfluous.[62]

In 1535 a number of Philipites—the followers of Philip Plener—fled toward Austria from Moravia. The news of Münster had sparked persecution even in their eastern havens. They were imprisoned in Passau. In the ensuing years these Philipites produced fifty-three hymns that were printed in 1564, in the first known published hymnal of the Swiss Brethren.[63] Many of these songs are saturated with exhortations to steadfastness and the expectation of suffering. It seems highly likely that, as the title of the collection stated, the prisoners not only composed, but also sang them (*geticht vnd gesungen*). "Love overcomes all things," wrote clothmaker Hans Betz, one of the group's leaders and himself responsible for at least twelve of the hymns:

"water, fire, sword do not conquer it, / their guide is eternal life."[64] Perhaps the most interesting for its social implications is a fourteen-stanza song about constancy and the hope of eternal joy. Each stanza is accompanied by the initials of the person who wrote it, one person per verse, several of whom can be identified.[65] Such a glimpse behind the song's authorship reveals group composition and points to collective singing. Together with interrogation records and reports like Reublin's, such songs imply that the Anabaptists who refused to recant shared the same views as their leaders.

This impression is reinforced if we recall how people became Anabaptists in central Europe. After attempts at civic reform failed, sustaining the movement depended on face-to-face contact with itinerant missionaries. During their interrogations, Anabaptists often mentioned these encounters. Frequently they noted who had taught or baptized them, but rarely did they attribute conversion to the reading of pamphlets. This direct interaction fostered solidarity and a sense of commitment lacking among typical Protestants and Catholics. Most Europeans learned as children that they were Christians, as they learned that they belonged to certain families and kingdoms. They had become Christians without their awareness or consent, as the result of a sacrament administered just days after birth. Not so for Anabaptists. For them, baptism implied the willingness to risk one's life for Christ, as his own apostles had done. Becoming an Anabaptist in Austria or Bavaria in the 1520s was, in terms of the resolve and danger entailed, more akin to becoming an Elizabethan missionary priest half a century later than to living as a politically protected lay Protestant or Catholic. Those who became Anabaptists were preselected for martyrdom.

As a result, for Anabaptists the ritual of baptism was itself linked to the prospect of suffering and martyrdom. It simultaneously testified to a covenant with God inspired by the Holy Spirit, signified participation in a community separated from a sinful world, and exposed one to hostile and powerful authorities. Early Anabaptists thus understood with a distinctive concreteness the threefold baptism by spirit, water, and blood mentioned in 1 John 5:6–7. By "baptism in blood," Hans Schlaffer explained, the Lord meant "the baptism of suffering and the shedding of his blood," which is why Jesus asked his followers if they could endure the same baptism as he.[66] A number of Upper Austrian Anabaptists questioned in the fall of 1527 said that "no one may be saved, except through suffering, that is genuine baptism by blood, into which they themselves consent through baptism by water."[67] If this seemed a brutal prospect, it paled in comparison to the alternative: certain damnation for failing to follow Christ. Those were lost who wallowed in Roman superstitions, or whom Protestants had seduced with promises of easy salvation—"faith alone" without transformation of life.

If the world rejected truth, then truth must reject the world. This was the bottom line once civic Anabaptism failed. In 1524 Grebel had put it bluntly to Müntzer: "It is much better that a few be rightly instructed through the Word of God, believing rightly and walking in virtues and [proper] practices, than that many believe deceitfully on the basis of false, adulterated doctrine" [*vermischter ler falsch*].[68] Anabaptism collapsed late medieval distinctions between status-quo, ordinary Christians and the saints to whom they appealed. Simply to become a Christian became extraordinary. Latter-day disciples would have to brace for the suffering described in scripture and which they saw all around them. Persecution heightened already keen apocalyptic expectations: with Antichrist on such a savage rampage, the end could not be far off.[69] Among early evangelicals, martyrdom helped *create* a sense of Protestant identity among the reform-minded. The martyrdom of Anabaptists *reinforced* a sense of separatism that was central to their identity after the collapse of civic reform and the decimation of the peasants.

Memorialization in the Early Years and Beyond

Early evangelicals exploited the printing press to memorialize their first martyrs. The logic of ecclesiological separatism suggested different strategies to Anabaptists. If the aim was no longer to reform Christendom per se, but rather to gather the Lord's flock before his imminent return, then memorialization should be directed towards the converted and spread by missionaries, not aimed at a wider audience and channeled through markets for printed matter. This in-group orientation helps explain the dearth of early Anabaptist publications about martyrs. The number of publications was also affected by low literacy rates among Anabaptists, as well as the deterrent effect for would-be printers of radical works following the Peasants' War and the execution of Nuremberg printer Hans Hergot in May 1527.[70] Indeed, apart from hymnals like the *Ausbund* or the *Schön Gesangbüchlein*, German-speaking Anabaptists, in contrast to Dutch Mennonites, published very few martyrological sources even later in the century.[71]

Yet print was not the only means to preserve and communicate word of the martyrs. Julius Lober, a former priest turned tailor after the Peasants' War, was apprehended in the duchy of Ansbach as he was on his way to Moravia in the spring of 1531. He had a list of over four hundred Anabaptists killed in fifty-two different towns and territories.[72] Combined with refugees' memories and oral accounts, such lists very likely contributed to the manuscript Hutterite chronicles in subsequent years. In the summer of 1527, Wilhelm Reublin did not rush to a printer with his handwritten account of recent martyrdoms, but rather sent copies to Anabaptist congregations in Zollikon,

Grüningen, Basel, and Appenzell.[73] Reports of Sattler's death were also spread via oral or written accounts that transcended Anabaptist circles: in Strasbourg, sixty miles west of Rottenberg-am-Neckar where the execution had occurred, Protestant reformer Wolfgang Capito and others had detailed information just eleven days after the event.[74] Johannes Faber, a Catholic theologian and the vicar general for the bishop of Constance, published a justification of Hubmaier's execution. Evangelicals as well as Müntzer's followers, he fumed, were proclaiming lawfully executed heretics to be "martyrs and holy before God."[75]

Only two early Anabaptist martyrs seem to have been publicized in print: Michael Sattler and Jörgen Wagner.[76] Like many of the early evangelical pamphlets, these accounts described the encounter between the martyr and authorities, recounted the manner of execution, and connected doctrines to deaths. Wagner, a cartwright, refused to have his child baptized, although the extent of his participation in Bavarian Anabaptism remains somewhat ambiguous.[77] Both his trial record, however, and the *New, Trustworthy, and Remarkable Story of Jörgen Wagner* make clear his willingness to die for his views. He explained that even though his wife and children were dear to him, he would leave them for the sake of his Lord.[78] As with the evangelical *Flugschriften,* the pamphlet about Wagner enumerated the articles he refused to recant. The author explicitly stated that Wagner "professed them publicly in front of the prison in the community" and "held them to his end," the four articles being "the reason for his death" [*vrsach seines tods*].[79]

Michael Sattler declined to abjure the articles brought against him and fellow Anabaptists unless biblically based arguments could persuade him to do so. Moreover, his execution ratified the seven Schleitheim Articles with a martyr's blood less than three months after the conference.[80] By 1529, Klaus von Graveneck's printed account of Sattler's trial and execution was circulating with the Schleitheim Articles and Sattler's letter to the Anabaptists at Horb—like the materials about Vos and van den Esschen assembled earlier in the *History of Two Augustinians* (1523), for example, and Luther's amalgamation of sources pertaining to Leonhard Keyser (1527).

As in evangelical sources, doctrines and deaths were linked in these pamphlets about Wagner and Sattler. It is virtually certain, as well, that similar accounts were carried via oral communication and/or manuscripts that are now lost. The later Hutterite codices, the Swiss Brethren's *Ausbund,* and the collections in the Dutch Mennonite tradition deliberately excluded Protestants and Catholics who were executed for their religious views.[81]

German-speaking Anabaptists preserved their martyrological legacy in the later sixteenth and seventeenth centuries. All but two of the fifty-three songs from the Swiss Brethren hymnal of 1564 reappeared as the second half of the

Ausbund, a hymnal likely published around 1570, although the oldest surviving edition dates from 1583.[82] Besides the many songs concerning patience and suffering as the way to salvation, the first half of the 1583 collection included twenty-four songs about martyrs among its total of eighty. Twenty-one of these describe in rhyming narrative the arrest, interrogation, responses, sentencing, and martyrdom of German- and Dutch-speaking Anabaptists put to death between 1527 and 1570. Nine of the twenty-four songs were adapted from the Dutch Mennonite martyrology *The Sacrifice unto the Lord.*[83] In fact, forty-two consecutive songs among the eighty in the first half of the hymnal are either about, or were written by or attributed to, martyrs.[84] All fifty-one of the songs from the second half of the *Ausbund* originated with the Anabaptists imprisoned in Passau in 1535, many of whom were executed.

Ursula Lieseberg has recently analyzed sixty-five different German-language songs about martyrs, drawn from among the Swiss Brethren, German Anabaptists, and Hutterites.[85] It is unknown when and by whom many of them were created, and this information is probably unrecoverable. Where evidence is available, however, it often points to composition within days or weeks after executions, usually by eyewitnesses or people privy to the judicial proceedings.[86] In other cases, such as the hymns about Felix Mantz and Jörgen Wagner in the *Ausbund,* the songs were crafted from letters by or pamphlets about the martyrs.[87] Most of the songs concern sixteenth-century Anabaptists, but others imply historical continuity with biblical and early Christian martyrs. The third song in the *Ausbund,* for example, traces the persecution of God's children from the Old Testament prophets through Christ, Stephen, and (complete with marginal references to Eusebius) early Christian martyrs such as Ignatius of Antioch, Polycarp, Agnes, and Martha.[88] Anabaptist songs about martyrs are linked to their songs about steadfast suffering, very much like Protestant martyrologies are related to their own anti-Nicodemite admonitions. Both memorialized for fellow believers those who had enacted the exhortations.

Besides producing and anthologizing songs, the Swiss Brethren and Hutterites memorized and sang them. With rare exceptions, sixteenth-century Anabaptist hymns, like most popular songs at the time, were printed without musical notation. A tune at the beginning of each song, the *contrafactum,* indicated the melody to singers. To provide a *contrafactum* therefore presupposed familiarity with it by the intended audience (or at least by a designated leader who could teach the rest). In the absence of musical notation, this implied memorization of the *contrafactum.* When martyr songs themselves were designated as *contrafacta,* it was assumed that their tunes had been memorized, which suggests as well a familiarity with the content of the songs.

The Hutterite songwriter who rendered Wolf Binder's martyrdom in 1571, for example, assumed that others knew the song about Hans Gurtzham, executed in Vienna in 1550, the melody of which was set as the *contrafactum*.[89] Judged by this criterion, the best-known martyr song was "Whoever Wants to Follow Christ Now," about Jörgen Wagner. No fewer than twelve other martyr songs, Hutterite as well as Swiss, indicated it as their melody.[90] Visitations by Lutheran officials in Urbach (Württemberg) in the spring of 1598 found that the mayor's son had "sung the 'Jörgen Wagner' at night for two years," while another young man, a tailor named Abraham Fouts, had "half learned by heart the song 'Jörgen Wagner, Anabaptist.'"[91] Catholic writers complained that the Hutterites often sang their martyr songs. Christoph Erhard, who lived in Nikolsburg for six years, bristled that they "always put their drowned and burned, obstinate and impervious, alleged martyrs into a song." Early in the seventeenth century, the Jesuit Christoph Andreas Fischer repeatedly ridiculed the singing of martyr songs by the Hutterites.[92] Such evidence, coupled with the large number of songs, implies that the martyrs remained very important to the Swiss Brethren and the Hutterites in the later sixteenth and into the seventeenth centuries.

In 1588 Andreas Gut, a member of the Swiss Brethren, addressed a statement of Anabaptist belief and practice to the mayor and city council of Zurich. His "Simple Confession" included numerous remarks about the reward for Christian suffering, plus scriptural examples of how the "children of the flesh" persecuted the "children of the spirit." Gut also compiled biblical passages about the blessedness of suffering, the persecution that comes from following Christ, and the difficulty of the narrow way that leads to eternal life.[93] "Since then the cross, suffering, and sadness has been foretold for us by Christ," he wrote, "and is also the genuine [*recht*] path and way to the Kingdom of God and eternal life, he thus says in the Revelation of John that whoever overcomes will inherit everything (Rev. 21[:7])."[94] This might have been written by Michael Sattler or any other early Anabaptist leader. If this document is any indication, third- or fourth-generation Anabaptist communities maintained the same attitudes toward persecution as their earliest predecessors.

Anabaptist Martyrs in the Low Countries

Beginning in 1530 Christianity based on adult commitment played an important role in the Netherlands. In the 1530s few would have guessed that within a generation, the followers of Menno Simons would be the leading Anabaptist group in the Low Countries. In the wake of the Münster debacle of 1534–1535, Obbe Philips—who later left the movement altogether—led this tiny band, which was one of the lesser of several Anabaptist sects. In the 1550s and 1560s their strength would be tested by schisms that would long outlast the sixteenth century. By the late sixteenth century the Mennonites had been toughened, too, by decades of repression by Catholic authorities.[95] Like the Swiss Brethren and the Hutterites, they embraced songs about martyrs and persecution with alacrity. The Mennonites, however, published much more concerning martyrdom than did other Anabaptists—probably because more of them could read, and they had easier access to printers. Moreover, Anabaptism was a broader movement, with a wider impact, in the Low Countries than in German-speaking lands.

Before and After Münster

Melchior Hoffman brought his apocalyptic message and practice of adult baptism from Strasbourg to Emden in 1530. Executions of his followers began almost immediately. In 1531 Sicke Frericx became the first Dutch Anabaptist martyr. Then another of Hoffman's disciples, Jan Volkerts Tripmaker, along with seven other Anabaptists whom Volkerts had converted in Amsterdam, were put to death in The Hague.[96] Wendelmoet Claes, a sacramentarian, had been burned in the same city in 1527; she was claimed as an Anabaptist martyr by 1570 at the latest.[97]

Yet no pre-Münster Anabaptist martyrological tradition seems to have crystallized in the Low Countries. Melchior Hoffman himself—in contrast to Luther, who responded jubilantly to the execution of the two Augustinians in Brussels in 1523—was shocked by Volkerts's death. He did not consider martyrdom the best way to promote the Gospel.[98] In fact, he suspended adult baptisms after the executions, hoping to avoid persecution, a moratorium that lasted for two years. Beginning in 1533, however, the course of Dutch Anabaptism far outstripped Hoffman's control. Jan Beukels van Leiden visited Münster in June 1533; Jan Matthijs baptized him in Leiden; the *Confession of Both Sacraments* by Münster reformer Bernhard Rothmann was distributed in the Netherlands; large-scale baptism resumed, and Anabaptists gained control of Münster in February 1534. With Hoffman imprisoned back in Strasbourg, apocalyptic expectancy surged in Münster. The city was soon under an episcopal siege. Melchiorites were becoming Münsterites. The process was complete once Jan van Leiden became the city's prophet-king after the death of Jan Matthijs.

The Münsterites found no memorialization as martyrs.[99] At first sight, this is ironic. Bernhard Rothmann's writings provide the only account of Münsterite self-perception before and after the Kingdom. Between the winter of 1534–1535 and June 1535, just before the regime's fall, the tone of his work shifted from crusading apocalypticism to suffering resignation.[100] Yet self-understanding is different from recognition by others; without the latter, no martyrological tradition forms. In 1539–1540, Menno Simons expressed sympathy for these "dear brothers" misled by a message of violence, who nevertheless "sought only Christ Jesus and eternal life." In 1558, however, when Menno reworked the same treatise, he deleted this passage.[101] The Münsterites might be pitied, but they never acquired a place among the Mennonite martyrs. Whatever the circumstances that helped create them, practices such as polygamy and the communal ownership of goods completely discredited the Münsterites in the eyes of virtually all Europeans.

Once the Kingdom was crushed, Dutch Anabaptism splintered. Sympathy for the Münsterites was scarce, especially since authorities now viewed *all* Anabaptists as inherently subversive, their professed pacifism as a pretense. Münster reinforced conclusions about religious radicals that rulers had drawn from the Peasants' War. Even before the city's demise, Menno too had excoriated the idea of a Christian regime imposed by violence.[102] David Joris and Obbe Philips, both Anabaptist leaders after Münster's fall, similarly opposed the regime and its values early in 1535. Joris, however, attempted to reconcile with Münsterite refugees in the later 1530s, although they failed to see eye to eye with him.[103] Throughout the sixteenth century and beyond, Mennonites would struggle to distinguish themselves from Münster and its legacy.

The Batenburgers were probably most likely to have viewed the Münsterites as martyrs. Jan van Batenburg's followers, however, did not write songs and gather stories about heroic victims. Instead, they waged an apocalyptic campaign of revenge against the destroyers of the Westphalian city.[104] In small, roving gangs they plundered churches, burned buildings, stole, and murdered as they waited for the site of the *real* New Jerusalem to be revealed. In certain respects they resemble the advocates of violence in the modern-day U.S. citizen militia movement. The Batenburgers were enraged by the killing of hundreds of Anabaptists, just as right-wing extremists are disgusted by the conflagration of the Branch Davidians in Waco, Texas. Like the Münsterite refugees who were biding their time in northern Westphalia, the Batenburgers did not value persecution. Martyrdom would have appeared to them, as it seems to have been at times for Thomas Müntzer, a perverse embrace of meek suffering. Christian duty impelled the just to eradicate the godless, not to suffer injustice at their hands.

David Joris, a glasspainter, was drawn to reforming ideas in the 1520s. He was baptized during the height of Münsterite ferment, emerging from the shambles as a charismatic, prophetic leader, the most important in Dutch Anabaptism in the later 1530s.[105] His followers, the Davidites,[106] seem to have comprised something of a stillborn tradition of martyrs within Dutch Anabaptism.

By 1540 the stage seemed set for martyrological celebration. At least one hundred Davidites, including Joris's own mother, were executed in 1539, in the harshest repression of Anabaptists since 1535.[107] Another victim was Anneken Jans, who was drowned in Rotterdam in January 1539. Her farewell letter to her infant son, jammed with biblical allusions, was published later the same year. Jans told him that Christ, the prophets, the apostles, the martyrs, and the elders from the book of Revelation, like her, "all had to drink from the chalice of bitterness."[108] Within weeks of her death, a song about her martyrdom was being sung on the streets of Hamburg.[109] After more than two dozen Davidites were executed in Delft in January 1539, Joris wrote (in typically rambling fashion), "I have given to no one the advice that he should seek to preserve his life here, or furthermore to run away from death or his enemy or to be afraid, but to meet it with ardor, indeed wide awake, which is the foundation of the spirit, when the Lord desires that we stand resigned and prepared, full of trust [*gelaeten voll betrouwens bereit staen*], according to God's will ready to surrender ourselves like sheep for the slaughter."[110] This was a call to constancy in the face of persecution. Judged alongside other sixteenth-century sources, Jans and Joris seem to indicate an emergent Davidite martyrological tradition.

Such a tradition withered, however, in part due to Davidite views about the willingness to die. During the 1540s, Mennonites and Davidites debated the issue of outward conformity to prescribed religious practices—the Nicodemism question. The chief Davidite participant was Nicolas Meynderts van Blesdijk, one of Joris's leading assistants.[111] In criticizing the Mennonites' willingness to die for their opposition to infant baptism, Blesdijk insisted on sufficient reason for martyrdom. His argument tended in a spiritualistic direction. According to Blesdijk, "although no one may enter God's kingdom or live a godly life without the cross or suffering," no external ceremony—infant baptism included—justified steadfastness unto death. Only if one were pressured to acknowledge a savior other than Christ, for example, or to deny that there is a God, a resurrection, a Last Judgment, and an eternal life—beliefs on which "the salvation of the soul depends"—was martyrdom justified. If interrogated on such matters, one was obliged to confess one's faith, as more than one hundred fifty Davidite martyrs had done. "If he is not willing joyfully and cheerfully to witness on the basis of this living hope which is in him," Blesdijk wrote, "that is a sure sign that his heart is not set right in faith."[112] If Blesdijk's views are typical, then the traditional distinction between Mennonite willingness to die and Davidite dissimulation is too crudely drawn. The difference between them turned rather on which aspects of Christian life warranted the witness of martyrdom.[113]

Had the Davidites set clear boundaries to this spiritualistic tendency, their martyrological tradition might have persisted. More people might have died for essential points of Christian faith, and fellow believers might have remembered them as they did Anneken Jans. In 1544, however, Joris left the Netherlands. He lived out his remaining twelve years under an assumed name as a conformist citizen in Protestant Basel. With so many of his followers executed, having endured years of severe hardship as one of the most hunted men in the Netherlands,[114] Joris either could not or would not sustain the tension between interior faith and its exterior expression. Blesdijk and others soldiered on, but the Davidites were bereft of Joris's charismatic leadership. A movement so reliant on the revelations of its Holy Spirit-filled prophet could not indefinitely survive his absence. Joris's growing spiritualism and voluntary exile, combined with an apparent Davidite reluctance to match the Mennonite celebration of martyrs, crippled any independent martyrological tradition.[115]

In terms of sustained martyrological traditions, the conventional contrast between Davidites and Mennonites is warranted. The Davidites and their nascent tradition waned as both the Mennonite movement and the celebration of their martyrs grew. Mennonite martyrology reached a first culmination in 1562–1563 with the published collection *The Sacrifice unto the Lord*. Ten subsequent editions, plus a flurry of lesser works about martyrs, appeared in the last third of the sixteenth century. They expressed ideas and values already cultivated for decades. In this respect the Mennonites closely parallel the Protestants, whose midcentury martyrologists extended ideas current in the early Reformation.

Mennonite Martyrological Sensibility before The Sacrifice unto the Lord

At the time of the Kingdom of Münster, Menno Simons struggled to free himself from a Frisian rural pastorate within a church whose claims he no longer believed. Even then he thought that Christian life entailed the willing embrace of suffering, in imitation of the Lord. Still earlier, in 1531, it had been Sicke Frericx's execution for "rebaptism" in nearby Leeuwarden that had led Menno to examine scripture, patristic writers, and contemporary evangelical authors concerning the validity of infant baptism.[116] Dissatisfied, he espoused believers' baptism as the external sign marking a life of Christian discipleship. In 1535 he wrote *Against the Blasphemy of Jan van Leiden* as a riposte to Bernhard Rothmann, the Münsterite apologist. The self-proclaimed King Jan championed a "Christian" violence; Menno battled back with a barrage of biblical quotations. Following Christ meant accepting persecution, not dishing it out. "Dear brothers," Menno admonished, paraphrasing James 5:10–11, "take as an example of suffering discomfort and of patience the prophets, who have spoken to you in the name of the Lord; see, we praise as blessed those who have suffered . . . And should we take the prophets as an example to suffer persecution, then the apostolic weapons must be donned, and the armor of David [that is, literal armor] must lie idle."[117] When he wrote his *Meditation on the Twenty-fifth Psalm* in 1537, Menno knew that he himself might be martyred. Like numerous Protestant writers, he thought that Antichrist and the world inevitably persecuted the truth.[118]

Menno's most important treatise was his *Foundation of Christian Doctrine* (1539–1540). It clustered ideas about persecution, suffering, martyrdom, and religious tyranny as a leitmotif against an apocalyptic backdrop.[119] Later Menno recalled that in 1539, the same year in which Anabaptists suffered so terribly, a man whom he had baptized, Tjard Reynerts, was executed for having sheltered him.[120] Beyond the general post-Münster difficulties, then, personal immediacy informed Menno's remark that "the word of God will be sealed with blood and defended with the cross. That lamb has been slain from the beginning of the world (Rev. 13:[8])."[121] The authorities who killed innocent Christians were Cain's murderous heirs. Menno provided biblical examples of God's judgment against such tyrants.[122] His own stubborn generation refused to accept the Lord's word, despite the teaching, living, and shedding of "the blood of the true witnesses and saints of God," despite the faithful who were "oppressed, plundered, and killed."[123]

The theme of Christian willingness to die recurs throughout the *Foundation*. Magistrates could not frighten Menno's followers from their faith by persecution; the faithful were prepared to forsake everything, including their lives, "for the testimony of Jesus"; and scripture witnessed that Christian freedom meant no exemption from suffering.[124] Even more explicitly than in the *Meditation,* Menno anticipated his own martyrdom. He situated himself in a tradition of scriptural predecessors. "I do not think better of my life than the dear fathers thought of theirs," he wrote, trusting in God's providence with reference to Matt. 10:29–30: "Not a hair shall and may be taken from my head apart from [*buyten*] my heavenly Father. If I lose my life for the sake of Christ and his Gospel, I will save it in eternal life."[125]

In the late 1530s and early 1540s the Mennonites were still a minority within Dutch Anabaptism. Yet from its outset, Menno's ministry was marked with a martyrological sensibility, long before *The Sacrifice unto the Lord* and the song collections of the 1550s and 1560s. His views were fundamentally identical to corresponding Protestant notions about the inevitability of Christian suffering, the awareness of other martyrs' sacrifice, the virtue of the willingness to die, the eternal reward promised to those who persevere, an identification with scriptural forebears, and God's eventual retribution against tyrants.

Such convictions are clear as well in the writings of Mennonite martyrs from the early 1540s. Wouter van Stoelwijck was burned in Brussels in March 1541 after more than three years in prison. Jan Claes, a bookseller, was beheaded in Amsterdam for having had six hundred copies of one of Menno's books printed in Antwerp, then distributed in Holland and Friesland.[126] Claes had in addition converted others to Menno's views, a charge verified by other Anabaptists questioned in Amsterdam. At least one of them, Quirijn Pieters, was also executed.[127]

Van Stoelwijck wrote a full-blown anti-Nicodemite treatise, *A Comforting Admonition and Very Pleasant Instruction on the Suffering and Glory of Christians.* Christians must do God's will, he argued, expressed in Christ's command to deny themselves, take up their crosses, and follow him. Scriptural directives made the matter as plain to him as it was to Protestants such as Calvin, Joye, and Bullinger. Paul said to Timothy that all who would live godly in Christ must suffer persecution; the Lord told his apostles that they would be hated for his sake. From this it "must irrefutably [*onwederspreke-lijck*] follow that all servants of God, all godly people, all the disciples of Jesus Christ, must suffer persecution for the sake of his name and be tried through many sorts of temptations." Van Stoelwijck condemned as hypocrites those alleged Christians who fled the cross by complying with Catholic practices, in stark contrast to "the true saints and servants of God, who would rather suffer death than break God's commandment." He linked Old Testament examples, including Daniel, Eleazar, and the Maccabees, directly to the present: "Yes, how many saints and witnesses of Jesus Christ are now still hated, persecuted, killed by the Babylonian whore, because they will not drink of the wine of her whoring [*hoerderie*] nor have community with her idolatrous works."[128] For van Stoelwijck as for Calvin, martyrs filled the same niche. They proved that the imperative to die rather than transgress God's commandments, while difficult and demanding, could be fulfilled.

To his wife, children, siblings, and other relatives, Jan Claes wrote prison letters packed with biblical quotations, paraphrases, and allusions. He told family members to model themselves on Christ, to focus on God's reward for perseverance, and to heed the reason why he was suffering. Combining James 5:10, 1 Pet. 2:21, and Acts 14:22, he directed his wife to "take Jesus Christ for an example, the way that he went before us, and that we must enter into the kingdom of heaven through much tribulation." He was not suffering as a wrongdoer (1 Pet. 4:15), he told his relatives, but for the fifteen-hundred-year-old teachings of Christ and the apostles, which Christ "sealed with his blood, and which the disciples preached and taught and confirmed with their blood."[129] Such convictions could only have pleased Menno. He would have approved, too, that stories about Mennonite martyrs were being "spread everywhere both orally and in writing [*ouer al mit mont ende schrift*] by some of his followers," as Blesdijk complained in the mid-1540s.[130]

As among Protestants, a martyrological sensibility among Mennonites long antedated a martyrology. Moreover, in a second parallel to the Protestant story, Menno and Dirk Philips, another important leader, wrote anti-Nicodemite works in the 1550s and early 1560s. Stiffer resistance greeted the expansion of Calvinism, with growing numbers of Protestants executed for their faith. The same was true for Mennonites in the Low Countries, particularly in the south, after Charles V promulgated the "Bloody Placard" of 1550. In Ghent, where no executions of *doopsgezinden* had occurred during the 1540s, there were thirty-eight in the 1550s and sixty-one in the following decade. Towns such as Bruges and Kortrijk followed a similar pattern.[131] Fully aware of the threat of violent death, Menno and Philips urged their followers to constancy, to avoid the contamination of idolatry. Indeed, their very awareness of Mennonite vulnerability made their admonitions especially important, for to recant was to risk damnation. Their arguments rested on scripture and its direct relevance to Dutch Anabaptist circumstances.

Menno left the Low Countries for northern Germany in 1543. Still, he remained primarily oriented toward his native Friesland, Holland, and the southern provinces.[132] To followers in the Low Countries he directed his *Comforting Admonition on the Suffering, Cross, and Persecution of the Saints for the Sake of God's Word and His Testimony,* published in Fresenburg in 1554 or 1555.[133] It is Menno's most extensive, detailed treatment of anti-Nicodemite themes.

Persecutors and martyrs stand in radical opposition throughout the treatise. The message to endure suffering and death is unambiguous. Menno left few adjectives unsaid when railing against those who assailed his followers. They were "an unbelieving, fleshly, earthly, malevolent, blind, obdurate, lying, idolatrous, degenerate, hostile, cruel, unmerciful, horrible, lionlike, and murderous people." Nevertheless, they deserved prayer and pity rather than hatred. Despite self-serving justifications, their actions sprang from an inability to abide true Christian doctrine and life; and so they raged against it, a perspective common, mutatis mutandis, among Protestant writers.[134]

The wicked had always persecuted the righteous, a claim Menno supported by a long litany of Old and New Testament figures, beginning with Cain and Abel. These biblical predecessors were explicitly invoked for the "consolation and refreshment of all miserable, anxious, sorrowful hearts, who for righteousness' sake have to suffer oppression and misery in their flesh." Whoever reflected on these examples, Menno wrote, would "undoubtedly not re-nounce, but rather in all his oppression, crosses, and suffering, keep standing through God's grace and remain unwavering, devout, and strong, to the end." The unjust affliction of the righteous was no distant memory for vague edification, but a daily reality that demanded a flesh-and-blood response. Menno catalogued the atrocities committed against his followers, as Foxe would do for English Protestants in 1563. The call for Mennonites to model themselves on previous martyrs, thereby becoming models in turn, could hardly have been clearer:

> See, my worthy brothers, if you prove yourselves in your oppression and temptations as mentioned here, and with all patience drink of the cup of the Lord, profess Christ Jesus truly and his holy Word orally, let your-selves suffer for witnessing to him with complete steadfastness as mild lambs for the butcher's block [*slachtbanc*], then the name of the Lord will through you be praised, made holy and glorious, the hope of the saints will be revealed, the kingdom of heaven enlarged, God's Word known, and your poor, weak brethren and companions in the Lord strengthened and instructed through your courage.[135]

Considering the circumstances, it would be difficult to imagine a more direct exhortation to Mennonite martyrdom.

Another important Mennonite leader, Dirk Philips, echoed these ideas in works first published in the late 1550s and early 1560s. They were reprinted in his *Handbook of Christian Doctrine and Religion* (1564).[136] Philips's par-ticipation in the movement, like that of his brother Obbe, antedated Menno's. He was baptized in late 1533 or early 1534, just before Münster came under Anabaptist control, and became Menno's trusted colleague until Menno died in 1561.[137] The two concurred entirely about Christian suffering and martyrdom, themes that recur in Philips's writings.

Philips regarded the persecution of Christians as the inevitable result of conflict between "the people of God and the people of the devil," whose pedigrees reached back to Abel and Cain. Accordingly, "the children of God must suffer persecution from the children of the devil and the congrega-tion of Christ must be oppressed, driven out, and killed by the Antichristian assembly."[138] Indeed, matters were worse for Dutch Mennonites than they had been for the first Christians, who could flee from one town to another (Matt. 10:23), a relative luxury lacking in the Netherlands.[139] Yet comfort came from scripture, which showed "how all good prophets and true teachers have been persecuted from the beginning, and shall be persecuted to the end of the world, yes, even as the most high prophet and master, Jesus Christ, the Son of the living God, had to suffer and thus enter into his glory."[140] Ecclesiologically, persecution was a sign with which Christ marked his congregation—a view that Philips supported, in typical fashion, with a host of scriptural passages.[141] Persecution utterly distinguished God's children from the devil's: the "great whore of Babylon" would suffer eternal retribution, while her victims, slain for Christ, would be rewarded with eternal joy, fulfilling the number of white-robed saints prophesied in the book of Revelation.[142]

Within this framework, Philips urged Mennonites to hold fast, most insistently in his *Three Fundamental Admonitions* (1564). After massing biblical verses on the eventual triumph of the righteous, he told readers to "comfort and admonish yourselves among one another with such and similar comforting quotations from holy scripture, and do not let yourselves be terrified by the tyrants and persecutors."[143] He was unmistakably explicit: "do not be terrified by the pain and sting of death, by tortures . . . But take comfort that the Lord is with you in all your distress, goes with you in prison, fire, and water, suffers with you, is with you in life and death, and never forsakes you."[144] In 1559 Philips offered individual encouragement by letter to a woman named Ariaentgen, who was imprisoned in Antwerp.[145] Like Calvin and Viret, he composed anti-Nicodemite treatises and wrote consolatory letters to imprisoned fellow believers. Pastoral attention personalized prescription.

Mennonite martyrs got the message. Imprisoned in Antwerp before he was burned on October 21, 1551, Peter de Bruyne wrote that it was "a grace from God" to suffer injustice. "So remain patient in your oppression," he said, "and share in [*weset deelachtich*] Christ's suffering, that you might inherit the promises, for there is only a brief period of scorn to suffer and endure compared to the eternal fruit."[146] Before her drowning in Friesland in March 1559, Claesken Gaeledochter displayed the same "scripture-speak" ability so characteristic of Menno and Philips. By letter, she told her friends to take Christ as an example and to follow in his footsteps, for "all of scripture compels [*dwingen*] us that we should give ourselves over to and prepare ourselves to suffer, as Paul also says: 'If we suffer with him, so shall we rejoice with him,' 'just as the suffering of Christ is great in us, so great consolation comes to us through Jesus Christ,' and when we read that all holy men of God are tested through much oppression and suffering, and how joyfully they would accept that suffering—yes, they rejoiced so much that they were worthy to suffer for the name of God."[147] Soetken van den Houte, decapitated in Ghent in 1560, was concerned about the upbringing of her children. She wanted them to hear the Lord's voice, "just as many who have suffered from the time of Abel to the present have done; they have been despised, condemned, persecuted, killed because they would not follow the wicked world with its false prophets." After this came a batch of biblical passages about the necessity and blessedness of suffering.[148] Such examples could be multiplied at great length. Mennonite martyrs translated prescriptions into practice, just as their spiritual cousins had done in Germanic lands beginning in the 1520s. To those who became Mennonites, as to those who became Anabaptists in Switzerland or Germany, the dangers were only too obvious. They grasped the implications of their commitment, which was sealed by baptism.

The Character of The Sacrifice unto the Lord

Besides their martyrological mentality and anti-Nicodemite writings, Mennonites shared with Protestants the project of martyrology itself. In 1562 Jan Hendricks van Schoonrewoerd anonymously published *The Sacrifice unto the Lord* in Franeker.[149] In some ways this work closely resembles the Protestant collections. In its gathering of materials by and about the "sacrificed children of God . . . for the comfort and strengthening of Christ's sacrificial lambs who are sent to their deaths," the publication was intended to serve a purpose similar to that of the works by Foxe, Crespin, van Haemstede, and Rabus.[150] Like the Protestant martyrologies, it was very popular, becoming "the most influential devotional literature of the Mennonites, surpassing if not superseding the writings of Menno."[151] There were eleven editions through 1599; and as with Foxe, Crespin, and van Haemstede, subsequent editions added material about other martyrs.

At the same time, *The Sacrifice unto the Lord* differed from the Protestant martyrologies in significant ways. Perhaps most conspicuously, songs were central to the Mennonite collection. The second half of the martyrology consisted of twenty-five songs in the first edition of 1563. Only nine of the 131 martyrs named in these songs overlap with the martyrs whose writings comprise the work's first half. This suggests that the *Songbook* was intended as a supplement.[152] Protestants wrote songs about their martyrs and about steadfastness and suffering, but in none of their martyrologies do these songs play an integral role.

We can infer the importance of singing to Mennonites from the remarkable number of song collections they published beginning in the 1550s.[153] In addition, several of the martyr hymns from the *Songbook* took their tunes from a collection entitled *Various Songs (Veelderhande Liedekens)*, first published around 1552 and appropriated by Mennonites by 1559, at which time it included over two hundred songs.[154] As with the hymns from the Swiss *Ausbund*, the indication of *contrafacta* in the absence of musical notation assumed familiarity with the tunes and songs among the intended audience. The self-standing, supplemental character of the *Songbook* points to the essential role of songs in the transmission of the Mennonite martyrological heritage. It was these songs, not printed narratives, that recounted the imprisonment, interrogation, defense of doctrine, and heroic deaths of the martyrs.

Songs could preserve the essence of sixteenth-century martyrology—the link between doctrines and deaths—with highly compact accuracy. Van Haemstede, a Reformed Protestant, carefully excluded the Anabaptists executed in Antwerp in the later 1550s. Mennonite memorialists were no less scrupulous in dividing up the dead. A hymn in the *Songbook* not only mentioned every one of the seventy-two Anabaptists executed in Antwerp between August 27, 1555, and April 3, 1560, but also, with one exception, gave them in chronological order. Protestants were carefully excluded—as were the only two Anabaptists who recanted but were executed anyway.[155] One of the two who abjured was Gillis van Aken, who after Menno had been probably the most important Mennonite leader in the preceding years, a man who had baptized hundreds. One of his converts was Vincken Verwee, who a year later in Bruges refused to alter her views in order to mitigate her sentence. Speaking of van Aken, she stated that "it would grieve her to die as he had died, for he forsook his faith."[156] Word got around. Whoever wrote the song about the Antwerp martyrs was not prepared to twist the record, even for such a prominent leader. A false claim about his constancy would have cheapened the martyrs' sacrifice.

A new series of songs accompanied the martyrology beginning in 1570. Unlike the *Songbook* hymns, these songs were based directly on the prose materials in the first half of *The Sacrifice unto the Lord,* the prison writings of the martyrs themselves. As selected versifications of the original writings, they added no new material about the martyrs. They must therefore have served a different purpose than the prose, one pursued through singing. The songs were made up of materials "thought to be the most important [*principaelste*] or the most instructive [*leerachtichste*]," which were "taken and selected from the preceding sources."[157] This comment, however, offers few clues about their function for Mennonites. To learn more, we must examine the songs alongside their prose entries.

The Sacrifice unto the Lord contains almost no interpretive commentary, even less than Rabus's *History.* The only exceptions are its concise preface and still shorter afterword, a brief account of the sentencing of Jan Claes, and a terse paragraph on the execution of Hans van Overdam and Jannijn Buefkijn.[158] In the first edition, the entries on only three other martyrs (Stephen, Michael Sattler, and Anneken Jans) are taken from third-person accounts (the first of these being the Acts of the Apostles). The remaining twenty prose entries consist entirely of letters, interrogation accounts, and confessions of faith written by the martyrs themselves.[159] The martyrologist(s) here were not storytellers, but the assemblers of documents produced by the martyrs, to which they added uniform marginal biblical citations. The lapidary introductions to each martyr's writings contrast sharply with the Protestant writers' heavily interpretive prose, the latter apparent as early as the evangelical pamphlets of the 1520s.[160] Perhaps the difference stemmed from a lesser concern by Mennonite writers, compared to Protestants, to employ martyrs as propaganda to win converts or woo magistrates. Believers' baptism and the separatist impulse precluded appeals to authorities to adopt and impose Anabaptism. Consequently, editors were not broadcasting the meaning of Mennonite martyrs for would-be converts, but providing models of steadfastness to those already converted.

Mennonites told their martyr stories through rhyming songs rather than narrative prose. Out of prison writings ill-suited to memorization, the songs crafted catchy stanzas set to well-known tunes. They turned written recollections of interrogations, for example, into verses that evoked events. Claes de Praet recounted his questioning in Ghent in 1556. The song opened like this:

> On the sixth day the authorities came,
> summoning Claes with fairness;
> then he was enkindled by joy
> all heaviness left his heart
> he delighted himself in God.
>
> They began with questions
> "Have you received a baptism other
> than in your infancy?"
> Claes plainly made known his conviction [*gront*],
> boldly before the magistrates.[161]

As the stanzas progressed, in this song and similar ones, de Praet and other martyrs defended their views on baptism, the Lord's Supper, and other contentious issues, providing the content for the relationship between doctrines and deaths. As a genre, the songs were better suited to the preservation and spread of the martyrs' stories than was the prose on which they were based. They permitted even illiterate Mennonites to recount the martyrs' experience through the song-singing central to the group's religious life. Far from being redundant, such songs were integral to passing on the martyrological patrimony.

The Sacrifice unto the Lord was more exclusively regional than any of the Protestant martyrologies. It is decidedly a *Dutch* Anabaptist collection, provided the term denotes the Low Countries from Friesland to the southern provinces, plus Holland and Zeeland. Only three of the more than one hundred fifty martyrs in the martyrology and its songbook are not Dutch. Two of these are Christ himself and Stephen. The third was Michael Sattler: a Dutch translation of materials from the German *Brotherly Union* had been published in 1560 and was appropriated in the collection.[162] This provinciality differed from the international character of the Protestant martyrologies and the circle of leaders and exiles who produced them. In contrast to Protestant vitality in France and the southern Netherlands, for example, sixteenth-century Anabaptists never really conquered the French linguistic divide.[163] This regional exclusivity was partly shaped by the doctrinal differences between Mennonites and other Anabaptists. Just three years before the *Sacrifice unto the Lord* appeared, Menno had banned Rhineland Mennonites who had associated with the Swiss Brethren, following conferences with members of both groups in Strasbourg in 1554, 1555, and 1557.[164] Not until the early seventeenth century would Dutch Anabaptist martyrology be internationalized.

Finally, *The Sacrifice unto the Lord* implied but did not offer, as did the Protestant martyrologies, an alternative reading of the Christian past. It was not martyrology as history. The preface stated that "the poor, innocent, peaceful, defenseless little lamb" had been at all times, including the present, "hated, persecuted, and killed in his chosen members." Examples from Abraham through Paul followed, showing God's powerful action in his children.[165] The martyrology itself, however, skipped from Stephen in the Acts of the Apostles to Michael Sattler in 1527, with no transition whatsoever, no hint of any medieval "precursors," and the *Songbook* jumped from Christ's passion to Frans van Boolsweert in 1545. Except for four entries in the first half and two songs in the second, the first edition concerned martyrs from 1550–1561 only, making it chronologically narrower than the Protestant martyrologies as well. Menno occasionally referred to Eusebius, which suggests that the editor(s) might have known about and included some pre-Constantinian martyrs, as Hans de Ries and other Mennonite martyrologists would do in the seventeenth century.[166] Yet none appeared in *The Sacrifice unto the Lord*.

The lack of early Christian martyrs is probably attributable in part to the work's intended audience. In addition, Mennonites were not—at this point at least—trying to best Catholic or Protestant controversialists over the correct interpretation of the Christian past. Unlike Eusebius or Foxe, the editor(s) simply added biblical references to documents without creating a larger narrative. Indeed, there *was* as yet no larger narrative. The point was not to document God's support of his afflicted flock through time, but rather to show how snugly present persecution fit its scriptural template. Intense apocalyptic expectations and an almost exclusive biblicism did not inspire the writing of church history. It was enough to show latter-day Mennonites that God had strengthened his own in biblical times, just as he had sustained his contemporary martyrs. It was tacitly assumed that in the wider world, somewhere between the first Christians and the present, things had gone terribly awry.

The preface, afterword, and songs in *The Sacrifice unto the Lord* revealed interpretive points about the martyrs, what lessons the editor(s) and song-writers thought they taught. Much of this overlapped with attitudes expressed by Menno, Dirk Philips, and the martyrs themselves. In fact, the first third of the martyrology's preface closely followed the preface to Menno's *Comforting Admonition*.[167] Without question, whoever wrote the preface to *The Sacrifice unto the Lord* had a copy of Menno's work at hand. This proves that the Mennonite martyrologist(s) linked anti-Nicodemism and martyrology in 1562.

The two prefaces began with the same argument. In these last days, after centuries of ignorance, God has opened the eyes of some and led them into new life, guiding hungry sheep away from faithless shepherds and their human doctrines to "their only and eternal shepherd, Jesus Christ." Accordingly, the gates of hell afflicted the Lamb, against whose members "the serpent's anger" raged with the sword, water, and fire. It has been so since the beginning and would remain so until Christ's return.[168] Here the two prefaces diverged, although they remained closely related: the martyrology provided a record of what Menno had encouraged in the *Comforting Admonition*.

Menno wrote that "especially in our time" the cross of Christ appeared to his children and exalted the Lord. He was compelled to admonish his "dear brothers and sisters" about the "suffering, cross, and persecution of the saints" so that they too might hold firm, as did the persecuted men and women of the Old and New Testaments. This constancy "many devout witnesses of our time at present demonstrate," and those who persevered would "receive the promised crown."[169]

The editor(s) of *The Sacrifice unto the Lord* began the same way, about the cross of Christ appearing again. It seemed fitting, the preface stated, "to gather together confessions of faith, letters, and testaments from some of the sacrificed children of God (for the comfort and strength of all lovers of the truth), in which one may perceive and understand how powerfully God still works in his chosen ones, and comforts, strengthens, and helps them in time of need, just as we also find abundantly with many examples in both the Old and New Testaments."[170] The martyrologist(s) described what Menno had prescribed. *The Sacrifice unto the Lord* carried forward his project by documenting the "many devout witnesses of our time," with the same practical objective: to strengthen and console fellow believers. The martyrology personalized the anonymity of Menno's allusion with names, writings, and songs—the testimony of real men and women who had made the supreme sacrifice for their faith.

The martyrology's preface continued. God's action in the martyrs was a specific instance of his power more broadly at work in his children. The biblical examples in the preface included those who were neither executed nor even persecuted in any obvious sense. The point was that God had comforted both Abraham, for example, as well as those executed in Flanders in the 1550s. A pragmatic directive followed: the "dear reader" was to "take an example" from these cases; encirclement by hundreds of thousands would not cause fear (Ps. 3:6–7), and the Lord forsook no one who hoped in him (Sir. 2:10).[171] Finally, a blend of eight biblical verses urged readers to seek God wholeheartedly, so that he might preserve them too through every difficulty, and that they too might receive the promised crown of eternal life. According to the martyrology's preface, then, the martyrs were to encourage persecuted Mennonites. Slain fellow believers dramatically displayed God's power.

A number of songs in the martyrology reinforced this theme. The songs about Anneken Jans and Stephen offered each as "a beautiful example" [*een schoon voorbeelt*].[172] From the martyrdom of Hans van Overdam and Jannijn Buefkijn, one was to "take an example from these servants, / that with them you receive the reward," understood as eternal life.[173] Since Joos 't Kindt, executed in Kortrijk in July 1553, had "devoutly carried out the struggle / as a bold, unperturbed fighter," others should "go forth in the same way with desire / that you might repose with God's friend."[174]

Another recurrent theme, one stressed in the afterword as well, is the sharp division between God and the devil, goodness and evil, darkness and light. These two cosmic forces clashed concretely in the encounter between martyrs and their persecutors. "Dear reader," the afterword intoned in commenting on the whole martyrology, "note the distinction, namely, which is the way of the Lord and the way of the devil, which the proper service of God and the service of devils and idols, who are the children of God and the children of the devil, who persecutes and who is persecuted."[175] This is the same biblical bipolarity that permeated the Protestant martyrological literature. Mennonite separatism reinforced it. The song about Stephen's martyrdom affirmed the Johannine idea that the "dark world cannot bear / the clear light of God's word and law." The last stanza about Peter van Wervick contrasted the "hypocrites" absorbed in the "teaching of Antichrist" with a directive to "remain by the word of the Lord."[176] Several hymns from the *Songbook* condemned authorities, asked them to stop persecuting God's innocent children, or both.[177] Others bemoaned the dreary sadness of an age burdened by persecution and martyrdom.[178] Unlike Protestants, Anabaptists did not anticipate a time when rulers would stop persecuting and start enforcing Anabaptist orthodoxy. Without the prospect or even desire for state support, Dutch Mennonites could at best hope for toleration as they waited for the apocalypse. Several decades' experience suggested little cause for optimism.

By the time their martyrology and its songbook appeared, the Mennonites were the most vigorous Anabaptist group in the Low Countries. Paradoxically, martyrdom might well have helped more than it hurt. It explained in compelling terms what was happening to them, and why. Persecution confirmed that the brothers and sisters really were the Lord's chosen flock, hated by a hostile world that could not bear his truth. In the mid- to late 1550s Tertullian's dictum looked as convincing to Mennonites as to Calvinists: members of both groups were being executed, yet their movements were growing. Just as doctrinal disagreements among Protestants made for friction over martyrs, however, analogous disputes among Dutch Mennonites did likewise. This contentiousness, plus the changes in Dutch society and the Mennonites' place within it, were the two principal forces that began to reshape the Mennonite martyrological tradition in the later sixteenth century.

The Transformation of the Dutch Mennonite Martyrological Tradition

The Sacrifice unto the Lord was a palm-sized collection of martyrs' letters and songs. From the 1560s to 1660 it grew into a huge folio, a chronicle of those persecuted for believers' baptism from biblical times to the seventeenth century. The position of Mennonites in Dutch society over the same period changed no less dramatically. Members of a once-hunted sect became respectable and frequently prosperous citizens in Holland's towns. The changing significance of Mennonite martyrs paralleled the group's altered place in Dutch society.

Martyrological Publications and Microconfessionalization in the Late Sixteenth Century

Scholars have largely ignored *The Sacrifice unto the Lord*. Consequently, they have neglected the relationship among its subsequent editions, other martyrological publications, and the schisms among Dutch Mennonites in the later sixteenth century. Most Protestant pamphlets concerning martyrs were published prior to the massive Protestant martyrologies. The large majority of Dutch Anabaptist martyrological publications, by contrast, appeared after the first edition of *The Sacrifice unto the Lord*. Only a handful were published before 1562, whereas at least thirty editions of no fewer than sixteen different works, by or about nineteen different martyrs, appeared between 1565 and 1595, twenty-two of them between 1577 and 1588.[179]

At least two factors help to explain this sudden profusion of print. First, the success of *The Sacrifice unto the Lord*, with four editions between 1562–1563 and 1570, indicated considerable demand for the genre. Mennonites, their numbers growing, wanted to read about their martyrs. Second, greater de facto religious tolerance in the north, especially after the Pacification of Ghent in 1576, diminished the danger for and permitted greater access to printers. Virtually all these publications appeared in the northern provinces, as did the editions of *The Sacrifice unto the Lord.*[180] Numerous printers and booksellers were among the Mennonites who migrated northward in these decades, a movement that accelerated after 1585, when Catholic rule was reestablished in the south.[181] The lesser publications resemble *The Sacrifice unto the Lord* in content: most are confessions of faith, prison letters by and to the martyrs, and songs, or some combination thereof.[182] However, they also include several treatises written by martyrs, such as Valerius Schoolmeester's *Test of Faith* and Thijs Joriaens's work on the incarnation of Christ, for which the martyrology offered neither precedent nor equivalent.[183]

A number of these sources were incorporated into subsequent editions of *The Sacrifice unto the Lord.* Like the martyrologies by Foxe, Crespin, and van Haemstede, the collection was in this respect a living book, whose editors were alert to the appearance of relevant publications.[184] Considering what was available to them, however, it is striking how much they chose *not* to include. The editors ignored, for example, collections of nineteen letters by Jacob de Roore and twenty-eight by Joos Verkindert, both of which were published more than once.[185] Given the movement of Mennonites in these decades and their interregional communication, it is implausible that the martyrology's additions reflect only the sources that happened to be available to the compilers. Indeed, such a hypothesis is disproved by the inclusion of a song about the Ghent martyrs in the Nicolaes (II) Biestkens edition of 1578, coupled with the exclusion of Herman Timmerman's *Confession of Faith* with which it was first published the previous year.[186] An active editorial hand was at work.

Why were so many of these sources absent from later editions of *The Sacrifice unto the Lord?* Samuel Cramer implied that adding them would have made the collection unwieldy,[187] but this explanation is unsatisfactory. The editors might have included only a letter or two from each of these other martyrs without appreciably swelling its size. Or they might have published successive installments of their martyrology, as Crespin did in the 1550s and early 1560s. Their selectivity was a function of the schisms among Dutch Mennonites, specifically the split between the Waterlanders and the rest of the Dutch Mennonites that unfolded between 1555 and 1557, and the division of the latter into Frisian and Flemish Mennonites in 1566–1567.[188] The Waterlanders were more lenient than Menno on the disciplinary practice of banning and shunning, and much more than Dirk Philips and Lenaert Bouwens. The disagreement resulted in schism. Disputes about congregational autonomy and church organization, compounded by cultural differences between southerners seeking refuge among their northern hosts, led to the mutual banning of Frisians and Flemish in 1566. In the following year, repeated attempts at reconciliation failed; the split hardened. Divisions ensued within Mennonite congregations throughout the Low Countries. "Frisian" and "Flemish" came to denote the side taken in the schism rather than geographical regions.[189]

The martyrs' blood helped to prevent the healing of this wound among the Dutch Mennonites. *The Sacrifice unto the Lord* might originally have been a nonpartisan collection, as Cramer argued, when published in 1562–1563, before the schism between Frisian and Flemish Mennonites. A look at some of the martyrs excluded from subsequent editions, however, suggests a Frisian appropriation of the martyrology. The editors ignored Jacob de Roore, an important Flemish Anabaptist leader who was baptized by Gillis van Aken in 1554 and executed in Bruges in June 1569.[190] They passed over letters, a song, and a treatise by Thijs Joriaens, who prior to his execution in Muiden had sided with the Flemish and strongly opposed the Frisians.[191] They disregarded letters by Joos Verkindert and Laurens Andries, members of Antwerp's important Mennonite congregation. After the Frisian-Flemish schism, this community made non-Flemish Anabaptists submit to (re)baptism in order to join them, a practice insulting to the Frisians.[192] In short, the editors of *The Sacrifice unto the Lord* excluded Flemish Mennonite martyrs, with whom they no longer shared fellowship.

In all likelihood, *The Sacrifice unto the Lord* never sought to include the Waterlanders. By the time the first edition appeared, they had already fallen afoul of the major Mennonite leaders. In 1560 Herman Timmerman, who seems to have been either an elder or a preacher in Antwerp's Waterlander congregation, publicly criticized both Menno and Philips on the ban, an action that could not have pleased the Frisians.[193] Timmerman's *Short Confession* (1577) found no place in any subsequent edition of *The Sacrifice unto the Lord*. A song about Gerrit Cornelis, however, who was apparently a Frisian, was included. He was baptized around 1563 by an advocate of strict banning and shunning, Lenaert Bouwens; this distinguished him from the Waterlanders.[194] Christiaen Rijcen, by contrast, apparently held such mild views about discipline that he was suspended from his preaching ministry in Leiden. This leniency, plus his paraphrasing of the Flemish leader Jacob de Roore, whom he mentioned by name, in one of his own letters, would not have endeared him to the Frisians.[195] None of Rijcen's letters appear in the four editions of the martyrology published after his execution in 1588.

In the late sixteenth century, the editors of *The Sacrifice of the Lord* construed the Dutch Mennonite martyrological tradition in ways that reflected the schisms of the 1550s and 1560s. The midcentury Protestant martyrologists overlooked doctrinal differences between Reformed and Lutheran to help strengthen the solidarity of an international movement. Frisian Mennonites favored the preservation of group identity in the wake of recent breaches within the brotherhood. Protestants used their martyrs to build bridges against an external threat; Frisian Mennonites wanted walls to preserve differences wrought by internal schism.

Non-Frisian Mennonites seem to have been erecting barriers of their own. Several collections of pamphlets, comprised of works mostly ignored by the editors of *The Sacrifice unto the Lord,* have survived in sixteenth-century bindings, proving that someone assembled them shortly after publication.[196] Two of these collections share the same six pamphlets (published by two or three different printers over a nine-year period) and virtually identical bindings. Accordingly, it is very likely that the pamphlets were purchased and gathered by the same person or group and bound by the same bookbinder, or perhaps assembled by the same bookseller (see Figure 19). These appear to be two exemplars of a do-it-yourself Mennonite martyrology, composed entirely of materials published after *The Sacrifice unto the Lord* first appeared. Delft printer Albrecht Hendricxs published six different martyrological pamphlets

Figure 19. Sixteenth-century bindings of two collections of Mennonite martyr pamphlets. Reproduced with permission of Amsterdam Doopsgezinde Bibliotheek (left) and Amsterdam University Library (right).

in 1577. The only new material in his 1578 edition of *The Sacrifice unto the Lord,* however, compared to the 1570 edition, was a song about two Delft martyrs of 1571. His edition of the martyrology, therefore, should probably be seen as a supplement to the 1577 pamphlets, intended primarily for Flemish Mennonites.[197] Because almost all of the martyrology's witnesses antedated the Frisian-Flemish schism, the Flemish had as much claim on them as did the Frisians. In his 1578 edition of the martyrology, Hendricxs bypassed materials about Hendrick Verstralen and Mayken Deynoots, since he had published their pamphlet the year before. But for Nicolaes Biestkens and the targeted Frisians of his 1578 edition, Verstralen and Deynoots were unobjectionable additions because nothing in their writings smacked of Flemish views.[198] Further research might disclose whether the anomalous 1592 edition of *The Sacrifice of the Lord*—which contains letters to Mennonites imprisoned in Ghent that are lacking in the 1595 and 1599 editions—is a non-Frisian printing, and whether the subsequent exclusion of these letters reflects a Frisian reaction.[199]

The divisions among Dutch Mennonites left traces in the publication history of *The Sacrifice unto the Lord* as well as other contemporary works about their martyrs. The eleven editions of the martyrology and their apparent corresponding group affiliations are summarized in Figure 20. Given the Mennonites' microconfessional antagonisms, the Frisians were probably no more likely to honor Jacob de Roore than John Foxe was to exalt Thomas More. The larger structure of martyrdom in early modern Christianity—the link between confessional affiliation and martyr recognition—was replicated on a smaller scale within one branch of Anabaptism.

The Triumph of Inclusivity and the Perils of Toleration

In the late sixteenth century the experience of all Mennonites began to change. Persecution ebbed, diminishing the possibility of martyrdom. The last person put to death in the north was Reytse Aysses van Oldeboorn, at Leeuwarden in 1574.[200] Executions persisted in the south, even reviving somewhat after 1585, when Alessandro Farnese assumed control of the region for Philip II. Anneken Emelt, who was buried alive outside of Brussels in July 1597, was the last person executed in the south.[201] In the heart of Brussels itself, Hendrik Vos and Johann van den Esschen had become the first two evangelical martyrs sixty-four years before. The eleventh and final edition of *The Sacrifice unto the Lord* was published in 1599. Greater religious toleration by the north's new government permitted Mennonites to do more than merely survive and brace for persecution.

The schisms, however, continued. The fundamental issue remained the

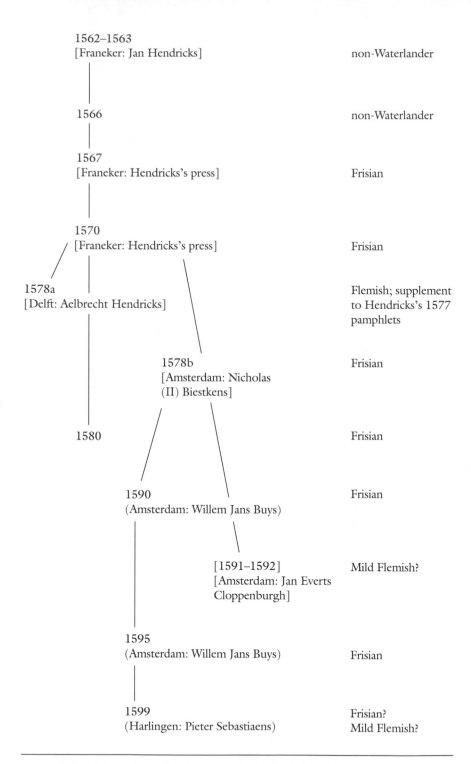

1562–1563
[Franeker: Jan Hendricks]   non-Waterlander

1566   non-Waterlander

1567
[Franeker: Hendricks's press]   Frisian

1570
[Franeker: Hendricks's press]   Frisian

1578a
[Delft: Aelbrecht Hendricks]   Flemish; supplement
                                                                              to Hendricks's 1577
                                                                              pamphlets

1578b   Frisian
[Amsterdam: Nicholas
(II) Biestkens]

1580   Frisian

1590   Frisian
(Amsterdam: Willem Jans Buys)

[1591–1592]   Mild Flemish?
[Amsterdam: Jan Everts
Cloppenburgh]

1595   Frisian
(Amsterdam: Willem Jans Buys)

1599   Frisian?
(Harlingen: Pieter Sebastiaens)   Mild Flemish?

Figure 20. Editions of *The Sacrifice unto the Lord* and their relationship to
Mennonite groups.

strictness and severity of discipline as applied within the group. The Flemish had split into "Old" and "Mild" (or simply "Flemish") factions by 1586, the Frisians into "Old" and "Young" Frisians by 1589.[202] The Waterlanders, more concerned about divisions within the broader movement than about uniformity of doctrine and practice, sought to reunify as many factions as possible. Leading this effort was Hans de Ries (1553–1638), whose initiative led to the union of the Waterlanders and High German Mennonites in 1591. Under de Ries, too, the Bevredigde Broederschap (Reconciled Brotherhood) was created in 1601, providing an umbrella organization for Waterlander congregations, High German Mennonites, and Young Frisians. Many of the Germans and Young Frisians, however, withdrew in 1613.[203] Lasting reconciliation proved elusive.

De Ries was the chief editor of the new Mennonite martyrology published at Haarlem in 1615, the *History of the Martyrs or Genuine Witnesses of Jesus Christ*.[204] This collection continued the tradition of *The Sacrifice unto the Lord*. Yet right from the elaborate title page, with its multiple images of executions, the *History* diverged from the earlier collection. The 1617 and 1626 editions bore the same title page design (see Figure 21).[205] By contrast, *The Sacrifice unto the Lord* contained no illustrations. The *History of the Martyrs* was much longer, with a larger format, than the first martyrology (1,000 double-column pages) with correspondingly more martyrs (over 600). De Ries's extensive preface more nearly resembled the introductory material in the Protestant martyrologies than the short preface in *The Sacrifice unto the Lord*. Moreover, his authorial presence was considerable throughout the work. Besides reprinting martyrs' writings, he offered comments and judgments as he shaped stories in his own narrative voice, one which would remain present decades later in van Braght's *Martyrs' Mirror*. New types of sources also appeared, such as legal documents relevant to the persecution of Anabaptists.[206] In these respects, and in drawing on Bernard of Clairvaux and others to argue that certain medieval Christians were executed for opposing infant baptism, de Ries operated much like Foxe or Crespin—both of whom he referred to in his preface.[207] A genuine history, rather than simply a compendium of martyrs' writings and songs, was taking shape.

In this new collection, de Ries dropped the songs that had been added in 1570 to the first half of *The Sacrifice unto the Lord*. Even more significantly, he changed the martyrology's *Songbook* hymns from rhyming poetry into prose. No information about the martyrs was lost; yet the displacement of one narrative genre by another reflected new realities in Mennonite life.[208] Martyr stories were no longer sung in clandestine gatherings, but rather read by increasingly educated Mennonites in newly secure surroundings. Not coincidentally, the early decades of the seventeenth century witnessed a growing Mennonite preference for psalm-singing, while the popularity of the earlier

Figure 21. Title page of *History of the Genuine Witnesses of Jesus Christ* (*Historie der Warachtighe getuygen Jesu Christi* [Hoorn: Zacharias Cornelisz, 1617]). Reproduced with permission of Amsterdam University Library.

song collections declined.[209] More than thirty years before, de Ries himself had noted "songs of the cross" [*cruyschliederen*] as a major category of Mennonite songs, which were "profitable to be sung at times when the congregation is burdened with the cross and suffering."[210] In the intervening generation, those times had passed. The direct relevance of such hymns and the closely related martyr songs dwindled with the waning threat of martyrdom. Now the narrative element of the martyrs' legacy was rendered in prose—and printed in a book available for the hefty price of three guilders.[211]

Another difference between the new martyrology and *The Sacrifice unto the Lord* was even more significant—and more controversial. By design, de Ries's collection was much more extensive than its predecessor. De Ries deconfessionalized and internationalized Anabaptist martyrology in pursuit of his reconciliatory aims. An important collaborator on the martyrology was Jacques Outerman (ca. 1547–1639), a Mild Flemish leader who also sought reunification among the Mennonite groups. It was Outerman's relatively lenient views on discipline that had fostered the split within the Flemish Mennonites in 1586.[212]

In the sixteenth century, the Dutch Mennonites were conspicuous among Anabaptists in not borrowing martyr songs from other groups. Although the Swiss Brethren adapted eleven hymns from *The Sacrifice unto the Lord* during or after 1570,[213] none of their own martyr songs was incorporated into the Dutch collection. Similarly, while the Hutterites borrowed numerous songs about early Swiss and south German martyrs from the Swiss Brethren,[214] the Dutch Mennonites adopted no songs from the Hutterites. To have done so would have implied doctrinal agreement with these martyrs, an issue vexing enough among the Mennonites themselves. In the mid- and late 1550s, German Mennonites from the Rhineland merged with the Swiss Brethren, using the memory of Michael Sattler and their shared experience of persecution to help effect the union. Menno responded by excommunicating the Rhinelanders.[215]

De Ries was sensitive to the martyrological heritage, having spent his youth "under the cross." As a young Waterlander convert returning from North Holland to his native Antwerp, he witnessed the burning of Hans Bret on January 4, 1577. The following year he spent a month imprisoned in Middelburg, Zeeland, for his religious views.[216] Likely recalling formative images from decades past, he wrote in the martyrology's preface of the "invincible power of God and of faith which bloomed forth, appeared, and was manifest in the holy martyrs . . . both men and women, servants or maids, no matter how young or old they were."[217] Much like earlier writers, de Ries emphasized the dichotomy between the martyrs and their persecutors; he deftly wove biblical verses into a linguistic fabric praising the martyrs' heroism; and he catalogued their many predecessors in the Old and New Testaments, from Abel through the apostles.[218]

Yet by recasting the Dutch Mennonite martyrological tradition in an inclusive, Waterlander mold, de Ries acted boldly. His initiative was a striking departure from the microconfessionalization of Mennonite martyrology. Throughout his preface he spoke revealingly of "those baptized according to Christ's ordinance" [*de gedoopten nae Christi ordeninghe*]. This was his broad doctrinal criterion that justified the inclusion of Anabaptists from different Mennonite factions as well as from the Swiss Brethren, the Hutterites, and other groups. For years prior to the work's publication, Mennonites had collected materials about martyrs unrepresented in *The Sacrifice unto the Lord.* The Waterlanders dispatched information gatherers to Germany, Austria, and Moravia for this purpose.[219]

De Ries was self-conscious about publishing the fruit of this work in his martyrology. "We might also be asked," he wrote,

> seeing that those baptized according to Christ's ordinance are divided into different peoples, why we have put all their martyrs in one book with the others without making any distinction, just as if all belonged to one church. To which we answer thus: we want to show ourselves in these [martyrs] not as sectarian but as nonpartisan [*onpartydige*] Christians, for we, having considered carefully the differences and the reasons for the division of these peoples, which [the martyrs] confessed in speech, we do not find that they differ concerning any article of Christian faith about which anyone might rightly be considered or judged as unbelieving, damned, or not saved.[220]

This was a contentious statement about religious truth and Christian identity. Essentially, de Ries claimed that none of the differences among the nonviolent sixteenth-century Anabaptist groups justified their mutual exclusiveness any more than differences among Roman Catholic religious orders kept them from belonging to the same church.[221] So much for all the effort spent on the Melchiorite doctrine of the incarnation or the proper application of Christian discipline! De Ries engaged the martyrologist's project of rightly linking doctrines and deaths ("it is true that suffering alone produces no martyrs, but the good cause for which they suffered")[222] but so wide was his range of *adiaphora* (indifferent matters) that it greatly altered Dutch Mennonite martyrology. Menno's followers now comprised only one branch of an Anabaptist tree that spread across Europe. After the collapse of the Bevredigde Broederschap in 1613, the new martyrology sought to unify the sects that espoused believers' baptism. It sought to mold the heroic heritage of past generations into a foundation for the future.

In the long run de Ries's vision carried the day. Most of the sixteenth-century material in van Braght's *Martyrs' Mirror* had appeared in the *History of the Martyrs* forty-five years earlier. To this extent, Kühler correctly argued that de Ries was more important than van Braght in shaping Mennonite martyrology.[223] It is de Ries's contours that have remained to the present. In 1615, however, he had to have known that remaking the relationship between doctrines and deaths would prove controversial. If specific doctrines and practices were highly esteemed, then a martyrology would stir dissent whose raison d'être depended on overlooking them. Objections to de Ries's work came from the strictest Mennonite group, the Old Frisians, especially from their most important leader at the time, Peter Jans Twisck (1565–1636).

In 1617 Twisck oversaw the publication of the *History of the True Witnesses of Jesus Christ*. A new preface and modified title accompanied this Old Frisian edition of the same martyrology that de Ries had published two years earlier.[224] Twisck did not, however, attack Waterlander inclusiveness directly, insisting on the differences that de Ries had minimized. Such would have required a laborious examination of the martyrs' views, one by one, pruning away those who failed to measure up. Instead, he and his colleague, Syvaert Pieters, simply claimed that all the martyrs in the new collection had believed alike: "in the reading of this book, one cannot find that any of those sacrificed made a wayward confession of faith in their fetters, but one finds each of them . . . unanimous [*een stemmich*] with the others."[225] The very next sentence in the preface specified, among others, Herman Timmerman and Jacob de Roore—respectively a critic of Menno on the ban and the Flemish Anabaptist leader whom the later editors of *The Sacrifice unto the Lord* had avoided.

Twisck was loath to dismember the impressive martyrological community that de Ries and others had assembled. Nevertheless, he rejected any implicit marginalization of Menno's and Dirk Philips's teachings, which he held in the highest regard. Accordingly, his colleague Pieters specified the purported content of the martyrs' confessional unanimity in a thirty-three-article, Old Frisian confession of faith. At length and in detail, it covered everything from the existence and nature of God the Father to the swearing of oaths and the practice of the ban.[226] In short, Pieters and Twisck contended that all the martyrs held views that harmonized with Old Frisian teachings as elaborated in this confession of faith.

Such a claim was dubious, though not necessarily inflammatory. Given the Waterlanders' powerful desire for reconciliation, they were perhaps disposed to overlook this proprietary claim by the Old Frisians. De Ries's endeavor had not been directly attacked. This changed in 1626, when the Old Frisians published another edition of the martyrology at Hoorn. After 1617, Flemish Mennonites had pointed out to them that in several places, de Ries and company had omitted Menno's doctrine of the incarnation from the martyrs' writings included in the 1615 edition of the *History of the Martyrs.* Twisck and his colleagues had unknowingly reproduced the deletions two years later.[227]

When the Old Frisians realized what had happened, they responded angrily. In the 1626 preface they accused the Waterlanders of intentionally corrupting the martyrs' writings to promote their own martyrological community, one that downplayed divisive doctrines. In addition to the "many noteworthy errors" in the 1615 and 1617 editions, there was "some falsification regarding the article of the incarnation of our dear Lord Jesus Christ." This deliberate tampering implied that "these witnesses might have had a different foundation regarding the aforementioned article than the one they confessed so clearly and openly to their examiners and murderers, and for which they died."[228] Along with the practice of banning and shunning, Menno's teaching about the incarnation, taken over largely from Melchior Hoffman, had indeed proved a stumbling block in meetings between Dutch Mennonites and other Anabaptists in the sixteenth century.[229] By altering this doctrine, the Waterlanders had jeopardized the meaning of the deaths, and therefore the status of the martyrs.

Unlike the Old Frisian appropriation of 1617, this attack directly impugned the Waterlanders' motivation and integrity. Probably because de Ries was otherwise occupied, a lay preacher, Hans Alenson, replied in 1630.[230] He defended the original compilers, asserting that the texts simply had been handled sloppily by typesetters. If they had sought to cut references to Menno's doctrine, Alenson asked, why would the editors have altered five texts but retained lengthier defenses of the doctrine in other martyrs' writings?[231] In addition, Alenson demolished the claim that all the martyrs' views harmonized with the Old Frisian confession of faith. He revealed the same critical abilities that Catholic controversialists used against the overarching Protestant martyrological community. Not all the martyrs could have held Menno's doctrine of the incarnation, for example, since some were executed before he converted and was baptized. Moreover, specific verses from the Swiss *Ausbund,* which Alenson quoted, directly contradicted Menno's view. Alenson noted, too, the inconsistency of including Flemish Mennonites such as Thijs Joriaens and Jacob de Roore while maintaining, as Old Frisians, that the contemporary Flemish were rightly banned and shunned. Perhaps most unsettling, Alenson used Menno himself against the Old Frisians. Menno adopted a view of banning and shunning that approached the Old Frisian teaching only in 1557 or 1558. Hence all Anabaptists executed earlier than this would have to be excluded.[232] In short, Alenson demonstrated that the Old Frisians could not have their cake and eat it too: they could not both accept the inclusive community of martyrs "baptized according to Christ's ordinance" and claim that all had held views consistent with Old Frisian teaching. The martyrs' own writings and the variegated Anabaptist past exploded Twisck's claim about what the martyrs had believed. If the Old Frisians—or anyone else—wanted to construe narrowly the doctrines for which their martyrs had died, they would have to shrink their martyrological community accordingly.[233]

As if to underscore Alenson's point, de Ries and the Waterlanders published a larger martyrology in 1631–1632. It was the first entitled the *Martyrs' Mirror.* In sketching the publication history of the previous collections, they noted the claim that "all the martyrs" in the work had "believed and felt" the same views specified in the Old Frisian confession of faith. "We indeed trust," they wrote, "that all these witnesses were unanimous in the necessary [*noodighe*] articles of faith," which they had backed up with their deeds. Such articles included belief in the one eternal God and his only son, deliverance from sins through Christ, the covenantal commitment of baptism, and a reward for following the Lord. "But we also know," they continued, "that concerning many and various points not every single one of them had the same view and opinion." Nevertheless, "the holy crown of the martyrs is not contingent on the variation among such points," but rather depended on the shared doctrinal fundamentals combined with their heroic actions.[234] The breadth of the community of martyrs was a function of de Ries's "necessary articles of faith." The key issue was not doctrinal disputes among Mennonite groups, but rather the commonalities that distinguished them from Catholics and Protestants: Anabaptist martyrs belonged to churches that were always oppressed, not to churches that legitimated persecution.[235]

This point fit nicely with a widening historical vision, one that continued to fill the gap between biblical times and the sixteenth century. The 1615 collection had somewhat randomly mentioned a few pre-Reformation, proto-Anabaptist martyrs. The new martyrology contained a lengthy, separate prologue elaborating "the conformity of the ancient, apostolic church with the church of these martyrs, as well as the lasting persecution of the suffering of the martyrs, from the time of Christ to the beginning of this *Martyrs' Mirror.*"[236] The same process occurred among Protestants in the increasingly detailed pre-Reformation treatments in Foxe between 1554 and 1570, and in Crespin between 1554 and 1582. For the ancient martyrs, de Ries and his collaborators drew primarily on Eusebius. For the medieval period their principal source was the monumental Counter-Reformation church history, the *Ecclesiastical Annals* of Caesar Baronius—which they turned against its author. Mennonite martyrology had become historical writing.

The title *Martyrs' Mirror* was new, reflecting another concern of Mennonite leaders. Many Mennonites now occupied niches in Dutch society that would have been inconceivable to their sixteenth-century forebears. They were secure, stable, and increasingly prosperous participants in the trade-based boom of the Dutch economy. Amsterdam's Waterlander community counted dozens of well-to-do Mennonites. Among them, for example, was Arent Dircks Bosch, whose entrepreneurial success helped him purchase a house on the Herengracht, the city's most exclusive street, by 1655, and whose son was deeply involved in the runaway tulip speculation of the 1630s. De Ries himself mentored the wealthy cloth merchant and lay preacher Cornelis Claes Anslo, who was painted by and patronized Rembrandt.[237] The burgeoning size and ever more luxurious presentation of the martyrologies themselves, from *The Sacrifice unto the Lord* through the second edition of van Bragt (1685), paralleled the socioeconomic rise of the Mennonites. The martyrologies metamorphosed from a concealable pocket book measuring about 3¾″ by 2¾″ by 1¼″, into a huge, two-volume "coffee table book" with detailed engravings by the artist Jan Luyken, measuring 14″ by 9½″ by 4″ (see Figure 22).

De Ries feared that material prosperity inevitably corroded religious commitment. He had said nothing about this in 1615. When he broached the issue in 1631, then, it is unlikely that he was simply parroting traditional clerical critiques of luxury and greed. Important changes were afoot in cities like Haarlem and Amsterdam. Considering the space he devoted to each concern, by 1631 Mennonite worldliness was more pressing than the reunification of Mennonite factions.[238] De Ries cautioned readers against "the idol of riches and avarice" and asked whether they held Christ as their greatest treasure. Indeed, he almost waxed nostalgic for the days of persecution and martyrdom, contrasting them with the creeping complacency of the present:

How many there are who, having lost the initial zeal and love, have become cold and careless in religious matters [*Godsdiensticheden*]. In previous times, in the times of the cross, when with danger to his life a person met with others, then zeal drove us at all hours of the night to corners and hidden spots, to fields and woods. How valuable then was an hour that could be used to arouse and confirm each other in godliness. How thirsty and hungry souls were then for godly nourishment . . . But how are things now? Temporal affairs assume first priority: the oxen must first be checked and the field inspected before one can come to the heavenly celebration. Wickedness is changed into pomp and splendor; goods are multiplied, but the soul is impoverished; clothes have become expensive, but interior beauty is gone; love has grown cold and diminished, and quarrels have increased.[239]

From this perspective, a new edition of the martyrology, the *Martyrs' Mirror,* would hold up a heroic legacy to increasingly assimilated Mennonites. They might then see how their own spiritual reflections compared to the commitment of the martyrs.

In 1660 a Flemish Mennonite minister from Dordrecht, Thieleman Jans van Braght (1625–1664), put the capstone on de Ries's project in his *Bloody Theater or Martyrs' Mirror of the Baptism-Minded or Defenseless Christians.* A martyrologist who himself was never threatened with martyrdom brought the tradition to its culmination. Jan Luyken, who had never witnessed an execu-

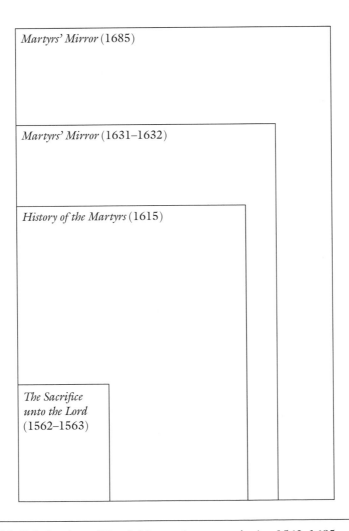

Figure 22. Relative sizes of Dutch Mennonite martyrologies, 1562–1685.

tion for heresy, provided 104 dramatic engravings for the second edition. Van Braght's distance from the martyrs' experience, however, did not preclude a profound affinity with them and their example. The trend toward affluence and assimilation continued. This sensitized van Braght still further to the gap between sixteenth-century single-mindedness and his own day's spiritual erosion amid material prosperity.

Van Braght articulated the peril of the present in terms as remarkable as they were unambiguous: "it is certainly *more dangerous now* [*nu gevaerlijcker*] than in the time of our fathers who suffered death for the witness of our Lord Jesus Christ."[240] Previously Satan had assaulted the faithful openly, "like a roaring lion," seeking to destroy their bodies, but now he came "as though in the night, or at dusk, in an unrecognized but nevertheless pleasing form." As such, he sought to destroy both bodies *and* souls by undermining faith and its outgrowth, "the true, separated Christian life." The devil's principal means were "lust of the flesh, lust of the eyes, and pride of life," which flourished now that the world was "very beautiful and lovely, more so than in any previous age."[241] Van Braght's targets were clear when he spoke of "wasteful and extensive transactions which stretch far across the sea to other parts of the world"; criticized the "many large, expensive, and beautiful houses, elaborately constructed"; lamented the "wearing of strange clothes from other regions, with their exotic fabrics, unusual colors, or rare shapes"; and attacked "enormous meals, excessive banquets, parties, and feasts." Seeing the conspicuous consumption required no more than opening one's eyes along the canals and docks of Amsterdam, where the second edition of the *Martyrs' Mirror* was published.[242] This was no "Golden Age"; it was a Dutch Babylon. The irony was profound. A century before, Mennonites had intoned, in song, the desire that magistrates might "let God's good children live in your lands." The *Ausbund* warned authorities not to abuse their power by persecuting innocent Christians. Now a Mennonite martyrologist, of all people, found toleration more dangerous than persecution to spiritual well-being.[243]

Too many Mennonites looked too much like the ungodly, preoccupied with worldly pleasures, whom Menno himself had caricatured in his *Comforting Admonition,* attacking those with "lovely, full, and ostentatious" houses who "dressed themselves with gold and silver, with silk and velvet."[244] Some sort of identity crisis was probably inevitable in a tradition that viewed persecution as a necessary sign of the true church (as Menno and Dirk Philips had written) and its historical continuity as a succession of martyrs (as de Ries had implied in 1631). If Mennonites were no longer persecuted, had they ceased to be Christ's flock? Van Braght seemed to think the sheep were threatening to wander away completely. The martyrs would provide inspiration for renewal. The martyrologist would make spiritually slack Mennonites look at themselves in the martyrs' mirror.

Whatever the prospects for the future, van Braght provided Mennonites with the fullest history of their martyrs' past. He dissociated the peaceful Anabaptists from violent Münsterites, tracing the lineage of the former forward from Christ to the sixteenth century. With the Protestant martyrologists he shared an Augustinian vision: "Just as there are two peoples, two congregations and churches," he wrote, "the one from God and heaven and the other from Satan and the earth, so there is also a twofold succession and continuation of the same."[245] Van Braght's framework emphasized the relationship between doctrines and deaths in identifying the "baptism-minded" community through time. He proceeded century by century, like the Magdeburg centuriators, one of the many Protestant and Catholic sources from which he quoted. Van Braght alternated sections on the doctrine and practice of adult baptism with sections on the martyrdom of "Anabaptist" Christians from the first through the sixteenth centuries. This exposition far transcended the superposition of sixteenth-century martyrs and biblical predecessors in *The Sacrifice unto the Lord.* It might be seen as extending de Ries's criterion of "those baptized according to Christ's ordinance."[246] Reaching back still further, van Braght was attempting to support claims by leaders like Menno, and martyrs like Jan Claes, about following a fifteen-hundred-year-old teaching.[247] Catholic attacks on the absence of Protestantism before Luther spurred the development of a Protestant historical vision. Similarly, the Catholic and Protestant tarring of all Anabaptists with the Münsterite brush eventually inspired a full-blown Mennonite version of Christian history.[248]

In his criteria for identifying the martyrological community, van Braght again showed himself the heir to de Ries. He was unwilling to define true martyrs narrowly. He spoke of the "baptism-minded in general" [*Doops-gesinde in 't gemeen*], noting that the martyrs confessed the same God, savior, and faith as his Mennonite readers. Adult baptism, he explained, was the key article and practice by which to identify true Christians and thus true Christian martyrs. This excluded Catholics and Protestants yet embraced all nonviolent Anabaptists. Van Braght went on to justify the term "baptism-minded" in his title. First, in every century, he claimed, some people taught and practiced Christian baptism of adults "in the same manner" as the Anabaptists. So he interpreted the Lollard refusal to have their infants baptized, for example, as an implicit affirmation of believers' baptism, rather than as generic anticlericalism.[249] Second, he claimed that no reliable authors reported anything about these martyrs that contradicted Anabaptist convictions. Only authors not "trustworthy or acceptable" made such allegations: they attributed preconversion beliefs to the martyrs, or failed to credit them with forsaking, prior to their deaths, any errors.[250] Here van Braght, like Protestant historians and martyrologists, seems to have maintained a blanket mistrust of Catholic sources. Anything unpalatable ascribed to "heretics" was ipso facto the product of malicious slander that sought to justify tyrannical wickedness.[251]

Yet van Braght seems not to have been wholly comfortable with the claim that his medieval martyrs believed the same things as sixteenth-century Anabaptists. He qualified his position: it applied to "things having some considerable importance [*merckelijck gewicht*] and which can be judged necessary for salvation." And he shielded his historical community against would-be detractors:

> Yet should it nevertheless turn out that one or the other [martyr] (of which we are unaware), whether in the faith or the knowledge of it was not properly enlightened, or had some noteworthy weakness or failing because of the earliness, decay, or darkness of previous times, and nonetheless maintaining the true ground of salvation, which is Christ, with a good intention, to the praise of God, the edification of his fellow brothers, and above all the preservation of his own soul, died, and although weak and faulty gave up his life through a violent death; such a person should (according to the nature of love) be excused therein and may be considered a true martyr, on account of his completely good intention, his total renunciation of both his possessions and his own self unto death; for which the Lord promised eternal life, indeed, the crown of life, Matt. 19:29 compared to Rev. 2:10, "be faithful unto death and I will give you the crown of life," etc.[252]

We have seen this before: the shortcomings in Foxe's and Crespin's medieval martyrs did not subvert their status. Van Braght thought they were not necessarily to be held to the same standards as sixteenth-century Anabaptists. Hence the Waldensians in particular, as well as the Lollards, were claimed as part of the Mennonite martyrological community.[253]

Van Braght did not write for readers facing martyrdom. It was rather the rising tide of affluence and cultural assimilation that was killing Mennonites, slowly, seductively, draining their spiritual identity. He wanted his martyrology to plug the leaking dike of Mennonite commitment. He instructed fellow believers to "read it through and reread it with the same attention and emotion as we had in the writing and rewriting of it; thus we firmly trust that it will not be unfruitful for you."[254] Yet van Braght himself eloquently bore witness to another aspect of the assimilation he sought to oppose. In his polyglot erudition that served a vast historical vision, he resembled Catholic and Protestant controversialists more than the editors of *The Sacrifice unto the Lord* or sixteenth-century Mennonite leaders, who had insisted on the self-sufficiency of scripture. Intellectually as well as socioeconomically and culturally, Mennonite respectability was superseding Anabaptist simplicity in Dutch towns.

Despite the increasing assimilation of Dutch Mennonites, the legacy of the martyrs outlived the seventeenth century. Van Braght was translated into German in the eighteenth century and brought to North America by German Mennonites. The *Martyrs' Mirror* was first translated into English in 1837. Joseph Sohm's English translation from the Dutch, first published in 1886, has been reprinted many times and continues to sell well. In the United States and Canada, Old Order Amish still sing from the *Ausbund* each week. Hutterites sing sixteenth-century hymns that are still recognizable after more than four hundred years of oral transmission.

From the earliest years of their movement, Anabaptists understood martyrdom as the anticipated result of commitment to Christian discipleship. It was never far from the essence of being Christian. The Lord had not established a "Christian society"—he had proclaimed the good news. He had baptized men and women who had accepted his word and who acknowledged their interior regeneration by God. From their beginnings in the 1520s, Anabaptists were experiencing exactly what Christ had foretold: "if they persecuted me, they will also persecute you" (John 15:20). Persecution confirmed their self-understanding and their perception of political power. It reinforced the separatist impulse that still echoes today in the Amish mistrust of government in the United States and Canada.[255] In the sixteenth century the executions of Anabaptists provided consolation and courage to fellow believers. They also deepened a chasm between Anabaptist groups and the Protestants and Roman Catholics around them—a rift that not even Hans de Ries sought to repair. Political vulnerability and severe persecution helped keep Anabaptist numbers small. Yet the ways in which they understood their suffering and remembered their martyrs strengthened the little flock.

CHAPTER SEVEN

The New Saints:
Roman Catholics and Martyrdom

"And I tell you, you are Peter, and on this rock I will build my church, and the gates of hell will not prevail against it. I will give you the keys of the kingdom of heaven, and whatever you bind on earth will be bound in heaven, and whatever you loose on earth will be loosed in heaven." . . . From that time on, Jesus began to show his disciples that he must go to Jerusalem and undergo great suffering at the hands of the elders and chief priests and scribes, and be killed, and on the third day be raised.

—MATTHEW 16:18–19, 21

Christ hath but one ship, that is, one Church, one in unity of faith, one in unity of profession, one in unity of sacraments, one in unity of head . . . To be of Christ's Church, in Christ's unity, is of such importance, that a constant Christian should rather choose to die, than to apart from it.

—THOMAS HIDE, *A CONSOLATORIE EPISTLE* (1579)

The values and virtues related to martyrdom were integral to late medieval Catholicism. The acts itself was alien, rendered dormant by Christianization. In the sixteenth century active Roman Catholic martyrdom reemerged, both in Europe and abroad. Yet its revival was less straightforward than might be supposed. Despite Catholic institutional, theological, and devotional continuities, both early evangelicals and Anabaptists celebrated their martyrs more avidly at first than did their Catholic counterparts. The broad lines of the Church's original emergence, establishment, and medieval dominance coincided with Catholic views of providence and history. Why God now allowed heresies to flourish with such variety and vigor, why he willed another era of Catholic martyrdom after such a lengthy hiatus, was not immediately clear. Lest the Lord contradict himself, heresy could not triumph over his mystical body, the Church. Yet resistance was real—as was the danger of death for the faith in some circumstances.

Within the European branch of this story of early modern Catholic martyrs, Britain, and especially England, occupies the primary position. Only in the British Isles were Catholics judicially tried and executed for religious commitments defined as treason under Henry VIII, Elizabeth I, and later, less extensively, in the seventeenth century. By definition the Henrician martyrs stood closer to the late medieval Church than did either Anabaptists or Protestants: the church for whose unity they died *was* the late medieval Church. Christians who remained loyal to traditional ways faced no obvious obstacles in assimilating new martyrs to existing saints. Still, the renaissance of martyrdom was initially perplexing because the Church had thrived for centuries without it. Whereas evangelicals and Anabaptists understood their martyrs as the victims of apocalyptic struggles, the Henrician martyrs hailed from a Church knocked back on its heels. Its leaders were appalled by the spread of heresy in northern and central Europe, yet frustrated by their inability to stop it. In the 1530s and 1540s the meaning of the present was ambiguous, the future hazy. Accordingly, the significance of the first executions was veiled.

Clarity returned by the last third of the sixteenth century. After the Council of Trent, several factors helped to produce widespread awareness and appreciation of martyrdom in Catholic Europe. Ecclesiastical leaders now concurred with their Protestant counterparts: the conflict of the age comprised no mere skirmish, but rather was a battle of overwhelming significance. At stake was Christian truth itself: what God had revealed to and expected of human beings. On this hung the eternal fate of millions of souls. The battle called for a resolute plan, required warriors, and presaged casualties. The same decades witnessed a powerful paleo-Christian revival, with ancient martyrs and their relics front and center. Enthusiasm for the early Christian martyrs was expressed in word, image, and object by a Church concerned to vindicate its historical claims against Protestant criticisms. Catholics revisited an era marked by a similar heroic urgency.

If the term "Counter-Reformation" denotes deliberate measures to counteract heresy and win back Protestants, it is especially well suited to European Catholic martyrological contexts. The reaffirmation of orthodoxy implied the commitment to re-Catholicize central, eastern, and northern Europe. Depending on local circumstances, this resolve led to deaths widely publicized as martyrdoms. Missionary work and diplomacy in Protestant lands, both to regain individual souls and to persuade rulers to reembrace Catholicism, were successful in parts of central and eastern Europe in the half century after Trent. In Elizabethan England by 1585, increasingly explicit laws defined all Catholic missionary priests as traitors. The priests, for their part, cultivated a martyrological sensibility and, along with recusant laity, celebrated the martyrs' sacrifice. Across Europe, members of religious orders, including the Jesuits, Franciscans, and Carthusians, devoted particular attention to their own recent martyrs. Hundreds (in early seventeenth-century Japan, thousands) more martyrs came from missions abroad. What early Christians had endured in the Roman Empire now, with overseas expansion, found its reprise as the living legacy of the paleo-Christian revival. As martyrs had helped convert ancient pagans in Europe, so they would do for modern pagans throughout the world. The universal Church was going global.

The missionaries and their converts killed abroad were much publicized in Catholic Europe. They extended a tradition of mendicant missionary martyrs in Asia and north Africa that dated back to the thirteenth century. Nevertheless, in addition to the Henrician and post-Tridentine martyrs in Europe, they comprise a third distinct group because of the remote theater of their deaths and the different relationship to their persecutors. In Europe, Catholic martyrs were put to death by Protestants; outside Europe, they were killed by non-Christians. The many sources, geographical diversity, and complexities of cultural interaction make these martyrs a major area of investigation in their own right. This chapter mentions them only in passing.

Catholic martyrological writers shared much with their Protestant and Anabaptist counterparts. The association between doctrines and deaths was essential. In particular, the English martyrs helped force the issue of papal authority and its implications for Catholic confessional identity, helping to pound some nails in the coffin of once-powerful conciliarism. Anti-Nicodemite arguments were no less applicable to Catholics than to Protestants or Anabaptists. And Catholic martyrological writers, too, saw a tradition reaching back through the early Christian martyrs to biblical witnesses for the truth.

In other respects the Catholic understanding of martyrdom was distinctive. Perhaps most obviously, the martyrs' status was dissimilar. Neither simply witnesses for the Gospel nor typical followers of Christ, the recent Catholic martyrs were new saints in heaven, instantly available as intercessors for potential supplicants. Official canonization in Rome was beside the point. Willem Hessels van Est, for example, a learned Franciscan theologian at Douai, reported how one Matthijs van Thore, seriously ill, prayed "with great trust" to the nineteen Gorcum martyrs shortly after their deaths in 1572 and recovered his health. Similarly, another man was cured of gout.[1] The new saints were venerated and prayed to, primarily by those who were not candidates for martyrdom.

Early modern popes, like their late medieval predecessors, were reluctant to canonize new saints in general and martyrs in particular. Not a single person killed for his or her religious commitments in the early modern period was canonized before 1700. Official proceedings were opened for some: the twenty-six Nagasaki martyrs of 1597 were beatfied thirty years after their death and the Gorcum martyrs in 1675.[2] Peter Burke has remarked "that other martyrs were unofficially regarded as saints seems likely." This supposition turns out to be overly cautious: virtually *all* of the Catholic martyrological sources imply their subjects' saintly status, pointing to a vigorous Catholic continuum between the "official" and the "popular."[3] Important continuities in Catholic hagiography, however, mask a major transformation between the early sixteenth and the early seventeenth centuries, from printed editions of the *Golden Legend* to the Bollandists. Traditional saints' lives were still published in abundance, as were liturgical martyrologies. Yet in the sixteenth century other forms of martyrological writing appeared. Narrative pamphlets and complex collections compiled from heterogeneous sources paralleled Protestant publications. One cannot simply contrast sixteenth-century Protestant "martyrology" with Catholic "hagiography," the latter understood as a mere perpetuation of its medieval antecedents.[4]

Early modern Catholics differed from Protestants and Anabaptists in their emphasis on visual representations of martyrs, continuing a centuries-old embrace of art and architecture for religious ends. As Émile Mâle put it, post-Tridentine art "unceasingly placed martyrdom before the eyes of the faithful and recalled, in this age of fire and blood, the virtue of sacrifice."[5] Here too was fundamental continuity between late medieval and early modern Catholicism. Ancient and recent martyrs abounded in paintings, single-sheet woodcuts, books of engravings, and illustrations that accompanied devotional and theological writings. German Lutherans used images more extensively than Catholics for overt propaganda,[6] but perhaps Catholics simply directed their energies elsewhere when it came to religion and the visual. Woodcuts of martyrs sometimes accompanied early evangelical pamphlets; they were integrated into Foxe's and Rabus's martyrologies, and later into van Haemstede's; and the second edition of van Braght's *Martyrs' Mirror* (1685) contained over one hundred engravings. Catholic martyrological images, however, overwhelm such expressions in both range and quantity.

Doctrinal differences among Protestants, as well as among Anabaptists, rendered unstable the criteria by which they identified their respective martyrological communities. In contrast, the persistent Catholic affirmation of one universal, visible Church produced a community with sharp boundaries. Whether Catholics had been killed for their religious convictions, and so deserved recognition as martyrs, might be an issue. Once this was determined, however, they belonged to the one and only Catholic martyrological community. In England the direct ecclesiological implications of the questions about papal authority put to suspected religious traitors sharpened all the more the boundaries of this community. Due to ambiguities, Anabaptists and Protestants occasionally ended up in one another's martyrologies by mistake—hence the "Anabaptist" Leonhard Keyser or the "Protestant" Jörgen Wagner. But neither Anabaptists nor Protestants ever appeared as martyrs in a Catholic source, nor did Catholics as martyrs in any of theirs. Members of religious orders sometimes devoted works exclusively to their own martyrs. Yet despite their frequent wrangling, I know of no instance in which a Jesuit, say, denounced a Franciscan or a secular priest condemned a member of a religious order as a "false martyr."[7] Insistence on the visible Church and unity of doctrine gave the Catholic martyrological community both internal flexibility and clear borders.

Of the three main traditions, Catholicism probably needed martyrdom least. For both Anabaptist and Protestant writers, from the outset of their movements, Christ's followers faced tribulation and risked death against an apocalyptic horizon. By contrast, it would be difficult to find a less apocalyptic indicator in the period than the liturgical calendar of the *Roman Martyrology* (1584). It duly calculates the movable feasts to beyond the year 4000— confidence indeed that the gates of hell would not prevail against Christ's church.[8] Although Catholicism did not especially need martyrs, post-Tridentine Catholics in particular seized on them with enthusiasm. The tradition's vast resources were mobilized to interpret and celebrate their deaths. Moreover, by the late sixteenth century devout Catholics probably *desired* martyrdom more than did Protestants or Anabaptists. Millions of Catholics perhaps experienced their faith as a less than arduous participation in the cultural status quo. For others, faith inspired intense devotion and the yearning to follow Christ in self-sacrifice. Such zeal was consistent with the aspirations of late medieval ascetics. Many of them would probably have envied the opportunities presented by a religiously divided Christendom.

Defensive Martyrdom: The Henrician Catholics

Unlike most of their Anabaptist and evangelical counterparts, Thomas More and John Fisher were famous before their deaths. A witty humanist and friend of Erasmus, More was a leading London lawyer, a king's counselor and Lord Chancellor, the author of *Utopia* (1516) and several works attacking heresy.[9] The bishop of Rochester, Fisher was internationally known as a first-rate theologian and highly respected in England as a model prelate, an excellent preacher, and the long-standing chancellor of the University of Cambridge.[10] When More and Fisher were executed in the summer of 1535, they died as perhaps the most distinguished layman and cleric, respectively, in the realm. Small wonder that such strenuous efforts were expended to make them change their views. More and Fisher appear to have been ideally suited to a Catholic campaign championing them and the cause for which they died. Yet little materialized.

No English account of More's life and death was even written until Mary's reign, twenty years after his death, when William Roper and Nicholas Harpsfield each assumed the task. No published account appeared until 1588, when Thomas Stapleton combined More with Thomas the Apostle and Thomas Becket in his Latin treatise *Three Thomases*. This work was not reprinted until 1612. No biography in English was published until 1626, when Roper's first appeared.[11] Fisher fared even worse: the earliest known manuscript account of his life and martyrdom dates from the late 1560s and early 1570s and remained unpublished until 1655.[12] At a time when obscure Anabaptists became the subjects of songs and undistinguished evangelical martyrs could inspire multiple *Flugschriften,* this should give us pause. Why this early neglect of More and Fisher?

The Reemergence of Catholic Martyrdom

In the 1520s and early 1530s Western Europe lacked the conditions to create Catholic martyrs. In England this changed with the measures set in motion by Henry VIII's desire to divorce Katherine of Aragon, which culminated in legislation that by 1535 had dismantled the medieval ties between England and Rome.[13] The capstone of this process, the Act of Supremacy, required of all adult male subjects an oath affirming that the king and his heirs would be accepted as "the only supreme head in earth of the Church of England," denial of which was made a treasonable offense effective February 1, 1535.[14] Final repudiation of papal authority came in 1536, but it was implied in the Act of Supremacy and intimated in earlier attacks on clerical privileges and jurisdiction. The course of events was deeply ironic: in 1521, Henry's support of papal authority in his *Defense of the Seven Sacraments* had led More to examine the issue more closely—after More had warned the king to temper his enthusiasm for papal authority, lest he come to regret it.[15] Henry's treatise won from Leo X the title "Defender of the Faith," a papal honorific the king had long craved.[16] When Johannes Eck visited England in 1525, he dedicated to Henry the first edition of his *Handbook of Commonplaces Against Luther and Other Enemies of the Church*—the first and third sections of which addressed the unity of the Church and papal primacy.[17] In the new political world of 1534, however, the bottom line was clear for prospective Roman Catholic martyrs: was papal primacy and authority unnecessary for salvation, as Henrician apologists argued and the vast majority of English subjects affirmed, or not?

The normal punishment for treason was public execution by hanging, drawing, and quartering. As with burning or drowning for heresy, the threat reduced any nuances of response to a binary "yes" or "no." The Act of Supremacy was designed this way in 1534 partly to force the issue with More and Fisher. They had been imprisoned in the Tower of London for refusing to swear to the Act of Succession, which legitimated Henry's marriage to Anne Boleyn. More famously declined to explain his refusal to take the oath. Yet the letters he wrote just before his imprisonment, to Thomas Cromwell, and just after, to his daughter, make quite clear that he thought it entailed "the jubarding [jeopardizing] of my soul to perpetual damnation" because it implicitly denied papal authority.[18]

At the yes-or-no level demanded by the oaths, the Henrician martyrs understood the denial of papal authority to violate the Church's essence—that it is one, holy, catholic, and apostolic. The royal supremacy undermined ecclesial unity and catholicity, rending Christ's mystical body by repudiating his earthly vicar, the guarantor of its corporate coherence and continuity. It trampled the Church's holiness by putting a layman, without the authority even to administer the sacraments, in command of liturgy and doctrine. It abrogated ecclesial apostolicity, abandoning the tradition that linked the present pope back to St. Peter himself and to Christ's words taken to support papal primacy (Matt. 16:18–19). Moreover, painfully aware of what had happened in Germany, More and Fisher feared that to spurn papal authority was to encourage the spread of heresy. Despite Henry's professed commitment to doctrinal orthodoxy, nothing could prevent him or subsequent monarchs from imposing heterodoxy via the royal supremacy. The religious importance of papal authority is essential for understanding early modern Catholic martyrs. At stake was the meaning and integrity of Christian truth, the genuine following and love of Christ, no less than in the Protestant insistence on justification by faith alone or in the Anabaptist commitment to believers' baptism.

Hence the Henrician martyrs of 1535 did not prepare for death by spinning defenses of papal primacy. Rather, when threatened for refusing the oaths, they reflected on Christ's passion and on the sacrifice of previous martyrs, turning prayerfully to scripture for consolation and strength. Such concerns were familiar to More. He was wary of Henry's voracious ambition even before his own entrance into political life in 1517—and resigned as chancellor when the king forced the submission of the clergy in May 1532, an action that presaged more extreme royal measures.[19] Between More's resignation and his imprisonment in April 1534, Roper said that he "would talk with his wife and children of the joys of heaven and the pains of hell, of the lives of holy martyrs, of their grievous martyrdoms, of their marvelous patience, and of their passions and deaths that they suffered rather than they would offend God; and what a happy and blessed thing it was, for the love of God, to suffer loss of goods, imprisonment, loss of lands and life also."[20] Likewise, More seems to have written his *Treatise upon the Passion,* a work deeply marked by late medieval imitation of Christ and devotion to Christ's suffering, largely if not entirely after he resigned as chancellor but before his imprisonment began.[21]

In the Tower of London, More composed his *Dialogue of Comfort against Tribulation* and his Latin treatise *On the Sadness of Christ*. He annotated his prayer book, singling out psalm verses to help maintain "trust" [*fiducia*] against temptations by "demons" [*demones*].[22] In the *Sadness of Christ* More combined devotion to Christ's passion with trepidation about martyrdom. Without a clear vocation to sacrifice himself for Christ, mindful that pride might make him covet a martyrdom he could not sustain, he felt fearful and feeble. Only circumstances from which he could not escape without endangering his salvation, then, could safely be understood as a providential dispensation making clear his call to martyrdom.[23] Traces of More's struggle with his timidity and his attempts to transcend it through trust in the Lord are evident throughout the *Sadness of Christ*. Jesus had known the same anguish in Gethsemane, in part "to lay down a fighting technique and a battle code for the faint-hearted soldier [*militi meticuloso*] who needs to be swept along, as it were, into martyrdom."[24] Such was God's love: Christ had shuddered in the depths of human terror to deflect despair from weak followers facing death.

From prison John Fisher wrote two devotional pieces to his half-sister Elizabeth, a nun, although he probably composed them at least as much for himself.[25] He was imprisoned for his outspoken opposition to Henry's divorce and his constant defense of papal authority. These were not, however, what sustained him in the Tower. Instead he ruminated on the intimate connection between Christ's love and the martyrs' utter refusal to forsake it:

> you should consider the love of your own spouse the sweet Jesu, how excellent it is, how sure, how fast, how constantly abiding, how many have much specially regarded it, martyrs innumerable both men and women have shed their blood, and have endured every kind of martyrdom were it never so cruel, were it never so terrible. No pain, no tormentry, might compel them to forsake his love . . . So dear and precious was that love to them, that all the honors, pleasures, and possessions of this life, they recounted as very trifles in comparison of that.[26]

This man said Mass with a skull on his altar as a *momento mori*. As he prepared for his own impending death, he would not sever love for Christ from unswerving allegiance to his earthly vicar.

Something similar is discernible in the response of the London Carthusians to the royal supremacy, as reported years later by one of the monks, Maurice Chauncy. After learning that the oath was compulsory, their prior, John Houghton, arranged a three-day period of mutual confession and reconciliation to prepare the monks for martyrdom. On the scaffold, Houghton coupled fidelity to God with fidelity to the Church: people in the crowd were his witnesses, he said, that he died not out of stubbornness, malice, or rebelliousness, but only lest he offend God's majesty and the Church's teachings.[27] He chose death over the delusion that Christ might be wrenched from his vicar or his Church.

Intersecting paths from the past helped sustain the martyrs of 1535. Respectful friends for well over a decade, Fisher and More exchanged letters in prison; the bishop told his examiners that they included "exhortations to patience, and prayers to God for grace."[28] As a young man More had spent four years living in close contact with the London Charterhouse, the same Carthusian monastery that produced four of the martyrs of 1535.[29] Himself the wearer of a hidden hair shirt, More remained their great admirer throughout his life. From a window in his cell, he watched Houghton and four others en route to execution two months before his own death. In Roper's words, he asked his daughter, who was visiting, "Dost thou not see, Meg, that these blessed fathers be now as cheerfully going to their deaths as bridegrooms to their marriage?"[30] Five weeks later, Fisher saw a batch of the monks' prison writings. (These were perhaps part of Houghton's notes about their interrogations that ended up in Chauncy's hands.) The bishop's servant, when questioned, said that Fisher prayed to God "that no vanity subvert [the monks]."[31] Another monk executed with Houghton was the erudite Richard Reynolds, a Bridgettine scholar and theologian from Syon Abbey near London. A graduate and fellow of Corpus Christi College at Cambridge, one of the university preachers during Fisher's tenure as chancellor, he was also a theological consultant to the bishop of Rochester and to More.[32] The few who refused the supremacy knew they did not stand alone. Indeed, the community that mattered most to them extended far beyond England's troubled present. Both More and Reynolds stated at their trials that tradition was on their side, and that the rest of Catholic Christendom had not broken with Rome.[33]

Between May 4 and July 6, 1535, ten men were publicly executed in London as traitors for "maliciously" denying the supremacy by refusing to take the oath. The first group of five included Houghton, Reynolds, secular priest John Hale, plus the priors of two other Carthusian houses, Augustine Webster and Robert Lawrence. On May 4 they were dragged on horse-drawn hurdles through the streets of London, from the Tower to Tyburn. Before a large crowd that included many nobles and members of Henry's Privy Council, they were hanged, drawn, and quartered. Conspicuously, there was no ritual degradation to lay status, the normal procedure when members of the clergy were punished as secular criminals. Their dismembered bodies were parboiled before the crowd and various parts displayed at visible points around the city. Three more Carthusians from the Charterhouse, Humphrey Middlemore, William Exmewe, and Sebastian Newdigate, were imprisoned for two weeks in the Marshalsea prison in standing position, bound to stone pillars with iron collars around their necks. They were similarly dispatched at Tyburn on June 19.[34] Three days later, on Tower Hill, John Fisher was beheaded—a concession to his episcopal status and perhaps his age. On July 6 Thomas More met the same end.

The Muted Early Response to the Martyrs of 1535

News of the English Catholics' demise spread quickly, and with it their recognition as martyrs. Using a standard analogy that went back to Innocent III, Richard Crowley, the curate of Broughton in Oxfordshire, asserted that the king derived his authority from the pope as the moon drew its light from the sun. The pope's power was undiminished despite the recent legislation, he said, and Fisher, Reynolds, and More had died for the true faith, "and so would I if it were put to me."[35] About the same time, in August, Gilbarte Rouse, the parson of Rouselynch in Worcestershire, was accused of claiming that those killed were martyrs before God and saints in heaven. Oliver Bromley, the curate of Exton, ignored commands to declare the pope's power usurped and to remove his name from the missal, because he had heard that Fisher and Reynolds had suffered death for it.[36] In 1536 two more clerics were investigated for esteeming More and Fisher, as was John Beche, the abbot of Colchester, in late 1539 before his own execution.[37] Considering the reputation of More and Fisher in particular, however, all this is not much response. True, Eustace Chapuys, the imperial ambassador in London, told Charles V that "the regret and compassion of the people" was "inconceivable" after Fisher's execution.[38] We will never know how many people regarded Fisher and the others as martyrs yet kept it to themselves. Perhaps authorities discovered these clerical sympathizers because they scrutinized the clergy more closely than the laity. They would not have been vigilant had they not perceived or at least feared a problem.

Unlike the response to executed evangelicals, however, evidently no vernacular pamphlets about the Catholic martyrs were secretly published. Nor were any songs set to folk tunes extolling their heroism. Interrogated about his remarks, Gilbarte Rouse deftly backed off: those executed were "unfortunate and unwise" for their opinion against the king, and "*if*" their views had been for God's faith, they would have been martyrs. The same day that he admitted his noncompliance, Oliver Bromley "repented his lewdness" and was willing to declare papal power a usurpation. In June 1536, the sub-prior of Woburn said that reading *The Glass of Truth* and Tyndale's *Obedience of a Christian Man* had quashed his previous estimate of More's and Fisher's death and ended his wish to have died with them.[39] Even some who sympathized with those executed were not disposed to follow their example.

In late 1546 or early 1547, shortly after he fled England for Bruges, Maurice Chauncy concluded an account of the Carthusian martyrs under Henry. He stated that "up until now the terror of princes constrained me from setting it forth."[40] The threat of capital punishment was probably the main reason for the tepid response to the martyrs of 1535, just as it influenced many Protestants and Anabaptists to recant. The Henrician regime was attentive to resistance and remarkably effective in quelling it between 1533 and 1540.[41] Just days after Fisher's execution, while More was yet in prison, Simon Matthew preached a sermon at St. Paul's in London justifying the executions, part of a stream of propaganda that favored the divorce, the remarriage to Anne, and the royal supremacy.[42] Yet the combination of concerted suppression, government propaganda, and fear of execution cannot sufficiently explain the meager response. Protestants and Anabaptists risked their lives to proclaim executed fellow believers as martyrs. They published accounts of the martyrs' deaths and smuggled pamphlets to spread the news. They too were subject to propaganda and threats.

Those favorably disposed towards the Henrician martyrs declined to publicize them mainly because of pervasive uncertainty about the recent developments in England. For early evangelicals and Anabaptists, martyrs were apocalyptic harbingers that confirmed Antichrist's hatred of the truth. The meaning of the Henrician martyrs of 1535 was much less evident. Because their deaths were unexpected, like the ecclesio-political revolution itself, there were no expectations to be confirmed. The martyrs thought that the supremacy issue involved the integrity of the Church and Christian faith, and therefore eternal salvation. However widespread this view might have been, few acted on it. Not even those closest to More understood his motivations and actions. Twenty years later, when his own son-in-law, William Roper, wrote about his life and death, he offered nothing interpretive about the significance of More's execution.[43] Unlike their early evangelical and Anabaptist counterparts, the Henrician martyrs had not died as part of a movement; rather, they had stood still while the world around them moved. Without a clear sense of the motion's direction, how long it would last, where it would stop, whether—as many thought—it might reverse, and what it meant, it was difficult to make sense of the sudden reappearance of Catholic martyrdom.

The continental reaction to their deaths was a somewhat different story, although not to the extent that some scholars have suggested.[44] It had two aspects: an initial burst of diplomatic commentary in the highest political circles that soon fizzled, and a round of manuscripts and publications about the executions. In the end, continental response did not result in sustained, widespread memorialization. Fisher and More were the only non-Frenchmen honored in the 1545 edition of Jean Bouchet's *Annals of Aquitaine,* for example, yet the poems about them were buried in the text and mild in tone.[45] By 1540, however, the executions had evoked comments and comparisons that would be further developed, with important implications, in subsequent decades.

In the spring and summer of 1535, diplomatic correspondence buzzed with news of the executions. Within weeks, the events in England were known at the papal, French, and imperial courts. Chapuys had written immediately to Charles V about the execution of the first five priests, "very cruelly put to death simply for having said and maintained that the pope was the true head and sovereign [*vray chefz et souverain*] of the universal Church." On May 17, the papal nuncio to France, Bishop Rodolfo Pio da Carpa, wrote to the papal secretary in Rome about the matter. His report was based on a London letter dated May 5, which included grisly details of the deaths. By the beginning of June the news was known in Rome, where Gregory da Casale, Henry's agent, reported to Cromwell that some cardinals envied the monks' deaths. An English merchant living in Venice, Edmond Harvel, wrote to Henry's chaplain, Thomas Starkey, that "all Venice was in great murmuration" on hearing of the deaths because they were "persuaded of the dead men's great honesty and virtues, and that their opinion was conforme[d] with the most part of all Christendom."[46] The reason for the monks' executions accompanied the news: doctrines and deaths were linked. His episcopal status and recent elevation to the cardinalate made Fisher's death even more provocative. King Francis I was outraged at Henry, with whom he said no friendship was possible. By his actions the English king had set himself against the honor of God and the Church. On July 18, the nuncio in France wrote the papal secretary about rumors of princely alliances that would aid the pope in retribution against Henry.[47]

Pope Paul III was incensed by Fisher's execution above all. On July 26 he wrote separate letters to King Ferdinand of Hungary and Francis I, calling on Habsburg and Valois to help deprive Henry of his kingdom.[48] The papal nuncio reported that Francis, a great patron of humanism and the arts, heard the news of More's death with tears in his eyes. By August 21, however, the French monarch had retreated and left any initiative to Charles, stating that Henry's treatment of Katherine of Aragon had wronged the emperor in the first place.[49] Charles, however, feared that attacking Henry might push France closer to England. Katherine's death in January 1536 removed some of the pressure on him to act.[50] Any prospects for political or military retribution foundered on the opposition between the King of France and the emperor. The Henrician executions were soon widely known and stirred rumors, yet produced no major disturbances in international politics.

The deaths also inspired manuscript and published accounts on the Continent. By far the most widespread of these was the so-called Paris Newsletter and the closely related *Trustworthy Account of the Death of Thomas More and Certain Other Distinguished Men in England* (the *Expositio fidelis*).[51] The Newsletter was a French translation of a Latin original that had reached Paris within about two weeks of More's death. The unidentified author of the original was perhaps a Frenchman associated with the imperial ambassador. Erasmus seems at least to have edited, if not written, the second half of the *Expositio* himself.[52] By 1536 multiple French manuscripts of the Newsletter were circulating, as were apparently a printed French edition (no longer extant) and two separate published German translations. There were also at least two Latin editions of the *Expositio* and two German translations, plus manuscript copies in Spanish and Italian.[53] Many Europeans must have learned of the executions, either directly or indirectly, through the printed editions of the *Expositio*.

The remarkable fact, given the nature of early evangelical and Anabaptist sources, is the interpretive restraint shown by the author-editor, whether it was Erasmus or Philippe Dumont. The Newsletter began abruptly and concerned only More's trial and execution, reflecting an interest in judicial procedure by someone who was present. There was neither praise for More nor denunciation of Henry. The *Expositio* added a brief introductory passage and continued beyond More's execution to remarks on the deaths of Fisher, the Carthusians, and Reynolds, derived "partly from friends' letters, partly from rumors." The author deplored More's death, yet compared his treatment not to the persecution of biblical or early Christian martyrs, but to the way that Cicero suffered under Antony, Seneca under Nero. (The latter choice is especially revealing, since St. Paul himself was another of Nero's victims.) As to suffering for or following Christ, the author merely mentioned that others said that Christ's spirit had been active in Fisher during his career.[54] That was all. In tone and content, the *Expositio* was worlds away from the prison writings of More and the martyrological writings by Protestants and Anabaptists.

The *Expositio* seems to have been a contemporary martyrological comment in a humanist vein. When Conrad Goclenius wrote to Erasmus from Louvain in August 1535, he compared More to Socrates—again, a humanist's analogy, and one that would have resonated with Erasmus.[55] There seem to have been humanists for whom the primary register of More's death was not Christian martyrdom, but rather something like classical virtue crushed by tyranny. Although the *Expositio* affirmed that More was killed "to protect the cause of the Church" [*ut Ecclesiae caussam tueretur*], it was conspicuously ambiguous about More's resolute willingness to die. "Those who serve monarchs ought to dissemble somewhat," the author wrote, "so that if they are not able to get what they think is best, by some means they will at least partially temper the passion of princes." The passage continued, directly confronting the anti-Nicodemite imperative not to renounce Christ:

> Someone else will say that one ought to die for the truth [*pro veritate mortem oppetendam*]. Yet not just any truth—if a tyrant commands one either to renounce Christ or to hang, one ought to hang. But it is one thing to be silent, another to renounce. If divine law permits you as a Christian to dissemble [*dissimulare*] without grave scandal, how much more would it permit being silent? But I am off base here, arguing about such difficult matters, I who have never taken part in the councils of rulers. Therefore I leave judgment of the entire affair to others [*Itaque de tota caussa iudicium alijs relinquo*].[56]

More *had* clung to silence for more than a year, refusing to explain his unwillingness to swear the oath of succession. In the end, silence was not enough. This excerpt from the *Expositio* is unusual for any early modern "martyrological" source. Leaving judgment of the affair to others was the antithesis of Protestant and Anabaptist responses, and very different from the post-Tridentine attitude toward Catholic martyrs. Such a comment implied either uncertainty about the meaning of their deaths, or a desire to avoid the either-or dichotomies that executions for religion were pressing upon Christendom.[57] And yet the *Expositio* was the most widely dispersed source about the Henrician martyrs of 1535.

Others, however, saw the new martyrs differently. In early 1536 Johannes Cochlaeus, an experienced German theologian, vigorously defended More and Fisher in a published Latin treatise. He had corresponded with both men and knew their writings. Cochlaeus left no doubt about their status as holy martyrs, nor about the wickedness of Henry and his advisors. Like the author of the *Expositio*, Cochlaeus compared the English king to Nero, but he added Herod to form a triumvirate. Against them he set More and Fisher along with John the Baptist and Paul—not Seneca. Then he quoted two classic New Testament passages, Luke 9:24 (whoever saves his soul will lose it, whoever loses it for my sake will save it) and Luke 12:4 (do not fear the one who can kill the body and do no more), evincing the same recourse to scripture so common in Anabaptist and Protestant sources, yet absent in the *Expositio*. "The apostles too," Cochlaeus wrote, "would have been able to avoid misfortunes, prisons, and the pains of death, had they wanted to remain silent about or dissemble [*tacere ac dissimulare*] the truth, which is Christ." Instead, Peter and the apostles said, "we must obey God more than men" (Acts 5 [:29]), and Paul cautioned himself, "woe to me if I do not preach the Gospel" [1 Cor. 9:16]. Addressing Henry, Cochlaeus saw More and Fisher in the same exalted company: "Therefore those most holy learned men, Fisher and More, feared that woe; thus they did not want to lose the truth either by remaining silent or by flattery [*neque tacendo, neque adulando*], even had they been able to attain massive amounts of all possible temporal goods from you, had they been willing either to agree with you or at least to dissemble."[58] For Cochlaeus, silence was not enough. His remarks little resembled the yearning for compromise implicit in the *Expositio.* Cochlaeus, however, was a professional controversialist, toughened by more than a decade of religious dispute in Germany.

Cochlaeus implied that adherence to papal primacy was necessary for salvation. He linked martyrdom to scriptural verses no less ably than did Protestant or Anabaptist writers. After quoting Matt. 5:10–11, Rom. 8:18, and 2 Cor. 4:17, he wrote that "those most learned and holiest of men, who lived in this age that the crown of martyrdom might deserve to be awarded, understood thoroughly [*optime*] these infallible sayings of God and countless others like them."[59] Parallels to other martyrs suggested themselves as well. Already in writing to Ferdinand and Francis I, Paul III had likened Fisher's death at the hands of Henry VIII to Becket's under Henry II in the twelfth century. Cochlaeus added More to the analogy: "if we consider the reason for death, we truly will discover that [More and Fisher] had greater and better reasons to be supposed martyrs than [Thomas Becket] did."[60] Becket defended the privileges and control of temporal goods in his particular church, but Fisher and More refused to "deny matrimony, approve divorce, justify adultery with a seductress, relinquish the Roman church, withdraw from obedience to the Roman pontiff, acknowledge as new head of the English church a king, profaner, and adulterer." Cochlaeus sounded deferential and disingenuous in stating that he "would not prefer these men to that most holy martyr," while adding that "in blamelessness of life they were either equal to him or at least close, but in talent and learning far superior."[61]

Cochlaeus's parallels were ancient and medieval Christian, not classical. The meaning of the deaths was unambiguous. Thomas Theobald, Cromwell's godson, wrote from the Continent in March 1536 after traveling through several German towns. He belittled Cochlaeus's book, yet acknowledged that it "doth and will do hurt."[62] To compare the recent martyrs to Becket was a powerful statement, considering his cult's popularity and significance in England. The analogies may well have influenced Henry's 1538 decision to obliterate the shrine to the slain Archbishop of Canterbury, whose death was "untruly called martyrdom."[63]

From his voluntary Italian exile, Reginald Pole wrote the most extensive and dramatic early response about More, Fisher, and the other martyrs. A cousin of Henry VIII himself, the erudite and devout Pole had left England for Padua in 1532 with the king's blessing, owing to his scruples about the divorce and remarriage. He played a leading role among the Italian *spirituali* and leaned toward a Lutheran view of justification prior to Trent. Yet the executions of 1535 resolved any doubts that Pole may have had about the importance of papal primacy and the Church's unity. Both are major themes in his *Defense of the Unity of the Church,* completed in the spring of 1536, a work that became a touchstone for his subsequent career.[64]

Thomas Starkey thought that the executions had decisively shaped Pole's views. He was in a position to know: he had belonged to Pole's household for two years in Padua before returning to England, where he became chaplain to Pole's mother and then to the king himself.[65] In early 1535 Starkey was asked to solicit Pole's approval of the royal supremacy, which he expected Pole to give.[66] The executions intervened. The *Defense* must have been a shock when it arrived in England in the late spring of 1536. Instead of support, Henry got a lengthy, impassioned plea to repent the wicked acts perpetrated in his name, lest he risk the destruction of his kingdom and the damnation of his soul. Due to the deaths, Starkey wrote, Pole regarded papal primacy not as a convention, but as Christ's institution: "after when he saw More and Rochester defend the cause with the shedding of their blood, pondering withal a consent of doctors agreeing to the same, with the practice of the church so ma[ny] years, then he leaned and formed his judgment thereby, as in his book he writeth plainly."[67] In the *Defense* Pole indeed made clear the meaning of the executions and the importance of the doctrines underlying them.

Pole wrote that the "astounding and unheard of cruelty" of the executions so stunned him that he was "left speechless for about a month, as though I were mute."[68] Finally able to compose himself, he understood that Christ was exhorting him to proclaim publicly what he had earlier kept to himself.[69] He implored Henry to acknowledge his outrageous evils, repent his crimes, and return to the Church. Although Pole softened the blow with the conventional implication that evil counsel had misled the king, his denunciations were severe. Executing such exemplary men surpassed any injury to the realm hitherto inflicted by any king; the crimes were worse than all the atrocities mentioned in scripture, a calamity greater than any war or pestilence; opposition to the monks was diabolical, Satan himself having presided over their trial; and Henry's actions exceeded anything ever done by Nero or Domitian, evils that even Luther, had he been king of England, would not have committed.[70] We can understand why the king, given to fits of rage, afterward tried to have Pole assassinated. According to his cousin, however, Henry had gone far too far and had sabotaged their relationship. Pole's affection for the king could not excuse the transgression of boundaries that even rulers had to respect.

Near the beginning of the work, with an allusion to Matt. 10:29–30 and the divine providence it implied, Pole declared his inability to believe that the deaths had been in vain:

> Can I let the idea pass or say that those who sustained hardship for the sake of the Church, and without recompense suffered death for the same, did so for nothing? Can I say this when I have so many times, with profound contentment in my soul, heard the voice of Christ say of such men that not a single hair from their heads can fall to the ground without God's providence? Can I now either think to myself or utter in speech the notion that those men, after putting up with so many hardships and tribulations, squandered their lives without purpose, for nothing [*uitam etiam illos temere ac sine fructu profudisse*]? I cannot, prince, I cannot. Let all such impiety be far from me.[71]

He could not vindicate the executions without eviscerating his convictions. Unable to believe their deaths were meaningless, Pole was obliged to defend the victims' views. Yet the doctrine behind their deaths—they preferred, as Pole put it, to lose their own heads than to admit that the Church's head should be severed from its body—pointed beyond itself, to the teachings and cause of the Church as such. Since these were identical with the teachings and cause of God and Christ, the Henrician victims were rightly understood as martyrs. The axe that killed them "truly brought them immortality." Despite his professed unworthiness to shed his own blood for Christian truth, Pole identified strongly with those whose only crime was holding the same views that he himself maintained.[72]

While Henry wallowed in wickedness, gravely jeopardizing his own redemption and England's future, the Christlike martyrs received their reward. More resembled Christ himself in his lack of animosity toward his persecutors, just as he paralleled Stephen in praying for them.[73] The recent martyrs were vessels of the Holy Spirit; in death they were filled with Christ's spirit, which had also moved the apostles.[74] Pole had not despaired of the king's salvation, but it depended on his penitence and return to the Church. The overall impression conveyed in the *Defense*, with Henry and his helpers on one side and the martyrs on the other, was a strong dichotomy of the sort abundantly present in both Protestant and Anabaptist sources.

Pole espoused the remarkable view that martyrdom was the preeminent manifestation of God's will, taking priority over even the Bible. This is especially striking given Pole's commitment, along with the other *spirituali*, to the direct reading of scripture for Christian life. According to Pole, God "writes his will for us in the blood of his son," which is apparent to the viewer who contemplates the crucifix. After Christ's death and resurrection, the persecuted members of his body, namely the apostles and disciples, replicated this primordial expression of God's will, such that

> whatever contains Christ's doctrine was written in their blood flowing out from Christ's wounds. They were living books in which learned and unlearned, wise and unwise, and finally the entire human race could read what the will of God and the way to happiness were. In these men the very beginnings of our religion were explicitly written down; through them the Church knows more about the will of God than it can learn through any books written by hand [*per hos ecclesia plus nouit de uoluntate Dei, quam per ullos manu scriptos libros cognosci possit*]. Even though what was written on paper was dictated by the same spirit (for there is no doubt that the memorials of the evangelists and the apostles in the New Testament were written by the Spirit of God), nevertheless, as the original always has more authority than the other books copied from it, so books written out in the blood of the martyrs are to be preferred above all others. For these alone were the original books in which the finger of God appeared . . . Through perverse human reasoning and interpretation [the written books] can be distorted and fashioned in many forms, whereas those that are written in the blood of the martyrs cannot be corrupted.[75]

This is a stunning passage. Implicitly, the unalterable certainty conveyed by the witness of Christ and his martyrs, which is "written out in blood, not in ink,"[76] provided an authoritative anchor for any problems raised by humanist biblical scholarship or wayward exegesis. Pole's historical picture of martyrdom differed from those of Protestant or Anabaptist writers. Neither a consequence of the Gospel's rediscovery nor a sign denoting Christ's flock, "the blood of the martyrs" had always been God's principal means for teaching his will. Throughout the Church's history, God in his great mercy "always brought forth his holy martyrs in bringing all great controversies to a close."[77] Pole did not elaborate. In the later sixteenth century, however, Catholic writers would amplify the view that latter-day martyrs were defending what early Christian martyrs had helped to establish.

Pole's dramatic exaltation of the new martyrs and extensive defense of papal authority were not part of a sustained celebration or veneration. Overall, it seems justified to contrast the continental Catholic response to the Henrician martyrs of 1535 with the early evangelical and Anabaptist response to their respective martyrs. Pole and Cochlaeus offered elegant formulations, but their treatises remained in Latin, apparently without much demand for reprints or vernacular translations. Pole's *Defense* was not reprinted until 1555, and then with Protestant rebuttals, while Cochlaeus and Richard Morison conducted in Latin their ensuing controversy about the executions and the nature of papal and royal authority.[78] Another Latin treatise attacking the Henrician innovations and executions, by Albertus Pighius, remained unpublished.[79] The one widely known account of the trials and deaths, the *Expositio,* interpreted the executions cautiously, if not ambiguously. It lacked any imperative for readers, any firm lesson to be drawn from their deaths.

In the mid-1530s the conditions were not right for widespread, popular recognition of the Henrician martyrs. More, Fisher, and the rest were not members of apocalyptic religious movements. They were profoundly devout men of the established church who found themselves in unprecedented circumstances. Early evangelical and Anabaptist expectations of martyrdom exploded immediately in a celebration of executed fellow believers; Catholic martyrdom in England was almost unthinkable even after the fact of the executions. The early response was accordingly restricted although, as we have seen, it could be intense. When Pole returned to England and became Mary's archbishop of Canterbury, he had not forgotten the shock of 1535. More than twenty years after the fact, he declaimed at length to Londoners about the heroic witness of the first Henrician martyrs.[80]

The Evolving Interpretation of the Henrician Martyrs

In 1541 Henry VIII ordered the execution of Pole's aged mother, Margaret, after her long imprisonment. Her son was forced to confront martyrdom anew, in the most personal way. According to his secretary, Pole thought God had greatly honored him. He took the news of her martyrdom as an occasion for rejoicing, "for we have another advocate in heaven."[81] Margaret Pole was one of at least forty English Catholics put to death for their refusal to subscribe to the supremacy between 1537 and 1544.[82] According to Thomas Stapleton (1535–1598), who was a child during these years, the martyrs were an inspiration, at least to some: "Without question More's reputation and the memory of his renowned martyrdom were much celebrated among us boys in England, which gave us incentive to embrace and maintain [*amplectendam et retinendam*] the Catholic faith; I remember very well and countless others will attest to it with me." Stapleton further noted that when Germain Gardiner, the nephew of Bishop Stephen Gardiner of Winchester, was executed in March 1544, "he was willing to give the people no other reason why he was suffering death for that cause, other than that the simple devotion of the Carthusians, the extraordinary learning of the bishop of Rochester, and the exceptional wisdom of Thomas More seemed to admonish him that he was to do this."[83]

Executed with Gardiner for refusing to acknowledge the supremacy were John Larke, who had been More's parish priest, and John Ireland, a family chaplain. Around this time the significance of More's death seems to have grown clearer among his intimates. This sense was shared by a number of scholars at Oxford and Cambridge, who, like the members of the "More circle" with whom they overlapped, chose continental exile rather than conformity in Edward VI's reign.[84] It now appeared that the royal supremacy and related events were not aberrations, but rather defined the new status quo. On the Continent, the attempted rapprochement at Regensburg between Protestants and Catholics had failed, and a council to meet at Trent had been convoked. Pressured in 1544, Gardiner, Larke, and Ireland refused to renounce papal authority and paid with their lives. Still, no celebration of the English Catholic martyrs rivaled Protestant and Anabaptist efforts.

Family and friends, above all, preserved the martyrs' memory between 1535 and Mary's reign. Remembrance transcended mere stories and recollections. When Maurice Chauncy made sure that John Houghton's prison notes found their way to Rome, he sent along part of the bloodstained shirt in which his prior had been slain.[85] Authorities fixed Houghton's dismembered arm above the door of the London Charterhouse, seeking to intimidate the remaining monks. They removed and concealed it as a relic after their monastery was suppressed.[86] In 1546 the future Marian Protestant martyr John Hooper told how a search for bibles in churches had turned up "the left arm of one of those Charterhouse monks, that died in the defence of the bishop of Rome, reverently hid in the high altar of the church, with a writing containing the day and cause of his death."[87] Margaret Roper, More's daughter, kept his hair shirt, which he had sent her shortly before his death. She also retained his severed head, for which she had bribed the executioner after it was removed from public display on London bridge. More's adopted daughter, Margaret Clements, gave to Stapleton a large piece of the shirt in which he was beheaded.[88] What bones and bloodied clothing lacked in distributability, they made up for in electrifying concretness. These remains had channeled the supernatural grace through which the martyrs had overcome temptation and sustained violent death.

The first published martyrological collection devoted to the Henrician Catholics was Maurice Chauncy's Latin work *A History of Some Martyrs of Our Age* (1550). His brother Carthusians executed between 1535 and 1541 occupied center stage, but the book also included sections on Fisher, More, and Richard Reynolds.[89] The Henrician martyrs were treated in themselves, not as adjuncts to issues of papal and royal authority, as in Cochlaeus and Pole. Throughout Chauncy's exposition, the meaning of their deaths was clear. With a gloss on John 10:11, for example, Fisher was called a "holy doctor of the Church, herald of God, defender of the faith, a true pastor laying down his life for his sheep, as well as for the thief and the robber." He was killed "for the sake of the unity of the faith and the Church" at a time when others in England were embarrassed to profess Christ and his words.[90] In their dedicatory preface, Mainz Carthusians Vitus van Dulken and Willem van Sittart identified the martyrs as among those "standing in the sight of the throne and the Lamb, clothed in white robes, with palm branches in their hands" [Rev. 7:9]. They compared their steadfastness and joyful bearing in death to that of ancient Christian martyrs, male as well as female—Lawrence, Vincent, Tiburtius, Agatha, and Catherine.[91] Martyrs' constancy and joy in dying, evidently, were not gender-specific aspects of their sanctity. In a graphic image that echoed Pole's view of martyrdom's incorruptible power, Chauncy wrote that "their dismembered heads or bodily members having been affixed to poles after death, they preach to us what sort of faith or love for Christ and the Church we ought to have unto death." The fate of Thomas Cromwell and Anne Boleyn, both executed at Henry's command, showed God's vengeance on those who persecuted his martyrs, whose own deaths were "precious in the sight of the Lord" (Ps. 116[:15]).[92] Chauncy's work, with its strong biblical and historical parallels to previous persecutors and martyrs, was published five more times under various titles between 1573 and 1608.[93]

Nicholas Harpsfield wrote his "Life and Death of Sir Thomas More" during Mary's reign, with Roman Catholicism restored in England. Completed by the spring of 1557, it remained unpublished, but eight extant manuscripts from the sixteenth and seventeenth centuries suggest a fairly wide, long-standing circulation.[94] Harpsfield saw God's providential hand in the martyrs. More was "the first of any whatsoever layman in England that died a martyr for the defense and preservation of the unity of the Catholic church." He was an "ambassador for the laity as was the good bishop of Rochester for the clergy" in leading England back to communion with Rome.[95] Because he died for the unity of the whole Church and not simply to save his soul, More's martyrdom was more glorious than those of St. Thomas of Dover and St. Thomas Becket. His intercession in heaven was correspondingly efficacious. After noting that More's head was displayed on London bridge, Harpsfield wrote that

> Sir Thomas More's head had not so high a place upon the pole as had his blessed soul among the celestial holy martyrs in heaven. By whose hearty and devout intercession and his foresaid co-martyrs, and of our protomartyr St. Alban, and other blessed martyrs and saints of the realm, I doubt not but God of late hath the sooner cast his pitiful eye to reduce us again by his blessed minister and queen, Lady Mary, and by the noble,

virtuous, excellent prelate, Cardinal Pole, to the unity of the Church that we had before abandoned.[96]

On the institutional level of the realm as a whole, the fruit of this intercession would prove to be short-lived. Elizabeth's accession was a bitter blow, but by no means incompatible with a Catholic providential framework. It simply meant that for whatever reason, God did not will England's lasting reconciliation with Rome at that moment.[97] Catholics needed to lament their ingratitude and repent their sins, just as committed Protestants had done under Mary.

The solidification of Elizabeth's reign suggested that no return to Rome was imminent. Situating English Catholicism within the universal Church and acknowledging the persistence of Protestantism highlighted the significance of the Henrician martyrs. Their meaning grew clearer in the context of major events on the Continent and in England: the imperial standoff with German Lutherans in the Peace of Augsburg, the growth of Calvinism and open conflict in France and the Netherlands, and the defeat of England's northern Earls in 1569. Already in Mary's reign, lay controversialist Miles Huggarde named many of the Henrician martyrs in a tradition that began with England's protomartyr, St. Alban. All had "died for the cause of the Catholic faith, that faith which hath ever continued from age to age, with the consent of all kingdoms Christian, even from the beginning, whose memory shall be magnified till the end of the world."[98] When John Young composed his life of Fisher in the late 1560s and the 1570s, he discerned multiple links between the bishop of Rochester as "a second Cyprian" and other Christian saints, including Thomas Becket, Bede, Ambrose, Chrysostom, and Stephen.[99]

Thomas Stapleton, inspired in boyhood by More's martyrdom, went to Oxford, then left for the Continent early in Elizabeth's reign. He matured into an erudite theologian who taught at the University of Douai in the southern Netherlands for nearly two decades.[100] Much as Young did for Fisher, Stapleton placed More alongside Thomas the Apostle and Thomas Becket as the third of his *Three Thomases* (1588). The Church's struggle against Protestantism sharpened the meaning of More's death. He had died for papal primacy and supremacy, upon which "the peace, order, and unity of the entire Church depend, for if it is removed the door is opened to all heresies, and without restraint the wolves ravage the flock, as even the one example of England can teach other countries."[101] More than a weary metaphor, this image was literally true of the Continent as well: Stapleton had been in Antwerp during the iconoclasm of 1566 and had seen the English College at Douai forced to relocate in Rheims due to a Dutch Protestant offensive in 1578.[102] In England, Henry VIII's break with Rome had proven to be the Trojan horse for English Protestantism. It was just as More and Fisher had feared. On this issue they had been right, Stephen Gardiner and the other proponents of Henrician Catholicism wrong.[103]

Once the Elizabethan executions began, the Henrician martyrdoms made even more sense within a larger story. They heralded a new era of Roman Catholic martyrdom. In 1574, writing from Douai, Richard Bristow connected the Henrician martyrs to other recently executed Catholics, such as John Felton and those who were involved in the rebellion of 1569.[104] Another leading controversialist, Nicholas Sander, smoothly integrated the Henrician martyrs into his *Origin and Growth of the Anglican Schism*. This counter-Foxean manuscript remained unfinished at his death in 1581. It was completed by Edward Rishton, a missionary priest trained at Douai who added the stories of the recent Elizabethan martyrs before having the work published in 1585.[105]

The Henrician martyrs found a place in pictorial narratives as well. In 1583 an Italian artist, Niccolo Circignani, was commissioned to do more than thirty paintings telling the story of English Catholicism through persecution and martyrdom. The cycle was to adorn San Tomaso di Cantorbery, the church of the new English College in Rome. Engravings based on these paintings were published in 1584. One of them, situated between an image of medieval martyrs and another of several Carthusians, depicted the execution of Fisher, More, and Margaret Pole (Figure 23).[106] It captured not a historical moment—More died more than two weeks after Fisher, and Margaret Pole six years later—but rather a martyrological truth. A bishop, a layman, and a laywoman were united in death for the teachings and tradition of the Church.

The Passion for Passion in Post-Tridentine Catholicism

Stapleton and others looked back to the Henrician martyrs from a different world. Guided by the Holy Spirit in accordance with Christ's promise, Trent's prelates had clarified contested doctrines and revamped the Church's internal regulations. While erudite Protestants worked out the lineage of their churches before Luther, their Catholic counterparts rediscovered the significance of the early Christian past, partly to justify beseiged practices. Now Rome as the cradle of European Christianity overshadowed Rome as the center of classical civilization. Counter-Reformation churchmen superseded earlier generations of humanists. From the 1560s, the renewed Church made Rome its primary showcase to the world.[107] The resolve of the church militant, faithful to Christ come what may, was dramatically epitomized in martyrdom, both ancient and modern. Pilgrims thrilled to the inscriptions, fres-

A. Ioannes Fischerus, epus Roffensis in Anglia Card. declaratus, uitæ et doctrinæ,
integerr. laude clariss. ab Henr. uiij. qd Pont. auctem tueretur capite plectitur.
B. Thomas Morus, eques auratᵒ, summo regni magratu perfunctᵒ, prudentia, eruditionæ,
morᵉ innocentia et suauitate insignis, ob eandem causam eiusdem Regis iussu percutitur.
Ambo Anglicanæ reipub. lumina; alter sacri, alter laici ordinis decus.
C. Margarita regiæ familiæ fœmina prudentiss, Comitissa Sar, Card. Poli mᵉ, ob gestatū
insigne quinq. plagar Christi, eadem morte, sub eodem Rege, plexa est.

2 7.

Figure 23. Martyrdom of John Fisher, Thomas More, and Margaret Pole,
engraving from *Ecclesiae Anglicanae trophaea* (Rome: Franciscus Zannettus, 1584),
engraving 27. Reproduced with permission of Brown University Library.

coes, and remains of the early Christian martyrs after the rediscovery of the Roman catacombs in 1578. The material realities of the subterranean city vivified saints' lives and preachers' sermons.[108] Despite lacking recent martyrs of its own, Rome was "Martyr Central," the hub from which spokes radiated to England, the Netherlands, France, and Catholic missions abroad. Having once struggled to establish itself in the Roman Empire, the Church now battled the greatest spread of heresy in over a millennium.

The muted early response to the Henrician martyrs stands in contrast to the mass of publications, letters, poems, and pictures about their post-Tridentine successors. Martyrdom was no longer a perplexing intrusion. Its prospect accompanied hundreds of missionary priests in England; it shadowed French and Dutch clergy during the Wars of Religion. The ethos of martyrdom had been transformed: seminarians and wider circles of the devout extolled it as the perfect culmination of trust in God, love for Christ, and commitment to his embattled Church. Martyrological sensibility was widespread in Counter-Reformation Europe, but where persecution was pressing, including the Netherlands and especially England, it was particularly intense.

The Dutch Catholic martyrs were overwhelmingly clergy killed by the Gueux, or Sea Beggars, during the conflict between Spain and the Netherlands. Around 130 priests perished between 1567 and 1591, with the peak in 1572, when the Gueux and William of Orange's forces regained territory previously subdued by the Duke of Alva.[109] The nineteen Gorcum martyrs, hanged and dismembered in Briel on July 9, 1572, are the best known, although multiple priests were also killed the same year in Alkmaar (June 24), Roermond (July 23), and Audenarde (October 4).[110] The Roermond Carthusians were tortured and slain while at prayer, an incident analogous to Catholic massacres of French Protestants.[111] The Gorcum martyrs, however, were not simply slaughtered: the Count of Lummen used Calvinist ministers and their family members to pressure them, sparing the two who denounced their Catholicism and hanging the rest from the beams in a barn.[112] Similarly, when priests such as Cornelius Musius (killed in Leiden, December 10, 1572) and Willem vander Gouwe (Sint Geertruidenberg, September 3, 1573) resisted quasi-judicial efforts to dissuade them of their views, they were executed.[113] The Dutch priests were martyrs because they had been singled out, threatened, and killed as Catholic priests, even though they were not formally tried and executed.

In England, Catholics were judicially tried and put to death as traitors.[114] In most of the Elizabethan treason trials of priests and their supporters, direct evidence of any conventionally treasonable activity is notoriously thin. Rather, executions followed the violation of new statutes that defined certain Catholic practices as treasonable. From the victims' perspective, as William Allen put it in 1582, this was "to make traitors and not to punish treasons."[115] Elizabethan authorities, however, had reason to be apprehensive. In 1569 the Earls of Westmorland and Northumberland led a serious Catholic uprising in Durham and Yorkshire. It was followed by Pius V's bull *Regnans in excelsis,* which excommunicated Elizabeth and threatened English subjects who obeyed her with the same action. Parliament retaliated by prohibiting the importation of papal bulls or Catholic religious objects.[116] In 1581, the year after Robert Parsons and Edmund Campion led the first Jesuit mission to England, new laws made it treason to reconcile anyone to the Roman Catholic church, and misprision of treason to assist anyone in such reconciliation.[117] In 1585, a year after the formation of the Catholic League in France and the startling assassination of William of Orange in the Netherlands, Parliament made it treason for a priest to be or remain in England, or for anyone to receive or aid any priest.[118] All this legislation conceived Roman Catholicism in strictly political terms, with the pope understood purely as a foreign ruler.

For Catholics, separation from the Church meant separation from Christ. To have observed these laws would have meant consigning all English non-Catholics to damnation. Catholic writers and the martyrs insisted that the missionaries' endeavors in England were apolitical—even though, between 1582 and 1585 in particular, Allen and Parsons were involved in negotiations on the Continent regarding the invasion of England.[119] In the tense international situation of the 1580s—with its multiple plots to replace Elizabeth with Mary Stuart, religious warfare in France and the Netherlands, and the threat of a Spanish invasion, realized in 1588—the English government was far from likely to concede that the missionaries had been dispatched solely to minister to Catholics and to reconcile others to the Church, even though it was likely true.[120] Those put to death were considered martyrs, killed by a duplicitous government without the decency to acknowledge the real reason for the executions.[121]

These circumstances incubated a strong martyrological sensibility among those likeliest to be killed: above all, seminarians and priests at the English College of Douai-Rheims, guided from its inception in 1568 by William Allen; and the members of the English College at Rome, founded by Gregory XIII in 1576 for the express purpose of training missionaries to save souls in England.[122] Additional seminaries were established in Spain at Valladolid (1589) and Seville (1592). Virtually all the Elizabethan and Jacobean Catholic martyrs were alumni from one of these institutions, or Jesuits, or laity who aided priests in violation of the laws of 1581 and 1585.[123] Members of this group, especially between 1580 and 1603, evinced the most intense martyrological sensibility in early modern Catholic Europe.

This sensibility, its enactment, and its celebration flowed from religious values shared among devout laity, committed clergy, martyrs, and martyrologists. Although Protestants and Anabaptists shared this basic sensibility, in

Counter-Reformation Catholicism the phenomenon assumed a distinctive cast: emphasis on the glory of martyrdom spurred the zeal to die for Christ, and the virtue of humility bridled the same desire.

Cultivation and Control: Channeling the Desire for Death

Early modern Catholics inherited the late medieval impulse to imitate Christ through the patient suffering of adversity. The ubiquitous image of cross-laden Christians processing behind their Lord depicted this desire. We find it, for example, on the title page of Luis de Granada's *Of Prayer and Meditation* (1582) and in John Bucke's *Instructions for the Use of the Beads* (1589) (Figure 24).[124] This image pictures the response elicited by Jesus in Matt.

OF
PRAYER, AND
MEDITATION. *Plompton.*
WHEREIN ARE CON-
TEINED FOVVERTIEN DEVOVTE
Meditations for the feuen daies of the weeke,
bothe for the morninges, and eueninges. And in
them is treyted of the confideration of the prin-
cipall holie Myfteries of our faithe.

WRITTEN FIRSTE IN THE SPANISHE
*tongue by the famous Religious father. F. LEWIS
de GRANADA, Prouinciall of the holie
order of preachers in the Pro-
uince of Portugall.*

*Si quis vult poft me venire, abneget femetipfum, & tollat crucem fuam
quotidie, et fequatur me: inc. 9 - verf. 23. Qui non fa in me manere debet
ficut ille ambulauit, et ipfe ambulare. 1 Johan. 2. verf. 6.*

Imprinted at Paris by Thomas Brumeau, at the figne of the
Olyue. Anno Domini. M.D.LXXXII.

---

for the vfe of the beades.   37

prayeth to her. For the more reuerence
and deuocion vve bear tovvardes her,
the greater helpe fhall vve receiue of
her fonne, in all our diftreffes. And this
vve may be fure of, that lyuing here according to her example in continence,
humilitie, pacience, and mortificacion
vve fhall arife at the laft daye in bodie
and foule to reft in heauen for euer. Vnto vvhiche Ioye God of his mercie bring
vs, vvhere that bleffed virgin refteth in
prefence of the Holie Trinitie, the Father, Sonne, and holy Ghooft. To vvhom
be all honor and glorie. Amen.

Figure 24. Christians bearing crosses in imitation of Christ, woodcuts from Luis de Grenada, *Of Prayer, and Meditation* (Paris: Thomas Brumeau, 1582) (left), and John Bucke, *Instructions for the use of the beades* (Louvain: [Jan Maes], 1589), p. 37 (right). Reproduced with permission of Scolar Press, from photostatic reproductions in the series *English Recusant Literature, 1558–1640*.

16:24 and Luke 9:23: "If any want to become my followers, let them deny themselves and take up their cross daily and follow me." In contrast to the late Middle Ages, however, circumstances provided real prospects for martyrdom. This helped transform the general directive to imitate Christ into an explicit desire to die for him.

To suffer and die for the Lord implied an intoxicating intimacy with him. In 1579, shortly after the first executions of missionary priests, expatriate cleric Thomas Hide assured English Catholics that "if you suffer for justice sake (as suffering for religion you cannot but suffer for justice) then may you take more comfort thereof, because you suffer upon Christ's own cross."[125] In his massive hagiographical collection published in the 1570s, Cologne Carthusian Laurentius Surius wrote that "Christ is the king of the martyrs, the form of the martyrs, the strength of the martyrs, and the victory of the martyrs" such that "the totality of the holy martyrs makes up the totality of Christ, from whom the nature of blessed martyrdom flows."[126] Christ as "king of the martyrs" echoed the title of a traditional hymn. In 1582 Circignani expressed the title, too, in the first in the series of martyr images that he painted for San Stefano Rotondo in the German-Hungarian College of Rome.[127] Female and male martyrs gesture toward the crucified Christ with palm-leaf crowns, while two of the Holy Innocents lie below his cross, which proclaims, "You conquer in martyrdom" (Figure 25).[128]

Period exegesis of Col. 1:24 sheds light on Surius's comment that the whole of the martyrs comprised the whole of Christ. Paul wrote to the Colossians, "I am now rejoicing in my sufferings for your sake, and in my flesh I am completing what is lacking in Christ's afflictions for the sake of his body, that is, the church." This verse is rare in Protestant martyrological sources; to imply that Christ's sufferings were incomplete might have opened a door to works righteousness. By contrast, it invited Catholic exegetes to discuss the relationship between Christ's passion and the meritorious sufferings of Christians. The Douai-Rheims New Testament (1582) glossed the verse accordingly:

> As Christ the head and his body make one person mystical and one full Christ . . . so the passions of the head and the afflictions of the body and members make one complete mass of passions . . . And not only those passions which he suffered in himself, which were fully ended in his death, and were in themselves fully sufficient for the redemption of the world and remission of all sins, but all those which his body and members suffer, are his also, and of him they receive the condition, quality, and force to be meritorious and satisfactory.[129]

The suffering of Christians, "and especially martyrs," comprised part of Christ's continuing passion in his mystical body, the Church. From here it

Figure 25. Christ as King of the Glorious Martyrs, from *Ecclesiae militantis triumphi* ([Rome: Franciscus Zannettus?] 1583), engraving 1. Reproduced with permission of Brown University Library.

was a short step to Rev. 6:11 and those to be slain before the Lord's second coming: "There is a certain number that God hath ordained to die for the testimony of truth and the Catholic faith, for conformity of the members to the head Christ our chief martyr."[130]

If martyrdom was the highest form of the imitation of Christ, then it was surpassingly valuable. Despite the transitory grief it might evoke, it was a magnificent good. Treatises, martyrologies, letters, and poems repeatedly described it as "glorious." A French translation of the *Roman Martyrology*, referring mostly to the early Christian martyrs, asserted that

> these great figures could find no means more beautiful, shorter, or more effective to witness to the ardent zeal for the honor and glory of God which burned in them, than joyously exposing their lives for the defense of his holy battle, willingly suffering all the torments that the injurious cruelty of tyrants, the fury of the barbarians, and the rage of hellish spirits were able to conceive . . . one can find no greater gift, more precious present, or more majestic sacrifice that the creature can offer to his creator, than the one the martyrs present to him in their deaths.[131]

Ignatius Loyola's remarks on the virtue of obedience implied a radical asceticism of the will that nurtured the self-denial integral to martyrdom, the holy indifference of Paul's claim that "living is Christ and dying is gain" (Phil. 1:21).[132] Even when prospects for its realization were nil, martyrdom was esteemed and desired by Counter-Reformation *dévots*. Teresa of Avila told her cloistered Carmelite sisters that "if someone is a true religious or a true person of prayer and aims to enjoy the delights of God, he must not turn his back upon the desire to die for God and suffer martyrdom."[133] François de Sales's *Introduction to the Devout Life* was one of the most popular devotional treatises of the seventeenth century. It urged readers to endure trivial nuisances as well as "many great afflictions for our Lord, even martyrdom," as a part of living as a Christian.[134]

The English clerical martyrs agreed that martyrdom was eminently desirable. In May 1582 William Allen told Alfonso Agazzari, the Jesuit rector of Rome's English College, that the recent spate of executions had *increased* the priests' ardor to be sent to England.[135] William Hart consoled his mother shortly before his execution at York in March 1583. Since his becoming a bishop or king would delight her, he wrote, she should be even happier "to see me a martyr, a saint, a most glorious and bright star in heaven. The joy of this life is nothing, and the joy of the afterlife is everlasting."[136] Robert Southwell's devotional reflections and *Epistle of Comfort* (1587 or 1588) disclose a burning desire for martyrdom.[137] The longest chapter in his *Epistle* treated the glory of martyrdom, its profit to the Church, and the honor it conferred on the martyrs. Southwell asked, "What greater preeminence is there in God's Church, than to be a martyr? What more renowned dignity, than to die in this cause of the Catholic faith?" Because it realized fortitude, charity, and obedience in the highest degree, martyrdom fulfilled and completed baptism.[138] Sometimes priests viewed martyrdom with eucharistic overtones. Edmund Campion, for example, referred to martyrs as "holy hosts and oblations" pleasing to God.[139]

Lay martyrs also yearned to die for Christ. Although he was not executed, George Gilbert's overwhelming desire for martyrdom impressed even Rome's seminarians. His unrequited aspiration brought him to grief as he lay dying from a mundane illness in 1583.[140] Margaret Clitherow was one of only three women besides Margaret Pole who suffered death for Catholic crimes in early modern England.[141] According to her spiritual advisor and martyrologist, the seminary priest John Mush, she considered herself unworthy of martyrdom, "but was most desirous and as willing to suffer as the enemy was to afflict her." She was the only English martyr to suffer death by *peine forte et dure,* crushed to death by heavy rocks for her refusal to stand trial. To prevent jeopardizing others whom a trial might have implicated, Clitherow repeatedly declined to be tried on the charge of harboring priests. Lying on her back as the massive weight was applied at York on the morning of March 25, 1586, her outstretched arms were bound to two posts by ribbons she had brought for that purpose, "so that her body and her arms made a perfect cross."[142]

In exalting martyrdom Catholic writers drew freely on patristic (and to a lesser extent, medieval) authors, especially Cyprian, Augustine, and Tertullian. Hide's *Consolatory Epistle* and Southwell's *Epistle* referred to them repeatedly. Henry Garnet, in his *Treatise of Christian Renunciation,* let them speak for themselves. His final chapter, "Of the necessary obligation to suffer martyrdom when otherwise God might be offended," consisted entirely of translated excerpts from Cyprian, Augustine, Ambrose, and Bernard, closing with the story of the seven Maccabees and their mother (2 Macc. 7).[143] Although Protestant anti-Nicodemite writers sometimes cited patristic authors, they did so less often and less zealously than their Catholic counterparts. The Protestant imperative to martyrdom was more exclusively negative: a duty not to compromise the Gospel rather than avidly to pursue the supreme act of self-sacrifice. For Protestants, coveting martyrdom could spoil a death for Christ with a self-regarding anticipation of merit. They could only have censured Cyprian's claim that imprisoned Christians would proceed "by the lingering of [their] torments to more ample titles of merit, and sure to have so many rewards in the heavenly payment as there are days reckoned in present pains."[144] Catholic writers, however, certain that good works played a part in salvation after the Tridentine decree on justification,[145] embraced and encouraged such views.

Thomas Hide implied a proportionalism of reward that would have rankled his Protestant contemporaries: "Doubtless you be daily crowned, the longer you fight, the more is your victory, the greater is your reward."[146] This idea informed the gory depictions and minute categorization of martyrs suffering virtually every conceivable torture and form of execution in Antonio Gallonio's *Treatise on the Instruments of Martyrdom* (1591, with many reprints). Similarly, Peter Biverus's *Holy Sanctuary of the Cross and the Sufferings of the Crucified* (1634) included seventy engravings of saints' crucifixions to accompany over seven hundred pages of devotional text.[147] The image of St. Tarbula sawn in two or of other martyrs suspended from crosses with their entrails hanging down (Figure 26) were harrowing reminders of what fidelity to Christ might demand—yet they also implied a heavenly reward condign to such suffering. A poem about Campion likely written by fellow Jesuit Henry Walpole (himself a future martyr) stated that "every wrinch some glory hath him won, / and every drop of blood which he did spend, / hath reaped a joy which never shall have end."[148]

Much more than their Protestant or Anabaptist counterparts, Catholic martyrs looked to the early Christian martyrs for inspiration. Martyrological writers encouraged them, drawing analogies to men and women who suffered in the early Church. Willem Hessels van Est compared the Gorcum martyrs to the forty Christian martyrs of Sebaste (d. 320), while Aert Swaens van Goerle likened Willem vander Gouwe to John the Baptist.[149] A poem about three seminary priests executed in Derby in July 1588 compared them to Andrew and Stephen:

> When Ludlam looked smilingly
> And joyful did remain
> It seemed St. Stephen was standing by
> For to be stoned again.
>   And afterward
> When Garlick did the ladder kiss
> And Simpson after high
> Me thought that there St. Andrew was
> Desirous for to die.[150]

With her cruciform death, Margaret Clitherow deliberately imitated the dying posture of Christ and early Christian martyrs. When Edward Geninges was taken off the sled to be hanged, drawn, and quartered in London on December 10, 1591, he exalted the gibbet as St. Andrew had praised the cross of his crucifixion.[151] After the jury pronounced Anthony Middleton guilty of treason, he said that just as the Roman soldier Mauritius refused to deny God by worshipping an idol, so "I rather submit myself to any death whatsoever, before I will forsake the Catholic faith."[152] These Catholics un-

Malo mihi tortor violet quàm membra Cytheris:
67.   Integra ſum ſecto corpore ſponſa Dei.

Figure 26. Martyrdom of St. Tarbula, engraving from Peter Biverus, *Holy Sanctuary of the Cross* (Antwerp: Balthasar Moret, 1634), p. 601. Reproduced with permission of University Library, Utrecht.

derstood themselves to be enacting the latest chapter in the history of Christian persecution, the same one depicted in Circignani's paintings in Rome. If the Church fathers provided an authoritative exhortation to martyrdom, the early Christian martyrs offered paradigms for its practice. Latter-day imitation of Christ encompassed multiple historical layers: by following the ancients, the moderns were imitating the imitators of Christ.

Every fresh martyrdom, too, created another model for mimesis. Thomas Alfield wrote that as Campion, Ralph Sherwin, and Alexander Briant "were in their lives lanterns of piety and virtue, so in their deaths [they] made themselves patterns and examples for all good Christian subjects to follow."[153] Campion's severed body parts solicited further warriors, in an image that recalled Pole's views about martyrdom's singular power in the proclamation of Christian truth:

> His quarters hung on every gate do show,
> his doctrine sound through countries far and near,
> his head set up so high doth call for more
> to fight the fight which he endured here,
> the faith thus planted thus restored must be,
> "Take up thy cross," sayeth Christ, "and follow me."[154]

At the English College in Rome, George Gilbert, a layman, "took great pains to learn the names of all the English martyrs of former and modern times." He financed Circignani's paintings in their honor, to stimulate the seminarians to follow their example.[155] Twenty-year-old Thomas Felton reportedly hoped that his imprisonment would end as it had for his father, John. The latter was executed in 1570 for having affixed the papal bull *Regnans in excelsis* to the bishop of London's gate. On August 28, 1588, his desire was fulfilled: son followed father in death for the Catholic faith.[156]

Martyrdom opened outward, most immediately toward those who witnessed the martyrs' deaths. Enthusiasts thought it uniquely efficacious for converting Protestants and confirming the faithful, once it became clear that no official return to Rome was imminent. Moreover, the martyrs' sacrifice would awaken God's mercy, placating his anger at Catholics for the sins that they believed had precipitated the English persecution.[157] In contrast to the defensive stance of the Henrician martyrs, the later English Catholics self-consciously deployed martyrdom as a tool of conversion, a Catholic recognition of Tertullian's dictum. In life, missionaries would minister to Catholics and seek to reconcile others to the Church; in martyrdom, they would move people to return to the faith. Sometimes it worked. Thomas Busbridge, for example, traveled from England to Rome, where in April 1582 he abjured his Protestantism and became a Catholic, citing Campion's eloquence and martyrdom. In 1601, an unjustly accused horse thief reportedly made a gallows conversion to Catholicism, having just witnessed the heroic death of the priest John Pybus.[158]

No one was more resolute than William Allen about martyrdom's potential for working conversion. As he wrote in his *Apology of the English Colleges* in 1581,

> blood so yielded maketh the forciblest mean[s] to procure mercy that can be. Every time that you confess Christ's name, every wrinch of any joint for it, every opprobrious scoff and scorn given by the popular,

when you be carried in the sacred vestments through the streets . . .
every villany and sacrilege done to your priesthood, every of your sores,
sorrows, and sighs, every of your wants and necessities, make a stronger
intercession for our country and afflicted Church, than any prayers
lightly in the world.

This is the way, by which we hope to win our nation to God again.[159]

In July 1582 Allen told Agazzari that martyrs' deaths affected people much
more powerfully than sermons; in March 1583 he proudly declared that the
first three martyrdoms in York had greatly confirmed the faithful.[160] Claudio
Aquaviva, the general of the Jesuit order, considered in 1584 whether Jesuits
ought to continue serving on the English mission. Allen defended its effectiveness with hyperbole: for fewer than thirty priests lost, he declared, over
one hundred thousand souls had been gained. "What did they do in the days
of the early Church under Diocletian, Maximinus, Julian, and Valens?" he
asked.[161] Even near the end of his life, in 1592, Allen expressed confidence
that the suffering was nearly finished and would soon usher in England's
return to the faith.[162] Obviously he was mistaken if judged by his criterion of
England's wholesale return to Catholicism—but he had also written that
saving even one soul was worth the price of all mortal pains.[163] Internal
disputes (above all the Appellant controversy) plagued English Catholicism
after Allen's death. There is little question, however, that their martyrs provided strength as English Catholics became increasingly sectlike in subsequent decades.

In the 1580s and 1590s Allen's views were widely shared. The social impact
of martyrdom paralleled the glory it conferred on the martyrs themselves.
Southwell expressed the idea with customary insight:

we find by experience that whosoever suffereth, though he suffer for
his offense is pitied, and naturally misery, though deserved, cannot but
breed remorse, and tenderness in the beholders. But now when such
men as be of innocent behavior, of virtuous conversation, learned and
grave persons, shall with comfort offer themselves to extremity, rejoice
when they are tormented, smile when they are dismembered, and go to
death as they would to a banquet; when such as neither want dignities to
withdraw them, nor friends and family to pull them back, nor powerable
enemies to affright them, shall be ready to change their dignity with
disgrace, to forsake their friends, and give themselves into the hands of
their mortal foes, only for the defense of their conscience, men must
needs say as they did in St. Cyprian's time . . . "It is a thing worthy to
be known and some virtue that deserveth deep consideration, for which
a man is content to suffer death" . . . And this is the comfort of those

that suffer, that their death raiseth many from death, and their patience maketh every one inquisitive of their religion.[164]

This social impressiveness made martyrdom "the seed of the Church." By conforming to culturally resonant models in the spectacle of their deaths, martyrs proselytized for Catholicism. God had designed things this way. "It is the blessed will of God," Thomas Hide wrote, "that the glory of his militant church should multiply in persecution, should increase under oppression, and that out of the blood of one Catholic suffering death for Christ, should arise many holy Christians."[165] One of Walpole's poems about Campion expected his influence to be greater after martyrdom than it had been in life:

> You thought perhaps when learned Campion dies,
> his pen must cease, his sugared tongue be still,
> but you forgot how loud his death it cries,
> how far beyond the sound of tongue and quill,
> you did not know how rare and great a good
> it was to write his precious gifts in blood.[166]

According to John Geninges, brother of the martyr Edmund, the phenomenon also worked the other way round. Catholics went to watch Edmund executed in London, "partly by the sight thereof to confirm their faith, and increase their charity, and to get courage to embrace all like assaults and combats, if like occasion should be offered; and partly to participate, although not in act, yet at least in desire, with him in his martyrdom."[167] We are back to solidarity in suffering—not only with Christ, "but also between one member and another" in the Church, for "the passions of the saints are always suffered for the common good of the whole body."[168]

Despite aspirations to imitate Christ in death, the English missionaries and their supporters were not carried away by an unrestrained rush to die for their faith. The evidence suggests that the yearning for martyrdom coexisted with a caution that was instilled during the missionaries' education and that remained part of their mentality.

The missionaries' casuistical training prepared them for situations they might face in England. A manual of cases of conscience, written between 1581 and 1585 and used in the English College in Rome, commented at length about what Catholics should do if they heard someone blaspheme against God, the saints, the Church, or the pope.[169] Especially if there were little hope of accomplishing anything beyond self-betrayal, usually it was best to remain silent. Not every dangerous situation was a summons to martyrdom:

> Where there is no hope of converting anyone and the need to avoid
> scandal and harm to the faith does not force one to speak, then it is

generally a sort of temerity to put oneself into open danger of death. Not everyone can claim for himself the honour of being a martyr, only one who is called to be a martyr by God. When, therefore, necessity compels us to speak out in order to avoid scandal or to maintain the faith of the weak, it can reasonably be believed that God calls us to martyrdom. But where neither of these two circumstances is to be found, we should not presume that God wants us to be martyrs, and so, to speak out in that case is directly to rush into martyrdom before receiving the vocation of God. Moreover, this boldness is justly censured because it is the action of a man who has no vocation, but nevertheless throws himself into something which he is perhaps unworthy to perform; and also because you presume you will be firm but perhaps will be deficient in bravery under torture. For, I can assure you, God is on hand to help both those he calls as well as those who rashly of their own accord push themselves forward, but sometimes he takes away grace from both sorts of men, or does not grant enough of it.[170]

This warning recalls Thomas More's caution half a century earlier. It suggests that the missionaries tempered their eagerness for martyrdom. Their behavior in England also implies discretion. They and their supporters did not brazenly denounce heresy in marketplaces or disrupt Protestant services. Rather they sought to avoid detection, employing false names and disguises—measures sanctioned, in certain circumstances, in their casuistical training.[171] Even Robert Southwell held that the desire for martyrdom was no sure sign from God that one was chosen to die. One was not, therefore, deliberately to court martyrdom in provocative ways, such as preaching to heretics or reprimanding the powerful.[172] George Gilbert, who seems to have lusted for martyrdom, abandoned the opportunity to shed his blood when in May 1581 he obeyed Parsons's order to leave England, owing to the perilous circumstances.[173] When Parsons was writing a life of Campion, Aquaviva cautioned him not to let the narration of Campion's death overshadow his missionary activity.[174] Caution and prudence balanced the passion for passion in the missionaries' milieu.

Ironically, the exaltation of martyrdom as the highest form of the imitation of Christ and the most perfect realization of Christian virtues helped *prevent* zeal for it from spinning out of control. Because the martyrs were greater in heaven than even doctors of the Church and virgins,[175] and because not everyone was called to such a glorious death, the virtue of humility militated against a presumption of holiness condign to such a vocation. Self-professed unworthiness was a widespread convention in early modern Catholic spiritual writing. Yet when prospective martyrs asserted it, they were grappling with a real tension: they were exhorted to martyrdom, an imitation of Christ that only spiritual arrogance could—mistakenly—make them think they merited.[176] No one could suffer for the faith "but by the gracious gift of God," Hide wrote, "and God giveth this gift to none but to his special friends."[177] For Anabaptists, the prospect of martyrdom was the inseparable shadow of simply being a Christian. For Catholics, martyrdom remained an extraordinary grace, bestowed only upon a "supremely brave athlete" [*fortissimus athleta*] for Christ.[178]

Misplaced pride could be deadly, as the casuistry manual warned: sometimes God withdrew his grace or did not bestow enough of it. This danger had led Thomas More to "squeeze" God's special providence, as it were, so that when loopholes collapsed despite his efforts to preserve them, the unfolding of God's will became clear. The casuists acknowledged how difficult the discernment of God's will could be.[179] Dying well was critically important. If there was any chance for martyrs to have the impact envisioned by Southwell, they could not be perceived as maniacal suicide seekers. When Catholics were executed, the martyrologists (who were sometimes also the casuists) did not fail to celebrate their heroism and its anticipated efficacy. Such deaths sometimes *did* inspire in others the desire for martyrdom: "Our constancy forceth men to look more into our cause, and then by seeking they find, by finding they believe, and believing are as ready to die as we ourselves."[180] Spiritual directors would have to monitor these aspirations, lest they become reckless presumption. The dialectic thus renewed itself; the delicate balancing act remained.

Communication and Publicization

Whatever the risk of inciting overzealousness, those associated with the English mission spread the news of the recent martyrdoms in the 1580s and 1590s. Unlike their Henrician predecessors, they knew what such deaths meant. God was punishing them for their sins and was also mercifully employing the martyrs to glorify the Church, to which he was recalling Englishmen and women. As the missionaries carried the desire for martyrdom into England, so the news of their deaths and the trail of their relics flowed back to the Continent. The primary axis ran from London to Douai-Rheims to Rome, with tributary branches along the way.

The communication process began with eyewitnesses and oral reports. Thomas Alfield, for example, was in the crowd when Campion, Sherwin, and Briant were killed. Also present, he noted, were "many good Catholic gentlemen desirous to be eyewitnesses of that which might happen in the speech, demeanor, and passage" of the three martyrs.[181] Similarly, a law student at

Gray's Inn in London named Dolman "did accompany Alfield to Campion's execution, took notes of his words and manner of execution and delivered the same to Roland [Verstegan] the printer in Smithfield."[182] Eyewitnesses also contributed to Dutch martyrological accounts. Some of the Roermond Carthusians were not slain with their fellow monks, for example, and a Franciscan novice who was reprieved by the Count of Lummen became an important source for the Gorcum martyrs. Aert Swaens van Goerle hid in water up to his neck for fourteen hours, ducking under when necessary, as he watched the Gueux ransack the town of Sint Geertruidenberg before they executed Willem vander Gouwe.[183]

Correspondence followed eyewitness encounters and oral reports. Between England and the Continent, the exchange of letters with news of the martyrs was frequent and extensive. Before Allen went to Rome in 1585, he received reports about the English martyrs in Rheims, sharing them in turn with Agazzari in Rome. For example, Allen sent Agazzari some of the poems honoring Campion in February 1582, just two months after the executions; he also explained in June how a young man (Samuel Kennet), a Catholic convert and caretaker in the Tower of London, had brought to Rheims letters from imprisoned priest John Hart; and the following month he wrote that people were "constantly" sending him "new material" about the martyrs.[184] During these very months Allen was writing his *Brief History of the Glorious Martyrdom of Twelve Reverend Priests,* which was completed and printed by the beginning of September.[185] Richard Barret, Allen's prefect of studies and his successor as president of the college, wrote to Agazzari in July 1584. He mentioned "a certain good and prudent man" who had come from Paris—presumably after being in England—"who was accustomed to observe most diligently [*diligentissime solebat observare*] everything about the martyrs, not only their words, but also their actions [*non solum dicta sed et facta*], to commit them to memory, and to write down what he knew either through himself or through someone else." Through this man's friend, Barret intended to solicit from him written accounts of the martyrs, including even the "very smallest" [*minutissima*] details, and to send them on to Agazzari.[186] We do not know whether Barret was successful in this instance. However, like Allen, he frequently updated Rome with news about the persecution and martyrdom of Catholics.[187]

Regular Jesuit correspondence constituted another direct link between England and Rome. Henry Garnet kept Aquaviva informed, as in a letter from early 1594 about martyrs from the previous two years. On February 22, 1595, he sent an account of Southwell's martyrdom, based on an eyewitness who had recounted it to him.[188] William Good, a Jesuit who was then confessor of the English College in Rome, preserved several of the letters from his martyred godson, William Hart. Father William Warford had corresponded with the Oxford-educated priest and martyr Edward Stransham and had kept some of his final letters.[189]

Other strands in the web of correspondence extended to Germany, the Low Countries, and Spain. An important member of this network during the 1580s was the Jesuit John Gibbons. He compiled and edited the most comprehensive Elizabethan Catholic martyrology, the *Struggle of the Catholic Church in England* (1583, expanded edition 1588). In Trier, Gibbons gathered materials from numerous informants, as a packet of letters intercepted by English officials in 1587 made clear.[190] Living in Antwerp from 1587 was Richard Verstegan, an English polymath of Dutch descent with a keen interest in the martyrs. In the 1590s he was a central link among English Jesuits such as Henry Garnet and Walpole in England, the Jesuit Robert Parsons in Spain, and William Allen in Rome through the latter's secretary, Roger Baynes.[191] English Catholic exiles in Antwerp also brought him fresh news of the martyrs' tribulations.[192]

In short, reports about the martyrs were plentiful. The writings often left England with little trouble, despite the watchful eye of authorities. This international Catholic circle closely resembled the network that had created the major Protestant martyrologies in the 1550s and 1560s. Allen in Rheims shuffled reports from England to Agazzari in Rome, just as Edmund Grindal in Strasbourg had supplied sources about the Marian martyrs to John Foxe in Basel. Such exchanges, built on shared religious commitments, lay behind printed martyrological sources intended for public consumption.

The publicization of Protestant martyrs had begun with early pamphlets and songs, which flowed into the midcentury martyrologies like so many rivulets. By the seventeenth century, multiple editions of the Protestant collections comprised powerful streams of martyrological expression. The publicization of Catholic martyrs by contrast, suggests not a river, but separate drops of rain, with the few sprinkles during the Henrician period becoming a downpour by the late sixteenth century. There were no comprehensive Catholic accounts of Christian history built around persecution and martyrdom that emphasized the sixteenth century. The number and variety of Catholic publications, however, compensated for the lack of a counterpart to the major Protestant martyrologies.

Between 1580 and 1640, at least 203 editions of more than 50 different works either about the English Catholic martyrs or in which they occupy an important place were published throughout Europe, in English, Latin, French, Italian, Spanish, German, and Dutch.[193] Of these, 95 appeared in the 1580s. They issued mainly from the major centers of Catholic publishing, such as Paris, Antwerp, Cologne, Ingolstadt, Rome, Madrid, and Seville. The publications vary in length from single-leaf French texts with supplementary engravings, as in Verstegan's *Brief Description of Various Cruelties That Catholics Suffer for the Faith in England* (Paris, 1583–1584), and single-subject Italian pamphlets such as the *Brief Account of the Martyrdom of Two Reverend Priests and Two Laymen at Oxford in 1589* (Rome and Brescia, 1590), to major compendia such as the Spanish history of the Elizabethan persecution compiled by Diego de Yepes, the bishop of Tarrasona, with help from the English Jesuit Joseph Cresswell (Madrid, 1599).[194] Eyewitness accounts, prison letters, exhortations to steadfastness, eulogies to martyrs, poems in Latin and the vernacular, engravings and woodcuts depicting the cruelties of English authorities—all were part of this storm of publicization. The sheer quantity suggests that by 1590 few literate Catholics, from Seville to Salzburg, from Bruges to Bologna, could have been unaware of the English martyrs.

Publications about Dutch martyrs swelled the volume of printed sources about martyrdom, persecution, and suffering in Counter-Reformation Catholicism. So did materials about foreign missionary martyrs, especially in Japan, particularly from the first decade of the seventeenth century.[195] The Church's new martyrology for liturgical use, the *Roman Martyrology*, first appeared in 1584. Its compressed accounts of the saints, many of them ancient martyrs, organized for day-by-day use the vast, venerable tradition that included the suffering of Christ in the members of his mystical body. Like the hagiographical compilation by Surius, the *Roman Martyrology* was widely excerpted and translated. It was supplemented by hundreds of lesser publications in Latin and every major European vernacular about martyr-saints and the wonders worked through their intercession. Sources about the recent martyrs both enriched and fed off a thriving industry of hagiographical publication.

Few works integrated Catholic martyrs from throughout Europe, and none combined foreign with European martyrs in a comprehensive, systematic way. Verstegan went furthest, in his *Theater of the Cruelties of the Heretics of Our Age* (1587), one of the best-known Catholic martyrological sources of the period. Twenty-nine engravings, accompanied by concise, didactic texts, recounted the stories of the Henrician martyrs, the Elizabethan martyrs, and the Catholics executed in France and the Low Countries during the Wars of Religion.[196] More often, however, Catholic martyrological sources were devoted to martyrs from one country or, if international, to those from a particular religious order.

Tracing the links of communication and publication about certain Dutch Franciscan martyrs conveys a good sense of how Latin facilitated internationalization.[197] In 1572, Willem Hessels van Est sent a preliminary report about the Gorcum martyrs to a friend (perhaps Surius) in Cologne, who without his permission published it as a Latin pamphlet.[198] This pamphlet was an important source for Florentius van Oyen, the provincial of the Observant Franciscans in the Netherlands (1570–1574), who used it for his own account of the eleven Franciscans among the Gorcum martyrs, which he dispatched to Rome. In 1580, van Oyen's account was supplemented with information about additional Dutch Franciscan martyrs, which in January 1581 was delivered to the general of the order, Franciscus Gonzaga, in Naples. Gonzaga had other news on hand about recent French Franciscan martyrs. The following month he published the combined accounts, in Latin, as *The History of the Suffering of Recent, Most Steadfast Martyrs from the Dutch Province of the Observant Franciscans.*[199] Wolfgang Eder published a second Latin edition the following year in Ingolstadt. He stated that "a certain devout and learned man," probably Valentius Friccius, a Franciscan from the Strasbourg province, had given him a copy of the Naples edition.[200] Also in 1582, in Paris, Thomas Bourchier, an exiled English Franciscan, published an independent Latin compendium of sixteenth-century Franciscans, the *Ecclesiastical History of the Martyrdom of Brothers From the Order of St. Francis.*[201] Bourchier's work was soon known in Austria: in Ingolstadt, Eder published it in another Latin edition in 1583. Friccius made the jump to the vernacular the following year with an abridged German version of both van Oyen's *History* and Bourchier's volume, the two of which Eder combined, published, and then reprinted in 1585.[202]

When it came to publicizing Franciscan martyrs, the shared language of Latin and the fact that the Franciscans were an international institution rendered linguistic and national boundaries superfluous. A line of transmission ran from Gorcum to Cologne, back to the Netherlands, then to Rome and Naples, and on to Ingolstadt; there another line joined it from Paris, and the two were fused and transformed in a linguistic shift from Latin to German. Knowledge of Latin enabled sources to move laterally among like-minded religious, regardless of their native tongue. Through preachers' sermons and vernacular translations they reached a larger audience, which included more laity. Catholic religious orders had an advantage over groups that faced vernacular boundaries, such as Anabaptists, who seem to have penetrated Francophone regions only lightly. In 1580, initial Latin reports were transmitted by Dutch Franciscans to Rome; four years later, translated and transformed, they were being sold in German by booksellers in Vienna and Ingolstadt.

The process also worked in the other direction: from the vernacular to Latin, and from one vernacular to another. Thomas Alfield's *True Report of the Death and Martyrdom of Mr. Campion,* for example, followed this pattern. We have seen how a law student accompanied Alfield to the execution of Campion, Sherwin, and Briant in London on December 1, 1581, and took notes on their words and deeds. Alfield undoubtedly used these notes plus his

own memory in composing the *True Report,* which Verstegan secretly published in London by early March 1582.[203] William Allen must have received a
copy of this pamphlet in Rheims. He followed it closely, at times verbatim, in
his *Brief History of the Glorious Martyrdom of Twelve Reverend Priests.*[204]
When Allen sent the *Brief History* to Agazzari that summer, he expressed
hope that someone in Rome would have time to translate it into Latin and
Italian.[205] An augmented Italian translation appeared in 1583 at Macerata,
with three more editions in the next two years.[206] A Latin edition was apparently published at Prague in 1583. The same year, in Trier, John Gibbons
incorporated an abridged Latin translation into his *Struggle of the English
Church,* combining it with a Latin rendering of a French publication, *The
History of the Death That Edmund Campion and Others Suffered in England
for the Roman Catholic Faith.*[207] The latter pamphlet had spread widely and
quickly: in 1582, French editions were published in Lyons and Paris, an
Italian translation in Turin and Venice, and a Latin translation—by Willem
Hessels van Est, the martyrologist of the Gorcum martyrs—in Louvain.[208]

Publications about the English martyrs crossed national and linguistic
boundaries as easily as did narratives about the Dutch Franciscans. From a
seminary priest and a London law student, the story traveled across the
English Channel to Rheims, where it branched out to Jesuits in both Rome
and Trier. In Trier, another account joined it by way of Paris and/or Lyons, a
rendition that veered south to Turin and Venice as well as north to Louvain.
Within a year of Campion's death, published accounts of his martyrdom were
available in English, French, Italian, and Latin. We cannot know whether, as
Henry Walpole claimed, "all Europe wonder[ed] at so rare a man"—but
much of Europe would have had the opportunity.[209]

The post-Tridentine martyrological sources reverberate with the Counter-
Reformation ethos of martyrdom. Stories of Protestant ministers and civil
authorities urging Catholics to renounce their views underscored the martyrs'
constancy. Rutger Hessels van Est, Willem's brother and also a Franciscan,
had been imprisoned with the Gorcum martyrs for a time. He versified in
song the Calvinist preachers' pressure: "In order to avoid death / they had
only to renounce / the pope, their supreme head. / But they could in no
sense / consent to that."[210] Publications about the English martyrs recorded
similar refusals, whether by priests such as Thomas Cottam and Edmund
Geninges, or laity such as John Rigby and Margaret Clitherow.[211] An engraving based on a Circignani painting captured the combination of devout resolve and futile disputation. As the priests are dragged on hurdles to the execution site, their hands folded in prayer, a "heretical minister" thrusts at them
an open book (the Bible?), seeking to wrest them from their Catholicism
(Figure 27).

Qui Summi Pontificis primatum Reginæ in Anglia negant tribui posse, tanquam Læsæ Maiestatis rei damnantur, et ad supplicij locum, Cratibus impositi, ministris interim hæreticis ad fidem Catholicam deserendam adhortantibus, per mediam Vrbem ignominiosè raptantur. Sic Edmundus Campianus cum socijs, alijque Catholici tum Sacerdotes tum laici ad mortem tracti sunt. Anno Domini 1581. 1582. 1583.

Figure 27. Attempts to make priests renounce their views en route to execution, from *Ecclesiae Anglicanae trophaea* (Rome: Franciscus Zannettus, 1584), engraving 32. Reproduced with permission of Brown University Library.

Resistance to heretical seduction paralleled the association of doctrines and deaths, another major theme in these sources. The martyrs rejected false teachings as they carried Catholic truth to the scaffold. As Walpole said of Campion, "his death confirmed his doctrine true," indeed, the very "streets, the stones, the steps you hauled them by, / proclaim the cause for which these martyrs die."[212] Papal authority was often part of this cause. Nicolas Pieck rebuffed the Protestant ministers who confronted him: renouncing the pope meant renouncing God, since the pope was the head of God's Church on earth.[213] Catholic interrogators often used transubstantiation as a litmus test of orthodoxy with accused heretics; Elizabethan authorities grilled suspected Catholics about papal and royal authority. When John Finch, for example, was asked about Elizabeth's ecclesiastical authority, he replied that the pope was "the head of the entire Church on earth," an office that neither a woman nor a layman could hold.[214]

In refusing to renounce papal authority, Catholic martyrs neither highlighted the essence nor proclaimed the totality of their faith. Nor did Protestants who denied transubstantiation or Anabaptists who rejected infant baptism. All such issues reflect the questions put to the martyrs, not autonomous expressions of their convictions. Still, these doctrines were related to comprehensive visions of Christian truth, whose integrity was violated if a part was rejected. For Catholics, to deny the pope was to deny Christ himself, because the Lord had delegated to Peter and his successors authority over his visible Church. Indeed, to reject the pope was to reject Christianity as such, as embodied in Roman Catholic liturgy, sacraments, and doctrines. We catch glimpses of the whole behind the part. Hide told persecuted English Catholics, "you suffer this affliction for [Christ's] honor, you suffer for the honor of his saints, you suffer for the honor of his sacraments, you suffer for the honor of the universal Church."[215] Similarly, Alfield wrote that Campion and company had suffered "for the honor, peace, and unity of the Church, for saving of their souls, and the souls of our beloved parents, children, and friends, for the defense of Christ's priesthood and sovereignty in earth, for his eternal sacrifice and sacraments." This was not "dying for the pope" in any narrow sense.[216] A reflection of interrogators' preoccupations, papal authority implied for the martyrs the whole of Roman Catholicism, which they believed was true Christianity. Elizabethan writers may have made of More "a martyr of Trent by anticipation" in editing his remarks about the Nun of Kent and his relationship with Erasmus. Yet the Henrician and post-Tridentine martyrs shared fundamentally the same views about the papacy's relationship to the Church and its tradition.[217] Neither before nor after Trent was the pope dispensable.

Martyrological sources portrayed the cruelty and bloodthirstiness of the

Catholics' persecutors. Writers usually and predictably softened their depictions with reference to the "evil counselors" who had led sovereigns astray. Nevertheless, they shared with their Protestant and Anabaptist counterparts the same dichotomous conception of innocent suffering and tyrannical oppression. Verstegan made this explicit in his works, including the *Theater of the Cruelties of the Heretics*. Its engravings showed "that the Church has never endured such a cruel and deadly plague, nor suffered more violent destruction, than this last, disastrous calamity wrought by this breed and generation of Calvin and Beza, having departed their cave of Geneva (or rather, Gehenna) that has deformed the whole world under a pretty pretense [*beau pretexte*] of the reformation of the Church."[218] One image illustrated the 1572 slaughter of the Roermond Carthusians (Figure 28). Another showed English priests and their lay supporters in various stages of being hanged, drawn, and quartered, from their appearance on hurdles to the boiling of their body parts (Figure 29). Peter Frarin enlisted a tradition of artistic didacticism that stretched back to Gregory the Great. He explained that woodcuts depicting the violence of heretics in his *Oration against the Unlawful Insurrections of the Protestants* (1566) were arranged according "to the eye and sight of the Christian reader, and of him also that cannot read."[219] Meanwhile, for the literate, texts bristled with denunciations. Robert Parsons wrote that heresy blinded men to mercy and compassion, driving them to commit outrageous acts. Allen hoped his *Brief History* would show "the whole Christian world . . . a spectacle of heretical cruelty and Machiavellian practices." And Adam Blackwood's French poem satirized "the virtues of the English Jezabel," Elizabeth, for her role in the execution of Mary Stuart.[220]

By the 1580s martyrs' glory and persecutors' cruelty were linked to more explicitly political martyrological claims. It would be misleading to characterize as purely political any Catholic military plans to invade England or to suppress continental Calvinists. Such actions, however, differed greatly from the saying of clandestine Masses and the reconciliation of people to the Church. Mary Stuart was trapped: her religious convictions made her central to plots aimed to overthrow Elizabeth.[221] After her execution, Catholics celebrated her as a martyr. Harder-edged were the publications that proclaimed the assassins of William of Orange and Henry III of France as martyrs. Horrific torture and execution were inflicted on Baltasar Gerard for murdering the Prince of Orange in 1584. Within months, sympathetic accounts of his suffering and death, some explicitly calling him a martyr, were published in Dutch, German, French, and Italian.[222] In 1589, Jacques Clément killed Henry III as a Catholic League retaliation for the murder of the Guises. After he was tortured and executed, several Parisian pamphlets and engravings described him as a martyr.[223] Insofar as the slain political leaders had been

Figure 28. Slaughter of the Roermond Carthusians, engraving from Richard Verstegan, *Theater of the Cruelties of the Heretics* (Antwerp: Adrien Hubert, 1588), p. 61. Reproduced with permission of Princeton University Library.

Figure 29. Stages in the execution of Elizabethan Catholics, engraving from Verstegan, *Theater of the Cruelties of the Heretics,* p. 83.

anti-Catholic, Gerard's and Clément's actions could hardly be wicked. The suffering they endured for their violent yet righteous actions was, as a Dutch pamphlet stated of Gerard in a phrase echoing the Mass, "like a holy and living sacrifice offered to God the Lord, his creator."[224] Before Welsh priest Richard Gwyn was executed at Wrexham on October 17, 1584, he wrote a poem praising Orange's murder. And in his own story of the Gorcum martyrs, Willem Hessels van Est wrote that Gerard "ended his life with a glorious martyrdom."[225] In some instances, at least, there was a porous membrane between praising the desire to die in the Church's cause and commending those willing to kill for it.

The Role of the Martyrs in Catholic Devotional Life

For the vast majority of post-Tridentine Catholics, the prospect of martyrdom remained as remote as it had been in the late Middle Ages. This was obviously so in Spain and Italy. In France and the Low Countries, extramilitary, anti-Catholic violence was sporadic and targeted mostly against the clergy. In England, even open recusancy did not entail the risk of martyrdom—unless one sheltered missionary priests, participated in secret Masses, fostered the reconciliation of Protestants to the Church, or associated with political subversives. Yet martyrs played a role in the lives of those who were themselves unlikely candidates for martyrdom. At one end of a spectrum stood the English seminarians and their lay supporters, the Roman Jesuits and Oratorians, and certain other religious, who avidly cultivated martyrological sensibilities. At the other end were rural peasants in Spain or Italy, who had perhaps never heard of Edmund Campion. They were far from indifferent, however, to traditional saints and their relics.[226]

Investigation of attitudes and practices along this spectrum makes it clear that the martyrs cut across neat distinctions between clergy and laity, elite and popular, devout and conformist. Catholics in all these categories widely remembered, honored, and prayed to the recent martyrs in the late sixteenth and seventeenth centuries. The dichotomy between extraordinary and ordinary, however, distinguished the place of martyrs in Roman Catholicism from the place of their Protestant and especially Anabaptist counterparts. Most Catholics related to their martyrs within the traditional, two-tier model, seeing themselves as frail human beings seeking help from powerful heavenly patrons. A world away were the Anabaptists, who constantly were at risk of martyrdom, a vulnerability that they understood as simply part of being Christian. Consequently, Catholics widely perceived their recent martyrs as new saints who were already in God's presence, regardless of the status of their canonization proceedings. Martyrs were not *conflated* with all the saints, but rather continued to be seen as one type of saint (along with virgins, doctors, apostles, and confessors), whose spectacular steadfastness betokened their status.

For most Catholics, the recent martyrs were above all new intercessors. Both clergy and laity participated in a dynamic that began with martyrs' material remains. It moved "upward," with the faithful venerating the martyrs in their presumed place in heaven, where they took their place alongside traditional intercessors. Then, in a "downward" movement, they responded, as supplicants discerned in manifold ways the new saints' favor with God.

From Earth to Heaven: Relics and Supplications

Clergy and laity alike coveted the martyrs' relics, continuing the practices of their Henrician predecessors. Writing about the English priests executed in 1582, William Allen stated that by

> the Catholics, of Italy, Spain, France, and namely (which is less to be marveled at) of England, more than the weight in gold would be given, and is offered for any piece of their relics, either of their bodies, hair, bones, or garments, yea or any thing that hath any spot or stain of their innocent and sacred blood. Wherein surely great diligence and honorable zeal hath been showed by divers noble gentlemen and virtuous people, that have to their great danger obtained some good pieces of them, to satisfy the godly greedy appetite of holy persons of divers nations making extreme suit for them.[227]

This "great diligence and honorable zeal" began at the gallows. Relics were dispatched to favored fellow believers, just like written accounts of the martyrs' deaths. Martyrs' remains were honored through ritual processions and at sites of final repose, in reliquaries and beneath church altars. Excitement over these relics ran high in the very decades when the archaeological exploration of the Roman catacombs was being undertaken.

A virtual frenzy for William Hart's remains and clothes followed his execution at York on March 15, 1583. He was barely dead when spectators began struggling among themselves to seize "either his shirt or shoes or some part of his clothes" and frustrated initial attempts at restraint by the authorities. Once order was restored, several of the enthusiasts were imprisoned.[228] At other executions, authorities thwarted the desires of Catholics who sought the martyrs' remnants.[229] Perhaps because of the danger, a young woman named Lucy Ridley proceeded discreetly at the 1591 execution of Edmund Geninges. After he and Swithun Wells had been dispatched in London, their body parts were hauled to Newgate prison. Their torn corpses would be boiled, as was customary, before they were placed on public display at various locations around the city. As the executioner hoisted Geninges's head for the crowd, Ridley positioned herself within reach of one of the martyr's thumbs, still attached to a bloodied quarter of his body that lay in a basket. She touched the thumb and it unexpectedly came off. Ridley stole it away and later smuggled it to Louvain, where she became a nun.[230] When Henry Garnet was executed in St. Paul's Churchyard, London, on May 3, 1606, a silk mercer named John Wilkinson was waiting beneath the scaffold. Garnet's blood "streamed down through the chinks of the boards, upon his hat and apparel," and Wilkinson "dipped such linen as he had prepared in the same."[231] The practice of cloth dipping was apparently long-lived and widespread: members of the crowd did likewise when Henry Burton lost his ears in 1637 for his vehement Puritan views. One verse of a song about the martyrdom of John Thulis, a Catholic priest executed at Lancaster on March 18, 1616, noted how "A hundred handkerchiefs / With his sweet blood was dight, / As relics for to wear / For this said blessed wight."[232]

Once martyrs' remains had been secured, the precious wealth was often shared. Sometimes members of a religious order dispersed the relics. In the early seventeenth century, for example, Dutch Franciscans preserved the bloodstained prayer book of Reijnier Linthers, one of their own killed at Roermond in 1572. Meanwhile, the Franciscan house at Aachen retained the hair shirt of the illustrious Nicolas Pieck.[233] In other instances, civic pride and hope of divine protection seem to have motivated the craving for relics: several towns in the southern Netherlands secured some remains of the Gorcum martyrs in the early seventeenth century.[234] Personal acquaintances could also be beneficiaries. The same John Wilkinson who brought linens beneath Garnet's scaffold gave to the wife of Hugh Griffin, a London tailor, the end of a bloodied wheat stalk with which he had departed the scene.[235]

Relics accompanied reports of the martyrs' trials and executions along familiar communication routes. From Rheims in the fall of 1581, Robert Parsons anonymously thanked a friend in England for "two printed papers" about the recently executed priest Everard Hanse. Additionally, he expressed gratitude "unfeignedly for his tooth, which came safely to my hands about ten days after the said books and your friend arrived. Much they make of the matter in these parts I assure you, not English only, but strangers most of all, being so enamored of the thing, that I shall have enough ado to keep it for your sake as you desire me: some, at the sight thereof, that were lately his familiars and equals, with godly emulation in a sort envying his incomparable preferment before them, and wondering at his so speedy felicity."[236] William Allen closely monitored the movement of the English martyrs' relics. Two months after Campion's execution, a nobleman had arrived from England with a fragment of his bone, he told Agazzari, "but it is so small it would not be possible to send it easily to any of you." The rector was not to worry, however: other English Catholics had bribed the executioner for one of his ribs, a piece of which Allen hoped soon to have and would pass on to Agazzari and Aquaviva.[237] He followed through. Three months later Allen wrote to George Gilbert, a devout layman living at the English College, "I send you here enclosed a little piece of Father Campion's holy rib. Take half to yourself and give the other half to Father Rector."[238] Allen shipped more relics to Rome in March 1583. That June, two people recently arrived from England—perhaps members of the frenzied crowd at William Hart's execution—had brought with them both Hart's bloodied shirt and several of his letters.[239]

Reginald Pole had asserted that the martyrs' blood proclaimed Catholic truth more eloquently than any linguistic formulation. Their relics, then, were even more desirable than their letters or stories about their deaths. Here were the stained garments that had covered the bodies, the very bones that had supported the flesh which, animated by saintly souls, had carried out heroic actions supernaturally sustained. Relics reinforced writings by and about the martyrs—both were *monumenta martyrum*.

The relics scuttled away from scaffolds or exhumed for distribution eventually reached stable destinations. Western Christians had venerated relics for more than a millennium when Ignatius Loyola commended the practice in his "Rules for Thinking with the Church" and when the Council of Trent formally approved it.[240] Rev. 6:9 authorized the placing of saints' relics beneath church altars: "I saw under the altar the souls of them that were slain for the word of God, and for the testimony which they had." The editors of the Douai-Rheims New Testament explained that the altar was Christ, under whom the martyrs' souls lived in heaven, "and for correspondence to their place or state in heaven, the Church layeth commonly their bodies also or relics near or under the altars, where our Savior's body is offered in the holy Mass."[241] The scholar chiefly responsible for this vernacular New Testament, Gregory Martin, was Allen's right-hand man at Douai and Rheims before Martin's death in 1582. Having traveled to Rome, he recounted in detail the city's sacred topography and religious practices. Its ancient martyrological past was present at every turn, revivified by the rediscovery of the catacombs. Martin enumerated the principal relics of the main churches, mostly from ancient martyr-saints, and marveled at the devotion they evoked from Roman crowds.[242] His description of Rome was written just before relics from the recent missionaries began arriving in the city. There the English College, like its counterpart at Rheims, had particular reason to preserve them.

The people of Brussels honored the relics of the Gorcum martyrs, beginning with elaborate public festivities on December 6, 1618.[243] First, the archbishop of Mechelen and the abbot of Louvain's prestigious Park Abbey concelebrated High Mass in the Franciscan convent. Then a ritual procession with thousands of torchbearers, including magistrates and members of the city's religious orders, and guilds made its way to the majestic St. Goedele's (now St. Michael's) Church. The procession featured two lavish, gilt chests bearing the relics. An image of each of the eleven Gorcum Franciscans was carried aloft by a member of the order. At St. Goedele's the chests were placed on either side of the tabernacle, emphasizing the martyrs' nearness to Christ. Organ music and a motet were performed in their honor. Afterwards the procession resumed, wending through the city's streets and main market-place (where ninety-five years earlier the first two Lutheran Augustinians had been burned) to the Franciscan church once more. There the reliquary chests flanked "both sides of St. Anne's altar in order to be honored publicly."[244] For eleven days—presumably to match the number of martyrs—the Franciscans preached about the martyrs' heroism and their triumph. Father Cornelius Thielmans reported that "in the church as well as in the streets" there were "not only women but also men crying out with devotion" [*van devotie schreyen*]. There was "an exceptional [*sonderlinghe*] devotion to be seen in the Franciscan church from men and women who from morning to evening poured forth their prayers before the relics."[245] By mid-December 1618, virtually every *Brusselaar* must have known about the Gorcum martyrs and the local repose of their relics. They drew attention and added prestige to the city's Franciscans. Paradoxically, martyrs' remains were most active in Catholic life once they were publicly laid to rest.

The desire to collect, distribute, and venerate the martyrs' relics was driven by the widespread conviction that the holy sacrifice of their deaths had made them saints in heaven. Blotches of blood and bits of bone were quasi-sacramental, traces of the grace that had sustained the martyrs seconds before they passed to eternity. Of all objects on earth (aside from the consecrated host), these relics were the closest to heaven. While various Christian virtues could make someone a candidate for canonization, martyrdom conferred instant sanctity. Augustine had said that Christians were to pray to the martyrs, not for them, since their sacrifice had assured their salvation.[246] As soon as More was decapitated, Stapleton wrote, his "soul flew to heaven," where he "immediately arrived in the sight of God and the angels."[247] In the late sixteenth and early seventeenth centuries, rather than waiting for papal approval, Catholics assumed the saintly status of the recent martyrs from whom they sought heavenly aid.[248]

Members of both the clergy and the laity recognized the new saints, whose own gender, age, and ecclesiastical status seem not to have mattered to those who celebrated or invoked them. The point was their consummate sacrifice and the power it bestowed, whether they were men or women, young or old, priests or laity. Margaret Clitherow's memorialist, the priest John Mush, implored her posthumous assistance.[249] Before her own death, Clitherow plus "two or three virtuous women" made secret nocturnal pilgrimages to Knavesmire, half a mile outside York. There, on bare knees, she prayed beneath the gallows where several missionaries had been executed in 1582.[250] Prior to the exhumation and translation of the Gorcum martyrs' remains, Catholic men and women "visited and devoutly frequented" their burial place to invoke their intercession.[251] A Latin poem honoring Richard Flower, a young layman executed in 1588 for assisting priests, explicitly linked the new martyr-saint to other martyrs and Catholics in general:

> O martyr of Christ, triumphing above the stars in heaven,
>   having continuously, utterly subdued all your enemies,
> Pray for all those joined to you in the bond of faith,
>   whose faith is true, witnessed to by your blood.
> Witnessed to together with the blood of a thousand saints,
>   with the holy blood of all the martyrs.[252]

One of Walpole's poems about Campion made clear the place of the new saints and their significance for the faithful. Of the martyred Jesuit in heaven, Walpole wrote

> From thence he prays and sings in melody
> for our recure, and calleth us to him,
> he stands before the throne with harmony
> and is a glorious suitor for our sin:
> with wings of love he jumped up so high,
> to help the cause for which he sought to die.
>   Rejoice, be glad, triumph, sing hymns of joy,
> Campion, Sherwin, Briant, live in bliss,
> they sue, they seek the ease of our annoy,
> they pray, they speak, and all effectual is,
> not like to men on earth as heretofore,
> But like to saints in heaven, and that is more.[253]

George Gilbert assumed just this when, as he lay dying in the English College at Rome on October 5, 1583, he "called to his assistance" these three martyrs, even as he lamented his unworthiness to share their fate.[254]

    Similar invocations continued in the early seventeenth century. John Geninges, for example, referring to his martyred brother and the latter's companions, told readers to "implore the suffrages of such holy saints, who in our miserable country have lost their lives for God's quarrel."[255] The Wallonian Franciscan Antoine Gambier praised the intercessory patronage of the

Gorcum martyrs to the magistrates of Mons, while the French Jesuit Louis Richeome implied the efficacious intercession of the forty Jesuits slain at sea in 1570.[256] The iconography of the Gorcum martyrs is highly suggestive: in both a 1620 engraving and a seventeenth-century panel painting, angels bestow on them martyrs' crowns like those held by Saints Peter and Paul in Circignani's image of Christ as the king of the martyrs (Figures 30 and 31; compare with Figure 25).

Remarks by clerical writers help explain why Catholics in this period regarded the recent martyrs as saints. First, traditional martyrologies were inclusive and open-ended, acknowledging unnamed and local saints for each day throughout the liturgical calendar.[257] Johannes Molanus explained that it was acceptable to add local saints to those invoked by the universal Church, "because we do not doubt that there are many martyrs, confessors, and virgins who have acquired the joys of heaven, even though in the Church they are not recorded [*non sint relati*] among the number of the saints."[258] Second, as noted earlier, there was a strong sense that martyrdom conferred automatic sanctity. Speaking of uncanonized Franciscan martyrs, Thielmans wrote that "although the Holy Church still maintains no special feast days for them, nevertheless they have received the reward of the martyrs and may be honored as saints [*heylighen*]. For the canonization of martyrs it is enough that one knows that they suffered for the Christian faith for the sake of the truth and righteousness."[259] The revision of canonization procedures between 1625 and 1634, during the pontificate of Urban VIII, implicitly endorsed the idea of martyrdom as a high road to sanctity.[260] In doing so, the papacy approved a view that members of the clergy had been articulating from the moment that each martyr died.[261]

The ultimate roots of this recognition lay in the spectacle at the scaffold, in spectators' reactions to the martyrs' embrace of death, such as, for example, the rush for William Hart's clothing. This unfettered response, in line with Allen's and Southwell's hopes about the social impact of martyrdom, recalled older forms of local veneration that took place centuries prior to papal preoccupation with canonization. To remain prayerful and calm while being torn apart denoted divine favor. And if God's grace had empowered the martyrs to sustain horrifying executions, could it not empower their relics to aid ordinary Christians? Was God not sovereign in the exercise of his providence?

In Heaven: Saints Old and New in Devotional Time

The new saints took their place among the old. In early modern Catholicism, however, traditional martyr-saints were more prominent than their recent counterparts. The latter's pictorial exposure, widespread as it was, paled in

Figure 30. Engraving of the Gorcum martyrs, from Cornelius Thielmans, *Cort Verhael, van het Leven Der Heijlighen van S[.] Franciscus Oirden* ('s Hertogen-bosch: Jan Scheffer, 1620), p. 227. Reproduced with permission of University Library, Utrecht.

comparison to that of the ancient martyrs. Acquaintance with the period's martyr images makes this clear. Among the eight martyrdom cycles painted in Rome between 1582 and 1603, for example, only the series in San Stefano Rotondo in the English College and San Andrea al Quirinale included sixteenth-century martyrs.[262] Federico Borromeo's portrait collection included paintings of at least eight early Christian martyrs, whereas the only recent ones were More and Fisher.[263] And the spate of graphic altar paintings of martyrdoms in the Catholic Netherlands between 1585 and 1610 was devoted exclusively to ancient martyrs.[264]

Catholic martyr images encapsulated central Counter-Reformation virtues, such as obedience and self-denial. Sometimes they encompassed scriptural allusions as well. In an oil painting by Adam Elsheimer, for example, St.

Figure 31. Gorcum martyrs, anonymous panel painting, seventeenth century. Reproduced with permission of Museum Catharijneconvent, Utrecht.

Lawrence, "robed in white" (Rev. 7:9), stands with arms spread in utter resignation. Exotically garbed executioners prepare the roaring fire beneath his gridiron. An angel gestures heavenward, poised to bestow the martyr's frond that will make Lawrence one of those "under the altar," "with palm branches in their hands" (Rev. 6:9, 7:9) (Figure 32).

In other media, too, Catholics were more likely to encounter early than recent martyrs. Ancient saints, many of them martyrs, predominated in the *Roman Martyrology* and in hagiographical collections. Dozens of the Jesuit plays produced and performed for large, mixed urban audiences from Lisbon to Vienna took ancient, and only occasionally recent, martyrs as their subjects.[265] The new martyr-saints were not competing with the old. In fact, the renewal of Catholic martyrdom seems to have accentuated, not displaced, the veneration of the early martyr-saints, strengthening the sense of an ancient tradition reborn.

That rebirth in Catholicism really meant continuity was the fundamental claim behind Baronius's massive ecclesiastical history, the *Ecclesiastical Annals*. He disputed categorically the degeneration alleged in the Lutheran

Figure 32. Adam Elsheimer, *St. Lawrence Prepared for Martyrdom*, oil on copper, ca. 1600. © National Gallery, London.

Magdeburg Centuries. In another sense, however, historical veracity was presumed but ceased to matter: exactly when and how the martyr-saints had died remained as irrelevant as ever to their role as celestial patrons. Pieck and Polycarp, Clitherow and Catherine—all were potential intercessors by virtue of their being in heaven. Although Catholic scholars themselves commonly denounced the *Golden Legend* as the "Leaden Legend," and a raft of Italian "local Baronios" did collaborative, diocesan ecclesiastical history in the seventeenth century,[266] prayers to the saints were little affected. Martyrs died in historical time, but they interceded for supplicants in devotional time, which was largely abstracted from history.

This suprahistorical regard was presupposed in the way that saints were inserted into the hagiographical collections and the liturgical martyrologies. Except for Rabus's first edition, the Protestant martyrologies were arranged historically, as a linear movement from biblical times to the present. By contrast, Surius's volumes and the *Roman Martyrology* were organized calendrically, day by day throughout the year. Unlike the abundant Catholic martyrological accounts and histories incorporating the martyrs, the liturgical martyrologies and hagiographical collections presumed a real historical past but were not conceived historically. Heribert Rosweyde, a Dutch Jesuit who built on the work of his Spanish predecessor, Pedro Ribadeneira, compiled entries in a large, vernacular collection of saints' vitae. For February 10, for example, Rosweyde followed an account of the twelfth-century French hermit William with St. Benedict's sister, Scholastica (sixth century), and then with two virgins from the Low Countries: Sura (fourteenth century) and Austreberta (seventh century).[267] The same phenomenon characterized works that were not arranged calendrically. In a collection by Cornelius Thielmans, for example, the Nagasaki martyrs of 1597 appeared before the Gorcum Franciscans of 1572, after which came several Franciscan martyrs from the thirteenth and fourteenth centuries, followed by the Franciscans who were killed in Prague in 1610.[268] A difference in genre—liturgical and devotional collections, as opposed to narrative accounts of the martyrs—reflected different conceptions, functions, and purposes. The two were neither in competition, nor mutually incompatible. To be sure, Catholic histories of the more recent martyrs, such as Willem Hessels van Est's, also sought to inspire readers' devotion. Yet to the men and women of Brussels who prayed within sight of the Gorcum martyrs' relics in December 1618, the historical details of their death probably did not matter much.

From Heaven to Earth: Providence, Intercession, and Miracles

Catholic trust in divine providence included belief in the saints' intercessory powers. Protestants and Anabaptists rejected such an idea as an infringement on the uniqueness and efficacy of Christ's intercession. They shared entirely with Catholic contemporaries, however, the broader conviction that God was active in the world. Like the wider providential framework it presupposed, the intercession of the saints was a doctrine incapable of refutation in principle. Nothing could count as evidence against it. If one sought healing and became well, one credited the saint's intercession. If recovery did not come, perhaps the supplicant was insufficiently purposeful, or too sinful—or perhaps God presently saw fit to have that person suffer, as discipline for one "whom he loves" (Heb. 12:6). In such a case God was offering an opportunity for merit through the patient endurance of affliction, patience being a virtue esteemed by the Lord. Even if improved health followed prayer sincerely directed to a fictitious saint, perhaps Christ had smiled on one's devotion and sympathetically covered for the saint's nonexistence.

Several sorts of intercession were attributed to the recent martyrs, whose stunning imitation of Christ made them particularly powerful patrons. The Gorcum martyrs were credited with healing miracles and visions. In Brussels, Thielmans wrote, the martyrs heeded parental pleas and cured a six-year-old who had been confined to a cradle. One woman's chronic arm pain was healed, another's dropsy disappeared, and a girl on the brink of death recovered her health, all after praying before the martyrs' relics. Two civic officials were on hand to authenticate the claims, a practice that reflected concern about fraud.[269] Besides recounting others' cures, Willem Hessels van Est wrote that his own maladies had been relieved through recourse to the Gorcum martyrs.[270] None of these cases—parallels to which can be found in professional medical literature today—resemble the grossly miraculous stories common in medieval hagiography: Saint Denis strolling with his severed head, or Saint Dorothy having her rent and scalded flesh perfectly restored.[271] There was nothing inherently unbelievable about praying to a saint for recovery and afterwards getting better; the saint's part in the cure could be neither confirmed nor disproved. The same applied to stories of divine retribution against persecutors, which are plentiful in both Catholic and Protestant sources.[272] Southwell explicitly noted that the understanding of such events was a hermeneutic endeavor—implying that although they were spurious, alternative readings were possible. After considering the demise of recent and ancient persecutors of Catholics, he wrote: "Which accidents though some will impute to other causes yet happening at such special times when so open and unnatural injustice was done they cannot be but interpreted as tokens of God's indignation."[273] When Thomas Cromwell was beheaded in 1540, how could one have disproved that God was retaliating against him for his role in procuring the deaths of the Henrician martyrs?

Other sorts of intercession by the new saints were interpreted analogously. An English nobleman credited his safe passage through dangerous seas to the fact that he was lying on a Campion relic.[274] John Geninges, who converted to Catholicism and himself became a priest on the Continent, "attributed his conversion wholly (next after God) to the intercession of his blessed brother."[275] On July 9, 1573, near the end of the siege of Haarlem and one year after the death of the Gorcum martyrs, many Catholics of Gorcum celebrated their martyrdom and prayed to them for deliverance from the Protestant Gueux. Three days later the siege ended and Spanish troops took the town. Hessels van Est attributed the victory to the martyrs' intercession.[276] They even were believed to have helped bring down William of Orange. On the twelfth anniversary of their death, Baltasar Gerard, along with several other Catholics, prayed fervently on his knees for an hour in a Delft church. Buoyed by the experience, he assassinated the prince the next day, July 10, 1584. According to Hessels van Est, Gerard's fortitude during his own martyrdom four days later also stemmed from the intercession and merits of the Gorcum martyrs.[277]

Another category of occurrences associated with the martyrs might be called "miracles of nature." A common feature of medieval hagiography as well, these viewed extraordinary natural phenomena as the product of God's favor toward the martyrs. Some cases are ambiguous: Geninges called it "miraculous" when his brother's bloodied thumb came off at Lucy Ridley's touch, but perhaps it was less secure than she had thought.[278] Two other examples, however, bear recounting for their more dramatic claims and their notoriety in the early seventeenth century.

On May 3, 1606, John Wilkinson departed his spot beneath Henry Garnet's scaffold with a bloodstained wheat stalk that had caught on his clothes.[279] He gave it to Hugh Griffin's wife, who put it in "a crystal case," the shape of which caused the grain kernels to bend around in a semicircle. Several days later a Catholic acquaintance saw a man's face on one of the kernels, a likeness the Griffins also discerned. The news spread and soon hundreds of people, both Catholic and Protestant, viewed the miniscule similitude of Garnet himself on the "miraculous ear of corn" (see Figure 33). The sensational image drew the attention of both the Royal Council and the archbishop of Canterbury, Richard Bancroft, who investigated the matter in November and December 1606. Painters testified that no artist could have produced the likeness. Unless the kernel bore something resembling a human face, this entire incident is unintelligible. To see the image as a miracle rather than a remarkable coincidence, however, depended on interpretation informed by faith. Hugh Griffin, the tailor to whose wife Wilkinson had given the wheat stalk, related the incident in detail and acknowledged the image. He added, "the said face is no more like Garnet's face than any other man's hath a beard . . . the face being so little, no man is able to say it is like Garnet . . . except one be told in which husk the face is, he will very hardly find it."[280]

Figure 33. "Miraculous ear of corn" with the likeness of Henry Garnet.
Reproduced from Henry Foley, ed., *Records of the English Province of the Society of Jesus,* vol. 4 (New York: Johnson Reprint, 1966), between pp. 132 and 133.

A second "miracle of nature" involved some white flowers that originally grew on the graves of the Gorcum martyrs outside Briel. According to Cornelius Thielmans, in 1615 one stem with three or four blossoms was picked from the grave and enclosed in a box. When it was removed from the box two years later it had nineteen blossoms—one for each of the Gorcum martyrs— "not without miracle."[281] Thielmans commissioned a copperplate engraving of the flower based on a previous engraving done in Holland; Thielmans's engraving was itself copied in a third engraving that appeared in Jan Boener's book on the Gorcum martyrs in 1623 (Figure 34). Judging from Thielmans's description, this episode turned on an event's facticity rather than its meaning: whether or not a stem with three or four flower blossoms inexplicably had nineteen blossoms two years later. From the perspective of Humean skepticism, this looks like an instance of pious fraud—it is easy to imagine someone replacing the original stem with another. The more salient point, in a cultural milieu that anticipated such miracles, was the link between the sanctity of the martyrs and the nineteen white blossoms: the natural world, guided by providence, proclaimed that the Gorcum martyrs numbered among the saints. This simply reinforced what Dutch Catholics already believed. More than the color of their heavenly robes, martyrs' white left an earthly trace.

The New Martyr-Saints as Models of Christian Virtue

We have traveled from earth to heaven and back, from martyrs' relics to pleas for intercession to the interpretation of the new saints' activity. The new intercessors joined the ancient martyr-saints from whom late medieval Christians had sought strength and succor. Appropriating the exhortations of their

Figure 34. White flower with nineteen blossoms, one for each of the Gorcum martyrs, from [Jan Boener], *Waerachtighe ende levende Figuren van de H. Martelaers van Gorcum* ('s Hertogenbosch: Antonius Scheffer, 1623), sig. [G4v]. Reproduced with permission of University Library, Utrecht.

humanist predecessors, post-Tridentine writers urged Catholics to imitate the martyrs' virtues. Writing for the Feast of All Saints, Surius told readers to apply themselves to the martyrs' example in order to learn "perfect faith, the love of God, an enormous sense of compassion, and a longing for what is to come."[282] In the Roman jubilee year of 1575, Carlo Borromeo informed the city's pilgrims that visiting the site of martyrs' executions would enhance their spiritual benefit: "That fiery flame of Christian religion which burned in the heart of St. Lawrence shall inflame your souls to the fervent love of God, when you shall contemplate the manifold memories of his martyrdom, in the place where he was roasted upon the gridiron."[283] The point was growth in love for God, not preparation for martyrdom. Images of the recent martyrs played a part here as well. Boener's work on the Gorcum martyrs combined head-and-shoulder portraits with the stories of their deaths, "so that through the attentive consideration [*merckelijck aensien*] of the lifelike figures and the diligent reading through [*neerstelijck over-lesen*] of the histories the hearts of devout people might be moved and enkindled to devotion and a burning love towards God, according to the common maxim, 'to look upon is to remember'" [*Aensien doet ghedencken*].[284] Like relics and stories, images and texts reinforced each other.

Perhaps that is why the Dutch priest Cornelius Musius carried paintings of More and Fisher with him, and why William Warford almost always described the physical appearance of the English missionary martyrs whose virtues he recounted.[285] Further, Boener wrote, the Church encouraged the sin-specific use of saints' images to help nurture contrary virtues. The greedy, for example, should gaze on St. Matthew, the converted tax collector, while the acquisitive should view the ascetic John the Baptist and St. Francis of Assisi. The martyrs filled a different niche: "If there are those who fear suffering persecution for the sake of righteousness and the public confession of their faith, then set the martyrdom of the holy martyrs clearly before their eyes, as though in a mirror [*als in eenen spiegel*], so as to inflame their souls, through considering their images and reflecting on their devotion, to follow their examples with God's grace."[286] The intention and imagery are striking: this is precisely what Jean Crespin had urged embattled Huguenots to pursue through texts alone more than half a century earlier. A few years after Boener, in 1631, Hans de Ries edited the first Mennonite martyrology entitled the *Martyrs' Mirror*. He, like van Braght in 1660, wanted readers to see themselves reflected against the Anabaptist martyrs in order to inspire their commitment.

The Catholic martyrs' post-Tridentine role was less exclusively intercessory than it had been on the eve of the Reformation. Partly this was because the new martyr-saints, compared to the ancient ones, were more familiar as real people. Willem Hessels van Est wrote about his uncle, Nicolas Pieck; John

Mush extolled the virtues of his spiritual advisee, Margaret Clitherow; William Allen assembled the stories of missionary martyrs he had trained. Such writers memorialized people with whom they had been intimate, so unlike the relationship between latter-day Catholics and early Christian martyrs. What did people really know about Sebastian or Blaise, Christopher or Barbara? Had Jacques de Voragine known any more? In addition, the emphasis on imitation of the martyrs' virtues served new objectives within the Church. The call to heed the martyrs as models for Christian living, if not necessarily patterns for dying, was part of a broad effort to make Catholic Europeans more self-consciously devout, to transform mere conformity into a vigorously practiced, explicit faith.

For the already devout who were unthreatened by persecution, the close relationship persisted between martyrdom and asceticism. Surius implied that rigorous ascetic practices were a form of martyrdom, while Teresa of Avila referred to the "life of a good religious" as "a long martyrdom."[287] Jacques Le Brun has shown how thoroughly a martyrological sensibility pervaded the lives of French female religious in the seventeenth and early eighteenth centuries, despite the remoteness of their prospects for martyrdom. The pain from illnesses, self-inflicted mortifications, and medical procedures directly paralleled the suffering of early Christian martyrs, while God's absence in prayer and mystical experience comprised a type of martyrdom.[288] Nor were ordinary Christians excluded from participation in martyrdom: Solier wrote that "all Christians" could "in truth be called martyrs" insofar as they bore adversity and injury patiently.[289] Gregory the Great had said this a thousand years earlier. As in the late Middle Ages, the dearth of opportunities for martyrdom inverted the hourglass. Impulses that would have nurtured an explicit martyrological mentality instead served ascetic discipline and the patient endurance of suffering, as they had for centuries.

Europe ceased to be an active arena of Roman Catholic martyrdom over the course of the seventeenth century. Ancient and recent martyr-saints, however, remained a vital part of Catholicism. The post-Tridentine Church more than compensated for the perplexities of the 1530s. Several hundred people in England, France, and the Low Countries were killed for their acknowledgment of a unique truth visibly embodied in the institutions and traditions of Roman Catholicism. Memorialized and publicized, honored and revered, the new martyrs offered something to everyone: models for the few facing violent death themselves; examples of asceticism for the devout; paradigms of virtue for ordinary people striving to become better Christians; additional intercessors for the most learned prelates through the least educated laity. All belonged to a Church reverberating with reminders of its ancient, heroic past.

In the present, the freshest history of the church militant was being written in blood as well as ink.

The witness of the new saints deepened cleavages between Catholics and other Christian groups. As both an outsider and former insider, the Englishman John Gee had been partial to Roman Catholicism before he spurned it, denouncing the seminary priests and Jesuits. In 1624 he described London Catholics on procession to honor their new saints. His words offer telling commentary about the martyrs' effect on Catholics in late Jacobean England:

> It was ancient, to visit *memorias martyrum;* and so, the sending of disciples to visit Tyburn, maketh a deep impression in their minds, of the saintship of some that have there paid their debt to our laws. We know, martyr and persecutor are correlations: and so, in this action of pretended humiliation, there is intended an increase of the Romanists' hatred against the Church and State of England, as persecuting, and guilty of the blood of those whom they adore. Thus every step in such pilgrimage, makes those penitents to walk further from us: nay, in every stripe [from self-flagellation] voluntarily received in such a processional journey, the confessor that enjoineth this performance, thinks he scourgeth the Protestants.[290]

Martyrs strengthened as they divided: they reinforced English Catholic identity *because* of the dichotomy between the martyrs and the authorities responsible for their deaths. The same was true of Roman Catholicism at large. Whether elsewhere in Europe or in distant mission fields, the contrast between the glorious and the wicked was plain to see.

CHAPTER EIGHT

The Conflict of Interpretations

And what I do I will also continue to do, in order to deny an opportunity to those who want to be recognized as our equals in what they boast about. For such boasters are false apostles, deceitful workers, disguising themselves as apostles of Christ. And no wonder! Even Satan disguises himself as an angel of light. So it is not strange if his ministers also disguise themselves as ministers of righteousness. Their end will match their deeds.

—2 CORINTHIANS 11:12–15

For if all were martyrs, that die for their religion, then many heresies both contrary among themselves, and repugnant to the evident doctrine of Christ, should be truths, which is impossible.

—ROBERT SOUTHWELL, *AN EPISTLE OF COMFORT* [1587 OR 1588]

Martyrs mattered deeply to early modern Protestants, Anabaptists, and Roman Catholics. All three traditions inherited late medieval sensibilities about patience and suffering, the art of dying well and imitation of Christ, which they appropriated according to their specific circumstances. All three were profoundly sensitive to martyrdom, nurtured a willingness to die, proclaimed the martyrs' witness to God's truth, affirmed the transcendent value of their sacrifice, and insured that their memory was preserved.

At the same time, the three groups of Christians diverged sharply. Not shared were the doctrines for which martyrs were willing to die. Fellow believers rightly associated these teachings with the martyrs' deaths no less than had the authorities who procured their executions. These doctrines articulated incompatible views of Christian truth: what God had revealed to human beings and consequently what they were bound to believe and do. Accordingly, martyrological traditions mirrored the distinct Christian communities that acknowledged and preserved them. Protestants, Anabaptists, and Catholics neither believed the same teachings, nor worshiped together, nor recognized the same martyrs.

Martyrologists and controversialists knew that their respective claims contradicted others in Western Christendom. Since all asserted propriety over the same domain—the witnesses to the one Christian truth—every declaration about martyrs challenged rival affirmations. Controversialists attacked these irritating, contrary allegations. Luther, for example, had to confront conflicting martyr claims once Müntzer and his followers, as well as Anabaptists,

315

were executed and found their sympathizers.[1] It has been suggested that Catholic writers were not much concerned with the denunciation of false martyrs until the seventeenth century,[2] yet they too addressed the issue as early as the 1520s and continued to do so in subsequent decades. By 1528, for example, Johannes Faber had seen how Lutherans celebrated heretics such as Caspar Tauber as "martyrs and holy before God." So he published a preemptive strike against "the leading Anabaptist and sacrament destroyer," Balthasar Hubmaier, just after his execution, which he called "a summary of his misdeeds based on his own writings and other documents."[3] The following year, Thomas More implied the existence of English public sympathy for punished heretics, whom he denounced as "the devil's martyrs, taking much pain for his pleasure."[4] Catholic opposition to Protestant martyr claims was present decades before the massive martyrologies rendered rebuttals still more urgent.

Numerous scholars have noted controversialists' disagreement about martyrs across confessional divides.[5] Yet the denunciations of false martyrs have not been seriously analyzed in relationship to the martyrological sources, without which both are less than well understood. Consequently, it is not entirely surprising that recent scholarship has sometimes missed the meaning of false martyrs.[6] Parallel to martyrology was antimartyrology, in which controversialists attacked those whom fellow believers celebrated. The phenomenon was persistent, widespread, and, in a context of religious controversy, inseparable from martyrdom.

The frequent mention of false martyrs in martyrological sources underscores this inseparability. Writers often distinguished true from false martyrs as they exalted their own witnesses, exhorted fellow believers to perseverance, or prepared for death from prison. Not merely aware of competing martyr claims, they evidently found it hard to forget about them.

As Thomas More readied himself for death from the Tower of London, heretical martyrs surfaced in the midst of his evocative prose about the willingness to die for Christ. He found a moment in the climactic, final chapter of his *Dialogue of Comfort* to condemn executed heretics: "The devil hath also some so obstinate heretics, that endure willingly painful death for vainglory."[7] After Reginald Pole returned to England in the 1550s, he was confronted by Marian Protestants whose refusal to renounce their religious views cost them their lives. While addressing the citizens of London, Pole praised the Henrician Catholic martyrs and curtly dismissed "these heretics pretending to die constantly for the faith of the church," who actually perished "for their own opinion."[8] A full-page engraving in the *Roman Martyrology* included, below the figure representing "Ecclesia," Cyprian's dictum "No one can be a martyr who is not in the Church" [*esse martyr non potest qui in Ecclesia non est*] (Figure 35). This implicit retort to competing martyr claims was made ex-

Figure 35. Frontispiece engraving from *Roman Martyrology* (Venice: Petrus Dusinellus, 1587), with Cyprian's dictum below the figure at left representing *Ecclesia*. Reproduced with permission of Ghent University Library.

plicit in the martyrologies and hagiographical collections of Catholic writers such as Johannes Molanus, Caesar Baronius, and Heribert Rosweyde.[9] Awareness of false martyrs shadowed the celebration of Catholic martyrdom.

Likewise, Protestants denounced executed Catholics and Anabaptists in their own martyrological writings. In 1544 John Bale, for example, just before introducing his proto-Protestant hero, John Oldcastle, condemned "the Papists . . . which have been slain, for the liberties, privileges, authority, honor, riches, and proud maintenance of their holy whorish church." Such included John Fisher, Thomas More, John Forest, Richard Reynolds, and the Carthusians, "with an infinite number more."[10] Reformed Protestant Joris Wybo was imprisoned in Antwerp with Christopher Fabri before the latter's execution in 1565. Wybo was likely the writer who sandwiched a discussion of true and false martyrs between exhortatory passages on the duty to suffer for Christ, in a preface to an account of Fabri's imprisonment and martyrdom.[11] By the 1570 edition of his martyrology, Jean Crespin did not finish even one page on the conformity of Protestant to ancient Christian martyrs without attacking executed Anabaptists as Satan's "martyrs of errors and lies."[12] Christoph Rab abridged Crespin's work, translated it into German, and published it in 1590. He explicitly condemned Anabaptists as Satan's "seeming saints [Scheinheiligen] and false martyrs," criticizing as well the "great stubbornness and presumptuous courage and constancy" of Baltasar Gerard, Edmund Campion, and other Catholics whom their fellow believers had publicized.[13] Protestant writers, like their Catholic contemporaries, were conscious of contrary martyr claims even as they memorialized their own martyrs.

Martyrological communities had to be monitored. Denouncing false martyrs defended a view of Christian truth and a corresponding religious identity. On the surface, however, this seems not to have been the case for Anabaptists. By and large, the wrangling about true and false martyrs was limited to Catholic and Protestant controversialists, with whom this chapter is primarily concerned. Yet it is important to consider why Anabaptist writers remained fundamentally aloof from direct participation in the interpretive struggle over martyrs.

At least three influences were involved. First, the separatist impulse that characterized Anabaptism very soon after the movement began was not generally conducive to serious involvement in religious controversy. Anabaptists simply ignored Protestant and Catholic martyr claims, having rejected both groups to pursue Christian truth as they understood it. After the earliest years of the movement this tendency intensified: most Anabaptist leaders, without university training, lacked the background in the learned culture of theological controversy that shaped both Protestant and Catholic theologians. Only in the late sixteenth and the seventeenth centuries did this begin to change for some of the Dutch Mennonites.

Second, all martyr claims were implicit criticisms of the ways in which authorities had interrogated, condemned, and executed fellow believers as heretics or traitors. When challenged, authorities defended their actions, part of which meant repudiating the claims that those executed were martyrs. In short, antimartyrology was closely related to the willingness to kill. Yet because nonmilitant Anabaptists were incapable of imposing orthodoxy, and indeed after some early attempts did not seek to become the official religion of states or cities, they executed no one. Therefore no martyr claims comprised a critique of Anabaptist actions. Accordingly, they had no need to view competing martyr claims as an attack on anything they had done, and could therefore simply ignore antimartyrology.

This leads to a third and in some ways the most important reason why Anabaptists avoided the debate. In contrast to Protestants and Catholics, their strongest ground for touting their martyrs as genuine lay in an external criterion: they had persecuted no one. They were true Christians, and their martyrs true Christian martyrs, because Anabaptists had not shed the blood of other Christians, as had Catholic and Protestant officials. This was the upshot of Hans de Ries's remarks on the persecution of Christians in his *Martyrs' Mirror* of 1631–1632. He did not explicitly denounce as false the martyrs from persecuting churches, but stated that "the cross is also a sure sign of those who serve and follow Christ, the captain of faith; and . . . conversely, those who inflict the cross and suffering on others belong not among these, but rather to another leader [that is, Satan]." True Christians had always been persecuted, not persecutors: "there is no surer indication of the false Church that fights against Christ than the killing of heretics, or rather alleged heretics, because as terrible as heresy is, this is the most terrible of all."[14] Why honor "martyrs" who belonged to Christian groups that defended their killing of people for so-called heterodoxy? Had Anabaptists directly debated true and false martyrs on the basis of doctrine, they would have argued on the same terms as their Catholic and Protestant contemporaries. Instead, their status as nonvictimizing victims allowed them to criticize Catholics and Protestants, and to exclude both groups' "martyrs" from their own martyrological communities.

Catholic and Protestant controversialists would not have been impressed by such arguments. The Anabaptist rejection of their martyrs seems not to have registered at all. Even if it had, they might well have thought that the Anabaptists' unwillingness to prosecute the heterodox compounded separatist arrogance with inattention to duty. In effect, self-absorbed Anabaptists were so lacking in charity that they neglected to make others follow the saving truth upon which they themselves insisted. The fact of nonpersecution was neither a virtue nor a means to discern genuine martyrs, if one saw persecution as prosecution and its absence as negligence.

Controversialists and martyrologists—including, implicitly, Anabaptists—distinguished true from false martyrs on the basis of right doctrine, the same criterion by which they identified their martyrological communities. Protestant and Catholic writers belabored the point for over a century, in part because they faced countervailing cultural impulses. Perhaps the strongest of these were assumptions about the good death drawn from the *ars moriendi* tradition. According to this tradition, determining whether a death was good was based fundamentally on appearances. Whether those afflicted were on a deathbed or at the stake, dying with steadfast resolve or patient resignation, evincing neither doubt nor fear regardless of the extent of their suffering, suggested that they were "right with God." The public endurance of excruciating torments often did impress people and, judging from controversialists' remarks, it also helped make converts. Without cultural receptivity to such comportment, martyrdom could not have been "the seed of the church."

It is here that Augustine's dictum—"not the punishment, but the cause, makes a martyr"—was critically important. Although proper behavior was normally a significant prerequisite for being considered a martyr, it was never a sufficient criterion by itself.[15] Attempts to find nondoctrinal criteria for telling true from false martyrs were hesitant and ultimately unsuccessful. Behavior yielded to beliefs. As a result, the divergent teachings for which the martyrs had died doubled as the only clear basis for criticizing contrary martyr claims. This satisfied whoever agreed with the respective protagonists. It solidified collective identities and strengthened distinct martyrological traditions. Since doctrinal compromise was not forthcoming, however, doctrinal criteria could only reinforce the impasse, not dissolve the deadlock, of competing martyr claims. Moreover, such compromise was virtually inconceivable precisely because men and women were dying for sharply contested doctrines and the distinct visions of Christian truth that they represented.

The Weaknesses of Nondoctrinal Criteria

If true and false martyrs had died in dissimilar ways, controversy about their status might have proceeded differently. Even antagonistic writers, however, admitted how difficult, even impossible, it was to distinguish between them based on their dying words and actions. Small wonder, since all sought to conform to the paradigm of their ancient predecessors. Yet to sensitized onlookers, martyrs' conformity to a model of edifying death remained a potentially disruptive, efficacious enactment of religious conviction. Controversialists sometimes proposed observable means by which to tell true martyrs from false. Decisive weaknesses, however, repeatedly emerged in their suggestions. For this reason there were no sustained, systematic efforts to differentiate between true and false martyrs based on behavioral criteria.

From the very first executions, the issue was unavoidable. In late August 1523 Erasmus wrote from Basel to Huldrich Zwingli, his humanist colleague in Zurich, about the recent burning of Hendrik Vos and Johann van den Esschen in Brussels. He touched on concerns upon which others would expand during the following century:

> I do not know whether I ought to deplore their deaths [*quorum mortem an deplorare debeam nescio*]. It is clear that they died with the greatest and unheard-of steadfastness [*summa et inaudita constantia*], not for the articles of Luther, but for his paradoxes—for which I would not want to die, because I do not understand them. I know that to die for Christ is a glorious thing. The devout have never lacked affliction, but the impious are also afflicted. He who repeatedly transforms himself into an angel of light is skilled in many crafts. And the discernment of spirits is a rare gift.[16]

Erasmus's characteristic caution mingled unstably with his assessment of the criteria for martyrdom. He accepted the value of martyrdom ("to die for Christ is a glorious thing") and stories about the monks' dying constancy. Yet he reserved judgment about whether this steadfastness betokened martyrdom, and hence whether their executions merited censure ("I do not know whether I ought to deplore their deaths"). Given his basic aversion to the coercion of belief, it is equally noteworthy that he did not simply condemn the executions. The wicked also suffered affliction; what mattered was what they had died for (Luther's "paradoxes"). Gesturing toward 2 Cor. 11:14 ("Even Satan disguises himself as an angel of light"), Erasmus, for whom the devil was far from ubiquitous by early sixteenth-century standards, hinted that the monks had perhaps been misled by Satan. Although he remained noncommittal, as most controversialists would not, Erasmus raised the central issue of how behavior and belief bore on the determination of genuine martyrs. His reluctance to condemn or commend reflected a deeper concern: these, the first willing deaths of Luther's followers, augured ill for his dreams of a gradual, education-based reform of Western Christendom.

More than twenty years later, in a different context, Nicolas Meynderts van Blesdijk disputed Menno Simons's claims about the link between persecution and holiness. His Davidite critique noted that Protestants and Henrician Catholics had died as willingly as the martyrs whom Menno championed:

in England . . . within the last ten years some of the most learned and noblest people of the country have been killed for the sake of the papist faith, indeed preferred to let their heads be chopped off rather than confess and consent to the king that he had the power to change the popish ceremonies without the pope's order. The same thing has been done by others for the sake of the freedom of the Gospel and water baptism; in Italy, France, Spain, Upper and Lower Germany, innumerable followers of Luther and Zwingli have been killed and are still being killed because they believe that their cause is just. Others with less common opinions, unnecessary and unworthy to mention here, do likewise; by their faith and profession that they have grasped from the scriptures . . . they joyfully and patiently [*vroolijck ende oock lijdtsamich*] risk body and life. And all of them, I say, although they all call upon the scriptures in the same measure, and however prepared they are to defend their cause with the scriptures, are nevertheless opposed to the others. It is not and cannot be that all of them have and follow a proper understanding of God [*eyghentlijcken sin Godes*].[17]

Like Erasmus, Blesdijk was concerned with how to determine the "blessedness" of those "persecuted for righteousness' sake" (Matt. 5:10). All claimed scriptural authority for the conflicting, incompatible views for which they were executed. Therefore martyrdom could not follow automatically from the mere fact of suffering death for one's religious convictions.

Beyond humanist correspondence and theological controversy, the issue also surfaced in confrontations between martyrs and those who urged them to capitulate. In 1586, for example, Margaret Clitherow refused to submit herself to a jury after being accused of treason. A Puritan minister, Giles Wigginton, told her she was "foully deceived" if she thought that death as a Catholic by *peine forte et dure* would be martyrdom: "In the time of Queen Mary were many put to death, and now also in this Queen's time, for two several opinions; both these cannot be martyrs."[18] Like Blesdijk and Erasmus, Wigginton separated the fact of punishment from the status of the punished.

Yet dying well remained important to both martyrs and martyrological writers. Without it, fellow believers would not have been edified nor potential converts moved. Moreover, to have ignored the martyrs' extraordinary courage would have slighted their witness. As their heroic deaths were celebrated, it was natural to suggest that their behavior could only be understood in ways that secured their status—and to look for ways in which "martyrs" from rival Christian groups failed to meet the same standards.

Working from the same scriptural and historical template, Christians in all three traditions understood persecution as a sign of divine favor. The world's violent scorn for latter-day martyrs highlighted their approval by God, as had been true for the Hebrew prophets, Christ's apostles, and the early Christian martyrs. Writers sometimes implied that only God's sustenance could explain their martyrs' steadfastness. John Bale, for example, stated that only Christ himself suffering in Anne Askewe, a "young, tender, weak, and sick woman," had enabled her to endure the torture to which she was subjected.[19] Reginald Pole wrote that only God's grace and strength could account for the calm, confident behavior of More and Fisher before their deaths.[20] Yet since both Protestant and Catholic apologists plausibly claimed God's support to explain the constancy of their respective martyrs, their contentions reinforced, rather than resolved, their disagreement.

Sometimes writers simultaneously implied and denied constancy in death as a criterion for telling true from false martyrs. Apparently, they struggled with the realization that their own martyrs did not have a monopoly on steadfast suffering. For example, Justus Menius stated that Anabaptists, Jews, and Moslems could die alongside believing (Lutheran) Christians, "each one of them being equally stalwart and tough in their courage" [*einen jeden jnn seinem mut, gleich hart vnd steiff sein*]—but he immediately insinuated that only someone who genuinely possessed God's word could stand firm against the devil.[21] Similarly, in his exhortatory sermon about suffering for the Lord, John Calvin said that the resolve to die for Christ's name and the Gospel's struggle could not exist "unless it is built on certainty of faith." This might have suggested that the willingness to die for one's views betokened certain faith. No—Calvin immediately added that some people "foolishly expose themselves to death in order to uphold some foolish opinions and dreams that they imagined in their heads."[22] He specified near the sermon's end that "the invincible steadfastness that *true* [*vrais*] martyrs exhibit is a more than adequate demonstration that God is powerfully at work in them."[23] Here the qualifier "true" undermined the possibility that behavior might distinguish those killed with "certainty of faith" from those executed for "foolish opinions and dreams," because it assumed who true martyrs were. The difficulty was how to repudiate competing claims without threatening one's own martyrs.

Steadfast dying behavior could not solve this problem for the reason adduced by Blesdijk and implied by Calvin and Menius even as they flirted with it: namely, men and women were willing to suffer and die for all sorts of incompatible views. Consequently, other Protestant writers warned that constancy in death for one's religious convictions was not enough. Luther, for example, stated that even if individuals were to die for the doctrine that good works contribute to salvation, and for human righteousness and free will, "they would not be God's martyrs, but rather their own and the devil's, just like pagans who died for the sake of temporal rights, possessions, and honor."[24] In principle the manner of their deaths would be irrelevant. Hugh Latimer denied that Anabaptists ought to be regarded favorably because they died impressively: "This is no good argument, my friends: A man seemeth not to fear death, therefore his cause is good. This is a deceivable argument: He went to his death boldly, *ergo,* he standeth in a just quarrel."[25] Prior to his own execution in 1567, the Wallonian Calvinist leader Guy de Brès similarly distinguished dying "boldly" [*hardiment*] from dying "well" [*bien*]. "Scripture in no way values those who died stubbornly and boldly," he asserted in his lengthy treatise against the Anabaptists, "but rather those who died in our Lord and those who died for his name."[26]

Catholic controversialists in particular attacked the criterion of suffering per se, starting especially in the 1550s. In some ways they had more at stake because of the deeply ingrained beliefs and practices associated with the veneration of the saints, which were challenged by Protestant and Anabaptist martyr claims. For Catholic writers the doctrinal unity of the one, visible Church exposed the fatal flaw of every heretical group—their mutually incompatible teachings—which simultaneously undermined the sufficiency of steadfast suffering as a means for discerning true martyrs. During Mary Tudor's reign the lay controversialist Miles Huggarde wrote that Arians, the radical Protestant Joan Boucher, and Anne Askewe would all have to be reckoned martyrs "if the stoutness of death be a just cause to prove a martyr."[27] In Louvain, Johannes Molanus challenged the idea that Anabaptists' impressive public deaths should lead one to embrace their beliefs. The same logic would dictate conversion to any and all doctrines for which people willingly died, despite their mutual contradictions.[28] Both Nicholas Harpsfield and Robert Parsons, in their respective treatises against John Foxe, denied that stalwart suffering necessarily denoted martyrdom. Disputing that the deaths of Foxe's subjects made them martyrs, Parsons listed steadfast heretics executed in England between the twelfth century and 1591, highlighting their incompatible views. This showed that "it is not enough for men or women to die resolutely for their opinions, thereby to prove themselves martyrs."[29] In effect, these Catholic controversialists concurred with Blesdijk: not all purported martyrs could be genuine, since they had died for conflicting doctrines. Using their Catholic convictions, however, these writers turned this argument against their opponents. The chaotic cacophony of heretical doctrines contrasted sharply with the coherence of the beliefs for which Roman Catholic martyrs had died.

Controversialists wielded a two-edged sword. Resolute suffering was an insufficient marker of martyrdom. Hence one could target rival martyr claims, but was exposed to adversaries' analogous attacks on one's own martyrs. Still, the meaning of heroic behavior was not undermined simply because it was challenged. Anabaptists, for example, seem to have been completely un-moved by Protestant and Catholic arguments that suffering alone did not denote sanctity. Such hostility revealed only that tyrannical antagonists re-mained blind to the martyrs' witness—hardly a surprising fact, given their murderous actions in the first place.

If steadfast death failed to sift true from false martyrs, then so did the amount of hardship a group had endured. That many people in a given group were executed for their religious convictions might simply mean that authori-ties were doing their job well. In 1554, the Dutch Protestant theologian Jan Gerrits Verstege (Veluanus) criticized the idea "that some views [*menongen*] are the best because they have the most persecution [*meeste verfolligung*] and the loveliest appearance of a good life."[30] He cited 2 Cor. 11:14, the same verse to which Erasmus alluded in his letter to Zwingli and one often adduced to repudiate martyr claims: "Even Satan disguises himself as an angel of light." Stanislaus Hosius, the Polish delegate to the Council of Trent, ridi-culed Calvin's claim that because more Calvinists than Lutherans were willing to suffer for their beliefs, Calvin's doctrine was preferable to Lutheran teach-ing. Reformed Protestants had begun "in these our days to brag and boast of their martyrs"—a reference to early editions of Crespin and Foxe. Yet "both for their number and also for the commendation of their sufferance and patience in punishment, the Anabaptists of old time [that is, the Donatists and Albigensians], and these of our age do so far surmount [them], that if they would make a martyrology of their brethren, they might make greater volumes then the Sacramentaries [that is, Reformed Protestants]."[31] Hosius rightly implied that Calvin would not favor Anabaptist views over his own simply because more Anabaptists than Calvinists had been executed, which in turn subverted Calvin's claim against the Lutherans.[32] How many had suf-fered, and how much they had endured, could not determine who had really witnessed to Christ.

A third attempt to discern genuine martyrs interpreted the fate of false martyrs and the demise of persecutors as the result of God's judgment. Im-plicitly and by contrast, one's persecuted fellow believers were true martyrs. In agreement for once, Luther and Thomas More both thought that Zwin-gli's early death in 1531 was the result of divine wrath.[33] "It amazes me," Luther wrote, "that the rest of the Müntzerites and Zwinglians remain so completely untransformed by such a beating from God, that they not only remain persistent in their error, but rather consider it a beating inflicted on martyrs [*rutten der Merterer*] and even justify themselves and compare them-selves to the holy martyrs."[34] Luther did not, of course, see his followers' deaths in the same terms. Still, his point was easily redirected by Catholic controversialists against Protestant martyrs, as when More used it against Thomas Bilney.[35] Yet More himself got the same treatment: in 1544 the

English Protestant exile George Joye implied that God had condemned him to hell, along with Fisher and others who had persecuted God's word and his martyrs.[36]

Parisian minister Antoine de la Roche Chandieu suggested, amid heavy persecution of Huguenots in the French capital, that the demise of certain Catholic authorities was God's judgment against them. Together with the martyrs' remarkable constancy and the Gospel's growth despite their deaths, the persecutors' downfall denoted the exalted status of the executed Protestants.[37] Had every, or even most, participating priests or magistrates met premature or terrible deaths, this argument might have been compelling. As matters stood, however, public executions of unrepentant heretics were equally easily seen as the fitting outcome of God's justice. This is how Antoine Du Val, a Catholic theologian in Paris during the same years, viewed the punishment of Calvinist heretics.[38] Thus, the same executions were alternately understood as the expression of divine wrath and divine blessing. Persecutors' deaths could no better distinguish true from false martyrs than could the fact or amount of steadfast suffering.

Equally weak was the hybrid criterion of social status and learning, a fourth would-be means to discern true martyrs. Robert Parsons, for example, implied that the lowly standing and/or meager education of Foxe's witnesses made them false martyrs. He disparaged Foxe's "rabblement, both of men, women, and children, artificers, sawyers, weavers, shoemakers, spinsters, yea some mad or distracted people." With naked willfulness they resisted their lawful superiors and died for their own opinions. Yet Parsons then played devil's advocate and undercut his own criterion:

> But you will say perhaps, that this very same may be objected to all martyrs, both old and new, as well of our side, that have died for [the] Cath[olic] religion in our days, as others of ancient times, whom we acknowledge for true martyrs, among whom there were divers simple people, maids and virgins that died constantly for Christian religion, though they were unlearned, and were not able to dispute of the points for which they died, and yet neither with the allurements, or terrors of the persecutors, could they be brought to yield in any one iota, in matters of their faith; and the like we confess, and do greatly commend in many simple Catholic people of our days, especially in our own country, who would rather suffer any loss and affliction, yea death itself, than go back in the confession of any least point of their faith, or communicate with heretics by going to their church, service, sermons, or the like.[39]

Believing something and being able to defend it were two different things. In itself, the latter meant nothing. An illiterate Catholic peasant woman might endure martyrdom although unable to articulate her beliefs, whereas a well-born, sophisticated theologian might dispute cleverly for weeks and yet die for heresy. Neither humble origin, nor low social status, nor lack of education were sure signs of false martyrs.

Catholic controversialists in particular argued that false martyrs lacked charity. Frequently bolstered by Augustine, Cyprian, or both, they cited 1 Cor. 13:3: "If I give away all my possessions, and if I hand over my body to be burned, but do not have love, I gain nothing." Protestant writers sometimes made the same accusation. Guy de Brès, for example, alleged that Anabaptist separatism implied a lack of charity.[40] However, the continuing Catholic emphasis on charity, rather than faith, as the greatest of the three theological virtues, made this argument predominantly a Catholic preserve. In commenting on 1 Cor. 13:3, the editors of the Douai-Rheims New Testament cited Augustine to argue that "Anabaptists and Calvinists," as well as "heretics and schismatics" who might die among non-Christians for defending some part of the Christian religion, could not be saved, because all lacked charity in breaking with the Church.[41] Huggarde, Hosius, Du Val, and Molanus argued similarly. Southwell amplified the same verse to provide a seamless lead into Cyprian: "For in truth as St. Paul sayeth, though I deliver my body to be burned, and have no charity *and union with God, and his true Church:* it availeth me nothing."[42] In the end, such remarks simply reiterated that non-Catholics could not be martyrs because they had rejected Roman Catholicism. Lack of charity was not an independent criterion for telling true martyrs from false, because separation from the Church was *defined* as uncharitable. From the perspective of those who left the Roman church, however, this separation was essential to escape the erroneous teachings, superstitious practices, and idolatrous worship that encumbered true Christian charity and jeopardized salvation.

The allegation that false martyrs were condemned for non-religious crimes comprised another attempt to distinguished false martyrs from true. It too proved impotent on both the Catholic and the English Protestant sides. Du Val claimed that some Calvinist martyrs had led dissolute lives or committed crimes prior to their time in Geneva, an accusation Jacques Sévert echoed in the early seventeenth century.[43] In England Thomas Harding, in the 1560s, and later Robert Parsons, leveled similar charges against some of Foxe's martyrs.[44] Even were all these instances conceded, however, no Catholic controversialist claimed that *all* false martyrs were false because they had suffered for nonreligious reasons. This was not a general criterion of exclusion, then, but only a means to rule out some purported martyrs while impugning the integrity of competing martyrological communities and their martyrologists.

In its English Protestant version, however, this argument *was* generalized.

It was claimed that all the Catholics executed under Henry VIII and Elizabeth were killed for treason, not religion. William Cecil formulated the classic statement of this position in his 1583 pamphlet *The Execution of Justice in England,* which followed the numerous executions of missionary priests in 1581–1582. Latin, French, Dutch, and Italian translations appeared in 1584, in an attempt to combat the continental proliferation of Catholic sources about the English martyrs. Cecil claimed that "secret" and "open" traitors differed only insofar as the former lacked the means to realize their intentions. The priests executed were "seedmen and sowers of rebellion" charged with "high treason, not being dealt withall upon questions of religion, but justly condemned as traitors."[45] The refusal to acknowledge the royal supremacy, however, was *defined* as treason. Hence the argument was as circular as the Catholic position that defined separation from the Church as uncharitable, then used lack of charity to identify false martyrs. To late Elizabethan Catholics, calling their martyred fellow believers traitors only reinforced their conviction that the new laws against their religion compounded tyranny with duplicity.

The absence of miracles was yet another way that Catholic writers attacked competing martyr claims. Heretical martyrs, they asserted, were neither in heaven nor favored by God, because he worked no posthumous miracles through them or their relics. By contrast, intercession by Catholic martyrs yielded abundant cures and other wonders. Both Baronius and Rosweyde invoked Tertullian's analogy of the bees and wasps, originally used against the Marcionites, to elucidate the difference: just as wasps mimicked bees by building hives but made no honey, so heretics imitated true martyrs but failed to produce posthumous miracles.[46] Harpsfield and Du Val, too, alleged that no genuine miracles had been worked through heretics.[47] Yet this merely displaced one contested issue—true and false martyrs—with another. Even if non-Catholic Christians had to leave room for miracles in their heavily providential worldviews, how would one tell genuine and false miracles apart, or discern whether miracles came through martyrs' intercession as opposed to God's direct action? With reference to the false prophets and messiahs foretold in Matt. 24:24, and the great signs and omens they would produce, John Bale derisively agreed that "the pope's martyrs indeed, were much fuller of miracles than ever were Christ's, as himself told us they should be so." By contrast, in "his own chosen martyrs, Christ looketh for none other miracle, but that only they persevere faithful to the end."[48] The marvel of the martyrs was their steadfastness in death, not purported wonders worked after it. Yet remarkable as such constancy was, it also failed to distinguish true from false martyrs.

Protestants were hardly disposed to believe stories about Catholic miracles when they could plausibly attribute them to a sinister symbiosis of clerical fraud and lay credulity. Indeed, unless one were open to the possibility of seeing God work wonders, by definition any purported miracle had to have an alternative explanation. Catholic apologists proceeded no differently: Miles Huggarde mocked sympathizers who claimed to see "the holy ghost in the likeness of a dove" when pigeons were roused by the smoke from the fire that consumed John Rogers, this being one of the "fancies" of "opinionative fools."[49] Moreover, considering the Catholic readiness to regard executed fellow believers as saints, it is extremely unlikely that miracles had to be used as an independent criterion for determining true martyrs: Catholics not were attentively waiting on or invoking all executed Christians to note who would work wonders. Rather they almost certainly looked for miracles only from those *already* considered martyrs.

On all sides, then, controversialists failed to isolate an observable, independent means to differentiate true from false martyrs. Constancy in death, how many had suffered and how much they had endured, the fates of false martyrs and persecutors, social status and educational level, the presence or lack of charity, punishment for nonreligious crimes, and the presence or absence of miracles—all exhibited fatal weaknesses. They could be turned back against their protagonists, or they were not generally applicable, or they were restatements of another criterion for identifying false martyrs. Consequently, genuine martyrs were discernible only by their doctrines, not their deeds: only by their convictions, not their comportment.

"Not the Punishment, but the Cause, Makes a Martyr"

In the early Reformation period it was sometimes claimed that other groups lacked people willing to die for their religious views. More and Tyndale, for example, leveled this indictment against each other.[50] Soon, however, the repeated spectacle of public executions before large crowds rendered this claim untenable. From the 1520s martyrological communities took shape based on what people died for, and its social cognate, the communities of belief to which they belonged. When controversialists seized on Augustine's dictum to criticize false martyrs, they simply applied a criterion already at work in determining their respective martyrological communities. Inclusion necessarily entailed exclusion.

Controversialists benefited from a resurgent interest in patristic authors. Spurred by humanist scholarship and printed editions of their works, this attention was perpetuated by competing claims to represent the fathers' legacy. Both Catholic and Protestant writers employed the criterion by which Augustine, heir to Tertullian, Eusebius, and especially Cyprian in this regard, had condemned Donatist martyrs in late antiquity: "not the punishment, but the cause, makes a martyr." Patristic writers had not concocted the principle themselves, but rather derived it from several New Testament passages, working out, for example, what it meant to be persecuted "for righteousness' sake" (Matt. 5:10) rather than for some other reason. The mocking thief was condemned, the other saved, even though both were crucified alongside Christ (Luke 23:39–43). Paul distinguished "wicked people and imposters" from those persecuted for living godly in Christ (2 Tim. 3:12–13). And it was laudable to suffer as a Christian but not as a wrongdoer (1 Pet. 5:14–16). Unlike nondoctrinal criteria, Augustine's dictum enabled controversialists to distinguish clearly between true and false martyrs. Yet it presupposed assent to the specific doctrines attached to it, and thus could not convince adversaries. Just as Christians from divergent traditions appropriated biblical verses about persecution, so Catholic and Protestant antimartyrologists harnessed scriptural and patristic passages to separate true from false martyrs.[51] Early modern controversialists thus rehashed the duels among martyrological communities in early Christianity, which had emerged as early as the second century.[52] When the early modern spectacle of steadfast deaths incited conversion, it did so against the efforts of Catholic and Protestant writers.

For more than a century in England and on the Continent, Catholic controversialists pummeled Protestant and Anabaptist martyrs for having died for false doctrines. Unless one belonged to the Roman Catholic church, believing its teachings and practicing the Christian faith as it prescribed, martyrdom was impossible. This stricture is less drastic than it sounds: it merely applied the principle that outside the Church—that is, apart from Christ; according to early modern Catholic views—there was no salvation. As Cyprian had remarked, one could not be a martyr if one was not in the Church; and it followed that heretical martyrs lacked charity, since they had rejected Christ's mystical body.[53]

From the late 1520s into the seventeenth century, English Catholic writers deprecated the new, false martyrs. More, for example, disparaged Thomas Hitton by listing "what wholesome heresies this holy martyr held," including the denial of several sacraments, repudiation of purgatory and prayers for the dead, and rejection of transubstantiation, for which he was "burned up in his false faith and heresies."[54] During the Marian restoration, Reginald Pole, Miles Huggarde, and the queen's confessor, John Christoferson, all claimed that purported Protestant martyrs had died for wayward reasons.[55] In 1566, Thomas Harding rebuked John Jewel's praise of the Marian martyrs' constancy, flatly stating that "patience in an evil cause is no sufficient trial of a true martyr. It is not suffering, but the cause of suffering, that maketh a martyr."[56] As a Jesuit missionary in England more than twenty years later, Robert Southwell concurred. He wrote that "Though martyrdom, if it be well used, be an act of singular virtue, yea of all virtues together, and turn to the incomparable glory of the martyr: yet when it is not taken for a right cause, and in a due sort, it is to the sufferer but the beginning of an eternal corruption."[57]

The same refrain resounded on the Continent well into the seventeenth century. Antoine Du Val sought to undermine Calvinist martyrs by exposing the erroneous convictions for which they had perished: only after a section entitled "That Calvin is a heretic" did he criticize Calvinist martyr claims.[58] Over half a century later, Jacques Sévert followed the logic of his Parisian predecessor when he organized his encyclopedic refutation of Crespin. First, Sévert laboriously enumerated and juxtaposed 160 Roman Catholic to 100 Calvinist articles of faith. Only then did he offer a painstaking, often person-by-person, treatment of Crespin's heroes, citing the specific heretical doctrines that disqualified them as martyrs.[59] This Catholic argument went unchanged regardless of its principal target. Christoph Andreas Fischer, for example, a Jesuit parish priest in Lower Austria near the Moravian border, disputed with the Hutterites and condemned Anabaptist martyrs with reference to Matt. 5:10. After naming several men whom they "praise and regard as martyrs," Fischer wrote that they did so "without reason, for the only ones esteemed and regarded as martyrs" would be those who suffered persecution "for righteousness' sake."[60] Similarly, in opposition to van Haemstede and Dutch Protestant martyrs, Arnoudt van Geluwe attacked competing martyr claims in the 1650s. If suffering alone made a martyr, he argued, *reductio ad absurdum,* then besides all manner of executed heretics, slain Jews and Moslems would also merit recognition as martyrs. Therefore "neither the pain nor the lamentable death makes a martyr, but the reason, or the 'why' [*maer de oorsake, often den waerom*], for which someone is suffering."[61]

Usually but not invariably, Protestant controversialists agreed, though naturally with their own ideas about the content of the "why." An exceptional case from the early Reformation highlights the fragility of cross-confessional martyr recognition. The preachers Martin Bucer and Wolfgang Capito helped make Strasbourg the most open of the leading evangelical cities in the 1520s. Shortly after Michael Sattler was executed in 1527, Bucer, Capito, and the city's other ministers wrote to the evangelicals of Worms. They distinguished Sattler from more objectionable Anabaptists such as Jakob Kautz and Hans Denck. With evident care, they noted Sattler's various errors and yet called him "a dear friend of God" [*eyn lieber frundt gots*]. Indeed, "we do not doubt that he is a martyr of Christ" [*eyn marterer Christi*]. Although Sattler and his followers erred regarding baptism, oath-taking, and the possibility of governments being Christian, they retained a foundation in Christ and therefore hope of salvation. Cyprian and Tertullian, too, the Strasbourgers wrote, had held many errors, but they were long and widely considered martyrs.[62]

By May 1535, however, the Strasbourgers had changed their tune. After persistent problems with Anabaptists and Pilgram Marpeck's arrival in the city, plus the deeply disturbing events in Münster, the preachers made the standard distinction between beliefs and behavior. They told the Strasbourg city council that a Christian government "should not always consider it a sign of conscience and faith when sometimes such people suffer much and die bravely. For not everything that goes by the name of conscience and faith really is. Satan can disguise himself as an angel of light and his own as apostles of Christ."[63] For all practical purposes, Münster destroyed the prospects for cross-confessional martyr recognition, even by the most lenient evangelical reformers. "Tolerable Anabaptist errors" became an oxymoron.

Luther was never disposed to make such distinctions in the first place, beginning with his denunciations of Anabaptists and Müntzer's followers in the 1520s. Later, in his *Appeal to Pastors to Preach against Usury* (1540), Luther implied that most purported martyrs, including "Anabaptists and the like," were really false martyrs whose place was in hell, not heaven. Noting Matt. 5:10 and Augustine's dictum, Luther stated that those who suffered for Christ's and righteousness' sake were blessed, but not those "who suffered for their wickedness, for the sake of their own will, for the sake of their praise, avarice, or glory, for their invented devotion and the sake of self-indulgent spirituality" [*erwelete geistlichkeit*].[64] Similarly, Guy de Brès listed many people who had died heroically, including the unrepentant thief crucified with Christ, many Jews, Arians, and Moslems, as well as "priests who suffered for their papacy." Yet this alone did not make "their doctrine and religion" laudable, "for the cause makes the martyr, and not the punishment." Neither could Anabaptists be martyrs, since they died not for "righteousness, for the truth, and for the name of Christ," but rather "for a doctrine of Antichrist," regrettable as that was.[65] Lamenting the demise of misguided, stubborn people, however, was not theological alchemy. It could not transform heresies into truths.

In England, the Protestant Latimer and the Catholic Huggarde agreed that to die for a teaching implied nothing about its truth or goodness. Conversely, God's truth depended not on whether people suffered for it—Catholics were not persecuted in Rome, nor Calvinists in Geneva. Crespin, a Genevan citizen, agreed that the truth alone, not suffering or apparent holiness, could separate true from false martyrs: "they delude themselves who fix their gaze on the crosses and punishments (which do not make the martyr) rather than on the infallible foundation of the truth, which alone shows the difference between the sufferings [*diuersité des souffrances*] of true and false Christians."[66] Nothing could make a false believer into a true martyr: not whether they suffered, their comportment in dying, or the horror of their torments. On this point Protestant controversialists agreed entirely with their Catholic counterparts. Both delineated and protected their respective martyrological communities with Augustine's dictum.

Consequently, controversialists' admonitions clashed with the conviction that good deaths were discernible by observation. Someone might seem to die with sanctity and grace and yet do nothing of the sort. Philipp Melanchthon drafted a justification for the execution of unrepentant Anabaptists in Electoral Saxony in 1536. He wrote that "each person should know, as Christians, to judge the great boldness and bravery [*große Kühnheit und Trotz*] that is noted in some Anabaptists in danger of death more according to God's Word rather than by such appearances [*solchen Schein*], and not let themselves err. For as long as the Anabaptists remain so stubborn in such errors and blasphemies in public as they have been, such boldness should be considered as nothing but a horrible obstinacy of the devil, as was in Saul and others."[67] Melanchthon had cause for concern, as popular attitudes toward relapsed Anabaptist Fritz Erbe made clear. Arrested in 1532 in western Thuringian lands under Philipp of Hesse's jurisdiction, Erbe was imprisoned for as long as he might maintain his views, since Philipp opposed the execution of non-seditious Anabaptists. Imprisoned in Eisenach, Erbe stood firm for the remaining sixteen years of his life. The common people in and around the city apparently came to view him as a prophet and martyr. The mayor and city council of Eisenach paraphrased popular opinion: "if he could be overcome by [arguments from] God's Word, he would not be a captive for so long a time."[68] Melanchthon and other controversialists wanted to dispel this sort of appearances-oriented, practical theology wherever it existed.

One writer, probably Joris Wybo, thought that the Gospel parable of the good and bad trees and their fruit (Matt. 12:33–35) supported Melanchthon's point: "where faith and doctrine are bad, how can the fruits be good and pleasing to God?" The upshot was a radical wariness of appearances in the assessment of purported holiness:

> Life and works are indeed like good fruits from a tree when they spring from a right [*goede*] faith, but are nevertheless sometimes deceptive, because a person with wicked faith also does works that are good in appearance, just as a wild tree bears fruit that resembles good fruit. For all heretics, or at least the majority, are always shrouded with an attractive appearance of holiness (just as false trees are adorned with wild fruit and leaves), by which they appear to be true Christians, *indeed even greatly surpassing true Christians* [*ia den warachtigen Christenen verre te bouen gaende*].[69]

Alarmingly, false martyrs might die even *more* steadfastly and heroically—in appearance—than true martyrs. According to Wybo, this was precisely what someone like Claes de Praet failed to grasp. De Praet explained that after having seen four Anabaptists burned in Ghent in 1551, "in time I began to investigate the belief for which these people had died so boldly, and I searched the scriptures." He converted and was himself executed several years later.[70]

Catholic apologist Florimond de Raemond invoked Origen's observation: seemingly holy heretics attracted more followers than dissolute heretics and were therefore more dangerous. Raemond admitted the impact of Protestant martyrs on people "who could not believe that a false doctrine could inhabit a life as Christian as theirs was in appearance" [*vne vie si Chrestienne comme estoit la leur apparence*].[71] When Reginald Pole praised the early Henrician martyrs in 1536, he contrasted the transparent testimony of martyrdom with the potential misuse of scripture.[72] Ultimately, however, this clarity depended on the doctrines for which they had died—themselves the product of a Catholic understanding of scripture, apprehended through tradition. By Mary's reign, Pole disparaged appearances per se and called "the constancy of those that willingly offer themselves to death for the defense of their opinion" among the Marian martyrs "mere obstinacy, and a devilish pertinac[it]y."[73] Henry VIII's apologists had argued just this about More and Fisher two decades earlier, when Pole thought it unimaginable that their deaths had been in vain.

Doctrinal differences prompted divergent descriptions: death for true Christianity was steadfastness, death for erroneous beliefs was stubbornness. Resoluteness and obstinacy turned on convictions, not comportment. As early as 1523 the *History of the Two Augustinians* coupled the twin possibilities—"constantia aut pertinacia"—in describing how Vos and van den Esschen had sustained their deaths.[74] A remark by Simon Renard, the imperial ambassador to England, captured perfectly the dichotomy: he told Charles V that the early Marian burnings had "hardened many hearts, for it has been seen how constant, or rather stubborn, these heretics prove at the stake."[75] The most seductive heretics might mimic the most devout martyrs. Unless the tendency to judge by appearances was rightly informed by doctrine, it could be disastrously misleading.

This concern is especially clear in Robert Parsons's *Treatise of Three Conversions of England*, where what began as an Aristotelian discussion of constancy and stubbornness ended as a reiteration of Augustine's dictum. Parsons began by noting that Foxe and company regarded Protestant martyrs' behavior "as a high point of fortitude," whereas Catholics "do most of all pity and condemn the same, as a special point of temerity and madness."[76] Virtue, Parsons stated, was a mean between two extremes of vice, here constancy between stubbornness and inconstancy. As Aristotle, Aquinas, and daily experience made clear, "obstinacy may be held for constancy, pertinacity for perseverance, self-will for steadfastness, and vainglory for true magnanimity." Consequently, "we must not believe presently the outer show or sound of matters, but must enter into the examinations of every one of these things, according to their natures, causes, motives, and effects, if we will not be deceived." This further analysis led to Gregory the Great's observation that obstinacy is the daughter of vainglory and the sister of presumption in novelties. From here Parsons argued that obstinacy is "so nearly conjoined in blood and kindred to heresy herself, as they cannot be separated," since heresy implied deliberate persistence in error.[77] The same stubbornness that had always made heretics cling to their own opinions, then, had led them to endure even death for their views. Hence "dying for opinions in religion, without other consideration, is not sufficient to make martyrs, for that it may be pertinacity and not constancy, sin and not virtue, instigation of the devil, and not inspiration of the spirit of God, and that it is, and hath been common to all heretics, and is incident to the nature of heresy itself, to have this pertinacity and stubbornness in defending their own fancies, censures, and opinions, upon pride and vainglory."[78] Informed observers ought to have *expected* heretics to die readily for their views. This was the logical extension of their essential stubbornness.

Yet as he often did, Parsons anticipated his reader's response and reopened the entire issue: "you will say perhaps, and how shall we be able to discern this matter, when it is true constancy, and when obstinacy? When perseverance, and when pertinacity?"[79] Observation fell short: Parsons ridiculed the lowly status and ignorance of many of Foxe's martyrs, but he acknowledged the same in some Catholic martyrs. Instead, Aristotle yielded to Augustine, behavior and background to beliefs. True martyrs died for "the name and confession of Jesus Christ" and the "Catholic doctrine of the universal Church," whereas Foxe's martyrs and other heretics "do not die for the name of Christ, but for particular opinions in Christian religion, contrary to the sense both of the ancient and present Catholic Church."[80] In other words, false martyrs were false because they were not Catholic. The cause made the martyr and dictated whether observable behavior was steadfastness or stubbornness.

If false martyrs might seem to die even more heroically than true martyrs, then it was imperative to explain the former's headstrong foolishness to those easily misled by appearances. Sometimes false martyrs' folly was the simple result of pride and vainglory. Closely associated with both these vices, however, was the devil. Catholic and Protestant controversialists repeatedly ascribed this deception to Satan, as we have seen in Melanchthon, Crespin, Pole, and Parsons. According to Luther, that false martyrs could pervert even Christian patience and suffering showed how utterly Satan had poisoned all the children of Adam.[81] The day after Rowland Taylor was burned in February 1555, his replacement preached that Satan had sustained him. John Christoferson wrote that if someone saw a heretic "gladly go to the fire, and patiently suffer it," he should "be right sorry in his heart and lament, that the devil was so great with him that he could make him suffer the hot flames of fire for his wicked opinion, and sold him straight to the fervent flames of everlasting fire."[82] Protestant and Catholic writers noted that if Satan could transform himself into an angel of light, then in his envy of God's martyrs, he could inspire heretics to die for false doctrines.[83] People routinely underestimated his power. As Bernard of Clairvaux had said and early modern controversialists often repeated, if Satan could move people to commit suicide, he could prompt people to die for heresy.[84] Just as martyrologists attributed their heroes' steadfastness to God's grace, controversialists imputed counterfeit, heretical stubbornness to Satan's envy.

Yet mutual denunciations of false martyrs were not strictly parallel. By noting the incompatible doctrines maintained within heretical martyrological communities, Catholic controversialists accused competing martyrologists of contradicting their own espousal of Augustine's dictum. Protestant controversialists were hard pressed to counter in kind. Catholic writers criticized the status of Wyclif and Hus as Protestant martyrs, since they had held numerous non-Protestant doctrines.[85] Parsons pointed out that together with English Protestants (who held divergent views among themselves) Foxe had lumped "Waldensians, Albigensians, Wyclifists, Lollards, Hussites, Taborites, Anabaptists, and Lutherans, who abhor and condemn expressly our English Protestant religion at this day."[86] In fact, Parsons splintered Foxe's martyrological community primarily by disclosing divergent doctrines as he moved methodically through the false martyrs included in the *Acts and Monuments*. A similar approach characterized Harpsfield's *Six Dialogues* and Sévert's *Anti-Martyrology*. The latter accused Crespin of subverting Augustine's dictum by including early evangelical martyrs with different eucharistic views.[87] Protestant writers, by contrast, found it difficult to turn the tables. Despite its variety and internal factions, Roman Catholicism's institutional hierarchy and confessional unity precluded analogous contradictory doctrines among latter-day Catholic martyrs.

In short, Catholic writers exploited the tension between specific confessions and broader martyrological communities. Evidently, their challenge elicited no direct response. Yet the Catholic attack did not directly undermine the doctrines of any particular confession—it implied only that martyrs' beliefs within a martyrological community could not contradict each other. This implication, if heeded, would have divided Protestant martyrs along denominational lines, a prospect glimpsed when German Lutheran pastors denounced Reformed Protestants as "the devil's martyrs" in the late sixteenth century.[88] Overwhelmingly, however, this did not happen: Crespin, Foxe, van Haemstede, and their continuators did not construe orthodoxy narrowly. Doing so would have changed considerably the face of Protestant martyrology. Instead, the acceptance of a broader tradition implied a rejection of the doctrinal congruence upon which Catholic critics insisted, *for the purposes of identifying the Protestent martyrological community*. A view of the Gospel's incremental restoration in the late Middle Ages could accommodate proto-Protestant martyrs from the pre-Reformation past. After the Reformation, various Protestant denominations might still dispute bitterly over the Lord's Supper and other issues, but they shelved these disagreements when identifying witnesses for the Gospel against radicals and Roman Catholics. In other words, in some contexts the groups within Lutheran and Reformed Christianity understood themselves simply as "Protestant." Still, this did not answer the deeper challenge of the Catholic critique, namely which among the conflicting sets of Protestant teachings was true Christianity.

Mennonite Waterlander Hans de Ries deliberately grabbed the other end of the stick when he assembled his Anabaptist martyrology in 1615. Despite Old Frisian protestations, what really mattered, he maintained, were not the disagreements among Swiss, German, and Dutch Anabaptist martyrs, but their practice of believers' baptism and their membership in nonpersecuting churches. *Doopsgezinde* identity lay in broad commonalities, not specific differences. By construing doctrinal disagreement less precisely than their Catholic critics, Anabaptist and Protestant writers skirted criticisms of the divergent doctrines maintained by their martyrs.

Paradoxically, the centrality of doctrine in identifying true martyrs relativized, if only to a degree, the behavioral prerequisites for martyrdom. Doubtless people still expected, in general, that martyrs would die with impressive steadfastness, but less than ideal comportment did not necessarily nullify their witness. Jesus himself was an impeccable model: as Pole noted, he showed "more heaviness and dolor at his dying hour, than did the thieves that hung beside him."[89] Hugh Latimer expressed the idea in its broadest terms: "will ye argue then, He goeth to his death boldly or cheerfully, *ergo*, he dieth in a just cause? Nay, that sequel followeth no more than this: A man seems to be afraid of death, *ergo*, he dieth evil. And yet our Saviour Christ was afraid of death himself."[90] In both cases, the root problem was interpretation that relied on appearances. In his *Epistle of Persecution*, Parsons conceded that Catholics sometimes cried out when being drawn and quartered, but he attacked Protestant claims that this disqualified them as martyrs.[91] Similarly, William Allen reported that John Shert grabbed the rope when he was hanged in 1582—yet this was merely a natural reflex, not a sign of cowardice. Likewise, John Geninges wrote that his brother Edmund blurted, "Oh it smarts," during his dismemberment in December 1591.[92] Since the cause, not the comportment, made the martyr, stoic impassivity was not required. The discriminating observer would look past appearances to the reasons for execution, allowing latitude for age, physical condition, and God's unpredictable dispensation of grace. No one would have acknowledged as a martyr anyone who went cursing, kicking, and screaming to the scaffold. Yet imperviousness to pain was not demanded when Jesus himself had cried from the cross, "My God, my God, why hast thou forsaken me?" (Matt. 27:46).

Why did controversialists endlessly repeat Augustine's dictum? Ironically, because they could not eradicate judgments based on appearances. Their reiterations make sense only if steadfast deaths for religion continued to impress, notwithstanding their admonitions. Indeed, their concern was justified. If a group of Leipzig burgers could discuss, in June 1525, whether recently slain peasants were martyrs, then Luther and Johannes Faber had reason to fear sympathy for Müntzer and his followers.[93] In 1555 Charles V received a letter claiming that "the foundation of the heretics," their arrogant presumption to know more than all the Church's theologians, was born of blindness, pride, and the fact that "simple people, seeing such heretics die publicly with firm steadfastness, and hearing their remarks and the prayers that they address to God before they die, fall into some vacillation and doubt of the [Catholic] faith."[94] Du Val wrote partly because he saw "many simple-minded men and women," presumably in Paris, "being deceived and seduced, astounded at the patience and steadfastness of some of [the Calvinists] when they are executed and burned."[95] The joyful endurance of death might overwhelm warnings not to judge based on behavior.[96] Here Tertullian's observation—"the blood of the martyrs is seed"—offered not a triumphalistic aphorism, but rather signified a persistent problem.

The spectacle of executions impressively endured could itself unsettle true doctrine, especially if the comportment of purportedly false martyrs shamed the moral conduct of one's own priests or ministers. Nor was the conflict of interpretations limited to learned theological debate. Indeed, it originated and was most concrete when the stake or scaffold were near. When Margaret Clitherow returned to prison after being sentenced to *peine forte et dure,* her "joyful countenance" became the subject of controversy: "some said 'It must needs be that she received comfort from the Holy Ghost,' for all were astonished to see her of so good cheer. Some said it was not so, but that she was possessed with a merry devil, and that she sought her own death."[97] In early modern Europe there were several thousand Margaret Clitherows. From 1523 into the seventeenth century, all told, hundreds of thousands of people must have seen them die, since at times thousands evidently witnessed particular executions. Given the far-flung communication and widespread publicization of their deaths, it seems safe to infer that over several generations, literally millions of Western Europeans had to decide for themselves, like Erasmus in his letter to Zwingli, how they understood the dying words and deeds of the executed, and whether or not they deplored their deaths.

Despite antagonists' efforts and authorities' orchestrations, executions for heterodoxy retained their capacity to affect onlookers. Hence controversialists reiterated their arguments for decades. Hence prospective martyrs pondered and planned in prison their final words and dying actions. Hence authorities sought to secure scripted control over executions and, when serious unrest threatened, opted for banishment or clandestine killings. As early as 1527, Holland's judicial court worried that executing relapsed heretic Cornelis Wouters of Dordrecht might evoke sympathy like that shown for Jan van Woerden in 1525.[98] Finally, some spectators at executions remained susceptible to the comportment of the condemned. Even if what moved specific individuals to pity, conversion, disgust, or contempt remains unrecoverable, collective tendencies are discernible: responses were likely to be divisive as sympathizers multiplied and consensus about orthodoxy dissolved. Executions in Paris affirmed communal Catholic values in the 1520s and 1530s; by the late 1550s, they provoked religious riots.[99] Even when a general drift is clear, however, the meaning of executions eluded imposition and control. Opposite perspectives were always available to individual observers.[100] The respective varieties of early modern Christianity offered different plausible interpretations, no matter what transpired.

Implications and Conclusions

Analytically, the denunciation of false martyrs should be seen in precisely the same light as the celebration of true martyrs. Considering the connection between doctrines and deaths, and the fact that Christian groups disagreed about God's teachings, false martyrs bore an *inextricable* relationship to true martyrs. There are no intellectual grounds for contrasting the (acceptable) celebration of martyrs as "victims" with the (objectionable) repudiation of false martyrs, as though the latter were patently a cruel unwillingness to sympathize with human suffering.[101] Simply by recognizing some martyrs and not others, all three traditions did both. As surely as contradictory doctrines could not both be true, martyrology necessarily excluded as it included. Moreover, to contrast celebration with denunciation would be to settle contentiously the unresolved early modern question of who the victims were—the men and women executed for their beliefs, or the general public threatened by dangerous criminals.

Martyrdom began and ended with divergent views of Christian truth. They underpinned the willingness to kill and die; they framed the dispute about the meaning of the executions. Paradoxically, the hardening of doctrinal differences made the criterion for identifying true martyrs simultaneously unassailable and utterly unconvincing. It was unassailable because Augustine's dictum radically severed belief from dying behavior: no stalwart display could make a heretic in hell into a martyr in heaven. This is why controversialists could and did acknowledge false martyrs' comportment in ways so similar to the descriptions by sympathetic writers. At the same time, Augustine's dictum was unconvincing because it presupposed the issue in question, namely Christian truth. As far as English Protestants were concerned, when Parsons appealed to "the universal visible Church" to distinguish true Catholic martyrs from Foxe's false martyrs, he merely begged central, disputed ecclesiological questions.[102] The only way to persuade people that someone was a true martyr was to convince them that he or she had died as a true Christian—that is, to convert them. But Protestants, Anabaptists, and Roman Catholics alike grew up with the stories of their respective martyrs, men and women who had shed their blood for the truth. Such witness was not to be taken lightly—yet conversion presupposed rejecting this witness, the martyrological tradition, and the beliefs of one's present Christian community for the sake of a different one. As a result, collectively and over the long term, martyrdom militated against conversion and reinforced confessionalization.

Divergent Christian teachings became fixed in part because of their irreducibly human connection to those who had died for them. After 1523, prospective doctrinal compromise never implied merely how to interpret scripture or understand tradition. It also meant reckoning with fellow believers who had sealed their interpretations and understandings in blood. Was not doctrinal compromise a retrospective negotiation of their convictions, a callous relativization of their witness? Eternal salvation was at stake even without martyrdom. Yet the deaths of men and women at the stake pushed disputed doctrines beyond the threshold of realistic prospects for compromise. If Christians within any one of these traditions had understood differently the scriptural admonitions about steadfastness and suffering—had not believed that God required fidelity to his truth—that entire tradition would almost certainly have evolved very differently. (Spiritualist sects that sanctioned dissembling, such as the Schwenkfeldians or Familists, claimed many fewer adherents than the Anabaptists and failed to exhibit the latter's staying power.) Devout Protestants, Anabaptists, and Roman Catholics all embraced these biblical passages and acted on them, forcing the issue of true and false martyrs. The identification of those "precious in the sight of the Lord" (Ps. 116:15) was as contentious as the Pauline "false apostles, deceitful workers, disguising themselves as apostles of Christ" (2 Cor. 11:13). Because martyrs perished similarly in all three traditions, "dying well" in imitation of ancient models, it is hard to see how the dispute could have turned on something besides doctrine. Because the deaths of fellow believers reinforced divergent doctrines, it is hard to see how the dispute could have ended in anything but deadlock. At the point where traditions coalesced and identities were forged, early modern Christians did not debate—they disagreed.

Shared faith and its practice in communities of belief, the answers that a particular commitment to Christ provided, the experiential fit between scripture and life, and the sacrifice of one's fellow believers in martyrdom—all these reinforced each other. They sliced paths through what otherwise might have been a hermeneutical jungle. Margaret Clitherow knew full well that Elizabethan Catholics and Marian Protestants could not both be true martyrs—but she had no doubts about who reposed with God. Menno Simons, too, was unfazed by Blesdijk's observation that Christians were dying for contrary convictions, not all of which could be true. Sure enough, not all could—but Christ's flock remained unchanged.

Conclusion:
A Shared and Shattered Worldview

Do not think that I have come to bring peace on earth; I have not come to bring peace, but a sword. For I have come to set a man against his father, and a daughter against her mother, and a daughter-in-law against her mother-in-law; and one's foes will be members of one's own household. Whoever loves father or mother more than me is not worthy of me; and whoever loves son or daughter more than me is not worthy of me; and whoever does not take up the cross and follow me is not worthy of me. Those who find their life will lose it, and those who lose their life for my sake will find it.

    —MATTHEW 10:34–39

The same cometh often to pass, when as men be of diverse opinions, concerning their faith and religion: for albeit that many other matters make one to hate another, yet nothing is there that breedeth so deadly hatred, as diversity of minds, touching religion.

    —JOHN CHRISTOFERSON, EXHORTATION TO BEWARE OF
    REBELLION (1554)

Martyrdom is a sharp wedge with which to penetrate the beliefs and behaviors of devout early modern Christians. It leads through distinct traditions, across national and linguistic boundaries, among the privileged and the humble, the learned and the unlettered, men and women, clergy and laity, into many types of sources, from the fifteenth century into the seventeenth. The previous chapters have reconstructed fundamental religious sensibilities of Protestants, Anabaptists, and Roman Catholics. It remains now to take a broad, analytical look at the whole.

What made sixteenth-century Christianity so explosive was the combination of shared and incompatible beliefs. Regardless of the group to which one belonged, one's adversaries were not an unknown "other." They were European contemporaries with whom one shared numerous religious convictions and other cultural assumptions. The nature of what was shared critically influenced the character and intensity of the disagreements.

Protestants, Anabaptists, and Roman Catholics agreed on many central beliefs within a traditional Christian worldview, fundamental convictions about the origins, purpose, meaning, and destiny of humankind. They all regarded the Bible as God's word, a unique and uniquely important revelation of his will. They all believed that God disposed occurrences on earth through his providence. This did not necessarily mean that events would transpire as one wished, but rather that God would preserve one from final ruin, no matter what happened. Protestants and Anabaptists rejected the notion of purgatory as a Romish money-making scam. Yet no less than their Catholic contemporaries, they believed that after death, the same God who had created them would either welcome them into heaven or damn them to hell. Christians in all three traditions held that human sinfulness had perverted God's created order, a corruption righted by Jesus Christ, his only son. It was only through Christ, God's incarnation and definitive revelation, that they could be saved. Right faith and action—adherence to God's teachings and the following of Christ—were prerequisites for the possibility of eternal salvation.

These were beliefs about the way the world is. People could heed them as facts in the hope of their salvation, or ignore them to their certain damnation. Properly understood, they were literally more than a matter of life and death.

At the same time, within this traditional, shared framework of faith, the content of God's truth was sharply disputed. Protestants, Anabaptists, and Catholics agreed that scripture was God's revelation to humanity, but they disagreed about its interpretation. Did it require an authoritative tradition to disclose its true meaning, elucidate implicit doctrines, and resolve apparent ambiguities? Or did the Bible interpret itself, God revealing himself through the Holy Spirit to the individual Christian who searched the scriptures? Did Christians play some role in assenting to and cooperating with the gift of God's grace that made salvation possible? Or was justification by faith alone the Bible's core teaching? If the latter, did this mean that adults alone should be baptized, since only they could grasp God's offer of faith and commit themselves to the rigors of following Christ? Or did infant baptism reaffirm, as a soteriological prefiguration, the doctrine of justification by faith alone? Scripture could be and was interpreted in incompatible ways, each bound to a vision of Christianity for which people proved themselves willing to die.

Christians in all three traditions agreed that all occurrences unfolded according to divine providence. Yet what did these occurrences mean? A sharp distinction between appearance and reality was embedded in the notion. Any given event or chain of events could be and was interpreted contradictorily. In the case of executions for religion, was God testing his beloved children through affliction that he might exalt them in heaven, or venting his wrath against those who obstinately resisted his truth? With the spread of Anabaptism or Calvinism, for example, was God restoring the purity of his truth after centuries of superstition? Or was he teaching his one, Roman Catholic church a stern lesson in the necessity of reform and renewal? Such questions could be extended indefinitely. All of them could be, and were, answered in terms as diametrically opposed as the bipolarities integral to the shared worldview. Neither the hermeneutical framework of providence nor the textual template of scripture yielded uniform interpretations of truth. Yet neither was dispensable.

Christians so vehemently defended the doctrines that divided them *because of their shared convictions* about what was at stake. Christianity was not a tissue of human invention, but the authoritative response to God's revelation. It concerned not a cultural identity, but believing in and rightly following Christ. It sought not a disciplinary regime as such, but the right ordering of human life, individually and collectively, such that eternal salvation remained possible.

Sixteenth-century Christians agreed that the Lord's Supper was one of at least two sacraments. When they disagreed about the manner in which one received Christ in the bread, they were not splitting hairs. They were disputing about the way in which humanity's one savior, who took away the world's sins, "through whom all things were made," was present to them; who had the authority to make him present in this special manner; and how they knew that this was so. The analogous point can be made for virtually every contested issue. *Doctrines were God's teachings.* Yet transubstantiation could not be both true and untrue. It was impossible that infants should be baptized because God could impart faith to them, *and* that adult awareness and commitment were prerequisites for faith and thus for baptism. Nor could scripture alone be sufficient to disclose God's revelation *and* an authoritative tradition be necessary in order to learn it. Indeed, such doctrinal contraries were, are, and always will be irreconcilable, because their incompatibility turns strictly on logic.

The answers to disputed doctrinal questions bore directly on eternal salvation. Disagreements that arose could not be taken lightly. To treat them indifferently showed that one did not grasp what was at stake. Nor did reference to certain disputed points as *adiaphora* (things indifferent) solve anything. It begged the question of where the line between essential and inessential was to be drawn—creating yet another arena for dispute, one that protagonists engaged within traditions as well as between them. Indeed, one could use the varied, shifting attitudes toward *adiaphora* as a theme around which to write the history of Protestantism and radical Protestantism from the sixteenth century to the present, with their countless reconciliations, attempted reconciliations, alliances, and ruptures. "Scripture alone" let the genie out of the bottle; he has never been put back in.

Even without a single execution for heterodoxy, the conviction that God's teachings were at stake, combined with disagreement about their content, would still have divided Western Christendom into distinct communities of faith along doctrinal lines. In fact, however, this conviction was integral to authorities' willingness to execute the heterodox, and to martyrs' willingness to die for their beliefs. Once Christians were put to death, their witness was linked—rightly—to the doctrines they had maintained. Accordingly, the teachings already considered so important acquired another, concretely human, dimension. With every martyr's death, chances for reconciliation diminished. The basic pattern was fixed by 1535, when the first executions of Henrician Catholics followed the deaths of dozens of evangelicals and hundreds of Anabaptists in the preceding decade. The respective celebration of martyrs helped insure that the three main traditions would diverge further in subsequent decades.

Historians of the Reformation and Counter-Reformation who slight doctrine and spirituality—who leave that to the historians of theology, while they do the social history of the Reformation—miss the character of early modern Christianity. Both approaches must be integrated: a scholarly division of labor will not do justice to the religious lives of sixteenth-century men and women. Social historians cannot afford to neglect theologians whose lives as preachers and pastors were intertwined with those of ordinary Christians. Sixteenth-century religious leaders were not marginalized intellectuals writing for a narrow, scholarly audience, preaching to the converted, with little if any impact on their society's wider culture or politics. True, such leaders were more often than not frustrated by the stubborn recalcitrance and sinful habits of the men and women whom they taught and exhorted, threatened and punished. Yet politically they often had the ear of princes and magistrates; as active pastors and moralists, their deep influence on the broader society and culture resounded for centuries; and, by the disagreements they engendered, they helped to shape fundamentally the subsequent course of Western, and indeed world, history. This is no small legacy for men whom some scholars seem to think were needlessly obsessed with minute points of doctrine. Regardless of how one judges the impact of these figures, the fact of their influence is undeniable. Reformation history that neglects them is inherently impoverished.

The religious ferocity of the sixteenth century baffles many people of today because the solution seems so obvious: religious toleration. If the various groups had simply agreed to disagree and left one another alone (as the relatively small number of Anabaptists and other radicals desired), a great deal of hatred and violence might have been avoided. That early modern Catholics and Protestants often did the opposite makes them seem to many people either foolish, or contemptible, or both. It also makes the voices of moderation and tolerance in the period, such as the Erasmians and the *politiques,* sound like murmurs of sanity in a din of madness. Yet those who disparaged toleration did so not for its inconceivability, as if unable to imagine communities in which people believed differently and went their separate ways. No, it was *because* the John Calvins and William Allens could envision this scenario that they inveighed so strenuously against it. The prospect of doctrinal pluralism horrified and disgusted them. They *preferred* a world in which truth did battle, come what may, to one swarming with ever-proliferating heresies. Although the former was far from ideal, it was less dangerous than the latter.

In fact, religious toleration would not have been in any respect a solution to the doctrinal disputes of the Reformation era. It bears not at all on the central concern of sixteenth-century Christianity, namely determining the content of God's truth for humanity. Toleration tacitly concedes that no agreement about religious truth can be reached. Thus it is a conceptual error to state or imply that religious toleration was the eventual solution to early modern religious disagreements—in fact, toleration could never address them. Similarly, it is mistaken to imagine that the shapers of early modern Christianity, being who they were, could have seized upon religious toleration or compromise as the solution to their strife. It is mistaken to think that they might have shelved their competing commitments to Christian truth for the sake of peaceful coexistence. All the major parties involved in martyrdom—authorities, martyrs, martyrologists, and controversialists—clearly could never have done so.

For *ecclesiastical and secular authorities* to have forsaken altogether the willingness to kill, they would have had to abandon their profound paternalism in a culture saturated with a sense of hierarchy and responsibility of the higher for the lower. They would have had to renounce several centuries of legal precedent in a culture horrified by the notion of innovation. And they would have had to decriminalize heresy sufficiently to permit obstinate heretics to go free, even as they thought that doing so would have imperiled others' eternal salvation.

For *martyrs* to have been unwilling to die for their beliefs, they would have had to consider ambiguous the many biblical passages that stipulated steadfastness in suffering. Or they would have had to believe that the Bible was not God's word. Or they would have had to think that, contrary to his words in verses such as Matt. 10:32–33, and despite the example of the biblical and early Christian martyrs, Christ would contradict himself and overlook dissimulation based on fear. Or they would have had to reckon that the particular Christian group to which they belonged was merely one among others and that they might as well have belonged to another group. That is, they would have had to think that God's teachings were not really so important after all. That any of these views might have gained wide acceptance in the sixteenth century is extremely implausible.

For *martyrological writers* not to have viewed and celebrated their executed co-believers as martyrs, they would have had to question whether in fact they had died for the truth. Or they would have had to doubt whether God would remain faithful to his promises to reward with eternal life those who persevered in his truth. Or they would have had to question the value of sacrificing one's life for Christ, even though scripture clearly attested that whoever loses his life for Christ's sake will gain it. In other words, they too would have had to doubt whether the Bible was God's word, an overwhelming improbability.

For *controversialists* not to have distinguished between true and false martyrs and excluded the latter on doctrinal bases, they would have had to find some nondoctrinal criterion by which to tell one from the other. Or they would have had to question fundamentally the willingness to kill and to die for God's truth. Or they would have had to consider God's teachings unimportant enough to think that deaths for contrary versions of Christianity were all equally valuable. Or they would have had to wonder whether Christian truth was articulable in a body of teachings—that is, whether God wanted people to know the truth when he revealed himself and showed them the way to salvation, or whether he wished sadistically to keep them guessing. Once again, that any of these views might have gained significant currency is a possibility so remote as to be inconceivable.

To imply that religious toleration was a sort of missed opportunity in the Reformation era implies that early modern Christian leaders should have made peaceful coexistence a priority over God's truth. This is a blatant anachronism: it is to imagine Luther, Calvin, Zwingli, Tyndale, Eck, Fisher, More, Loyola, Sattler, Hubmaier, Huter, Menno, plus dozens of other leaders and the martyrs not as they were, but as one wishes they had been. To suggest that the course and character of early modern Christianity might have been completely different—with the divergences and intensity, but without the disagreements, conflict, and violence—is to imagine early modern Christians who never existed in a world that never was. What chance did Erasmian moderation have when martyrs were dying for disputed doctrines?

Specific authorities might have been more lenient. Fewer people might have been willing to die. Particular martyrologists might have refrained from writing. And individual controversialists might not have addressed the issue of true and false martyrs. But given the character of Christians' shared and divergent religious beliefs, it is inconceivable that in the sixteenth century in general, *no* authorities would have been willing to kill, *no* devout men and women willing to die, *no* fellow believers disposed to memorialize, *no* controversialists willing to defend and attack. This does not imply that the Reformation itself was inevitable, or that any particular individual was fated to become an Anabaptist or a Protestant. Rather, it means that, contextually understood, devout Protestants and Anabaptists, like their Roman Catholic counterparts, were real candidates for martyrdom in circumstances of persecution.

Another analytical issue remains. How did martyrdom come to seem so strange in the modern West? To early modern Europeans, the willingness to suffer and die was part of the spiritual air they breathed; today the idea baffles many people, religious believers as well as unbelievers. Yet as this book has shown, religious behavior that at first sight appears to be impenetrable on closer examination becomes compellingly lucid, revealing a tight fit between commitment and comportment, across the confessional traditions that took shape in the sixteenth century. Still, long-term institutional and intellectual developments, partly set in motion by early modern religious disagreements, have made martyrdom inaccessible to many. Indeed, they have profoundly affected the way that most scholars approach the study of religion in general.

In certain incontestable ways, sixteenth-century Protestants, Anabaptists, and Roman Catholics were completely mistaken in their expectations for the future. The apocalypse did not come. Catholic leaders wrongly thought that the new heretics, like their medieval predecessors, would quickly be eliminated or at least controlled. Instead, heterodoxy thrived and proliferated. Protestant and Anabaptist leaders wrongly thought that the Synagogue of Antichrist would soon collapse as a prelude to Christ's second coming. Instead, the papists reemerged, steeled and strengthened, in the later sixteenth and seventeenth centuries. Christian pluralism emerged de facto, much to the chagrin of all the parties involved. Heresy flourished, Babylon prospered, and God's truth remained the subject of heated disagreement.

From the perspective of Christians within each of the confessions involved, this did not necessarily pose serious conceptual difficulties. The apocalypse did not come—but God, as ever, had his own timetable. Moreover, they all knew that truth was necessarily unitary and could not contradict itself, whereas error comes in countless forms. There were myriad ways to be mistaken, to twist the meaning of scripture, to misread providential dispensation. Pluralism as such does not necessarily entail skepticism or relativism. To someone who judges the issues to be ambiguous, however, or who views the entire phenomenon from the outside and looks for a means to adjudicate among competing religious truth claims, pluralism presents problems. One response might be to search for a different foundation for truth. Another might be to move away from truth altogether, toward skepticism, relativism, or both. Another might be to invent comparative religion as a scholarly discipline. It would be an exaggeration to say that unresolved religious disagreement caused the Enlightenment, the rise of modern science and philosophy, the early modern renaissance of skepticism, and the birth of modern relativism. Yet its important influence on all these major trajectories in modern thought is clear.

Moreover, the clash of religious absolutisms in early modern Christianity was fertile soil for the growth of secular political thought and secular political institutions. Such was the logical extension of the *politique* views articulated in the sixteenth century, as for example during the French Wars of Religion. Because the prospects for peaceful coexistence among Christians were tenuous at best, and none of the parties would capitulate to the others, only nonreligious values could serve as the basis of stable social and political life. *Individuals* would eventually have the right to believe and worship as they saw fit. Or they might choose not to worship at all. Or they might, eventually, campaign against religion as a source of intolerance and oppression throughout human history. All these activities would be protected by the modern state, which permits virtually anything that it has rendered private and that it can control. At the most fundamental level, the choices were a Hobbesian religious war of all against all, or a secular, state-supported religious pluralism that allowed each person a freedom of belief and expression at a level consistent with the same for everyone else.

Consequently, modern Westerners (with the possible, complicated exception of Northern Ireland) do not live in a world in which religious dogmas trump religious toleration. In different ways, with varying degrees of success, modern Western states are long-term experiments in the institutionalization of religious toleration. Laws and authorities were created and remain in force that enable those who believe contradictory things about central questions of human values and meaning to coexist with minimal disharmony, at least by comparison to the sixteenth century. Religious pluralism is protected and, overwhelmingly, the laws that permit religious freedom are treasured as a great good. Catholics and Protestants in the United States today, for example, do not kill each other out of religious commitment, and seldom even act in a hostile manner toward one another on religious grounds. They are often close friends. It is this experience of living amiably among people with whom one disagrees—what we might call "social ecumenism"—that understandably inspires the wish that the dominant forces in the sixteenth century, too, might have been more like those at the millennium's end. If we can be friends despite disagreeing about what is ultimately true, can doctrine really be all that important?

Social ecumenism, however, should not be confused with doctrinal consensus; religious toleration is not agreement about religious truth. It is rather a shared agreement to disagree. Distortion arises when this latter-day attitude toward doctrine is used either to analyze or to judge the meaning and importance of doctrine for sixteenth-century Christians. The more ecumenically minded Christians are, the more likely they are to wring their hands and condemn the intransigence and intolerance of early modern Christians. To kill over transubstantiation? To die for denying it? The more doctrine seems relative, or negotiable, or at least bracketable for the sake of social concord, the more difficult it will be to understand people who, because they believed it to be God's absolute truth, were willing to kill and die for it. Thus martyrdom grows opaque for many modern Christians, who dearly wish the sixteenth century had unfolded very differently.

Yet desiring a different past cannot unmake its realities. This misdirected impulse exposes the real danger involved in contemporary attempts to "construct a usable past." Usable by whom? And for what? A variant of this temptation serves up historical role models for present emulation or inspiration—a sort of latter-day hagiography. The figures chosen merely express the values, whether religious or secular, of the historian making the selections. Values "A" will yield one set of heroes, values "B" another. Yet we understand the dominant convictions that shaped early modern Christianity not one whit better by wishing that they had included more of Erasmus, and less of More.

Even to certain religious sensibilities, then, martyrdom can seem bizarre. For the most part, however, ecumenically minded Christians would rather forget than explore the searing crucible of early modern Christianity. They tend to confine themselves to exhorting Christians today to further tolerance and cooperation—which is not, of course, historical investigation.

It is scholars who deploy reductionist theories who go further—in the wrong direction. When they consider martyrdom at all, they seem uninterested in exploring what it meant to the martyrs and their contemporaries. Instead, modern or postmodern beliefs underpin explanatory theories that assume a post-Enlightenment, materialist, and atheistic metaphysic, one now in its afterlife, characterized mostly by an indifference toward religious claims. Consequently, these scholars' assumptions remain largely implicit and seem to operate almost unconsciously. Careful reflection about martyrdom, however, should help raise awareness. *No* social scientific or cultural theory undergirded by a tacit atheism, the historical imagination of which is restricted to people competing for influence, striving for power, resisting the exercise of power, "constructing" themselves, "reinventing" themselves, manipulating symbols, and the like, can explain martyrdom. The act of martyrdom makes no sense whatsoever unless we take religion seriously, on the terms of people who were willing to die for their convictions. When we do, the intelligibility of martyrdom hits us like a hammer. Given its quantity and clarity, the evidence for the understanding of martyrdom presented in this book is not merely suggestive, or piecemeal, or promising of future research—it is overwhelming. What would it even mean to read the sources "against the grain?" That Christians did not really believe what they died for? That Catholics, Protestants, and Anabaptists were really much closer to each other than they thought? That martyrs were not really esteemed as highly or as widely as the superabundance of sources over more than a century indicates? Perhaps other scholars can find another way of reading the evidence. Before they make the effort, however, they might consider something rarely heard in these days of historians' infatuation with literary and anthropological theory: that insofar as one wants to learn what life in the past meant to the people who lived it, such theories are not the answer. They are the problem.

Not all aspects of religious belief and practice necessarily resist explanation in the same manner as martyrdom. Nevertheless, the martyrs were not eso-teric. They simply believed—seriously and single-mindedly—what their re-spective versions of Christianity taught. The convictions of devout Genevan Calvinists differed neither in content nor in character from those of Calvinists facing martyrdom. What distinguished them was context: security as opposed to persecution. Martyrdom exposes the shortcomings of many methodologi-cal assumptions in the recent practice of the history of religion. Accordingly, scholars should think twice before assuming they see what they think they see in the religious convictions and actions of the past. A given theory might well render some aspect of religion intelligible based on atheistic presuppositions. That it can do so, however, does not necessarily mean that it tells us anything about past, lived experience. It might simply mean that those who agree with the argument hold the same assumptions as those who make it.

A critical attitude and close assessment of evidence are necessary prereq-uisites for doing history; thoroughgoing suspicion and cynicism are inimical to doing it well. Present-day commitments of whatever kind can never substi-tute for evidence in assessing the motives of past people, including—*espe-cially*—those whose words and actions might offend us personally. We should not, for example, ascribe to Protestant reformers in general a self-serving duplicity insofar as they quoted scripture to urge the need for control in self, household, town, and state. Is it plausible that men committed to scripture as God's word used it merely to justify social control and to reinforce patriarchal ideology? Can we imagine them believing that the Bible revealed God's truth for humanity, but not thinking it relevant for every domain of human life on which it could be brought to bear? If so, again we meet sixteenth-century Christians who never existed. It is dubious history to locate past people who did things one finds offensive, suspect them of ulterior motives, apply the theory that explains what they were "really up to," and present one's findings as a building block in the ongoing quest for post-Enlightenment liberation, understood in secular terms. In the end, such an approach reflects a self-indulgent presentism that cannot see past its own political agenda.

Yet, ironically and indirectly, martyrdom itself played a significant role in shaping the world in which such presentist scholarship flourishes. The com-mitments of the differently devout fostered developments that they all would have deplored. By adamantly rejecting religious pluralism, they helped make religious pluralism a prerequisite for the stable ordering of society. By insisting that religious truth was more important than all temporal concerns, they helped render all religious considerations irrelevant to the secular preoccupations of the modern state. Through their willingness to die for contrary doctrines, which they understood as the very expression of God's will, they helped to render problematic the knowability of his will and to call into question the value of religion. Incompatible, deeply held, concretely expressed religious convictions paved a path to a secular society.

The principled atheism that Lucien Febvre argued was unthinkable in "a century that wanted to believe" has emerged and run its course. Nietzsche is not shocking; he is passé. Meanwhile, the aftermath of indifference has helped embed atheistic assumptions so deeply in the status quo that skepticism and unbelief are mistaken for neutrality. Institutionally and intellectually, our world is one that committed early modern Christians scarcely could have imagined. I am certain they would not have wanted to live in it.

Appendix

In this appendix are two versions of Maeyken Wens's letter to her son Adrien written the day before she was burned in Antwerp, on October 6, 1573. On the left is a transcription of her holograph, transcribed by and reprinted from Samuel Cramer, "Het eigenhandig laatst adieu van Maeyken Wens aan haar kind," *DB*, 44 (1904), 119–120. On the right is the same letter from Van Braght 1685, vol. 2, pp. 663–664.

Och mijn lievc sonc, al ben ick u hier ontnomen, scict u van joncs om Godt te vreesen ~~sult~~ so sult ghij u moeder wel wederomme hebben hierboven in het niewe Jerusalem: daer en sal geen sceijden meer sijn sal. Mijn lieve sone, ick hope u nu voor te gaene; ——— mij so na af al so lief ende [?] ulieden [?] ——ele hebt; want daer en sal geen anderen wech bevonden sijn totter salicheyt dan desen. So wel ick ulieden nu den Heere gaen bevelen. De Heere wel ulieder bewaeder sijn: ick betrout den Heere ~~ick~~ dat hijt doen sal, ist dat ghylieden souct. Hebt malcander lief alle de daghen uws levens onder malcaderen. Nemt Hansken altemet in uwen aerme voor mij; ende oft uwen vader u ontnomen waere, so wilt toch voor macanderen suerghe draeg. De Heere bewaere u alle ghelijck, mijn lieve kinders, cust malcander eens voor mij tot eender ghedijnkenisse. Adieu, mijn lie lieve kinders alle ghelijck. Mijn lieve sone,

Ooh! mijn lieven Sone / al ben ik u hier ontnomen / schikt u van jonks op om God te vresen / soo sult gy uw Moeder wederom hebben hier boven in het nieuwe Jerusalem / daer geen scheyden meer zijn sal: mijn lieven Sone / ik hope u nu voor te gaen / volgt my soo na / alsoo lief als gy uwe ziele hebt / want daer en sal geen anderen weg bevonden zijn tot de saligheyd dan desen / soo wil ik u-lieden den Heere nu gaen bevelen / de Heere wil u-lieden bewaerder zijn / ik betrouwe het den Heere dat hy 't doen sal / is 't dat gy-lieden hem soekt / hebt malkanderen lief alle de dagen uwes levens / neemt Hansken al te met in uwen arm voor my / en of uwen Vader u ontnomen ware / soo wilt doch voor malkanderen sorge dragen / de Heere beware u alle gelijk / mijn lieve Kinders / kust malkanderen eens voor my tot een gedachtenis. Adieu mijn lieve kinderen alle gelijk. Mijn lieve Sone / en vreest doch niet voor dit lijden / 't en en vreest toch niet voor dit lieden, ten heeft niet te bedieden bij dat eewich dueren sal. De Heer nemt de vreese al wech; ick en wiste van vrueden niet wat doen, doen ick verwesen was. Daeromme en laet Godt niet te vreesen om sulken tijtelicke doot; ick en can mijnen Godt niet te vole edancken van de ———— Godt an mij bewesen heeft. Noch een adieu, mijn lieve sone Arijaen, sijt toch uwen bedruecte vader vriedelijke alle daghen uws levens, en doet hem toch geen verdriet an; dat bidde ick ulieden alle ghelijck: want wat ick tot den houste segghe, daer meen ick den ————jonste oock me. Hiermede wel ick ulieden den Heere noch eens beve [len] Dit hebbe ick gheschreven, nadat ick verwesen was ende ~~ick~~ doen ick most sterven om het ghetughenisse Iesus Christus, den 5 dach van october int jaar ons heere Iesu Christus 1573.

Bij mij Maeyken Weens, ulieder moeder, die ulieden gebaert heeft in veel smerten ———— ghed————-tenisse. Bewaert dit wel, den adieu, die u vader an u moeder schreef doen sij verwesen was ende den adieu van u moeder.

heeft niet te bedieden by dat eeuwig dueren sal / de Heere neemt de vreese al wech / ik en wist niet van vreugden wat ik doen soude / als ik verwesen was. Daerom en laet God niet te vreesen / om alsulken tijdelyken dood / ik en kan mijnen God niet ten vollen danken van de groote genade die hy aen my bewesen heeft: noch eens Adieu mijn lieve Sone Adriaen, zijt doch uwen bedrukten Vader altijd vriendelijk alle de dagen uwes levens / ende en doet hem doch geen verdriet aen / dat bidde ik u-lieden alle gelijk / want dat ik tot den oudste schrijve / daer meen ik de jongste ook mede. Hier mede wil ick u-lieden den Heere noch eens bevelen / dit hebbe ik geschreven na dat ik verwesen was / en als ik moeste sterven om het getuygenisse Jesu Christi / den vijfden dag van October / in 't jaer onses Heeren Jesu Christi / 1573.

By my Maeyken Wens, u-lieder Moeder, die u-lieden gebaert heeft in veel smerten, tot een gedachtenisse, bewaert dit wel, den Adieu die uw Vader aen uw Moeder schreef als sy verwesen was, en den Adieu van uw Moeder.

[Oh, my dear son, even though I've been taken away from you here, see to it that from your childhood on you fear God, so that you will again have your mother above in the New Jerusalem, where there will be no more separation. My dear son, I now hope to go before you; follow after me thus just as you love your own soul, for there is and shall be found no other way to salvation than this, hence I will commend you all to the Lord; may the Lord be your keeper, I trust that the Lord will do it, if you seek him. Love one another all the days of your life, take little Hans up in your arms for me, and if your father is taken away from you, still keep caring for one another; may the Lord preserve all of you alike, my dear children; give one another a kiss for me as a remembrance. Farewell, my dear children, all of you alike. My dear son, don't be afraid in the face of this suffering, it is as nothing compared to what lasts forever; the Lord removes fear entirely; out of joy, I didn't know what to do when I was sentenced. Therefore don't stop fearing God on account of any sort of temporal death; I can't thank God enough for the great grace that he has shown me. Once more, farewell, my dear son Adriaen, be kind to your oppressed father all the days of your life, and don't cause him any grief; I ask this of all of you, for although I'm writing to the oldest, I mean to include the youngest as well. Herewith I commend you all once more to the Lord. I've written this after I was sentenced and when I had to die as a witness to Jesus Christ, on the fifth day of October, in the year of our Lord Jesus Christ, 1573.

By me, Maeyken Wens, your mother, who gave birth to you with much pain, as a remembrance; preserve this well, both the farewell that your father wrote to your mother when she had been sentenced, and the farewell from your mother.]

Notes

Abbreviations

AA	*Antwerpsch Archievenblad*
AAW	Archive of the Archbishops of Westminster
AB	*Analecta Bollandiana*
ADB	*Allgemeine Deutsche Biographie*
A & R	*The Contemporary Printed Literature of the English Counter-Reformation between 1558 and 1640.* Ed. A. F. Allison and D. M. Rogers. Vol. 2, Works in English. Aldershot: Scolar Press, 1994.
A & R Foreign	*The Contemporary Printed Literature of the English Counter-Reformation between 1558 and 1640.* Ed. A. F. Allison and D. M. Rogers. Vol. 1, Works in languages other than English. Aldershot: Scolar Press, 1989.
ARB	Algemeen Rijksarchief, Brussels
ARG	*Archiv für Reformationsgeschichte*
Ausbund 1583	*Aussbund: Etlicher schöner Christlicher Geseng* . . . N.p., 1583.
BL	British Library
BMPN	*Bibliographie des martyrologes protestants neerlandais.* 2 vols. Ed. Ferdinand Vander Haeghen, Th.-J.-I. Arnold, and R. Vanden Berghe. The Hague: Martinus Nijhoff, 1890.
BRN	*Bibliotheca Reformatoria Neerlandica. Geschriften uit den tijd der hervorming in de Nederlanden.* 10 vols. Ed. S. Cramer and F. Pijper. The Hague: Martinus Nijhoff, 1903—1914.
BSHPF	*Bulletin de la Société de l'Histoire du Protestantisme Français*
CDN	*Corpus documentorum inquisitionis haereticae pravitatis neerlandicae.* 5 vols. Ed. Paul Fredericq. Ghent: J. Vuylsteke; and The Hague: Martinus Nijhoff, 1889–1902.
CO	John Calvin. *Joannis Calvini opera quae supersunt omnia.* 59 vols. Ed. G. Baum et al. Brunswick: C. A. Schwetschke and Son, 1863–1900.
CR	*Corpus Reformatorum*
Crespin 1554	Jean Crespin. *Recveil de plvsievrs personnes qui ont constamment enduré la mort pour le Nom de nostre Seigneur Iesus Christ* . . . [Geneva: Jean Crespin], 1554.

Crespin 1555	Jean Crespin. *Recveil de plvsievrs personnes* . . . [Geneva: Jean Crespin], 1555.
Crespin 1564	Jean Crespin. *Actes des Martyrs dedvits en sept livres, depuis le temps de Wiclef et de Hus, iusques à present* . . . [Geneva]: Jean Crespin, 1564.
Crespin 1570	Jean Crespin. *Histoire des vrays Tesmoins de la verite de l'Evangile* . . . [Geneva]: Jean Crespin, 1570.
Crespin and Goulart 1582	Jean Crespin [and Simon Goulart]. *Histoire des Martyrs persecvtez et mis a mort pour la verité de l'Euangile* . . . [Geneva: Eustace Vignon], 1582.
CRS	Catholic Record Society
CTM	*The Correspondence of Sir Thomas More.* Ed. Elizabeth Frances Rogers. Princeton: Princeton University Press, 1947.
CWTM	*The Complete Works of St. Thomas More.* New Haven: Yale University Press. 1963–.
DAN	*Documenta Anabaptistica Neerlandica*
DB	*Doopsgezinde Bijdragen*
DNB	*Dictionary of National Biography.* Ed. George Smith et al. Oxford: Oxford University Press, 1973.
Foxe 1554	John Foxe. *Commentarii rervm in ecclesia gestarum* . . . Strasbourg: Wendelin Rihel, 1554.
Foxe 1563	John Foxe. *Actes and Monuments of these latter and perilous dayes, touching matters of the Church* . . . London: John Daye, 1563.
Foxe 1570	John Foxe, *The First [Second] Volume of the Ecclesiastical history contaynyng the Actes and Monumentes* . . . 2 vols. London: John Daye, 1570.
Foxe 1576	John Foxe. *The First Volume of the Ecclesiastical History* . . . London: John Daye, 1576.
Foxe 1583	John Foxe. *Actes and Monuments* . . . 2 vols. London: John Daye, 1583.
Foxe 1610	John Foxe. *Actes and Monuments* . . . 3 vols. London: for Stationers' Company, 1610.
Herminjard	*Correspondance des Réformateurs dans les pays de langue française.* 9 vols. Ed. A.-L. Herminjard. Geneva: H. Georg et al., 1866–1897.
Isambert	*Recueil Général des anciennes lois françaises depuis l'an 420, jusqu'a la Révolution de 1789.* Ed. François André Isambert et al. Paris, 1821–1833.
JEH	*Journal of Ecclesiastical History*
LP	*Letters and Papers, Foreign and Domestic, of the Reign of Henry VIII.* 22 vols. Ed. James Gairdner et al. London: Longman, Green, Longman, and Roberts, 1862–1932.
ME	*The Mennonite Encyclopedia.* 5 vols. Scottdale, Pa.: Mennonite Publishing House; and Herald Press, 1955–1959, 1990.
MQR	*Mennonite Quarterly Review*
MSOO	Menno Simons. *Opera omnia theologica, of Alle de godtgeleerde wercken van Menno Symons* . . . Amsterdam: Joannes van Veen, 1681.

OH	*Dit Boec wort genoemt: Het Offer des Heeren, om het inhout van sommighe opgheofferde kinderen Godts . . .* [Franeker: Press of Jan Hendricks van Schoonrewoerd], 1570.
OHL	*Een Lietboecxken, tracterende van den Offer des Heeren . . .* [Franeker: Press of Jan Hendricks van Schoonrewoerd], 1570.
OL	*Original Letters Relative to the English Reformation . . .* 2 vols. Ed. and trans. Hastings Robinson. Cambridge: Cambridge University Press, 1846–1847.
PL	*Patrologia Latina*
P&P	*Past and Present*
QGT	*Quellen zur Geschichte der (Wieder)Täufer*
QGTS	*Quellen zur Geschichte der Täufer in der Schweiz*
RAB	Rijksarchief, Bruges
Rabus 1–8	Ludwig Rabus, *Historien Der Heyligen Außerwölten Gottes Zeügen, Bekennern vnd Martyrern . . .* Pts. 1–8. Strasbourg: Samuel Emmel, 1552–1558.
RAG	Rijksarchief, Ghent
REPSJ	*Records of the English Province of the Society of Jesus.* 7 vols. Ed. Henry Foley. 1877–1880; reprint, New York: Johnson, 1966.
ROPB	*Recueil des ordonnances des Pays-Bas.* 2nd ser., 1506–1700. Vols. 1–6. Ed. Ch. Laurent and J. Lameere. Brussels: J. Goemaere, 1893–1922.
SAA	Stadsarchief, Antwerp
SAB	Stadsarchief, Bruges
SAG	Stadsarchief, Ghent
SCJ	*Sixteenth Century Journal*
STC 1475–1640	*A Short-Title Catalogue of Books Printed in England, Ireland, Scotland and Wales, 1475–1640.* 2nd ed. 3 vols. Ed. A. W. Pollard, G. R. Redgrave, et al. London: Bibliographical Society, 1976–1991.
STC 1641–1700	*A Short-Title Catalogue of Books Printed in England, Scotland, Ireland, Wales and British America and of English Books Printed in Other Countries, 1641–1700.* 2nd ed. 3 vols. Ed. Donald Wing et al. New York: Modern Language Association of America, 1972–1994.
Van Braght 1660	Thieleman Jans van Braght. *Het Bloedigh Tooneel der Doops-gesinde, en Weereloose Christenen . . .* Dordrecht: Jacob Braat, 1660.
Van Braght 1685	Thieleman Jans van Braght. *Het Bloedig Tooneel, of Martelaers Spiegel der Doops-Gesinde of Weereloose Christenen . . .* 2 vols. Amsterdam: J. vander Deyster et al., 1685.
Van Haemstede 1559	Adriaen Cornelis van Haemstede. *De Gheschiedenisse ende den doodt der vromer Martelaren . . .* [Emden: Gilles van der Erve], 1559.
WA	Martin Luther. *D. Martin Luthers Werke. Kritische Gesamtausgabe.* Weimar: Hermann Böhlau, 1883–.
Wackernagel	Philipp Wackernagel. *Das deutsche Kirchenlied von der ältesten Zeit bis zu Anfang des XVII. Jahrhunderts.* Leipzig: B. G. Teubner, 1864–1877.

1. A Complex of Martyrs

1. It is often appropriate to refer to the Protestant martyrological tradition as including the early evangelicals of the 1520s, Lutherans, and Reformed Protestants (including the regimes in England under Edward VI and Elizabeth I). My own research has confirmed Jean-François Gilmont's tripartite division of Christian martyrological traditions (Protestant, Anabaptist, and Roman Catholic) in the early modern period. Gilmont, "Un instrument de propagande religieuse: les martyrologes du XVIe siècle," in *Sources de l'histoire religieuse de la Belgique: Moyen âge et Temps moderne* (Louvain: Publications universitaires de Louvain, 1968), p. 379. Yet I agree with Robert Kolb that the Lutheran tradition's course and character in certain respects distinguish it as a separate phenomenon, particularly from the 1550s, when Ludwig Rabus compiled the period's first (and only) Lutheran martyrology. Kolb, *For All the Saints: Changing Perceptions of Martyrdom and Sainthood in the Lutheran Reformation* (Macon, Ga.: Mercer University Press, 1987).

2. Frederik Pijper, *Martelaarsboeken* (The Hague: Martinus Nijhoff, 1924), pp. 3–4; Léon-H. Halkin, "Hagiographie protestante," *AB*, 68 (1950), 458; Halkin, "Les martyrologes et la critique: Contribution à l'étude du Martyrologe protestant des Pays-Bas," in *Mélanges historiques offerts à Monsieur Jean Meyhoffer* (Lausanne: L'Imprimerie La Concorde, 1952), p. 57; Gilmont, "Instrument," pp. 379–380; Jean-Marie Valentin, *Le théâtre des Jésuites dans les pays de langue allemande (1554–1680)*, vol. 1 (Berne: Peter Lang, 1978), pp. 375–376; Kolb, *For All the Saints*, p. 6; Victor Houliston, "St. Thomas Becket in the Propaganda of the English Counter-Reformation," *Renaissance Studies*, 7 (1993), 63–64; John R. Knott, *Discourses of Martyrdom in English Literature, 1563–1694* (Cambridge: Cambridge University Press, 1993), p. 10; Thomas M. McCoog, "'The Flower of Oxford': The Role of Edmund Campion in Early Recusant Polemics," *SCJ*, 24 (1993), 913.

3. See Helen White, *Tudor Books of Saints and Martyrs* (Madison: University of Wisconsin Press, 1963), who discusses Voragine's *Golden Legend* in Caxton's English translation, Foxe, and sixteenth-century Catholic sources, but limits her study to England; see also A. G. Dickens and John Tonkin, "Weapons of Propaganda: The Martyrologies," in *The Reformation in Historical Thought* (Cambridge, Mass.: Harvard University Press, 1985), pp. 39–57, who briefly treat both Protestant and Catholic martyrs (though they scarcely mention Anabaptists), but emphasize John Foxe and consider only English Catholics.

4. Gilmont, "Instrument," p. 380.

5. Kreider, "'The Servant Is Not Greater Than His Master': The Anabaptists and the Suffering Church," *MQR*, 58 (1984), 9 n. 27.

6. Gilmont, "Les martyrologes du XVIe siècle," in *Ketzerverfolgung im 16. und frühen 17. Jahrhundert*, ed. S. Seidel Menchi (Wolfenbüttel: Harrassowitz, 1992), pp. 189–191; idem, "Books of Martyrs," in *The Oxford Encyclopedia of the Reformation*, ed. Hans J. Hillerbrand, vol. 1 (Oxford: Oxford University Press, 1996), pp. 195–200.

7. Henri Meylan, "'Martyrs du Diable'," *Revue de théologie et de philosophie*, 9

(1959), 114–130. See also David Loades's remarks in the introduction to *Martyrs and Martyrologies*, ed. Diana Wood, vol. 30 of *Studies in Church History* (Oxford: Blackwell, 1993), pp. xv–xvi.

8. For groups such as the Old Order Amish in North America, the legacy of the Anabaptist martyrs remains vibrant. For the Mennonite tradition more generally, see Alan Kreider, "The Relevance of *Martyrs' Mirror* to Our Time," *Mennonite Life*, 45:3 (1990), 9–17. The dust jacket of the most recent reprint of van Braght's *Martyrs' Mirror* reads: "Martyrs Mirror has timeless value in the teaching of the position of Christians in human conflict today . . . The testimonies of these thousands of martyrs disclose a heart in likeness of our Savior. Martyrs Mirror is for today!" Thieleman Jans van Braght, *The Bloody Theater or Martyrs Mirror of the Defenseless Christians . . .* , trans. Joseph F. Sohm (1886; reprint, Scottdale, Pa.: Herald Press, 1990). In the Catholic and Protestant traditions, sixteenth-century martyrs remain significant in certain national and local contexts rather than as part of a broad sensibility, as with the English Catholic martyrs. Thus the neo-Gothic Church of Our Lady and the English Martyrs, Cambridge, with sculptures and stained glass befitting its name, enthusiastically celebrated its centennial in 1990. In London the medieval chapel of St. Etheldreda's was redecorated in the 1960s with images of the English Catholic martyrs, and Westminster Cathedral displays the encased body of St. John Southworth, the last English priest executed as a Catholic traitor (June 28, 1654). In 1979 a *Gedenkwoche* celebrated the 450th anniversary of the martyrdom of the evangelicals Adolf Clarenbach and Peter Fliesteden in Cologne, the city where they were burned (September 28, 1529) and in which several twentieth-century monuments honoring them have been erected. See *Bekenner und Zeugen: Zum Gedenken an den 450. Todestag der Märtyrer Adolf Clarenbach und Peter Fliesteden*, ed. J. F. Gerhard Goeters, Albert Stein, and Friedrich Gerhard Venderbosch (Düsseldorf: Landeskirchamt der Evangelische Kirche im Rheinland, 1979).

9. To mention only a few recent scholarly contributions, beginning with research on Anabaptist martyrs: Victor G. Doerksen, "The Anabaptist Martyr Ballad," *MQR*, 51 (1977), 5–21; T. Alberda-van der Zijpp, "'Het Offer des Heeren': Geloof en getuigenis van de martelaren," in *Wederdopers, menisten, doopsgezinden in Nederland 1530–1980*, ed. S. Groenveld, J. P. Jacobszoon, and S. L. Verheus (Zutphen: Walburg Press, 1980), pp. 46–61; Kreider, "'Servant Is Not Greater'"; Cornelius J. Dyck, "The Suffering Church in Anabaptism," *MQR*, 59 (1985), 5–23; John Klassen, "Women and the Family among Dutch Anabaptist Martyrs," *MQR*, 60 (1986), 548–571; Werner O. Packull, "Anna Jansz of Rotterdam, a Historical Investigation of an Early Anabaptist Heroine," *ARG*, 78 (1987), 147–173; Jenifer Hiett Umble, "Women and Choice: An Examination of the *Martyrs' Mirror*," *MQR*, 64 (1990), 135–145; Piet Visser, "Het doperse mirakel van het onverbrande bloempje: Terug naar de bron van een onbekend lied over martelaar Leonhard Keyser (overl. 1527)," *DB*, n.s., 17 (1991), 9–30; Brad S. Gregory, "Particuliere martelaarsbundels uit de late zestiende eeuw," *DB*, n.s., 19 (1993), 81–106; idem, "Weisen die Todesvorbereitungen von Täufermärtyrern geschlechtsspezifische Merkmale auf?" *Mennonitische Geschichtsblätter*, 54 (1997), 52–60.

The Protestant martyrs and particularly martyrologists have been studied more extensively than their counterparts in the other two traditions. Noteworthy recent contributions dealing primarily with John Foxe and/or the English martyrs include David Loades, *The Oxford Martyrs* (1970; reprint, Bangor: Headstart History, 1992); V. Norskov Olsen, *John Foxe and the Elizabethan Church* (Berkeley: University of California Press, 1977); Patrick Collinson, "Truth and Legend: The Veracity of John Foxe's Book of Martyrs," in *Clio's Mirror: Historiography in Britain and the Netherlands,* ed. A. C. Duke and C. A. Tamse, vol. 8 of *Britain and the Netherlands* (Zutphen: Walburg Press, 1985), pp. 31–54; Jane Facey, "John Foxe and the Defence of the English Church," in *Protestantism and the National Church in Sixteenth Century England,* ed. Peter Lake and Maria Dowling (New York: Croom Helm, 1987), pp. 162–192; Knott, *Discourses of Martyrdom in English Literature;* and the collection of articles in *John Foxe and the English Reformation,* ed. David Loades (Aldershot: Scolar Press, 1997). To these should be added two significant older studies, J. F. Mozley, *John Foxe and His Book* (1940; reprint, New York: Octagon Books, 1970), and William Haller, *Foxe's Book of Martyrs and the Elect Nation* (London: J. Cape, 1963). On Jean Crespin, see Gilmont's biographical study of him as a printer in *Jean Crespin: Un éditeur réformé du XVIe siècle* (Geneva: Droz, 1981); and David Watson, "Jean Crespin and the Writing of History in the French Reformation," in *Protestant History and Identity in Sixteenth-Century Europe,* ed. Bruce Gordon, vol. 2 (Aldershot: Scolar Press, 1996), pp. 39–58. Other studies of Protestant martyrdom and martyrology in France include David Nicholls, "The Theatre of Martyrdom in the French Reformation," *P&P,* 121 (1988), 49–73; Catharine Randall Coats, *(Em)bodying the Word: Textual Resurrections in the Martyrological Narratives of Foxe, Crespin, de Bèze, and d'Aubigné* (New York: Peter Lang, 1992); Charles H. Parker, "French Calvinists as the Children of Israel: An Old Testament Self-Consciousness in Jean Crespin's *Histoire des Martyrs* before the Wars of Religion," *SCJ,* 24 (1993), 227–247; and David El Kenz, *Les buchers du roi: La culture protestante des martyrs 1523–1572* (Seyssel: Champs Vallon, 1997). The standard work on Adriaen Cornelis van Haemstede, who is much less well known in the world of English-speaking scholars than either Foxe or Crespin, is A. J. Jelsma, *Adriaan van Haemstede en zijn martelaarsboek* (The Hague: Boekencentrum N.V., 1970); see also Andrew Pettegree, "Adriaan van Haemstede: The Heretic as Historian," in *Protestant History and Identity,* ed. Gordon, vol. 2, pp. 59–76. The most important work to date on Ludwig Rabus and Lutheran martyrs is Kolb, *For All the Saints.*

There exists relatively less recent scholarship on early modern Catholic martyrs, especially any that takes a broad compass; the best overview remains the chapter on martyrdom in Émile Mâle, *L'art religieux de la fin du XVIe siècle, du XVIIe siècle et du XVIIIe siècle: Etude sur l'iconographie après le concile de Trente,* 2nd ed. (Paris: Armand Colin, 1951), pp. 109–149. For a brief sketch, see R. Po-chia Hsia, *The World of Catholic Renewal 1540–1770* (Cambridge: Cambridge University Press, 1998), pp. 80–91. An extensive, older body of scholarship on the Dutch Catholic martyrs seems virtually unknown in the world of English language research (see Chapter 7). On the English Catholic

martyrs, aside from the abundant work on Thomas More, recent contributions
include Geoffrey F. Nuttall, "The English Martyrs 1535–1680: A Statistical
Review," *JEH*, 22 (1971), 191–197; Houliston, "Becket in the English
Counter-Reformation"; and McCoog, "Campion in Early Recusant Polemics."
The subject of martyrs in Counter-Reformation art has been a fruitful domain
for research. In addition to Mâle, see David Freedberg, "The Representation of
Martyrdoms during the Early Counter-Reformation in Antwerp," *Burlington
Magazine*, 118 (1976), 128–138; Thomas Buser, "Jerome Nadal and Early
Jesuit Art in Rome," *Art Bulletin*, 58 (1976), 424–433; Leif Holm Monssen,
"*Rex gloriose martyrum:* A Contribution to Jesuit Iconography," *Art Bulletin*,
63 (1981), 130–137; idem, "Triumphus and Trophaea Sacra: Notes on the
Iconography and Spirituality of the Triumphant Martyr," *Konsthistorisk
Tidskrift*, 51 (1982), 10–20; and Alexandra Herz, "Imitators of Christ: The
Martyr-Cycles of Late Sixteenth-Century Rome Seen in Context," *Storia
dell'arte*, 62 (1988), 53–70.

10. For example, Phyllis Mack Crew, with only a passing reference to van Braght
and no mention of the flood of published Dutch Anabaptist martyrs' songs and
letters in the last third of the sixteenth century, claims that Calvinists "exploited
the heroic suffering of their adherents most successfully." Mack Crew, *Calvinist
Preaching and Iconoclasm in the Netherlands, 1544–1569* (Cambridge: Cambridge University Press, 1978), p. 73, 73 n. 74. Alexandra Herz, in her fine
article on Catholic martyrological iconography in late sixteenth-century Rome,
unfairly condemns the Protestant martyrologists as having "no idea of the theory underlying the ancient martyrs' deeds" and falsely claims that Foxe's collection was "the only [Protestant] martyrology illustrated in the sixteenth century"—Rabus's martyrology was also illustrated, as eventually was van
Haemstede's. Herz, "Imitators of Christ," p. 57. As a final example, in her
recent study of Reformed Protestant martyrology, Catharine Randall Coats
relies exclusively on secondary sources in treating Catholic hagiography, and
consequently exaggerates both its homogeneity and the originality of Protestant
martyrology; the continuing, indeed renewed, significance of Catholic martyrological writing in the late sixteenth and seventeenth centuries is entirely ignored. Coats, *(Em)bodying the Word.*

11. *Der actus vnd handlung der degradation vnd verprenung der Christlichen Ritter
vnd merterer Augistiner ordens geschehen zu Brussel . . .* , in *BRN*, vol. 8, ed.
F. Pijper (The Hague: Martinus Nijhoff, 1911), pp. 13–19; *Eyn warhafftig
geschicht wie Caspar Tawber, Burger zü Wien in Osterreich für ein Ketzer, unnd
zü dem todt verurtaylt und auß gefürt worden ist; Histori oder dz warhafftig
geschicht, des leydens vnd sterbens Lienhart Keysers seligen . . .; Warhaffte hystorien: Von dem frummen zeügen vnd marterer Christi Johansen Heüglin von
Lindaw . . . .* For the number of editions, as well as meticulous identification of
the various printers, places, and dates of publications (where known), see the
appendix in Hildegard Hebenstreit-Wilfert, "Märtyrerflugschriften der Reformationszeit," in *Flugschriften als Massenmedium der Reformationszeit*, ed.
Hans-Joachim Köhler (Stuttgart: Klett-Cotta, 1981), pp. 432–436, 439–442,
444–446; and *WA* 23, pp. 443–445.

12. Lucien Febvre and Jean-Henri Martin suggest an average of 1,000–1,500 for

early sixteenth-century books, "with occasional figures below that." Febvre and
Martin, *The Coming of the Book: The Impact of Printing, 1450–1800,* trans.
David Gerard (London: Verso, 1990), p. 218. Gilmont has recently given
1,000–1,350 as an average for sixteenth-century books. Gilmont, "L'imprimerie à l'aube du XVIe siècle," in *La Réforme et le livre: L'Europe de l'imprimé (1517–v.1570),* ed. idem (Paris: Editions du Cerf, 1990), p. 28. Michael
Schilling has estimated 1,500 as an average for illustrated German *Flugblätter.*
Schilling, *Bildpublizistik der frühen Neuzeit: Aufgaben und Leistungen des illus-
trierten Flugblatts in Deutschland bis um 1700* (Tübingen: Max Niemeyer Verlag, 1990), p. 25.

13. *STC 1475–1640,* vol. 1, p. 496; *STC 1641–1700,* vol. 2, p. 95. The English
editions were published in 1563, 1570, 1576, 1583, 1596, 1610, 1632, 1641,
and 1684, with an abridged edition (of some 800 pages) in 1589.

14. *Bibliotheca Belgica,* vol. 1, ed. Ferdinand Vander Haeghen and Marie-Thérèse
Lenger (Brussels: Culture et civilisation, 1964), pp. 966–982; Gilmont, *Jean
Crespin,* pp. 166–182; idem, "Une édition inconnue du martyrologe de Jean
Crespin," *Bibliothèque d'Humanisme et Renaissance,* 30 (1968), 363–371.

15. *Bibliotheca Belgica,* vol. 3, ed. Vander Haeghen and Lenger (Brussels: Culture
et civilisation, 1964), pp. 374–394; *BMPN,* vol. 2, pp. 271–364.

16. The figures for publications about the English martyrs in this paragraph are
derived from A & R and A & R Foreign.

17. *The National Union Catalogue: Pre-1956 Imprints,* vol. 99 (London: Mansell,
1970), pp. 451–452, 454–455; *British Museum: General Catalogue of Printed
Books,* vol. 139 (London: K. G. Saur, 1982), pp. 352–354.

18. For discussion of five do-it-yourself collections in relation to *Het Offer des
Heeren,* see my "Particuliere martelaarsbundels."

19. See the bibliography in F. Wieder, *De schriftuurlijke liedekens: De liederen der
nederlandsche hervormden tot op het jaar 1566* (The Hague: Martinus Nijhoff,
1900), pp. 125–178; and Bert Hofman, *Liedekens vol gheestich confoort: Een
bijdrage tot de kennis van de zestiende-eeuwse Schriftuurlijke lyriek* (Hilversum:
Verloren, 1993). Piet Visser is currently completing a comprehensive bibliography of all known editions, their songs, and the songs' *contrafacta,* which will
supersede Wieder.

20. For the songs, see *Die Lieder der Hutterischen Brüder* (Scottdale, Pa.: Mennonitische Verlagshaus, 1914); for the oldest Hutterite chronicles, in which martyrs
are prominent, see A. J. F. Zieglschmid, ed., *Die älteste Chronik der Hutterischen Brüder* (Ithaca, N.Y.: Cayuga Press, 1943).

21. Wieder, *Schriftuurlijke liedekens,* pp. 88–117; Rudolf Wolkan, *Die Lieder der
Wiedertäufer: Ein Beitrag zur deutschen und niederländischen Litteratur- und
Kirchengeschichte* (Berlin: B. Behr, 1903); A. J. Ramaker, "Hymns and Hymn
Writers among the Anabaptists of the Sixteenth Century," *MQR,* 3 (1929),
93–131; Rosella Reimer Duerksen, "Anabaptist Hymnody of the Sixteenth
Century: A Study of Its Marked Individuality Coupled with a Dependence
upon Contemporary Secular and Sacred Musical Style and Form" (Doctor of
Sacred Music diss., Union Theological Seminary, 1956), pp. 195–201, 220–
229; Harold S. Bender, "The Hymnology of the Anabaptists," *MQR,* 31

(1957), 5–10; N. van der Zijpp, "The Hymnology of the Anabaptists in the Netherlands," *MQR*, 31 (1957), 11–15; Doerksen, "Anabaptist Martyr Ballad"; Ursula Lieseberg, *Studien zum Märtyrerlied der Täufer im 16. Jahrhundert* (Frankfurt am Main: Peter Lang, 1991).

22. Thomas Freeman's important, continuing work on Foxe is a good example. See his articles "Research, Rumour and Propaganda: Anne Boleyn in Foxe's 'Book of Martyrs,'" *Historical Journal*, 38 (1995), 797–819, and "The Importance of Dying Earnestly: The Metamorphosis of the Account of James Bainham in 'Foxe's Book of Martyrs,'" in *The Church Retrospective*, ed. R. N. Swanson, vol. 33 of *Studies in Church History* (Woodbridge, Suffolk: Boydell Press, 1997), pp. 267–288.

23. See Robert Chazan, *European Jewry and the First Crusade* (Berkeley: University of California Press, 1987), and Miri Rubin, "Choosing Death? Experiences of Martyrdom in Late Medieval Europe," in *Martyrs and Martyrologies*, ed. Wood, pp. 178–180.

24. Donald R. Kelley, "Martyrs, Myths, and the Massacre: The Background of St. Bartholomew," *American Historical Review*, 77 (1972), 1323–42; Robert M. Kingdon, *Myths about the St. Bartholomew's Day Massacres, 1572–1576* (Cambridge, Mass.: Harvard University Press, 1988).

25. Van Haemstede 1559 [p. 455]; Crespin 1570, fol. 308v.

26. A. L. E. Verheyden, "De Martyrologia in de optiek van de hedendaagse Martelaarslijsten," in *Sources de l'histoire religieuse de la Belgique*, p. 358.

27. William Monter, "Heresy Executions in Reformation Europe," in *Tolerance and Intolerance in the European Reformation*, ed. Ole Peter Grell and Bob Scribner (Cambridge: Cambridge University Press, 1996), pp. 48–65.

28. Nuttall, "English Martyrs," pp. 191–197.

29. É. de Moreau, *Histoire de l'Église de Belgique*, vol. 5 (Brussels: L'Edition universelle, 1952), pp. 172–206. To these should be added the six priests judicially executed by Calvinist regimes in Bruges and Ghent (three each) in 1578. Ibid., pp. 199–200.

30. Based on an estimate of 3.8 million deaths in 1941–1942, an average of 5,205 per day. See Raul Hilberg, *The Destruction of the European Jews*, student ed. (New York and London: Holmes and Meier, 1985), p. 339. The actual distribution of industrialized killing in these years, of course, was not spread evenly across 730 days.

31. Mack P. Holt, *The French Wars of Religion, 1562–1629* (Cambridge: Cambridge University Press, 1995), p. 2, here citing John Bossy, *Christianity in the West, 1400–1700* (Oxford: Oxford University Press, 1985), "passim, but especially pp. 170–1." Ibid., n. 1.

32. Social analyses of sixteenth-century religious allegiance have their limitations. Records sometimes permit us to determine the social and occupational distribution of Protestants, for example, in a given city during a certain period of time, but nothing whatsoever about why they became Protestant. Speaking of Parisian Calvinists, Barbara Diefendorf rightly notes that "it is easier to show that Protestantism exerted its greatest appeal among certain social groups than to explain just what it was in the Protestant message that appealed to these peo-

ple." Diefendorf, *Beneath the Cross: Catholics and Huguenots in Sixteenth-Century Paris* (New York: Oxford University Press, 1991), p. 112. To show that most French Calvinists came from the ranks of middling officials, entrepreneurs, and better-off artisans explains nothing about the appeal of Protestantism, because numerous people from these ranks remained Catholic. Examples of such social analyses of French Protestants in various cities include Joan Davies, "Persecution and Protestantism: Toulouse, 1562–1575," *Historical Journal,* 22 (1979), 31–51; Philip Benedict, *Rouen during the Wars of Religion* (Cambridge: Cambridge University Press, 1980), pp. 71–81; Natalie Zemon Davis, "The Sacred and the Body Social in Sixteenth-Century Lyon," *P&P,* 90 (1981), 47–48; Diefendorf, *Beneath the Cross,* pp. 108–110. Similarly, pointing to the humble background of most Anabaptists makes clear that almost all of the socially privileged avoided Anabaptism, but not why most humble lay Catholics and Protestants also avoided it, nor why those who became Anabaptists embraced it.

33. These remarks are meant to apply especially to early modern Christianity, but much in them pertains, mutatis mutandis, to other periods and religious traditions.

34. Patrick Collinson, *The Religion of Protestants: The Church in English Society, 1559–1625* (Oxford: Clarendon Press, 1982), p. x.

35. Stephen Greenblatt's commentary on the session, "Religion, Literature, and Psychology in Early Modern England," American Historical Association Convention, San Francisco, January 8, 1994. I thank Prof. Greenblatt for sending me a printed copy of his comments on this session, here quoted from p. 3 of his text.

36. Aviad M. Kleinberg, "Proving Sanctity: Selection and Authentication of Saints in the Later Middle Ages," in *Viator: Medieval and Renaissance Studies,* vol. 20 (Berkeley: University of California Press, 1989), p. 185.

37. "But if we are truly to appreciate the context of belief, death, and witness in the later Middle Ages . . . we *must* relativize the notion of faith, because issues of truth and faith were contested in these centuries as never before." Rubin, "Choosing Death?" p. 172 (italics in original).

38. For the quoted phrase, see Paul Ricoeur, *Freud and Philosophy: An Essay on Interpretation,* trans. Denis Savage (New Haven: Yale University Press, 1970), pp. 28–36.

39. I have made this point with reference to the most popular devotional treatise in late sixteenth-century England. See my article "The 'True and Zealouse Seruice of God': Robert Parsons, Edmund Bunny, and *The First Booke of the Christian Exercise,*" *JEH,* 45 (1994), 260.

40. For these two basic depictions applied to early seventeenth-century English Puritans, see respectively William Hunt, *The Puritan Moment: The Coming of Revolution in an English County* (Cambridge, Mass.: Harvard University Press, 1983), p. 81, and Eamon Duffy, "The Godly and the Multitude in Stuart England," *The Seventeenth Century,* 1 (1986), 31–33.

41. James D. Tracy, "With and Without the Counter-Reformation: The Catholic

Church in the Spanish Netherlands and the Dutch Republic, 1580–1650," *Catholic Historical Review,* 71 (1985), 571.

42. Examples include Crespin 1555, sig. *2; van Haemstede 1559, p. [3]; *OH*, in *BRN*, vol. 2, p. 54; and [Richard Verstegan], *Theatre des Cruautez des Heretiques de nostre temps* (Antwerp: Adrien Hubert, 1588), p. 15.

43. *QGT*, vol. 5, *Bayern*, pt. 2, ed. Karl Schornbaum (Gütersloh: Bertelsmann, 1951), p. 137/18–26.

44. Luther, *WA Tischreden* 2, no. 1444, p. 102/9–10.

45. Johannes Fabri von Heilbronn, *Von dem Ayd Schwören: Auch von der Widertauffer Marter, vnd wo her entspring, das sie also frölich vnnd getröst die peyn des tods leyden . . .* ([Ingolstadt?] 1550), sigs. E3v–E4.

46. [Joris Wybo?], *Historie ende ghesciedenisse van de verradelicke gheuangenisse der vromer ende godsaligher mannen, Christopher Fabritij . . .* [n.p., 1565], repr. in *BRN*, vol. 8, pp. 288–289. For Wybo, a prisoner with Fabri and Oliver Bock in Antwerp, as the likely author of this treatise, see *BRN*, vol. 8, pp. 272–274. Also in 1565, Guy de Brès confirmed Anabaptists' "constance à souffrir et à mourir" which Calvin had implied more than twenty years earlier; see de Brès, *La racine, sovrce et fondement des Anabaptistes ov rebaptisez de nostre temps* ([Rouen]: Abel Clemence, 1565), sigs. a4, [a6] (quotation on [a6]); Calvin, *Brieve instruction pour armer tous les bons fideles contre les erreurs de la secte commune des anabaptistes* (Geneva: Jean Girard, 1544), in *CO* 7, cols. 140–142.

47. Johannes Eck, *Warhafftige handlung, wie es mit her Lienhart Keszer zu Scherding verbrannt, ergangen ist . . .* [Ingolstadt: Peter and Georg Apianus, 1527], sig. [A4]; compare with *Histori des leydens vnd sterbens Lienhart Keysers,* sig. [A4v]. Bernd Moeller also notes this confirmation; see his "Inquisition und Martyrium in Flugschriften der frühen Reformation in Deutschland," in *Ketzerverfolgung,* ed. Seidel Menchi, p. 39.

48. Antoine Du Val, *Mirover des Calvinistes et armvre des Chrestiens, pour rembarrer les Lutheriens et nouueaux Euangelistes de Genéue . . .* (Paris: Nicolas Chesneau, 1562), fols. 31v, 33v; see also fols. 34v, 36. The work was first published in 1559.

49. Reginald Pole, "Speech to the citizens of London, in behalf of religious houses," in John Strype, ed., *Ecclesiastical Memorials,* vol. 3, pt. 2 (Oxford: Clarendon Press, 1822), p. 498. The speech is not dated, but Pole's remarks imply that it was delivered in 1557 or 1558. Ibid.

50. Florimond de Raemond, *L'histoire de la naissance, progrez et decadence de l'heresie de ce siecle* (Rouen: Estienne Vereul, 1622), p. 864. The work was first published in 1605. On Raemond, see Barbara Sher Tinsley, *History and Polemics in the French Reformation: Florimond de Raemond, Defender of the Church* (Selinsgrove, Pa.: Susquehanna University Press, 1992).

51. Penny Roberts, "Martyrologies and Martyrs in the French Reformation: Heretics to Subversives in Troyes," in *Martyrs and Martyrologies,* ed. Wood, p. 228. Roberts offers no evidence for this claim.

52. The most important contradictory accounts are to be found, respectively, in Thomas More, *The Confutation of Tyndale's Answer* [1532], in *CWTM*, vol. 8,

pt. 1, ed. Louis A. Schuster et al. (New Haven: Yale University Press, 1973), pp. 22–25, and Foxe 1563, sigs. [UU7v–UU8]. For more detailed consideration of Bilney's and similar cases, see my "Anathema of Compromise: Christian Martyrdom in Early Modern Europe," vol. 1 (Ph.D. diss., Princeton University, 1996), pp. 283–286.

53. *Eyn new warhafftig vnd wunderbarlich geschicht oder hystori, von Jörgen Wagner zu München in Bayern als eyn Ketzer verbrandt im Jar M. D. xxvii* [Nuremberg: Hans Hergot, 1527], sig. A3v.

54. J. A. Sharpe, "'Last Dying Speeches': Religion, Ideology and Public Execution in Seventeenth-Century England," *P&P,* 107 (1985), 144–167.

55. Munday's work, *A Discouerie of Edmund Campion, and his Confederates, their most horrible and traiterous practises, against Maiesties most royall person, and the Realme . . .* (London: for Edward White, 1582), was printed on Jan. 29. Alfield's *True Report* must have appeared shortly thereafter: at some point in February, Richard Topcliffe said he "had received six of the traitorous books of Campion's, Sherwin and Bryant's martyrdom as they term it." John Hungerford Pollen, ed., *Unpublished Documents Relating to the English Martyrs,* vol. 1, 1584–1603, vol. 5 of CRS (London: Catholic Record Society, 1908), p. 27.

56. [Alfield], *A true reporte of the death and martyrdome of M. Campion Iesuite and preiste, and M. Sherwin, and M. Bryan preistes . . .* [London: Richard Verstegan, 1582], sigs. [B4v]–C1; M[unday], *Discouerie,* sigs. [F7v–F8].

57. M[unday], *Discouerie,* sigs. [F8v], G1v.

58. Ibid., sigs. G1v, G1v–G2v (quotations on G2v). For Campion's repeated denial of treason, compare ibid., sigs. G2v–G3, with [Alfield], *True reporte,* sig. C1.

59. [Alfield], *True reporte,* sig. [C2r-v]; M[unday], *Discouerie,* sig. G3r-v.

60. For a more detailed discussion, see my "Anathema of Compromise," vol. 1, pp. 256–287.

61. Ibid., pp. 297–314.

62. For the published pamphlet, see *Troys Epistres de Godefroy de Hamaelle, natif de niuele en Brabant: Le quel Souffrit martyre pour Iesu Christ, en la uile d Tournay le. 23. de Iullet, lan 1552. Auecq; troys belles chansons Faictes pay luy mesmes estant en prison* (n.p., ca. 1552). Erroneous dates are common in the martyrological sources. For June 22, not July 23, as the date of his execution, see Gérard Moreau, *Histoire du Protestantisme à Tournai jusqu'à la veille de la Révolution des Pays-Bas* (Paris: Société d'Édition "Les Belles Lettres," 1962), p. 126, and Leiden University Library, MS Vulcanius 98 D, fol. 20. This manuscript, which includes the letter at fols. 13–20, is reprinted and analyzed in H. T. Oberman, "De betrouwbaarheid der martelaarsboeken van Crespin en Van-Haemstede," *Nederlands archief voor kerkgeschiedenis,* n.s., 4 (1907), 74–110.

63. Leiden University Library, MS Vulcanius 98 D, fol. 14r–v; de Hamaelle, *Troys Epistres,* sig. [B6]; Crespin 1570, fol. 189. The translated passage: "I know that I will not be condemned to death for such belief and true articles of faith, but rather only for not following and wanting to believe the commandments of men. Yet to the good, the Lord's will is clear to me; I am his both in life and in death. I have written you this only so that if I have to suffer, at least I will not be judged a heretic. For I am not ignorant of Christian belief and articles of faith,

but rather believe them with all simplicity, according to the meager capacity for faith which the Lord has granted me by his grace, as you will hear." Gérard Moreau compares several passages from the Leiden manuscript to the 1554 and 1619 versions of Crespin's martyrology. Moreau, "Contribution à l'Histoire du Livre des Martyrs," *BSHPF,* 103 (1957), pp. 180–181. This was not the manuscript Crespin used, since it includes most of only one of the three letters that he reprinted in toto, as well as many biographical details that he surely would have included had he known them. Ibid., p. 179. Oberman persuasively argues that the Leiden manuscript was made from another, now-lost manuscript, not the pamphlet. Oberman, "Betrouwbaarheid," pp. 88–89. This makes the Leiden manuscript even more valuable, providing evidence about how accurately manuscript copies were reproduced as fellow believers disseminated them.

64. Arthur Piaget and Gabrielle Berthoud, *Notes sur Le Livre des Martyrs de Jean Crespin* (Neuchâtel: Secretariat de L'Université, 1930), pp. 32–66.

65. For their execution sentence, see SAA, Vierschaar, V150 (1571–1574), fols. 112v–113v, repr. in *AA,* vol. 13, pp. 129–131.

66. Samuel Cramer, "Het eigenhandig laatst adieu van Maeyken Wens aan haar kind," *DB,* 44 (1904), 115–133. On the front side of the leaf is a letter from Maeyken's husband in a clearly different hand; if they were copies, one would expect that the same person would have copied both brief letters, and thus the handwriting would match. Ibid., p. 125.

67. Cramer, "Maeyken Wens," pp. 117, 123.

68. For example, note her redundancies such as "sal" at the end of the first sentence, and "onder malcanderen" at the end of the fifth.

69. Van Braght 1685, vol. 2, p. 283.

70. Samuel Cramer's century-old, detailed study of van Braght's reliability remains the most comprehensive of its kind for this martyrologist. Cramer, "De geloofwaardigheid van van Braght," *DB,* 39 (1899), 65–164, and idem, "Nogmaals de geloofwaardigheid van van Braght: Tevens antwoord op de kritiek van den Heer W. Wilde," *DB,* 40 (1900), 184–210. Like van Braght, William Allen might have written a rousing conclusion to a reprinted letter from Ralph Sherwin, instead of admitting that "three or four of the latter lines are wanting"; see his *Briefe Historie of the Gloriovs Martyrdom of XII. Reverend Priests . . .* ([Rheims: Jean Foigny], 1582), sig. f2v.

71. Susan Wabuda, "Henry Bull, Miles Coverdale, and the Making of Foxe's *Book of Martyrs,*" in *Martyrs and Martyrologies,* ed. Wood, pp. 255–256. The three collections are Emmanuel College, Cambridge, MSS 260, 261, and 262. Wabuda and Thomas Freeman are currently producing a critical edition of these letters for publication.

72. See J. W. Martin, "Sidelights on Foxe's Account of the Marian Martyrs," in *Religious Radicals in Tudor England* (London: Hambledon Press, 1989), p. 177; David Loades, "Anabaptism and English Sectarianism in the Mid-Sixteenth Century," in *Reform and Reformation: England and the Continent, c. 1500–c. 1750,* ed. Derek Baker (Oxford: Blackwell, 1979), p. 65; John F. Davis, *Heresy and the Reformation in the South-East of England, 1520–1559* (London: Royal Historical Society, and Atlantic Highlands, N.J.: Humanities

Press, 1983), pp. 143–147; Patrick Collinson, "Cranbrook and the Fletchers: Popular and Unpopular Religion in the Kentish Weald," in *Godly People: Essays on English Protestantism and Puritanism* (London: Hambledon Press, 1983), pp. 403–404; Collinson, "Truth and Legend," pp. 39–44; Thomas Freeman, "Notes on a Source for John Foxe's Account of the Marian Persecution in Kent and Sussex," *Historical Research,* 67 (1994), 206–207.

73. Wabuda, "Henry Bull," p. 256.

74. On the concrete activity behind the writing and distribution of these letters, see also the excellent discussion by Thomas Freeman, "'Great Searching Out of Bookes and Autors': John Foxe as an Ecclesiastical Historian" (Ph.D. diss., Rutgers University, 1995), pp. 367–377.

75. Piaget and Berthoud, *Notes sur Le Livre des Martyrs,* pp. 47–49. It does seem valid, as they suggest, that precise references to patristic and conciliar sources allegedly recalled from memory must have been added by an editor (assuming that specific prisoners had no access to the quoted books in prison, as some of the Marian martyrs did). Not even learned theologians memorized these at length; their use in theological exposition and controversy did not depend on this.

76. Philippe Muret, "François Varlut et Alexandre Dayke, martyrs calvinistes à Tournai en 1562," *BSHPF,* 110 (1964), 33–43.

77. Cramer, in *BRN,* vol. 2, pp. 22, 26–27.

78. Most scholarship on the reliability of martyrological sources has compared them with surviving archival records. For a more detailed discussion, see my "Anathema of Compromise," vol. 1, pp. 318–333.

79. Van Braght 1685, vol. 2, p. 366.

2. The Late Medieval Inheritance

1. Margery Kempe, *The Book of Margery Kempe,* ed. Sanford Brown Meech, Early English Text Society, no. 212 (London: Oxford University Press, 1940), pp. 29/32–30/6.

2. In this chapter, broad designations such as "Christian society" and "late medieval Christians" are not meant to imply that late medieval Christianity was homogeneous, but rather that it was Christian across its spectrum of diversity. In contrast to earlier scholarship and consistent with the work of historians such as John Van Engen and Eamon Duffy, late medieval Christianity is better understood as a diverse, multilayered continuum rather than as two distinct cultures of "elite" and "popular" religion. See Van Engen, "The Christian Middle Ages as an Historiographical Problem," *American Historical Review,* 91 (1986), 519–552; Duffy, *The Stripping of the Altars: Traditional Religion in England, c. 1400–c. 1580* (New Haven: Yale University Press, 1992). A term such as "late medieval Christians" is misleading if taken to mean that more than a small minority nourished their spirituality with Latin devotional prose, but fitting if it denotes those who knew to pray to the saints for help, or who were familiar with the crucifix.

3. André Vauchez, *La sainteté en occident aux derniers siècles du moyen age d'après*

les procès de canonisation et les documents hagiographiques, 2nd ed. (Rome: École Française de Rome, 1988), p. 482.

4. Richard Kieckhefer, *Unquiet Souls: Fourteenth-Century Saints and Their Religious Milieu* (Chicago: University of Chicago Press, 1984), p. 67.

5. Vauchez, *Sainteté,* pp. 197–203.

6. Ghent University Library, HS 1761, fol. 225.

7. William Caxton, trans., *Here begynneth the book of the pylgrimage of the sowle late translated oute of Frensshe in to Englysshe* (London: William Caxton, 1483), fol. 95v.

8. Ghent University Library, HS 1761, fol. 223.

9. [John Mirk], *The festyuall* (London: Wynkyn de Worde, 1519), fol. 148.

10. Ibid., fol. 2.

11. [Thomas à Kempis], *A full deuoute and gostely treatyse of the Imytacyon and folowynge the blessed lyfe of our moste mercyfull Sauyour cryste . . .* (London: Richard Pynson, 1517), 1.23, sig. [C4r–v]. For the *Imitatio Christi,* the *Legenda aurea,* and the *Ars moriendi* I have used contemporary English translations from the early sixteenth century to preserve a period sense of language, even though they are not always particularly close translations of the Latin.

12. See Johan Huizinga, *The Autumn of the Middle Ages,* trans. Rodney J. Payton and Ulrich Mammitzsch (Chicago: University of Chicago Press, 1996), pp. 164–172; Philippe Ariès, *The Hour of Our Death,* trans. Helen Weaver (New York: Vintage, 1981). On the sensibility of the macabre in general from the fourteenth through the sixteenth centuries, see Jean Delumeau, *Sin and Fear: The Emergence of a Western Guilt Culture, 13th–18th Centuries,* trans. Eric Nicholson (New York: St. Martin's, 1990), pp. 35–114.

13. See Georg Schreiber, *Die Vierzehn Nothelfer in Volksfrömmigkeit und Sakralkultur: Symbolkraft und Herrschaftsbereich der Wallfahrtskapelle, vorab in Franken und Tirol* (Innsbruck: Wagner, 1959). Other saints sometimes included as part of these fourteen were Anthony, Leonard, Nicholas, Roche, Sebastian, Dorothy, Martha, local saints, and frequently the Virgin Mary. See Pierre Rézeau, *Les prières aux saints en français à la fin du moyen âge,* vol. 1 (Geneva: Droz, 1982), p. 216.

14. For example, after the story of the martyred brothers Sts. Cosmas and Damian, one is encouraged to "pray to these holy martyrs for to be our succor and help in all our hurts, blechours [wounds], and sores, and that by their merits after this life we may come to everlasting bliss in heaven." As for the martyred saints Primus and Felician, "let us pray to these saints that we may come to everlasting bliss in heaven." [Jacques de Voragine], *The Golden Legende,* trans. Wynkyn de Worde (London: Wynkyn de Worde, 1512), fols. 267, 138v. For similar examples, see the exhortations to invoke Thomas Becket (fols. 66, 174), Marcellinus (122), Peter Martyr (124v), Philip (125), King Edward (138v), Margaret (176v), Stephen (200v), Quentin (305v), Cecilia (345v), Dorothy (361), and Erasmus (400).

15. See the many prayers reprinted in both volumes of Rézeau, *Prières aux saints.*

16. Ibid., vol. 2 (Geneva: Droz, 1983), pp. 461, 462.

17. At least 114 Latin editions were printed in England (or on the Continent for

sale in England) between 1477 and the first wholly English vernacular editions in the 1530s, while 760 dated editions were published in France (predominantly in Paris) between 1485 and 1530. See Duffy, *Stripping of the Altars,* p. 212; Albert Labarre, "Heures (Livres d'Heures)," in *Dictionnaire de spiritualité ascétique et mystique,* vol. 7, pt. 1 (Paris: Beauchesne, 1969), col. 420. Both Duffy and Paul Saenger have argued that liturgical familiarity would have enabled many more or less literate laypeople to use Latin prayers despite a lack of formal training in the language. Duffy, *Stripping of the Altars,* pp. 221–222; Saenger, "Books of Hours and the Reading Habits of the Later Middle Ages," in *The Culture of Print: Power and the Uses of Print in Early Modern Europe,* ed. Roger Chartier, trans. Lydia G. Cochrane (Princeton: Princeton University Press, 1989), pp. 142, 148, 149.

18. See, for example, *Hore beate marie virginis ad vsum insignis ac praeclare ecclesie Sarum* (London: Wynkyn de Worde, 1514), sigs. [e7–e8v].

19. Prayer sheets for plague protection formed an entire subgenre within woodcuts of the saints; see Paul Heitz and W. L. Schreiber, *Pestblätter des XV. Jahrhunderts* (Strasbourg: J. H. E. Heitz, 1901). Several scholars have recently discussed the importance of Christ's matrilineal kin relations in late medieval Europe. See John Bossy, *Christianity in the West, 1400–1700* (Oxford: Oxford University Press, 1985), pp. 8–10; Clarissa W. Atkinson, *The Oldest Vocation: Christian Motherhood in the Middle Ages* (Ithaca: Cornell University Press, 1991), pp. 160–161; and the essays in *Interpreting Cultural Symbols: Saint Anne and Late Medieval Society,* ed. Kathleen Ashley and Pamela Sheingorn (Athens: University of Georgia Press, 1990), esp. Sheingorn, "Appropriating the Holy Family: Gender and Family History," pp. 169–198, which includes a discussion of the *Anna Selbdritt* at pp. 175–176.

20. *The crafte to lyue well and to dye well,* trans. [Andrew Chertsey] (London: Wynkyn de Worde, 1505), fol. [55].

21. Rézeau, *Prières,* vol. 1, pp. 146, 149.

22. *Les louenges a Nostre Seigneur, a Nostre Dame et aux benoitz sains et saintes de paradis* (Paris: for A. Vérard, n.d.), repr. in Rézeau, *Prières,* vol. 1, p. 159.

23. Besides the more than 170 printed editions that appeared between 1470 and 1499 in Latin, English, French, High and Low German, Dutch, Italian, and Bohemian, the *Golden Legend* survives in more than 1,000 Latin manuscripts (which as of 1986 had not yet been catalogued, let alone collated) in addition to a great many vernacular manuscripts and adaptations. Robert Francis Seybolt, "Fifteenth Century Editions of the *Legenda aurea,*" *Speculum,* 21 (1946), 327–338; Barbara Fleith, "Le classement des quelque 1000 manuscrits de la *Legenda aurea* latine en vue de l'établissement d'une histoire de la tradition," in *Legenda aurea: Sept siècles de diffusion,* ed. Brenda Dunn-Lardeau (Montreal: Éditions Bellarmin; Paris: J. Vrin, 1986), pp. 19–24. Sherry L. Reames has overstated the work's declining popularity from the 1490s under criticism from learned churchmen and humanist scholars, although she acknowledges that Caxton's English translation constituted an exception to this trend. Reames, *The Legenda aurea: A Reexamination of Its Paradoxical History* (Madison: University of Wisconsin Press, 1985), pp. 27–29. Her figures for sixteenth-century French

vernacular editions, derived from the *National Union Catalogue* and the catalogues of the British Library and the Bibliothèque Nationale, are incomplete. The work continued to see at least five editions in French every decade from the 1480s through the 1520s. See Brenda Dunn-Lardeau and Dominique Coq, "Fifteenth- and Sixteenth-Century French Editions of the *Légende dorée*," *Bibliothèque d'Humanisme et Renaissance*, 47 (1985), 88–93. For the various manuscript branches produced in the filiation of German vernacular translations, see Konrad Kunze, "Jacobus a Voragine," in *Die deutsche Literatur des Mittelalters: Verfasserlexikon*, ed. Kurt Ruh et al., vol. 4 (Berlin: W. de Gruyter, 1982), cols. 456–463.

24. This conclusion is based on the following late medieval manuscripts and early sixteenth-century printed editions of the *Golden Legend:* BL, Additional MS 11,565; BL, Additional MS 18,162; BL, Additional MS 20,034; BL, Harleian MS 630; BL, Stowe MSS 50–51; *Passionael twinter stuc Datmen hiet die gulden legende,* and the second half of this Dutch version, *Hier beghint tsomer stuc vanden passionale* (Antwerp: Henrick Eckert, 1505); *La legende doree et vie des Saincte et Sainctes translatee de latin en francoys* (Paris: Jean de la Roche, 1513); *Der heiligen leben neüw getruckt . . .* and *Der heiligen leben winterteil mit sein figuren legenden exemplen vnd geschichten . . .* (Strasbourg: Johannes Knoblouchs, 1517); and *Golden Legende* (1512). For example, in BL, Additional MS 20,034, a Dutch manuscript that belonged to the Convent of St. Ursula in Delft and was completed in 1465, St. Alban is simply "Albaen mit sinen gesellen" [Alban with his companions] in the table (fol. 4v), but a "maertelaer" [martyr] at the end of his story in the text (fol. 155v).

25. For prayers to St. Barbara that address her as "martyr" or refer to her passion, see Rézeau, *Prières,* vol. 2, pp. 72–73, 74–75, 78–79, 82–84, 85–86, 87, 88–89, 90–91, 95–96, 98–102, 108–110, 111–112; for those that do not, see ibid., 76–77, 80, 81, 92–93, 97, 103–106.

26. In the following manuscripts and editions St. George is called a martyr: BL, Additional MS 20,034, fol. 2v; BL, Additional MS 11,565, fol. 98 (although at the end of his story he is simply "seint George" [fol. 99v]); and *Golden Legende* (1512), fol. 106v. He is not referred to as a martyr in the tables or rubrics of any of the following manuscripts or printed editions: BL, Additional MS 18,162; BL, Stowe MSS 50–51; BL, Harleian MS 630; the 1505 Dutch edition of the *Passionael;* or *Legende doree* (1513).

27. Vauchez, *Sainteté,* p. 484.

28. Caroline Walker Bynum, "The Female Body and Religious Practice in the Later Middle Ages," in *Fragmentation and Redemption: Essays on Gender and the Human Body in Medieval Religion* (New York: Zone Books, 1991), p. 231. More recently Bynum has noted the "increasing visual emphasis on Christ's suffering in crucifixion, although depictions of the saints show them impassive and impassible under torture . . . It is as though—at least visually—Christ, because he is God, takes on all the culture's obsession with torture and partition, while the saints are guaranteed (by their participation in beatific vision and blessedness) to be free of pain and fragmentation." Bynum, *The Resurrection of the Body in Western Christianity, 200–1336* (New York: Columbia University

Press, 1995), p. 314 n. 129. This might be amended somewhat: it seems to me that the contrast rightly noted here depends not on Christ being *God,* but rather on his being a *human savior,* that is, both God *and* man. Late medieval depictions of the suffering Christ would seem to represent the fullest visual expression of the view—one not understood, necessarily, with theological precision—that only a God-man could have redeemed fallen humanity. This is a major theme in Ellen M. Ross, *The Grief of God: Images of the Suffering Jesus in Late Medieval England* (New York: Oxford University Press, 1997). The martyrs, as the beneficiaries of Christ's supremely efficacious redemption, feel no pain regardless of their torments. He, on the other hand, bearing all humanity's sins and offering them up in perfect sacrifice, had to suffer utterly.

29. For example, when St. Agatha was being "drawn and stretched on a tree and tormented," she said, "I have as great delection in these pains as he that hath found great treasure"; St. Primus drank the "boiling lead" poured in his mouth "as sweetly as it had been cold water." *Golden Legende* (1512), fols. 95, 138v. On the same point, see Bynum, "Bodily Miracles and the Resurrection of the Body in the High Middle Ages," in *Belief in History: Innovative Approaches to European and American Religion,* ed. Thomas Kselman (Notre Dame, Ind.: University of Notre Dame Press, 1991), p. 79; Miri Rubin, "Choosing Death? Experiences of Martyrdom in Late Medieval Europe," in *Martyrs and Martyrologies,* ed. Diana Wood, vol. 30 of *Studies in Church History* (Oxford: Blackwell, 1993), pp. 169–170.

30. Familiar with St. Lawrence's story, late medieval Christians would have viewed such an image and recalled his famous taunt to his torturers: "That side that is roasted enough eat thereof while the other side roasteth." [Mirk], *Festyuall,* fol. 130v.

31. A similar rendering of the same subject by Bellini belongs to the collection of the Warburg Institute, London. The close parallel that Jacques de Voragine drew between the deaths of Christ and Peter Martyr might suggest Dominican envy of Francis of Assisi as *alter Christus* (another Christ). See *Golden Legende* (1512), fol. 123v. On the importance of Peter Martyr to Jacques de Voragine, see André Vauchez, "Jacques de Voragine et les saints du XIIIe siècle dans la *Légende dorée,*" in *Legenda aurea: Sept siècles de diffusion,* ed. Dunn-Lardeau, pp. 51–52.

32. For the quotation, see BL, Additional MS 18,162, fol. 3; for two-thirds of the saints being martyrs, see Reames, *Legenda aurea,* pp. 98, 256 n. 44. On this point with specific reference to bodily dismemberment, see Bynum, "Bodily Miracles," p. 79; Helen White, *Tudor Books of Saints and Martyrs* (Madison: University of Wisconsin Press, 1963), pp. 41–43. In his analysis of the narrative structures of the Latin text of the *Golden Legend,* Alain Boureau has found 81 different kinds of tortures in the 91 chapters devoted to martyrs, with a total of 131 martyrdoms depicted. Alain Boureau, "Les structures narratives de la *Legenda aurea:* De la variation au grand chant sacré," in *Legenda aurea: Sept siècles de diffusion,* ed. Dunn-Lardeau, p. 62. See also Boureau's full-length study of the work's narrative structures and logic, *La Légende Dorée: Le système narratif de Jacques de Voragine (+ 1298)* (Paris: Éditions du Cerf, 1984), esp. pp. 111–133.

33. *Golden Legende* (1512), fols. 138, 160v.

34. [Richard Whitford], *The Martiloge in englysshe after the vse of the chirche of salisbury, and as it is redde in Syon, with addicyons* (London: Wynkyn de Worde, 1526), fols. 9, 12v, 13, 14v, 15-16v, 20v, 23, 26, 29, 34v, 37v (for the first quarter of the year alone). For the distinction among calendars (which indicate the names and types of saints day by day throughout the liturgical calendar, but without the place or time of their deaths), martyrologies (which add this minimal information), and legendaries (collections of saints' vitae, not necessarily arranged calendrically), see Jacques Dubois, *Martyrologes d'Usuard au Martyrologe romain* (Abbeville: F. Paillart, 1990), p. 3. The classic study of the development of the Western martyrology in the critical eighth and ninth centuries is Henri Quentin, *Les martyrologes historiques du moyen age: Étude sur la formation du Martyrologe romain* (Paris: Victor Lecoffre, 1908).

35. [Whitford], *Martiloge,* fol. 16v. Both Whitford's description and this woodcut are relatively unusual, as St. Apollonia's teeth were usually said to have been wrenched out with a pair of pincers.

36. Klaus P. Jankofsky, "*Legenda aurea* materials in *The South English Legendary*: Translation, Transformation, Acculturation," in *Legenda aurea: Sept siècles de diffusion,* ed. Dunn-Lardeau, p. 326; Osbern Bokenham, *Legendys of Hooly Wummen,* ed. Mary S. Serjeantson, Early English Text Society, no. 206 (London: Oxford University Press, 1938).

37. [Mirk], *Festyuall,* fol. 70.

38. For example, see the reproductions from a number of deluxe medieval Books of Hours in Roger S. Wieck, *Time Sanctified: The Book of Hours in Medieval Art and Life* (New York: George Braziller, 1988), pp. 111–123.

39. On this robust popular veneration and the negotiation over sanctity claims in the late medieval period, see Aviad M. Kleinberg, *Prophets in Their Own Country: Living Saints and the Making of Sainthood in the Later Middle Ages* (Chicago: University of Chicago Press, 1992).

40. Vauchez, *Sainteté,* pp. 174–180, 480–489; Jean-Claude Schmitt, *The Holy Greyhound: Guinefort, Healer of Children since the Thirteenth Century,* trans. Martin Thom (Cambridge: Cambridge University Press, 1983). Rubin, "Choosing Death?" pp. 162–169, discusses the reluctance of the papacy and high ecclesiastical officials to recognize child martyrs during the later Middle Ages.

41. Vauchez, *Sainteté,* pp. 482–483 n. 12, 483 n. 13. Vauchez erroneously gives 1216 rather than 1220 as the year of their death; for the correct date, see John Moorman, *A History of the Franciscan Order from Its Origins to the Year 1517* (Oxford: Clarendon Press, 1968), p. 22; "Frati minori francescani," *Enciclopedia cattolica,* vol. 5 (Vatican City: Enciclopedia cattolica and Libro cattolica, 1950), col. 1726; "Passio sanctorum martyrum fratrum Beraldi, Petri, Adinti, Accursii, Othonis in Marochio martyrizatorum," *Analecta Franciscana sive chronica aliaque varia documenta ad historiam Fratrum Minorum . . . ,* vol. 3 (Quaracchi: S. Bonaventura, 1897), p. 590. Miri Rubin was apparently unaware of these five martyrs when she recently wrote that "the earliest Franciscan martyrs are the group of seven who arrived in Morocco in the late summer of 1227." Rubin, "Choosing Death?" p. 160.

42. Examples include the followers of Peter John Olivi at the beginning of the fourteenth century, and those inspired by the four *fraticelli* burned in Marseilles in 1318 or executed in Sicily around 1372. Rubin, "Choosing Death?" pp. 159–161, 171; Malcolm Lambert, *Medieval Heresy: Popular Movements from the Gregorian Reform to the Reformation*, 2nd ed. (Oxford: Blackwell, 1992), pp. 209–211; Vauchez, *Sainteté*, p. 104.

43. For the Dominicans see R. Loenertz, "Un catalogue d'écrivains et deux catalogues de martyrs dominicains," *Archivum Fratrum Praedicatorum*, 12 (1942), 279–303. In 1226 the Franciscans received local permission to build and staff five churches in North Africa, honoring the five martyrs of 1220 killed in Marrakesh. Moorman, *Franciscan Order*, p. 229. See also the numerous accounts of thirteenth- and fourteenth-century Franciscan missionary martyrs in *Analecta Franciscana*, vol. 3.

44. P. Grosjean, "Thomas de la Hale, moine et martyr à Douvres en 1295," *AB*, 72 (1954), 167–191; Vauchez, *Sainteté*, p. 299.

45. John W. McKenna, "Popular Canonization as Political Propaganda: The Cult of Archbishop Scrope," *Speculum*, 45 (1970), 608–623; idem, "Piety and Propaganda: The Cult of Henry VI," in *Chaucer and Middle English Studies in Honour of Rossell Hope Robbins*, ed. Beryl Rowland (London: Allen and Unwin, 1974), pp. 72–88; *The Miracles of King Henry VI*, ed. Ronald Knox and Shane Leslie (Cambridge: Cambridge University Press, 1923); Duffy, *Stripping of the Altars*, p. 195.

46. Quoted in Kieckhefer, *Unquiet Souls*, p. 68 (Kieckhefer's trans.).

47. "I thank thee, daughter, that thou wouldst suffer death for my love, for as often as thou thinkest so, thou shalt have the same mede in Heaven as though thou suffered the same death." *Book of Margery Kempe*, p. 30/7–10.

48. See Robert Markus's eloquent treatment in *The End of Ancient Christianity* (Cambridge: Cambridge University Press, 1990), pp. 70–72.

49. Alfred C. Rush, "Spiritual Martyrdom in St. Gregory the Great," *Theological Studies*, 23 (1962), 574–575.

50. Gregory the Great, *Homiliae in evangelia*, 1.3.4 and 2.35.7, quoted in Rush, "Spiritual Martyrdom," pp. 579, 580 (Rush's trans.). Spiritual martyrdom was embedded within Gregory's notion of Christian life as a multifaceted sacrifice offered for love of Christ. Carole Straw, *Gregory the Great: Perfection in Imperfection* (Berkeley: University of California Press, 1988), pp. 179–193, esp. 187–188.

51. See the classic overview of the desire for martyrdom from the church fathers through the late Middle Ages, including the distinctions between different sorts of martyrdom, in Louis Gougaud, *Dévotions et pratiques ascétiques du moyen age* (Paris: Desclee de Brouwer, 1925), pp. 200–219. See also E. Randolph Daniel, "The Desire for Martyrdom: A *leitmotiv* of St. Bonaventure," *Franciscan Studies*, 32 (1972), 74–87.

52. [Mirk], *Festyuall*, fol. 71. With a wealth of evidence, patience has been described as "in many ways the key virtue in fourteenth-century spirituality." Kieckhefer, *Unquiet Souls*, p. 52. See the whole of Kieckhefer's Chapter 3, "Patience," pp. 50–88.

53. *STC 1475–1640,* vol. 2, pp. 156–157.

54. *Golden Legende* (1512), fol. 310.

55. John Van Engen, ed. and trans., *Devotio Moderna: Basic Writings* (New York: Paulist Press, 1988), pp. 41, 84–91, quotations on pp. 84, 86–87. See also Kieckhefer, *Unquiet Souls,* pp. 80–83, which refers to this letter and the presence of the same theme in Grote's correspondence.

56. Van Engen, ed., *Devotio Moderna,* p. 212.

57. Roger Lovatt, "The *Imitation of Christ* in Late Medieval England," *Transactions of the Royal Historical Society,* 5th ser., 18 (1968), 113; Augustin De Backer, *Essai bibliographique sur le livre "De imitatione Christi"* (1864; reprint, Amsterdam: Desclee de Brouwer, 1966), pp. 1–9, 34–35, 107–111, 127–129, 149, 155–156, 174; *STC 1475–1640,* vol. 2, p. 303.

58. [à Kempis], *Imytacyon* (1517), 2.12, sigs. [F4v–F5].

59. Ibid., sigs. [F5, F6v].

60. Sister Mary Catharine O'Connor, *The Art of Dying Well: The Development of the Ars Moriendi* (New York: Columbia University Press, 1942), pp. 114–115, 134, 147, 149–150, 157, 162, 164; Henri Zerner, "L'Art au morier," *Revue de l'Art,* 11 (1971), 7; Roger Chartier, "Texts and Images: The Arts of Dying, 1450–1600," in *The Cultural Uses of Print in Early Modern France,* trans. Lydia G. Cochrane (Princeton: Princeton University Press, 1987), pp. 35, 37; Erik Lips, "Sur la popularité de l'*Ars moriendi* aux Pays-Bas (1450–1530)," *Revue du Nord,* 70 (1988), 495. O'Connor's abbreviations for the two texts (CP, QS), now standard in the scholarship, are based on the initial letters of their opening Latin words. O'Connor, *Art of Dying Well,* p. 7.

61. O'Connor, *Art of Dying Well,* pp. 142–143.

62. Chartier, "Arts of Dying," p. 42. See also Lips, "Popularité de l'*Ars moriendi,*" pp. 498–499. On the stability and small range of variation of the eleven woodcut images in the shorter, QS text, see Zerner, "L'Art au morier," p. 15.

63. *Here begynneth a lityll treatise shorte and abredged spekynge of the arte and crafte to knowe well to dye,* trans. William Caxton (London: William Caxton, 1490), sigs. A1v, A2.

64. [à Kempis], *Imytacyon* (1517), 1.23, sig. C3v.

65. O'Connor, *Art of Dying Well,* pp. 7–9; Zerner, "L'Art au morier."

66. *Arte and crafte to dye,* sigs. A2–A4v.

67. Ibid., sigs. A3v–A4. The author here incorporated a paraphrase of Rom. 8:18: "I consider that the sufferings of this present time are not worth comparing with the glory about to be revealed to us."

68. A 1507 woodcut of the wounded Jesus prior to his crucifixion, printed in Augsburg or Nuremberg, hails him as "O marter groß" in the first of several invocations. Richard S. Field, *Fifteenth Century Woodcuts and Metalcuts from the National Gallery of Art, Washington, D.C.* (Washington, D.C., n.d.), no. 129. In 1510 an Albrecht Dürer prayer accompanying one of his crucifixion woodcuts mentioned the Lord's "great martyrdom" [*groß marter*]. Max Geisberg, *The German Single-Leaf Woodcut: 1500–1550,* rev. and ed. Walter L. Strauss, vol. 2 (New York: Hacker, 1974), no. G.750, p. 700. For references to Christ's martyrdom in John Hus's correspondence, see *The Letters of John*

Hus, trans. Matthew Spinka (Manchester: Manchester University Press, 1972), no. 20, p. 60; no. 41, p. 115.

69. [à Kempis], *Imytacyon* (1517), 2.12, fol. [F6v].

70. Medieval exegetes derived many of the graphic details about Christ's passion, from his apprehension through his removal from the cross, from patristic and ultimately biblical sources, especially certain of the psalms and Isaiah. F. P. Pickering, "The Gothic Image of Christ," in *Essays on Medieval German Literature and Iconography* (Cambridge: Cambridge University Press, 1980), pp. 3–30.

71. Gougaud, *Dévotions,* pp. 74–78; André Wilmart, *Auteurs spirituels et textes dévots du moyen age latin: Études d'histoire litteraire* (1932; reprint, Paris: Etudes Augustiniennes, 1971), pp. 505–522; R. W. Southern, *The Making of the Middle Ages* (New Haven: Yale University Press, 1953), pp. 231–241. For England in particular, see Ross, *Grief of God.*

72. Duffy, *Stripping of the Altars,* pp. 234–235.

73. Huizinga, *Autumn of the Middle Ages,* p. 220.

74. Michel-Jean Picard, "Croix (chemin de)," *Dictionnaire de spiritualité ascétique et mystique,* vol. 2 (Paris: Beauchesne, 1953), col. 2584.

75. Ibid., col. 2588. Margery Kempe mentioned that when she was in Jerusalem, friars led pilgrims through the stages of Christ's passion. *Book of Margery Kempe,* p. 68/2–10.

76. *Dit is een devote meditacie op die passie ons liefs heeren . . . ,* repr. in *Bijdragen voor de geschiedenis van het Bisdom van Haarlem,* 11 (1884), 325. Composed in the late fifteenth century, this pamphlet was reprinted five times between 1518 and ca. 1525. Picard, "Croix," cols. 2584–2585.

77. Ibid., cols. 2585–2588.

78. Wieck, *Time Sanctified,* pp. 89–90. The meditative subject for Matins was the betrayal; for Prime, usually Christ before Pilate; for Terce, most commonly the flagellation; for Sext, typically Christ carrying the cross; for None, the crucifixion; for Vespers, the deposition from the cross; and for Compline, the entombment.

79. Sarah McNamer, "Further Evidence for the Date of the Pseudo-Bonaventuran *Meditationes vitae Christi,*" *Franciscan Studies,* 50 (1990), 235–261. McNamer dates the work to ca. 1336–ca. 1364 rather than the traditional "early fourteenth century."

80. Michael G. Sargent, ed., *Nicholas Love's "Mirror of the Blessed Life of Jesus Christ"* (New York: Garland, 1992), pp. 161–190, and idem, "Introduction," pp. ix, xxv, xxx. In England, Love's translation "was probably the most popular vernacular book of the fifteenth century," surviving in fifty-six complete or originally complete manuscripts. Duffy, *Stripping of the Altars,* p. 235 (quotation); Sargent, "Introduction" to *Nicholas Love's "Mirror",* p. lxiii.

81. On Christ as the Man of Sorrows see Romuald Bauerreiss, *Pie Jesu: Das Schmerzensmann-Bild und sein Einfluss auf die mittelalterliche Frömmigkeit* (Munich: K. Widmann, 1931); Gert von der Osten, *Der Schmerzensmann: Typengeschichte eines deutschen Andachtsbildwerkes von 1300 bis 1600* (Berlin: Deutscher Verein für Kunstwissenschaft, 1935); Sixten Ringbom, *Icon to Narrative: The Rise of*

the Dramatic Close-Up in Fifteenth-Century Devotional Painting, 2nd ed. (Doornspijk: Davaco, 1984), pp. 66–69, 142–147.

82. Gougaud, *Dévotions,* pp. 78–90. Caroline Walker Bynum notes the significance of devotion to Christ's wounds among women, although it seems to me that she somewhat understates its prevalence among men. Bynum, *Holy Feast and Holy Fast: The Religious Significance of Food to Medieval Women* (Berkeley: University of California Press, 1987), pp. 249, 271–272.

83. Duffy, *Stripping of the Altars,* pp. 238–248; McKenna, "Henry VI," p. 78. Specific devotion to the wound in Christ's side, the entrance to his wounded heart, reached a high pitch in the fifteenth century, a precursor to the later devotion to the Sacred Heart. Gougaud, *Dévotions,* pp. 99–101.

84. *Devote meditacie,* p. 338.

85. On Mary's importance as paradigm of compassion, see Wilmart, *Auteurs spirituels,* pp. 505–522; Kieckhefer, *Unquiet Souls,* pp. 106–107; Ross, *Grief of God,* pp. 52, 87.

86. [Fisher], *A spirituall consolation, written by Iohn Fyssher Bishoppe of Rochester . . .* [London: Thomas East, 1578], sigs. F5v–[F6]. On the reciprocity between devotional images and practices in the fifteenth century, see Ringbom, *Icon to Narrative;* Ross, *Grief of God;* Michael Baxandall, *Painting and Experience in Fifteenth Century Italy* (Oxford: Oxford University Press, 1972), pp. 45–56.

87. Thomas More, *A Dialogue of Comfort against Tribulation* [1534–1535], in *CWTM,* vol. 12, ed. Louis L. Martz and Frank Manley (New Haven: Yale University Press, 1976), p. 312/13–23.

88. [Fisher], *Spirituall consolation,* sig. [F6v].

89. Ross, *Grief of God,* p. 78, criticizes interpretations that see too exclusively Christ's humanity in late medieval devotion to his passion: "The suffering of Jesus Christ derives its power and meaning from the fact that it is God who suffers." Ross also stresses that the graphic character of passion depictions and devotions was meant to animate love of God and neighbor.

90. More, *Dialogue of Comfort,* p. 313/3–4.

91. For Fisher, see Eamon Duffy, "The Spirituality of John Fisher," in *Humanism, Reform and the Reformation: The Career of Bishop John Fisher,* ed. Brendan Bradshaw and Eamon Duffy (Cambridge: Cambridge University Press, 1989), pp. 205–231.

92. More, *Dialogue of Comfort,* p. 312/1–3.

93. [à Kempis], *Imytacyon* (1517), 2.12, sig. F3v.

94. Anne Hudson, *The Premature Reformation: Wycliffite Texts and Lollard History* (Oxford: Clarendon Press, 1988), p. 172 (quotation); John A. F. Thomson, *The Later Lollards, 1414–1520* (Oxford: Oxford University Press, 1965), p. 29.

95. Matthew Spinka, "Introduction" to *John Hus at the Council of Constance* (New York: Columbia University Press, 1965), pp. 41–42. Howard Kaminsky writes that "it would be a great mistake . . . to attach less than the greatest importance to the action of the three young men against indulgences, and to the tragic sequel that provided the *de facto* Hussite church with its first martyrs, who were venerated as such." Kaminsky, *A History of the Hussite Revolution* (Berkeley: University of California Press, 1967), p. 121.

96. Lambert, *Medieval Heresy,* pp. 153, 309 n. 38.

97. Ibid., pp. 289–296; Spinka, "Introduction," *Hus at Constance,* pp. 30–31.

98. Spinka, trans., *Letters of John Hus,* p. 213 (I have used Spinka's translations throughout in references to Hus's correspondence). Several years earlier, in 1407, two Czechs had been in England looking for manuscripts of Wyclif's works. Anne Hudson, ed., *English Wycliffite Sermons,* vol. 1 (Oxford: Clarendon Press, 1983), p. 197.

99. *Letters of John Hus,* pp. 213–214.

100. Ibid., pp. 214, 215. All biblical citations in Hus's correspondence, given by Spinka in footnotes, are here placed in brackets.

101. This idea was also central to Waldensian self-understanding. Jean Gonnet and Amedeo Molnár, *Les Vaudois au moyen age* (Turin: Claudiana, 1974), pp. 425–427.

102. *Letters of John Hus,* no. 15, pp. 46, 45.

103. Ibid., pp. 40, 46–47 (the reply to Richard Wyche), 54, 62, 84, 89, 102, 119.

104. Ibid., no. 10, p. 39.

105. Ibid., no. 16, p. 50. This passage combines a paraphrase of 1 Pet. 1:7 with other New Testament echoes, such as the synoptic parallel of Matt. 10:22, Mark 13:13, and Luke 21:19 ("But the one who endures to the end will be saved").

106. See Spinka, "Introduction," *Hus at Constance,* pp. 50, 55–56, 73–74; idem, *John Hus' Concept of the Church* (Princeton: Princeton University Press, 1966).

107. In the fall of 1412 he wrote to the Praguers, setting John 10:11–12 ("A good shepherd lays down his life for his sheep . . .") next to Matt. 10:23 ("When they persecute you in one town, flee to the next"), admitting "which of the two opposites to choose I know not." *Letters of John Hus,* no. 25, p. 75. The same autumn he quoted Phil. 3:21–24 ("For me to live is Christ and to die is gain . . ."), on which he commented: "I would choose to die with Christ and to be with Him; yet I yearn to labour with you for your salvation. 'But what to choose I know not', awaiting the mercy of God." Ibid., no. 28, p. 85. By the time he wrote to them again, shortly before Christmas, he combined his flight "in accordance with Christ's teaching" (that is, Matt. 10:23) with a professed willingness to die for the truth: "Hold firmly that in whatever way the Lord will dispose of me, so it will happen. If He will find me worthy of death, He will be pleased to call me to it; if, however, He will be pleased to prolong my preaching to His people, all these things rest in His power and will." Ibid., no. 32, p. 93. Hus later repeated this holy indifference to life and death, including one instance less than two weeks before he was burned—and this after having several times expected his imminent execution. Ibid., pp. 123, 142, 197.

108. Ibid., no. 27, pp. 80–81; no. 37, p. 108. For other applications of biblical passages on persecution and suffering to concrete circumstances during the exile period, see ibid., pp. 82, 88, 103, 106–107. After stringing together four such verses, Hus wrote: "These are my foundations and food, by which my spirit is refreshed, that it may be strong against all adversaries of the truth." Ibid., no. 35, p. 103.

109. Ibid., no. 27, p. 84 (quotation); pp. 107–108, 115, 119, 123. See also no. 52, p. 134, written just after his arrival in Constance.

110. Ibid., no. 27, p. 83.

111. For conflicting assessments, see Paul de Vooght, *L'Heresie de Jean Huss* (Louvain: Publications universitaires de Louvain, 1960), pp. 466–468; and Spinka, "Introduction," *Hus at Constance,* pp. 73–78, which assails de Vooght. Francis Oakley contends that Hus's religious commitment itself was "within a hairs-breadth of being orthodox in actual fact," but was overshadowed by his increasingly provocative style in his writings and confrontations. Oakley, *The Western Church in the Later Middle Ages* (Ithaca: Cornell University Press, 1979), p. 300.

112. *Letters of John Hus,* no. 26, p. 78. Hus argued that abjuration implied admission that one had maintained the heresies in question, and that inwardly to retain views one outwardly abjured was sinful because perjurious. For the same views expressed during the last three weeks of his life, see ibid., pp. 176, 180, 183.

113. Ibid., no. 66, p. 156; no. 69, p. 161; no. 70, p. 162 (quotations).

114. Hus acknowledged that despite his best intentions, he might fall and repudiate Christ: "I am not better than St Peter: since he had thrice denied the Lord Jesus, if I also deny, do not follow my example, dear Czechs, being without an excuse before God and men." Ibid., no. 66, p. 156.

115. Ibid., no. 63, p. 153. Hus's Latin reads: "Primo nunc disco psalterium intelligere, debite orare, contumelias Christi et martirum passiones pensare." *M. Jana Husi: Korespondence a dokumenty,* ed. Václav Novotný (Prague: Nakl. komise pro vydavani pramenu nabozenskeho hnuti ceskeho, 1920), no. 118, p. 255.

116. Hus mentioned these Old Testament examples in letters written in early January, March (when he crafted them into verse), and on June 25, when he added the examples of Lazarus's resuscitation from the dead (John 11) and Peter's liberation from prison by an angel (Acts 12). *Letters of John Hus,* pp. 142, 152, 193. For the number of sermons given by Hus in Prague, see Lambert, *Medieval Heresy,* p. 296.

117. *Letters of John Hus,* no. 78, pp. 174; no. 80, pp. 176–177; no. 91, p. 197; no. 97, pp. 204–205.

118. Ibid., no. 94, pp. 200–201.

119. Ulrich von Richental, *Chronik des Constanzer Concils 1414 bis 1418,* ed. Michael Richard Buck (Tübingen: Litterarische Verein in Stuttgart, 1882), p. 81. Peter of Mladoňovice wrote that Hus sang three (specified) songs in a loud voice until the wind blew the flame into his face, then moving his lips silently, he seemed to move for about as long as it takes to recite quickly two or three Our Fathers before he expired. Franciscus Palacký, ed., *Documenta Mag. Joannis Hus vitam, doctrinam, causam . . . motas illustrantia* (1869; reprint, Osnabrück: Biblio, 1966), p. 323 (English trans. in Spinka, *Hus at Constance,* p. 233). Drawing on this discrepancy and others between the two accounts, Hubert Herkommer has argued that the writers' perceptions were so shaped by their values and assumptions that one cannot distinguish between the experience of events and their meaning ("Their experience of *reality* is *identical* with the experience of the meaning of this reality"). Herkommer, "Die Geschichte vom Leiden und Sterben des Jan Hus als Ereignis und Erzählung," in *Literatur und Laienbildung im Spätmittelalter und in der Reformationszeit,* ed. Ludger

Grenzmann and Karl Stackmann (Stuttgart: J. B. Metzler, 1981), p. 119 (my emphasis). Herkommer's remark seems to imply an epistemology in which perceptions not only interpret reality, but *constitute* it. Strictly understood, this implies a flat contradiction in this case: Hus both cried out and did not cry out depending on who was perceiving his execution. We can grant radically different evaluations of the execution, but implying both that A and not-A actually happened makes no sense. Either or both writers, of course, could have been embellishing or inventing, and both had their ideological axes to grind, but further evidence tends against Ulrich's veracity: he gets the date of Hus's execution wrong (July 8 instead of July 6), seems to confuse it with Jerome of Prague's execution (which he places in September 1415, eight months too early), and claims that Jerome of Prague also cried out ("schrayt vast grülich") when he was burned, even though Poggio Bracciolini, who came from a very different world than Peter of Mladoňovice, suggests nothing of the sort in his account of Jerome's execution, noting instead his remarkable steadfastness. Spinka, ed., *Hus at Constance,* p. 233 n. 27; Richental, *Chronik,* p. 83; Poggio Bracciolini, *Lettere,* ed. Helene Harth, vol. 2 (Florence: Leo S. Olschki, 1984), pp. 162–163 (English trans. in *The Portable Renaissance Reader,* ed. James Bruce Ross and Mary Martin McLaughlin [New York: Viking Press, 1953], pp. 623–624). Nor, as Herkommer implies, do the parallels between Christ's trial and passion and Hus's trial and death in Peter of Mladoňovice's narrative necessarily indicate a willingness to sacrifice accuracy. Herkommer, "Geschichte," pp. 117–118. The pattern of accusation, interrogation, condemnation, and execution comprised a formal parallel to Christ's story in the Gospels, as it did to the treatment of all men and women judicially tried and executed for heresy or religious treason. Moreover, Hus's correspondence unmistakably reveals his self-conscious imitation of Christ, a fact Peter would have known as part of the circle in Constance that received multiple prison letters from him. We cannot be certain that Peter's account is closer to what happened than Ulrich's at points where the two are contradictory, but we can be reasonably confident that this is so for the reasons adduced here.

120. *Letters of John Hus,* no. 99, p. 207.
121. See Siegfried Hoyer, "Jan Hus und der Hussitismus in den Flugschriften des ersten Jahrzehnts der Reformation," in *Flugschriften als Massenmedium der Reformationszeit,* ed. Hans-Joachim Köhler (Stuttgart: Klett-Cotta, 1981), pp. 291–307. On the appropriation of late medieval heretics by Protestant martyrologists and historians in general, see Euan Cameron, "Medieval Heretics as Protestant Martyrs," in *Martyrs and Maryrologies,* ed. Wood, pp. 185–207.
122. Kaminsky, *Hussite Revolution,* pp. 141–142. For the appeal of the Hussite professors to Lacek of Kravaří, see Palacký, ed., *Documenta Joannis Hus,* no. 78, pp. 561–562.
123. Kaminsky, *Hussite Revolution,* pp. 143–144.
124. Palacký, ed., *Documenta Joannis Hus,* no. 108, pp. 647–648. Palacký dates the document with the conciliar grievances to November or December 1416. See also the complaint by the council earlier in the year, which also mentioned the three young men beheaded in Prague in 1412. Ibid., no. 105, pp. 638–639.

125. Kaminsky, *Hussite Revolution*, pp. 162–163 (quotation on 163, Kaminsky's trans.).

126. Ibid., pp. 165–168. For Kozí Hradek, Kaminsky translates an anonymous letter written in 1416, apparently by a local Catholic. Ibid., pp. 165–167. For the Latin original, see Palacký, ed., *Documenta Joannis Hus*, no. 104, pp. 636–638.

127. Kaminsky, *Hussite Revolution*, p. 142 n. 3; Gonnet and Molnár, *Vaudois*, p. 220, 220 n. 45. For Novotný's redaction of the manuscripts of this Latin sermon, see *Fontes rerum bohemicarum*, vol. 8 (Prague: N. F. Palackeho, 1932), pp. 231–242.

128. My trans. from the Latin quoted in Kaminsky, *Hussite Revolution*, p. 121 n. 80.

129. Kaminsky, *Hussite Revolution*, p. 364; Lambert, *Medieval Heresy*, pp. 331–332.

130. Thomas J. Talley, "A Hussite Latin Gradual of the XV Century," *Bulletin of the General Theological Seminary*, 48:5 (1962), 11.

131. Ibid., pp. 10–11. The text of the sung Alleluia reads: "Laetetur in domino mater ecclesia que tempore concilii in cristi constancia parturiens per ignem Johannes cum Jeronimo transmissit ad celestia. Alleluia." Ibid., p. 10.

132. Peter Brock, *The Political and Social Doctrines of the Unity of the Czech Brethren in the Fifteenth and Early Sixteenth Centuries* (The Hague: Mouton, 1957), pp. 60–61; Murray L. Wagner, *Petr Chelčický: A Radical Separatist in Hussite Bohemia* (Scottdale, Pa.: Herald Press, 1983), p. 127; Gonnet and Molnár, *Vaudois*, pp. 233–234.

133. Hoyer, "Hus und der Hussitismus," pp. 297–298, 295.

134. *Quellen zur Ketzergeschichte Brandenburgs und Pommern*, ed. Dietrich Kurze (Berlin: De Gruyter, 1975), p. 300, cited in Robert Kolb, *For All the Saints: Changing Perceptions of Martyrdom and Sainthood in the Lutheran Reformation* (Macon, Ga.: Mercer University Press, 1987), p. 24 n. 39.

135. Lambert, *Medieval Heresy*, pp. 243–251, 259–260.

136. Hudson, *Premature Reformation*, p. 158. For example, not one of the forty-five examined refused to abjure during the trials in the diocese of Coventry and Lichfield in 1511–1512. John Fines, "Heresy Trials in the Diocese of Coventry and Lichfield, 1511–12," *JEH*, 14 (1963), 161–162.

137. Thomson, *Later Lollards*, pp. 228–235; Hudson, *Premature Reformation*, p. 164; Lambert, *Medieval Heresy*, p. 261.

138. Thomson, *Later Lollards*, pp. 148–150; Hudson, *Premature Reformation*, p. 172.

139. Thomson, *Later Lollards*, p. 39; Hudson, *Premature Reformation*, pp. 172, 458.

140. J. L. Morison, ed., *Reginald Pecock's Book of Faith: A Fifteenth Century Theological Tractate* (Glasgow: J. Maclehose and Sons, 1909), pp. 11–12, 191, 192 (quotations on 191, 192). By implying that those who died outside the Church were not martyrs, Pecock argued as many Catholic controversialists would in the sixteenth and seventeenth centuries. He also noted that heretics might believe their errors just as staunchly as Catholics believed their truths, another point frequently made by early modern Catholic writers. Ibid., p. 165.

141. Quoted in Hudson, *Premature Reformation,* p. 172. See also Thomson, *Later Lollards,* p. 156; Susan Brigden, *London in the Reformation* (Oxford: Clarendon Press, 1989), p. 86.

142. Thomson, *Later Lollards,* pp. 156, 161.

143. Euan Cameron, *The Reformation of the Heretics: The Waldenses of the Alps, 1480–1580* (Oxford: Clarendon Press, 1984), pp. 83, 268.

144. Hudson, *Premature Reformation,* pp. 158–159. Matt. 10:23: "When they persecute you in one town, flee to the next; for truly I tell you, you will not have gone through all the towns of Israel before the Son of Man comes."

145. *English Wycliffite Sermons,* vol. 2, ed. Pamela Gradon (Oxford: Clarendon Press, 1988), no. 66/40–55, quotations at lines 41, 46–48, pp. 61–62. The sermons very likely date from the late 1380s or 1390s. See ibid., vol. 4, ed. Pamela Gradon and Anne Hudson (Oxford: Clarendon Press, 1996), pp. 10–20. For another sermon that stresses steadfastness despite danger to one's life, see vol. 2, no. 122/166–180, pp. 326–327 (on Matt. 5:10 during the sermon for the Feast of All Saints). By and large, sermons addressing persecution and suffering do not apply biblical passages at length to the contemporary context (for some brief applications, see vol. 2, no. 65/105–113, p. 58; no. 66/85–89, p. 63; no. 67/58–61, p. 67), nor press the imperative to remain faithful to death. They were written prior to the enactment of *De haeretico comburendo* in 1401 and before the execution of any Lollards. Thus one sermon makes the traditional distinction between martyrdom of body and martyrdom of will (or blood martyrdom and spiritual martyrdom). Another, for the Feast of the Holy Innocents, uses the traditional classification of martyrs in will, martyrs in deed, and martyrs in both will and deed. Ibid., vol. 2, no. 59/89–103, p. 24; no. 93/38–43, p. 222.

146. For Christ as the head of martyrs, see *Wycliffite Sermons,* vol. 2, no. 74/29, p. 107 (quotation) and no. 93/38–39, p. 222; for the other quotation, see ibid., no. 72/104–106, p. 98. A similar passage is in the sermon on Rom. 8:18–23, vol. 1, no. E34/66–69, p. 625.

147. For Hudson's remark plus the quoted passage from the commentary itself, see her *Premature Reformation,* p. 263.

148. On the Lollard understanding of Antichrist and apocalypticism, I am indebted to Curtis V. Bostick, *The Antichrist and the Lollards: Apocalypticism in Late Medieval and Reformation England* (Leiden: E. J. Brill, 1998).

149. See *Wycliffite Sermons,* vol. 2, pp. 38, 41, 65, 81, 94, 96–98.

150. A. Dondaine, ed., *Un traité néo-Manichéen du XIIIe siècle: Le liber de duobus principiis* (Rome: Istituto storico domenicano, 1939), pp. 10, 19, 143–147, quotation on 144.

151. This family resemblance among the Lollards, Hussites, and Waldensians is noted in A. J. Lamping, "Een school voor martelaren: De plaats van de dresdener school in de boheemse kerkstrijd," *Nederlands archief voor kerkgeschiedenis,* n.s., 56 (1975–1976), 279–280.

152. My trans. from the Latin quoted in Rubin, "Choosing Death?" p. 181, from G. G. Merlo, "Pietro di Verona-S. Pietro martire: Difficoltà e proposte per lo studio di un inquisitore beatificato," in *Culto dei santi, instituzioni e classi sociali*

in età preindustriale, ed. S. Boesch-Gajano and L. Sebastiano (L'Aquila and Rome: L. U. Lapadre, 1984), pp. 473–474.

153. Thomson, *Later Lollards,* pp. 126–127.

3. The Willingness to Kill

1. Victor Houliston, "St. Thomas Becket in the Propaganda of the English Counter-Reformation," *Renaissance Studies,* 7 (1993), 63.

2. Urbanus Rhegius, "Der Leunebergischen bedenken der widertaufer halb, ob die mit dem schwert zu straffen seien, durch Urbanum Regium gestelt," in *Wiedertäuferakten 1527–1626,* ed. Günther Franz, vol. 4 of *Urkundliche Quellen zur hessischen Reformationsgeschichte* (Marburg: N. G. Elwert, 1951), p. 111. Heinrich Bullinger made the same point with reference to Anabaptism in *Der Widertöufferen vrsprung, fürgang, Secten, wäesen . . .* (Zurich: Christoph Froschauer, 1561), fol. 166.

3. See Peter Brown, "St. Augustine's Attitude to Religious Coercion," *Journal of Roman Studies,* 54 (1964), 107–116.

4. Malcolm Lambert, *Medieval Heresy: Popular Movements from the Gregorian Reform to the Reformation,* 2nd ed. (Oxford: Blackwell, 1992), pp. 10–16, 26; R. I. Moore, *The Formation of a Persecuting Society: Power and Deviance in Western Europe, 950–1250* (Oxford: Blackwell, 1987), pp. 12–16. Lambert disputes Moore's interpretation of the Orléans incident as an instance of court politics and faction. The monastic chronicler's report that the crowd wanted to lynch those who rejected orthodoxy (Lambert, *Medieval Heresy,* p. 12) accords ill with Moore's main thesis, that whatever wider societal hatred of heretics existed in medieval Europe was created by princes and prelates from the later eleventh and especially twelfth centuries.

5. Lambert, *Medieval Heresy,* pp. 44–61, 66–68, 91–146; Moore, *Formation,* pp. 19–27; Joseph Lecler, *Toleration and the Reformation,* trans. T. L. Westow, vol. 1 (New York: Association Press; London: Longmans, 1960), pp. 80–81. On the misnomer of "the Inquisition" as a medieval institution—as opposed to a range of locally varied measures by papal and episcopal inquisitors against heresy—see Richard Kieckhefer, *Repression of Heresy in Medieval Germany* (Philadelphia: University of Pennsylvania Press, 1979), esp. pp. 1–10.

6. James Given, "The Inquisitors of Languedoc and the Medieval Technology of Power," *American Historical Review,* 94 (1989), 352–356.

7. Teresa of Avila, *The Story of Her Life,* 1.4, in *The Collected Works of Teresa of Avila,* trans. Kieran Kavanaugh and Otilio Rodriguez, vol. 1 (Washington, D.C.: ICS Publications, 1976), pp. 33–34.

8. Natalie Zemon Davis, "The Rites of Violence," in *Society and Culture in Early Modern France* (Stanford: Stanford University Press, 1975), pp. 152–187; Denis Crouzet, *Les guerriers de Dieu: La violence au temps des troubles de religion (vers 1525–vers 1610),* 2 vols. (Paris: Champ Vallon, 1990).

9. See John O'Malley, *The First Jesuits* (Cambridge, Mass.: Harvard University Press, 1993), pp. 288–290.

10. Winfried Trusen, "Rechtliche Grundlagen des Häresiebegriffs und des Ketzer-

verfahrens," in *Ketzerverfolgung im 16. und 17. Jahrhundert,* ed. S. Seidel Menchi (Wolfenbüttel: Harrassowitz, 1992), p. 3.

11. Thomas More, *A Dialogue Concerning Heresies* [1529], in *CWTM,* vol. 6, pt. 1, ed. Thomas M. C. Lawler, Germain Marc'hadour, and Richard C. Marius (New Haven: Yale University Press, 1981), p. 416/23–26.

12. John Calvin, *Declaration povr maintenir la vraye foy que tiennent tous Chrestiens de la Trinité des personnes en vn seul Dieu* . . . (Geneva: Jean Crespin, 1554), pp. 48–49.

13. See the London examples from 1515–1532 mentioned in Susan Brigden, *London and the Reformation* (Oxford: Clarendon Press, 1989), pp. 162–163.

14. Beginning with Thomas Cromwell's chancellorship, torture was widely practiced as well in England for treason trials, including ones involving Catholic priests and their protectors in the latter half of Elizabeth's reign. John Bellamy, *The Tudor Law of Treason (London: Routledge and Kegan Paul, 1979),* pp. 109–118; John H. Langbein, *Torture and the Law of Proof: Europe and England in the Ancien Régime* (Chicago: University of Chicago Press, 1976), pp. 73–139.

15. Raymond F. Mentzer, *Heresy Proceedings in Languedoc, 1500–1560* (Philadelphia: American Philosophical Society, 1984), p. 101. For Paris, Mentzer relies on Bernard Schnapper, "La justice criminelle rendue par le Parlement de Paris sous le règne de François Ier," *Revue historique de droit français et étranger,* 52 (1974), 258–265.

16. Suspects before the Languedoc Inquisition, for example, had to answer questions based on depositions they had not seen, without benefit of counsel, under strong presumption of guilt, and sometimes without being able to call witnesses on their behalf. Mentzer, *Heresy Proceedings in Languedoc,* pp. 73, 83, 93. In English ecclesiastical courts, suspects could be made to abjure heretical doctrines which they might not have held, without learning by whom they had been accused or who had witnessed against them. [John A. Guy], "The Legal Context of the Controversy: The Law of Heresy," in Thomas More, *The Debellation of Salem and Bizance* [1533], in *CWTM,* vol. 10, ed. Guy et al. (New Haven: Yale University Press, 1987), p. lv.

17. Not only legal records, but also martyrological sources, indicate many capitulations under pressure. Foxe, for example, listed well over one hundred people who abjured in England and Scotland "in King Henry's days after the first beginning of Luther," but gives only nineteen martyrs in these countries between 1520 and 1533. For the list of those who abjured, see Foxe 1563, pp. 418–420. For another example, see Wilhelm Reublin's acknowledgment of recantations in his accounts of the trials and executions of Michael Sattler and fellow Anabaptists in May 1527. *QGTS,* vol. 1, ed. Leonhard von Muralt and Walter Schmid (Zurich: S. Hirzel, 1952), p. 253. On dissimulation in general in the period, see Perez Zagorin, *Ways of Lying: Dissimulation, Persecution, and Conformity in Early Modern Europe* (Cambridge, Mass.: Harvard University Press, 1990).

18. Penry Williams, *The Tudor Regime* (Oxford: Oxford University Press, 1979), pp. 234–235; John Bellamy, *Crime and Public Order in England in the Later Middle Ages* (London: Routledge and Kegan Paul, 1973), pp. 181–185;

J. Scheerder, *De Inquisitie in de Nederlanden in de XVIe eeuw* (Antwerp: N. V. De Nederlandsche Boekhandel, 1944), p. 59; Langbein, *Torture and the Law of Proof,* pp. 27–28; Albrecht Keller, ed., *A Hangman's Diary, Being the Journal of Master Franz Schmidt, Public Executioner of Nuremberg, 1573–1617,* trans. C. A. Calvert and A. W. Gruner (New York: D. Appleton, 1928).

19. Mentzer, *Heresy Proceedings in Languedoc,* pp. 122 (quotation), 127.

20. See Pieter Spierenberg, *The Spectacle of Suffering: Executions and the Evolution of Repression: From a Preindustrial Metropolis to the European Experience* (Cambridge: Cambridge University Press, 1984); David Nicholls, "The Theatre of Martyrdom in the French Reformation," *P&P,* 121 (1988), 49–73; Richard van Dülmen, *Theatre of Horror: Crime and Punishment in Early Modern Germany,* trans. Elisabeth Neu (Cambridge: Polity Press; Cambridge, Mass.: Blackwell, 1990); Lionello Puppi, *Torment in Art: Pain, Violence, and Martyrdom* (New York: Rizzoli, 1991), pp. 11–69.

21. A[nthony] G[ilby], *An answer to the deuillish detection of Stephane Gardiner . . .* ([London? Steven Mierdman for John Day?] 1548), fol. 4.

22. In English Roman Catholicism, both Mary Tudor and her bishop of London, Edmund Bonner, for example, expressed their willingness to die, although neither was threatened with execution (Bonner, however, was imprisoned for most of Edward VI's reign). For Mary, see *Sources of English Constitutional History,* rev. ed., ed. Carl Stephenson and Frederick George Marcham, vol. 1 (New York: Harper and Row, 1972), pp. 334–335. In 1555, the year the first Marian Protestants were executed, Bonner quoted 2 Macc. 7:37 in his catechism: "We are ready rather to die, than to break or transgress the laws of God which our fathers kept." Quoted in Eamon Duffy, *The Stripping of the Altars: Traditional Religion in England, c. 1400– c. 1580* (New Haven: Yale University Press, 1992), p. 535.

23. More, *Dialogue Concerning Heresies,* p. 410/8–12. If intermittent abuses implied the wholesale abolition of heresy executions, Heinrich Bullinger argued, then the occasional misuse of wine would entail its complete prohibition. Bullinger, *Widertöufferen vrsprung,* fol. 170v.

24. See John Tedeschi, *The Prosecution of Heresy: Collected Studies on the Inquisition in Early Modern Italy* (Binghamton, N.Y.: Medieval and Renaissance Texts and Studies, 1991).

25. *ROPB,* vol. 2, p. 580. See also ibid., vol. 3, p. 69; and, for Jan. 1539, ibid., vol. 4, pp. 104–105.

26. *CDN,* vol. 4, pp. 80–81, 88–96.

27. *QGTS,* vol. 1, pp. 252–253; C. Arnold Snyder, *The Life and Thought of Michael Sattler* (Scottdale, Pa.: Herald Press, 1984), p. 104.

28. Claus-Peter Clasen, "The Anabaptists in Bavaria," *MQR,* 39 (1965), 252, 259 (quotation).

29. Mentzer, *Heresy Proceedings in Languedoc,* pp. 122, 169–170; William Monter, "Les exécutés pour hérésie par arrêt du Parlement de Paris (1523–1560)," *BSHPF,* 142 (1996), 220–222. Similarly, the infamous medieval inquisitor Bernard Gui sentenced to the stake only 42 (4.5 percent) of the 930 heretics whom he convicted during the course of his career. Given, "Inquisitors," p. 353.

30. Hans H. T. Stiasny, *Die strafrechtliche Verfolgung der Täufer in der freien Reichsstadt Köln 1529 bis 1618* (Münster: Aschendorff, 1962), pp. 55–59. Although the records of Cologne's *Hohen Gericht* are missing for this period, the tower secretary's sentences, where executions were always noted, record none. Ibid., p. 59.

31. Johan van de Wiele, "De inquisitierechtbank van Pieter Titelmans in de zestiende eeuw in Vlaanderen," *Bijdragen en mededelingen betreffende de geschiedenis der Nederlanden*, 97 (1982), 59–61. Van de Wiele notes "the enormous exertions that the inquisitor continuously made in order to get imprisoned heretics to abjure their beliefs." Ibid., p. 60.

32. Johan Decavele, *De dageraad van de Reformatie in Vlaanderen (1520–1565)*, vol. 1 (Brussels: Paleis der Academiën, 1975), pp. 26, 26 n. 77, 439, 440–442, 449. A. L. E. Verheyden's characterization of Titelmans is completely untenable: "Titelman considered it useless to combat the Reformation by trying to convert the heretics with religious discussions and disputes. His strategy allowed only one means to make a final purification; namely, brutal extermination." Verheyden, *Anabaptism in Flanders, 1530–1650: A Century of Struggle* (Scottdale, Pa.: Herald Press, 1961), p. 45. Decavele calls the traditional stereotype of Titelmans as a "bloodthirsty bogeyman" who let interrogated suspects be murdered without due process a "serious misrepresentation." *Dageraad*, vol. 1, p. 26. Indeed, "no one who had abjured his beliefs was ever handed over by the inquisitor to the secular authorities." Van de Wiele, "Inquisitierechtbank van Titelmans," p. 25. Verheyden's mistaken contention misses the real issue at hand—namely, what was to be done with heretics who refused every effort made to coax them back to orthodoxy.

33. *Eyn warhafftig geschicht wie Caspar Tawber, Burger zü Wienn in Oesterreich für ein Ketzer, unnd zü dem todt verurtaylt und auß gefürt worden ist* ([Nuremberg: Jobst Gutknecht], 1524), sigs. [A2, A4, B2r-v, B4v].

34. *Ein wunderliche geschycht newlich geschehen jn dem Hag in Holland . . . von einr frawen geheissen Wendelmut Clausen dochter, einr witwe, die do verprendt ist* [n.p., n.d.], repr. in *CDN*, vol. 5, p. 276.

35. Brigden, *London and the Reformation*, p. 607.

36. J. B. Cannaert, *Bydragen tot de kennis van het oude strafrecht in Vlaenderen* (Ghent: F. and E. Gyselynck, 1835), pp. 248–267; Louis Antoine de Rycker, "Een proces voor ketterij, te Gent. 1560–1561," *Jaarboek van het Willems-fonds* (Ghent: n.p., 1878), pp. 3–18. Soetken was executed on November 20 along with Martha Baert and Lijnken Pieters; the fourth woman, Lijnken Claeys, was beheaded on August 14, 1561. SAG, Boeken van den Crime, vol. 3 (1555–1561), fols. 237–240, 245v-246; A. L. E. Verheyden, *Het Gentsche martyrologium (1530–1595)* (Bruges: "De Tempel," 1945), pp. 26–27.

37. Bullinger, *Widertöufferen vrsprung*, fol. 168v.

38. Puppi, *Torment in Art*, pp. 30, 59. Donald Kelley misleadingly portrays the views of French authorities, too, as "an almost totalitarian, off-with-their-heads attitude towards heresy and disobedience that was hardly less intense than the fanaticism of the Huguenots themselves." Kelley, "Martyrs, Myths and the Massacre: The Background of St. Bartholomew," *American Historical Review*, 77 (1972), 1329.

39. Nicholls, "Theatre of Martyrdom," pp. 50–51; Brigden, *London and the Reformation*, p. 607. Mentzer makes the same point for the inquisition in Languedoc, in *Heresy Proceedings in Languedoc*, p. 71.

40. Puppi, *Torment in Art*, p. 56. Puppi pronounces his judgment: "the difference is only one of concept, not of substance." Ibid. Doubtless Sixtus V would have been surprised to learn that nothing substantive distinguished truth from error, nor martyrdom for Christ from death as a criminal. Puppi fails to ask what criteria might have prompted Sixtus V—and so many others—to draw such distinctions.

41. On the continuity of the legal basis for the execution of heretics among Protestant writers and magistrates, see Trusen, "Grundlagen," pp. 11–15.

42. Tilmann Smeling, Eck's Dominican colleague in Cologne, edited and expanded the work beginning in 1529; Eck amended later editions as well. See Johannes Eck, *Enchiridion locorum communium adversus Lutherum et alios hostes ecclesiae (1525–1543)*, ed. Pierre Fraenkel, vol. 34 of *Corpus Catholicorum* (Münster: Aschendorff, 1979), pp. 35*–42*. For a meticulous description of the many editions, see ibid., pp. 63*–96*. Some authors essentially reproduced long passages from the *Enchiridion* without acknowledging Eck. See, for example, Antoine Du Val, *Mirover des Calvinistes et armvre des Chrestiens, pour rembarrer les Lutheriens et nouueaux Euangelistes de Genéue: Renouuellé et augmenté . . .* (Paris: Nicolas Chesneau, 1562), fols. 15–31.

43. On Augustine's understanding of the Old Testament in this context, see Brown, "St. Augustine's Attitude," pp. 112 114.

44. Eck, *Enchiridion*, pp. 271–272. Following Eck, Du Val quoted the same passage. *Mirover des Calvinistes,* fol. 16.

45. Calvin, *Declaration*, pp. 44–46.

46. Eck, *Enchiridion*, p. 272.

47. *QGT*, vol. 1, *Herzogtum Württemberg*, ed. Gustav Bossert (Leipzig: Heinsius, 1930), p. 166/25–30. For another Protestant example of Deut. 13, 17, 18 and Lev. 24 applied to the execution of Anabaptists, see Bullinger, *Widertöufferen vrsprung,* fol. 171v.

48. The Houghton Library copy of Calvin's *Declaration* at Harvard University contains marginal comments in a sixteenth-century hand to this effect. Calvin noted the esteem for Moses despite his having delivered God's command about executing blasphemers. This reader wrote: "He was [a] Jew, but Calvin [is a] Christian; it's a different thing" [*Il etoit Juif Mais Calvin Chretien: cest autre chose*]. Calvin, *Declaration*, p. 49 (shelf mark *FC5.C1394.Eh554d).

49. Balthasar Hubmaier, *Uon ketzern vnd iren verbrennern . . .* ([Constance: Johann Schäffler], 1524), in idem, *Schriften*, ed. Gunnar Westin and Torsten Bergsten, vol. 9 of *QGT* (Gutersloh: Gerd Mohn, 1962), p. 97. See also Roland H. Bainton, "The Parable of the Tares as the Proof Text for Religious Liberty to the End of the Sixteenth Century," *Church History*, 1 (1932), 67–89.

50. Rhegius, "Leunebergischen bedenken," pp. 106 (with 1 Pet. 2), 108, 110 (with 1 Pet. 2), 112, 113 (with 1 Tim. 1:9).

51. Since the thirteenth century heresy had been judicially understood as a crime against God's majesty and honor (*crimen laesae maiestatis divinae*). Trusen, "Grundlagen," pp. 6–7.

52. Josse Damhouder, *La praticqve et enchiridion des cavses criminelles* . . . (Louvain: Estienne Wauters and Jean Bathen, 1554), p. 101. See also Du Val, *Mirover des Calvinistes,* fol. 17r-v; Calvin, *Declaration,* p. 16.

53. Du Val, *Mirover des Calvinistes,* fol. 17v.

54. Eck repeated the a fortiori argument about heretics and counterfeiters formulated by Aquinas in the *Summa Theologicae* (2a 2ae, q. 11, a. 3). Eck, *Enchiridion,* p. 276. See also Rhegius, "Leuneburgischen bedenken," p. 109; Calvin, *Declaration,* p. 42; Bullinger, *Widertöufferen vrsprung,* fol. 171r-v; and Huggarde, who during Mary Tudor's reign had asked the same question as Du Val: "If Emperors do punish theft, murder, rape, adultery, and perjury, why should they not as well punish heresy and sacrilege?" Huggarde, *The displaying of the Protestantes, and sondry their practises, with a description of diuers their abuses of late frequented* . . . (London: Robert Caly, 1556), fol. 44.

55. Trusen, "Grundlagen," pp. 11–15.

56. John Fisher, *A sermon had at Paulis by the commandment of the most reuerend father in god my lord legate* . . . (London: Thomas Berthelet, [1526?]), repr. in *The English Works of John Fisher,* ed. John E. B. Mayor, Early English Text Society, extra series, no. 27 (London: N. Trubner, 1876), p. 434. For the sermon's date and occasion, see Richard Rex, "The English Campaign against Luther in the 1520s," *Transactions of the Royal Historical Society,* 5th ser., 39 (1989), 102.

57. Thomas More, *The Confutation of Tyndale's Answer* [1532], in *CWTM,* vol. 8, pt. 1, ed. Louis A. Schuster et al. (New Haven: Yale University Press, 1973), p. 38/21–22. In his last extant letter to Erasmus (ca. June 1533), More confirmed his attitude towards heretics: "As to the statement in my Epitaph that I was a source of trouble to heretics—I wrote that with deep feeling [*hoc ambitiose feci*]. I find that breed of men absolutely loathsome, so much so that, unless they regain their senses, I want to be as hateful to them as anyone can possibly be; for my increasing experience with those men frightens me with the thought of what the world will suffer at their hands." *St. Thomas More: Selected Letters,* ed. Elizabeth Frances Rogers (New Haven: Yale University Press, 1961), p. 180 (Rogers's trans.). For the Latin, see *Opus epistolarum Des. Erasmi Roterodami,* vol. 10, 1532–1534, ed. P. S. Allen (Oxford: Clarendon Press, 1941), no. 2831, p. 260/60–64.

58. Eck, *Enchiridion,* pp. 272, 273–274; Du Val, *Mirover des Calvinistes,* fol. 16v; Rhegius, "Leunebergischen bedenken," pp. 106–107; Huggarde, *Displaying of the Protestantes,* fol. 61; Bullinger, *Widertöufferen vrsprung,* fol. 172v. For Jerome's original use of the rancid flesh image, see his commentary on Gal. 5:9 in *PL,* vol. 26, col. 430.

59. Latimer, sermon on Phil. 3:17–18, repr. in *Sermons by Hugh Latimer, Sometime Bishop of Worcester, Martyr, 1555,* ed. George Elwes Corrie (Cambridge: Cambridge University Press, 1844), p. 525.

60. Fisher, *Sermon had at Paulis,* p. 434.

61. John Christoferson, *An exhortation to all menne to take hede and beware of rebellion* . . . (London: John Cawood, 1554), sig. Y6v. Christoferson was a product of Fisher's college, St. John's, Cambridge. *DNB,* vol. 4, p. 293.

62. Isambert, vol. 13, p. 136.

63. *ROPB,* vol. 4, p. 228.

64. Calvin, *Declaration,* pp. 35–36.

65. Gina Alexander, "Bonner and the Marian Persecutions," *History,* 60 (1975), 388–390.

66. Edmund Bonner, *Homelies sette forth by the righte reuerende father in God, Edmunds Byshop of London . . .* (London: John Cawood, 1555), fol. 26v.

67. Eck, *Enchiridion,* p. 274; Du Val, *Mirover des Calvinistes,* fols. 17v–18. Pole held this view even before returning to England to become Mary's Archbishop of Canterbury. See Dermot Fenlon, *Heresy and Obedience in Tridentine Italy: Cardinal Pole and the Counter Reformation* (Cambridge: Cambridge University Press, 1972), pp. 252–253, 253 n. 1.

68. "As for David George [Joris], and Servete the Arian, and such other the like, they were yours, M. Harding, they were not of us. You brought them up, the one in Spain, the other in Flanders. We detected their heresies, and not you. We arraigned them. We condemned them. We put them to the execution of the laws. It seemeth very much to call them our brothers, because we burnt them." John Jewel, *An Answer to a Certain Book Lately Set Forth by M. Harding, and Entituled, A Confutation of the Apology of the Church of England* [1567], repr. in *The Works of John Jewel,* ed. John Ayre, vol. 3 (Cambridge: Cambridge University Press, 1848), p. 188.

69. Clasen, "Anabaptists in Bavaria," pp. 244–252.

70. More, *Dialogue Concerning Heresies,* p. 408/30–34; see also pp. 415/32–416/9.

71. Eck, *Enchiridion,* p. 274; Du Val, *Mirover des Calvinistes,* fol. 18. For Jerome's original passage, see his commentary on Gal. 5:9, in *PL,* vol. 26, col. 430.

72. Isambert, vol. 13, p. 199.

73. N. M. Sutherland, *The Huguenot Struggle for Recognition* (New Haven: Yale University Press, 1980), pp. 104–105, 113–114, 133–135; Isambert, vol. 14, pp. 24–26, 31–33, 124–129. Geoffrey Parker, *The Dutch Revolt* (1977; reprint Harmondsworth: Penguin, 1981), pp. 70–71.

74. Calvin, *Declaration,* pp. 22–23. Lecler was surprised by Calvin's position, apparently because he did not see that whether such an argument was articulated by Protestants of Catholics, it depended on the distinction between true and false doctrine, not on any general right or obligation of magistrates to prosecute people who offended against established religion. Lecler, *Toleration and the Reformation,* vol. 1, p. 334.

75. Stanislaus Hosius, *A Most Excellent Treatise of the begynnyng of heresyes in oure tyme . . . ,* trans. Richard Shacklock (Antwerp: Aeg Diest, 1565), fol. 47r-v. The Latin original appeared in 1559. For a brief sketch of Hosius's life and theology, see George H. Williams, "Stanislaus Hosius (1504–1579)," in *Shapers of Religious Traditions in Germany, Switzerland, and Poland,* ed. Jill Raitt (New Haven: Yale University Press, 1981), pp. 157–174.

76. Thomas Hide, *A Consolatorie Epistle to the afflicted Catholikes: set foorth by Thomas Hide Priest* ([East Ham: Stephen Brinkley], 1580), sig. E1r-v, quotation on E1v.

77. Ibid., sig. E2v (my emphasis). See also William Allen's argument contrasting the legitimate prosecution of Marian Protestants with the unjust persecution of

Elizabethan Catholics, in his *Trve, Sincere, and Modest Defence, of English Catholiqves that Svffer for Their Faith* . . . [Rouen: Robert Parsons's press, 1584], pp. 34–58. When missionary priest Anthony Middleton was interrogated in May 1590, he alleged that the executions of Marian Protestants had been charitably enacted "by a law made and received and put in execution by all Princes Christian whatsoever" after multiple attempts to "reduce them to their mother Catholic Church," whereas Elizabethan Catholics were "butchered by a peculiar law made by herself and never heard of before, without all charity." John Hungerford Pollen, ed., *Unpublished Documents Relating to the English Martyrs,* vol. 1, 1584–1603, vol. 5 of CRS (London: Catholic Record Society, 1908), p. 185.

78. More, *Dialogue Concerning Heresies,* pp. 406–407, 409.

79. For the quoted phrase, see Thomas A. Brady, Jr., *The Politics of the Reformation in Germany: Jacob Sturm (1489–1553) of Strasbourg* (Atlantic Highlands, N.J.: Humanities Press, 1997), p. 3.

80. Isambert, vol. 12, p. 819. See also the 1551 comments by the Paris Parlement, issued shortly after the Edict of Châteaubriand, in ibid., vol. 13, pp. 207–208.

81. Justus Menius, *Wie ein iglicher Christ gegen allerley lere, gut vnd böse nach Gottes befelh, sich gebürlich halten sol* (Wittenberg: Nickel Schirlentz, 1538), sig. D4v; Du Val, *Mirover des Calvinistes,* fols. 28v-29.

82. Huggarde, *Displaying,* fols. 60–61, quotation on 60v–61. The "cutting off" referred to derives from Tit. 3:10–11, combined with 1 Tim. 1:8–11 (about the legitimate use of the law). Ibid., fol. 59r-v. Smeling included this Augustinian reading of the same parable beginning in the 1529 edition of Eck's *Enchiridion.* Eck, *Enchiridion,* p. 278. For Augustine's original passage, see his *Contra epistolam Parmeniani,* 3.13, in *PL,* vol. 43, col. 92.

83. Calvin, *Declaration,* p. 36. Urbanus Rhegius used Gal. 5:19–21 to support the view that "heresy is also reckoned among the fruits of the flesh," and as such was subject to punishment by the sword. Rhegius, "Leunebergischen bedenken," p. 109. "Heresy" [*ketzrei*] is not explicitly mentioned in Gal. 5:19–21; by using it, Rhegius implied that it had the same force as "idolatry." Luther translated εἰδωλολατρία [Latin Vulgate: *idolorum servitus*] as "abgötterey" [idolatry], not "Ketzerei." Luther, *WA Deutsche Bibel* 7, p. 187.

84. Eck, *Enchiridion,* pp. 272–273; Calvin, *Declaration,* p. 35; Bullinger, *Widertöufferen vrsprung,* fol. 168v. According to Bullinger, the fact that Ananias and Sapphira died as the result of spoken words rather than the sword was irrelevant, for "to kill is to kill." Ibid., fol. 172.

85. More, *Dialogue Concerning Heresies,* pp. 146/30–147/22, quotations at lines 147/1, 20–21, 3–4. See also pp. 153/9–11, 239/11–20, 355/15–20.

86. Sebastian Castellio, *De haereticis an sint persequendi et omnino quomodo sit cum eis agendum* . . . ([Basel: Johannes Oporinus], 1554), facsimile reprint with introduction by Sape van der Woude (Geneva: E. Droz, 1954), pp. 122–123.

87. Calvin, *Declaration,* p. 17. In writing to Poitiers's Reformed Protestants on February 20, 1555, Calvin derided Castellio's "belle maxime" that fundamental Christian doctrines might be subject to disputation and scripture itself a "nez de cire." *CO* 15, no. 2118, col. 441.

88. For a more detailed discussion of the legal and institutional channels of prosecution in France, the Low Countries, and England, see my "Anathema of Compromise: Christian Martyrdom in Early Modern Europe," vol. 1 (Ph.D. diss., Princeton University, 1996), pp. 208–243.

89. The most important sources for this paragraph are Isambert, vols. 12–14; Barbara Diefendorf, *Beneath the Cross: Catholics and Huguenots in Sixteenth-Century Paris* (New York: Oxford University Press, 1991); James K. Farge, *Orthodoxy and Reform in Early Reformation France: The Faculty of Theology of Paris, 1500–1543* (Leiden: E. J. Brill, 1985); P. Imbart de la Tour, *Les origines de la Réforme*, vol. 3, *L'Évangelisme (1521–1538)* (Paris: Hachette, 1914); R. J. Knecht, *Francis I* (Cambridge: Cambridge University Press, 1982); and Sutherland, *Huguenot Struggle*.

90. On the basis of careful archival research, William Monter has discovered that executions for heresy surged in 1544 and continued through 1549, only a minority of which were recorded by Crespin. Monter, "Parlement de Paris," pp. 219–222, and more extensively, idem, *Judging the French Reformation* (Cambridge, Mass.: Harvard University Press, 1999). I am grateful to Professor Monter for allowing me to read his book in manuscript.

91. This paragraph is based most importantly on *CDN*, vols. 4–5; *DAN*, vol. 5, *Amsterdam (1531–1536)*, ed. A. F. Mellink (Leiden: E. J. Brill, 1985); *ROPB*, vols. 2–6; Alastair Duke, "Salvation by Coercion: The Controversy Surrounding the 'Inquisition' in the Low Countries on the Eve of the Revolt," in *Reformation and Revolt in the Low Countries* (London: Hambledon Press, 1990), pp. 152–174; Parker, *Dutch Revolt*; Scheerder, *Inquisitie*; James D. Tracy, "Heresy Law and Centralization under Mary of Hungary: Conflict between the Council of Holland and the Central Government over the Enforcement of Charles V's Placards," *ARG*, 73 (1982), 284–307; idem, *Holland under Habsburg Rule, 1506–1566: The Formation of a Body Politic* (Berkeley: University of California Press, 1990); and Paul E. Valvekens, *De Inquisitie in de Nederlanden der zestiende eeuw* (Brussels: De Kinkhoren, 1949).

92. [Louis P.] Gachard, *Correspondance de Philippe II sur les affaires des Pays-Bas*, vol. 1 (Brussels: Muquardt, 1848), August 12, 1566, no. 448, p. 446.

93. For this paragraph, I have relied primarily upon *Tudor Royal Proclamations*, 3 vols., ed. Paul L. Hughes and James F. Larkin (New Haven: Yale University Press, 1964–1969); Bellamy, *Tudor Law of Treason*; Brigden, *London and the Reformation*; Christopher Haigh, *English Reformations: Religion, Politics, and Society under the Tudors* (Oxford: Clarendon Press, 1993); I. B. Horst, *The Radical Brethren: Anabaptism and the English Reformation to 1558* (Nieuwkoop: De Graaf, 1972); Geoffrey F. Nuttall, "The English Martyrs 1535–1680: A Statistical Review," *JEH*, 22 (1971), 191–197; Rex, "English Campaign"; and J. J. Scarisbrick, *Henry VIII* (Berkeley: University of California Press, 1968).

94. On Forest, see Peter Marshall, "Papist as Heretic: The Burning of John Forest, 1538," *Historical Journal*, 41 (1998), 351–374.

95. The same was true in medieval Languedoc. Given, "Inquisitors," pp. 356–358.

96. Alexander, "Bonner and the Marian Persecutions," p. 381.
97. *Acts of the Privy Council of England,* new series, vol. 6, 1556–1558, ed. John Roche Dasent (London: H. M. Stationery Office, 1893), p. 361. In July 1557 the Privy Council sent the same message to the sheriffs of Essex, Kent, Suffolk, and Staffordshire, the mayor of Rochester, and the bailiffs of Colchester. Ibid., p. 135. Haigh refers to these and other examples illustrating the erratic, regional variability of heresy prosecution in Mary's reign, in *English Reformations,* p. 232.
98. *CO* 15, February 10, 1554, no. 1904, col. 20. Lecler discusses this letter and Zerkinden's relatively moderate application of antiheresy laws in *Toleration and the Reformation,* vol. 1, pp. 335–336. Zerkinden seems not to have grasped Calvin's explicit distinctions among different degrees of error. Servetus could scarcely have been characterized as a "simple misbeliever" by anyone.
99. Isambert, vol. 13, p. 496.
100. A. F. Mellink, "Anabaptism at Amsterdam after Munster," in *The Dutch Dissenters: A Critical Companion to Their History and Ideas,* ed. I. B. Horst (Leiden: E. J. Brill, 1986), pp. 138–139; *DAN,* vol. 2, *Amsterdam (1536–1578),* pp. xvii-xviii.
101. Claus-Peter Clasen, *Anabaptism: A Social History, 1525–1618* (Ithaca: Cornell University Press, 1972), pp. 382–383.
102. Mentzer, *Heresy Proceedings in Languedoc,* p. 103.
103. David Nicholls, "The Nature of Popular Heresy in France, 1520–1542," *Historical Journal,* 26 (1983), 263.
104. Verheyden, *Gentsche martyrologium,* pp. 13–18; Decavele, *Dageraad,* vol. 1, p. 439. See also Scheerder, *Inquisitie,* p. 65.
105. Decavele, *Dageraad,* vol. 1, pp. 449, 449 n. 69.
106. John Oyer, *Lutheran Reformers against Anabaptists: Luther, Melanchthon and Menius and the Anabaptists of Central Germany* (The Hague: Martinus Nijhoff, 1964), pp. 59–60.
107. James Martin Estes, *Christian Magistrate and State Church: The Reforming Career of Johannes Brenz* (Toronto: Toronto University Press, 1982), p. 135.
108. Ibid., pp. 128–129; Oyer, *Lutheran Reformers against Anabaptists,* pp. 136–138, 142–144, 154–155.
109. CRS, vol. 5, pp. 102–103; Bellamy, *Tudor Law of Treason,* pp. 119–120.
110. The proportion of women ranges from about one-third of the total in van Braght, to one-fifth (of the Marian martyrs) in Foxe, 13 percent in the 1570 edition of Crespin, and one-tenth in Rabus, to just 4 of the 314 English Catholics recognized as saints, blessed, or venerable for the period 1535–1680. See Jeannine E. Olson, "Jean Crespin, Humanist Printer among the Reformation Martyrologists," in *The Harvest of Humanism in Central Europe: Essays in Honor of Lewis W. Spitz,* ed. Manfred P. Fleischer (St. Louis: Concordia, 1992), p. 334; Nuttall, "English Martyrs," p. 194.
111. CRS, vol. 5, p. 200.
112. Olson, "Jean Crespin," p. 227; Joan Davies, "Persecution and Protestantism: Toulouse, 1562–1575," *Historical Journal,* 22 (1979), 48–49; I. M. J. Hoog, *De martelaars der hervorming in Nederland tot 1566* (Schiedam: H. A. M. Roelants, 1885), p. 93.

113. Decavele, *Dageraad*, vol. 1, p. 439.

114. Alexander, "Bonner and the Marian Persecutions," p. 381.

115. Duke, "Salvation by Coercion," pp. 159, 170.

116. Tracy, *Holland under Hapsburg Rule*, pp. 200–202; Alastair Duke, "Building Heaven in Hell's Despite: The Early History of the Reformation in the Towns of the Low Countries," in *Reformation and Revolt*, p. 76.

117. See Nicholls, "Theatre of Martyrdom," pp. 65, 72–73. For the same dynamic in Scotland, where by 1558 the prosecutorial system had entirely broken down, see Jane E. A. Dawson, "The Scottish Reformation and the Theatre of Martyrdom," in *Martyrs and Martyrologies*, ed. Diana Wood, vol. 30 of *Studies in Church History* (Oxford: Blackwell, 1993), pp. 259–270.

4. The Willingness to Die

1. The story is taken from Foxe 1563, pp. 1619–1621. All quotations are from these pages. Foxe streamlined the paragraphing of the story in 1570, slightly altered a few words and phrases, and added two biographical details: that Lewis had previously been married to a man named Appleby before wedding Thomas Lewis of Manchester, and that the second friend who accompanied her to the stake was Augustine Bernher. Foxe 1570, vol. 2, pp. 2206–2208. Otherwise, the 1563 and 1570 accounts are the same in every respect. The 1583 edition follows the 1570 edition almost verbatim, with only three words altered. Compare Foxe 1570, vol. 2, pp. 2206–2208, with Foxe 1583, vol. 2, pp. 2012–2013. On Ralph Baynes, Lewis's questioner, see *DNB*, vol. 3, p. 456.

2. The "stuff" referred to was almost certainly gunpowder, which was frequently used in executions to bring immediate death rather than prolonging the agony. The final sentence quoted varies slightly in Foxe 1570, p. 2207, the most important difference being that the later version has Lewis lifting her hands "towards heaven" rather than "towards God."

3. Seymour Byman, "Ritualistic Acts and Compulsive Behavior: The Pattern of Tudor Martyrdom," *American Historical Review*, 83 (1978), 625, 626, 627.

4. Ignoring the deep suspicion of innovation and originality common in the sixteenth century, Byman writes that Tudor martyrs intoned "the proper words and gestures they believed Jesus might have used during His martyrdom. There was no need to be original; they merely had to re-enact the battle against Satan that had been fought a millennium and a half before." Ibid., p. 636; see also p. 642. Their point was precisely not to be original, but to conform as nearly as possible to Christ and other heroic predecessors. Byman's reading of John Bradford's prayer routine is equally misguided: "Since the anxiety was so great, he expanded the ritualistic mechanism to include communal prayer. Now he needed the reassurance of others to maintain his self-esteem" (ibid., p. 634)—as if an ardent Protestant like Bradford was seeking "self-esteem" rather than proper understanding of himself as a sinner before God! Communal prayer was an integral part of Christian religiosity in early modern Europe, not the psychological crutch of people riddled with pathological anxiety.

5. Richard Marius, *Thomas More: A Biography* (New York: Alfred A. Knopf, 1984), pp. 517–518.

6. Marius, *Thomas More,* p. xxii. Marius is technically correct: this *may* indeed be argued—but not if the distinction between believing and wanting to believe means anything at all. How then could one distinguish between martyrs who resisted all attempts to dissuade them from views they did not believe but only "wanted to believe," and martyrs who resisted in exactly the same way but believed in fact? Marius simply transforms *his* incomprehension into a distorting statement about More, consistent with his remark that "most of our lives have been robbed of any sense of the sacred, and when we search for it, we are like color-blind people looking for green." Ibid., p. 517, and more generally, pp. 515–520. Alastair Fox indulges in the same sort of contentious projection: "as with Shelley, one feels, More had to die to satisfy the requirements of his own myth." Fox, *Thomas More: History and Providence* (New Haven: Yale University Press, 1982), p. 252.

7. John Frith, *A boke made by John Frith prisoner in the tower of London, answeringe vnto M[.] mores lettur* . . . ([Antwerp: Christoffel Ruremond's widow?], 1533), sigs. [L6v-L7].

8. Penny Roberts, "Martyrologies and Martyrs in the French Reformation: Heretics to Subversives in Troyes," in *Martyrs and Martyrologies,* ed. Diana Wood, vol. 30 of *Studies in Church History* (Oxford: Blackwell, 1993), p. 228.

9. Crucial verses in Matthew about the willingness to die rather than deny Christ (Matt. 10:28–33) come almost immediately after the exhortation to flee persecution: "When they persecute you in one town, flee to the next" (Matt. 10:23). Therefore Christians had good reason to think about the two together and to base the legitimacy of flight on Christ's own words, as long as in so doing they did not overtly deny him.

10. *QGTS,* vol. 1, *Zürich,* ed. Leonhard von Muralt and Walter Schmid (Zurich: Theologischer Verlag, 1952), p. 176. For the escape from prison, see ibid., pp. 191–193.

11. In *Een Testament ghemaecket by Jan Gheertsen, Gheuanghen wesende in Sgreuen Haeghe, die welcke aldaer omme het ghetuychenisse Jhesu Christi, verbrandt is* . . . [n.p., ca. 1566], fols. 15v–16.

12. [William Allen], *Briefe Historie of the Gloriovs Martyrdom of XII. Reverend Priests* . . . ([Rheims: Jean Foigny], 1582), sig. f3.

13. Willem Hessels van Est, *Histoire veritable des bienhevrevx martyrs de Gorcum en Hollande* . . . (Douai: Marc Wyon, 1618), pp. 421, 423. Hessels van Est's work was first published, in Latin, in 1603.

14. Alphonsus Agazzari to Allen, in *The Letters and Memorials of William Cardinal Allen (1532–1594),* ed. Thomas F. Knox (London: David Nutt, 1882), June 13, 1579, no. 236, p. 398. Still more than four months away from his execution in London, Luke Kirby wrote from prison that he was afraid "lest our unworthiness of that excellent perfection and crown of martyrdom, shall procure us a longer life." [Allen], *Briefe Historie,* sig. B4v.

15. Marie de l'Incarnation, *Correspondance,* ed. G. Oury (Solesmes: Abbaye Saint-Pierre, 1971), Sept. 4, 1641, no. 56, p. 133.

16. David Bagchi, "Luther and the Problem of Martyrdom," in *Martyrs and Martyrologies,* ed. Wood, p. 212.

17. [Willem Voldersgraft (Gnapheus)], *Een suuerlicke ende seer schoone disputacie,*

welcke gheschiet is in den Haghe in Hollant, tusschen die kettermeesters ende eenen christelijcken priester ghenaemt Jan van Woorden . . . (n.p., ca.1526), repr. in *CDN*, vol. 4, pp. 479, 487, 488.

18. *Calendar of State Papers and Manuscripts, Relating to English Affairs, Existing in the Archives and Collections of Venice, and in Other Libraries of Northern Italy*, vol. 6, pt. 1, ed. Rawdon Brown (London: H.M. Stationery Office, 1877), no. 489, p. 455 (Brown's trans. from the Italian original).

19. Van Haemstede 1559, p. 448.

20. These two different ways of dying are combined under the term "voluntary death" by Arthur J. Droge and James D. Tabor in their recent study of martyrdom and suicide in antiquity: "By this term we mean to describe the act resulting from an individual's intentional decision to die, either by his own agency, by another's, or by contriving the circumstances in which death is the known, ineluctable result." Droge and Tabor, *A Noble Death: Suicide and Martyrdom among Christians and Jews in Antiquity* (San Francisco: Harper Collins, 1992), p. 4; see also pp. 156, 187–188. Distinctions based on agency are crucial in a consideration of the early modern period; it seems to me that Droge and Tabor too easily elide them for antiquity as well.

21. Foxe, however, mentioned several ancient martyrs who took their own lives in his discussion of James Hales, a judge who drowned himself in 1555 after being reconciled to the Roman Catholic church. Hales had laudably recognized his sinful capitulation, but he wrongly took his own life as a result. Foxe accordingly placed Hales in an intermediate category between the martyrs and the lost—an impulse toward a Protestant recognition of purgatory? Foxe 1563, pp. 1116–1117.

22. [Voldersgraft], *Suuerlicke disputacie*, in *CDN*, vol. 4, p. 491.

23. Thomas More, *Dialogue of Comfort against Tribulation*, in *CWTM*, vol. 12, ed. Louis L. Martz and Frank Manley (New Haven: Yale University Press, 1976), p. 12/8–24 (my emphases).

24. *Canons and Decrees of the Council of Trent*, ed. H. J. Schroeder (St. Louis: B. Herder, 1941), p. 296.

25. For example, the preface to the Dutch Anabaptist martyrology *The Sacrifice unto the Lord* contains fifty-four scriptural references on four tiny pages. A letter from Claesken Gaeledochter in the same collection includes one sentence with twelve marginal biblical citations, which is not atypical. *OH*, in *BRN*, vol. 2, pp. 53–55, 334.

26. *OL*, vol. 2, Aug. 24, 1554, no. 353, p. 750.

27. *The Bible and Holy Scriptvres Conteyned in the Olde and Newe Testament* . . . (Geneva: Rowland Hall, 1560), New Testament, fol. 2.

28. In Herminjard, vol. 1, pp. 135–136 (italics in original).

29. William Tyndale, *The Obedience of a Christen man and how Christen rulers ought to governe* . . . ([Antwerp: Jacob Hoochstraten], 1528), fol. 4v.

30. More, *Dialogue of Comfort*, pp. 230/31–231/6 (italics in original).

31. Henrick Alewijnsz, *Een vaderlijck Adieu, Testament ende sorchuuldighe onderwijsinge wt der H. Schrift, ghemaeckt door Henrick Alewijnsz* . . . ([Amsterdam]: Nicholas Biestkens, 1578), sig. A6.

32. For an extensive compilation of New Testament passages about the endurance

of persecution and suffering, see my "Anathema of Compromise: Christian Martyrdom in Early Modern Europe," vol. 3 (Ph.D. diss., Princeton University, 1996), pp. 1054–1066.

33. Dutch Anabaptist Jeronimus Segers specifically invoked this verse in a letter to his wife, with reference to the endurance of persecution and the way in which God had delivered his own people from dire straits. *OH,* in *BRN,* vol. 2, p. 165.

34. More, *Dialogue of Comfort,* p. 12/22–24.

35. Henri-Léonard Bordier, ed., *Le chansonnier Huguenot du XVIe siècle,* vol. 2 (Paris: Librairie Tross, 1870), pp. 368–369.

36. *OL,* vol. 2, Apr. 3, 1554, no. 241, p. 515.

37. Barret to Alphonsus Agazzari, August 2, 1584, in *Letters of William Allen and Richard Barret, 1572–1598,* ed. P. Renold, vol. 58 of CRS (Oxford: Catholic Record Society, 1967), no. 41, p. 105.

38. Foxe 1563, pp. 1619–1621. For a useful discussion of the Marian Protestant community under affliction, see John R. Knott, *Discourses of Martyrdom in English Literature, 1563–1694* (Cambridge: Cambridge University Press, 1993), pp. 84–116.

39. Luther, *Von Er Lenhard Keiser ynn Beyern vmb des Euangelij willen verbrandt Eine selige geschicht* (Wittenberg: Hans Lufft, 1528 [1527]), in *WA* 23, p. 473/11–16. Luther's letter also appeared in another contemporary pamphlet, with slight variations in the text that suggest different manuscript copies. See *Histori oder dz warhafftig geschicht, des leydens vnd sterbens Lienhart Keysers seligen . . .* [n.p., 1527], sig. B1r-v.

40. Calvin, June 10, 1552, *CO* 14, no. 1631, cols. 331–334 (all the following letters are from this volume); no. 1679, 423–425; no. 1680, 425–428; no. 1700, 469–471; no. 1708 (Mar. 7, 1553), 490–492; no. 1746, 544–547; no. 1754, 561–564; no. 1776 (Aug. 22, 1553), 593–596. Several of these letters appeared in Crespin's martyrology beginning with the 1555 edition. See Crespin 1555, pp. 721–725, 725–728, [729]-733, 738–741, 741–743.

41. Foxe 1563, pp. 520, 521 (my emphasis). Writing from continental exile in 1544, English Protestant George Joye also had a strong sense of the international community of the persecuted. He applied Heb. 13:3 to the present: "if one of us suffer for Christ's sake in England, all the true brethren and sisters in the same land, in France, in Germany or elsewhere, suffer the same." G[eorge] J[oye], *A present consolation for the sufferers of persecucion for rughtwysenes* ([Antwerp: S. Mierdman], 1544), sig. [E5r-v]. Heb. 13:3: "Remember those who are in prison, as though you were in prison with them; those who are being tortured, as though you yourselves were being tortured."

42. Crespin 1564, p. 162. Crespin erroneously gives 1541 rather than 1544 as the year of Jusbergh's execution. For the correct date (January 7, 1544), see ARB, Rekenkamer, vol. 12,531, fol. 5v; A. L. E. Verheyden, *Le martyrologe courtraisien et le martyrologe bruxellois* (Vilvorde: R. Allecourt, 1950), p. 63.

43. Crespin 1564, pp. 162–163. Tielemans was executed in Brussels on January 27, 1544. See ARB, MS 14,896–14,898, fol. 132v (new foliation numbers). Verheyden omits one and a half lines in his transcription of this passage about Tielemans's execution in his *Martyrologe courtraisien et bruxellois,* p. 64. Nei-

ther Jusbergh's nor Tielemans's words should be taken as verbatim transcripts; nor are prison events technically part of the martyrs' public behavior. But considering everything else we know about the martyrs, there is no reason to doubt the substance of either their words or actions as reported by Crespin.

44. Foxe 1563, pp. 1142, 1250, 1468.

45. Van Haemstede 1559, p. 446. For their execution sentence, see SAA, Vierschaar, V147 (1555–1559), fols. 97v–98; *AA,* vol. 8, pp. 457, 472.

46. Crespin 1564, p. 965.

47. *QGTS,* vol. 1, p. 55. Brötli also requested that they send him a Bible, urged them to stand firm, and praised the constancy of other leaders among the early Swiss Brethren, including Felix Mantz, Jörg Blaurock, and Conrad Grebel.

48. [Michael Sattler], *Brüderlich vereynigung etzlicher kinder Gottes, sieben Artickel betreffend. Item, Eyn sendtbrieff Michael Satlers, in eyn gemeyn Gottes . . .* ([Strasbourg: Jacob Cammerlander], 1533), ed. Walter Köhler, repr. in *Flugschriften aus den ersten Jahren der Reformation,* ed. Otto Clement, vol. 2 (Leipzig: Rudolf Haupt, 1908), p. 319. On Sattler's arrest and his role at Schleitheim, see C. Arnold Snyder, *The Life and Thought of Michael Sattler* (Scottdale, Pa.: Herald Press, 1984), pp. 97–100.

49. Hohenwart was a parish where Anabaptists from the Tirol often stopped on the trek to Moravia. This particular group to whom Huter wrote was led by Bastel Glaser, who was executed in January 1538. Jacob Hutter, *Brotherly Faithfulness: Epistles from a Time of Persecution* (Rifton, N.Y.: Plough Publishing, 1979), p. 49; Werner O. Packull, *Hutterite Beginnings: Communitarian Experiments during the Reformation* (Baltimore: The Johns Hopkins University Press, 1995), pp. 270, 392 n. 75.

50. In Hans Fischer, *Jakob Huter: Leben, Froemmigkeit, Briefe* (Newton, Kans.: Mennonite Publication Office, 1956), p. 22.

51. Huter told them that the kingdom of heaven was theirs (Matt. 5:10–12); as Christ's own they faced persecution (John 16:33); through much pain and tribulation they must enter the kingdom of God (Acts 14:22), and through suffering with Christ they would become co-heirs with him (Rom. 8:17); to them had been granted the opportunity not only to believe in Christ, but also to suffer for him (Phil. 1:29–30); it was a grace from God when they suffered for doing right (1 Pet. 2:20, 1 Pet. 4:14); James called those blessed who endured chastisement (James 5:11); Paul highly esteemed persecutions suffered for Christ (2 Cor. 12:9–10); both Peter and James said it was a joy to suffer as a Christian (1 Pet. 4:15–16, James 1:2); and Christ said that the one who endures to the end will be saved (Matt. 24:13). In Fischer, *Jakob Huter,* pp. 23–24.

52. John Klassen gives numerous examples of spousal affection and concern among Anabaptist martyrs, although without particularly emphasizing the centrality of scripture in their letters. Klassen, "Women and the Family among Dutch Anabaptist Martyrs," *MQR,* 60 (1986), 556–564.

53. *OH,* in *BRN,* vol. 2, pp. 126–134, 144–167, 170–173, specific verses on p. 156. All their letters are loaded with biblical quotations and allusions. For their execution sentences, issued on September 1, 1551 (Segers) and February

19, 1552 (Aerts), see SAA, Vierschaar, V146 (1548–1554), fols. 50v, 61; *AA*, vol. 8, pp. 402, 409.

54. In *Sommige belijdinghen schriftlijcke Sentbrieuen, ende Testamenten geschreuen door Jan Wouterszoon van Cuyck . . .* (n.p., 1579), sigs. [K8] (quotation), [K8v]–L1v. Among the passages Jan quotes, paraphrases, or draws on in this particular string, all of which are noted in the margins (some incorrectly), are Ps. 22:6, Isa. 53:3, Phil. 2:6,8, 1 Pet. 4:1–2, 2 Tim. 3:12, Heb. 11:37, Ps. 7:1, and Ps. 31:4. This is typical of the way in which disparate texts were understood topically and applied to circumstances of persecution in the sixteenth century.

55. In Samuel Cramer, "Het eigenhandig laatst adieu van Maeyken Wens aan haar kind," *DB*, 44 (1904), 119–120, quotation on 119.

56. *Een Testament, gemaeckt by Soetken van den Houte, het welcke sy binnen Gendt in Ulaenderen metten Doodt beuesticht heeft . . .* [Rees: Dirck Wylicx van Zanten, ca. 1582], sigs. [B7v], C2v (she says specifically that this letter strengthened her: "my mede gesterckt hebt"). *Tgetuygenisse ende de nae-ghelaeten Schriften van den Godvruchtigen Christiaen Rijcen, die nu in dese laetste dagen een ghetrouwe Getuyghe binnen Hontschoote in Vlaenderen is gheweest . . .* (Haarlem: Gillis Rooman for Franchoys Soete, 1588), pp. 56, 64, 88. Mayken Boosers thanked her parents for having remembered and written her in prison, "on account of which I greatly rejoiced." *OH*, in *BRN*, vol. 2, p. 413.

57. Rijcen, *Schriften*, p. 56.

58. *OH*, in *BRN*, vol. 2, p. 83. Jan Claes requested this of his wife before his execution in Amsterdam in 1544. For his death sentence, see *DAN*, vol. 2, *Amsterdam (1536–1578)*, ed. A. F. Mellink (Leiden: E. J. Brill, 1980), pp. 47–48.

59. V[alerius] S[chool] M[eester], *Proba fidei: Oft, de Proeue des Gheloofs. Waerinne een yegelijck mensche, van wat Opinie dat hy sy, van woorde te woorde, en wercken te wercken, hem proeuen mach, oft hy int Ghelooue recht staet oft niet . . .* (n.p., 1569), fol. 30v. On Valerius, see S. Voolstra, "Valerius Schoolmeester (overleden omstreeks 1569): Leven en leer van een menniste hageprediker in Zeeland in de reformatietijd," in *Rond de kerk in Zeeland: Derde verzameling bijdragen van de Vereniging voor Nederlandse kerkgeschiedenis*, ed. P. H. A. M. Abels et al. (Delft: Eburon, 1991), pp. 106–133.

60. For Anabaptist practices at their (usually clandestine) meetings, including singing, see Claus-Peter Clasen, *Anabaptism: A Social History, 1525–1618* (Ithaca: Cornell University Press, 1972), pp. 343–348.

61. This song initially appeared in the first edition of the *Veelderhande Liedekens* (1556), and was also included in the songbook of *Het Offer des Heeren*. Bert Hofman, *Liedekens vol gheestich confoort: Een bijdrage tot de kennis van de zestiende-eeuwse Schriftuurlijke lyriek* (Hilversum: Verloren, 1993), p. 334; Frederik C. Wieder, *De schriftuurlijke liedekens: De liederen der nederlandsche hervormden tot op het jaar 1566* (The Hague: Martinus Nijhoff, 1900), pp. 181, 185; *OHL*, in *BRN*, vol. 2, pp. 594–603.

62. *OHL*, in *BRN*, vol. 2, pp. 594–595.

63. In Philipp Wackernagel, ed., *Lieder der niederländischen Reformierten aus der*

Zeit der Verfolgung im 16. Jahrhundert (1867; reprint, Nieuwkoop: B. de Graaf, 1965), p. 85.

64. None of these letters survives, but ten days before his execution in 1535, Fisher told his examiners that they included "exhortations to patience, and prayers to God for grace." *LP*, vol. 8, no. 858, p. 332. Simon Matthew's sermon, given at St. Paul's in London between the executions of Fisher and More, said that the two "in prison write to their mutual comfort in their damnable opinions." Matthew, *A Sermon made in the cathedrall church of saynt Paule at London, the XXVII. day of June, Anno 1535* (London: Thomas Berthelet, 1535), sig. [C8].

65. More, *Dialogue of Comfort,* pp. 293/28–294/5 (italics in original).

66. Aert Swaens van Goerle, "Die Martirie ende Confessie van broeder Willem vander Gouwe," in *Een salighe vermaninghe* . . . ('s-Hertogenbosch: Jan Scheffer, 1574), sigs. [E7–E8], quotation on [E7]. The biblical verses include Christ's promise to forsake whoever forsakes him and confess whoever confesses him (Matt. 10:32–33); that Christians must not only be patient in suffering, but rejoice in it, "knowing with certainty" [*seecker wetende*] that it is the way to salvation (Acts 14:22); and Paul's statement that earthly suffering is not to be compared to heaven's eternal glory (Rom. 8:18).

67. Gijsbertus Hesse, "Het lied van Rutger Estius op de H.H. martelaars van Gorcum, gedrukt bij Willem Jacobszoon te Amsterdam in 1575," *De Katholiek,* 145 (1914), 307. The song was published anonymously by Willem Jacobszoon. Ibid., p. 294.

68. William Weston, *An Autobiography from the Jesuit Underground,* trans. Philip Caraman (New York: Farrar, Straus, and Cudahy, 1955), p. 119. This was about the same time that Southwell wrote his *Epistle of Comfort,* secretly published in Arundel house in London under a false Paris imprint, ca. 1587 or 1588.

69. Ingram to fellow prisoners, July 1594, in John Hungerford Pollen, ed., *Unpublished Documents Relating to the English Martyrs,* vol. 1, 1584–1603, vol. 5 of CRS (London: Catholic Record Society, 1908), p. 283.

70. Swaens van Goerle, "Martirie," in *Salighe vermaninghe,* sig. E3v.

71. [John Geninges], *The Life and Death of Mr Edmund Geninges Priest, Crowned with Martyrdome at London, the 10. day of Nouember, in the yeare M.D.XCI* (St. Omers: Charles Boscard, 1614), pp. 76–77 (italics in original).

72. Richard Bristow, *A Briefe Treatise of diuerse plaine and sure wayes to finde out the truthe in this doubtful and dangerous time of Heresie* . . . (Antwerp: John Fowler, 1574), fol. 140v.

73. [Wouter van Stoelwijck], *Een Trostelijcke vermaninghe ende seer schoon onderwysinghe van het lyden ende Heerlicheyt der Christenen* ([Groessen: Nicolaes Biestkens van Diest], 1558), sig. C3v.

74. Donald R. Kelley, "Martyrs, Myths, and the Massacre: The Background of St. Bartholomew," *American Historical Review,* 77 (1972), 1328.

75. Foxe 1563, p. 1159.

76. Crespin 1564, p. 816.

77. Richard Tracy, trans., *Of the Preparation to the Crosse, and to Deathe, and of the*

comforte vnder the crosse and deathe . . . (London: Thomas Berthelet, 1540), sig. [F8r-v].

78. John Calvin, *Petit traicté monstrant que c'est que doit faire un homme fidele congnoissant la verité de l'Evangile, quand il est entre les papistes* . . . ([Geneva: Jean Girard], 1543), in *CO* 6, cols. 573–574 (my emphases).

79. John Scory, *An Epistle wrytten by John Scory the late bishope of Chichester vnto all the faythfull that be in pryson in Englande, or in any other troble for the defence of Goddes truthe* . . . ([Emden: Gilles van der Erve], 1555), sigs. [A8]-B2.

80. *Ausbund* 1583, pp. 9–26. Menno Simons, *Eyne Troestelijke Vermaninge van dat Lijden, Cruyze, vnde Vervolginge der Heyligen, vmme dat woort Godes, vnde zijne getuichenisse* [Fresenburg: "B. L."? 1554 or 1555], sig. F3. Two Hutterite songs incorporated the early Christian martyrs in the manner of the song from the *Ausbund*. See *Die Lieder der Hutterischen Brüder* (Scottdale, Pa.: Mennonitische Verlagshaus, 1914), pp. 669–675, 770–781.

81. For this point, see my "Prescribing and Describing Martyrdom: Menno's *Troestelijke Vermaninge* and *Het Offer des Heeren,*" *MQR,* 71 (1997), 605–606.

82. See Werner O. Packull, "Anna Jansz of Rotterdam, a Historical Investigation of an Early Anabaptist Heroine," *ARG,* 78 (1987), 147–173.

83. Anneken [Jans], *Hier begint dat Testament dat Anneken zeliger gedachtenisse, Esaias haren Sone bestelt heefft* . . . (n.p., ca. 1566), sig. A1.

84. *OH,* in *BRN,* vol. 2, p. 148.

85. In Wouters van Cuyck, *Sentbrieuen,* sig. [K6r-v]. There are four scriptural citations in the margins of this passage: Job 1:21, James 5:11, Acts 12:2, and Luke 23:32.

86. John Fisher, *A spirituall consolation, written by Iohn Fyssher Bishoppe of Rochester, to hys sister Elizabeth, at suche tyme as hee was prisoner in the Tower of London* . . . [London: Thomas East, 1578], sig. [D8].

87. More, *Dialogue of Comfort,* p. 311/15–17, 26–28. Compare with Thomas à Kempis, *A full deuoute and gostely treatyse of the Imytacyon and folowynge the blessed lyfe of our moste mercyfull Sauyour cryste* . . . (London: Richard Pynson, 1517), 2.12, sigs. [F4v–F5].

88. More, *Dialogue of Comfort,* pp. 313/2–6, 316/10–12. In general, see the entire final chapter, pp. 312–320. About two months before he was beheaded on July 6, 1535, More wrote to his daughter, Margaret Roper, that "my whole study should be, upon the passion of Christ and mine own passage out of this world." *CTM,* May 2 or 3, 1535, no. 214, p. 552/66–68.

89. [Allen], *Briefe Historie,* sig. [D6].

90. Ibid., sig. f3v (italics in original). Persecuted by her neighbors after converting to Catholicism in York, Margaret Clitherow was consoled by the story of Christ himself, who was betrayed by his own apostle, and comforted by "the example of Abel and Joseph, which were not persecuted by strangers, but by their own brethren." John Mush, "A True Report of the Life and Martyrdom of Mrs. Margaret Clitherow," in *The Troubles of Our Catholic Forefathers Related by Themselves,* ed. John Morris, third series (London: Burns and Oates, 1877), p. 406.

91. Thomas Hide, *A Consolatorie Epistle to the afflicted Catholikes* ([East Ham: Stephen Brinkley], 1580), sigs. B3–B4v, quotations on B3, B3v.

92. [William Allen], *An Apologie and Trve Declaration of the Institution and endeuours of the two English Colleges . . .* ([Rheims: Jean Foigny], 1581), fol. 116. For other examples of Allen's linking ancient and contemporary martyrs, see ibid., fols. 108v, 109, 110v-111, 121r-v.

93. *Ausbund* 1583, pp. 27–34; Calvin, *Petit traicté,* in *CO* 6, cols. 569–570; [Allen], *Briefe Historie,* sig. [c7v].

94. More, *Dialogue of Comfort,* p. 297/6–8; J[oye], *Present consolation,* sig. G4; Wouters van Cuyck, *Sentbrieuen,* sig. [B7v].

95. *Ein Warhaffte grausamme Geschicht, So geschehen ist zü Mechel in Brabandt . . .* (n.p., 1556), repr. in *Duitse vlugschriften van de tijd over het proces en de terechtstelling van de Protestanten Frans en Nikolaas Thys te Mechelen (1555),* ed. Robert Foncke (Antwerp: "De Sikkel," 1937), p. 127.

96. Scory, *Epistle vnto all the faythfull,* sigs. B2v–B3. See also ibid., sig. A3, where several of the recent martyrs are mentioned by name.

97. Van Haemstede 1559, p. 452. Van Haemstede provided a marginal gloss: "The death of martyrs strengthens the weak" *(Der Martelaren doodt versterct den swacken).* For the proceedings against Halewijn and Janssens between September 2, 1558, and February 27, 1559, see SAA, Vierschaar, V147, fols. 90v, 92–97, 98–99v; *AA,* vol. 8, pp. 448–460, 471, 472.

98. Crespin 1564, p. 997.

99. Ibid. Crespin referred the reader to the following passage, from a short letter by Oguier to his "Treschers Freres": "Now is not the time to sleep and take it easy, while we who are your members are in torment and in pain. Take heart, my brothers, be valiant, and help us by your prayers; help us to remain vigilant one more night, for we do not hope to live past tomorrow." Ibid., p. 819.

100. V[alerius] S[chool] M[eester], *Proba fidei,* fol. 18. Compare with Hans van Overdam's line in *OH,* in *BRN,* vol. 2, p. 116: "And the Spirit declares this [*dit betuycht den Geest*], that this is at the door and is the beginning."

101. Rijcen, *Tgetuygenisse ende nae-ghelaeten Schriften,* p. 15. He refers to a passage in the sixteenth letter of *In dit teghenwoordighe Boecxken zijn veel schoone ende lieflijcke Brieuen, van eenen ghenaemt Jacob de Keersmaecker . . .* ([Delft: Aelbrecht Hendricxsz], 1577), fols. 138v–139. I thank Mr. Paul Valkema Blouw for identifying this printer. De Roore's correspondence was republished in 1584. For the correct date of his execution as June 8, see RAB, Brugse Vrije, registers, 17,041/2, fol. 22v; A. L. E. Verheyden, *Het Brugsche martyrologium* (Brussels: Wilco, [1944]), p. 58.

102. Van den Houte, *Testament,* sig. [B7r-v]. For the name of her husband, as well as his arrest and execution in 1554, see Johan Decavele, *De dageraad van de Reformatie in Vlaanderen (1520–1565),* vol. 1 (Brussels: Paleis der Academiën, 1975), pp. 374–376.

103. Hessels van Est, *Histoire des Martyrs de Gorcum,* p. 423.

104. AAW, Series A, vol. 3, no. 59, p. 238.

105. *A True Report of the Inditement, Arraignment, Conviction, Condemnation, and Execution of Iohn Weldon, William Hartley, and Robert Sutton . . .* (London:

Richard Jones, 1588), repr. in *Miscellanea*, vol. 32 of CRS (London: Catholic Record Society, 1932), p. 417.

106. Fisher, *Spirituall consolation*, sig. A2v.

107. More, *Dialogue of Comfort*, pp. 109/2–7, 198/5–7, 247/9–10, 290/15–25.

108. Van Haemstede 1559, p. 451; Crespin 1564, pp. 997–1003.

109. Wouters van Cuyck, *Sentbrieuen*. For Matt. 10:24 and John 13:16, see sigs. [B8], [C6], E5, [F8v]-G1, G3r-v, H2r-v; for Heb. 12, see sigs. B3v-B4, J4, [J6]; for 4 Esd. 7:7, Matt. 7:13, and Luke 13:24, see sigs. [B7r-v], [C6], G1r-v.

110. Crespin 1564, p. 997. All scriptual citations in the martyrs' writings, given by Crespin in the margins, are here placed in brackets. (Crespin erroneously gives 2 Pet. 4 for 1 Pet. 4:13–14.)

111. *Eenen Troostelijcken Sentbrief, voor alle die om derwaerheyt, ende om Christus naem veruolcht worden* [Antwerp: Matthias Crom, ca. 1530; reprint, Wesel: Hans de Braeker, 1558], repr. in *BRN*, vol. 8, p. 127. In 1540 Pierre Viret similarly noted the inferiority of academic detachment in comparison to a concrete hermeneutic born of persecution. See Viret, *Epistre consolatoire, envoyée aux fideles qui souffrent persecution pour le Nom de Jesus et Verité evangelique* ([Geneva: Jean Girard], 1541), in Herminjard, vol. 6, p. 431.

112. Crespin 1564, p. 1001.

113. *The Letters of John Hus*, trans. Matthew Spinka (Manchester: Manchester University Press, 1972), no. 63, p. 153.

114. More, *Dialogue of Comfort*, pp. 75/6–76/3, quotation at 75/25; 198/5–21, quotations at 198/5–7, 11–21 (my emphases). More's *Dialogue* is filled with metaphors about what to *do* with the scriptural admonition to sustain persecution for the truth. In the work's last few pages alone, for example, he wrote, "let it sink into our heart"; a man should "well weigh those words, and let them sink as they should do down deep into his heart"; we should "deeply ponder the sample [example] of our savior himself" such that it take "deep a place in our breast"; and there should be "deep considering of the joys of heaven." Ibid., pp. 296/21, 303/23–24, 312/8, 314/21, 319/19–20.

115. See *Thomas More's Prayer Book: A Facsimile Reproduction of the Annotated Pages*, ed. Louis L. Martz and Richard S. Sylvester (New Haven: Yale University Press, 1969).

116. More, *Dialogue of Comfort*, p. 308/9–14.

117. Heinrich Bullinger, "A Sermon of the confessing of Christe," in [Peter Martyr Vermigli and Bullinger], *A Treatise of the Cohabitacyon of the faithfull with the vnfaithfull. Wherunto is added. A sermon made of the confessing of Christe and his gospell, and of the denyinge of the same*, trans. Thomas Becon? ([Strasbourg: Wendelin Rihel], 1555), fol. 85v.

118. [Jans], *Testament*, sig. A3v. Jans wove two biblical passages into the admonition itself, Deut. 6:8 ("Bind them as a sign on your hand, fix them as an emblem on your forehead") and Ps. 1:2 ("their delight is in the law of the Lord, and on his law they meditate day and night"). Another woman, Claesken Gaeledochter, drowned in Friesland for persisting in her Anabaptist views, began numerous paragraphs with imperatives about the scriptures like "take it to heart" and "consider it well." See *OH*, in *BRN*, vol. 2, pp. 331–334. For her execution

sentence of March 14, 1559, see *DAN*, vol. 7, *Friesland (1551–1601) and Groningen (1538–1601)*, ed. A. F. Mellink (Leiden: E. J. Brill, 1995), p. 109.

119. CRS, vol. 5, p. 283.

120. "Nicodemus Martyr," *Von dem warhafftigen Creutz Christi, wo man dasselbig finden, wie man auch solchs eeren, tragen vnd erheben sol* . . . (n.p., 1528), sig. B1.

121. Calvin, *Petit traicté*, in *CO* 6, col. 571.

122. J[oye], *Present consolation*, sig. D2. For further instances of similar language, see ibid., sigs. F1v, G2v.

123. Foxe 1563, p. 1160.

124. [John Bradford], *A godlye Medytacyon composed by the faithfull and constant seruant of God J. B. Precher who latlye was burnte in Smytfelde for the testimonie of Jesus Christ* . . . (London: William Copland, 1559), sigs. B4, [C5].

125. [Van Stoelwijck], *Trostelijcke vermaninghe*, sig. C4r-v.

126. More, *De tristitia Christi*, in *CWTM*, vol. 14, pt. 1, ed. and trans. Clarence Miller (New Haven: Yale University Press, 1976), p. 171/6–13.

127. John Gerard, *The Autobiography of a Hunted Priest*, trans. Philip Caraman (New York: Pellegrini and Cudahy, 1952), pp. xvii, 116 (quotation).

128. Van Haemstede 1559, p. 421. Diericks was recalling the promise of Matt. 10:19–20: "When they hand you over, do not worry about how you are to speak or what you are to say; for what you are to say will be given to you at that time; for it is not you who speak, but the Spirit of your Father speaking through you."

129. [Allen], *Briefe Historie*, sig. [f6v].

130. As Thomas Hide put it in 1579, "certain it is, that prayer is the valor either to take away tribulation, or to give strength to bear it." Hide, *Consolatorie Epistle*, sig. F8. See also ibid., sig. G2: "We must persevere eager and fervent in prayer, not doubting but in time we shall receive what we ask, in time we shall find what we seek, and after we have knocked, the door will be opened."

131. In Rijcen, *Schriften*, p. 129 (my emphasis).

132. Gerard, *Autobiography*, p. 109.

133. Menno, *Troestelijke Vermaninge*, sig. P4.

134. Calvin, *Petit traicté*, in *CO* 6, col. 579.

135. More, *Dialogue of Comfort*, p. 319/19–25, quotation at lines 23–25.

136. Johannes Bugenhagen, ed., *Artickel der Doctorn von Louen, zu welchen, Wilhelm von Zwollen* . . . *Christlich hat geantwort* . . . *dar auff er zu Mechelen ym Niderlande verbrand ist* . . . (Wittenberg: Joseph Klug, 1530), repr. in *BRN*, vol. 8, p. 176; Crespin 1564, p. 1068.

137. See Luther's emphasis on "pro me" in his *In epistolam S. Pauli ad Galatas Commentarius ex praelectione D. Martini Lutheri collectus* [1535], in *WA* 40, pp. 295–300.

138. Fisher, *Spirituall consolation*, sig. D3 (my emphasis).

139. More, *Dialogue of Comfort*, pp. 247/5, 316/19–20 (my emphasis).

140. Foxe 1563, p. 1536 (my emphasis). Compare with Etienne Gravot's remark, written before his death in 1553: "Therefore *cast all your cares on him* [God]; for he cares for us, and we are also as precious as the apple of his eye." Crespin 1564, p. 451 (my emphasis).

141. Rijcen, *Schriften*, p. 94 (my emphasis). See also, for example, Jan Gheertsen's comment about how the Lord bore his pain when he was being tortured, thus preventing him from divulging the names of fellow Anabaptists, in his *Testament*, fol. 3.

142. Donald Weinstein and Rudolph M. Bell, *Saints and Society: The Two Worlds of Western Christendom, 1000–1700* (Chicago: University of Chicago Press, 1982), p. 160 (my emphasis).

143. [Allen], *Briefe Historie*, sig. f3.

144. All quotations are from [Geninges], *Life and Death of Edmund Geninges*, pp. 105–106.

145. *Warhaffte grausamme Geschicht*, in *Duitse vlugschriften*, ed. Foncke, pp. 122–123, 126, 130.

146. Wackernagel, vol. 5, no. 1590, p. 1364.

147. For a brief overview of the importance of the psalms to the Huguenots, see Roger Zuber, "Les psaumes dans l'histoire des Huguenots," *BSHPF*, 123 (1977), 350–361.

148. Crespin 1564, p. 1084. For additional examples of Protestant martyrs singing psalms, see ibid., pp. 310, 452, 815, 965, and sig. Kkk2.

149. *Eyn warhafftig geschicht wie Caspar Tawber, Burger zü Wienn in Osterreich für ein Ketzer, unnd zü dem todt verurtaylt und auß gefürt worden ist* ([Nuremberg: Jobst Gutknecht], 1524), sigs. [B4v], C1v.

150. *OHL*, in *BRN*, vol. 2, p. 517. For their execution sentence, issued on April 11, 1551, see RAG, Raad van Vlaanderen, secrete camere, vol. 7613, fols. 137v–138; A. L. E. Verheyden, *Het Gentsche martyrologium (1530–1595)* (Bruges: "De Tempel," 1945), pp. 13–14.

151. Hessels van Est, *Martyrs de Gorcum*, p. 250.

152. *Der actus vnd handlung der degradation vnd verprenung der Christlichen Ritter vnd merterer Augistiner ordens geschehen zu Brussel . . .* [Speyer: Johann Eckhart, 1523], repr. in *BRN*, vol. 8, pp. 15–16.

153. *Historia de duobus Augustinensibus, ob Euangelij doctrinam exustis Bruxellae . . .* [n.p., 1523], repr. in BRN, vol. 8, pp. 36–37.

5. Witnesses for the Gospel: Protestants and Martyrdom

1. By "evangelical" I mean the early Reformation movement that coalesced around the doctrine of justification by faith alone and neither sought socioreligious revolution (as did the protagonists of the Peasants' War) nor embraced separatism (as did the Anabaptists). At least twenty-four editions of Luther's sermon about meditating on Christ's passion were published between 1519 and 1524. See *Ein Sermon von der Betrachtung des heiligen Leidens Christi* [1519], in *WA* 2, pp. 131–142. His sermon on preparation for death saw twenty-two editions between 1519 and 1525. See *Ein Sermon von der Bereitung zum Sterben* [1519], in *WA* 2, pp. 685–697. For examples of Luther's letters to persecuted Christians, see *Eyn missive allen den, szo von wegen des wort gottes verfolgung leyden an Hartmutt von Cronberg geschrieben* [1522], in *WA* 10.II, pp. 43–60, and *Ein christlicher Trostbrief an die Miltenberger, wie sie sich an*

ihren Feinden rächen sollen, aus den 119 Psalm [1524], in *WA* 15, pp. 69–78. Luther's martyrological pamphlets from the 1520s include the following: on Vos and van den Esschen, *Ein Brief an die Christen im Niederland* [1523], in *WA* 12, pp. 77–80; on Hendrik van Zutphen, *Von Bruder Henrico in Ditmar verbrannt samt dem zehnten Psalmen ausgelegt* [1525], in *WA* 18, pp. 224–240; on Georg Winkler, *Tröstung an die Christen zu Halle über Herr Georgen ihres Predigers Tod* [1527], in *WA* 23, pp. 402–434; and *Von Er Lenhard Keiser ynn Beyern vmb des Euangelij willen verbrandt Eine selige geschicht* [1527], in *WA* 23, pp. 452–476.

2. On this point see Hugh R. Boudin, "Les martyrologes protestants de la Reforme: Instruments de propagande ou documents de temoignage?" in *Sainteté et martyre dans les religions du livre*, ed. J. Marx, vol. 19 of *Problèmes d'Histoire du Christianisme* (Brussels: Editions de l'Université de Bruxelles, 1989), p. 68; Léon H. Halkin, "Les martyrologes et la critique: Contribution à l'étude du Martyrologe protestant des Pays-Bas," in *Mélanges historiques offerts à Monsieur Jean Meyhoffer* (Lausanne: L'Imprimerie La Concorde, 1952), pp. 53–56.

3. Jane Campbell Hutchison, *Albrecht Dürer: A Biography* (Princeton: Princeton University Press, 1990), pp. 164–165, quotation on 165 (Hutchison's trans.).

4. See Siegfried Hoyer, "Jan Hus und der Hussitismus in den Flugschriften des ersten Jahrzehnts der Reformation," in *Flugschriften als Massenmedium der Reformationszeit*, ed. Hans-Joachim Köhler (Stuttgart: Klett-Cotta, 1981), pp. 291–307; Robert W. Scribner, *For the Sake of Simple Folk: Popular Propaganda for the German Reformation*, 2nd ed. (Oxford: Clarendon Press, 1994), pp. 27, 28.

5. Poggio Bracciolini, *Eyn sendt brieff wie Hieronimus eyn Junger Joannis huß Im concilio czu Costentz für ein ketzer vorbrandt von Pogio des babst tzuerzeyt secretarienn . . .* (n.p., 1521), esp. sigs. A2, A3, B1v.

6. Luther, *Missive an Hartmutt von Cronberg geschrieben*, in *WA* 10.II, pp. 54/2–4 (quotation), 59/25–34.

7. Hildegard Hebenstreit-Wilfert, "Märtyrerflugschriften der Reformationszeit," in *Flugschriften als Massenmedium*, ed. Köhler, pp. 397–446; Bernd Moeller, "Inquisition und Martyrium in Flugschriften der frühen Reformation in Deutschland," in *Ketzerverfolgung im 16. und frühen 17. Jahrhundert*, ed. S. Seidel Menchi (Wiesbaden: Harrassowitz, 1992), pp. 21–48.

8. Moeller, "Inquisition und Martyrium," pp. 40–41, 44–45.

9. Judging from the disdainful manner in which she expressed her views about the Lord's Supper, Claes seems to have been some sort of sacramentarian rather than a Lutheran or Zwinglian evangelical. A German pamphlet with a heavily apocalyptic introduction, probably based on a now lost Dutch original, was published shortly after her death, which recounted the story of her interrogations and execution. See *Ein wunderliche geschycht newlich geschehen jn dem Hag in Holland jm jar MDXXVII . . .* [n.p., n.d.], repr. in *CDN*, vol. 5, pp. 274–279. For contemporary references to a Dutch publication about her, see ibid., pp. 279, 370–371, 381. Later in the century both Lutherans and Dutch Anabaptists claimed Claes as their martyr, a development apparently facilitated by her belonging to neither group. See Rabus 3, fols. 120v–124; *OH*, in *BRN*, vol.

2, pp. 422–427; and J. C. van Slee, "Wendelmoet Claesdochter van Monniken-dam, 20 november 1527," *Nederlands archief voor kerkgeschiedenis,* n.s., 20, (1927), 121–156.

10. *Der actus vnd handlung der degradation vnd verprenung der Christlichen Ritter vnd merterer Augistiner ordens geschehen zu Brussel . . .* [Speyer: Johann Eckhart, 1523], repr. in *BRN,* vol. 8, pp. 15–19. For the editions, see Hebenstreit-Wilfert, "Märtyrerflugschriften," pp. 432–436. Other publications about Vos and van den Esschen include Luther's *Brief an die Christen im Niederland,* in *WA* 12, pp. 77–80, and his first hymn, *Eynn hubsch Lyed von denn zcweyen Marter-ern Christi, zu Brussel von den Sophisten zcu Louen verbrandt* [1524], in *WA* 35, pp. 411–415. See also the anonymous Latin pamphlet *Historia de duobus Augustinensibus, ob Euangelij doctrinam exustis Bruxellae . . .* [n.p., 1523], repr. in *BRN,* vol. 8, pp. 35–54; and Martin Reckenhofer, *Dye histori, so zwen Augustiner Ordens gemartert seyn tzü Bruxel yn Probant, von wegen des Euan-gelij . . .* [Erfurt: Wolfgang Stürmer, 1523], repr. in *BRN,* vol. 8, pp. 66–114.

11. *Eyn warhafftig geschicht wie Caspar Tawber, Burger zü Wienn in Osterreich für ein Ketzer, unnd zü dem todt verurtaylt und auß gefürt worden ist* ([Nuremberg: Jobst Gutknecht], 1524). For the seven editions, see Hebenstreit-Wilfert, "Märtyrerflugschriften," pp. 439–442. Other contemporary publications about Tauber include Leonhardt Guttman, *Verantworttung Casper Taubers, der zü Wien verprant ist worden. Vnd eyn kurze vnterricht, wer Gottes wort vervolgt* [Nuremberg: Hans Hergot, 1524]; and *Eyn erbermlich geschicht So an dem frommen christlichen man Tauber von Wien in Osterreich gescheen ist . . .* [n.p., 1524]. At least two versions of a song about Tauber were published, including *Ein hüpsch new lied von einen Christlichen man mit namen Caspar Tauber* [n.p., 1525?]; it has twenty-five verses rather than the twenty-six of the version dis-cussed by Hebenstreit-Wilfert, "Märtyrerflugschriften," pp. 413–415, 443.

12. On Keyser, see the *Histori oder dz warhafftig geschicht, des leydens vnd sterbens Lienhart Keysers seligen . . .* [n.p., 1527]. For the editions, see *WA* 23, pp. 443–445. Johannes Eck published a Catholic response to this pamphlet, the *Warhaf-ftige handlung, wie es mit her Lienhart Keszer zu Scherding verbrannt, ergangen ist . . .* [Ingolstadt: Peter and George Apianus, 1527]. Luther's pamphlet on Keyser, a collection of documents similar in its composite nature to the later martyrologies, went through two printings. *WA* 23, p. 448. On Heuglin, see the *Warhaffte hystorien: Von dem frummen zeügen vnd marterer Christi Johan-sen Heüglin von Lindaw . . .* [Nuremberg: Jobst Gutknecht, 1527]. For all four editions, see Hebenstreit-Wilfert, "Märtyrerflugschriften," pp. 444–445. There was a Catholic response to this pamphlet: Peter Speyser and Christoph Golter, *Warhafft verantwurttung über dz lugenhafft schmachbüchlein . . . von wegen Hannsen Heüglins von Lindaw . . .* [Tübingen: Ulrich Morhart the Elder, 1527?]. Heuglin was burned in Meersburg, in the diocese of Constance, on May 10, 1527; Keyser at Schärding, in Bavaria, on July 10, 1527.

13. There were two editions of [Johannes Lange], *Eyn Historie odder geschicht wie eyn Christlicher Euangelischer prediger von wegen des Evangelions, gemartert vnnd getödtet worden ist . . .* ([Erfurt: Johan Loersfeld], 1525); three editions of [Jakob Probst], *Ein erschreckliche geschicht wie ein etliche Ditmarschen den Christlichen prediger Heinrich von Zutfeld* [sic] *newlich so jemerlich vmb gebracht*

haben . . . [n.p., ca. 1525] (at least one of the other two editions was published by Heinrich Steiner in Augsburg, 1525; see Moeller, "Inquisition und Martyrium," p. 47); one printing of [Johannes Lange and Wenceslaus Linck], *Histoira* [sic] *wie S. Heinrich von Zutphan newlich yn Dittmars, vmbs Euangelions willen gemartert vnd gestorben erlitten haben* . . . [Altenburg: Gabriel Kantz, 1525]; and six German editions, plus one Low German translation, of Luther's pamphlet about Hendrik, *Von Bruder Henrico in Ditmar verbrannt* (for all seven editions, see *WA* 18, pp. 219–220).

14. "Theodulus Philadelphus" [François Lambert?], *Epistre chrestienne enuoyee a tresnoble Prince monseigneur le duc de Lorayne* ([Strasbourg: J. Preus], 1526). For Lambert as the probable author, see Moeller, "Inquisition und Martyrium," p. 24 n. 10.

15. [Willem Voldersgraft (Gnapheus)], *Een suuerlicke ende seer schoone disputacie, welcke geschiet is in den Haghe in Hollant, tusschen die kettermeesters ende eenen christelijcken priester ghenaemt Jan van Woorden, aldaer gheuanghen ende oock verbrant* . . . [n.p., ca. 1526], repr. in *CDN*, vol. 4, pp. 452–496.

16. Following Georg Winkler's murder, six editions of Luther's consolatory letter were published in late 1527; see Luther's *Tröstung an die Christen zu Halle*, a work that triggered three different Catholic responses. *WA* 23, pp. 391–395.

17. [Theodor Fabricius], *Ernstliche handlung zwischen den hochgelehrten Doctorn inn der gotheyt (als mann sie zu Cölln nennt) oder ketzermeyster, vnnd eynem gefangnen genant, Adolph Clarenbach* . . . [Cologne: Hiero Fuchs, 1529]; [Fabricius], *Histori von Adolff Clarenbach und Peter Flysteden* (1530); [Fabricius], *Alle Acta Adolphi Clarenbach* . . . [Cologne: Eucharius Hirtzhorn? ca. 1531]. For a Catholic defense of their condemnation and execution, see Johann Romberg von Kierspe, *Epistola Johannis Romberch Kyrspensis theologi . . . in qua narratur universa tragoedia Adolphi Clarenbach una cum Petro Flysteden nuper Coloniae exusti* (Cologne: Eucharius Hirtzhorn, 1530), repr. in *Theologische Arbeiten aus dem rheinischen wissenschaftlichen Predigerverein*, n.s., 2, ed. E. Bratke and A. Carsted (Freiburg, 1898).

18. Johannes Bugenhagen, ed., *Artickel der Doctorn von Louen, zu welchen, Wilhelm von Zwollen . . . Christlich hat geantwort . . . dar auff er zu Mecheln ym Niderlande verbrand ist* . . . (Wittenberg: Joseph Klug, 1530), repr. in *BRN*, vol. 8, pp. 149–176.

19. John Frith, *A boke made by John Frith prisoner in the tower of London . . .* ([Antwerp: Christoffel Ruremond's widow?], 1533).

20. For Chastellain, see François Lambert, *In primvm dvodecim prophetarum, nempe Oseam, Francisci Auenionensis Commentarij . . .* (Strasbourg: Johan Hervagius, 1525), sigs. A3–[A5v]. For le Clerc, see idem, *Francisci Lamberti Auenionensis Commentarij, in Micheam, Naum, et Abacuc* (Strasbourg: Johan Hervagius, 1525), fols. 2–3v. For briefer passages about Chastellain in yet another work, see idem, *Farrago omnium fere rerum Theologicarum, quarum catalogum sequenti pagella reperies* [Strasbourg? 1525], fols. 25v–26, 51v. For Berquin, see Erasmus, *Opus epistolarum Des. Erasmi Roterodami*, ed. P. S. Allen and H. M. Allen, vol. 8 (1529–1530) (Oxford: Clarendon Press, 1934), no. 2188, pp. 209–216.

21. For a list of twenty-five such evangelicals executed between 1525 and 1534, see

my "Anathema of Compromise: Christian Martyrdom in Early Modern Europe," vol. 2 (Ph.D. diss., Princeton University, 1996), p. 482 n. 25.

22. On the importance of oral communication in the early Reformation, see Robert W. Scribner, "Oral Culture and the Transmission of Reformation Ideas," in *The Transmission of Ideas in the Lutheran Reformation,* ed. Helga Robinson-Hammerstein (Dublin: Irish Academic Press, 1989), pp. 83–104, esp. 84–93.

23. *Hüpsch new lied von Caspar Tauber,* sig. [A1v]. On the importance of the *Zeitungslied* in late medieval and sixteenth-century Germany, see Helga Robinson-Hammerstein, "The Lutheran Reformation and Its Music," in *Transmission of Ideas in the Lutheran Reformation,* p. 155.

24. Luther, *Den Auszerwelten lieben Freunden gottis, allen Christen zu Righe, Reuell vnd Tarbthe* [1523], in *WA* 12, p. 147/7. For September as the likely month of composition, see ibid., p. 145. For Luther's letter to Georg Spalatin that first mentions the two Augustinians, at which time he thought that a third, Lambert (Thorn), had also been executed, see *WA Briefwechsel* 3, no. 635, p. 115/9–16.

25. *Journal d'un bourgeois de Paris sous le règne de François Premier (1515–1536),* ed. Marie Ludovic Lalanne (Paris: Jules Renouard, 1854), p. 185. The detail about the *Te Deum laudamus* might suggest that the author based his information on the *Historia de duobus Augustinensibus,* which mentioned the hymn. *BRN,* vol. 8, pp. 36–37. But because the journal writer tended to give specific dates when he knew them, and the *Historia* provided dates for the execution of Vos and van den Esschen not mentioned by the diarist, it would seem either that the author got this detail from oral reports that were circulating, or that perhaps he derived it from an independent written source that mentioned the hymn.

26. The first line of the song about Jan van Woerden is "Nu heffen wy een nieu Liedt aen"; compare with Luther's "Eyn newes lied wir heben an." See Frederik C. Wieder, *De schriftuurlijke liedekens: De liederen der nederlandsche hervormden tot op het jaar 1566* (The Hague: Martinus Nijhoff, 1900), pp. 92–93.

27. Toussain to Farel, February 11, 1525, in Herminjard, vol. 1, no. 140, p. 338. In the summer of 1525 Farel was still spreading word of Chastellain's martyrdom, along with mention of Wolfgang Schuch's execution. See his letter to Nicolas d'Esch in Metz, written from Strasbourg, July 31, 1525, in Herminjard, vol. 5, no. 154a, p. 389. At least twice in October 1527 Luther wrote to Michael Stiefel, an evangelical pastor near Schärding in Bavaria, thanking him for materials by and about Leonhard Keyser. *WA Briefwechsel* 4, October 8, 1527, no. 1156, p. 263/1–3; ibid., October 22, 1527, no. 1161, p. 270/1–2. For further epistolary references to early evangelical martyrs, see Gerard Roussel to Farel in Strasbourg, September 25, 1525, about Jean le Clerc (Herminjard, vol. 2, no. 162, p. 390); Nicolas Cop from Basel to Martin Bucer in Strasbourg, April 5, 1534, apparently referring to Jean Pointet (ibid., vol. 3, no. 458, pp. 159, 162 n. 16); and Oswald Myconius from Basel to Bullinger in Zurich, April 8, 1534, also about Pointet (ibid., vol. 3, no. 459, p. 162, 162 n. 16).

28. See Joye's reference to "Sei[n]te Thomas mar[tyr]" for February 23 in the calendar of saints of his *Ortulus anime. The garden of the soule: or the englisshe primers* ([Antwerp: Marten de Keyser], 1530), sig. A3v. For the likely date of publication as late June or July, see Charles C. Butterworth and Allan G. Ches-

ter, *George Joye, 1495?-1553: A Chapter in the History of the English Bible and the English Reformation* (Philadelphia: University of Pennsylvania Press, 1962), p. 61.

29. [Lange], *Historie eyn Christlicher prediger,* sig. [A2].

30. On the composition of Probst's pamphlet in Antwerp, see [Probst], *Erschreckliche geschicht,* sig. 3v. The close correspondence between the narrative leading up to and including Hendrik's burning, as well as Probst's use of Lange's phrase in describing the crowd's treatment of the martyr's corpse, implies that Probst derived his account from Lange. On the latter point, compare [Probst], *Erschreckliche geschicht,* sig. 3v ("Dan den strumpff als man sagt haben sie begraben"), with [Lange], *Historie ein Christlicher prediger,* sig. A4r-v ("den strumpff aber begruben"). For Probst's recantation of thirty articles in February 1522, see the documents in *CDN,* vol. 4, pp. 88–98, 99–100. On Probst's regret and grief, see *Erschreckliche geschicht,* sig. 3v.

31. Luther, *Von Bruder Henrico,* in *WA* 18, pp. 215–240; for the editions, see ibid., pp. 219–220.

32. *Actus und handlung,* in *BRN,* vol. 8, pp. 15, 15–16. This pamphlet is not highly interpretive insofar as it purports to describe a "spectacle" [*spectaculam*] without passing judgment on it.

33. *Historia de duobus Augustinensibus,* in *BRN,* vol. 8, pp. 39–43. Frederik Pijper hypothesized that perhaps a lesser official was bribed to allow the copying of these articles. Ibid., p. 25. The articles as printed bear traces of the transcription of the Augustinians' responses. Moeller, "Inquisition und Martyrium," pp. 27–28 n. 33, with reference to articles 4, 21, 23, 42, 51, 60.

34. See articles 1, 12, 29, 34, 35, in *Historia de duobus Augustinensibus,* in *BRN,* vol. 8, pp. 39–41. The explicitly Lutheran character of these articles jibes with the immediately preceding history of the Observant Augustinian monastery in Antwerp. Along with the houses in Ghent and Dordrecht, the Antwerp monastery was one of the earliest channels whereby Luther's doctrines reached the Low Countries. Between 1516 and 1520, sixteen monks from one of these three houses had studied with Luther in Wittenberg before the dissolution of the Antwerp house in early October 1522. See Alphonsus De Decker, *Les Augustins d'Anvers et la Réforme* (Antwerp: A. de Decker, 1884), pp. 5–11; Julius Boehmer, "Die Beschaffenheit der Quellenschriften zu Heinrich Voes und Johann van den Esschen," *ARG,* 28 (1931), 130; Alastair Duke, "The Origins of Evangelical Dissent in the Low Countries," in *Reformation and Revolt in the Low Countries* (London: Hambledon Press, 1990), pp. 15–16; *CDN,* vol. 4, pp. 138–142.

35. Reckenhofer, *Histori zwen Augustiner Ordens,* in *BRN,* vol. 8, p. 66.

36. Bugenhagen, ed., *Artickel der Doctorn von Louen,* in *BRN,* vol. 8, pp. 166–167, 167–171, 151–165, respectively. Bugenhagen passed over van Zwolle's understanding of the Eucharist in silence, almost certainly since it sounded much less Lutheran than Zwinglian or sacramentarian, and instead stressed his advocacy of lay reception of the sacrament in both species. Ibid., pp. 155–156. Willem wrote, "that the Mass is nothing else [*nicht anders*] than a testament, remembrance, or thanksgiving [*Testament, gedechtnis, odder dancksagunge*], or if one

wants to call it such, one may also consider it a representation [*representacio*], but not a work, sacrifice, or satisfaction [*kein werck, Opffer odder gnugthuunge*] for human beings who have died or souls that have been separated from their corpses; and thus for the soul's justification the shedding of Christ's blood alone suffices." Ibid., p. 169. That Bugenhagen allowed such a statement to stand when he might easily have "Lutheranized" it implies both that he respected the integrity of his sources and that van Zwolle's view did not disqualify him from the ranks of genuine martyrs.

37. Bugenhagen, ed., *Artickel der Doctorn von Louen*, in *BRN*, vol. 8, pp. 168, 169, 171.

38. In addition to the examples mentioned in this paragraph, see the eighteen "haubt artickel" publicly defended by Leonhard Keyser, in *Histori des sterbens Lienhart Keysers*, sig. A3v. Michael Stiefel listed twenty-one articles in a section of Luther's pamphlet on Keyser, which divide differently the eighteen given in the aforementioned pamphlet. In Luther, *Von Er Lenhard Keiser*, in *WA* 23, p. 463/12–37. See also the twelve articles that Johannes Heuglin refused to abjure, in *Hystorien Johansen Heüglin*, sigs. A3v–B1v; the summary description of Matthias Weibel's views in Rabus 2, fol. 152v; and the twenty-two articles brought against Adolph Clarenbach, first printed around 1531 in *Alle Acta Adolphi Clarenbach*, and repr. in Rabus 3, fols. 237v-238v.

39. *Warhafftig geschicht Caspar Tawber*, sigs. [A2v], [A3r-v]. Caspar Tauber's eucharistic views were closer to a Zwinglian/sacramentarian than to a Lutheran interpretation, much like those of Willem van Zwolle: "the true body and blood of Jesus Christ is not present [*nicht sey der war leyb vnd das war plut Jesu Christi*] under the form of bread and wine after the consecration by the priest." Ibid., sig. [A2v].

40. [Voldersgraft], *Suuerlicke disputacie*, in *CDN*, vol. 4, pp. 456–458, 460–461, 473, 475, 481. For the brief account of events on the day of his execution (September 15, 1525), which comprises less than a tenth of the work, see ibid., pp. 494–495.

41. For Frith's extended argument against the idea that transubstantiation is a necessary article of faith, see *A boke made by John Frith*, sigs. A3v–L3; for his repudiation of purgatory, see ibid., sig. L4r-v; for the connection between his refusal to affirm transubstantiation and his anticipated death, see ibid., sigs. [L6v–L7].

42. Luther, *Brief an die Christen im Niederland*, in *WA* 12, p. 80/4–5; idem, *Eynn hubsch Lyed von denn zcweyen Marterern Christi*, in *WA* 35, p. 414/25–27. These two analogies seem to have been the most common at the time. For further instances, see Reckenhofer, *Histori zwen Augustiner Ordens*, in *BRN*, vol. 8, p. 114; [Lange], *Historie eyn Christlicher prediger*, sig. A3; Guttman, *Verantworttung Casper Taubers*, sig. A2v; Luther, *Tröstung an die Christen zu Halle*, in *WA* 23, p. 403/19–20; and the Dutch song about Jan van Woerden, quoted in Wieder, *Schriftuurlijke liedekens*, p. 93.

43. Lambert, *Oseam Commentarij*, sig. A3r-v (Cardinal of Lorraine's decrees); idem, *Commentarij in Micheam, Naum, et Abacuc*, fol. 3 (persecutors), 3v (Lawrence and Vincent).

44. See Halkin, "Martyrologes et la critique," p. 56. Jean-François Gilmont has argued, however, that this controversy is better explained by reference to the two contemporary political factions in Geneva than by any fundamental opposition to the term "martyr." Gilmont, *Jean Crespin: Un éditeur réformé du XVIe siècle* (Geneva: Droz, 1981), pp. 169–170.

45. Luther, *Brief an die Christen im Niederland,* in *WA* 12, p. 78/17–19.

46. *Histori des sterbens Lienhart Keysers,* sig. B1. See also the reference to "S[anctus]" Hendrik van Zutphen in the title of one of the pamphlets about him: [Lange and Linck], *Histoira* [sic] *S. Heinrich von Zutphen.*

47. Johannes Faber, *Ursach warumb der widerteuffer patron vnnd erster Anfenger Doctor Balthasar Hübmayer zü Wienn . . . verbrennet sey* [Vienna: n.p., 1528], sig. A2; [Joye], *Ortulus anime,* sig. A3v.

48. *Histori des sterbens Lienhart Keysers,* sig. B1.

49. Lambert, *Farrago omnium rerum Theologicarum,* fol. 26.

50. Luther, *Brief an die Christen im Niederland,* in *WA* 12, pp. 77/6, 78/2–8. Luther expressed similar views in letters written immediately before this pamphlet, which suggests that his words were not merely a rhetorical show for publication. See *WA Briefwechsel* 3, July 22 or 23, 1523, no. 635, p. 115/14–16; ibid., July 26, 1523, no. 637, p. 117/9–11.

51. Luther, *Von Bruder Henrico in Ditmar verbrannt,* in *WA* 18, p. 224/20–24.

52. Luther, *Tröstung an die Christen zu Halle,* in *WA* 23, p. 423/7–9.

53. On this point in general, see Heiko A. Oberman, *Luther: Man between God and the Devil,* trans. Eileen Walliser-Schwarzbart (New Haven: Yale University Press, 1989), pp. 265–269.

54. [Lange], *Historie eyn Christlicher prediger,* sig. A2. See also *Hystorien Johansen Heüglin,* sig. A2.

55. Tyndale, *The Obedience of a Christen man and how Christen rulers ought to governe . . .* ([Antwerp: Jacob Hoochstraten], 1528), fols. 2 (quotation), 7v–8.

56. William Tyndale, *An answere vnto Sir Thomas Mores dialoge made by Willyam Tindale* [Antwerp: Symon Cock or Martinus de Keyser? 1531], fol. 69r-v.

57. Cited in Susan Brigden, *London and the Reformation* (Oxford: Clarendon Press, 1989), p. 83.

58. [Lange], *Historie eyn Christlicher prediger,* sig. A4v. Luther expressed this idea several times in his martyrological writings. See his *Tröstung an die Christen zu Halle,* in *WA* 23, p. 403/19–26; *Von Er Lenhard Keiser,* in ibid., p. 476/9–11; and *Von Bruder Henrico in Ditmar verbrannt,* in *WA* 18, p. 226/5–11.

59. *Hystorien Johansen Heüglin,* sig. B3.

60. Wolfgang Capito, *In Hoseam prophetam V. F. Capitonis Commentarius* (Strasbourg: Johann Hervagius, 1528), sig. 1²v. The work is dedicated to Marguerite de Navarre.

61. *Historia de duobus Augustinensibus,* in *BRN,* vol. 8, pp. 44–45, 49–54, quotation on 44.

62. *Warhafftig geschicht Caspar Tawber,* sig. C2. A few lines later, at the very end, the author quoted Matt. 10:28.

63. Luther, *Von Er Lenhard Keiser,* in *WA* 23, p. 452/27–29.

64. *Eenen Troostelijcken Sentbrief, voor alle die om derwaerheyt, ende om Christus*

naem veruolcht worden ([Antwerp: Matthias Crom, ca. 1530]; reprint, Wesel: Hans de Braeker, 1558), repr. in *BRN,* vol. 8, p. 125.

65. "Nicodemus Martyr," *Von dem warhafftigen Creutz Christi, wo man dasselbig finden, wie man auch solchs eeren, tragen vnd erheben sol . . .* (n.p., 1528), sig. A4.

66. Foxe 1563, pp. 486, 494. Tyndale, *Obedience of a Christen man,* fols. 2–11v. For example, Tyndale used Matt. 5:10 to relativize persecution in the light of eternal life: "Tribulation is a blessing that cometh of God, as witnesseth Christ. Matt. 5. 'Blessed are they that suffer persecution for righteousness' sake, for theirs is the kingdom of heaven.' Is this not a comfortable word? Who ought not rather to choose and desire to be blessed with Christ in a little tribulation, than to be cursed perpetually with the world for a little pleasure?" Ibid., fol. 7.

67. Herminjard, vol. 2, July 9, 1532, no. 384, p. 427. Rom. 8:38–39 are the verses paraphrased. The second letter came from Guillaume Farel less than three weeks later. He used Rom. 8:31 to ask the Genevans who would be against them if God were for them, reminding them that Christ threatens to deny before the Father those who deny him on earth. Ibid., July 26, 1532, no. 387, p. 437.

68. Anémond de Coct, in François Lambert, *Evangelici in Minoritarum Regulam Commentarij, Quibus, palàm sit, tam de illa, quàm de alijs Monachorum Regulis et constitutionibus sentiendum sit . . .* [Wittenberg: n.p., 1523], sig. a3r-v.

69. Luther, *Tröstung an die Christen zu Halle,* in *WA* 23, p. 427/1–18, quotations at lines 3, 15–16.

70. See, for example, Rabus 1, sig. ☞5; Rabus 2, sig. [6]; Rabus 4, sigs. [*4v]-)(1v; Rabus 5, sig.)(4; Rabus 8, sig. 3; Crespin 1555, sigs. *3, *4; Crespin 1564, sigs. α2, α3r-v, γ1.

71. At several points in his *Trostbrief an die Miltenberger* Luther advocated pity towards persecutors. See *WA* 15, pp. 71/17–19, 72/16–19, 77/1–3. For the praise of Winkler's murderers, see idem, *Tröstung an die Christen zu Halle,* in *WA* 23, p. 425/1–3, 9–14. With reference to Matt. 5:44–45, Luther told the Christians of Halle to pray for Winkler's murderers, not to grow angry or seek revenge. Ibid., p. 429/11–33.

72. See Scribner, *For the Sake of Simple Folk,* esp. pp. 148–189.

73. Luther, *Von Er Lenhard Keiser,* in *WA* 23, p. 474/20–23. In the preface to the same work, he simultaneously called them tyrants and asked Christ to forgive them. Ibid., p. 452/29–30.

74. Reckenhofer, *Histori zwen Augustiner Ordens,* in *BRN,* vol. 8, p. 89; for analogous attacks, see ibid., pp. 85, 86, 102. *Warhafftig geschicht Casper Tawber,* sig. [A1v]; for similar remarks, see ibid., sigs. [B2], [C2]. See also [Lange], *Historie eyn Christlicher prediger,* sigs. [A2], [A3]; [Probst], *Erschreckliche geschicht,* sig. 2v.

75. [Voldersgraft], *Suuerlicke disputacie,* in *CDN,* vol. 4, pp. 456, 463, 465, 470, 477.

76. On anticlericalism, see most recently the articles in *Anticlericalism in Late Medieval and Early Modern Europe,* ed. Peter Dykema and Heiko A. Oberman (Leiden: E. J. Brill, 1993).

77. *Actus und handlung,* in *BRN,* vol. 8, pp. 16–17 (my emphasis).

78. For example, see David Nicholls, "The Nature of Popular Heresy in France, 1520–1542," *Historical Journal,* 26 (1983), 261–275; Cornelius Augustijn, "Anabaptism in the Netherlands: Another Look," *MQR,* 62 (1988), 197–210.

79. *WA Briefwechsel* 5, July 13, 1530, no. 1643, p. 471/13–18.

80. For recent treatments of Calvin's anti-Nicodemism, see Carlos M. N. Eire, *War against the Idols: The Reformation of Worship from Erasmus to Calvin* (Cambridge: Cambridge University Press, 1986), pp. 234–275; Eugénie Droz, *Chemins de l'hérésie,* vol. 1 (Geneva: Slatkine Reprints, 1970), pp. 131–171; Perez Zagorin, *Ways of Lying: Dissimulation, Persecution, and Conformity in Early Modern Europe* (Cambridge, Mass.: Harvard University Press, 1990), pp. 63–82. The intricate publication history of Calvin's anti-Nicodemite works in French and Latin can be followed in Rodolphe Peter and Jean-François Gilmont, *Bibliotheca Calviniana: Les oeuvres de Jean Calvin publiées au XVIe siècle,* vol. 1 (Geneva: Droz, 1991), pp. 41–43, 132–134, 165–166, 168–169, 195–198, 303–307, 356–358, 368–369, 427–429, 456–462, 463–466, 477–479; ibid., vol. 2 (Geneva: Droz, 1994), pp. 590–591, 592–593, 600–601, 675–676, 932–934, 1017–1019.

81. For this point with respect to England in particular, see Andrew Pettegree, "Nicodemism and the English Reformation," in *Marian Protestantism: Six Studies* (Aldershot: Scolar Press, 1996), pp. 86–117.

82. See Peter Matheson, "Martyrdom or Mission? A Protestant Debate," *ARG,* 80 (1989), 154–171.

83. Ibid., p. 167. The language of Calvin's letter of Sept. 12, 1540 (printed along with the *Petit traicté* of 1543), suggests that he was expressing his own view, which he indeed saw no way around, but which is not presented with the same inflexible detachment that characterizes the *Petit traicté.* He speaks in the 1540 letter, for example, of "*ma* raison qui *m'*induit à ainsi iuger" and "à *ma* part," phrases the likes of which are lacking in the *Petit traicté. CO* 6, cols. 584, 586 (my emphasis).

84. Eire, *War against the Idols,* pp. 245–247, 247 n. 51. Bucer's preface to Enzinas's Latin treatise on the murder of Juan Diaz also exemplifies the shift. See [Francisco de Enzinas], *Historia vera de morte sancti viri Ioannis Diazij Hispani . . .* ([Basel: Johannes Oporinus], 1546), sigs. α2–[γ7].

85. Sometime in 1543 or early 1544, for example, Valérand Poullain sent to embryonic Calvinist communities in Wallonia a manuscript copy, then more than two hundred printed copies, of Calvin's *Petit traicté.* See Herminjard, vol. 9, Poullain to Calvin, March 9, 1544, no. 1334, p. 178. Manuscript copies of Pierre Viret's *Epistre enuoyee avx fideles conversans entre les Chrestiens Papistiques* (n.p., 1543) had also been made prior to its publication in 1541. See ibid., sig. A2r-v; Herminjard, vol. 6, no. 933, p. 429 nn. 1–2.

86. For the specific editions in these languages, see Peter and Gilmont, *Bibliotheca Calviniana,* vol. 1, pp. 70–73, 221–223, 288–290, 375–377, 424–426, 469–471, 474–476, 517–518, 534–536; ibid., vol. 2, pp. 660–662, 814–817; Eire, *War against the Idols,* p. 273 n. 154; Droz, *Chemins de l'hérésie,* vol. 1, pp. 139, 142; Andrew Pettegree, *Emden and the Dutch Revolt: Exile and the Development of Reformed Protestantism* (Oxford: Clarendon Press, 1992), p. 253.

87. Richard Tracy, trans. *Of the Preparation to the Crosse, and to Deathe, and of the comforte vnder the crosse and deathe* . . . (London: Thomas Berthelet, 1540); G[eorge] J[oye], *A present consolation for the sufferers of persecucion for rughtwysenes* ([Antwerp: Steven Mierdman], 1544); [Wolfgang Musculus], *Proscaerus: Liceatne homini Christiano, euangelicae doctrinae gnaro, papisticis superstitionibus ac falsis cultibus externa societate communicare, Dialogi quatuor* (Basel: J. Kündig, 1549), which also appeared in a French translation by Valérand Poullain as *Le temporiseur* (1550) and an English translation, based on the French, by Robert Pownall, *The Temporysour* (1555); Giulio della Rovere, *Esortazione al martirio* (Zurich, 1552); [John Hooper], *Whether christian faith maye be kepte secret in the heart, without confession therof openly* ([London? John Daye?] 1553); Thomas Becon, *A confortable Epistle, too Goddes faythfull people in Englande* . . . ([Wesel? J. Lambrecht?] 1554); [John Bradford], *An Exhortation to the carienge of Chrystes crosse wyth a true and brefe confutation of false and papisticall doctryne* [Wesel? H. Singleton? 1555?]; [Peter Martyr Vermigli and Heinrich Bullinger], *A Treatise of the Cohabitacyon of the faithfull with the vnfaithfull. Wherunto is added. A Sermon made of the confessing of Christe and his gospell, and of the denyinge of the same*, trans. Thomas Becon? ([Strasbourg: Wendelin Rihel], 1555); John Scory, *An Epistle wrytten by John Scory the late bishope of Chichester vnto all the faythfull that be in pryson in Englande* . . . ([Emden: Gilles van der Erve], 1555).

88. Urbanus Rhegius, *Trostbrieff an alle Christen zü Hildeshaim, die vmbs Euangeliums willen yetzt schmach vnd verfolgung leyden* . . . ([Magdeburg: Hans Walther], 1531). To the best of my knowledge, no one has noted this appropriation of Rhegius by Joye, who was very likely working from the 1543 Latin edition of Rhegius's work, published in Frankfurt by Peter Braubach.

89. See Anne Jacobson Schutte, *Pier Paolo Vergerio: The Making of an Italian Reformer* (Geneva: Droz, 1977), pp. 239–244; Michael McDonald, "*The Fearefull Estate of Francis Spira:* Narrative, Identity, and Emotion in Early Modern England," *Journal of British Studies*, 31 (1992), 32–34; Jean-François Gilmont, "Les martyrologes protestants du XVIe siècle" (license thesis, Catholic University of Louvain, 1966), pp. 34–40. M. A. Overell mistakenly assumes that Spiera could not have held Calvinist views in the Italy of the 1540s because of the general swirl of competing and often confused theological ideas; see Overell, "The Exploitation of Francesco Spiera," *SCJ*, 26 (1995), 619–637. For Melanchthon's account of Spiera, see his *Warhaftige Historia von einem Doctor in Italia welchen die feind des heligen Euangelij gezwüngen die erkandte warheit zuuerleugnen* . . . (Wittenberg: Joseph Klug, 1549), repr. in *CR*, vol. 20, cols. 613–632.

90. Schutte, *Pier Paolo Vergerio*, pp. 244–246.

91. See the songs about martyrdom in Henri-Léonard Bordier, *Le chansonnier Huguenot du XVIe siècle*, vol. 2 (Paris: Librairie Tross, 1870), including verse renditions about the temptation to renounce one's faith, the danger of giving in to fear, and the consolation and strength that comes from Christ amid persecution. For the period ca. 1540–1555, see pp. 336–337, 341, 350–351, 354–363, 368–369, 374–378.

92. For example, see the pastors of Geneva to the pastors of Zurich, Basel [and

Berne?], November 13, 1537, in Herminjard, vol. 4, no. 668, pp. 318–319; Farel in Geneva to Conrad Pellican in Zurich, Feb. 22, 1538, ibid., no. 686, p. 371; Bucer in Strasbourg to Marguerite de Navarre, July 5, 1538, ibid., vol. 5, no. 721, pp. 40–41; Jean Collassus in Geneva to Farel in Neuchâtel, Sept. 2, 1538, ibid., no. 740, p. 100; Farel in Neuchâtel to Christophe Fabri in Thonon, Feb. 8, 1540, ibid., vol. 6, no. 848, p. 178.

93. For example, see Johannes Anastasius Veluanus [Jan Gerrits Verstege], "Van verfolligung om dat Euangelium" and "Van versaken [of faith]," in *Kort Bericht in allen principalen punten des Christen geloues . . . genant der Leken Wechwyser* (Strasbourg: Balthasar von Klarenbach, 1554), repr. in *BRN*, vol. 4, ed. Frederik Pijper (The Hague: Martinus Nijhoff, 1906), pp. 340–345; A[nthony] G[ilby], *An answer to the deuillish detection of Stephane Gardiner, Bishoppe of Wynchester . . .* ([London: Steven Mierdman for John Daye?] 1547 or 1548), fols. 48v–49, 167–168, sig. Ff4v; Hugh Latimer, *Sermons by Hugh Latimer, Sometime Bishop of Worcester, Martyr, 1555,* ed. George Elwes Corrie (Cambridge: Cambridge University Press, 1844), pp. 222, 347, 361, 379, 380, 436–437, 466, 487; Roger Hutchinson, "Two Sermons of Oppression, Affliction, and Patience, Preached by Roger Hutchynson," in *The Works of Roger Hutchinson* (Cambridge: Cambridge University Press, 1847), pp. 289–340.

94. Calvin, *Petit traicté monstrant que c'est que doit faire un homme fidele congnoissant la verité de l'Evangile, quand il est entre les papistes* ([Geneva: Jean Girard], 1543), in *CO* 6, col. 544. Calvin also quoted Rom. 10:10 on this issue. Ibid., col. 545. In the 1540 letter written from Strasbourg and printed together with the *Petit traicté* in 1543, Calvin used this same passage (Rom. 10:9–10) along with 1 Cor. 6:20 to make the same point. *CO* 6, col. 580. Given these explicit references to scripture, Carlos Eire's contention that Calvin's anti-Nicodemite views were grounded especially in "his metaphysical interpretation of the nature of reverential acts and on a strong rejection of the separation of body and spirit in worship" seems misleading. Eire, *War against the Idols,* pp. 256–259, quotation on 256. Eire says nothing about the relationship between this "metaphysical interpretation" and the specific scriptural passages on which Calvin based it.

95. Viret, *Epistre avx fideles,* pp. 36–37, quotation on 37. See also ibid., pp. 61–62. Bullinger also stressed the clarity of Rom. 10:8–10 in this context. See his "Sermon of the confessing of Christe," in [Vermigli and Bullinger], *Cohabitacyon of the faithfull,* fol. 77.

96. *Chansonnier Huguenot,* ed. Bordier, vol. 2, p. 359.

97. Calvin resented accusations that he was being gratuitously severe or intentionally malicious towards persecuted Protestants. He always insisted that he sought their ultimate well-being. See, for example, *Petit traicté,* in *CO* 6, cols. 573, 575; idem, *Excuse de Iehan Calvin a Messieurs les Nicodemites, sur la complaincte qu'ilz font de sa trop grand' rigueur* ([Geneva: Jean Girard], 1544), in *CO* 6, cols. 596, 602, 607–608, 610. In his *Epistre avx fideles,* Viret acknowledged the serious hardships of voluntary exile, recognized the power of the fear of death, expressed solidarity with those suffering in prison, and said he had written to exhort people to follow God's spirit and word, not to trouble afflicted consciences. Ibid., pp. 47–53, 64, 118, 134–135.

98. Calvin, *Excuse,* in *CO* 6, col. 597. For the same remark made eleven years later

in a letter to the Reformed community at Poitiers, see *CO* 15, February 20, 1555, no. 2118, col. 444.

99. Calvin, *Excuse*, in *CO* 6, cols. 596, 599, 601.

100. Ibid., col. 604.

101. Droz, *Chemins de l'hérésie*, vol. 1, p. 154.

102. Calvin, *Petit traicté*, in *CO* 6, cols. 570–571.

103. Viret, *Epistre avx fideles*, p. 79. Viret saved his greatest condemnation for those who sought to justify their participation in the Mass and other Catholic practices, rather than feeling utter sorrow and desire to amend their ways. Ibid., esp. pp. 121–123, 128–135. See also Zagorin, *Ways of Lying*, pp. 104–105.

104. [Bullinger], "Sermon of the confessing of Christe," in [Vermigli and Bullinger], *Cohabitacyon of the faithfull*, fol. 68. See also ibid., fol. 73v: "He which doth deny that all these sayings must be understood of persecutors, he sayeth that darkness is light."

105. Calvin, *Petit traicté*, in *CO* 6, cols. 544, 549, 569–570, 573–574.

106. Calvin, *Excuse*, in *CO* 6, col. 604.

107. Calvin, "Le second sermon, contenant exhortation a souffrir persecution pour suyvre Iesus Christ et son evangile," in *Quatre sermons de M. Iehan Calvin, traictans des matieres fort utiles pour nostre temps* (Geneva: Robert Estienne, 1552), in *CO* 8, cols. 395–396, 403–404, 407–408, quotation on 407. On Destoubequin, see Gérard Moreau, *Histoire du Protestantisme à Tournai jusqu'à la veille de la Révolution des Pays-Bas* (Paris: Société d'Édition "Les Belles Lettres," 1962), p. 117. Crespin, who refers to him as "Michel dit Miquelot," erroneously puts his death in 1547. Crespin 1570, fol. 171.

108. For Viret's invocation of the Hebrew youths, Daniel, the apostles, and the early Christian martyrs, see his *Epistre avx fideles*, pp. 33–34, 127. Viret had previously invoked the examples of the three youths from Dan. 3, as well as Daniel himself. See his *Epistre consolatoire*, repr. in Herminjard, vol. 6, pp. 434–435. Latimer mentioned the apostles, martyrs, and the same three young men from Dan. 3 to indicate that latter-day Christians must "likewise offer ourselves unto the cross, content to suffer whatsoever [God] shall lay upon us." Latimer, *Sermons*, p. 347. For Bullinger's reference to the examples from Daniel and the early Christian martyrs from book eight of Eusebius's *Ecclesiastical History*, see his "Sermon of the confessing of Christe," in [Vermigli and Bullinger], *Cohabitacyon of the faithfull*, fols. 78–80. The early Christian martyrs were also invoked in Lutheran settings: after Charles V's victory over the Schmalkaldic League, two anonymously edited works published in Lutheran Magdeburg drew martyrs' stories from the ancient church historians Sozomen, Socrates, and Theodoret. See Robert Kolb, *For All the Saints: Changing Perceptions of Martyrdom and Sainthood in the Lutheran Reformation* (Macon, Ga.: Mercer University Press, 1987), p. 37.

109. Calvin, *Excuse*, in *CO* 6, col. 604. Veluanus attributed the apostles' and martyrs' courage to their "certain knowledge" [*gewis weten*] that after death they would remain forever with Christ. *Leken wechwyser*, in *BRN*, vol. 4, p. 345.

110. The very beginning of the "Second Sermon" baldly stated that all exhortations to suffer for Christ were pointless without the proper certainty and resolve:

"such steadfastness cannot be in us unless it is founded on certainty of faith." Calvin, "Second sermon," in *CO* 8, col. 393. See also J[oye], *Present consolation,* sig. D4; parallel passage in Rhegius, *Trostbrieff an christen zü Hildeshaim,* sig. [a7v].

111. Calvin, *Petit traicté,* in *CO* 6, col. 571.

112. Ibid., col. 576. See also ibid., col. 568; idem, *Excuse,* in *CO* 6, col. 602.

113. Viret, *Epistre consolatoire,* in Herminjard, vol. 6, p. 434. See the same idea in the *Epistre aux fideles,* pp. 82–83.

114. This verse was frequently quoted to console afflicted Christians. For just a few Protestant examples, see Viret, *Epistre consolatoire,* in Herminjard, vol. 6, p. 430; Calvin, "Second sermon," in *CO* 8, col. 406; Latimer, *Sermons,* p. 466; Scory, *Epistle,* sig. [A6]; Rabus 8, sig. [6]; Guillaume Farel's letter to afflicted Protestants in Metz, in Crespin 1564, p. 257.

115. Calvin, *Excuse,* in *CO* 6, col. 604.

116. [Bradford], *Exhortation to the carienge of Chrystes crosse,* repr. in *Remains of Myles Coverdale, Bishop of Exeter,* ed. George Pearson (Cambridge: Cambridge University Press, 1846), p. 235. See more generally the entire second chapter from which this remark is taken, entitled "Persecution is not Strange." Ibid., pp. 233–235. The work is now attributed to Bradford rather than Coverdale. *STC 1475–1640,* vol. 1, p. 158.

117. Viret, *Epistre consolatoire,* in Herminjard, vol. 6, p. 430.

118. J[oye], *Present consolation,* sig. [C8].

119. Tracy, trans., *Preparation to the Crosse,* sig. [F7v]; Calvin, "Second Sermon," in *CO* 8, cols. 397–398, quotation on 397.

120. Calvin, "Second sermon," in *CO* 8, cols. 394–395.

121. Calvin, *Petit traicté,* in *CO* 6, col. 570. Calvin's remark is a hybrid paraphrase of the two verses from Isaiah.

122. Viret, *Epistre consolatoire,* in Herminjard, vol. 6, p. 431.

123. Calvin, *Petit traicté,* in *CO* 6, cols. 544, 571.

124. [Robert Crowley], *The confutation of .xiii. Articles wherunto Nicolas Shaxton, late byshop of Salisburye subscribed and caused be set forthe . . .* (London: John Daye and William Seres, [1548]), sigs. [A7v, A8].

125. J[oye], *Present consolation,* sigs. D2, D4, D4v, [D8v], E3v, F1v.

126. Calvin, *Petit traicté,* in *CO* 6, col. 568; idem, "Second sermon," in *CO* 8, col. 401.

127. Anne Askewe was born into a prominent Lincolnshire family around 1520. Her Protestant views at Henry VIII's court led to an interrogation by the bishop of London, Edmund Bonner, in the spring of 1545. Freed, she was questioned again the following year, condemned for her denial of transubstantiation, and burned along with three other Protestants at Smithfield on July 16, 1546. The song as well as accounts of her interrogations and torture found their way to the exiled John Bale in Wesel, who published them. For a recent overview of Askewe and her case, see Elaine V. Beilin's introduction to *The Examinations of Anne Askew,* ed. idem (New York: Oxford University Press, 1996), pp. xv–xlii.

128. "The Balade whych Anne Askewe made and sange whan she was in Newgate," stanzas 1–4, in John Bale, *The lattre examinacyon of Anne Askewe, latelye mar-*

tyred in Smythfelde, by the wycked Synagoge of Antichrist, with the Elucydacyon of Johan Bale ([Wesel: Dirik van der Straten], 1547), fol. 63. Same passage in *Examinations,* ed. Beilin, p. 149.

129. Crespin 1564, pp. 232–233. This letter (and two others by Brully) appeared in the first edition of Crespin's martyrology. Crespin 1554, pp. 201–205.

130. Crespin 1564, p. 233; Crespin 1555, p. 209.

131. See the final Latin edition of the *Institutio religionis Christianae* (1559), in *CO* 2, 3.24.7, 3.24.9, cols. 718, 719–720.

132. See Harro Höpfl's concise analysis of Calvin's notion of predestination and election in *The Christian Polity of John Calvin* (Cambridge: Cambridge University Press, 1982), pp. 227–239, esp. p. 235. As Calvin put it in the *Institutio,* in *CO* 2, 3.24.6, col. 717: "we are sufficiently taught by experience itself that a call [*vocationem*] and faith are insignificant unless perseverance is added, which does not happen to everyone."

133. Calvin, "Second sermon," in *CO* 8, col. 404. In a letter to the Lyons prisoners written around December 1552, Calvin said that "you know that in departing from this world, we do not go on an adventure; not only because of the certainty that you have that there is a heavenly life, but also because, being *assured* of unmerited adoption by our God [*estans asseurez de l'adoption gratuite de nostre Dieu*], you are headed there as to your inheritance." *CO* 14, no. 1679, col. 424 (my emphasis). See also another letter to the same prisoners from early July 1553, in *CO* 14, no. 1754, col. 563.

134. J[oye], *Present consolation,* sig. D3. More than two decades earlier, William Tyndale had written that suffering patiently for God's sake was a "sure" sign of being "sealed with Gods spirit unto everlasting life." Tyndale, *Obedience of a Christen man,* fols. 7v–8.

135. Emmanuel College, Cambridge, MS 260, fol. 166v. For the same passage verbatim in print, see Foxe 1570, vol. 2, p. 2105, and Miles Coverdale [and Henry Bull], *Certain most godly, fruitful, and comfortable letters of such true Saintes and holy Martyrs . . .* (London: John Daye, 1564), p. 630.

136. J[oye], *Present consolation,* sig. B4r-v.

137. Bale, *Lattre examinacyon of Anne Askewe,* fol. 67r-v, quotation on 67v.

138. From Estienne's *Apologie pour Hérodote,* quoted in Arthur Piaget and Gabrielle Berthoud, *Notes sur le Livre des Martyrs de Jean Crespin* (Neuchâtel: Secretariat de L'Université, 1930), p. 220 n. 3.

139. Viret, *Epistre consolatoire,* in Herminjard, vol. 6, p. 437.

140. Calvin, *Petit traicté,* in *CO* 6, col. 572.

141. [Crowley], *Confutation of Shaxton,* sig. [B8v]. Ironically, prior to recanting his Protestant views, Shaxton had said that "if it had not been for this broiling" of the early English Protestant martyrs—he goes on to mention Lambert and Frith by name—"I should never have looked so diligently upon the matter, but have slept on both sides soundly as I did before, and been still wrapped in mine old ignorance." Ibid., sig. C4v.

142. In a work justifying Barnes's execution for heresy, John Standish referred to "the great number of copies that be in writing of this his *Protestation,*" a work Barnes had written just before his death. Standish, *A Lytle treatyse . . . againste*

the protestacion of Robert barnes at ye time of his deth (London: Robert Redman, 1540), sig. A2v. From the Continent Miles Coverdale attacked Standish and Barnes's execution in his rebuttal, *A confutacion of that treatise, which one John Standish made agaynst the protestacion of D. Barnes* . . . [Zurich: Christoph Froschauer? 1541?]. Luther's work is entitled *Bekantnus Deß Glaubens, die Doctor Robertus Bar[n]s der hailigen schrifft Doctor . . . zü Lunden in Engelland gethon hat . . . do er züm fewr, on Vrtel vnd Recht, vnschuldig, vnuerhörter sach, gefürt, vnd verbrendt worden ist* (Augsburg: Melchior Ramminger, [1540]). This was one of the four High German editions published without Luther's preface. For the four editions, plus the two with his preface (one each in German and Low German), see *WA* 51, pp. 446–447. Luther's preface is reprinted in ibid., pp. 448–451. For evidence that this pamphlet was known in England, see Richard Hilles's letter written to Bullinger sometime in 1541, which refers to "a little book printed in German, concerning the protest of the said Robert Barnes at the stake." *OL,* vol. 1, no. 105, p. 211.

143. [Jean Calvin], *Histoire d'un meurtre execrable: commis par un Hespagnol, nommé Alphonse Dias, Chambellan du Pape, en la personne de Jehan Dias son frere, le 17 de mars, 1546* . . . ([Geneva: Jean Girard], 1546), repr. in Francis Higman, "Calvin, le polar et la propagande: L'*Histoire d'un meurtre execrable*," *Bibliothèque d'Humanisme et Renaissance,* 54 (1992), 111–123; Philipp Melanchthon, *Ware Historia newlich zu Newberg an der Tonaw ein Spanier, genant Alphonsus Diasius . . . seinen leiblichen bruder Johannem . . . grausamlich ermördet habe* (n.p., [1546]); [Francisco de Enzinas], *Historia vera de morte Diazij*. Melanchthon's pamphlet is dated April 17, 1546, just three weeks after Diaz's assassination. Melanchthon, *Ware Historia,* sig. [A4]. Bucer's extensive preface to Enzinas's treatise, a sterling example of how the calumniation of persecutors was paired with the celebration of martyrs, occupies sigs. α2–[γ7] in the *Historia vera*. For Higman's argument for Calvin's authorship of the *Histoire d'un meurtre execrable* see idem, "Calvin," pp. 116–117. One point Higman does not mention is the striking similarity between Calvin's description of the devil as the father of the Roman church in the last paragraph of this treatise (ibid., p. 123) and a passage from a letter of April 16, 1546, three weeks after Diaz's death, where Calvin said the same thing (alluding to John 8:44) in commenting on his demise: "Clearly the wretched papists show more and more that they are led by the spirit of their father, who from the beginning has been a murderer." Calvin, *CO* 12, to Monsieur de Falais, no. 790, col. 333.

144. Bale, *The first examinacyon of Anne Askewe, latelye martyred in Smythfelde, by the Romysh popes vpholders, with the Elucydacyon of Johan Bale* ([Wesel: Dirik van der Straten], 1546); idem, *Lattre examinacyon of Anne Askewe*. Writing from Winchester in June 1547, Stephen Gardiner complained that these works "were in these parts common, some with leaves unglued . . . and some with leaves glued. And I call them common because I saw at least four of them." Gardiner to Somerset, June 6, [1547], in James Arthur Muller, ed., *The Letters of Stephen Gardiner* (Cambridge: Cambridge University Press, 1933), no. 121, p. 293. Lambert's *Farrago* was translated as *The summe of christianitie gatheryd out almoste of al placis of scripture, by that noble and famouse clerke Francis Lambert*

of Auynyon . . . ([London: Robert Redman], 1536), with the account of Chastellain's martyrdom at fols. 19v–20.

145. Gnapheus, *Johannis Pistorii a Worden, ob evangelicae doctrinae assertionem, apud Hollandos primo omnium exusti, vita* . . . (Strasbourg: Wendelin Rihel, 1546). Part of this edition, excluding the treatise defending clerical marriage, is reprinted in *CDN,* vol. 4, pp. 406–452. See also *BMPN,* vol. 1, pp. 287–288.

146. William Monter, "Les exécutés pour hérésie par arrêt du Parlement de Paris (1523–1560)," *BSHPF,* 142 (1996), 218–222.

147. *Troys Epistres de Godefroy de Hamaelle, natif de niuele en Brabant: Le quel Souffrit martyre pour Iesu Christ* . . . (n.p., ca. 1552). On Godefroy de Hamaelle, see further Moreau, *Histoire du Protestantisme à Tournai,* pp. 120–127.

148. [Calvin], *Histoire d'un meurtre execrable,* in Higman, "Calvin," p. 118.

149. Bale, *First examinacyon of Anne Askewe,* preface, fol. 5r-v.

150. Veluanus, *Leken Wechwyser,* in *BRN,* vol. 4, p. 341.

151. So far as I am aware, scholars have not explicitly noted these parallels. For treatments of the major Protestant martyrologists as a group, see A. G. Dickens and John Tonkin, "Weapons of Propaganda: The Martyrologies," in *The Reformation in Historical Thought* (Cambridge, Mass.: Harvard University Press, 1985), pp. 41, 44, 49–50, 51; Boudin, "Martyrologes protestants," pp. 69–70; and Gilmont, "Les martyrologes du XVIe siècle," in *Ketzerverfolgung,* ed. Seidel Menchi, pp. 176–189 (including Heinrich Pantaleon). For Foxe, Crespin, and van Haemstede, see Andrew Pettegree, "European Calvinism: History, Providence, and Martyrdom," in *The Church Retrospective,* ed. R. N. Swanson, vol. 33 of *Studies in Church History* (Woodbridge, Suffolk: Boydell Press, 1997), pp. 227–252. Gilmont's unpublished thesis remains the most complete treatment of the major Protestant martyrologies. Gilmont, "Martyrologes protestants du XVIe siècle," pp. 141–374. Gilmont rightly notes the *different* reasons that led each of these martyrologists to produce their works, characterizing Foxe as a humanist historian, Crespin as a contemporary journalist, and van Haemstede and Rabus fundamentally as pastors. Gilmont, "Un instrument de propagande religieuse: les martyrologes du XVIe siècle, in *Sources de l'histoire de la Belgique: Moyen age et Temps modernes* (Louvain: Publications universitaires de Louvain, 1968), pp. 383–384.

152. For this paragraph, see Kolb, *For All the Saints,* p. 42; Gilmont, *Jean Crespin,* pp. 27–28; A. J. Jelsma, *Adriaan van Haemstede en zijn martelaarsboek* (The Hague: Boekencentrum, 1970), pp. 5–10; J. F. Mozley, *John Foxe and His Book* (1940; reprint, New York: Octagon Books, 1970), pp. 12–16.

153. Kolb, *For All the Saints,* pp. 41–43; Gilmont, *Jean Crespin,* pp. 31–32; Jelsma, *Adriaan van Haemstede,* pp. 10–11, 16–17; Mozley, *Foxe and His Book,* pp. 14–18, 20, 24–25.

154. Kolb, *For All the Saints,* pp. 43–45.

155. Ibid., pp. 46–47. Emmel continued to publish the volumes despite Rabus's move to Ulm in late 1556. The martyrologist had accepted the city council's offer to become the town's superintendant of churches, a post he held until his death in 1592. Ibid., pp. 49, 52.

156. Gilmont, *Jean Crespin,* pp. 32–39, 41–44. For Crespin's letters to Calvin during this period, see Calvin, *CO* 12, April–May 1545, no. 637, cols. 72–74; July 1546, no. 808, cols. 357–359; July 20, 1547, no. 928, cols. 556–557; September 13, 1547, no. 945, cols. 588–589.

157. As Crespin stated in the preface to the first folio edition, "Regarding the five students who came from the school in Lausanne and were burned in the city of Lyons, with good reason can I say that they provided me the first occasion to apply myself to the gathering of the writings of those who have died steadfast in the Lord." Crespin 1564, sig. γ2v. For the complicated publication history of his martyrology, from the successive installments of the 1550s, to the Latin editions of 1556 and 1560, to the first folio edition of 1564, see Gilmont, *Jean Crespin,* pp. 165–182.

158. Jelsma, *Adriaan van Haemstede,* pp. 28–81. Jelsma downplays the relationship between van Haemstede's preaching and the crackdown by authorities. Ibid., p. 67. But the house of the congregation's leader, Gaspar van der Heyden, was raided just days after van Haemstede preached, which strongly suggests a direct connection between the two events. See Andrew Pettegree, *Emden and the Dutch Revolt,* pp. 63–64. For the prolonged, detailed proceedings against Janssens and Halewijn between September 2, 1558, and their execution sentences on February 27, 1559, see SAA, Vierschaar, V 147 (1555–1559), fols. 90, 92–97, 98–99v; *AA,* vol. 8, pp. 448–460, 471, 472.

159. Pettegree, *Emden and the Dutch Revolt,* pp. 93–94, 275. The first edition is dated March 18, 1559, so the work must have been essentially complete, save for the February 1559 events narrated, by the time van Haemstede left Antwerp in late January.

160. Mozley, *Foxe and His Book,* pp. 17–30, 37–52, 118–122; Christina H. Garrett, *The Marian Exiles* (Cambridge: Cambridge University Press, 1938), pp. 155–157; David Loades, *The Oxford Martyrs* (1970; reprint, Bangor: Headstart History, 1992), pp. 151–153. For Foxe's conception of his initial two-part martyrological project, the first part comprising Wyclif to 1500 and the second "from the initial undertakings of Martin Luther," see his dedicatory preface to Duke Christoph of Württemberg in Foxe 1554, sig. [a6r-v].

161. Donald Kelley has described the network that included Crespin, Johannes Sleidan, Matthias Flacius Illyricus, Foxe, and Heinrich Pantaleon as "something approaching a literary circle, a kind of Protestant pleiade of the the exile circuit, which drew upon a common fund of experience, a common ideological commitment, a common historical perspective, and a common reliance upon what Foxe called the 'miracle' of printing." Kelley, "Martyrs, Myths, and the Massacre: The Background of St. Bartholomew," *American Historical Review,* 77 (1972), 1325. See also Dickens and Tonkin, "Weapons of Propaganda," p. 44.

162. Kolb, *For All the Saints,* p. 47; Gilmont, *Jean Crespin,* p. 149.

163. Calvin, *CO* 15, no. 1940, cols. 111–112. For their earliest known exchange, see Sleidan to Calvin, May 22, 1539, in Herminjard, vol. 5, no. 791, pp. 320–321.

164. Gilmont, *Jean Crespin,* pp. 32–38.

165. Ibid., pp. 43, 246–260.

166. Moreau, *Protestantisme à Tournai,* pp. 90–94; Mozley, *Foxe and His Book,* p. 43.

167. Foxe 1554, sig. a2; Kolb, *For All the Saints*, p. 47.
168. Leslie P. Fairfield, *John Bale: Mythmaker for the English Reformation* (West Lafayette, Ind.: Purdue University Press), pp. 150–153; Mozley, *Foxe and His Book*, pp. 50–51, 122–123; William Haller, *Foxe's Book of Martyrs and the Elect Nation* (London: Jonathan Cape, 1963), pp. 58, 64–65. Foxe conceived the 1559 *Rerum*, devoted to British martyrs, as the first part of a two-volume work; the second volume was to cover continental martyrs. Upon his return to England the vernacular *Acts and Monuments* absorbed all his energy; Heinrich Pantaleon compiled the second volume.
169. Haller, *Foxe's Book of Martyrs*, pp. 112–113; [Crowley], *Confutation of Shaxton*.
170. Mozley, *Foxe and His Book*, pp. 23, 25.
171. Ibid., pp. 35–37; David Daniell, *William Tyndale: A Biography* (New Haven: Yale University Press, 1994), p. 201.
172. See especially Grindal's letter from Strasbourg to Foxe in Basel dated June 18, 1557, in *The Remains of Edmund Grindal, D.D.*, ed. William Nicholson (Cambridge: Cambridge University Press, 1843), pp. 224–227. On November 28, 1557, Grindal told Foxe that he would send an account of the theological disputations involving Thomas Cranmer and Nicholas Ridley at Oxford. In an undated letter sent perhaps the following month, Foxe acknowledged Grindal's diligence in collecting and supplying him with materials relevant to the martyrs. Ibid., pp. 229–231.
173. See Foxe's letters to Bullinger of May 13, June 17, August 2, and September 26, 1559, in *The Zurich Letters, Comprising the Correspondence of Several English Bishops . . .*, 2nd ed., ed. Hastings Robinson (Cambridge: Cambridge University Press, 1847), pp. 35, 47, 57.
174. Susan Wabuda, "Henry Bull, Miles Coverdale, and the Making of Foxe's *Book of Martyrs*," in *Martyrs and Martyrologies*, ed. Diana Wood, vol. 30 of *Studies in Church History* (Oxford: Blackwell, 1993), pp. 245–258; Mozley, *Foxe and His Book*, pp. 129–130.
175. BL, Harleian MS 416, no. 61, fol. 106.
176. See Théodore Agrippa d'Aubigné, *Histoire Universelle*, ed. Joseph Étienne Alphonse de Ruble, vol. 1, 1553–1559 (Paris: Librarie Renouard, 1886), p. 202.
177. For de Brès (and before him, perhaps Charles de Nielles) as Crespin's informant for Tournai, see Gérard Moreau, "Contribution à l'Histoire du Livre des Martyrs," *BSHPF*, 103 (1957), 196–199. The first edition of Crespin's martyrology begins with Hus and proceeds chronologically through Fanini Fanino (Crespin 1554, pp. 615–626), after which follow brief entries on Wolfgang Schuch (d. 1525) and Pierre Gaudet (d. 1534) (p. 627), and then two longer series of entries as further addenda to the main text, each of which is substantially chronological within itself. The first begins with Jean le Clerc, covers 1524 to 1551, and ends with Thomas de Sainct Paul (pp. 627–644); the second begins with François Bribard, covers 1543-July 1554, and concludes with Richard le Feure (pp. 644–687). Crespin apparently typeset and printed the main text as he was receiving more materials, which he clustered several at a time and printed at the end. This is consistent with his own remarks to the reader: "We have since bit by bit collected numerous letters, confessions [of faith], interrogation pro-

ceedings, and certain attestations of numerous holy people who were subsequently executed, which we have added here without much attention given to
the sequence of the years." Crespin 1555, sig. [*8v].

178. Jelsma, *Adriaan van Haemstede,* pp. 257–258; van Haemstede 1559, [p. 455].
Although Rabus drew heavily on previously published accounts, he too integrated oral and manuscript sources for some of his martyrs. For example, for
Matthias Weibel, he used "some trustworthy oral and handwritten testimonies
[*Mündtlicher vnd Schrifftlicher Zeügnuß*] from honorable people (who are still
alive and with whom I have had much interaction), which were recorded in
brief, but faithfully and truthfully." Rabus 2, fol. 151.

179. Van Haemstede 1559, [p. 455]; Crespin 1570, fol. 709. See also Crespin's
exhortation to the faithful in Hainaut "to do their duty" in gathering information about local martyrs, and his prefatory exhortation to all the faithful, from
his earliest editions, to "collect . . . their [the martyrs'] words and writings, their
responses, the confession of their faith, their speeches and final exhortations."
Crespin 1570, fol. 308v; Crespin 1555, sig. *4v.

180. There were four printings of *Ein Warhaffte grausamme Geschicht, So geschehen
ist zü Mechel in Brabandt . . .* (n.p., 1556). See the careful treatment plus texts
in *Duitse vlugschriften van de tijd over het proces en de terechtstelling van de
Protestanten Frans en Nikolaas Thys te Mechelen (1555),* ed. Robert Foncke
(Antwerp: "De Sikkel," 1937). For its inclusion in the martyrologies, see
Crespin, *Troisieme partie du recueil des martyrs . . .* ([Geneva]: Jean Crespin,
1556), pp. 86–97; Rabus 6, fols. 202v–209v; van Haemstede 1559, pp. 348–
354. Three more German editions appeared ca. 1557–1558 in pamphlet form,
which were derived from Rabus's account. A Low German translation without
place or date of publication also appeared. *Duitse Vlugschriften,* ed. Foncke,
pp. 134–185.

181. Bordier, *Chansonnier Huguenot,* vol. 2, for example, pp. 360–363, 368–369,
374–378, 386–392, 413–414. For four works concerning Anne du Bourg, see
Gilmont, "Martyrologes protestants du XVIe siècle," pp. 118–121.

182. [Antoine de la Roche Chandieu], *Histoire des persecvtions, et martyrs de l'Église
de Paris depuis l'An 1557. iusques au tepms* [sic] *du Roy Charles neufuiesme . . .*
(Lyons: [Claude Senneton], 1563). Crespin's extensive use of Chandieu can be
followed in Matthieu Lelièvre's notes to the nineteenth-century edition of
Crespin's martyrology. See Crespin, *Histoire des Martyrs,* ed. Daniel Benoit, vol.
2 (Toulouse: Société des libres religieux, 1887), pp. 542–628, 639–648, 657–
699, 705–706. See also Piaget and Berthoud, *Notes sur le Livre des Martyrs,*
pp. 50–58; Gilmont, "Martyrologes protestants du XVIe siècle," pp. 124, 264–
265; idem, *Jean Crespin,* pp. 180–181.

183. [Joris Wybo?] *Historie ende ghesciedenisse van de verradelicke gheuangenisse der
vromer ende godsaligher mannen, Christophori Fabritij . . . ende Oliuerij Bockij
. . .* (n.p., 1565), repr. in *BRN,* vol. 8, pp. 281–460; [Wybo?] *Histoire notable de
la trahison et emprisonnement de deux bons et fideles personnages en la ville
d'Anuers: . . . Christophle Fabri Ministre . . . et d'Oliuier Bouck Professeur . . . ,*
trans. Guy de Brès, (n.p., 1565). For Wybo as the likely author, see Pijper's
introduction in *BRN,* vol. 8, pp. 272–274. For the abundant archival materials

about Fabri's imprisonment, interrogations, and execution, see SAA, Vier-schaar, V139.

184. Marten Microen, *Een Waerachteghe Historie, van Hoste (gheseyt Jooris) vander Katelyne, te Ghendt . . . ghebrandt ten grooten nutte ende vertroostinghe aller Christenen gheschreven . . .* [Emden: Gillis van der Erve, ca. 1556], repr. in *BRN,* vol. 8, pp. 187–253. Van der Erve may also have published Pierre du Val, *Petit dialogue d'un consolateur consolant l'Eglise en ses afflictions, tiré du pseaume CXXIX* [ca. 1555?]. For both works, see Pettegree, *Emden and the Dutch Revolt,* pp. 262, 264. He was also perhaps responsible for Carolus de Koninck's Dutch translation of the story of Francesco Spiera, of which no copies survive. Ibid., p. 258. Van Haemstede referred to this translation in his entry on de Koninck, who had spent time in both England and Emden as a refugee. Van Haemstede 1559, p. 417.

185. Andrew Pettegree, *Foreign Protestant Communities in Sixteenth-Century London* (Oxford: Oxford University Press, 1986), pp. 89–90; idem, *Emden and the Dutch Revolt,* p. 88.

186. These include John Knox, *A Faythfull admonition made by Iohn Knox, unto the professours of Gods truthe in England . . .* (1554); Scory, *Epistle* (1555); Nicholas Ridley, *A Brief declaracion of the Lordes Supper . . .* (1555); Nicholas Ridley and Hugh Latimer's *Certein godly, learned, and comfortable conferences . . .* (1556), which they exchanged in prison prior to their deaths; Thomas Cranmer, *The copy of certain lettres sent to the Quene . . .* (1556), also written from prison prior to his execution; the lengthy *Examinacion of the constaunt Martir of Christ, John Philpot . . .* (ca. 1557), Philpot's own account of his multiple interrogations; and two printings of Cranmer, *Defensio verae et catholicae doctrinae de Sacramento corporis et sanguinis Christi Servatoris nostri . . .* (1557). For complete bibliographical descriptions of these works, see Pettegree, *Emden and the Dutch Revolt,* pp. 255, 260, 261, 265, 266, 269, 270.

187. Rabus rearranged his ancient martyrs chronologically in the second edition of 1571–1572.

188. Hence Rabus devoted most of vol. 4 of his work to Luther, a critically important witness to the Gospel, but not one who was executed for it. Rabus 4, fols. 1–264. On Rabus's work as more a book of confessors than a martyrology per se, see Kolb, *For All the Saints,* pp. 8–9, 63.

189. On Foxe as a Eusebian ecclesiastical historian rather than a martyrologist in the narrow sense, see Thomas S. Freeman, "'Great Searching Out of Bookes and Autors': John Foxe as an Ecclesiastical Historian" (Ph.D. diss., Rutgers University, 1995).

190. For the figures, see Jean-François Gilmont, "Les centres d'intérêt du martyrologe de Jean Crespin (1554–1570) révélés par la cartographie et les statistiques," *Miscellanea historiae ecclesiasticae,* vol. 5 (Louvain: Publications universitaires de Louvain, 1974), p. 366; idem, "La genèse du martyrologe d'Adrien van Haemstede (1559)," *Revue d'histoire ecclésiastique,* 63 (1968), 401.

191. Van Haemstede 1559, sig. +3v. The title of another brief, prefatory section repeats this idea and provides the Old Testament overview that precedes the

body of the text: "That the Righteous from the Beginning of the World Have Always Been Persecuted." Ibid., sig. [+7v].

192. Rabus 6, sigs. 2–[*4v], quotation on sig. [4]. That Rabus did not organize his first edition chronologically does not mean that he lacked a vision of the history of Christian persecution.

193. Crespin 1555, sig. *2.

194. Foxe 1554, sig. [a6]; Foxe 1563, sigs. B1–B2v. Foxe paraphrased 2 Tim. 3:12 in making a similar, transhistorical claim in his entry on Patrick Hamilton, one of many such remarks in the *Acts and Monuments:* "In all things and in all ages, the saying of St. Paul is verified. Whosoever doth desire and study to live godly in Christ, he shall suffer persecution as a companion of his godliness." Foxe 1563, p. 460.

195. This is how English Protestants understood their predicament under Mary. In 1555 the exiled Bishop of Chichester, John Scory, encouraged afflicted believers at home: "although God seemeth now to defer us, and to suffer the bloody and cruel adversaries, too long to triumph over us: yet let us not despair, but continue in prayers, being fully persuaded, that though he seem now to be far off, that yet he will certainly come, and deliver us." Scory, *Epistle,* sig. B5. In August of the same year, Richard Morison expressed the same idea to Bullinger: "Since he [God] is our Father, he cannot for ever be angry with his children. Nay rather, when he has an assurance of our improvement, he will then certainly think of punishing both his enemies, and ours for his sake." *OL,* vol. 1, no. 75, p. 150. The providential understanding of Mary's death and Elizabeth's accession was not contrived as an ex post facto, Elizabethan "myth" (*pace* Haller and Loades), but rather comprised a consistently interpreted realization of a Marian Protestant longing. There is every reason to think Thomas Brice meant it when in 1559 he concluded each of his seventy-plus verses about the Marian martyrs with the line "we wished for our Elizabeth." As Brice wrote in his preface to the reader, "the same just and righteous God, which (for our sins) corrected us and gave us over into the hands of the most bloody and viperous generation, to be eaten like bread, hath now (of his mercy alone) exalted the horn of his people." Brice, *A compendious Register in Metre, conteining the names, and pacient suffryngs of the membres of Jesus Christ, and the tormented, and cruelly burned within Englande . . .* (London: John Kyngston for Richard Adams, 1559), sig. [A8v].

196. BL copy of Crespin 1555, shelf mark 847.a.29.

197. In this sense Rabus's first edition, even though not arranged calendrically, is closer to traditional collections of saints' lives than are the other three martyrologies.

198. I agree fundamentally with such scholars as Auke Jelsma and Hugh Boudin concerning the martyrologists' objectives. Jelsma, *Adriaan van Haemstede,* pp. 230–250; Boudin, "Martyrologes protestants," pp. 70–71. I have tried to tie these aims to their target audiences, however, and to provide explicit evidence for their goals by quoting directly from all four martyrologists.

199. Foxe 1563, sig. [B6v].

200. Crespin 1555, sig. *2.
201. Crespin 1555, sigs. *4v–*5; Crespin 1564, sig. [β6v]; Rabus 1, sig. ☞3r-v.
202. Rabus 1, sigs. ☞2–☞3v, quotations on sig. ☞2. For another instance where Rabus cited Rom. 10:10 in the same way, see Rabus 6, sig. *4. For similar ideas, see Rabus 2, sig. 4v; Rabus 7, sig.)(3.
203. Rabus 6, sigs. *1–*2v. Similarly, another preface derived twelve explicit "consolations" [Trosten] from Matt. 10:15–32, a text including the admonition not to fear those who can kill the body, but rather the one who can cast both body and soul into hell. Rabus 8, sigs. 2–[7].
204. Foxe 1563, sig. [B6].
205. Crespin 1555, sig. *2v.
206. Crespin 1555, sig. *4r-v. For Crespin's criticism of previous "lukewarmness," see sig. *3.
207. Crespin 1555, sig. *3; Foxe 1563, sig. [B6].
208. Foxe 1563, sig. [B6v]. He expressed a particular obligation to preserve the martyrs' memory: "I thought it not to be neglected, that the precious monuments of so many matters, and men most meet to be recorded and registered in books, should lie buried by my fault in the pit of oblivion." Ibid.
209. The best treatment of the woodcuts in Foxe, which situates them solidly in continental iconographical traditions, is Margaret Aston and Elizabeth Ingram, "The Iconography of the Acts and Monuments," in John Foxe and the English Reformation, ed. David Loades (Aldershot: Scolar Press, 1997), pp. 66–142.
210. Foxe 1563, sig. [B6]. Rabus and Crespin, too, were aware of the ancient veneration of Christian martyrs, and maintained the common Protestant view that originally legitimate practices had later degenerated into superstition. Rabus 1, sig. ☞4r-v; Crespin 1570, sig. α5v.
211. Foxe 1570, vol. 1, sig. *3v: "In probation whereof we see with what admiration, and almost superstition, not only the memory, but also the relics of those good martyrs were received and kept amongst the ancient Christians." Similarly, the 1563 calendar, in which Foxe had replaced traditional Catholic saints with Protestant martyrs, was omitted in 1570, although he brought it back in the fourth edition of 1583 (the last before his death) and it remained in subsequent editions. Foxe 1563, sigs. [*3–*6v]; Foxe 1583, vol. 1, sigs. §2–[§4v].
212. One engraving depicted the execution of martyrs at the hands of Catholic ecclesiastics as the border image for a sonnet, the other portrayed Noah's ark. Crespin 1564, sigs. [α4v], [γ4v]. The same engravings appear in Crespin 1570, sig. [β6r-v].
213. Robert Scribner, "Incombustible Luther: The Image of the Reformer in Early Modern Germany," P&P, 110 (1986), 36–68. For more on Lutheran memorialization of the reformer after his death, see Kolb, For All the Saints, pp. 103–138.
214. Crespin 1564, p. 173. On the public disturbance at Tielemans's execution, see the report by a sixteenth-century chronicler in ARB, MS 14,896–14,898, fol. 132v (new foliation), which is reprinted (with omissions) in A. L. E. Verheyden, Le martyrologe courtraisien et le martyrologe bruxellois (Vilvorde: R. Allecourt, 1950), pp. 63–64.

215. Miles Huggarde, *The displaying of the Protestantes* . . . (London: Robert Caly, 1556), fol. 62v.

216. *Acts of the Privy Council of England,* new series, vol. 5, ed. John Roche Dasent (London: H.M. Stationary Office, 1892), p. 120. For Foxe's account of William Pygot, see Foxe 1563, pp. 1111–1112.

217. For Hullier, see Foxe 1570, vol. 2, pp. 2086, 2196–2197, quotation on 2197. This story is not in the first edition of the *Acts and Monuments,* which included just one prayer and one letter by Hullier. Foxe 1563, pp. 1513–1516. For Miln, see John Knox, "The History of the Reformation in Scotland," in *The Works of John Knox,* ed. David Laing, vol. 1 (1895; reprint, New York: AMS Press, 1966), p. 308. Knox added that initial efforts by ecclesiastical authorities to remove the cairn were unsuccessful. Ibid. Additionally, not only did Foxe recount that Nicholas Ridley gave away small possessions to people near him just before his execution, but he stated that "some plucked the points of his hose. Happy was he that might get any rag of him." Foxe 1570, vol. 2, p. 1937. See also the report by the imperial ambassador, Simon Renard, to Philip II, concerning the crowd's actions after the execution of John Rogers in February 1555: some of the people present "gathered the ashes and bones and wrapped them up in paper to preserve them." *Calendar of Letters, Despatches and State Papers Relating to the Negotiations between England and Spain,* vol. 13, ed. Royall Tyler (1954; reprint, Nendeln: Kraus, 1978), no. 148, pp. 138–139, quotation on 138 (Tyler's trans. from French original).

218. Van Haemstede 1559, p. 444. Gillis was executed on December 24, 1558, Anthonius on January 12, 1559. For the documents detailing the expenses of their interrogations and executions, see ARB, Rekenkamer, vol. 12,709, fols. 130v–131, 152v–154, 157; Verheyden, *Martyrologe courtraisien et bruxellois,* p. 70.

219. For example, when Henry Burton lost his ears for his outspoken Puritan views in June 1637, an underground pamphlet described how "the blood ran streaming down upon the scaffold, which divers persons standing about the pillory seeing, dipped their handkerchiefs in, as a thing most precious." See *A Briefe Relation Of certain speciall and most materiall passages, and speeches in the Starre-Chamber* . . . *at the censure of those three worthy Gentlemen, Dr.* BASTWICKE, *Mr.* BVRTON *and Mr.* PRYNNE . . . (Amsterdam: [J. F. Stam], 1637), p. 30, repr. in *Harleian Miscellany,* vol. 4 (London: for R. Dutton, 1809), p. 237. I thank Alastair J. Bellany for calling this reference to my attention. For the Catholic convert Sir Kenelm Digby's sarcastic comments on such devotional practices, see John R. Knott, *Discourses of Martyrdom in English Literature, 1563–1694* (Cambridge: Cambridge University Press, 1993), p. 140.

220. Catherine Randall Coats, a literary scholar, is apparently unaware of such examples and fails to distinguish prescription from practice. This leads her to contrast Catholic cultic practices involving the veneration of relics with a Protestant attitude toward their martyrs that she contends remained exclusively textual. For example, contrasting Catholic attitudes and practices with Crespin's, she claims that "because Protestants did not acknowledge or venerate enclosed presence, it was impossible that portions of the Protestant martyrs' bodies

function in the sense of relics." Coats, *(Em)bodying the Word: Textual Resurrections in the Martyrological Narratives of Foxe, Crespin, de Bèze and d'Aubigné* (New York: Peter Lang, 1992), p. 61. See also ibid., p. 6.

221. Foxe 1563, sig. [B6].

222. Rabus 4, sigs. [4–*4]. See also his reference to the many holy patriarchs, fathers, kings, and prophets from the Old Testament, Christ and his followers in the New Testament, and the "Herrlicher Martyrer" of the early Church. Rabus 1, sig. ☞4. Rabus also mentioned persecuted witnesses from scripture and the early Church by name—Isaiah, Jeremiah, Peter, Lawrence—plus "several thousand other martyrs." Rabus 7, sig.)(2.

223. Van Haemstede 1559, pp. 1–29 (for Christ through the martyrs of the 330s), sigs. [+7v–+8v] (for persecution victims in the Old Testament).

224. Ibid., sig. [+6]. Note the paraphrase of John 15:20. Foxe's allegorical Latin play, *Christus triumphans,* was published in 1556 while he was gathering materials on the Marian martyrs in Basel. For him, "the major events and most significant periods in ecclesiastical history are as acts and scenes in a theater." V. Norskov Olsen, *John Foxe and the Elizabethan Church* (Berkeley: University of California Press, 1973), p. 58.

225. Foxe 1563, sig. B2. In a frequently quoted passage, Foxe wrote that "if martyrs are to be compared with martyrs, I see no cause why the martyrs of our time deserve not as great commendation as the other in the primitive church, which assuredly are inferior to them in no point of praise, whether we look upon the number of them that suffered, or the greatness of their torments, or their constancy in dying, or also consider the fruit that they brought to the amendment of mens' lives, and the increase of the Gospel." Ibid., sig. [B6v]. He employed the same Tertullianesque metaphor as George Joye: The ancient martyrs "did, like famous husbandmen of the world, sow the fields of the church, that first lay unmanured and waste. And these [recent martyrs] with the fatness of their blood did cause it to battle and fructify." Foxe 1563, ibid. Compare with J[oye], *Present consolation,* sig. B4r-v.

226. Foxe 1563, p. 1694.

227. Crespin 1555, sig. *3v; Crespin 1564, sig. α3v (see also p. 1); Crespin 1570, sig. α4.

228. Crespin 1570, sigs. α4v–α5v.

229. Crespin and Goulart 1582, fols. 8–36v. Goulart also added a tenth book covering the St. Bartholomew's Day massacres. Ibid., fols. 712–732.

230. Crespin 1564, sig. γ1.

231. Ibid., p. 71. Crespin added that the problems with four of Saube's articles were attributable to the ignorance of the times. Moreover, ambiguities surrounded her trial and responses due to a lack of information. Ibid., p. 72.

232. Foxe 1563, p. 347. These Lollards had followed Wyclif, who "by God's providence, sprang and rose up, through whom the Lord would first wake up again the world." Ibid., p. 87. See the very similar view in van Haemstede 1559, p. 44.

233. Foxe 1563, p. 41. Speaking of the articles alleged against fifteenth-century Lollards from Norfolk and Suffolk, Foxe stated that "many of them either were

falsely objected against them, or not truly reported of the notaries, according as the common manner is of these adversaries." Foxe 1570, vol. 1, p. 784. For more on the Protestant accusation of medieval Catholic falsification, see Euan Cameron, "Medieval Heretics as Protestant Martyrs," in *Martyrs and Martyrologies,* ed. Wood, p. 205.

234. See J. A. F. Thomson, "John Foxe and Some Sources for Lollard History: Notes for a Critical Appraisal," in *Studies in Church History,* vol. 2, ed. G. J. Cuming (London: Thomas Nelson and Sons, 1965), pp. 251–257. See also Foxe's complaints about Catholic chroniclers' partiality in his "Protestation to the whole Church of England." Foxe 1570, vol. 1, sig. ☞2v. Elsewhere Foxe mentioned Lollard shortcomings but qualified them, as for example when he discussed Londoner Joan John's views about the saints, based on her 1511 interrogation. Foxe 1570, vol. 2, pp. 927–928.

235. Cameron, "Medieval Heretics," p. 194. See also Jane Facey, "John Foxe and the Defence of the English Church," in *Protestantism and the National Church in Sixteenth Century England,* ed. Peter Lake and Maria Dowling (New York: Croom Helm, 1987), pp. 168–170.

236. Van Haemstede 1559, sig. +5v.

237. Foxe 1563, sig. [B4v].

238. Crespin 1564, sig. α4. Both sonnets appear on this page. The one addressed to the Catholics first appeared on the verso of the title page of Crespin's *Quatrieme partie* (1561). *BMPN,* vol. 2, p. 133.

239. Van Haemstede 1559, sigs. +2–[+7], quotations on sigs. +3, +4, +4v, [+5], [+5v], [+7].

240. Foxe 1563, sigs. [B4v–B5v].

241. Van Haemstede 1559, [p. 455]. He did not elaborate on the meaning of the latter phrase, but any hostile preacher who had felt faint, passed out, or suffered a stroke or heart attack would have been readily understood to have been struck down by God.

242. Foxe 1563, pp. 1694–1703, 1703–1707. Foxe explicitly stated his purpose in the latter as "only to set forth God's manifest scourge and judgment upon such, whose punishment may engender a terror in all other persecutors to beware hereafter of spoiling innocent blood." Ibid., p. 1704.

243. Crespin 1570, sig. [α6v], fols. 67, 673, quotation on sig. [α6v].

244. Mozley, *Foxe and His Book,* pp. 163–1   David Nicholls, "The Theatre of Martyrdom in the French Reformation," *P&P,* 121 (1988), 66.

245. Mozley, *Foxe and His Book,* p. 164.

246. Foxe 1563, p. 444.

247. Ibid., p. 1706. Foxe reported that William Fenning was "yet alive" despite his role in procuring the death of John Cooper. Ibid., p. 1705.

248. For an overview of Calvin's dispute with Westphal, see François Wendel, *Calvin: Origins and Development of His Religious Thought,* trans. Philip Mairet (1963; reprint, Durham, N.C.: Labyrinth Press, 1987), pp. 102–105.

249. Foxe is best understood as a "moderate Puritan" after Elizabeth's accession. See Peter Lake, *Moderate Puritans and the Elizabethan Church* (Cambridge: Cambridge University Press, 1982). I thank Prof. Lake for discussion on this point.

250. Cranmer to Melanchthon, in *OL,* vol. 1, March 27, 1552, no. 15, pp. 25–26. The letters to Bullinger and Calvin are dated March 20, 1552. Ibid., pp. 22–24, 24–25.

251. For general remarks on the way in which early modern martyrologies excluded as they included, see Jean Meyhoffer, *Le Martyrologe protestant des Pays-Bas 1523–1597: Étude critique* ([Brussels?] Nessonvaux, 1907), pp. 75–76; Halkin, "Hagiographie protestante," p. 458; A. L. E. Verheyden, *Le Martyrologe Protestant des Pays-Bas du Sud au XVIe siècle* (Brussels: Editions de la Librairie des éclaireurs unionistes, 1960), pp. 47–48; Alan F. Kreider, "'The Servant Is Not Greater than His Master': The Anabaptists and the Suffering Church," *MQR,* 58 (1984), 9. The fact that Rabus otherwise systematically excluded Anabaptists from his martyrology implies that the presence of sisters-in-law Maria and Ursula van Beckum (Rabus 3, fols. 180v–184) stemmed from ambiguities in sources such as the song about their deaths, *Ein New Lied von zweien Jungkfrawen, vom Adell zu Delden, drey meil von Deuenter vorbranth* (n.p., 1545). When asked about rebaptism, the women responded as interrogated Anabaptists often did, saying that they had been baptized "rightly" [*recht*] only once— which could be taken to refer to their infant baptisms (as Rabus apparently understood it) or (as Anabaptists meant it) that because infant baptism was an empty ceremony, they had been baptized once as adults, after having made a commitment to Christ: "Ein mahl wir seynt getauffet recht / Das ist noch Christus lere." *New Lied von zweien Jungkfrawen,* fols. [2v–3]. Given the notable lack of Anabaptists in Rabus's work despite ample opportunity to include many others, Pijper's contention that he consciously sought to acknowledge them as martyrs cannot be sustained. Pijper, *Martelaarsboeken,* p. 132. For Maria and Ursula van Beckum, see *ME,* vol. 1, pp. 260–261; John Oyer, "Maria and Ursula van Beckum," in *Profiles of Anabaptist Women: Sixteenth-Century Reforming Pioneers,* ed. C. Arnold Snyder and Linda A. Huebert Hecht (Waterloo, Ont.: Wilfred Laurier University Press, 1996), pp. 352–358; *OHL,* in *BRN,* vol. 2, pp. 509–516. As for Foxe, he indexed Nicholas Ridley's remarks about Anabaptists as "Anabaptists justly condemned." When Foxe included Peter Franke ("Peter, a German"), who was burned in November 1538, he carefully noted that although he and a companion "constantly endured death by the fire at Colchester for the Lord's supper . . . it is reported that they defiled this good quarrel with another foul error, touching the incarnation of Christ of his mother." Foxe 1563, sig. QQQQ1, p. 571. For Peter Franke, an Anabaptist refugee from Bruges, see Irvin B. Horst, *The Radical Brethren: Anabaptism and the English Reformation to 1558* (Nieuwkoop: De Graaf, 1972), pp. 87–89. Five radicals from Essex were burned at Smithfield in London in April 1557, who maintained, among other views, that all men's wives should be held in common. Foxe probably knew about them, but they did not appear in his work. Brigden, *London and the Reformation,* p. 615.

252. Foxe 1563, p. 1161 (referring to Thomas Haukes); van Haemstede 1559, p. 348 (referring to Hoste van der Katelyne); Rabus 3, fol. 124v (referring to Georg Winkler); Crespin 1564, p. 305 (in the entry on Florent Venot).

253. *Eyn new warhafftig vnd wunderbarlich geschicht oder hystori, von Jörgen Wagner*

zu München in Bayern als eyn Ketzer verbrandt im Jar M. D. xxvii [Nuremberg: Hans Hergot, 1527], sig. A1v.

254. Crespin 1564, p. 109 (my emphasis).

255. Foxe 1563, p. 436 (my emphasis). Foxe's double negative here carries the force of the original single. Van Haemstede, who derived the account from Rabus's direct reprinting of the *New geschicht von Jörgen Wagner,* left the article alone in his translation: "Dat het Doopsel des Waters gheen saligheyt en gheeft" [That baptism by water offers no salvation]. Van Haemstede 1559, p. 96.

256. The song, "Wer Christo jetzt wil folgen nach," later appeared in the Swiss Brethren's hymnal, the *Ausbund* (1583). The ninth stanza is as follows (note the care to articulate the Anabaptist sequence of saving grace followed by baptism, a precision not found in the *New geschicht von Jörgen Wagner*): "Baptism is proper, as Christ teaches / when the order is not inverted, / meaning that his bitter death / is a cleansing of our sins / through which we obtain grace" ["Der Tauff ist recht, wie Christus lehrt, / wenn die ordnung nit wirt verkehrt, / bedeut sein bitter sterben, / Ist ein abwäschung vnser Sünd, / dardurch wir gnad erwerben"]. Wackernagel, vol. 3, p. 455. For the relationship between pamphlet and song, see Ursula Lieseberg, *Studien zum Märtyrerlied der Täufer im 16. Jahrhundert* (Frankfurt am Main: Peter Lang, 1991), pp. 70–73.

257. A brief account of the two Augustinians in Crespin's first edition was replaced a decade later by a much longer entry based on the Latin *History of the Two Augustinians* (1523). Compare Crespin 1554, pp. 152–154, with Crespin 1564, pp. 87–96.

258. Rabus 2, fols. 117v–121v.

259. Crespin omitted articles 16, 17, 18, 26, 35, 39, 41, 46, 55, and 56. Compare *Historia de duobus Augustinensibus,* in *BRN,* vol. 8, pp. 40–42, with Crespin 1564, pp. 88–90. In addition, he changed the original "responderet" to "consentir" in article 51, altering the meaning of the monks' remark to their interrogators. Compare *Historia,* p. 42, with Crespin 1564, p. 90.

260. On Rabus's accuracy in reproducing his sources, see Pijper, *Martelaarsboeken,* pp. 125, 132; Jelsma, *Adriaan van Haemstede,* p. 251; Kolb, *For All the Saints,* pp. 54–56, 64, 66. For Willem van Zwolle, compare Bugenhagen, ed., *Artickel der Doctorn von Louen,* in *BRN,* vol. 8, p. 169, with Rabus 3, fol. 168; for Wendelmoet Claes, compare *Ein wunderliche geschicht von Wendelmut Clausen,* in *CDN,* vol. 5, p. 275, with Rabus 3, fol. 121.

261. Kolb, *For All the Saints,* pp. 55–56. This unacknowledged borrowing from Crespin applies not only to the stories in Rabus 5, as Kolb notes, but also to Rabus 6, including his accounts of Nicolas of Antwerp (fols. 36–37), Louis de Berquin (37–38), Jean de Cadurque (106v–108v), and Jean Pointet (108v–109v). Between these entries he reprinted Urbanus Rhegius's *Trostbrief* to the Christians of Hildesheim and identified Rhegius as the author (fols. 81v–106 at 81v), and immediately after the Pointet entry identified Lutheran historian Johannes Sleidan as his source for the ensuing story (109v–110). It seems clear that Rabus deliberately avoided mention of Crespin.

262. For example, both Humphrey Middleton and Nicholas Shetterton, burned at Canterbury in mid-1555, had been active in Henry Hart's separatist group

known as the Freewillers. Thomas Avington had signed a Freewiller confession of faith less than six months before he was burned in June 1555, no hint of which appears in Foxe. J. W. Martin, "Sidelights on Foxe's Account of the Marian Martyrs," in *Religious Radicals in Tudor England* (London and Ronceverte: Hambledon Press, 1989), p. 177. For analogous examples, see the sources cited in Chapter 1, n. 72.

263. Foxe 1563, p. 1249.

264. Ibid., p. 1244.

265. On the disproportionate influence of the well-documented, well-educated Marian martyrs, see Haller, *Foxe's Book of Martyrs*, pp. 44–47.

266. See van Haemstede's title ("by een vergadert op het kortste"), as well as similar remarks in his preface. Van Haemstede 1559 [p. 3]. Jelsma's comment that van Haemstede's work is the "the least trustworthy" of the major martyrologies is misleading, since abridgment need not entail distortion or misrepresentation. Jelsma, *Adriaan van Haemstede*, pp. 252–253. Except for martyrs from the circles in Antwerp and Brussels with which he was familiar, van Haemstede did not provide nearly as much detail about most contemporary martyrs as could be found in various *Flugschriften*, or in Crespin, Rabus, or Foxe. His work is less untrustworthy, however, than compressed—a sort of *Reader's Digest* version of Protestant martyrologies. In this it resembles later abridgments of the other martyrologies, such as Timothy Bright's *Abridgement of the Booke of Actes and Monumentes* (London: J. Windet, 1589); Christoph Rab's German translation and abridgment of Crespin, entitled simply *Märtyrbuch* (Herborn: [Christoph Rab], 1590); and Daniel DesMarest's shorter version of Crespin, *Histoire abregée des martirs francois du tems de la Reformation* (Amsterdam: Andre de Hoogenhuyse, 1684).

267. See van Haemstede 1559; SAA, Vierschaar, V147 (1555–1559), fols. 32v–98; *AA*, vol. 14, pp. 20–25. The five martyrs whom van Haemstede included were Jan des Champs ("de Schoolmeester"), Adriaen Coreman ("de Schilder"), Henrick Snoelaecke ("de Kleermaker"), Cornelis Halewijn ("Slotemaker"), and Herman Janssens ("Bussemaker"). Van Haemstede 1559, pp. 422–423, 444–447, 449–450.

268. Foxe to members of Magdalen College, May 2, 1563, quoted in Mozley, *Foxe and His Book*, p. 136.

269. With its extensive annotations, this second edition was apparently intended for a more scholarly, clerical audience than the first. See Kolb, *For All the Saints*, p. 95.

270. Ibid., pp. 85–96.

271. Moeller, "Inquisition und Martyrium," pp. 29–32.

272. There is a significant difference in both stance and tone between Luther and Calvin on the anti-Nicodemite issue: where Luther exhorts, Calvin demands. For example, compare Luther's supplicatory tenor in his pamphlet on Leonhard Keyser—"O dear Lord Jesus Christ, help us through your spirit to likewise confess you and your word according to such an example"—with Calvin's uncompromising insistence in the *Petit traicté*, *Excuse*, and "Second sermon." For Luther's German original, see *Von Er Lenhard Keiser*, in *WA* 23, p. 452/ 27–29.

273. Henry J. Cohn, "The Territorial Princes in Germany's Second Reformation, 1559–1622," in *International Calvinism, 1541–1715,* ed. Menna Prestwich (Oxford: Clarendon Press, 1985), pp. 135–165; R. Po-chia Hsia, *Social Discipline in the Reformation: Central Europe, 1550–1750* (London: Routledge, 1989), pp. 26–38.

274. [Jean Crespin and Simon Goulart], *Märtyrbuch: Darinnen merckliche, denckwürdige Reden vnd Thaten viler heiligen Märtyrer beschriben werden . . . ,* ed. and trans. Christoph Rab (Herborn: [Christoph Rab], 1590), sig. [ ]:(7]. Rab's condensed translation is based on Crespin and Goulart 1582.

275. Rab's abridgment was published again in 1591, 1595, 1597 (2), 1603, 1608, 1617, 1641, and 1682; Crocius's translation appeared in 1606, 1617, and 1682, with a final edition in 1722. *BMPN,* vol. 2, pp. 205–250.

276. *BMPN,* vol. 2, pp. 285–364. Most of the editions after 1566 were printed in Dordrecht (10), Amsterdam (5), or Delft (3), with others appearing at Enkhuizen, Gouda, and Briel. Ibid. Jan Gailliart anonymously printed the 1565 edition in Emden. Pettegree, *Emden and the Dutch Revolt,* pp. 288–289. The 1566 edition was published anonymously by Goosen Goebens in Sedan. Gilmont, "Martyrologes protestants du XVIe siècle," p. 339 n. 57. For the date of van Haemstede's death, see Jelsma, *Adriaan van Haemstede,* p. 205.

277. [Van Haemstede], *Historie oft Gheschiedenissen der vromer Martelaren . . .* ([Sedan: Goossen Goebens], 1566), p. 652.

278. *BMPN,* vol. 2, pp. 288–297, 301–302, 325–329, 335–339. In 1604 Abraham Conin published in Dordrecht the first edition with illustrations, which was also the first folio edition. Ibid., pp. 309, 311. Gilmont convincingly argues that Guy de Brès was not responsible for the additions of 1566, which are Flemish rather than Wallonian and hence do not correspond to the region around Tournai and Valenciennes where he worked. Gilmont, "Martyrologes protestants du XVIe siècle," pp. 337–339.

279. Pijper, *Martelaarsboeken,* pp. 50–51; *BMPN,* vol. 2, pp. 296–297. It is unclear whether Cubus was responsible for the actual addenda to the 1579 edition, since he died the same year.

280. *Acta van de nederlandsche synoden der zestiende eeuw,* ed. F. L. Rutgers (Utrecht: Kemink and Zoon, 1889), pp. 267–268.

281. *BMPN,* vol. 2, pp. 295, 299, 301, 303–307, 309.

282. Matt. 10:32 appears on the title pages of the editions of 1608, 1616, 1633, 1643–1644, and 1657 (Amsterdam: G. Willemsz Doornick), but not on those of 1609, 1612 (2), 1634, 1657 (Dordrecht: Jacob Braat for Jacob Savry), 1658, 1659, or 1671. See *BMPN,* vol. 2, pp. 313–314, 317, 323, 325–326, 331–332, 335–336, 341, 343, 345–346, 349–350, 357, 361, 363.

283. Pijper, *Martelaarsboeken,* pp. 49–50.

284. Van Haemstede 1559, p. 430; *BMPN,* vol. 2, pp. 290–292. Later editors were similarly scrupulous about exactly whom they included in the martyrology. The author of the 1579 preface, for example, carefully distinguished the many Christians killed "through the cruelty of the Duke of Alva" in general, about whom he had "no certainty of their Christian confession" [*bekentenisse*], from the martyrs about whose particular views "we have received assured testimony [*sekere getuygenissen*] from other Christian communities." The aim was not indis-

criminately to pad the ranks of the martyrs, but to include only those who were genuine. [Van Haemstede], *Historien oft gheschiedenissen der vromer Martelaren . . .* (Dordrecht: [Jan Canin], 1579), sig. [*8v].

285. On the debate over congregationalist versus presbyterian forms of ecclesiastical government, see Robert M. Kingdon, *Geneva and the Consolidation of the French Protestant Movement, 1564–1572* (Geneva: Droz, 1967), pp. 62–137.

286. C. Paillard, *Histoire des troubles religieux de Valenciennes,* vol. 4 (Brussels: Société de l'histoire de Belgique, 1876), pp. 185–191, cited in Jean-François Gilmont, "Une édition inconnue du martyrologe de Jean Crespin: Cinquieme partie du recueil des martyrs (1564)," *Bibliothèque d'Humanisme et Renaissance,* 30 (1968), 363. For Crespin at Calvinist services in Normandy, see Glenn Sunshine, "From French Protestantism to the French Reformed Churches: The Development of Huguenot Ecclesiastical Institutions, 1559–1598" (Ph.D. diss., University of Wisconsin–Madison, 1992), p. 164, cited in David Watson, "Jean Crespin and the Writing of History in the French Reformation," in *Protestant History and Identity in Sixteenth-Century Europe,* vol. 2, ed. Bruce Gordon (Aldershot: Scolar Press, 1996), p. 38 n. 2. See also the case of Jeanne Gayant, the wife of a silk garment merchant, who lost a copy of the 1556 edition of Crespin on the street in Tournai in April 1564, for which she was arrested. Moreau, *Protestantisme à Tournai,* p. 373. A Calvinist arrested during a service near Bilstain at Pentecost in 1568 admitted that he had sung and discussed a psalm "and that after that a chapter of the *Book of Martyrs* was read." Halkin, "Martyrologes," p. 63.

287. Jacques Sévert, *L'Anti-Martyrologe, ov Verite Manifestee contre les Histoires des Svpposes Martyrs de la Religion pretendue reformée . . .* (Lyons: Simon Rigaud, 1622), pp. lxix-lxx.

288. Philip Benedict, "Bibliothèques protestantes et catholiques à Metz au XVIIe siècle," *Annales E.S.C.,* 40 (1985), 348–351, 354.

289. *BMPN,* vol. 2, pp. 153–171; Leonard Chester Jones, *Simon Goulart, 1543–1628* (Geneva: Georg and Cie, 1917), pp. 37–38, 111, 215, 231. Subsequent editions were published in 1582, 1597, 1608, and 1619.

290. On Goulart's *Mémoires,* published five times in three editions between 1576 and 1579, see Robert M. Kingdon, *Myths about the St. Bartholomew's Day Massacres, 1572–1576* (Cambridge, Mass.: Harvard University Press, 1988), pp. 2–4. For Goulart's treatment of the St. Bartholomew's Day massacres in the martyrology, see Crespin and Goulart 1582, fols. 712–732.

291. Foxe 1563, p. 1387.

292. In 1555 Crespin greatly expanded the brief entry in his first edition. Compare Crespin 1554, pp. [656]–666, with Crespin 1555, sigs. AA1-[II8v]. In 1555 he also published an independent work on the massacres, the *Histoire memorable de la persecution de Merindol et Cabrieres.* Gilmont, *Jean Crespin,* p. 249; see also Crespin 1564, pp. 189–221. On the massacres themselves, see Paul Gaffarel, "Les massacres de Cabrières et de Mérindol en 1545," *Revue historique,* 107 (1911), 241–271; Daniela Boccassini, "Le massacre des Vaudois de Provence: échos et controverses," *ARG,* 82 (1991), 257–286.

293. Crespin and Goulart 1582, sig. *.3.

294. Ibid., fol. 732v.

295. Ibid., fol. 704v.

296. For the identification of DesMarest as the editor, see Piaget and Berthoud, *Notes sur le Livre des Martyrs,* pp. 71–72.

297. [DesMarest, ed.], *Histoire abregée des martirs francois.* The sermon was delivered on November 7, 1680; for the year, see Piaget and Berthoud, *Notes sur le Livre des Martyrs,* p. 72.

298. [DesMarest, ed.], *Histoire abregée des martirs francois,* sig. +6.

299. Ibid., p. 5.

300. Jacob Verwey, ed., *De eerste Hollandsche Martelaer, ofte Historie van het Liiden ende de Doodt aengedaen Jan de Backer, geboortigh van Woerden . . .* (Leiden: Willem Christiaens vander Boxe, 1652). This printing is a translation of the 1546 Latin edition.

301. See, most importantly, Haller, *Foxe's Book of Martyrs,* and Leslie Mahin Oliver, "The Acts and Monuments of John Foxe: A Study of the Growth and Influence of a Book" (Ph.D. diss., Harvard University, 1945). See also Collinson, "Truth and Legend," p. 31; Mozley, *Foxe and His Book,* p. 180; Frances Yates, "Foxe as Propagandist," in *Ideas and Ideals in the North European Renaissance,* vol. 3 of her collected essays (London: Routledge and Kegan Paul, 1984), p. 33; A. G. Dickens, *The English Reformation* (1964; reprint, London: Fontana, 1967), p. 416. The eight editions after 1563 were published in 1570, 1576, 1583, 1596, 1610, 1632, 1641, and 1684. *STC 1475–1640,* vol. 1, p. 496; *STC 1641–1700,* vol. 2, p. 95.

302. BL, Lansdowne MS 10, fols. 211–212v.

303. Edward Cardwell, ed., *Synodalia: A Collection of Articles of Religion, Canons, and Proceedings of Convocations in the Province of Canterbury . . .* (Oxford: Oxford University Press, 1842), vol. 1, pp. 115, 117. In 1604 Robert Parsons, a Jesuit, remarked on how the work was "obtruded to be read in very many parish churches, and other public places." [Parsons], *The Third Part of a Treatise Intituled: Of Three Conuersions of England . . . ,* vol. 3 ([St. Omers: F. Bellet], 1604), p. 401.

304. Foxe 1576; Bright, ed., *An Abridgement of the Booke of Actes and Monvmentes,* [p. i]. The *Acts and Monuments* returned to a multivolume format in 1583, perhaps due to dissatisfaction with the cheaper edition of 1576. In 1582 Foxe's friend, Simon Parrett, wrote to him from Oxford, having heard that another edition was imminent. He hoped that "it may be printed in good paper, and a fair and legible print, and not in black, blurred, and torn paper, as your last edition is: being neither good paper, nor good print." Parrett to Foxe, February 3, 1582, BL, Harleian MS 416, no. 131, fol. 203.

305. See Clement Cotton, *The mirror of martyrs . . .* (London: T. P[urfoot] for J. Budge, 1613), which used anecdotes and remarks mostly from the Marian martyrs to create a devotional work. It was republished in 1614, 1615, 1625, 1631, 1633, 1639, 1658, and 1685. *STC 1475–1640,* vol. 1, p. 263; *STC 1641–1700,* vol. 1, p. 648. Another adaptation was Thomas Mason, *Christs victorie over Sathans tyrannie* (London: G. Eld and R. Blower, 1615), a collection emphasizing the doctrines held by the martyrs. Samuel Clarke produced

A Martyrologie, containing a collection of all the persecutions which have befallen the Church of England since the first plantation of the Gospel to the end of Queen Maries reign (London: A. M. for Thomas Underhill and John Rothwell, 1651), fundamentally an abridged version of Foxe with only minor additions from other sources. It was reprinted three times by 1677. STC 1641–1700, vol. 1, p. 577. For observations on all these abridgments, see Oliver, "Acts and Monuments," pp. 151–156, 168–172.

306. [Parsons], Third Part of a Treatise of Three Conuersions, vol. 3, p. 400. Among its other enticements, Parsons mentioned Foxe's pious phrases, the speeches he attributed "to sectaries at their deaths," and the size of the book itself. Ibid., pp. 400–401.

307. Thomas Fuller, "Mixt Contemplations," Good Thoughts in Bad Times (Exeter: R. C. for Andrew Cook, 1645), quoted in Oliver, "Acts and Monuments," p. 137. On Fuller, see DNB, vol. 7, pp. 755–760.

308. Wallington, quoted in Paul S. Seaver, Wallington's World: A Puritan Artisan in Seventeenth-Century London (Stanford: Stanford University Press, 1985), p. 74. For a partial list of commonplace books with excerpts from Foxe, see Peter Beal, ed., Index of Literary Manuscripts, vol. 1, 1450–1625 (New York: R. R. Bowker, and London: Mansell, 1980), p. 94.

309. For the plays, see Oliver, "Acts and Monuments," pp. 221–331. For the broadside ballads and woodcut, see Tessa Watt, Cheap Print and Popular Piety, 1550–1640 (Cambridge: Cambridge University Press, 1991), pp. 90–96, 158.

310. Robert Walton, A catalogue of divers maps, pictures etc (1666), quoted in Watt, Cheap Print, p. 159.

311. "Edward Bulkeley to the Christian Reader," in Foxe 1610, vol. 2, p. 1950.

312. Ibid., p. 1952.

313. The quoted passages come near the end of his "Protestation to the whole Church of England," Foxe 1570, vol. 1, sig. ☞4v. For Cartwright, Whitgift, and the debate over clerical offices and ministry in the church with respect to Foxe, see Olsen, John Foxe and the Church, pp. 153–158.

314. Foxe 1583, vol. 1, sig. ¶2v.

315. Knott, Discourses of Martyrdom in English Literature, pp. 134–144.

316. Ibid., pp. 119–134, 151–255.

317. For the celebration of Vos and van den Esschen, see Ter gedachtenis van de eerste martelaren voor de Hervorming: Hendrik Voes and Jan van Esschen (Brussels: Evangelisatie-Drukkerij, 1923). For Clarenbach and Fliesteden, see Axel Blum, ed., Allein Gottes Wort: Vorträge, Ansprachen, Predigten, Besinnungen anläßlich des 450. Todestages der Märtyrer Adolf Clarenbach und Peter Fliesteden (Cologne: Rheinland-Verlag, 1981).

6. Nachfolge Christi: Anabaptists and Martyrdom

1. I have emphasized Dutch Anabaptist martyrs for several reasons. Their martyrological sources are richer and more plentiful than those for Swiss, German, or Austrian Anabaptists, and Hutterite manuscripts, many of which date from the seventeenth century, raise complex questions of origin and transmission if used

as sources for the sixteenth century. Moreover, although hundreds of Anabaptists were executed in Switzerland and the Holy Roman Empire between 1527 and 1535, executions thereafter dropped dramatically, whereas in the Low Countries numerous executions continued into the 1570s. In addition, Dutch Protestants and Catholics were killed and understood as martyrs by their fellow believers, providing a geographical cross-confessionality that stands in contrast to German-speaking lands, where few Protestants or Catholics were put to death. Finally, the Dutch Mennonite martyrological tradition culminated in Thieleman Jans van Braght's *Martyrs' Mirror*, the most important martyrological source for subsequent Mennonite identity in Europe and North America.

2. Abraham Friesen, *Erasmus, the Anabaptists, and the Great Commission* (Grand Rapids, Mich.: Eerdmans, 1998).

3. On the relationship between Anabaptists' understanding of justification by faith alone and their rejection of infant baptism, see C. Arnold Snyder, *Anabaptist History and Theology: An Introduction* (Kitchener, Ont.: Pandora Press, 1995), pp. 83–99.

4. Cornelius J. Dyck, "The Suffering Church in Anabaptism," *MQR*, 59 (1985), 5.

5. Some of the most significant older contributions include J. de Hoop Scheffer, "Onze martelaarsboeken," *DB*, 4 (1870), 45–89; Samuel Cramer, "De geloofwaardigheid van van Braght," *DB*, 39 (1899), 65–164; idem, "Nogmaals de geloofwaardigheid van van Braght: Tevens antwoord op de kritiek van den Heer W. Wilde," *DB*, 40 (1900), 184–210; Frederik Pijper, "Een nieuw ontdekt doopsgezind martelaarsboek," *Nederlands archief voor kerkgeschiedenis*, n.s., 2 (1903), 286–300; Cramer, introduction to *OH*, in *BRN*, vol. 2, pp. 3–40; Pijper, *Martelaarsboeken* (The Hague: Martinus Nijhoff, 1924), pp. 73–119; W. J. Kühler, *Geschiedenis der nederlandsche doopsgezinden in de zestiende eeuw* (Haarlem: H. D. Tjeenk Willink, 1932), pp. 245–277; Ethelbert Stauffer, "The Anabaptist Theology of Martyrdom," *MQR*, 19 (1945), 179–214; A. Orley Swartzentruber, "The Piety and Theology of the Anabaptist Martyrs in van Braght's *Martyrs' Mirror*," *MQR*, 28 (1954), 5–26, 128–142. Dutch Anabaptist works are also included in *BMPN*, vols. 1–2.

6. See, for example, Rosella Reimer Duerksen, "Anabaptist Hymnody of the Sixteenth Century: A Study of Its Marked Individuality Coupled with a Dependence upon Contemporary Secular and Sacred Musical Style and Form" (Doctor of Sacred Music diss., Union Theological Seminary, New York, 1956); Harold S. Bender, "The Hymnology of the Anabaptists," *MQR*, 31 (1957), 5–10; N. van der Zijpp, "The Hymnology of the Mennonites in the Netherlands," *MQR*, 31 (1957), 11–15; Duerksen, "Doctrinal Implications in Sixteenth Century Anabaptist Hymnody," *MQR*, 35 (1961), 38–49; Helen Martens, "Hutterite Songs: The Origins and Aural Transmission of their Melodies from the Sixteenth Century" (Ph.D. diss., Columbia University, 1969); Victor G. Doerksen, "The Anabaptist Martyr Ballad," *MQR*, 51 (1977), 5–21; Ursula Lieseberg, *Studien zum Märtyrerlied der Täufer im 16. Jahrhundert* (Frankfurt am Main: Peter Lang, 1991); Bert Hofman, *Liedekens vol gheestich confoort: Een bijdrage tot de kennis van de zestiende-eeuwse Schriftuurlijke lyriek* (Hilversum:

Verloren, 1993), which attempts to relate Dutch song collections to various Protestant and Anabaptist groups in the sixteenth century; and idem, "Gereformeerden en doopsgezinden in de spiegel van de Schriftuurlijke liederen in de zestiende eeuw," *DB*, n.s., 20 (1994), 61–69.

7. Reliance on van Braght has been especially true of scholarship in English, since Sohm's translation of the *Martyrs' Mirror* is so readily available. Recent scholarship in the *MQR* that relies almost entirely on van Braght includes Alan F. Kreider, "'The Servant Is Not Greater Than His Master': The Anabaptists and the Suffering Church," *MQR*, 58 (1984), 5–29; Dyck, "Suffering Church in Anabaptism"; John Klassen, "Women and the Family among Dutch Anabaptist Martyrs," *MQR*, 60 (1986), 548–571; and Jenifer Hiett Umble, "Women and Choice: An Examination of the *Martyrs' Mirror*," *MQR*, 64 (1990), 135–145. Exceptions to this heavy reliance on the *Martyrs' Mirror* have generally been studies of individual martyrs. See Werner O. Packull, "Anna Jansz of Rotterdam, A Historical Investigation of an Early Anabaptist Heroine," *ARG*, 78 (1987), 147–173; M. J. Reimer-Blok, "The Theological Identity of the Flemish Anabaptists: A Study of the Letters of Jacob de Roore," *MQR*, 62 (1988), 318–331; S. Voolstra, "Valerius Schoolmeester (overleden omstreeks 1569): Leven en leer van een menniste hageprediker in Zeeland in de reformatietijd," in *Rond de kerk in Zeeland: Derde verzameling bijdragen van de Vereniging voor Nederlandse kerkgeschiedenis*, ed. P. H. A. M. Abels et al. (Delft: Eburon, 1991), pp. 106–133. For a broader treatment intended for a more general audience and not primarily dependent on van Braght, see T. Alberda-van der Zijpp, "'Het Offer des Heeren': Geloof en getuigenis van de martelaren," in *Wederdopers, menisten, doopsgezinden in Nederland 1530–1980*, ed. S. Groenveld, J. P. Jacobszoon, and S. L. Verheus (Zutphen: Walburg Press, 1980), pp. 46–61.

8. Cramer, "Geloofwaardigheid van van Braght" and "Nogmaals de geloofwaardigheid van van Braght."

9. The frequently cited essay that both summarized the existing scholarship and framed much subsequent research was James M. Stayer, Werner O. Packull, and Klaus Deppermann, "From Monogenesis to Polygenesis: The Historical Discussion of Anabaptist Origins," *MQR*, 49 (1975), 83–121. Another landmark was Claus-Peter Clasen's extensive social history of German-speaking Anabaptism, which also noted the disagreements (and in numerous cases, mutually hostile relations) among various Anabaptist groups. Clasen, *Anabaptism: A Social History, 1525–1618* (Ithaca: Cornell University Press, 1972), pp. 36–48. For a synthetic overview that convincingly balances recent research on the distinctiveness of different groups with the broader, sixteenth-century Anabaptist tradition, see Snyder, *Anabaptist History and Theology*.

10. I am producing a critical edition of these letters, as well as several songs and relevant archival sources, for the series *Documenta Anabaptistica Neerlandica*.

11. See especially James M. Stayer, "Anabaptists and Future Anabaptists in the Peasants' War," *MQR*, 62 (1988), 100–113, and the literature cited there on p. 100 n. 4. From their very different starting points, Harold Bender and Claus-Peter Clasen had argued that the two movements were fundamentally separate.

See Harold S. Bender, "The Anabaptist Vision," *Church History,* 13 (1944), 8; Clasen, *Anabaptism,* pp. 152–157.

12. James M. Stayer, "Die Anfänge des schweizerischen Täufertums im reformierten Kongregationalismus," in *Umstrittenes Täufertum 1525–1975: Neue Forschungen,* ed. Hans-Jürgen Goertz (Göttingen: Vandenhoeck and Ruprecht, 1975), pp. 19–49; Martin Haas, "Der Weg der Täufer in die Absonderung: Zur Interdependenz von Theologie und sozialem Verhalten," in *Umstrittenes Täufertum,* ed. Goertz, pp. 50–78; C. Arnold Snyder, *The Life and Thought of Michael Sattler* (Scottdale, Pa.: Herald Press, 1984), pp. 66–71.

13. Torsten Bergsten, *Balthasar Hubmaier: Anabaptist Theologian and Martyr,* trans. Irwin J. Barnes and William R. Estep, ed. Estep (Valley Forge, Pa.: Judson Press, 1978), pp. 210–214, 228–269; James M. Stayer, *Anabaptists and the Sword,* 2nd ed. (Lawrence, Kans.: Coronado Press, 1976), pp. 105–110.

14. Stayer, *Anabaptists and the Sword,* pp. 109–110; Snyder, *Sattler,* p. 72.

15. Figures derived from Claus-Peter Clasen, "Executions of Anabaptists, 1525–1618: A Research Report," *MQR,* 47 (1973), 118–119.

16. So far as I know, the term "anti-Nicodemism" was not used in Anabaptist circles, but Anabaptist leaders and martyrs articulated views about the Christian duty to externally profess and maintain faith despite threats of persecution and death. The similarity of their arguments to those of Protestants (and Roman Catholics) justifies my broader use of the term.

17. Grebel to Müntzer, September 5, 1524, in *QGTS,* vol. 1, *Zürich,* ed. Leonhard von Muralt and Walter Schmid (Zurich: S. Hirzel, 1952), p. 17.

18. Grebel to Müntzer, sent with letter of Sept. 5, 1524, in *QGTS,* vol. 1, p. 20.

19. Grebel to Joachim Vadian, May 30, 1525, in *QGTS,* vol. 1, p. 78.

20. For Eberli and his anonymous companion, see *QGTS,* vol. 2, *Ostschweiz,* ed. Heinold Fast (Zurich: Theologischer Verlag, 1973), pp. 606–607 (from Johannes Kessler's "Sabbata," ca. 1533). For Krüsi, see ibid., pp. 262–265, 607–608. Most scholars have followed Kessler's mistake in placing Eberli's family name first. For the correction, see *The Sources of Swiss Anabaptism: The Grebel Letters and Related Documents,* ed. and trans. Leland Harder (Scottdale, Pa.: Herald Press, 1985), p. 376.

21. *QGTS,* vol. 1, p. 125.

22. For the sentence against Mantz and Blaurock in Zurich on January 5, 1527, see *QGTS,* vol. 1, pp. 224–226, 227–228. For Blaurock's activity in the South Tirol, see Werner O. Packull, *Hutterite Beginnings: Communitarian Experiments during the Reformation* (Baltimore: The Johns Hopkins University Press, 1995), pp. 181–186. For Blaurock's execution (along with Hans Langegger's), see *QGTS,* vol. 13, *Österreich,* pt. 2, ed. Grete Mecenseffy (Gütersloh: Gerd Mohn, 1972), p. 286/17–19.

23. John H. Yoder, *The Legacy of Michael Sattler* (Scottdale, Pa.: Herald Press, 1973), pp. 27–33; Stayer, *Anabaptists and the Sword,* pp. 117–131; Snyder, *Sattler,* pp. 97–100, 104–105.

24. [Sattler], *Brüderlich vereynigung etzlicher kinder Gottes, sieben Artickel betreffend. Item, Eyn sendtbrieff Michael Sattlers . . .* ([Strasbourg: Jacob Cammerlander], 1533), ed. Walter Köhler, repr. in *Flugschriften aus den ersten Jahren der*

Reformation, ed. Otto Clement, vol. 2 (Leipzig: Rudolf Haupt, 1908), pp. 306, 318.

25. Ibid., p. 318.

26. Repr. in Wackernagel, vol. 3, no. 405, stanzas 1, 4, p. 341. Another version of this song was printed in Michael Weiss's German hymnal of the Bohemian brethren, *Ein New Geseng buchlen* (1531), before appearing in the *Ausbund* (1583). It is unclear, however, whether Sattler wrote the song and Anabaptist refugees carried it east or whether it originated in Bohemia or Moravia and was appropriated by the Swiss Brethren after Sattler's death. See Wackernagel, vol. 3, pp. 229, 340–341; Rudolf Wolkan, *Die Lieder der Wiedertäufer: Ein Beitrag zur deutschen und niederländischen Litteratur- und Kirchengeschichte* (Berlin: B. Behr, 1903), p. 9; Snyder, *Sattler,* pp. 220–221 n. 9. Whether written by Sattler or not, the song illustrates separatism wedded to a martyrological mentality in Anabaptism's formative years.

27. Clasen, "Executions of Anabaptists," p. 119.

28. Werner O. Packull, *Mysticism and the Early South German-Austrian Anabaptist Movement, 1525–1531* (Scottdale, Pa.: Herald Press, 1977). After Müntzer's death, under the principal leadership of Melchior Rink, central German Anabaptists seem to have cultivated a martyrological sensibility less assiduously, perhaps partly because Philipp of Hesse showed himself unwilling to execute Anabaptists. See John S. Oyer, *Lutheran Reformers against Anabaptists: Luther, Melanchthon and Menius and the Anabaptists of Central Germany* (The Hague: Martinus Nijhoff, 1964), p. 91. Certain of the central German Anabaptists, such as the followers of Hans Römer, seem also to have retained from Müntzer a less sympathetic attitude towards nonresistance. Stayer, "Anabaptists and the Peasants' War," pp. 121–122.

29. Müntzer, *Außlegung des andern vnterschyds Danielis . . .* [1524], repr. in idem, *Schriften und Briefe: Kritische Gesamtausgabe,* ed. Günther Franz (Gütersloh: Gerd Mohn, 1968), pp. 259/20–25, 259/28–260/4.

30. Müntzer, *Schriften,* ca. July 20, 1524, no. 55, pp. 411/22–36, 412/36–413/7, 413/22–414/2. God would bestow on them the same spirit he bestowed on Job and the martyrs. Ibid., p. 414/3–6.

31. Ibid., July 25, 1524, no. 59, p. 423/9–11.

32. See, for example, the passage to the people of Allstedt in a letter written from Mühlhausen, to which he fled after leaving Allstedt, in ibid., August 15, 1524, no. 67, p. 435/3–9.

33. For Müntzer's appeal, see his letter to the people of Allstedt of April 26 or 27, 1525, written immediately after he had heard about the peasant uprising in Langensalza on April 24. Müntzer, *Schriften,* no. 75, pp. 454–456. For the events leading up to the battle of Frankenhausen and Müntzer's response to it, see Abraham Friesen, *Thomas Muentzer, a Destroyer of the Godless: The Making of a Sixteenth-Century Religious Revolutionary* (Berkeley: University of California Press, 1990), pp. 237–263.

34. Oyer, *Lutheran Reformers against Anabaptists,* p. 108; Stayer, "Anabaptists and the Peasants' War," pp. 124–125.

35. Stayer, *Anabaptists and the Sword,* pp. 150–162; Packull, *Mysticism,* pp. 62–76,

88–106; Gottfried Seebass, "Hans Hut: The Suffering Avenger," in *Profiles of Radical Reformers: Biographical Sketches from Thomas Müntzer to Paracelsus,* ed. Hans-Jürgen Goertz (Scottdale, Pa.: Herald Press, 1982), pp. 54–61.

36. [Hans Hut], *Ain Christliche vnderrichtung, wie die Götlich vergleycht vnd geurtaylt soll werden . . .* [Augsburg: Philipp Ulhart the Elder, 1527], repr. in *Flugschriften vom Bauernkrieg zum Täuferreich (1526–1535),* vol. 1, ed. Adolf Laube et al. (Berlin: Akademie Verlag, 1992), p. 692/8–11, 20–23. See also the interrogation of Hut from late 1527, in which he expressed the same idea. *QGT,* vol. 2, *Bayern,* pt. 1, ed. Karl Schornbaum (Leipzig: Heinsius, 1934), p. 42/11–15.

37. Hut, "Von dem geheimnus der tauf . . . ," in *QGT,* vol. 3, *Glaubenszeugnisse oberdeutscher Taufgesinnter,* pt. 1, ed. Lydia Müller (Leipzig: Heinsius, 1938), p. 22. Hut's biblical citations, given in the margins of the manuscript used by Müller with reference to book and chapter, are here given in brackets with verses added. Earlier in the same work, Hut quoted perhaps the most important New Testament verse about the suffering of Christ's followers in solidarity with him, Col. 1:24. Ibid., p. 16.

38. Leonhard Schiemer, "Ein Epistl an die gmain zu Rottenburg geschrieben," in *QGT,* vol. 3, p. 51.

39. Schiemer, "Wir bitten dich ewiger Gott" ["Wie köstlich ist der Heilgen todt"], in Wackernagel, vol. 3, no. 523, stanzas 5–6, p. 464. Without giving a specific date, Wolkan notes that this song was printed early (ca. 1530?) along with a song attributed to either Jörg Steinmetz (executed in Pforzheim, 1530) or Eucharius Binder (burned in October 1527). Wolkan, *Lieder der Wiedertäufer,* pp. 10–11. The song subsequently appeared in *Ausbund* 1583, pp. 189–193.

40. Schiemer, "Lienharten Schiemers epistl an die gmain Gottes zu Rattenburg, geschriben 1527," in *QGT,* vol. 3, p. 69.

41. On the split between *Schwertler* and *Stäbler* and the formation of the earliest Moravian communities, see A. J. F. Zieglschmid, ed., *Die älteste Chronik der Hutterischen Brüder* (Ithaca: Cayuga Press, 1943), pp. 86–92; Packull, *Hutterite Beginnings,* pp. 61–66; Stayer, *Anabaptism and the Sword,* pp. 167–173; Leonard Gross, *The Golden Years of the Hutterites: The Witness and Thought of the Communal Moravian Anabaptists during the Walpot Era, 1565–1578* (Scottdale, Pa.: Herald Press, 1980), pp. 27–28.

42. See letters 3, 5–8, in Hans Fischer, *Jakob Huter: Leben, Froemmigkeit, Briefe* (Newton, Kans.: Mennonite Publication Office, 1956), esp. pp. 20–25, 35–39, 41–43, 45–46, 54–59, 63–72.

43. Ibid., no. 3, pp. 19–20.

44. Ibid., no. 6, pp. 45–46.

45. Hubmaier's case reveals the force of Augustine's dictum ("martyrem non facit poena, sed causa") within Anabaptism, even if it was infrequently articulated. Judging from extant sources, the Swiss Brethren did not honor Hubmaier's memory. The oldest Hutterite chronicle paid tribute to him, but only along with the unlikely story that from prison in Vienna, Hubmaier had withdrawn the views about magistracy and the sword that divided him from Hut. Zieglschmid, ed., *Älteste Chronik der Hutterischen Brüder,* pp. 50–52; Bergsten,

Hubmaier, pp. 384–385. He was not mentioned in the Dutch Mennonite martyrological tradition until 1615, and then only very briefly. See van Braght 1685, vol. 2, p. 62.

46. Balthasar Hubmaier, *Ain Summ ains gantzen Christlichen lebens . . .* ([Augsburg: Melchior Ramminger], 1525), repr. in idem, *Schriften,* ed. Gunnar Westin and Torsten Bergsten, vol. 9 of *QGT* (Gütersloh: Gerd Mohn, 1962), p. 112. Near the end of this pamphlet, Hubmaier quoted Matt. 10:32–33 and Matt. 10:28, Christ's warning to deny those who deny him and not to fear the one who can kill the body. Ibid., p. 115. This pamphlet also formed the seventh chapter of Hubmaier's best known theological work, *Von der Christlichen Tauff der gläubigen* ([Strasbourg: Matthias Schürer Erben], 1525), the opening chapter of which reiterated the theme of baptism as the doorway to Christian suffering. *Schriften,* p. 122.

47. Hubmaier, *Ettlich beschlußreden von Doktor Paltus Fridberger zü Waltzhüt allen christen von vnderricht der meß* ([Ulm: Matthias Hoffischer], 1525), repr. in idem, *Schriften,* p. 102. For Hubmaier's teaching on the Lord's Supper, see Christof Windhorst, "Das Gedächtnis des Leidens Christi und Pflichtzeichen brüderlicher Liebe: Zum Verständnis des Abendmahls bei Balthasar Hubmaier," in *Umstrittenes Täufertum,* ed. Goertz, pp. 111–137.

48. For the prayers from prison, see Hubmaier, *Die zwelf Artickel Christenlichs glaubens, zü Zurichs im Wasserthurn in Bettweis gestelt* (Nikolsburg: [Simprecht Sorg], 1527), repr. in idem, *Schriften,* p. 220. See also the similar prayer in *Ein kurtzes Vatervnser* (Nikolsburg: [Simprecht Sorg], 1526), written during the same period of imprisonment. Ibid., p. 223. The second quotation is taken from one of Hubmaier's most important writings, *Ein Christennliche Leertafel* (Nikolsburg: Simprecht Sorg, 1526 or 1527), a catechetical summary of Christian faith in dialogue form. Ibid., p. 325.

49. See, for example, Linda A. Huebert Hecht, "Anabaptist Women in Tirol Who Recanted," in *Profiles of Anabaptist Women: Sixteenth-Century Reforming Pioneers,* ed. C. Arnold Snyder and Linda A. Huebert Hecht (Waterloo, Ont.: Wilfred Laurier University Press, 1996), pp. 156–163. For a case study on the related issue of Anabaptist accommodation to prescribed (in this case, Lutheran) worship and belief in the later sixteenth century, see John Oyer, "Nicodemites among Württemberg Anabaptists," *MQR,* 71 (1997), 487–514.

50. *Eyn new warhafftig vnd wunderbarlich geschicht oder hystori, von Jörgen Wagner zu München in Bayern als eyn Ketzer verbrandt im Jar M. D. xxvii* [Nuremberg: Hans Hergot, 1527], sigs. A2v–A3.

51. Ibid., sig. A3r-v.

52. *QGTS,* vol. 1, pp. 252–253.

53. Ibid., p. 277. This hearing took place between August 2 and September 5, 1528. For the Grüningen community as an addressee of Reublin's account, see ibid., p. 250.

54. For the others in Grüningen, see *QGTS,* vol. 1, p. 284. For Mether, see *QGT,* vol. 8, *Elsaß,* pt. 2, ed. Manfred Krebs and Hans Georg Rott (Gütersloh: Gerd Mohn, 1960), pp. 296/30–297/1. Katherina Seid, the wife of Andres Klaibers, had been baptized two years prior to her 1534 interrogation in Strasbourg.

Authorities described her as "an obstinate Anabaptist woman" [*eine hartnäckige widertäufferin*] in reporting her resolve. Ibid., pp. 309/15, 309/33–310/4.

55. *QGT,* vol. 2, *Bayern,* pt. 1, ed. Karl Schornbaum (Leipzig: Heinsius, 1934), pp. 16/32–17/1. For his baptism by Hans Hut, see a later interrogation, Jan. 17, 1529, ibid., p. 134/37–39.

56. See, for example, the response of Wolfgang Wüst to his interrogation on Jan. 3, 1528, in *QGT,* vol. 2, *Bayern,* pt. 1, p. 73/28–34. Two women questioned about the sacrament sometime in 1528 said that Christ's words about the "chalice" were "that is the chalice of my blood; that is suffering" [*das ist der kelich in meinem plüt. Das sei das leiden*]. Ibid., pp. 95/41–96/1. For Hans Ritter, see ibid., p. 139.

57. See Gerald Strauss, *Luther's House of Learning: Indoctrination of the Young in the German Reformation* (Baltimore: Johns Hopkins University Press, 1978). For Protestants as being generally less effective than Catholics in their catechetical methods, see Geoffrey Parker, "Success and Failure during the First Century of the Reformation," *P&P,* 136 (1992), 51–76.

58. In addition to the more recent literature cited in note 4 earlier, see Frederik C. Wieder, *De schriftuurlijke liedekens: De liederen der nederlandsche hervormden tot op het jaar 1566* (The Hague: Martinus Nijhoff, 1900); Wolkan, *Lieder der Wiedertäufer;* and Albert J. Ramaker, "Hymns and Hymn Writers among the Anabaptists of the Sixteenth Century," *MQR,* 3 (1929), 93–131.

59. For the tradition of late medieval popular songs, both religious and secular, in Germanic lands, see Rolf Wilhelm Brednich, *Die Liedpublizistik im Flugblatt des 15. bis. 17. Jahrhunderts,* vol. 1 (Baden-Baden: Valentin Koerner, 1974), pp. 31–78, 190–194, 248–250; and Jan H. Rahmelow, "Das Volkslied als publizistisches Medium und historische Quelle," *Jahrbuch für Volksliedforschung,* 14 (1969), 11–26. For reference to an early Anabaptist singing, see Johannes Brötli's letter to Fridli Schumacher and other Anabaptists in Zollikon, from early February 1525, in *QGTS,* vol. 1, p. 45. See also the anonymous letter by an imprisoned Anabaptist man to the "brothers and sisters" in Zollikon, from March 1525, in which he asked that someone "tell my wife to send me the song 'Christ is Risen.'" Ibid., p. 70.

60. Schiemer, "Wir bitten dich ewiger Gott," in Wackernagel, vol. 3, no. 523, stanza 9, p. 465. Another song, written by either Jorg Steinmetz or Eucharius Binder and printed together with Schiemer's, shows that the uncompromising anti-Nicodemite verses of Matt. 10:32–33 and Luke 12:8–9 were not restricted to the prose of early Anabaptist leaders. See ibid., no. 540, stanzas 8–9, p. 488.

61. Sattler, "Als Christus mit seinr waren lehr," in Wackernagel, vol. 3, no. 405, stanza 10, p. 341.

62. See stanzas 1 and 5 of Hätzer, "Solt du bey got dein wonung han," in Wackernagel, vol. 3, no. 536, pp. 480–481.

63. *Etliche schöne Christliche Geseng, wie sie in der Gefengkniß zu Passaw im Schloß von den Schweitzer Brüdern durch Gottes gnad geticht vnd gesungen worden* (n.p., 1564; reprint, Amsterdam and Nieuwkoop: [F. Knuf? 1972]). On these songs and the circumstances of their composition, see Packull, *Hutterite Beginnings,* pp. 89–98; Wolkan, *Lieder der Wiedertaufer,* pp. 27–43.

64. H[ans] B[etz], "O Menschen kind vernimm mich wol," in *Etliche schöne Christliche Geseng,* no. 12, stanza 5, fols. 18v–19. On Betz, see Wolkan, *Lieder der Wiedertäufer,* pp. 32–35; Packull, *Hutterite Beginnings,* pp. 92–93.

65. "Mit freuden wölln wir singen," in *Etliche schöne Christliche Geseng,* no. 22, fols. 38v–40v. The final verse, by Bernhard Schneider, speaks of "der Brüder sein viertzehen die das beschlossen hon / dz Lied haben sie gsungen / in einer Gefengknuß schwer." Ibid., fol. 40v. For the identification of "BER. S." as Bernhard Schneider, plus the identification of four of the other fourteen co-writers of the song, see Wolkan, *Lieder der Wiedertäufer,* p. 39. The initials "H. R." for the sixth verse are not identified by Wolkan, though this may have been Hans Ruemmich von Marbach, whom Wolkan elsewhere identifies as one of the Passau prisoners. Ibid., p. 30; *Etliche schöne Christliche Geseng,* fol. 39r-v.

66. Hans Schlaffer, "Ein Kurzer Underricht zum Anfang Eines Recht Christlichen Lebens . . . ," in *QGT,* vol. 3, p. 93. See also Leonhard Schiemer, "Die dritt epistel Leonhart Schiemers, darinnen wirt begriffen von dreyerley Tauf im Neuen Testament ganz clärlich entdeckt," in ibid., pp. 77–79, esp. p. 78.

67. *QGT,* vol. 11, *Österreich,* pt. 1, ed. Grete Mecenseffy (Gütersloh: Gerd Mohn, 1964), p. 43. Hans Hut stated that the waters penetrating the soul in baptism were "tribulation, affliction, anxiety, trembling, and worry, therefore baptism is suffering"; to find oneself persecuted, forsaken by God, and facing death was to experience "genuine baptism" [*rechten tauf*]. Hut, "Geheimnus der tauf," in *QGT,* vol. 3, pp. 25, 25–26. For the same idea in a song by Hans Betz, one of the Philipites who produced the songs at Passau, see the twelfth stanza of "Christus das Lamb / auff Erden kam," in *Etliche schöne Christliche Geseng,* no. 30, fol. 64v.

68. Grebel to Müntzer, September 5, 1524, in *QGTS,* vol. 1, p. 16.

69. See esp. Walter Klaassen, *Living at the End of the Ages: Apocalyptic Expectation in the Radical Reformation* (Lanham, Md.: University Press of America, 1992). Klaassen suggests that Anabaptist ecclesiologies may have been short-term measures undertaken in anticipation of an imminent second coming, which persisted and hardened when these expectations went unfulfilled. Ibid., pp. 117–118. I concur with Cornelius Dyck's assessment that Anabaptist apocalyptic expectations are "a constant backdrop in the martyr accounts" but "not the compelling reason for martyrdom." Dyck, "Anabaptists and the Suffering Church," p. 20.

70. Hergot was executed in Leipzig for publishing and selling *Von der newen wandlung eynes Christlichen lebens,* a pamphlet that he probably wrote as well. See Ferdinand Seibt, "Johannes Hergot: The Reformation of the Poor Man," in *Profiles of Radical Reformers,* ed. Goertz, pp. 97–100; John L. Flood, "Le livre dans le monde germanique à l'époque de la Réforme," in *La Réforme et le livre: L'Europe de l'imprimé (1517–v. 1570),* ed. Jean-François Gilmont (Paris: Éditions du Cerf, 1990), p. 41.

71. The hymnal apparently used by Anabaptists in northwest Germany, *Ein schön Gesangbüchlein Geistlicher Lieder zusamen getragen Auss dem Alten und Newen Testament,* was first published shortly before or around 1565, with a second edition around 1569 and a third around 1589–1593. It borrowed many Dutch

hymns and translated them into German, whence a number of them passed into the 1583 *Ausbund*. Only a handful, at the very end of the collection, were about martyrs. See Duerksen, "Anabaptist Hymnody," pp. 64–71.

72. *QGT,* vol. 5, *Bayern,* pt. 2, ed. Karl Schornbaum (Gütersloh: Bertelsmann, 1951), pp. 278–279; Clasen, *Anabaptism,* pp. 370, 486 n. 15; Packull, *Hutterite Beginnings,* pp. 84–85.

73. *QGTS,* vol. 1, p. 250.

74. See the letter from Capito and others to the *Bürgermeister* and city council of Horb, May 31, 1527, in *QGT,* vol. 7, *Elsaß,* pt. 1, ed. Manfred Krebs and Hans Georg Rott (Gütersloh: Gerd Mohn, 1959), pp. 80–87, esp. pp. 81/5–14, 83/11–33.

75. Johannes Faber, *Ursach warumb der widerteuffer patron vnnd erster Anfenger Doctor Balthasar Hübmayer zü Wienn auff den zehendten tag Martij. Anno. M. D. xxviij. verbrennet sey* [Vienna, n.p., 1528], sigs. [A1v]–A2.

76. In 1527, before his own execution, Hans Hergot published the first edition of the anonymous *New geschicht von Jörgen Wagner,* a work reprinted at least three times with slightly variant texts and titles. A second, longer pamphlet about Wagner's martyrdom also appeared: *Ein Seltzame wunderbarlich geschicht, zu München im Bayerlandt, deß Jars, als man zalt 1527 . . .* [Strasbourg: Jakob Frölich, ca. 1532–1540], which perhaps had been published previously. It is reprinted in the *Jahrbuch für die evangelisch-lutherische Landeskirche Bayerns,* 6 (1905), 16–20. On these publications about Wagner, see *Flugschriften vom Bauernkrieg zum Täuferreich,* vol. 2, ed. Laube et al., pp. 1526–1527; Lieseberg, *Märtyrerlied,* pp. 70–72. One who reissued the *New geschicht von Jörgen Wagner* was Hans Eichenauer, a Nuremberg printer. In 1528, he also published, anonymously, Klaus von Graveneck's account of the trial and execution of Sattler, *Ayn newes wunderbarliches geschicht von Michel Sattler zü Rottenburg am Neckar.* This work appeared in substantially the same form, together with the Schleitheim articles and Sattler's prison letter to the congregation at Horb, in the *Brüderlich vereynigung etzlicher kinder Gottes, sieben Artickel betreffend . . .* [Worms: Peter Schöffer the Younger, ca. 1527–1529]. This compilation was in turn reprinted, along with a tract on divorce, by Jacob Cammerlander in Strasbourg in 1533. Köhler reprinted Cammerlander's edition, with an introductory essay, in *Flugschriften aus des ersten Jahren der Reformation,* ed. Clement, vol. 2, pp. 277–337. On these publications about Sattler, see *Flugschriften vom Bauernkrieg zum Täuferreich,* vol. 2, ed. Laube et al., pp. 1557–1558; C. Arnold Snyder, "The Influence of the Schleitheim Articles on the Anabaptist Movement: An Historical Evaluation," *MQR,* 63 (1989), 336–337, 336 n. 42.

77. See Hans Rössler, "Wiedertaufer in und aus München 1527–1528," *Oberbayerisches Archiv,* 85 (1962), 42, 54 n. 3; Lieseberg, *Märtyrerlied,* pp. 69–70; *Flugschriften vom Bauernkrieg zum Täuferreich,* vol. 2, ed. Laube et al., p. 1527. According to both the pamphlet and the legal record of his trial and sentencing, Wagner did not, for example, contrast a rejection of infant baptism to adult baptism, as so many interrogated Anabaptists did. Rather, he seemed to repudiate the significance of any external rite of baptism. See the trial summary reprinted in Georg Müller, "Zur Geschichte des Wiedertäufers Georg Wagner,"

Beiträge zur bayerische Kirchengeschichte, 2 (1896), pp. 299–301. See also the *New geschicht von Jörgen Wagner* (sig. A2v): although Christ's baptism in the Jordan was necessary, Wagner stated, the savior's status had rendered subsequent baptisms of Christians superfluous.

78. *New geschicht von Jörgen Wagner,* sig. A2. The trial summary also noted the attempts to persude Wagner to renounce his views. Müller, "Geschichte Georg Wagner," p. 300.

79. *New geschicht von Jörgen Wagner,* sigs. [A1v], A2.

80. According to Arnold Snyder, "The teachings of Schleitheim were unquestionably reinforced by Sattler's heroic death at Rottenburg." Snyder, *Sattler,* p. 100. On May 18, 1527, the second day of his trial at Rottenburg-am-Neckar, Sattler defended the articles alleged against him and fellow Anabaptists. He denied they had done anything contrary to imperial mandate, which prohibited only "Lutheran teaching"; rejected the presence of Christ in the bread and wine of the Eucharist; denied the efficacy of infant baptism; rejected the priests' use of oil (in the sacraments); said Mary was to be praised above all women (but not as an intercessor); claimed that "saints" referred to living believers; affirmed that Christians should not swear oaths; justified leaving the Benedictines and taking a wife; and finally said that the commandment "Thou shalt not kill" should apply to nonresistance to the Turks, should they invade. [Klaus von Graveneck], *Newes wunderbarliches geschicht von Michel Sattler,* sigs. A3v–[A4v]. For these responses having been made on May 18 rather than May 17, as Graveneck indicated in his pamphlet, see C. Arnold Snyder, "Rottenburg Revisited: New Evidence Concerning the Trial of Michael Sattler," *MQR,* 54 (1980), 226.

81. As in the case of the Protestant martyrologists, mistakes were sometimes made and Protestants were included as Anabaptists. For a well-documented study of how Leonhard Keyser, the Lutheran pastor executed in 1527, ended up in Hutterite sources and the Dutch Mennonite martyrologies of the seventeenth century, see Piet Visser, "Het doperse mirakel van het onverbrande bloempje: Terug naar de bron van een onbekend lied over martelaar Leonhard Keyser (overl. 1527)," *DB,* n.s., 17 (1991), 9–30.

82. One of the two deleted songs referred to the communal ownership of goods, espoused by the Hutterites and Philipites but sharply rejected by the Swiss Brethren, which raises questions about its presence in the 1564 collection in the first place. See "Wir schreyen zu dir Herre Gott," in *Etliche schöne Christliche Geseng,* no. 17, stanza 4, fol. 28v. The other omitted song, "Lobt den Herren jr Heyden all," a versification of Psalm 117 (itself only two verses), was probably deleted because of its unusual brevity. Ibid., fol. 9. A reference to "the *Ausbund,* or book of spiritual songs" during the 1571 Frankenthal disputation between Anabaptists and Reformed Protestants seems to imply an earlier edition published around 1570–1571 (ten songs in the 1583 *Ausbund* were adapted from the first half of *Het Offer des Heeren,* where they appeared for the first time in the 1570 ed.). Wolkan, *Lieder der Wiedertäufer,* p. 56 (quotation); Duerksen, "Anabaptist Hymnody," p. 28. Or perhaps a manuscript version of the song collection circulated. None of the martyr songs in the 1583 *Ausbund* concerns anyone executed after 1570, evidence that corroborates the existence of an earlier edition or manuscript version, produced ca. 1570–1571. Chronologically,

the four Maastricht martyrdoms of 1570 are the latest recounted in the collection. See "Nun hört, ihr Freunde ehrsame," *Ausbund* 1583, pp. 165–178.

83. *Ausbund* 1583, pp. 9–34, 51–185, 238–241; Lieseberg, *Märtyrerlied,* pp. 81–95, 273–299; Duerksen, "Anabaptist Hymnody," pp. 28–30.

84. *Ausbund* 1583, pp. 9–246, the last song in the series being "Merckt auff jr Völcker alle," about Joriaen Simons, a Dutch martyr executed in Leiden in April 1557. This was one of the songs adapted from *The Sacrifice unto the Lord.*

85. Lieseberg, *Märtyrerlied.* For a list of all sixty-five songs plus the collections and manuscripts in which they are found, see ibid., pp. 273–299.

86. Wieder gives several examples of Dutch songs for which this was the case. Wieder, *Schriftuurlijke liedekens,* pp. 106–109. See also Duerksen, "Anabaptist Martyr Ballad," pp. 198–199. For instance, according to the final stanza of the song about Frans van Boolsweert's (Dammassoon's) execution, it was first sung the day after his death, Palm Sunday (March 29), 1545: "Alsmen dit liedeken eerstmael sanck / Dat was op Palmen daghe." *OHL,* in *BRN,* vol. 2, pp. 505 n. 2, 509 (quotation); Wieder, *Schriftuurlijke liedekens,* p. 107; *DAN,* vol. 1, *Friesland en Groningen (1530–1550),* ed. A. F. Mellink (Leiden: E. J. Brill, 1975), p. 74, 74 n. 1. A song about five Anabaptists burned in Ghent on April 11, 1551, was written by Hans van Overdam, who was present at their executions and was himself put to death in the same city on July 9 or 10. He must have written the song within this three-month period. *OH, OHL,* in *BRN,* vol. 2, pp. 100, 516–521; Johan Decavele, *De dageraad van de Reformatie in Vlaanderen (1520–1565),* vol. 1 (Brussels: Paleis der Academiën, 1975), p. 439; RAG, Raad van Vlaanderen, sententies, Registers van de secrete camere, vol. 7613 (1549–1554), fol. 160r-v; A. L. E. Verheyden, *Het Gentsche martyrologium (1530–1595)* (Bruges: "De Tempel," 1945), pp. 13–15.

87. The song about Mantz, "Mit lust so wil ich singen," is probably a versification of Mantz's letter to his co-believers, and thus very likely a reworking by other Anabaptists after his death. Gottfried Locher, however, has argued that the letter is a prose adaptation of the song. *QGTS,* vol. 1, p. 220 n. 1; *Ausbund* 1583, pp. 40–45, repr. in Wackernagel, vol. 3, no. 514, pp. 451–452; Gottfried W. Locher, "Felix Manz' Abscheidsworte an seine Mitbrüder vor der Hinrichtung 1527: Spiritualität und Theologie. Die Echtheit des Liedes 'Bei Christo will ich bleiben,'" *Zwingliana,* 17 (1986), 11–26. The song about Wagner, "Wer Christo jetzt wil folgen nach," was based on the *New geschicht von Jörgen Wagner.* Lieseberg, *Märtyrerlied,* pp. 71–72; *Ausbund* 1583, pp. 59–65, repr. in Wackernagel, vol. 3, no. 517, pp. 455–456.

88. *Ausbund* 1583, pp. 9–26. One of the longest Hutterite songs, by Jacob Pruchmair, recounts martyrs from the Old Testament through the Hutterites in 105 stanzas. *Die Lieder der Hutterischen Brüder* (Scottdale, Pa.: Mennonitische Verlagshaus, 1914), pp. 770–781. Anabaptists may have gotten their knowledge of Eusebius through Sebastian Franck (whose *Chronica* was widely read among the Hutterites), Balthasar Hubmaier, or other pamphlets with excerpts from the early church historian. *ME,* vol. 2, p. 262.

89. For a description of the two songs and their *contrafacta,* see Lieseberg, *Märtyrerlied,* pp. 274–275, 306.

90. Lieseberg, *Märtyrerlied,* pp. 275, 277–278, 284–286, 288, 293, 296–297,

306. So familiar was the song that it was indicated as "Jörg Wagners Ton," rather than by the customary first line.

91. *QGT*, vol. 1, *Herzogtum Württemberg*, ed. Gustav Bossert (Leipzig: Heinsius, 1930), pp. 708/16–17, 25–26, 725/11–17.

92. Christoph Erhard, *Gründliche kurtz verfaste Historia. Von Münsterischen Widertauffern: vnd wie die Hutterischen Brüder so auch billich Widertauffer genent werden* . . . (Munich: Adam Berg, 1589), p. 34, quoted in Wolkan, *Lieder der Wiedertäufer*, p. ii. For Fischer, see his *Antwort auff die Widerlegung Clauß Breütel* . . . (Bruck an der Teya, 1604), sig. E2, where he mentions eight songs by their *contrafacta*, and idem, *Hutterischen Widertauffer Taubenknobel* . . . (Ingolstadt: Andreas Angermeyer, 1607), p. 47, both cited in Wolkan, *Lieder der Wiedertäufer*, pp. iii-iv. See also Christoph Andreas Fischer, *Vier vnd funfftzig Erhebliche Ursachen, Warumb die Widertauffer nicht sein im Land zu leyden* (Ingolstadt: Andreas Angermeyer, 1607), p. 79.

93. Andreas Gut, "Einfaltig bekanntnus: An Burgermeister und Ratth der Statt Zürich was die ursach des grossen zwyspalts und zwytrachts sye under allen die sich Christy und des H. Evangeliums rümend," Staatsarchiv Zürich, sig. EII 443, pp. 125, 140, 143, 147–150, 166a. I am most grateful to Arnold Snyder for sharing with me lengthy excerpts from this source.

94. Gut, "Einfaltig bekanntnus," p. 166a.

95. I use the term "Mennonites" to denote the followers of Menno Simons from the group's beginnings under Obbe Philips into the seventeenth century, understanding them as one of several groups of Dutch Anabaptists in the period 1530 to around 1560. This avoids cumbersome descriptions like "early Dutch followers of Menno" as contrasted to later "Mennonites."

96. For Sicke Frericx, see *DAN*, vol. 1, *Friesland en Groningen (1530–1550)*, p. 4; for Jan Volckerts Tripmaker and the others executed in The Hague in December, see *DAN*, vol. 5, *Amsterdam (1531–1536)*, ed. A. F. Mellink (Leiden: E. J. Brill, 1985), pp. 1–4.

97. Claes appeared in *Het Offer des Heeren* beginning in 1570, the entry based on the ca. 1527 German pamphlet *Ein wunderliche geschycht newlich geschehen jn dem Hag in Holland jm jar MDXXVII*, . . . *von einr frawen geheissen Wendelmut Clausen dochter* . . . , repr. in *CDN*, vol. 5, pp. 274–279. *OH*, in *BRN*, vol. 2, pp. 422–429. Claiming Claes as an Anabaptist martyr reflects the fluid relationship between sacramentarians and Anabaptists in the Netherlands from 1530 until about 1560. Sacramentarians were loosely organized groups of men and women who denied transubstantiation and met to read and discuss scripture, without developing formal ecclesiastical structures. By about 1560 they seem to have been largely absorbed by the Mennonites, not unlike the way that the Lollards were absorbed by the English Protestants. On the coexistence of sacramentarians and Anabaptists, see A. F. Mellink, "The Beginnings of Dutch Anabaptism in the Light of Recent Research," *MQR*, 62 (1988), 220. Cornelius Augustijn has recently criticized the older contention of W. J. Kühler and Cornelius Krahn that sacramentarians contributed significantly to the origins of Dutch Anabaptism; according to Augustijn, they were simply one part of the general reform-minded climate of the 1520s. Augustijn, "Anabaptism in the

Netherlands: Another Look," *MQR*, 62 (1988), 197–210; Kühler, *Geschiedenis der nederlandsche doopsgezinden in de zestiende eeuw*, pp. 43–48; Krahn, *Dutch Anabaptism: Origin, Spread, Life, and Thought*, 2nd ed. (Scottdale, Pa.: Herald Press, 1981), pp. 39–40, 44–79. Other scholars have criticized Augustijn, however, and the question of the precise relationship between sacramentarians and early Dutch Anabaptists remains unresolved. For the most recent debate, see the contributions in *DB*, n.s., 15 (1989), 121–147.

98. Klaus Deppermann, *Melchior Hoffman: Social Unrest and Apocalyptic Visions in the Age of Reformation*, trans. Malcolm Wren, ed. Benjamin Drewery (Edinburgh: T. and T. Clark, 1987), pp. 330–331.

99. This applies both to those in the city itself and to the Münsterites who more than once attempted armed takeovers of Amsterdam and had briefly overrun the Cistercian monastery of Oldeklooster near Bolsward (Friesland) at Easter 1535.

100. W. J. de Bakker, "Bernhard Rothmann: Civic Reformer in Anabaptist Münster," in *The Dutch Dissenters: A Critical Companion to Their History and Ideas*, ed. Irvin B. Horst (Leiden: E. J. Brill, 1986), pp. 105, 112.

101. Compare Menno Simons, *Dat Fundament des Christelycken leers* (n.p., 1539 [–1540]), repr. and ed. H. W. Meihuizen (The Hague: Martinus Nijhoff, 1967), pp. 202–203, with idem, *MSOO*, fol. 66v.

102. That is, if Menno's *Gantsch duydelyck ende klaer bewys . . . tegens . . . de blasphemie van Jan van Leyden* (repr. *MSOO*, fols. 619–631), not known in any printed edition until 1627, was in fact written by him in 1535. Because it was a deliberate response to Bernhard Rothmann's *Van der Wrake* (December 1534), a work with almost no currency in the sixteenth century after the fall of Münster, and because its language and style are congruent with Menno's other writings, recent scholarly opinion has generally, if tentatively, affirmed the work's authenticity. For an overview of the question, see James M. Stayer, "Menno and Oldeklooster," *SCJ*, 9 (1978), 59, 65–66. See also Irvin B. Horst, *A Bibliography of Menno Simons* (Nieuwkoop: B. de Graaf, 1962), pp. 117–118.

103. Stayer, *Anabaptists and the Sword*, pp. 267–268. For Joris's attempts at reconciliation with the Batenburgers and Münsterite refugees in Oldenburg, see Gary K. Waite, *David Joris and Dutch Anabaptism, 1524–1543* (Waterloo, Ont.: Wilfred Laurier University Press, 1990), pp. 113–126.

104. On the Batenburgers, see Stayer, *Anabaptists and the Sword*, pp. 284–297; Gary K. Waite, "From Apocalyptic Crusaders to Anabaptist Terrorists: Anabaptist Radicalism after Münster, 1535–1545," *ARG*, 80 (1989), 180–191.

105. Waite, *David Joris;* S. Zijlstra, *Nicolaas Meyndertsz van Blesdijk* (Assen: Van Gorcum, 1983), p. 19.

106. I follow the new convention in English-language nomenclature for Joris's followers, who have also been called "Davidjorists," "Davidjorites," and "Davidians." James Stayer coined the term "Davidite" as a deliberate parallel to "Mennonite"; Gary Waite has followed Stayer in his recent biography of Joris. Stayer, "Davidite vs. Mennonite," in *The Dutch Dissenters*, p. 143 n. 1; Waite, *David Joris*, p. 157 n. 1.

107. On the execution of Davidites in 1539, see A. F. Mellink, *De wederdoopers in de noordelijke nederlanden, 1531–1544*, 2nd ed. (Leeuwarden: Gerben Dykstra, 1981), pp. 399–401; Zijlstra, *Blesdijk*, pp. 17–19; Waite, *David Joris*, p. 73.

108. Anneken [Jans], *Hier begint dat Testament dat Anneken zeliger gedachtenisse, Esaias haren Sone bestelt heefft* . . . [n.p., ca. 1566], sigs. A1–A2, quotation on A2. For the first edition of the *Testament* (1539), printed with an apocalyptic song by Jans that probably dates from the Münster period, see Packull, "Anna Jansz of Rotterdam," p. 152. Packull's evidence linking Jans to Joris is convincing even if one accepts James Lowry's view that she might have repudiated Joris at the very end of her life. Lowry, "Stierf Anna van Rotterdam als volgeling van David Joris?" *DB*, n.s., 18 (1992), 113–118. Her willingness to die does not by itself demonstrate that she was no longer a Davidite.

109. Van der Zijpp, "Hymnology of the Mennonites in the Netherlands," p. 11.

110. Karel Vos, "Brief van David Joris, 1539," in "Kleine bijdragen over de Doopersche beweging in Nederland tot het optreden van Menno Simons," *DB*, 54 (1917), 164–165.

111. Stayer, "Davidite vs. Mennonite."

112. Nicolas Meynderts van Blesdijk, *Weder-antwoort Nicolaes Meynaertsz, van Bleesdijck op zekeren Brief by Gellium onderteeckent . . . Geschreuen in 't Jaer 1545* (n.p., 1607), fols. 11r-v, 16r-v, 18v–19, quotations on 11, 11r-v, 16v. At one point Blesdijk quoted the Gospel verse about not fearing those who can kill the body but cannot harm the soul (Matt. 10:28, Luke 12:4), referring to situations in which magistrates call one to account for one's faith. Ibid., fols. 19v–20.

113. For an overview of the traditional perspective, see S. Zijlstra, "Menno Simons and David Joris," *MQR*, 62 (1988), 249–256.

114. On the latter point, see Gary K. Waite, "Staying Alive: The Methods of Survival as Practiced by an Anabaptist Fugitive, David Joris," *MQR*, 61 (1987), 46–57.

115. Davidites were perhaps wary of being identified with what they considered a Mennonite *over*willingness to die. Something of this comes across in another of Blesdijk's treatises from the mid-1540s, his *Christelijcke Verantwoordinghe* . . . (n.p., 1607), fols. 19v, 28v–29v, 31v.

116. Menno, *Een klare beantwoordinge, over een schrift Gellii Fabri, prediker tot Emden* . . . [1554], repr. in *MSOO*, fol. 256.

117. Menno, *Tegen Jan van Leyden*, in *MSOO*, fol. 628. Menno also quoted the New Testament image of martial engagement par excellence, Paul's exhortation to put on the armor of God (Eph. 6:10–17). Ibid., fol. 627.

118. Menno, *Voele goede vnd chrystelycke leringhen op den 25. Psalm* . . . (n.p., 1539 [1540]), in *MSOO*, fols. 163–165.

119. At the outset of the preface, Menno made clear the role of scripture and recent events as the basis for his apocalyptic hermeneutic. Menno, *Fundament*, p. 5.

120. Menno, *Klare beantwoordinge over een schrift Fabri*, in *MSOO*, fol. 234.

121. Menno, *Fundament*, p. 13. Menno's marginal reference to Rev. 13, to which the editor Meihuizen added the verse, is here indicated in parentheses. Menno followed this passage immediately with several crucial New Testament verses about how Christ's followers will necessarily suffer (Luke 24:26, Matt. 10:25,

2 Tim. 3:12, and Matt. 24:24). Ibid. In the 1558 revision of the *Fundament,* published near the end of his life, he slightly altered this passage. If anything, another twenty years had confirmed his views about the bond between the Gospel and persecution: "It [the Lord's Word] is the word of the cross, and in my view it shall indeed remain such until the very end. For it shall be set forth with much suffering and sealed with blood. That lamb has been slain from the beginning of the world." Menno, *Fundament* (1558), in *MSOO,* fol. 6.

122. Menno, *Fundament,* p. 21. For the retribution against tyrants from the "bloodguzzling Cain" through Pontius Pilate, Nero, and other "tyrants and bloodthirsty dogs," see ibid., pp. 178–180.

123. Ibid., pp. 23, 56. By 1558 Menno's awareness of the geographically widespread nature of Anabaptist martyrdom is reflected in his subtle modifications of both these passages: "with the blameless blood of the witnesses of Jesus, that so over-flowingly, indeed like water, is squeezed out and shed in many lands" [*in vele landen*]; "we poor outcast people are by each and every one in many lands [*in veel Landen*] so miserably blamed, outlawed, plundered and like innocent sheep throttled and put to death." Menno, *Fundament* (1558), in *MSOO,* fols. 8, 17.

124. Menno, *Fundament,* pp. 30, 40–41, 156.

125. Ibid., pp. 166–167.

126. A. L. E. Verheyden states that van Stoelwijck was executed in 1541 after being arrested on February 11, 1538, though archival evidence of the execution seems not to have survived. Verheyden, *Le martyrologe courtraisien et le marty-rologe bruxellois* (Vilvoorde: R. Allecourt, 1950), pp. 49, 62. According to van Braght, he was burned at Vilvoorde, where he had been imprisoned, on March 24, 1541. Van Braght 1685, vol. 2, p. 51. A narrative account of the sentencing of Jan Claes in *Het Offer des Heeren,* first published eighteen years after his death, closely coheres with the record of his sentence by the Amsterdam *Vier-schaar.* Compare *OH,* in *BRN,* vol. 2, pp. 86–88, with *DAN,* vol. 2, *Amsterdam (1536–1578),* ed. A. F. Mellink (Leiden: E. J. Brill, 1980), pp. 47–48.

127. For other Anabaptists' references to Claes, see *DAN,* vol. 2, *Amsterdam (1536–1578),* pp. 47, 49, 55, 56, 61, 63, 74. For Pieters's interrogations and his execution on April 16, 1545, see ibid., pp. 52–57, 58–59, 61–62, 65.

128. [Wouter van Stoelwijck], *Een Trostelijcke vermaninghe ende seer schoon onderwys-inghe van het lyden ende Heerlicheyt der Christenen* ([Groessen: Nicolaes Biest-kens van Diest], 1558), sigs. A3v, A4r-v, A4v–A5 (final quotation on A5).

129. *OH,* in *BRN,* vol. 2, pp. 79, 84.

130. [Blesdijk], *Christelijcke Verantwoordinghe,* fol. 29v.

131. For Ghent, see Verheyden, *Gentsche martyrologium,* pp. xxiv, 5–31. In Bruges, no Anabaptists were executed in the 1540s, but eight were put to death in the 1550s and twenty-five in the 1560s. In Kortrijk, none were put to death in the 1540s, but six were in the 1550s, and seventeen in the 1560s. These figures are derived from Verheyden, *Het Brugsche martyrologium (12 October 1527–7 Augustus 1573)* (Brussels: "Wilco," [1944]), pp. 33–60; idem, *Martyrologe courtraisien et bruxellois,* pp. 31–40.

132. Menno had spent two years ministering in Holland in the early 1540s. For

Flanders, Johan Decavele convincingly replaces Verheyden's view of continuous Anabaptist growth through the 1540s with a picture of discontinuity between the late 1530s and the Mennonite rebuilding of the movement in the 1550s. Decavele, *Dageraad van de Reformatie in Vlaanderen*, vol. 1, pp. 435–437; Verheyden, *Anabaptism in Flanders 1530–1650: A Century of Struggle* (Scottdale, Pa.: Herald Press, 1961), pp. 23–29.

133. Menno Simons, *Eyne Troestelijke Vermaninge van dat Lijden, Cruyze, vnde Vervolginge der Heyligen, vmme dat woort Godes, vnde zijne getuichenisse* [Fresenburg: "B. L."? 1554 or 1555]. Other scholars have noted this work's significance for Mennonite martyrdom in the sixteenth century. See, for example, Stauffer, "Anabaptist Theology of Martyrdom," pp. 184, 189, 200, 204, 212, 213; Dyck, "Suffering Church in Anabaptism," p. 10.

134. Menno, *Troestelijke Vermaninge*, sigs. B3 (quotation), C1, C2.

135. For the quotations, see ibid., sigs. C3v, E2, Q1r-v. The section with biblical examples occupies ibid., sigs. [C4]–J2. For the atrocities, see ibid., sig. H2r-v; Foxe 1563, sig. [B4v].

136. For the publication information, see Marja Keyser, *Dirk Philips 1504–1568: A Catalogue of His Printed Works in the University Library of Amsterdam* (Amsterdam: University Library of Amsterdam, 1975), pp. 41–43, 93, 96, 97, 101–102; Paul Valkema Blouw, "Drukkers voor Menno Simons en Dirk Philips," *DB*, n.s., 17 (1991), 50–57, 74.

137. J. ten Doornkaat Koolman, *Dirk Philips: Vriend en medewerker van Menno Simons 1504–1568* (Haarlem: T. J. Tjeenk Willink, 1964), pp. 3–4.

138. D[irk] P[hilips], *Van de Gemeynte Godts . . .* ([Groessen]: Nicolaes Biestkens van Diest, 1562), repr. in *Enchiridion Oft Hantboecxken van de Christelijcke Leere ende Religion . . .* ([Franeker?], 1564), and in *BRN*, vol. 10, ed. Frederik Pijper (The Hague: Martinus Nijhoff, 1914), pp. 382–383.

139. D[irk] P[hilips], *Van der Sendinge der Predicanten oft Leeraers . . .* ([Groessen: Nicolaes Biestkens van Diest], 1559), repr. in *Enchiridion* and in *BRN*, vol. 10, p. 245.

140. Ibid., pp. 223–224, quotation on 224. The same idea recurs in other works. See, for example, his *Drie grondighe Vermaningen ofte Sendtbrieuen . . .*, printed as an appendix to the *Enchiridion* in 1564, in *BRN*, vol. 10, pp. 421, 457.

141. P[hilips], *Van de Gemeynte Godts*, in *BRN*, vol. 10, pp. 404–405. Menno, too, saw persecution as "a sure sign of Christ's Church," witnessed to by scripture, Christ, the prophets, the apostles, and God's faithful children, "especially in our Netherlands." Menno, *Klare beantwoordinge, over een schrift Schrift Gellii Fabri*, in *MSOO*, fol. 300.

142. D[irk] P[hilips], *Een lieffelijcke vermaninghe wt des Heeren woordt . . .* [Franeker: Jan Hendricks van Schoonrewoerd, 1558], repr. in *Enchiridion* and in *BRN*, vol. 10, pp. 250–251, quotation on 251. Twice in the *Three Fundamental Admonitions*, to console and strengthen afflicted Mennonites, Philips referred to those who have "washed their robes in the blood of the Lamb" (Rev. 7:14). In *BRN*, vol. 10, pp. 419–420, 458–459.

143. P[hilips], *Drie grondighe Vermaninghen*, in *BRN*, vol. 10, pp. 418–420, quotation on 420.

144. Ibid., p. 424.

145. Dirk Philips, "Eenen seer schoonen troostelijcken ende Christelijcken Sendt-brief . . . ," in a collection of several different Mennonite writings with continuous signatures that begins with Thomas van Imbroeck, *Confessio: Een schoone Bekentenisse . . .* ([Leeuwarden: Pieter Hendricks], 1579), fols. 125–139, repr. in *BRN,* vol. 10, quotation on p. 679. See Cramer's introduction to this letter in *BRN,* vol. 10, p. 669, 669 n. 3; *BMPN,* vol. 1, pp. 195–203. For Ariaentgen as the woman's name, see ten Doornkaat Koolman, *Dirk Philips,* p. 103. Her husband, Joachim de Suikerbaker, was an important Mennonite elder in Antwerp who had baptized many people but eventually recanted. This explains why the letter to his wife was not published until well after Philips's death in 1568. Ibid., pp. 103–104.

146. *OH,* in *BRN,* vol. 2, p. 179. For his execution sentence, see SAA, Vierschaar, V146 (1548–1554), fol. 55.

147. *OH,* in *BRN,* vol. 2, p. 334. Nine marginal scriptural references accompany this sentence. The editor(s), not the martyrs themselves, provided the uniform marginal biblical references by chapter and verse throughout *Het Offer des Heeren.* This can be inferred from the occasional references to chapters alone in the texts of the martyrs' letters (for example, see ibid., pp. 374, 381). Usually Mennonite martyrs simply quoted or paraphrased a verse or two without indicating the fact, or with cues like "as Paul says," or "as Peter has written." They seem to have been indifferent to memorizing the references to the scriptural verses that they absorbed.

148. Soetken van den Houte, *Een Testament, gemaeckt by Soetken van den Houte . . .* [Rees: Dirck Wylicx van Zanten, ca. 1582], sig. [A8v]. The biblical verses included Matt. 11:12, Acts 14:22, Ps. 44:11–22, John 16:20, Rev. 2:10, and John 16:33. Ibid., sig. B1. I thank Paul Valkema Blouw for the approximate date of publication as 1582; the *Bibliotheca Belgica* gives 1580. *Bibliotheca Belgica,* vol. 3, ed. Ferdinand Vander Haeghen and Marie-Thérèse Lenger (Brussels: Culture et civilisation, 1964), p. 518.

149. After Hendricks's death (apparently in 1564), whoever took over his press printed the 1567 and 1570 editions of the martyrology. Paul Valkema Blouw, "Een onbekende doperse drukkerij in Friesland," *DB,* n.s., 15 (1989), 57–59. There may have been an earlier edition published in 1561, perhaps by Nicolaes Biestkens van Diest in Groessen. Valkema Blouw, "Nicolaes Biestkens van Diest, *in duplo,* 1558–83," in *Theatrum Orbis Librorum: Liber Amicorum Presented to Nico Israel on the Occasion of His Seventieth Birthday,* ed. Ton Croiset van Uchelen, Koert van der Horst, and Günther Schilder (Utrecht: HES Publishers, 1989), p. 324.

150. The quotation comes from the lengthy title of *Het Offer des Heeren* itself. *OH,* in *BRN,* vol. 2, p. 51.

151. Stayer, *Anabaptists and the Sword,* p. 326.

152. Three of these nine (Willem Droochscheerder, Adriaen Pan, and Lenaert Plovier) are mentioned only in passing in the song about seventy-two Anabaptists executed in Antwerp between 1555 and 1560, "Aenhoort Godt hemelsche Vader." *OHL,* in *BRN,* vol. 2, pp. 564, 566, 567. The other six represented in

both the first half of the work and in the *Liedtboecxken* are Peter de Bruyne and Jan/Hans vanden Wouwere ("de oude cleercooper"), two of the three martyrs who were executed in Antwerp (1551) and celebrated in "Ick sal met vruechden singen een Liet"; Hans de Vette, one of the twelve martyrs from Ghent in 1559 who was memorialized without being named in "Ick moet een liet beginnen"; Joriaen Simons, one of the two martyrs depicted in "Hoort vrienden al / hier in dit aertsche dal" after he was burned in Haarlem in 1557; Peter van Olmen of Wervick, who was executed in Ghent in 1552 and who wrote the song that begins "Een eewige vruecht die niet en vergaet"; and Jacques d'Auchy, drowned in Leeuwarden in March 1559, whose betrayal and imprisonment is recounted in "Och siet hoe droeue dingen." *OHL,* in *BRN,* vol. 2, pp. 521–526, 521–522 n. 2, 556–559, 586–591, 594–603, 608–611.

153. Bert Hofman has amended the view in his monograph on Dutch spiritual songs in the sixteenth century, now arguing that the first Mennonite edition of the *Veelderhande Liedekens* was that of 1559 rather than 1566. Hofman, *Liedekens vol gheestich confoort,* pp. 169–202, 244–245, 247; idem, "Gereformeerden en doopsgezinden," 63–65. Only three editions of the *Veelderhande liedekens* (1554, 1556, 1558) originated outside of Mennonite circles. Between 1554 and 1600, however, Wieder inventoried no fewer than twenty-four editions of the work, plus eleven editions of the *Liedtboecxken* from *Het Offer des Heeren* and six additional Mennonite hymnals. Hofman, *Liedekens vol gheestich confoort,* ibid.; idem, "Gereformeerden en doopsgezinden," ibid.; Wieder, *Schriftuurlijke liedekens,* pp. 134–171. Piet Visser, who is compiling a comprehensive catalogue of Dutch Mennonite hymnals and their contents, informs me that their total number for the sixteenth and seventeenth centuries is considerably higher than indicated by Wieder.

154. For example, a song entitled "O Syon wilt v vergaren" was the designated *contrafactum* for no fewer than four songs in the *Liedtboecxken. OHL,* in *BRN,* vol. 2, pp. 516, 526, 538, 581. For the song itself, see *Veelderhanden Liedekens, gemaeckt wt den ouden ende nieuwen Testamente, nv derdewerf gecorrigeert ende meer ander daer by gheset . . .* ([Antwerp]: Frans Fraet, 1556), sigs. X1v–X2v. Before Pieter van Olmen of Wervick was executed in Ghent in 1552, he used "In doots ghewelt lach ick gheua[ng]en" as the *contrafactum* for his own hymn, "Een eewige vruecht die niet en vergaet." *OHL,* in *BRN,* vol. 2, p. 594; *Veelderhande Liedekens,* sigs. O–O2v. A final example: whoever wrote the song in the *Liedtboecxken* about the woman named Anneken executed in Antwerp, "Verhuecht verblijt groot ende cleyn," used a song from the *Veelderhande liedekens* for the tune, "Ick roepe v o hemelsche Uader aen." *OHL,* in *BRN,* vol. 2, p. 552; *Veelderhande liedekens,* sigs. [O5v–O6v]. All three of these *contrafacta* appeared in the 1559 Mennonite edition of the *Veelderhande liedekens* (printed by Jan Hendricks van Schoonredewoerd, who first printed *Het Offer des Heeren* as well); the three songs were part of the martyrology's *Liedtboecxken* beginning with the first edition of 1563. Hofman, *Liedekens vol gheestich confoort,* pp. 346–347.

155. Compare "Aenhoort Godt hemelsche Vader," in *OHL,* in *BRN,* vol. 2, pp. 563–568, with SAA, Vierschaar, V147 (1554–1559), fols. 32v–100; V148

(1559–1565), fols. 3v–14; and *AA*, vol. 14, pp. 20–29. The only exception to exact chronological order is "Nohele" (Noëlle Mazille), who was executed on August 19, 1558, but is placed in the song before Frans Thybault and Dierick Jonckhans, who were executed on July 6, 1558. Compare *OHL*, in *BRN*, vol. 2, p. 565, with SAA, Vierschaar, V147, fols. 88v, 90, and *AA*, vol. 14, pp. 24–25. For the two who recanted and were beheaded, rather than drowned or burned, see SAA, Vierschaar, V147, fols. 74 (Gillis van Aken), 84v, 85v–86v (Anthonis de Rocke); *AA*, vol. 8, pp. 435, 438, 444–447, 464. Because the song does not include the Anabaptists executed on August 9 or October 4, 1560, though it carefully enumerated every martyr for nearly five years, it is extremely likely that the song was composed between April 3 (the day of the last recorded executions) and August 9, 1560. *BRN*, vol. 2, p. 568 n. 1.

156. Quoted in Verheyden, *Anabaptism in Flanders*, p. 38 (Verheyden's trans.); idem, *Brugsche martyrologium*, p. 44. For the record of her hearing and sentencing, see SAB, Bouc van den steene (1558–1559), fols. 90v–91.

157. *OH*, in *BRN*, vol. 2, p. 55.

158. Ibid., pp. 53–55, 86–88, 123, 615–616.

159. Among the additions to the 1570 edition, the entries on Wendelmoet Claes, and on Feije Baucke and Elcke Foucke, are third-person narratives. *OH*, in *BRN*, vol. 2, pp. 422–427, 430–433.

160. For example, this introduction to the entry on Adriaen Cornelis, executed in Leiden in November 1552 (erroneously given here as 1551), is typical of *The Sacrifice unto the Lord:* "Hereafter follows a prayer, admonition, and confession of faith by Adriaen Cornelis, glassmaker, from when he was imprisoned in Leiden, and there was killed for his witness to Jesus in the year 1551." *OH*, in *BRN*, vol. 2, p. 195.

161. "De Werelt op de Christen verstoort," stanzas 3–4, *OH*, in *BRN*, vol. 2, p. 254. For Claes de Praet's own account, on which the song was based, see ibid., pp. 238–239. For payment of the costs of Claes de Praet's execution, see SAG, Stadsrekeningen, vol. 64 (1556–1557), fol. 177; Verheyden, *Gentsche martyrologium*, p. 23.

162. *Broederlicke vereenige van sommighe kinderen Gods . . .* (n.p., 1560), repr. (n.p., 1565), repr. in *BRN*, vol. 5, ed. Samuel Cramer (The Hague: Martinus Nijhoff, 1910), pp. 585–650.

163. French-speaking Anabaptists were not unknown, however. For the handful from Wallonia who ended up in Antwerp, see Guido Marnef, *Antwerp in the Age of Reformation: Underground Protestantism in a Commercial Metropolis, 1550–1577*, trans. J. C. Grayson (Baltimore: The Johns Hopkins University Press, 1996), pp. 75–76, 157–158.

164. John S. Oyer, "The Strasbourg Conferences of the Anabaptists, 1554–1607," *MQR*, 58 (1984), 218–219; Stayer, *Anabaptists and the Sword*, pp. 327–328. In at least one instance this exclusivity seems to have surfaced regarding the Mennonite-Davidite opposition. It seems likely that the editor(s) would have known about Jorien Ketel's admonition to his children published in the mid-1540s, but deliberately excluded it because Ketel (in contrast to Anneken Jans) was one of David Joris's most important followers. See [Jorien Ketel], *Heilsame*

Leere ende nutte onderwysinge van enen Godvruchtigen man . . . (n.p., ca. 1544); Waite, *David Joris,* pp. 153–157. If this is so, it qualifies Cramer's assertion that the editor(s) of *Het Offer des Heeren* included all the martyrological sources available to them. Cramer, in *BRN,* vol. 2, pp. 20, 38.

165. *OH,* in *BRN,* vol. 2, pp. 53–54.

166. The editor(s) of *Het Offer des Heeren,* after mentioning the examples of the chosen men and women in whom God worked powerfully, stated simply, "and so forth with so many others, whom it would take too long to mention." *OH,* in *BRN,* vol. 2, p. 54. For Menno's references to Eusebius, see, for example, *Fundament,* pp. 71, 173–174, 199; *Troestelijke Vermaninge,* sig. F3.

167. See my "Prescribing and Describing Martyrdom: Menno's *Troestelijke Vermaninge* and *Het Offer des Heeren,*" *MQR,* 71 (1997), 603–613.

168. Menno, *Troestelijke Vermaninge,* sigs. [A1v]–A2v; *OH,* in *BRN,* vol. 2, pp. 53–54.

169. Menno, *Troestelijke Vermaninge,* sig. A3r-v.

170. *OH,* in *BRN,* vol. 2, p. 54.

171. Ibid.

172. Ibid., pp. 61, 77.

173. Ibid., p. 120.

174. Ibid., p. 237. See also the final stanza of the song about Adriaen Cornelis, ibid., p. 218. For Joos 't Kindt, see also Verheyden, *Martyrologe courtraisien et bruxellois,* pp. 31–32.

175. *OHL,* in *BRN,* vol. 2, p. 615.

176. *OH,* in *BRN,* vol. 2, pp. 60, 194.

177. See, for example, *OHL,* in *BRN,* vol. 2, pp. 521, 581, 591.

178. See, for example, ibid., pp. 526, 538, 547–548, 560, 608.

179. For a complete list of the sixteen works and their editions, see my "Anathema of Compromise: Christian Martyrdom in Early Modern Europe," vol. 2 (Ph.D. diss., Princeton University, 1996), p. 740 n. 197. Most of these works are also catalogued in *BMPN,* vol. 1, albeit with less complete publication information. Up to 1560, except for the inclusion of Anabaptist songs in early editions of *Various Songs,* the only known publications are Davidite Anneken Jans's *Testament* (1539), Davidite Jorien Ketel's *Blessed Doctrine* (ca. 1544), Wouter van Stoelwijck's *Comforting Admonition* (1558), and a Dutch translation of material about Michael Sattler (1560). For the term "microconfessionalization" in the context of this section I am indebted to William Monter.

180. Some of the printers of these works remain anonymous and the places of publication unknown, but none are known to have been printed in the southern provinces. For only one has a southern city of origin been proposed, the *Christelijcke seynntbrieuen gheschreuen door eenen vromen christen genaemt Hans Bret* . . . ([Antwerp?] 1582). See *BMPN,* vol. 1, pp. 689–702.

181. See J. G. C. A. Briels, *Zuidnederlandse boekdrukkers en boekverkopers in de Republiek der Verenigde Nederlanden omstreeks 1570–1630* (Nieuwkoop: B. de Graaf, 1974).

182. Typical is the *Sommige belijdingen, schriftlijcke sentbrieuen, ende Christelicke vermaningen, Gheschreuen door Reytse Aysseszoon, van Oldeboorn* . . . (Leeuwar-

den? Pieter Hendricksz? ca. 1577), a compilation that included Reytse's accounts of his interrogations, fourteen letters sent to family members and fellow believers, a letter of consolation written to him in prison, and two songs.

183. V[alerius] S[chool] M[eester], *Proba fidei: Oft, de Proeue des Gheloofs* . . . (n.p., 1569). Thijs Joriaens, *Een Christelijcke Sentbrief, van de Sendinghe, Inleydinghe, ende coemste Jesu Christi in deser Werelt* . . . ([Haarlem: Gillis Rooman for] Willem Jans Buys in Amsterdam, 1586).

184. For a more detailed treatment of these additions, see my "Anathema of Compromise," vol. 2, pp. 743–744.

185. Jacob de Roore, *In dit teghenwoordighe Boecxken zijn veel schoone ende lieflijcke Brieuen, van eenen ghenaemt Jacob de Keersmaecker* . . . ([Delft: Aelbrecht Hendricxs], 1577), repr. 1579(?), 1581, 1584. There seems to have been an earlier edition (ca. 1571) of which no copies have survived. Joos Verkindert and Mayken Deynoots, *Sommige Brieuen, Testamenten, ende Belijdingen geschreuen door Joos Verkindert* . . . (n.p., 1572), repr. 1577.

186. Herman Timmerman, *Een corte Bekentenisse ende grondige aenwijsinge wt der H. Scrift* . . . *noch is hier achter gedaen een nieu Liedeken, inhoudende van sommige opgeofferde kinderen Gods, die om tgetuygennise Christi haer leuen te Ghent ghelaten hebben* ([Delft: Aelbrecht Hendricxs], 1577), fols. 13–16; the song "Alsmen schreef duyst vijfhondert Jaer / Ende twee en tsestich mede," is reprinted in *BRN*, vol. 2, 649–654. For the identification of Biestkens as the printer of Cramer's "1578b," rather than the other 1578 edition (as Cramer reported in *BRN*, vol. 2, p. 11), see Valkema Blouw, "Nicolaes Biestkens van Diest," pp. 321, 330 n. 73.

187. Cramer acknowledged that the editor(s) of the later editions of *Het Offer des Heeren* must have been familiar with these publications, but implied that they wanted to keep the work within manageable proportions. *BRN*, vol. 2, pp. 21, 621–624.

188. See my "Particuliere martelaarsbundels uit de late zestiende eeuw," *DB*, n.s., 19 (1993), 100–104, for an earlier version of the material in the following paragraphs. Frederik Pijper argued long ago that the editors of *Het Offer des Heeren* had made decisions based on differences among the Mennonite factions. Pijper, "Nieuw ontdekt doopsgezind martelaarsboek"; idem, *Martelaarsboeken*, pp. 107–112. Long before the social history of the Reformation, however, he looked too exclusively for specific doctrinal indicators in the sources themselves. Mennonites were not only bearers of doctrines, but members of concrete communities of belief. They could well have been excluded on this basis, even without objectionable "tags" in their writings.

189. Kühler, *Geschiedenis der Nederlandsche doopsgezinden in de zestiende eeuw*, pp. 395–435, esp. 399–425. For a detailed account of the origins and development of the split in Frisian towns between 1560 and 1567, see J. G. de Hoop Scheffer, "Het verbond der vier steden," *DB*, 33 (1890), 1–90.

190. Reimer-Blok, "Letters of Jacob de Roore," pp. 318–319; Verheyden, *Anabaptism in Flanders*, pp. 67–69. De Roore was executed along with Herman Vleckwick on June 8, 1569. For the proceedings and sentences against De Roore in the two preceding months, see RAB, Brugse Vrije, registers, vol. 17,041/2,

Crimbouck (1568–1573), fols. 7v–8, 9v, 14–16v, 18v–19v, 22v; Verheyden, *Brugsche martyrologium*, pp. 57–60. For translated excerpts from these proceedings, see Verheyden, *Anabaptism in Flanders*, pp. 125–133.

191. *ME*, vol. 4, p. 713; Hans Alenson, *Tegen-Bericht Op de voor-Reden vant groote Martelaer Boeck der Doops-Ghesinde Ghedruckt tot Hoorn 1626*. . . . (Haarlem: Jan Pieters Does, 1630), repr. in *BRN*, vol. 7, ed. Samuel Cramer (The Hague: Martinus Nijhoff, 1910), pp. 259–261.

192. Karel Vos, *De Doopsgezinden te Antwerpen in de zestiende eeuw* (Brussels: Kiessling and Co., 1920), pp. 66–69. Vander Haeghen concluded, on the basis of Verkindert's remarks about the ban's importance, that he was a Frisian. *BMPN*, vol. 1, p. 453. This is inconclusive, however, because the Flemish also held banning in high esteem. On the Anabaptists in Antwerp, see also Marnef, *Antwerp*, pp. 72–80, 153–170, 188–194.

193. *ME*, vol. 2, p. 710; Vos, *Doopsgezinden te Antwerpen*, pp. 19, 23, 42–44.

194. For Cornelis's baptism by Bouwens, see *DAN*, vol. 2, *Amsterdam (1536–1578)*, p. 301. For the song about him, included in later editions of *OH*, see *BRN*, vol. 2, pp. 654–658.

195. *ME*, vol. 1, p. 577; Alenson, *Tegen-Bericht*, p. 249. For Rijcen's mention of de Roore, see Christiaen Rijcen and Adriaen Jans, *Tgetuygenisse ende de de naeghelaeten Schriften van den Godvruchtigen Christiaen Rijcen* . . . (Haarlem: Gillis Rooman for Franchoys Soete, 1588), p. 15.

196. Three collections are in the Amsterdam University Library: two in the collection of the Doopsgezinde Bibliotheek (shelf marks OK 65–180, OK 65–181), the other in the general university library collection (shelf mark 976 D 8). A fourth collection is in the Leiden University Library (shelf mark 1499 G 17); I thank Paul Valkema Blouw for calling this volume to my attention. A fifth volume belonged to the State and University Library of Hamburg, but was destroyed in World War II. Its contents are known from a nineteenth-century catalogue description, a photocopy of which Richard Gerecke kindly sent to me. See my "Particuliere martelaarsbundels" for a detailed description and analysis of these five collections.

197. For the six pamphlets, see my "Anathema of Compromise," vol. 2, p. 740 n. 197, nos. 4–9. I thank Paul Valkema Blouw for identifying Hendricxs as the printer.

198. Conversely, Hendricxs had not previously published the only addition to his 1578 printing of *Het Offer des Heeren*, the song about two Ghent martyrs of 1571.

199. The letters to unnamed Ghent prisoners by Joos Meulenaar, Francis Lochtemer, and "N. N. Jonge dochter," plus the letters by Mattheus Panten are (except for the extremely short letter to Mayken Boosers from her children printed with the 1566 but not the 1567 edition) the only materials that were left out of subsequent editions. *Het Offer des Heeren* ([Amsterdam]: I[an] E[verts] C[loppenburgh], 1591 [1592?]), fols. 282–300. For the puzzle regarding this edition's date of publication, see *BRN*, vol. 2, p. 15. Cramer's remark that nothing in these letters would disqualify them is unconvincing if group affiliation, rather than any comments in the letters per se, determined their unacceptability—if,

for example, Frisian editors knew or suspected that they were written by Flemish Mennonites. Ibid. At the same time, in introducing these letters, the editor(s) mentioned the *Confession* of the lenient Christiaen Rijcen. *Het Offer des Heeren* (1591/1592), fol. 282. The 1599 edition, however, included letters from Joos de Tollenaer (who was part of the Mennonite community in Ghent before his execution there in 1589), one of which referred to Jacob de Roore's letters. *ME*, vol. 3, p. 120; Verheyden, *Gentsche martyrologium*, pp. 68–69. This could suggest that if this final edition was aligned with a specific group, it was the Flemish—or perhaps the Waterlanders.

200. For his execution sentence (April 23, 1574), see *DAN*, vol. 7, *Friesland (1551–1601) and Groningen (1538–1601)*, ed. A. F. Mellink and S. Zijlstra (Leiden: E. J. Brill, 1995), pp. 131–132.

201. See F. van Dijk, "Het laatste ketterproces in de Nederlanden (19 Juli 1597, Anneke Emelt buiten Brussel levend begraven)," *Gereformeerd Theologisch Tijdschrift*, 49 (1949), 219–231.

202. *ME*, vol. 2, pp. 338, 413.

203. *ME*, vol. 2, p. 413; ibid., vol. 4, p. 330; Kühler, *Geschiedenis van de doopsgezinden in Nederland*, pt. 2, first half, 1600–1735 (Haarlem: H. D. Tjeenk Willink and Son, 1940), pp. 71–94.

204. [Hans de Ries, Jacques Outerman, et al.], *Historie der Martelaren ofte waerachtighe Getuygen Jesu Christi die d'Evangelische waerheyt in veelderley tormenten betuygt ende met haer bloet bevesticht hebben sint het Jaer 1524 tot desen tyt toe* . . . (Haarlem: Jacob Pauwels Hauwert for Daniel Keyser, 1615). For older scholarship on the "Hoorn" and "Haarlem" martyrologies, that is, the four Mennonite martyrologies published between *Het Offer des Heeren* and van Braght, see De Hoop Scheffer, "Onze martelaarsboeken," 63–89, and Kühler, *Geschiedenis van de doopsgezinden*, pt. 2, first half, pp. 97–115.

205. The only difference between the ten title-page images in the 1615 martyrology on the one hand and the 1617 and 1626 collections on the other is the 1615 bottom-center depiction of the alliance between the papacy and worldly powers. In 1617 and 1626 it was replaced by an angel watching over a flock of sheep (representing Mennonite Christians).

206. For example, in his preface de Ries reprinted both the imperial decree of June 10, 1535, and a 1530 Zurich decree against the Anabaptists. *Historie der Martelaren*, sigs. (*3)v–[(*4)v], **2. The French version of the imperial decree is reprinted in *ROPB*, second series, 1506–1700, vol. 3, ed. J. Lameere (Brussels: J. Goemaere, 1902), pp. 477–478.

207. For Bernard of Clairvaux, see [de Ries], "Voor-reden," *Historie der Martelaren*, sig. [*8v]; for the 1570 ed. of Crespin's martyrology, see ibid., sigs. [*8v]–**1; for Foxe (from whose martyrology de Ries erroneously turned Joan Boucher into a man, "Johan"), see ibid., **2v.

208. Kühler says nothing about the change in genres and accompanying practices vis-à-vis the martyrological tradition; instead, he emphasizes the care with which the information from the songs was preserved in the new prose. Kühler, *Geschiedenis van de doopsgezinden*, pt. 2, first half, pp. 99–101.

209. I am assuming that the decline in the number of editions reflected a decline in

popularity. Van der Zijpp, "Hymnology of the Mennonites in the Netherlands," pp. 12–13; Duerksen, "Anabaptist Hymnody," p. 61. In contrast to the twenty-four editions of the *Veelderhande liedekens* published between 1554 and 1600, Wieder lists further editions only for 1608 (2), 1611, 1624, 1630, 1637, and 1664. Wieder, *Schriftuurlijke liedekens,* pp. 171–175.

210. [Hans de Ries], "Vorreden," *Lietboeck Inhoudende Schriftuerlijcke Vermaen Liederen, Claech Liederen, Gebeden, Danck Liederen, Lofsanghen, Psalmen, ende andere stichtelijcke Liederen* . . . (Rotterdam: Dierick Mullem, 1582), repr. in Philipp Wackernagel, ed., *Lieder der niederländischer Reformierten aus der Zeit der Verfolgung im 16. Jahrhundert* (1867; reprint, Nieuwkoop: B. de Graaf, 1965), pp. 38–39, 66–71, quotation on 67. For de Ries as the editor of this collection and the author of its preface, see *ME,* vol. 1, p. 331.

211. For the price of the *Historie der martelaren,* see Alenson, *Tegen-Bericht,* in *BRN,* vol. 7, p. 160. Around 1620, journeyman bricklayers in Leiden made less than six guilders per week, and in 1637 even master carpenters there earned less than ten. Jan de Vries, "An Inquiry into the Behavior of Wages in the Dutch Republic and the Southern Netherlands, 1580–1800," in *Dutch Capitalism and World Capitalism,* ed. Maurice Aymard (Cambridge: Cambridge University Press, 1982), pp. 40–42, 54–55.

212. Samuel Cramer, introduction to Alenson, *Tegen-Bericht,* in *BRN,* vol. 7, p. 144; *ME,* vol. 4, pp. 98–99.

213. Wolkan, *Lieder der Wiedertäufer,* pp. 126–136; Duerksen, "Anabaptist Hymnody," pp. 28–30; Lieseberg, *Märtyrerlied,* pp. 81–95.

214. Duerksen, "Anabaptist Hymnody," pp. 37–44.

215. Stayer, *Anabaptists and the Sword,* pp. 327–328; Oyer, "Strasbourg Conferences," p. 219.

216. Cornelius J. Dyck, "Hans de Ries and the Legacy of Menno," *MQR,* 62 (1988), 401–402; *ME,* vol. 4, p. 330.

217. [de Ries], "Voor-reden," *Historie der Martelaren,* sig. *2v.

218. Ibid., sigs. *2v (quotation), *2v–*3, *4v, [*6v–*7v], [**4].

219. For example, Jacques Outerman traveled away from Haarlem to collect materials, especially about Flemish martyrs; from Amsterdam, Joost Goverts and his assistants concentrated on Brabant; from Hoorn, the Old Frisians searched local archives. [Syvaert Pieters], "Voor-reden tot den Christelijcken Leser," in [Pieter Jans Twisck et al.], *Historie van de Vrome Getuygen Iesu Christi* . . . (Hoorn: Isaac Willems for Zacharias Cornelis, 1626), sig. A2v; Kühler, *Geschiedenis van de doopsgezinden,* pt. 2, first half, pp. 98–99. For the Waterlander activities in German-speaking lands, see Kühler, ibid.; Alenson, *Tegen-Bericht,* in *BRN,* vol. 7, pp. 160, 184.

220. [de Ries], "Voor-reden," *Historie der Martelaren,* sig. **1.

221. De Ries himself made this analogy. Ibid.

222. Ibid. Augustine was far from revered by Anabaptists, yet his dictum could be derived anew directly from scripture. De Ries referred in the margin to 1 Pet. 4:15–16: "But let none of you suffer as a murderer, a thief, a criminal, or even as a mischief maker. Yet if any of you suffer as a Christian, do not consider it a disgrace, but glorify God because you bear this name."

223. Kühler, *Geschiedenis van de doopsgezinden*, pt. 2, first half, p. 115.

224. Certain elements were retained from de Ries's preface. For example, the Old Frisians reprinted both the 1535 imperial placard and the 1530 Zurich ordinance against the Anabaptists, both of which they set within the argument that Catholics as well as Protestants had persecuted them. [Syvaert Pieters], "Voorreden tot den Christelijcken Leser," in [Pieter Jans Twisck et al.], *Historie der warachtighe getuygen Jesu Christi* . . . (Hoorn: Zacharias Cornelis, 1617), sigs. [*6–*7], ‡1v.

225. [Syvaert Pieters], "Tot den Leser," *Historie der Warachtighe getuygen Jesu Christi*, sig. [*1v]. On Pieters's authorship of the prefatory material to the 1626 martyrology (the second edition of the Old Frisian version), including "de kleyne Voorreden . . . staende voor de Articulen des Geloofs," see Alenson, *Tegen-Bericht,* in *BRN*, vol. 7, pp. 155–156.

226. Syvaert Pieters was probably the author of the confession of faith itself, although it reflects Twisck's views as well. Archie Penner, "Pieter Jansz. Twisck— Second Generation Anabaptist/Mennonite Churchman, Writer and Polemicist" (Ph.D. diss., University of Iowa, 1971), pp. 256–261. Penner fundamentally accepts the veracity of Twisck's response to Alenson after the latter asked Twisck about the authorship of the confession of faith. Ibid.; Alenson, *Tegen-Bericht,* in *BRN*, vol. 7, pp. 155–156. For the confession of faith itself, which runs to more than fifty pages, see [Twisck et al.], *Historie der warachtighe getuygen Jesu Christi*, sigs. *2–**3.

227. Kühler, *Geschiedenis van de doopsgezinden*, pt. 2, first half, p. 111; Penner, "Twisck," pp. 244–245.

228. [Pieters], "Voor-reden," in [Twisck et al.], *Historie van de Vrome Getuygen Iesu Christi*, sigs. A2v–A3. Five instances of alleged tampering regarding the doctrine of the incarnation were listed, with specific folio references to the 1615 edition. Ibid., sig. A3.

229. Oyer, "Strasbourg Conferences," pp. 218–219.

230. For de Ries's controversy with fellow Waterlander Nittert Obbes between 1625 and 1628 and the broader context of the dispute, see Sjouke Voolstra, "The Path to Conversion: The Controversy between Hans de Ries and Nittert Obbes," in *Anabaptism Revisited: Essays on Anabaptist/Mennonite Studies in Honor of C. J. Dyck*, ed. Walter Klaassen (Scottdale, Pa.: Herald Press, 1992), pp. 98–114.

231. Alenson, *Tegen-Bericht,* in *BRN*, vol. 7, pp. 156–158.

232. Ibid., pp. 181–182, 187–189, 198; 214–218 (see also 195, 259–261); 231– 234, 242.

233. Ibid., p. 217.

234. [Hans de Ries], "Voor-reden tot den Leser," in *Martelaers Spiegel der Werelose Christenen t'zedert A°. 1524* . . . (Haarlem: Hans Passchiers van Wesbusch, 1631[–1632]), pp. 3–4.

235. This is one of the major preoccupations of the preface, continuing the attacks against Roman Catholic and Protestant persecution in the preface to the 1615 edition. Ibid., pp. 9–16.

236. [de Ries et al.], *Martelaers Spiegel*, pp. 21–56.

237. There is still no full-length study of this process of Mennonite economic, social, and cultural assimilation from the mid-sixteenth through the late seventeenth centuries. The subject is touched on in several of the contributions in *From Martyr to Muppy (Mennonite Urban Professionals): A Historical Introduction to Cultural Assimilation Processes of a Religious Minority in the Netherlands: The Mennonites*, ed. Alastair Hamilton, Sjouke Voolstra, and Piet Visser (Amsterdam: Amsterdam University Press, 1994). For the Amsterdam Waterlanders in the seventeenth century, including Arent Dircks Bosch and his son, see Mary Sprunger, "Waterlanders and the Dutch Golden Age: A Case Study on Mennonite Involvement in Seventeenth-Century Dutch Trade and Industry as one of the Earliest Examples of Socio-economic Assimilation," in *From Martyr to Muppy*, pp. 133–148, esp. 136, 140–142; see also idem, "Hoe rijke mennisten de hemel verdienden: Een eerste verkenning van de betrokkenheid van aanzienlijke doopsgezinden bij het Amsterdamse zakenleven in de Gouden Eeuw," *DB*, n.s., 18 (1992), 39–52. For the links among de Ries, Anslo, and Rembrandt, see Stephanie S. Dickey, "Doop door water en het zwaard: Doopsgezind martelaarschap in de kunst van Rembrandt en zijn tijdgenoten," *DB*, n.s., 21 (1995), 55–56. On the complex relationship between economic prosperity and culture in general in the seventeenth-century Dutch Republic, see Simon Schama, *The Embarrassment of Riches: An Interpretation of Dutch Culture in the Golden Age* (New York: Alfred A. Knopf, 1987), esp. pp. 289–371.

238. Whereas de Ries devoted only about two pages to the dispute with the Old Frisians about the relationship between martyrs' doctrines and deaths, he spent nearly four on growing spiritual complacency and worldliness. [de Ries], "Voorreden," *Martelaers Spiegel*, pp. 3–4, 16–20.

239. Ibid., pp. 17–18, quotations on 17.

240. Van Braght 1660, sig. [(*)4v] (my emphasis).

241. Ibid., sigs. [(*)4v], (**)1.

242. Ibid., sig. (**)1v.

243. "Hoort vrienden al / hier in dit aertsche dal," stanza 12, *OHL*, in *BRN*, vol. 2, p. 591. *Ausbund* 1583, "Vorred," sigs. (???)–[(????)v].

244. Menno, *Troestelijke Vermaninge*, sig. P1v.

245. Van Braght 1660, sig. a3.

246. Van Braght's first book, rather than the second book on the sixteenth-century martyrs, constitutes his most original and important contribution to the Mennonite martyrological tradition. To the best of my knowledge, no one has examined how he read and used the dozens of sources that went into his version of the history of Anabaptism from the first through the fifteenth centuries. His unusually precise references to sources would permit a detailed study of this sort. Samuel Cramer's important discussion of van Braght's reliability addressed the question only very briefly, and it appeared long before the emergence of recent interest in the history of reading and narrative. Cramer, "Nogmaals de geloofwaardigheid van van Braght," pp. 185–187.

247. Menno, *Fundament*, p. 163; *OH*, in *BRN*, vol. 2, p. 84.

248. Van Braght 1660, sig. [(***)4].

249. See, for example, van Braght 1685, vol. 1, p. 388, on Thomas Walsingham's report of Louis Clifford.

250. For both these points, see van Braght 1660, sig. [(***)4].

251. For this view among Protestant writers, see Euan Cameron, "Medieval Heretics as Protestant Martyrs," in *Martyrs and Martyrologies,* ed. Diana Wood, vol. 30 of *Studies in Church History* (Oxford: Blackwell, 1993), pp. 203–205.

252. Van Braght 1660, sig. (****)1.

253. For the Waldensians and Lollards, see van Braght 1685, vol. 1, pp. 302–323, 332–334, 338, 342–349, 360–363, 373–375, 378–384. Van Braght's exclusion of the Hussites as he understood them, although confused in its groupings and terminology like many other sixteenth- and seventeenth-century accounts (for example, he identified the Taborites as pacifistic rather than as militant Hussites), remained consistent with his guiding criteria: military activity after the deaths of Hus and Jerome of Prague coupled with capitulation to much of Roman Catholic doctrine precluded them from the ranks of true martyrs. Ibid., pp. 390–391.

254. Van Braght 1660, sig. [(*)4].

255. I am grateful to David Luthy for a conversation on this point.

7. The New Saints: Roman Catholics and Martyrdom

1. Willem Hessels van Est, *Histoire veritable des bienheureux martyrs de Gorcum en Hollande, la plus part freres mineurs, qui pour la foy Catholique ont esté mis à mort à Brile l'an 1572 . . .* (Douai: Marc Wyon, 1618), pp. 392–394, quotation on 393. The work was first published, in Latin, in 1603.

2. Peter Burke, "How to Be a Counter-Reformation Saint," in *Religion and Society in Early Modern Europe, 1500–1800,* ed. Kaspar von Greyerz (London: German Historical Institute, 1984), pp. 46, 48, 51. Only two martyr-saints were canonized between 1523 and 1767: Jan Nepomuk, the fourteenth-century bishop of Prague, in 1729; and Fidelis of Sigmaringen (1577–1622), a Capuchin missionary killed by peasants at Protestant instigation in Seewiss, Switzerland, in 1746. Ibid., p. 51; David Hugh Farmer, *The Oxford Dictionary of Saints* (Oxford: Oxford University Press, 1978), p. 149. On the paucity of martyr-saints canonized by late medieval popes, see André Vauchez, *La sainteté en occident aux derniers siècles du moyen age d'après les procès de canonisation et les documents hagiographiques,* 2nd ed. (Rome: École française de Rome, 1988), p. 482.

3. Burke, "Counter-Reformation Saint," p. 51. Many historians have recognized the insufficiency of a sharply divided, two-tier model of early modern Catholicism such as William A. Christian, Jr., suggests. He postulates "two levels of Catholicism—that of the Church Universal, based on the sacraments, the Roman liturgy, and the Roman calendar; and a local one based on particular sacred places, images, and relics, locally chosen patron saints, idiosyncratic ceremonies, and a unique calendar built up from the settlement's own sacred history." Christian, *Local Religion in Sixteenth-Century Spain* (Princeton: Princeton University Press, 1981), p. 3. The veneration of uncanonized Catholic martyrs across national boundaries further blurs this overdrawn dichotomy.

4. For a recent example of this juxtaposition posed too sharply, with no consideration of sixteenth-century Catholic martyrological sources, see Catharine Ran-

dall Coats, *(Em)bodying the Word: Textual Resurrections in the Martyrological Narratives of Foxe, Crespin, de Bèze and d'Aubigné* (New York: Peter Lang, 1992), esp. pp. 2, 4–5, 9, 10, 17, 19, 38, 49, 103.

5. Émile Mâle, *L'art religieux de la fin du XVIe siècle, du XVIIe siècle, et du XVIIIe siècle: Etude sur l'iconographie après le concile de Trente,* 2nd ed. (Paris: A. Colin, 1951), p. 122.

6. See Robert W. Scribner, *For the Sake of Simple Folk: Popular Propaganda for the German Reformation,* 2nd ed. (Oxford: Clarendon Press, 1994).

7. The closest parallel to the German Lutheran denunciation of Reformed martyrs, or the microconfessionalization of Mennonite martyrology, is perhaps the selectivity that religious orders displayed in memorializing their own martyrs. Mâle provides a noteworthy example. Of the twenty-six Catholics crucified in Nagasaki in 1597, three were Jesuits, six Franciscan missionaries, and seventeen converts. The three Jesuits but not the others were painted in the refectory of a Jesuit church in Rome, San Andrea al Quirinale, while in an engraving by Jacques Callot probably commissioned by the Franciscans of Lorraine in the late 1620s, the crucifixion scene included only twenty-three martyrs—the Franciscans and the converts but not the Jesuits. Mâle, *L'art religieux après Trente,* pp. 117–119. For similar tension between English secular priests and religious in the late sixteenth and early seventeenth centuries, see Peter Lake and Michael Questier, "Agency, Appropriation and Rhetoric under the Gallows: Puritans, Romanists and the State in Early Modern England," *P&P,* 153 (1996), 93–94.

8. Caesar Baronius, ed., *Martyrologium Romanum ad novam kalendarii rationem, et Ecclesiasticae historiae veritatem restitutum . . .* (Venice: Petrus Dusinellus, 1587), pp. xvii–xviii.

9. The secondary literature on More is massive, spurred in recent decades by the Yale critical edition of More's works and the forum provided by the journal *Moreana.* The following scholarship is relevant to More the martyr and the response to his death: R. W. Chambers, *Thomas More* (1935; reprint, Harmondsworth: Penguin, 1963); Henry de Vocht, *Acta Thomae Mori: History of the Reports of His Trial and Death with an Unedited Contemporary Narrative* (1947; reprint, Nendeln: Kraus, 1966); J. Duncan M. Derrett, "Neglected Versions of the Contemporary Account of the Trial of Sir Thomas More," *Bulletin of the Institute of Historical Research,* 33 (1960), 202–223; Derrett, "The Trial of Sir Thomas More" (1964), repr. in *Essential Articles for the Study of Thomas More,* ed. R. S. Sylvester and G. P. Marc'hadour (Hamden, Conn.: Archon, 1977), pp. 55–78; James K. McConica, "The Recusant Reputation of Thomas More" (1964), repr. in *Essential Articles,* pp. 136–149; W. Gordon Zeeveld, "Apology for an Execution" (1967), repr. in *Essential Articles,* pp. 198–211; Giovanni Santinello, "Thomas More's *Expositio passionis*" (1969), repr. in *Essential Articles,* pp. 455–461; Thomas Wheeler, "An Italian Account of Thomas More's Trial and Execution," *Moreana,* 26 (1970), 33–39; Paul D. Green, "Suicide, Martyrdom, and Thomas More," *Studies in the Renaissance,* 19 (1972), 135–155; R. S. Sylvester, "Roper's Life of More" (1972), repr. in *Essential Articles,* 189–197; Henri Meulon, "Thomas More et la souffrance," *Moreana,* 37 (1973), 53–60; Michael A. Anderegg, "The Tradition of Early

More Biography," in *Essential Articles,* pp. 3–25; Dermot Fenlon, "Thomas More and Tyranny," *JEH,* 32 (1981), 453–476. The voluminous introductory material and critical commentary in *CWTM* are also invaluable. For two recent full-length studies see Alastair Fox, *Thomas More: History and Providence* (New Haven: Yale University Press, 1982), trenchant criticisms of which appear in Brendan Bradshaw, "The Controversial Sir Thomas More," *JEH,* 36 (1985), 537–545; and Richard Marius, *Thomas More: A Biography* (New York: Alfred A. Knopf, 1984), a useful corrective to which is Louis L. Martz, *Thomas More: The Search for the Inner Man* (New Haven: Yale University Press, 1990). The most astute recent biography is Peter Ackroyd, *The Life of Thomas More* (New York: Nan A. Talese, 1998).

10. See Edward Surtz, *The Works and Days of John Fisher (1469–1535)* (Cambridge, Mass.: Harvard University Press, 1967); *Humanism, Reform and the Reformation: The Career of Bishop John Fisher,* ed. Brendan Bradshaw and Eamon Duffy (Cambridge: Cambridge University Press, 1989); Richard Rex, *The Theology of John Fisher* (Cambridge: Cambridge University Press, 1991).

11. William Roper, More's son-in-law, wrote his biography around 1555, partly to assist a longer account by the Marian archdeacon of Canterbury, Nicholas Harpsfield, who completed his work in 1557 and dedicated it to Roper. For modern critical editions, see William Roper, *The Lyfe of Sir Thomas Moore, knighte,* ed. Elsie Vaughan Hitchcock, Early English Text Society, no. 197 (London: Oxford University Press, 1935); Nicholas Harpsfield, *The life and death of Sr Thomas Moore, knight, sometymes Lord high Chancellor of England,* ed. Elsie Vaughan Hitchcock, Early English Text Society, no. 186 (London: Oxford University Press, 1932). For Stapleton's work, see his *Tres Thomae: Seu De S. Thomae Apostoli rebus gestis. De S. Thoma Archepiscopo Cantuariensi et martyre. D. Thomas Mori Angliae quondam Cancellari . . .* (Douai: Joannis Bogardi, 1588; repr. Cologne: Bernard Gualter, 1612). For the 1626 edition of Roper's biography, see *The mirrour of vertue in worldly greatnes: Or the life of syr Thomas More knight . . .* ([St. Omers: English College], 1626). For an overview of these and the other early accounts of More's life and death, see Anderegg, "Tradition of Early More Biography," in *Essential Articles,* pp. 3–25.

12. See Franciscus van Ortroy, ed., "Vie du bienheureux martyr Jean Fisher Cardinal, Évêque de Rochester (+1535): Texte anglais et traduction latine du XVIe siècle," *AB,* 10 (1891), 186–192; and *AB,* 12 (1893), 97–287. According to van Ortroy, this biography's principal author was John Young, vice chancellor of Cambridge University during Mary's reign. Van Ortroy, "Vie," *AB,* 10, pp. 200–201. It was first edited and published with interpolations by Thomas Baily as *The Life and Death of that renowned John Fisher, Bishop of Rochester . . .* (London: n.p., 1655). Rex, *Theology of Fisher,* p. 2.

13. For a standard narrative of the events, see G. R. Elton, *Reform and Reformation: England 1509–1558* (Cambridge, Mass.: Harvard University Press, 1977), pp. 103–200.

14. 26 Henry VIII, c. 1, 13, in *The Tudor Constitution: Documents and Commentary,* ed. G. R. Elton (Cambridge: Cambridge University Press, 1972), pp. 62, 355, quotation on 355.

15. More pointed this out to Thomas Cromwell in a March 1534 letter. *CTM*, no. 199, p. 498/203–214.

16. J. J. Scarisbrick, *Henry VIII* (Berkeley: University of California Press, 1968), pp. 115–117.

17. Johannes Eck, *Enchiridion locorum communium adversus Lutherum et alios hostes ecclesiae (1525–1543)*, ed. Pierre Fraenkel, vol. 34 of *Corpus Catholicorum* (Münster: Aschendorff, 1979), pp. 2–4, 17–34, 48–75. See also Rex, *Theology of Fisher*, p. 85.

18. *CTM*, to Margaret Roper, ca. April 17, 1534, no. 200, p. 502/16–17. Cromwell must have known this: he was present along with Thomas Cranmer and others when More refused the oath at Lambeth on April 13, 1534, and received a letter written March 5 in which More made clear his opinion concerning papal primacy. See ibid., no. 199, pp. 498/200–499/247. For a thorough treatment of More's view of the legal and doctrinal status of papal primacy, see Brian Gogan, *The Common Corps of Christendom: Ecclesiological Themes in the Writings of Sir Thomas More* (Leiden: E. J. Brill, 1982), pp. 251–262.

19. Fenlon, "Thomas More and Tyranny."

20. Roper, *Life of More*, pp. 55/17–56/3.

21. See Garry E. Haupt, "Introduction," in Thomas More, *Treatise on the Passion, Treatise on the Blessed Body, Instructions and Prayers,* in *CWTM*, vol. 13, ed. Haupt (New Haven: Yale University Press, 1976), pp. xxxvii–xli, lxxxiii–cxxii.

22. *Thomas More's Prayer Book: A Facsimile Reproduction of the Annotated Pages,* ed. Louis L. Martz and Richard S. Sylvester (New Haven: Yale University Press, 1969); J. B. Trapp, *Erasmus, Colet and More: The Early Tudor Humanists and Their Books* (London: British Library, 1991), pp. 43–45.

23. Numerous scholars have made this point, including Green, "Suicide, Martyrdom, and Thomas More," pp. 149–154. For More's distinction between eager and fearful martyrs, see *De tristitia Christi,* in *CWTM*, vol. 14, ed. and trans. Clarence H. Miller (New Haven: Yale University Press, 1976), pp. 63–71, 241–257.

24. More, *De tristitia Christi,* p. 109/2–5 (Miller's trans.).

25. Surtz, *John Fisher,* p. 374.

26. John Fisher, *A spirituall consolation, written by Iohn Fyssher Bishoppe of Rochester, to hys sister Elizabeth, at suche tyme as hee was prisoner in the Tower of London . . .* [London: Thomas East, 1578], sig. [D8].

27. Chauncy (ca. 1513–1581) wrote five versions of the passion of the English Carthusians between 1546 and 1570. For an overview of them and their circumstances of composition, see *Cause of the Canonization of Blessed Martyrs . . . Put to Death in England in Defence of the Catholic Faith (1535–1582): Official Presentation of Documents on Martyrdom and Cult* (Vatican City: Polyglot Press, 1968), pp. 12–13; E. Margaret Thompson, *The Carthusian Order in England* (London: Society for Promoting Christian Knowledge, 1930), pp. 345–352. The second through the fifth versions (I have not examined the first) included Houghton's remarks about preparedness to die, an account of the Carthusians' three-day reconciliation, and his scaffold comment. See Franciscus van Ortroy, ed., "Opusculum R. P. Mauritii Chauncy de beatis martyri-

bus anglicis ordinis Carthusiensis Joanne Houghton et sociis ejus," *AB*, 6 (1887), 39–40, 43; *Historia aliquot nostri saeculi martyrum cum pia tum lectu jucunda* . . . (Mainz: Franciscus Behem, 1550), fols. 45–46v, 51r-v; van Ortroy, ed., "Martyrium monachorum Carthusianorum in Anglia passio minor, auctore Mauritio Chauncy," *AB*, 22 (1903), 60–61, 64; *The Passion and Martyrdom of the Holy Carthusian Fathers: The Short Narration*, ed. G. W. S. Curtis (London: Society for Promoting Christian Knowledge, 1935), pp. 66–70, 90–92. It is uncertain whether Chauncy or any of the other monks were present at the executions on May 4, 1535. If not, Chauncy might have gotten a report from Antonius Recsius, a Dominican friend of Houghton's, who was there. Thompson, *Carthusian Order in England*, p. 400 n. 2.

28. Edward Surtz, "More's Friendship with Fisher," in *Essential Articles*, pp. 169–179. For Fisher's remarks, see *LP*, vol. 8, no. 858, p. 332. A Henrician apologist, Simon Matthew, confirmed that Fisher and More "in prison write to their mutual comfort in their damnable opinions." Matthew, *A Sermon made in the cathedrall churche of saynt Paule at London, the XXVII. day of June, Anno 1535* (London: Thomas Berthelet, 1535), sig. [C8].

29. Roper, *Lyfe of Moore*, p. 6/9–11. The Carthusians ordinarily did not allow nonmembers to live in the monastery, but in 1490 special provisions permitted unmarried men to live in a building on the grounds of the London house. More might have resided there during this period. Thompson, *Carthusian Order in England*, pp. 311–312; see also Ackroyd, *Life of More*, pp. 97–98.

30. Roper, *Lyfe of Moore*, p. 80/9–19, quotation at lines 16–19.

31. *LP*, vol. 8, no. 856, p. 328. In prison Houghton made notes of his interrogations, which he gave to William Exmewe, the procurator of the monastery, who gave them to Chauncy, who in turn gave them to a Florentine from the Bardi family, who promised to send them to the pope and the papal court. Chauncy, *Historia*, fol. 53. Here "Bardin" was described as a Spaniard, but in both the 1564 and the 1570 versions of the martyrdoms, Chauncy wrote that he gave them "cuidam spectabili Florentino nomine Petro de Berdes." *Martyrdom of Carthusian Fathers*, ed. Curtis, p. 104; "Passio minor," p. 65/40–41. For these notes as the ones probably seen by Fisher in prison, see David Knowles, *The Religious Orders in England*, vol. 3 (Cambridge: Cambridge University Press, 1959), p. 231.

32. Knowles, *Religious Orders in England*, vol. 3, pp. 214–215. More gave the impression that he was a regular visitor to Syon Abbey. *CTM*, More to Cromwell, March? 1534, no. 197, pp. 484–485.

33. For More, see Derrett, "Trial of More," in *Essential Articles*, pp. 72–73; compare with Roper, *Lyfe of Moore*, pp. 94/17–95/9. For Reynolds, see *Cause of the Canonization*, p. 21; summary in *LP*, vol. 8, no. 566, p. 214.

34. Chauncy, *Historia*, fols. 50v–52v, 53v–54. See also the letter from Eustace Chapuys to Charles V, May 5–8, 1535, in *Cause of the Canonization*, pp. 28–29 (English summary in *LP*, vol. 8, no. 666, p. 250).

35. This was reported by Humfrey Schokborough to Sir Thomas Inglefield, justice of assize in Oxfordshire, on August 7, 1535. *LP*, vol. 9, no. 46, p. 12. For subsequent testimony against Crowley by Schokborough, see *LP*, vol. 12, pt. 2,

August 14, 1537, no. 518, pp. 196–197. For the analogy by Innocent III in a letter from 1198, see *The Crisis of Church and State 1050–1300,* ed. Brian Tierney (1964; reprint, Toronto: University of Toronto Press, 1988), p. 132.

36. For Rouse, see the second-hand report by three men (including one laborer and one farmer) to justice of the peace John Russel in *LP,* vol. 9, August 13, 1535, no. 84, p. 23. For Bromley, see the report by Thomas Clerk and William Vowell to Cromwell in ibid., August 15, 1535, no. 100, pp. 28–29.

37. In August 1536 William Hoo, vicar of Eastbourne, Sussex, was accused of referring to the new "preachers of the devil," bewailing the loss of More, and lamenting the loss of Fisher as the most learned man in the kingdom. *LP,* vol. 11, no. 300, p. 126. The next month a certain John Heseham was imprisoned for treasonable words, saying "that the bishop of Rochester and Sir Thomas More died martyrs." Ibid., no. 486, p. 197. For the abbot of Colchester, see the testimonies of Thomas Nuthake, a physician and mercer from Colchester, in *LP,* vol. 14, pt. 2, November 3, 1539, no. 454, p. 166; and of Robert Rouse, another Colchester mercer, in ibid., November 4, 1539, no. 458, p. 167. John Beche was executed at Colchester on December 1, 1539.

38. Chapuys to Charles V, June 30, 1535, in *LP,* vol. 8, no. 948, p. 372. On the same day he wrote to Granvelle, asserting that people were complaining that the continuous rain ever since the executions was God's vengeance. Ibid., no. 949, p. 373. On disaffection in London immediately following the executions, see also Susan Brigden, *London and the Reformation* (Oxford: Clarendon Press, 1989), pp. 230–231.

39. *LP,* vol. 9, no. 84, p. 23 (my emphasis); ibid., no. 100, p. 29; ibid., vol. 10, no. 1239, p. 517. On the anonymous *Glass of the Truth* [1532], a work about the limitations of papal dispensations, in which the king himself seems to have had a hand, see G. R. Elton, *Policy and Police: The Enforcement of the Reformation in the Age of Thomas Cromwell* (Cambridge: Cambridge University Press, 1972), pp. 176–178.

40. Chauncy, "De Martyribus Carthusiensibus," *AB,* 14, p. 283. For the dates of Chauncy's departure from England and his composition of this particular account, plus his time at the Val de Grace monastery in Bruges, see Thompson, *Carthusian Order in England,* pp. 343–346.

41. See Elton, *Policy and Police;* Derrett, "Neglected Versions," p. 203.

42. Matthew, *Sermon at London.* The sermon was printed on July 30, a little more than three weeks after More's execution. Ibid., sig. D2v. For more about its tone and the circumstances in which it was preached, see Zeeveld, "Apology for an Execution," in *Essential Articles,* pp. 199–201.

43. He stated simply, "so passed Sir Thomas More out of this world to God, upon the very same day in which himself had most desired." Roper, *Lyfe of Moore,* p. 103/15–17.

44. For instance, de Vocht gives many examples of the reception of More's death, both in England and on the Continent, but neither analyzes the specific terms in which More's death was understood, nor addresses the lack of sustained understanding of More as a martyr after the initial responses in 1535–1536. De Vocht, *Acta Thomae Mori,* pp. 21–31.

45. See Jennifer Britnell, "Jean Bouchet's Epitaphs for Thomas More and John Fisher, 1545," *Moreana*, 85 (April 1985), 45–55. See also the dearth of references to More's martyrdom in works prior to the 1580s, in *St. Thomas More: A Preliminary Bibliography of His Works and of Moreana to the Year 1750*, ed. R. W. Gibson (New Haven: Yale University Press, 1961), p. 475.

46. For the quoted passage in Chapuys's letter, see *Cause of the Canonization*, p. 28 (English summary of entire letter in *LP*, vol. 8, no. 666, pp. 250–254). Pio da Carpa's letter explicitly noted that they refused to believe that the king could be the "true head" [*vero capo*] of the English Church, a position that, as the rest of Catholic Christendom believed, could belong only to the pope. *Cause of the Canonization*, p. 31 (English summary in *LP*, vol. 8, no. 726, p. 272). For da Casale's report, see *Cause of the Canonization*, p. 33. They were put to death "because they claimed that the king could not be supreme in the Church of England" [*propterea quod asserebant non posse Regem supremum esse in Ecclesia Anglicana*]. Ibid. For Harvel's letter to Starkey, dated June 15, 1535, see ibid., p. 34.

47. For Francis, see *LP*, vol. 8, no. 985, p. 389. Pio da Carpa [bishop of Faenza] to Ambrosius [de Recalcatis], in *LP*, vol. 8, no. 1060, p. 418.

48. Paul III to Ferdinand, July 26, 1535, in *LP*, vol. 8, no. 1116, p. 437; Paul III to Francis I, July 26, 1535, in ibid., no. 1117, p. 437.

49. Bishop of Faenza to Ambrosius, July 29, 1535, in *LP*, vol. 8, no. 1141, p. 446; bishop of Faenza to Ambrosius, August 21, 1535, in *LP*, vol. 9, no. 148, p. 43.

50. Hubert Jedin, *A History of the Council of Trent*, vol. 1, trans. Ernest Graf (London: Nelson, 1957), p. 304.

51. [Philippe Dumont and Erasmus?] *Expositio fidelis de morte D. Thomae Mori, et quorundam aliorum insignium virorum in Anglia* (Antwerp: Ioannes Steelsius, 1536), first published in Basel by Froben in late 1535. The text of the Paris Newsletter, based on eight manuscripts, is printed in Harpsfield, *Life and death of Moore*, pp. 258–266. The most convincing account of the relationship among the various early manuscript and printed accounts of More's trial and death is Derrett, "Neglected Versions." Derrett meticulously reconstructs the now missing Latin original that was the basis for the Paris Newsletter and for two other Latin texts, one of which was printed (perhaps in Paris) in 1536 as the *Novitates quaedam ex diversorum praestantium epistolis desumptae. De Sanctorum in Angliae persequutione ac martyrii constantia* . . . The other Latin account, the "Ordo condemnationis Thomae Morj," remained in manuscript until this century. See de Vocht, *Acta Thomae Mori*, pp. 145–163. Derrett's reconstruction supersedes earlier proposals about the relationships among these sources by Hitchcock, in Harpsfield, *Life and death of Moore*, pp. 254–256, and by de Vocht, in his *Acta Thomae Mori*, pp. 31–96.

52. The other person most often mentioned as the possible author of the second part of the *Expositio* is Philippe Dumont, a former student of Erasmus's. See Hitchcock in Harpsfield, *Life and death of Moore*, p. 256; Derrett, "Neglected Versions," pp. 207–208, 211–212.

53. Hitchcock in Harpsfield, *Life and death of Moore*, pp. 254–257; de Vocht, *Acta Thomae Mori*, pp. 40–52, 59–60, 89–91, 138; Derrett, "Neglected Versions,"

p. 210. For one of the two German translations of the *Expositio,* see *Ein glaub-wirdige anzaygung des tods, Herrn Thome Mori, vnnd andrer treffenlicher män-ner inn Engelland, geschehen im jar M.D.xxxv* ([Augsburg: H. Steiner], 1536).

54. [Dumont and Erasmus?] *Expositio,* sigs. [A6], [A8v], [A7].

55. Goclenius to Erasmus, August 10, 1535, quoted in de Vocht, *Acta Thomae Mori,* p. 24. Something of the same attitude characterized Melanchthon's lament for More the humanist rather than More the controversialist or martyr. See Dermot Fenlon, *Heresy and Obedience in Tridentine Italy: Cardinal Pole and the Counter-Reformation* (Cambridge: Cambridge University Press, 1972), p. 41. For Melanchthon's remarks see his letters to Joachim Camerarius of August 31 and December 24, 1535, in *CR,* vol. 2, no. 1309, cols. 918–919, and no. 1381, cols. 1027–1028.

56. [Dumont and Erasmus?] *Expositio,* sig. [A8]. On More killed for the cause of the Church, see ibid., sig. B2v. The remark about the importance of imperfectly tempering the passion of princes recalls More's own comments in *Utopia.* See More, *Utopia,* in *CWTM,* vol. 4, ed. Edward Surtz and J. H. Hexter (New Haven: Yale University Press, 1965), pp. 98–103.

57. The cautious attitude concerning the imperative to lay down one's life for Christ is strongly reminiscent of Erasmus's comments to Zwingli twelve years earlier, shortly after the execution of the first two Augustinian monks in Brussels. See *Opus epistolarum Des. Erasmi Roterodami,* vol. 5, ed. P. S. Allen and H. M. Allen (Oxford: Clarendon Press, 1924), no. 1384, p. 327/3–9.

58. Cochlaeus, *Antiqva et in signis Epistola Nicolai Pape .i. . . . Defensio Ioannis Episcopi Roffensis et Thomae Mori, aduersus Richardum samsonem Anglum . . .* (Leipzig: Melchior Lotther, 1536), sigs. Q3v–Q4. Biblical citations in parentheses are given by Cochlaeus in the margins; I have added the ones in brackets.

59. Ibid., sig. Aa3v.

60. For the pope's letters, see *LP,* vol. 8, no. 1095, p. 429, and ibid., no. 1117, p. 437. Cochlaeus, *Defensio,* sig. Aa4. John Young, the author of the Elizabethan life of Fisher, had seen a copy of Paul III's letter comparing Fisher to Becket and Henry VIII to Henry II, from which he paraphrased extensively. "Vie du Jean Fisher," *AB,* 12, pp. 215–218.

61. Cochlaeus, *Defensio,* sig. Aa4.

62. Theobald to [Earl of Wiltshire], [March 12, 1536], in *LP,* vol. 10, no. 458, p. 188.

63. *Tudor Royal Proclamations,* vol. 1, ed. Paul L. Hughes and James F. Larkin (New Haven: Yale University Press, 1964), p. 276.

64. For the tension between Pole's affirmation of *sola fide* justification and his obedience to ecclesiastical authority, brought into conflict and then pressured into resolution by the Tridentine decree on justification, see Fenlon, *Heresy and Obedience.* John O'Malley argues that Pole's view of justification was less opposed to the Tridentine decree than Fenlon implies and that the latter's dramatization of the "anxieties" inherent in the *spirituali* exaggerates the disparity between the two doctrines of justification. O'Malley, review of Fenlon, in *Catholic Historical Review,* 61 (1975), 105. On Pole's *De unitate* in the context of his career, see Georges Blond, "Le Cardinal Reginald Pole et l'Unité de l'Église," *Moreana,* 17 (1968), 33–46.

65. Fenlon, *Heresy and Obedience*, p. 36.
66. Starkey to [Pole], February 15, 1535, in *LP*, vol. 8, no. 218, pp. 84–86.
67. Starkey to Cromwell, [ca. July 1536], quoted in Fenlon, *Heresy and Obedience*, p. 38 n. 1 (summary in *LP*, vol. 11, no. 73, p. 36).
68. Reginald Pole, *Reginaldi Poli Cardinalis Britanni, ad Henricum Octauum Britanniae Regem, pro ecclesiasticae unitatis defensione, libri quatuor* (Rome: Antonius Bladus, ca. 1538), fol. 107v. By scholarly convention the work is abbreviated *De unitate*.
69. Pole ostensibly wrote the work for Henry alone, and apparently tried to suppress copies of the first edition printed without his approval in Rome around 1538. Yet several passages suggest that he wanted a wider readership at some point. Most dramatically, he wrote that after the initial shock of their deaths, "having pulled myself together, I considered that I had always been of the same mind as those men, and I was convinced that, not only should my view not be kept secret any longer, but that if heretofore I was sometimes wont to whisper it in the ear of a friend, now I ought to proclaim it from the rooftops as if by the command of Christ [*tum supra tecta depraedicandam, quasi iubente Christo, mihi persuadebam*] (Matt. 10[:27]). Then I judged that those words in Isaiah pertained to me no less than to the prophet himself: 'Raise your voice like a trumpet' (Isa. [58:1]), so that it might be heard, if possible, not only in the kingdom but throughout the whole world [*per uniuersum orbem*] wherever the name of Christ is revered." Pole, *De unitate*, fol. 107v (Isa. 38 rather than 58 is erroneously given in the margin); see also fols. 15v, 18. This docs not sound like someone writing for an audience of one. On Pole intending the work for Henry alone and his attempts to remove printed copies from circulation, see Noëlle-Marie Egretier, "Introduction," in Pole, *Défense de l'Unité de l'Église en quatre livres*, trans. Egretier (Paris: J. Vrin, 1967), p. 47, and Joseph G. Dwyer, in Pole, *Pole's Defense of the Unity of the Church*, trans. Dwyer (Westminster, Md.: Newman Press, 1965), pp. 341–342.
70. Pole, *De unitate*, fols. 2v–3; 27, 95; 84v, 89; 106v.
71. Ibid., fol. 1v.
72. For the preference to lose their own heads, see ibid., fol. 2. On the identity between the teachings and cause of the Church and the teachings of God and Christ, see ibid., fols. 3v, 99, 101v, 103. Quotation in ibid., fol. 2v. On holding the same view as the martyrs, see ibid., fols. 1v, 106. In May 1540, John Legh told the English Privy Council that in Rome, Pole talked to him about More and Fisher and said he would have died with them. *LP*, vol. 15, May 31, 1540, no. 721, pp. 336–337.
73. Pole, *De unitate*, fol. 93.
74. Ibid., fols. 99, 116, 125v.
75. Ibid., fol. 96. The Latin of the pertinent passage of the second from the last sentence quoted is: "ut archetypus maiorem semper authoritatem habet reliquis omnibus, qui inde descripti sunt, libris: sic qui sanguine martyrum perscripti sunt libri aliis omnibus praeferendi sunt. Hi enim archetypi libri fuerunt, in quibus solus Dei digitus apparet." See also fols. 103, 103v, 104v.
76. Ibid., fol. 104v.
77. Ibid., fol. 96.

78. For the second edition of Pole's *De unitate,* published by Vergerio together with opposing arguments from leading Protestant theologians on Matt. 16:18, see Egretier in Pole, *Défense,* pp. 47–48, and Dwyer in Pole, *Pole's Defense,* p. 342. The most complete Henrician justification for the 1535 executions was Richard Morison, *Apomaxis calumniarum . . .* (London: Thomas Berthelet [1536–1538]), to which Cochlaeus responded in 1538 with his *Scopa Ioannis Cochlaei Germani, in Aranea Ricardi Morysini Angli* (Leipzig: Nicolaus Wolrab, 1538). For an overview of Morison's work, see Zeeveld, "Apology for an Execution," pp. 205–211.

79. Albertus Pighius, "Adversus furiosissimum libellum Henrici Angliae regis et senatus eius," in *Concilii Tridentini Tractatuum . . . ,* pt. 1, vol. 12, ed. Vincentius Schweitzer (Freiburg-im-Breisgau, 1930), pp. 774–810, esp. 782–785, 799–801.

80. See "Cardinal Pole's speech to the citizens of London, in behalf of religious houses," in John Strype, ed., *Ecclesiastical Memorials,* vol. 3, pt. 2 (Oxford: Clarendon Press, 1822), pp. 490–497. According to internal evidence, this address was given late in Mary's reign, in 1557 or 1558. Ibid., p. 498. Speaking of More and Fisher, Pole used the same corporeal imagery that he had employed in *De unitate.* Compare "Speech," p. 496, and Pole, *De unitate,* fol. 2.

81. Quoted in Martin Haile, *Life of Reginald Pole* (London: Sir Isaac Pitman and Sons, 1910), pp. 282–283.

82. For a list of those executed during these years and later officially recognized as saints, blessed, or venerable by the Roman Catholic church, see Philip Caraman, "Martyrs of England and Wales," *New Catholic Encyclopedia,* vol. 9 (New York: McGraw-Hill, 1967), pp. 323–324. Of the total of fifty who perished during Henry's reign, forty-two were clergy (eighteen Carthusians, including brothers; seven Benedictines; five Franciscans; one Bridgettine; one Augustinian; and ten secular priests) and eight were laity. Margaret Pole was the only woman among those put to death. London saw the most executions by far, twenty-five (another eleven men starved to death in the city's prisons); three martyrs each were killed at Southwark, Glastonbury, and Reading; two at York; and one each at Dublin, Colchester, and Canterbury. Approaching the matter from the side of the Henrician regime, Elton says that about sixty-five people were executed as traitors for refusing to acknowledge the supremacy between 1535 and Cromwell's death in 1540. Elton, *Reform and Reformation,* pp. 191–192. See also idem, *Policy and Police,* pp. 383–400.

83. Stapleton, *Tres Thomae* (1612), pp. 360, 360–361.

84. McConica, "Recusant Reputation of Thomas More," in *Essential Articles,* pp. 137–138.

85. Chauncy, *Historia,* fol. 52v; "Passio minor," *AB,* 22, p. 65/40–43; *Martyrdom of Carthusian Fathers,* ed. Curtis, p. 104.

86. For the placement of the arm and its procurement by the monks, see Chauncy, *Historia,* fol. 52v; "Passio minor," *AB,* 22, p. 65/23–31; *Martyrdom of Carthusian Fathers,* ed. Curtis, p. 98; Thompson, *Carthusian Order in England,* pp. 400–401. In 1547, Thomas Monday, parson of St. Leonard's in Foster Lane, and Thurstan (or Tristram) Hickman, previously procurator of the

Witham Charterhouse, attempted to send Houghton's arm and other relics to a former London Carthusian living in Louvain. Thompson, ibid., p. 498.

87. John Hooper, *An Answer unto my lord of Wynchesters booke intytlyd a detection of the devyls Sophistrye* . . . (Zurich: A. Fries, 1546), quoted in *Cause of the Canonization*, p. 53.

88. For the hair shirt, see Roper, *Lyfe of Moore*, p. 99. For his head, see Stapleton, *Tres Thomae* (1612), p. 357. For the bloodstained shirt, see ibid., pp. 358–359. Margaret Clements once showed Stapleton a lifelike image of More going to his execution, which implies that pictures of the martyrs were made as well as relics preserved. Ibid., p. 353.

89. Chauncy, *Historia*, fols. 1–10. For the relationship between Chauncy's sources for More, Fisher, and Reynolds and the accounts in the *Historia*, see my "Anathema of Compromise: Christian Martyrdom in Early Modern Europe," vol. 3 (Ph.D. diss., Princeton University, 1996), p. 842 n. 109.

90. Chauncy, *Historia*, fol. 3.

91. In ibid., sig. a2v (quotation). For the comparison to the ancient martyrs, see ibid., sigs. a2v–[a4].

92. Ibid., fols. 11v, 64v–65. Chauncy cites the psalm in the margin, fol. 65.

93. A & R Foreign, nos. 1455, 235–240. The 1606 and both 1608 editions do not include the accounts of Fisher and More.

94. See Hitchcock's description of the manuscripts in her critical edition, Harpsfield, *Life and death of Moore*, pp. xiii-xx. The work is dedicated to William Roper, who had written his own biography of his father-in-law shortly before this, partly to aid Harpsfield. Both works should be seen in relation to the Marian edition of More's English writings (1557), which was edited by his nephew, William Rastell, whose own life of More did not survive.

95. Harpsfield, *Life and death of Moore*, pp. 209–213, quotations at pp. 209/9–11, 211/23–24. Pole, too, said that More was for the laity what Fisher was for the clergy when he addressed the people of London during Mary's reign. Pole, "Speech to the citizens of London," in Strype, ed., *Ecclesiastical Memorials*, vol. 3, pt. 2, pp. 495–496.

96. Harpsfield, *Life and death of Moore*, pp. 217/23–218/6. For the superior cause of More's martyrdom and the comparison to Dover and Becket, see ibid., pp. 214–217.

97. Thus John Christoferson, Mary Tudor's chaplain and confessor, explained early in her reign (with reference to the book of Job) that God sometimes sends a wicked ruler either because of past sins or to try the patience of people. Christoferson, *An exhortation to all menne to take hede and beware of rebellion* . . . (London: John Cawood, 1554), sigs. [D7v]–E1.

98. Miles Huggarde, *The displaying of the Protestantes, and sondry their practices, with a description of diuers their abuses of late frequented* . . . (London: Robert Caly, 1556), fols. 66v–69v, quotation on fol. 69v.

99. [Young], "Vie du Jean Fisher," *AB*, 12, pp. 225–226. Immediately after this, Young developed an extensive comparison between Fisher and St. John the Baptist: they shared the same name, were ascetics, preached diligently, were imprisoned for opposing an unlawful marriage, exercised multiple offices, and,

like Fisher's head, the Baptist's finger was preserved uncorrupted after his death. Ibid., pp. 226–229.

100. Marvin R. O'Connell, *Thomas Stapleton and the Counter Reformation* (New Haven: Yale University Press, 1964), pp. 26–43.

101. Stapleton, *Tres Thomae* (1612), p. 355.

102. O'Connell, *Thomas Stapleton,* pp. 31–33, 39–41.

103. This particular contrast between More and Fisher on the one hand and Gardiner on the other was inspired by a comment by Andrew Pettegree.

104. Richard Bristow, *A Briefe Treatise of diuerse plaine and sure wayes to finde out the truthe in this doubtful and dangerous time of Heresie . . .* (Antwerp: John Fowler, 1574), fols. 72v–73.

105. Nicholas Sander and Edward Rishton, *De Origine ac Progressu Schismatis Anglicani . . .* ([Rheims: Jean Foigny], 1585), fols. 76–84 (martyrs of May–July 1535); 89v (John Forest); 91r–v (Hugh Faringdon, Richard Whiting, John Beche, John Rugg, and John Eynon); 96 (Thomas Abel, Edward Powell, and Richard Fetherston); 96v–97 (Clement Philpot and Margaret Pole); and 98v (Germaine Gardiner, John Larke, John Ireland, and Thomas Ashby). For Edmund Campion and the other Elizabethan clerical martyrs of 1581–1584, see ibid., fols. 191v–196.

106. *Ecclesiae Anglicanae trophaea siue Sanctorum martyrum, qui pro Christo Catholicaeque fidei Veritate asserenda, antiquo recentiorique Persecutionum tempore, mortem in Anglia subierunt . . .* (Rome: Franciscus Zannettus, 1584), engr. 27. For the circumstances in which Circignani created the paintings, see Thomas Buser, "Jerome Nadal and Early Jesuit Art in Rome," *Art Bulletin,* 58 (1976), 424–433. For the more precise date of completion of June or July 1583, see Leif Holm Monssen, "*Rex gloriose martyrum:* A Contribution to Jesuit Iconography," *Art Bulletin,* 63 (1981), 131.

107. See Frederick J. McGinness, *Right Thinking and Sacred Oratory in Counter-Reformation Rome* (Princeton: Princeton University Press, 1995); Herwarth Röttgen, "Zeitgeschichtliche Bildprogramme der katholischen Restauration unter Gregor XIII, 1572–1585," *Münchner Jahrbuch der Bildenden Kunst,* 26 (1975), 89–122; Torgil Magnuson, *Rome in the Age of Bernini,* vol. 1 (Stockholm: Almqvist and Wiksell International, 1982).

108. See G. J. Hoogewerff, "De Romeinse catacomben," *Nederlands archief voor kerkgeschiedenis,* n.s., 44 (1961), 220–224; Gisella Wataghin Cantino, "Roma sotteranea: Appunti sulle origini dell'archeologia cristiana," *Ricerche di Storia dell'arte,* 10 (1980), 5–14; Simon Ditchfield, *Liturgy, Sanctity and History in Tridentine Italy: Pietro Maria Campi and the Preservation of the Particular* (Cambridge: Cambridge University Press, 1995), pp. 86–90. On the Jesuit and Oratorian appropriation of the martyrological iconography of the catacombs in Rome in the 1580s and 1590s, see Alexandra Herz, "Imitators of Christ: The Martyr-Cycles of Late Sixteenth Century Rome Seen in Context," *Storia dell'arte,* 62 (1988), 68–69.

109. É. de Moreau, *Histoire de L'Église en Belgique,* vol. 5 (Brussels: L'Édition universelle, 1952), pp. 172–206.

110. Valuable research on these martyrs from the late nineteenth and early twentieth

centuries seems virtually unknown among English-speaking scholars. On the Gorcum martyrs, see E. H. J. Reusens, *Iconographie des bienheureux martyrs de Gorcum* (Louvain: C. Peeters, 1867); G. v. d. Elsen, "Iets over de geschiedenis van de HH. martelaren van Gorcum," *De Katholiek,* 88 (1885), 58–63; Gijsbertus Hesse, "De oudere historiographie der HH. martelaren van Gorcum," *Collectanea Franciscana Neerlandica,* 2 (1931), 447–498; D. de Lange, *De martelaren van Gorcum* (Utrecht: Het Spectrum, [1954]); P. W. Lampen, "Notae de SS. Nicolao et sociis O.F.M. martyribus Gorcomiensibus," *Collectanea Franciscana,* 28 (1958), 404–411. On the Alkmaar martyrs, see Willibrordus Lampen, "De martyribus Alcmariensibus P. Daniele ab Arendonck et sociis O.F.M.," *Archivum Franciscanum Historicum,* 16 (1923), 453–468; and 17 (1924), 13–29, 169–182; W. Nolet, "De historische waarheid aangaande de Alkmaarsche martelaren," *Studia Catholica,* 5 (1928–1929), 171–199. On the martyrs of Roermond, see Hesse, "De martelaren van Roermond," *Limburg's Jaarboek* (1911), 170–209, 264–290. On the Audenarde martyrs, see the report of archpriest Pierre Simons in *Analectes pour servir a l'histoire ecclésiastique de la Belgique,* ed. Edmond Reusens et al., vol. 7 (Louvain, 1870), pp. 49–77. For a brief overview of all four groups of martyrs, see Moreau, *Histoire de L'Église en Belgique,* vol. 5, pp. 185–198.

111. Arnoldus Havensius, *Historica relatio duodecim martyrum Cartusianorum qui Ruraemundae In Ducatu Geldriae Anno M. D. LXXII. Agonem suum feliciter compleverunt* . . . ([Ghent: Gualterus Manilius?] 1608), pp. 20–38. For a meticulous account of Havensius's sources, their reliability, and his care in using them, see Hesse, "Martelaren van Roermond," pp. 174–194.

112. Hessels van Est, *Histoire des martyrs de Gorcum,* pp. 210–211, 249–264.

113. For Musius, see ibid., pp. 428–429, 432–433. For Willem vander Gouwe, see Aert Swaens van Goerle, "Die Martirie ende Confessie van broeder Willem vander Gouwe . . . ," in idem, *Een salighe vermaninghe: Om werdelyck te ontfanghen het H. Sacramente des outaers* . . . ('s Hertogenbosch: Jan Scheffer, 1574), sigs. E3v–E4.

114. For the Elizabethan prosecution of Catholics for treason, see Philip Hughes, *Rome and the Counter-Reformation in England* ([London]: Burns and Oates, 1942); John Bellamy, *The Tudor Law of Treason: An Introduction* (London: Routledge and Kegan Paul, 1979); Peter Holmes, *Resistance and Compromise: The Political Thought of the Elizabethan Catholics* (Cambridge: Cambridge University Press, 1981), esp. pp. 35–78. For overviews of the Elizabethan martyrs themselves, see Hughes, *Rome and the Counter-Reformation,* pp. 240–267; Helen White, *Tudor Books of Saints and Martyrs* (Madison: University of Wisconsin Press, 1963), pp. 196–276.

115. [William Allen], *Briefe Historie of the Gloriovs Martyrdom of XII. Reverend Priests* . . . ([Rheims: Jean Foigny], 1582), sig. c4v.

116. 13 Eliz. I, ca. 2, "An Act against the bringing in and putting in execution of bulls and other instruments from the see of Rome," in *Tudor Constitution,* ed. Elton, pp. 418–421.

117. 23 Eliz. I, ca. 1, "An Act to retain the Queen's Majesty's subjects in their due obedience," in ibid., pp. 422–423. On the mission see E. E. Reynolds, *Cam-*

pion and Parsons: The Jesuit Mission of 1580–1 (London: Sheed and Ward, 1980). Parsons and Campion were the only two Jesuits among the total of fifteen priests who left for England in 1580. Ibid., pp. 32–33. A few missionary priests had begun coming from Douai to England as early as 1574.

118. 27 Eliz. I, ca. 2, "An Act against Jesuits, seminary priests, and other such like disobedient persons," in *Tudor Constitution,* ed. Elton, pp. 424–425.

119. For Allen's and especially Parsons's political activities during these years, see John Bossy, "The Society of Jesus in the Wars of Religion," in *Monastic Studies: The Continuity of Tradition,* vol. 1, ed. Judith Loades (Bangor: Headstart History, 1990), pp. 232–233. For a more detailed account of Parsons's endeavors in 1582, see A. Lynn Martin, *Henry III and the Jesuit Politicians* (Geneva: Droz, 1973), pp. 65–74, 80–82. The most extensive narrative of Jesuit activities in the British Isles between 1580 and 1588, set within the intricate institutional and international context, is Thomas M. McCoog, *The Society of Jesus in Ireland, Scotland, and England, 1541–1588: "Our Way of Proceeding?"* (Leiden E. J. Brill, 1996), pp. 129–264.

120. It has recently been argued that the mission of 1580–1581, and indeed the English Catholic mission in general, was overwhelmingly "political" rather than "pastoral" and sought the forcible conversion of England. Michael L. Carrafiello, "English Catholicism and the Jesuit Mission of 1580–1581," *Historical Journal,* 37 (1994), 761–774; idem, *Robert Parsons and English Catholicism, 1580–1610* (Selinsgrove, Pa.: Susquehanna University Press, 1998). Yet it remains far from clear that individual missionaries dispatched to England—as opposed to men such as Parsons, Allen, and others who on the Continent worked in favor of military invasion—were involved in explicit, subversive political machinations. More fundamentally, this argument, like those it criticizes, implies an almost mutually exclusive—and misleading—distinction between "spiritual and individual" as opposed to "political and collective" conversion. Carrafiello, "English Catholicism," p. 765. Continental negotiations which sought to place a Catholic ruler on the English throne were not necessarily "political" rather than "religious" actions; monarchical rulers could dictate religion, and right religion could save souls. On the relationship between politics and religion in this context, Thomas McCoog is nearer the mark than Carrafiello: "Because of his concern for the spiritual well-being and salvation of his compatriots, Parsons could have argued that his involvement in such enterprises was a spiritual pursuit harmonious with the Society's Institute." McCoog, *Society of Jesus,* p. 266. See also ibid., p. 279 and (on Ignatius Loyola's counsel regarding the spiritual importance of cultivating political elites) pp. 22–23.

121. [Robert Parsons], *An Epistle of Persecution of Catholickes in Englande . . .* ([Rouen: Parsons's press], 1582), p. 75; [Allen], *Briefe Historie,* sig. [a5].

122. The English College at Douai moved to Rheims in 1578 due to disruptions in the Low Countries, then returned to Douai in 1593. During the years of the most intense prosecution of missionary priests as traitors, it was located in Rheims. The English College at Rome was placed under Jesuit guidance in 1579.

123. Among the Elizabethan and Jacobean martyrs canonized, beatified, or declared

venerable by the Roman Catholic church (several of whom died in prison), 189 died between 1570 and 1603, and another 25 from 1604 to 1618. A total of 51 more were executed up to 1681, all but four in the years 1641–1646 and 1678–1680. See Geoffrey F. Nuttall, "The English Martyrs 1535–1680: A Statistical Review," *JEH*, 22 (1971), 191–192; Caraman, "Martyrs of England and Wales," *New Catholic Encyclopedia*, vol. 9, pp. 324–332.

124. On the ubiquity of the same image in Dutch Catholicism, see John B. Knipping, *Iconography of the Counter-Reformation in the Netherlands: Heaven on Earth*, vol. 2 (Nieuwkoop: B. de Graaf, 1974), p. 95. For the iconographic development of this image in northern Italy in the fifteenth century, see Sixten Ringbom, *Icon to Narrative: The Rise of the Dramatic Close-Up in Fifteenth-Century Devotional Painting*, 2nd ed. (Doornspijk: Davaco, 1984), pp. 147–155.

125. Thomas Hide, *A Consolatorie Epistle to the afflicted Catholikes: set foorth by Thomas Hide Priest* ([East Ham: Stephen Brinkley], 1580), sig. [C8]. The first seminary priest executed was Cuthbert Mayne (November 30, 1577), followed by John Nelson (February 3, 1578) and layman Thomas Sherwood (February 7, 1578). Hide's first work appeared in 1579.

126. Laurentius Surius, *De probatis sanctorvm historiis . . . nunc recèns optima fide collectis per F. Laurentivm Svrivm*, vol. 5 (Cologne: Gervinus Calenius, 1574), pp. 982–983.

127. Leif Holm Monssen, "Triumphus and Trophaea Sacra: Notes on the Iconography and Spirituality of the Triumphant Martyr," *Konsthistorisk Tidskrift*, 51 (1982), 11–13. The German-Hungarian College was under Jesuit direction.

128. *Ecclesiae militantis triumphi sive Deo amabilium martyrum gloriosa pro Christi fide Certamina . . .* ([Rome: Franciscus Zannettus?] 1583), engr. 1. The scriptural quotation is an adaptation of Isa. 53:10–12, about the suffering servant, understood in Christianity as a prophetic reference to Christ. For a detailed iconographic analysis of the painting on which this engraving was based and its relation to Jesuit devotion, see Monssen, "Contribution to Jesuit Iconography," pp. 133–137.

129. *The New Testament of Iesvs Christ, Translated Faithfvlly into English . . .* [ed. Gregory Martin et al.] (Rheims: Jean Foigny, 1582), p. 538.

130. Ibid., pp. 538, 712.

131. *Le Martyrologe Romain . . . tourné en François par le R. P. Francois Solier de la Compagnie de Iesvs . . .* (Douai: Baltazar Beller, 1600), sigs. *2r-v, *2v–ā3 [*sic*].

132. See, for example, Ignatius's famous "Letter on Obedience," originally addressed to the Jesuit province of Portugal, March 26, 1553, repr. in *St. Ignatius of Loyola: Personal Writings*, trans. Joseph A. Munitiz and Philip Endean (Harmondsworth: Penguin, 1996), pp. 251–260. As missions to India and China assumed a larger role in Jesuit ministry from the 1550s, many members of the Society expressed a desire to suffer persecution and death for Christ. See James Brodrick, *The Progress of the Jesuits (1556–1579)* (1947; reprint, Chicago: Loyola University Press, 1986), pp. 207–235, esp. 208–214.

133. Teresa of Avila, *The Way of Perfection*, in *The Collected Works of Teresa of Avila*, trans. Kieran Kavanaugh and Otilio Rodriguez, vol. 2 (Washington, D.C.: ICS Publications, 1980), ch. 12.2, p. 82.

134. François de Sales, *Introduction à la Vie Devote* (1609), vol. 3 of *Oeuvres* (Annecy: J. Nierat, 1893), 3.35, p. 254.

135. Allen to Agazzari, May 28, 1582, in *The Letters and Memorials of William Cardinal Allen (1532–1594)*, ed. Thomas F. Knox (London: David Nutt, 1882), p. 136. Richard Barrett, prefect of studies at Rheims, repeatedly corroborated the seminarians' desire to go to England. See, for example, his letters to Agazzari of December 28, 1583, in *The First and Second Diaries of the English College, Douay . . .*, ed. Francis Thomas Knox et al. (London: David Nutt, 1878), p. 333; April 16, 1584, in *Letters of William Allen and Richard Barret, 1572–1598*, ed. P. Renold, vol. 58 of CRS (Oxford: Catholic Record Society, 1967), p. 94; August 2, 1584, in ibid., p. 104. In 1579 Agazzari had written to Allen about the Roman seminarians' desire to die for the faith. Allen, *Letters and Memorials*, ed. Knox, June 13, 1579, p. 398. Twelve priests were executed from December 1, 1581, through May 30, 1582, whom Allen memorialized in his *Brief History*.

136. AAW, Series A, vol. 3, no. 59, p. 237. This letter is not among the nine by Hart reprinted in the 1588 edition of the most comprehensive Elizabethan Catholic martyrology, [John Gibbons and John Fenn], *Concertatio Ecclesiae Catholicae in Anglia Adversvs Calvinopapistas et Pvritanos sub Elizabetha Regina quorundam hominum doctrina et sanctitate illustrium renouata . . .* (Trier: Henricus Bock, 1588), fols. 105v–107, 110v–116. Subsequent references to the *Concertatio* are to this edition unless otherwise noted.

137. See J.-M. de Buck, ed., *Spiritual Exercises and Devotions of Blessed Robert Southwell, S.J.*, trans. P. E. Hallett (New York: Benziger Brothers, 1931), pp. 146, 155–157, 168, 176, 179–180; [Southwell], *An Epistle of Comfort, to the Reverend Priestes, and to the Honorable, Worshipful, and other of the Laye sort restrayned in Durance for the Catholicke Fayth* [London: Arundel house, 1587 or 1588], fols. 24v, 25v, 26v–27, 28v–29, 38v–39, 40v–41, 99, 104v, 134v, 160–161, 193v, 213v.

138. [Southwell], *Epistle of Comfort*, fols. 137v–142, quotation on fol. 137v. See also fols. 131v, 133, 136v, 159v, 192v–193, 195v.

139. In [Allen], *Briefe Historie*, sig. [e7]. See also Allen's remark to priests serving on and preparing for the English mission, in [Allen], *An Apologie and Trve Declaration of the Institution and endeuors of the two English Colleges . . .* ([Rheims: Jean Foigny], 1581), fols. 119v–120.

140. See Agazzari's letter to Claudio Aquaviva, written just after Gilbert's death in October 1583, in *REPSJ*, vol. 3 (1878), pp. 691–700. William Allen expressed a regret similar to Gilbert's as he lay dying in Rome in 1594: "His greatest pain was to see that whereas God had given him grace to persuade so many to suffer prison, persecution and martyrdom in England, his sins had merited for him to end his life on that bed." Duke of Sesa [Spanish ambassador to the Roman Court] to Philip II, October 24, 1594, in Allen, *Letters and Memorials*, ed. Knox, no. 220, pp. cxxii, 364 (Knox's trans. from Spanish original). For another lay example of the desire for martyrdom, see the description of John Finch, executed at Lancaster on April 10, 1584, in John Hungerford Pollen, ed., *Unpublished Documents Relating to the English Martyrs*, vol. 1, 1584–1603, vol. 5 of CRS (London: Catholic Record Society, 1908), p. 84.

141. The other two were Margaret Ward (Tyburn, August 30, 1588) and Anne Line (Tyburn, February 27, 1601), both hanged for aiding priests. Authorities' concentration on missionary priests was probably the chief reason why so many more men than women were executed. Many more women were involved in sheltering priests than were prosecuted, however. As mentioned in Chapter 3, authorities were predisposed to treat women more leniently than men and to make them less than fully responsible for their actions under the law. The discrepancy between the numbers of male and female English Catholic martyrs does not necessarily imply that the desire for martyrdom was an overwhelmingly male phenomenon. See the case discussed in Chapter 3, p. 95, from CRS, vol. 5, p. 200.

142. John Mush, "A True Report of the Life and Martyrdom of Mrs. Margaret Clitherow," in *The Troubles of Our Catholic Forefathers Related by Themselves,* ed. John Morris, 3rd ser. (London: Burns and Oates, 1877), pp. 397–398, 432, 436, quotations on 397, 432. Internal evidence shows that Mush must have written his account within three months of her execution. Ibid., p. 358. An abbreviated version of the three chapters covering her apprehension, trial, and martyrdom was printed decades later as *An abstract of the life and martirdome of Mistres Margaret Clitherowe* (Mechelen: Henry Jaey, 1619). Claire Cross has recently argued that "Mush can be seen at the very least as an accessory to her death," insofar as he and other priests imparted to her the views of martyrdom that they had internalized in the seminaries. "Confronted with her decision [not to be tried and so to endure *peine forte et dure*], Mush subsequently had no choice but to defend it." Cross, "An Elizabethan Martyrologist and His Martyr: John Mush and Margaret Clitherow," in *Martyrs and Martyrologies,* ed. Diana Wood, vol. 30 of *Studies in Church History* (Oxford: Blackwell, 1993), pp. 275–281, quotations on 281, 280. Cross seems to imply that Mush did not want to be an "accessory" to Clitherow's martyrdom and that he was somehow ambivalent about her death and refusal to be tried, but she presents no evidence for either implication. The "True Report" suggests that Mush felt honored for having helped to mold a martyr's resolve. For more on Margaret Clitherow and the context in York at the time, see Katharine M. Longley, *Saint Margaret Clitherow* (Wheathampstead, England: Anthony Clarke, 1986).

143. [Henry Garnet], *Treatise of Christian Renunciation . . .* [London: Garnet's press, 1593], sig. A2v (quotation), pp. 111–144.

144. Quoted in [Southwell], *Epistle of Comfort,* fol. 109r-v.

145. See the "Decretum de justificatione," esp. ch. 16 and canons 24 and 26, in *Canons and Decrees of the Council of Trent,* ed. H. J. Schroeder (St. Louis: B. Herder, 1941), pp. 319–320, 323.

146. Hide, *Consolatorie Epistle,* sig. [D7v]. See also Christoferson, *Exhortation,* sig. G2v: "he that suffereth most, getteth the most noble victory."

147. Antonio Gallonio, *Trattato de gli instrumenti di martirio e delle varie maniere de martoriare usate da'gentili contro christiani, descritte et intagliate in rame* (Rome: n.p., 1591). Peter Biverus, *Sacrvm sanctvarivm crvcis et patientiae crvcifixorvm et crvciferorvm, emblematicis imaginibvs laborantivm et aegrotantivm ornatvm . . .* (Antwerp: Balthasar Moret, 1634). Like his friend Caesar Baronius, Gallonio was an Oratorian. Besides editing the *Martyrologium Ro-*

manum, Baronius was the Counter-Reformation's leading historian and an important architectural patron of the martyrological iconography of the Church of Saints Nereus and Achilleus in Rome in 1597. Herz, "Imitators of Christ," pp. 54, 59–65.

148. In [Thomas Alfield], *A true reporte of the death and martyrdome of M. Campion Iesuite and preiste, and M. Sherwin, and M. Bryan preistes, at Tiborne the first of December 1581* . . . [London: Richard Verstegan, 1582], sig. F1. For Walpole as the likely author of this poem, see A. G. Petti, "Richard Verstegan and Catholic Martyrologies of the Later Elizabethan Period," *Recusant History,* 5 (1959–1960), 68.

149. Hessels van Est, *Martyrs de Gorcum,* pp. 274–276; Swaens van Goerle, "Martirie van Willem vander Gouwe," in *Salighe vermaninghe,* sig. [E5v].

150. AAW, Series A, vol. 4, no. 1, p. 9. Nicholas Garlick, Robert Ludlam, and Richard Simpson, all missionary priests educated at Douai-Rheims, were executed at Derby on July 24, 1588, the first of at least twenty-seven executions between July and October at the height of the Armada scare.

151. [John Geninges], *The Life and Death of Mr Edmund Geninges Priest, Crowned with Martyrdome at London, the 10. day of Nouember, in the yeare M.D.XCI* (St. Omers: Charles Boscard, 1614), pp. 83–84. James Young, an eyewitness to the executions who in 1595 sent his account of them to Robert Parsons (then in Spain), does not record this detail, but he does say that Geninges kissed the rope after mounting the ladder. John Hungerford Pollen, ed., *Acts of English Martyrs Hitherto Unpublished* (London: Burns and Oates, 1891), p. 109.

152. CRS, vol. 5, p. 184. Middleton was executed at Clerkenwell on May 6, 1590.

153. [Alfield], *True reporte,* sig. A2v.

154. "A Dialogue betwene a Catholike, and Consolation," in [Alfield], *True reporte,* sig. F4. For Stephen Vallenger as the poem's possible author, see Petti, "Richard Verstegan and Catholic Martyrologies," p. 68.

155. Agazzari to Aquaviva, October 14, 1583, in *REPSJ,* vol. 3, pp. 697–698, quotation on 697. Gilbert specifically recommended to them the examples of Campion, Sherwin, and Briant. Ibid., p. 693.

156. Southwell to Aquaviva, August 31, 1588, in CRS, vol. 5, p. 324. An account of John Felton's apprehension and execution was published as early as 1571 in Nicholas Sander's massive defense of the papacy. Sander, *De visibili Monarchia Ecclesiae* . . . (Louvain: John Fowler, 1571), pp. 734, 736. The lay joiner of Dorchester, William Pikes, was taught the Catholic faith by a seminary priest, Thomas Pilchard. After Pilchard's execution in Dorchester in March 1587, Pikes reverenced his memory and followed his example in martyrdom. Pollen, ed., *Acts of English Martyrs,* p. 267.

157. As among the Marian Protestants, this view was common, *mutatis mutandis,* among Elizabethan Catholics. See, for example, [Parsons], *Epistle of Persecution,* p. 139; [Allen], *Apologie of the English Colleges,* fol. 112; Mush, "Life and Martyrdom of Margaret Clitherow," in *Troubles,* ed. Morris, 3rd ser., p. 363; [Adam Blackwood], *Martyre de la Royne d'Escosse Dovairiere de France* . . . (Antwerp: Gaspar Fleysben, 1588), sig. ā2v, p. 482.

158. For Busbridge, see John Tedeschi, "The Dispersed Archives of the Roman

Inquisition," in *The Prosecution of Heresy: Collected Studies on the Inquisition in Early Modern Italy* (Binghamton, N.Y.: Center for Medieval and Early Reformation Studies, 1991), p. 31. See also the text accompanying Cavallieri's engraving of the execution of Campion, Sherwin, and Briant, which claimed that because of their steadfast death, "several people have converted to the Roman church." *Ecclesiae Anglicanae trophaea,* engr. 33. For the conversion of the accused thief executed with Pybus at Southwark on February 18, 1601, see [Richard Verstegan], *Brief et veritable discovrs, de la mort d'avcvns vaillants et glorievx Martyrs, lesquelz on à faict mourir en Angleterre, pour la Foy et Religion Catholicque, l'An passé de 1600* . . . (Antwerp: Hierome Verdussen, 1601), sig. [D7]. Verdussen published a Dutch version of this work in 1601.

159. [Allen], *Apologie of the English Colleges,* fols. 109v–110.

160. Allen to Agazzari, July 17, 1582, in *Letters and Memorials,* ed. Knox, no. 70, p. 148; idem, March 14, 1583, in ibid., no. 92, p. 181. Allen was referring to the execution of three missionary priests: William Lacey, Richard Kirkman (August 22, 1582), and James Thompson (November 28, 1582). Word of the deaths of Campion and the other martyrs of 1581–1582 had spread, he noted, "and hath pierced the very heretics' hearts in France, Geneva, and Germany." [Allen], *Briefe Historie,* sig. [c7].

161. Allen to Agazzari, August 5, 1584, in *Letters and Memorials,* ed. Knox, no. 131, pp. 236–238, quotation on 238. In a letter to Allen dated July 15, 1584, Aquaviva explained how he had reiterated to Gregory XIII the importance of Jesuit missionary support in England. *Miscellanea VII,* vol. 9 of CRS (London: Catholic Record Society, 1911), p. 96. See also Renold in CRS, vol. 58, pp. 101–102 n. 1; Bossy, "Society of Jesus," p. 238.

162. Allen to the Catholics in England, December 12, 1592, in *Letters and Memorials,* ed. Knox, no. 209, p. 344.

163. [Allen], *Apologie of the English Colleges,* fol. 107.

164. [Southwell], *Epistle of Comfort,* fols. [146]-147. For other passages that express or imply the efficacy of martyrdom, see ibid., fols. 93v–94, 136, 137, 154–155, 156r-v, 196–197. See also Southwell's letter to Agazzari written shortly after his arrival in England, December 22, 1586, in CRS, vol. 5, 315.

165. Hide, *Consolatorie Epistle,* sig. C2.

166. [Walpole], in [Alfield], *True reporte,* sig. [E4].

167. [Geninges], *Life and Death of Edmund Geninges,* pp. 90–91, quotation on 91.

168. Douai-Rheims *New Testament,* p. 538, commentary on Col. 1:24.

169. Peter Holmes, ed., *Elizabethan Casuistry* (Thetford: Catholic Record Society, 1981), pp. 1, 7, 9, 72–73.

170. Ibid., pp. 72–73 (Holmes's trans.); I have corrected the misprint "reasonable" to read "reasonably." The continuation of this passage acknowledged that the Holy Spirit sometimes moved people to "throw themselves into mortal danger even if there is no necessity, in order to confirm the infirm and those who are hesitant in faith," examples of which were plentiful in saints' lives. At the same time, however, as implied in 1 John 4:1, not every impulse "which comes into the mind is the vocation and election of God." Ibid., p. 73.

171. Giving a false name was legitimate if the presumptive motivation of one's inter-

rogator was not hostility to the Catholic faith per se. If this was the presumptive motivation, then denial of one's status or faith was a mortal sin. Holmes, ed., *Elizabethan Casuistry,* pp. 54–55. Changing one's appearance was acceptable as long as it did not provoke scandal—for example, as long as it did not cause unsophisticated Catholics to think that in so doing a priest was denying his faith. Ibid., p. 64.

172. Southwell, *Spiritual Exercises and Devotions,* ed. de Buck, p. 185.

173. *REPSJ,* vol. 3, p. 675; Agazzari to Aquaviva, October 14, 1583, ibid., p. 691. For Parsons's letter to Gregory XIII (June 14, 1581) commending Gilbert and explaining how Parsons had recently persuaded him to leave England, see *Letters and Memorials of Father Robert Persons, S.J.,* vol. 1 (to 1588), ed. Leo Hicks, vol. 39 of CRS (London: Catholic Record Society, 1942), pp. 64–66.

174. Discussed by John Bossy, who suggests that Parsons's "difficulty on knowing exactly what Aquaviva wanted him to do about Campion's death" may have been the reason he never finished the manuscript. Bossy, "Society of Jesus," p. 234. Judging from the evidence that Bossy cites in this article, however, he seems to overestimate the extent to which Aquaviva sought to restrain the missionaries' desire for martyrdom, and exaggerates "the depth and importance of the view that what he wanted in England was living missioners and not dead martyrs." Ibid., p. 240. Bossy states that "martyrdom, Aquaviva conceded in a letter to Allen, was more meritorious than a life of toil, but the salvation of the missionary's soul was not the purpose of his mission." Ibid., p. 234. The latter part of this claim may well have been Aquaviva's view, but the letter with Aquaviva's concession to Allen does not contain it. In fact, immediately after extolling the value of martyrdom to Allen, Aquaviva himself anticipated the efficacy of Campion's steadfastness and martyrdom, even concluding with an echo of Matt. 10:28 and Luke 12:4 about not fearing those who can kill the body. The relevant passage is as follows: "We even hope that, inasmuch as there is more merit in enduring torture rather than toil, so for the conversion of that people Father Campion will have greater influence in prison or being racked, than on the platform or by preaching, or any of his former occupations [*ad istorum populorum conversionem maiorem vim habeat Pater Campianus in carcere, vel in equuleo, quam in suggestu, aut concione ceterisque occupationibus pristinis*]. May our Lord, as we hope and ask of Him with most earnest prayers, only grant him strength and fortitude to make a good confession for His name's sake. But we, nowise dismayed at this event [*nihilo hac re territi*], will not (with God's grace) cease on that account from sending thither fresh reinforcements; until our Lord shall grant us labourers with courage so great that they have no fear at all for 'those who kill the body'" [*donec nobis Dominus et operarios, et tales animos dederit, qui minime eos timeant qui occidunt corpus*]. Aquaviva to Allen, October 14, 1581, in CRS, vol. 9, pp. 80–83 (Patrick Ryan's trans.). Aquaviva here seems to agree with Allen, not to caution him or steer him in another direction.

175. [Southwell], *Epistle of Comfort,* fol. 195v.

176. For two examples, see Mush, "Life and Martyrdom of Margaret Clitherow," in *Troubles,* ed. Morris, 3rd ser., p. 398; Agazzari to Aquaviva, October 14, 1583,

in *REPSJ,* vol. 3, pp. 699–700. More than half a century later, Marie Guyart Martin expounded on this theme in a remarkable letter written to her son: "I am in a very tender consolation from the nice wish [*bon souhait*] that you expressed for me (that is, martyrdom). Alas, my dearest son, my sins will deprive me of this good; I have done nothing up till now that would be capable of having won God's heart for, you know, one must have worked very hard to be found worthy to shed one's blood for Jesus Christ; I dare not set my pretensions so high." Marie de l'Incarnation, *Correspondance,* ed. G. Oury (Solesmes: Abbaye Saint-Pierre, 1971), September 4, 1641, no. 56, p. 133.

177. Hide, *Consolatorie Epistle,* sig. [A7v].

178. Willem Hessels van Est used this term for Willem vander Gouwe in his *Historiae martyrvm Gorcomiensvm, maiori nvmero fratrvm minorvm; qui pro fide Catholica à perduellibus interfecti sunt anno Domini M. D. LXXII* . . . (Douai: Baltazar Beller, 1603), p. 300. Similarly, he described the forty ancient martyrs of Sebaste and the Gorcum martyrs as "generous athletes of Jesus Christ." Idem, *Martyrs de Gorcum.* p. 276.

179. Holmes, ed., *Elizabethan Casuistry,* p. 73.

180. [Southwell], *Epistle of Comfort,* fol. 197.

181. [Alfield], *True reporte,* sig. [A4r-v], [A4], quotation on [A4].

182. Reprinted in *Cause of the Canonization,* pp. 317–318.

183. Hesse, "Martelaren van Roermond," p. 177; Hessels van Est, *Martyrs de Gorcum,* pp. 374–375; Swaens van Goerle, "Martirie van Willem vander Gouwe," in *Salighe vermaninghe,* sigs. E2v–E3.

184. Allen to Agazzari, February 7, 1582, in *Letters and Memorials,* ed. Knox, no. 52, pp. 110, 113; June 23, 1582, in ibid., no. 69, pp. 146–147, 146 n. 4; July 17, 1582, in ibid., no. 70, p. 148.

185. Allen to Agazzari, September 3, 1582, in *Letters and Memorials,* ed. Knox, no. 77, p. 160. For additional examples of Allen sending information about or letters by the martyrs to Agazzari, see his correspondence of August 8, 1581, in ibid., no. 45, p. 103; December 20, 1581, in CRS, vol. 58, no. 23, p. 37; August 16, 1582, in *Letters and Memorials,* ed. Knox, no. 74, p. 156; March 2, 1583, in ibid., no. 89, pp. 176–177; June 10, 1583, in ibid., no. 102, p. 197; August 8, 1583, in ibid., no. 107, pp. 202–203; March 6, 1584, in CRS, vol. 58, no. 34, pp. 73–74; March 1584, in *Letters and Memorials,* ed. Knox, no. 282, p. 453. See also Robert Parsons's letter to Agazzari about the trial and execution of Campion, Sherwin, and Briant, sent from Rouen on December 23, 1581, in *Cause of the Canonization,* pp. 300–306.

186. Barret to Agazzari, July 10, 1584, in CRS, vol. 58, no. 40, p. 102.

187. For examples, see Barret to Agazzari (the addressee in all these cases), May 3, 1583, in *Douay Diaries,* ed. Knox, no. 23, pp. 327–328 (English trans. in CRS, vol. 58, no. 28, pp. 50–51); December 28, [1583], in *Douay Diaries,* no. 27, p. 333 (English trans. in CRS, vol. 58, no. 31, pp. 59–60); April 6, 1584, in CRS, vol. 58, no. 37, pp. 88–90; September 15, 1584, in ibid., no. 42, pp. 106–107; November 8, 1584, in ibid., no. 44, p. 113; August 8 and 15, 1585, in ibid., no. 67, p. 167.

188. For the letter about the martyrs of 1592 and 1593, see CRS, vol. 5, pp. 227–

230; the letter of February 22, 1595, written from London, is translated in *REPSJ*, vol. 1 (1877), pp. 376–377. The following year Garnet wrote a longer, more formal account of Southwell's execution that was translated into Italian and published in Spanish translation in Diego de Yepes, *Historia particula de la persecucion de Ingalterra, y de los martirios que en ella ha auido, desde el año del Señor, 1570* (Madrid: Luis Sanchez, 1599); repr. in *REPSJ*, vol. 1, pp. 364–375. For further examples of Jesuit correspondence from England to Rome about the English martyrs, see Southwell to Agazzari, December 22, 1586, in CRS, vol. 5, p. 315; Southwell to Aquaviva, August 31, 1588, in ibid., pp. 321–325; Southwell to Aquaviva, January 16, 1590, in ibid., pp. 328–330 (partial English trans. from Challoner in *REPSJ*, vol. 1, p. 324); Southwell to Aquaviva, March 8, 1590, in CRS, vol. 5, pp. 330–332 (English trans. in *REPSJ*, vol. 1, pp. 325–326); Garnet to Aquaviva, July 15, 1598, in CRS, vol. 5, pp. 371–374.

189. See "Father Warford's Recollections," written between 1594 and 1599, in Pollen, ed., *Acts of English Martyrs*, pp. 252, 257. Stransham was executed at Tyburn on January 21, 1585. For his interrogation and condemnation, see CRS, vol. 5, pp. 121–125, 129.

190. CRS, vol. 5, pp. 140–144.

191. For examples of Verstegan's correspondence pertaining to the English martyrs, see Verstegan to Parsons, March 5, 1592, in *The Letters and Despatches of Richard Verstegan (c. 1550–1640)*, ed. Anthony G. Petti, vol. 52 of CRS (London: Catholic Record Society, 1959), no. 3a, pp. 39–40 (subsequent references in this note are to this work); to Roger Baynes, August 1, 1592, no. 6a, p. 51; to Parsons, August 3, 1592, no. 7, pp. 57–59; to Parsons (a copy of Garnet's letter to Verstegan dated July 26, 1592, from London), mid-August 1592, no. 9, pp. 67–68; to Parsons (from a [Jesuit?] in England), October 15, 1592, no. 12, p. 79; to Baynes, October 18, 1592, no. 13, p. 83; to Parsons, ca. early June 1593, no. 37, p. 164; to Parsons, March 30, 1595, no. 58, p. 228; to Baynes, May 20, 1595, no. 61, p. 233; to Parsons, May 25, 1595, no. 62, pp. 238–239; to Baynes, June 30, 1595, no. 63, pp. 242–243; to Baynes(?) October 12, 1595, no. 64, p. 246; to Parsons, late 1595, no. 65, p. 247; to Baynes, January 10, 1597, no. 67, p. 250. Petti surveys Verstegan's network of correspondents in England, France, Spain, Italy, and the Low Countries. Ibid., pp. xvi-xxi.

192. See Verstegan to Baynes, June 25, 1594, in CRS, vol. 52, no. 54, p. 214.

193. These publication figures are derived A & R and A & R Foreign. They include the 11 editions of Sander and Rishton's *De origine ac progressu schismatis Anglicani* in Latin, French, and German, as well as 26 editions of works derived from it in Latin, Italian, Spanish, and German. A & R Foreign, nos. 972–1011. The figures also include exhortations to martyrdom and letters of consolation, such as Hide's *Consolatory Epistle* and Southwell's *Epistle of Comfort*.

194. See A & R Foreign, nos. 1283–1285, 896–898, 284. For Cresswell's role in compiling the *Historia particula de la persecucion de Ingalterra*, see A. J. Loomie, *The Spanish Elizabethans* (New York: Fordham University Press, 1963), pp. 206–207.

195. Works about the Japanese martyrs were plentiful between 1600 and 1640 in Latin, Italian, and French. See, for example, Louis Cerquera and François Pas-

sio, *Histoire veritable de la glorievse mort, qve six nobles Chrestiens Iaponois, ont constamment enduré pour la Foy de Iesvs-Christ* . . . (Arras: Guillaume de la Riviere, 1608); *La glorievse mort de nevf Chrestiens Iapponois martyrizez povr la foy catholiqve royavmes de Fingo, Sassvma et Firando* . . . (Douai: Pierre Auroy, 1612); *Histoire de l'estat de la Chrestienté av Iapon, et dv glorievx martyre de plvsievrs Chrestiens en la grande persecution de l'an 1612, 1613, et 1614* . . . (Douai: Baltazar Beller, 1618).

196. [Verstegan], *Theatre des Cruautez des Heretiques de nostre temps: Traduit du Latin en François* (Antwerp: Adrien Hubert, 1588). Latin editions were published in 1587, 1588, 1592, and 1604, other French editions in 1587, 1588 (a different edition than Hubert's), and 1607. A & R Foreign, nos. 1297–1304.

197. The story in this paragraph is derived from Jeroen Doedens, "Florentius Leijdanus (Van Oyen) en zijn *Novorum martyrum historia,*" *Collectanea Franciscana Neerlandica* (1927), 267, 272–276, 280–283; and Hesse, "Oudere historiographie der martelaren van Gorcum," pp. 448–450, 453–456, 460–463. Among religious orders, the Jesuits were most involved in celebrating the English martyrs and the Franciscans the Dutch martyrs, reflecting the predominance of their respective martyrs in these countries. Between 1567 and 1591, thirty-three Franciscans were killed in the Low Countries, but no Jesuits; in England, thirty Jesuits were executed between 1570 and 1680, but only eight Franciscans. Moreau, *Histoire de L'Église en Belgique,* vol. 5, p. 205; Nuttall, "English Martyrs," p. 193. In modern scholarship too, Franciscans from the Low Countries (Hesse, Doedens, Lampen) have tended to concentrate on the Dutch martyrs, English Jesuits (Morris, Foley, Pollen, Caraman) the English martyrs.

198. Willem Hessels van Est, *Novorum in Hollandia constantissimorvm martyrvm passionis historia, anno M. D. LXXII* . . . (Cologne: Henricus Aquensis, 1572). In 1579 Simon Calvarin reprinted this Latin edition and published a French translation at Paris. See [Hessels van Est], *Brevis narratio certarvm victoriarvm spiritualium in Hollandia et Zelandia* (Paris: Simon Calvarin, 1579), and [idem], *Brief discovrs de certaines victoires spiritvelles advenves en Hollande et Zelande* (Paris: Simon Calvarin, 1579). The Latin of the 1572 edition is reprinted, with a modern Dutch translation, in [J. W. L. Smit], "Over de 'Novorum martyrum historia' van W. Estius," *De Katholiek,* 45 (1864), 163–187. (Hessels van Est's brief report of 1572 should not be confused with his extensive work on the Gorcum martyrs published in 1603, the *Historiae Martyrum Gorcomiensum.*)

199. Florentius Leijdanus, *Novorum, in Inferioris Germaniae Provintia Constantissimorum Martyrum, Ordinis Sancti Francisci ex Obseruantia, passionis historia* . . . (Naples: Horatio Salvianus, 1581).

200. Quoted in Doedens, "Florentius Leijdanus," p. 281. Doedens also convincingly suggests that Friccius was the man to whom Eder referred. Ibid.

201. Thomas Bourchier, *Historia Ecclesiastica de Martyrio Fratrvm Ordinis Divi Francisci, Doctorvm de Observantia* . . . (Paris: [bookseller] Jean Poupy, 1582). This major collection is over three hundred pages long. On Bourchier, who died in Rome ca. 1586, see *DNB,* vol. 2, pp. 926–927.

202. Bourchier, *Catalogus vnd ordentliche Verzeichnuss der newgekroenten andert-*

halbhundert streitbarn Barfusser Martyrer . . . (Ingolstadt: Wolfgang Eder, 1584). A & R Foreign, no. 109. For the 1585 edition, see ibid., no. 110. Yet another Latin edition of Bourchier's work was published at Paris in 1586, and an abridged Italian translation at Bologna in 1607. A & R Foreign, nos. 108, 111.

203. The date can be determined by William Fleetwood's letter to Lord Burghley of April 14, 1582, which referred to the work's availability during the "first week of Lent" in a year when Ash Wednesday fell on February 28. CRS, vol. 5, pp. 27–28.

204. Compare [Alfield], *True reporte,* sigs. [B3]-D4, with [Allen], *Briefe Historie,* sigs. [c8v–f8v], esp. d1-d2v, [e7v–e8], f4-[f7].

205. Allen to Agazzari, August 16, 1582, in *Letters and Memorials,* ed. Knox, no. 74, p. 156. On September 3 Allen reiterated his desire that someone translate the work into Latin. Ibid., no. 77, p. 160.

206. Allen, *Historia del glorioso martirio di sedici sacerdoti martirizati in Inghilterra* . . . (Macerata: Sebastiano Martellini, 1583). This edition included six engravings that influenced Circignani's paintings in the English College at Rome the same year. Buser, "Nadal and Early Jesuit Art," p. 429. For this and the other three Italian editions, two from 1584 and one from 1585, see A & R Foreign, nos. 8–11.

207. [John Gibbons and John Fenn], *Concertatio Ecclesiae Catholicae in Anglia, adversvs Caluinopapistas et Puritanos* . . . (Trier: Edmond Hatot, 1583), pp. 153–302. *L'histoire de la mort que le R. P. Edmund Campion, et autres ont souffert en Angleterre pour la foy Catholique et Romaine* . . . (Lyons: Jean Pillehoute, [1582]) and (Paris: Guillaume Chaudiere, 1582). For these two editions and a third published under a different title, see A & R Foreign, nos. 196–198. The Prague Latin edition of 1583 is not listed in A & R Foreign, but is mentioned in Allen, *Letters and Memorials,* ed. Knox, p. 160 n. 1.

208. *Martirio del Reuer. P. Emondo Campione* . . . *patito in Inghilterra per la fede Catholica* . . . (Turin: Bevilacqua, 1582). For this and the Venice edition, see A & R Foreign, nos. 199, 202. There may have been a third 1582 edition published at Milan by Giacomo Piccaria. Ibid., no. 200. For Hessels van Est's Latin translation, see A & R Foreign, no. 203.

209. In [Alfield], *True reporte,* sig. [E4v].

210. In Gijsbertus Hesse, "Het Lied van Rutger Estius op de H.H. martelaars van Gorcum," *De Katholiek,* 145 (1914), 303.

211. For Thomas Cottam, who remained unmoved by five days of conferences with various ministers, see [Allen], *Briefe Historie,* sigs. C2v–C3. For multiple attempts to dissuade Edmund Geninges and his companions, see [Geninges], *Life and Death of Edmund Geninges,* pp. 78–80. For the repeated efforts to sway John Rigby, executed at Southwark on June 21, 1600, see [Verstegan], *Glorievx Martyrs en Angleterre,* sigs. B3, B4, [B7r-v]. For Margaret Clitherow's refusals to agree to be tried for treason, despite reassurance that she would probably be found innocent, see Mush, "Life and Martyrdom of Margaret Clitherow," in *Troubles,* ed. Morris, 3rd ser., pp. 420–424.

212. In [Alfield], *True reporte,* sig. [E4v].

213. Hessels van Est, *Martyrs de Gorcum*, p. 238.

214. [Gibbons and Fenn], *Concertatio Ecclesiae Catholicae in Anglia*, fol. 170r-v.

215. Hide, *Consolatorie Epistle*, sig. E3v.

216. [Alfield], *True reporte*, sig. D4. Similarly, Johannes Molanus quoted from a sermon by Ambrose about how faith was the "mother of martyrdom" and was itself venerated when the faithful venerated the martyrs. Molanus, *Vsvardi Martyrologivm, qvo Romana Ecclesia, ac permvltae aliae vtuntur* . . . (Louvain: Hieronymus Wellaeus, 1573), fol. 248v.

217. The quoted phrase is McConica's, in "Recusant Reputation of Thomas More," p. 147. For alterations in editions of More's writings in the mid- and late sixteenth century, see ibid., pp. 139–148. Insofar as the papacy was only a part within the whole, Richard Marius correctly writes of More that "it is a critical error to say that he died for the authority of the pope in England and to leave it at that." Marius, *Thomas More*, p. 517. Of course, it would be a critical error to say this about any of the Catholic martyrs. To be sure, Nicholas Sander was unconcerned with the nuances of More's and Fisher's positions on papal authority in his sweeping history of the Church's "papal monarchy." Yet his claim that the Henrician martyrs had shed their blood in defense of papal primacy was neither misleading nor inaccurate. Sander, *De visibili Monarchia Ecclesiae*, pp. 588, 590, 592. The same is true of Stapleton's claims in his *Tres Thomae* about More's dying for papal authority.

218. [Verstegan], *Theatre des Cruautez des Hereticques*, p. 15. See also [Verstegan], *Glorievx Martyrs en Angleterre*, sigs. A4r-v, [D7v], E3v–E4 (his address "Aux Deformez"). Thomas Clancy also notes the prevalent theme of persecutors' cruelty in Elizabethan Catholic martyrological publications. Clancy, *Papist Pamphleteers: The Allen-Persons Party and the Political Thought of the Counter-Reformation in England, 1572–1615* (Chicago: Loyola University Press, 1964), pp. 129–130.

219. Peter Frarin, *An Oration against the Vnlawfull Insurrections of the Protestantes of our time, vnder the pretence to Refourme Religion* . . . (Antwerp: John Fowler, 1566), sig. [K4].

220. [Parsons], *Epistle of Persecution*, p. 86; [Allen], *Briefe Historie*, sig. a2v; [Blackwood], *Martyre de la Royne d'Escosse*, p. 655.

221. In a letter to Allen, Mary proclaimed her willingness to risk her life for her faith. See Mary Stuart to Allen, August 3, [1577], in Allen, *Letters and Memorials,* ed. Knox, no. 11, p. 30.

222. The *Historie Balthazars Gerardt, alias Serach, die den Tyran van tN'ederlandt den Prince van Orangie doorschoten heeft* . . . (n.p., 1584) stated that Gerard received the sentence of death "like St. Cyprian" and shed "his blood to earn an eternal reward from the Lord." Ibid., sig. b2v. The *Warhafftige vnnd eigentliche beschreibung was gestalt Graff Wilhelm von Nassauw, Printz von Arangien vmbkommen* . . . (Cologne: Niclaus Schreiber, 1584), after enumerating Gerard's tortures, mentioned his response "with St. Cyprian" and noted his "imperturbable spirit in his immortal and glorious triumph" at death. Ibid., sigs. A3, [A4]. Most explicitly, *Les cruels et horribles tormens de Balthazar Gerard, Bourguignon, vrai martyr, souffertz en l'execution de sa glorieuse et memorable*

mort, pour avoir tué Guillaume de Nassau . . . (Paris: Jean du Carroy, 1584; reprint, Ghent, n.d.) called Gerard a "true martyr [*vray martyr*] and father of the country," the writer usurping the Prince of Orange's popular title as the "father of the country." Ibid., p. 28. This pamphlet also appeared in Italian translation as *Avviso dell'aspra, et crvdel morte data a Baldassarre Borgognene in Delfi d'Hollandia, et la sua constantia* (Bologna: Alessandro Benacci, 1584). For a lengthy Latin poem in praise of Gerard published several years later, see "T. G. A. V. B.," *In honorem inclyti herois, Balthasaris Gerardi, tyrannidis Auraicae fortissimi vindicis, carmen* . . . (Louvain: Johannes Maes, 1589).

223. See Philip Benedict, "Of Marmites and Martyrs: Images and Polemics in the Wars of Religion," in *The French Renaissance in Prints from the Bibliothèque Nationale de France* (Los Angeles: Grunwald Center for the Graphic Arts, 1995), p. 129.

224. *Historie Balthazars Gerardt,* sig. b3v.

225. CRS, vol. 5, pp. 98–99; Hessels van Est, *Martyrs de Gorcum,* p. 400.

226. For the place of saints' relics in the life of sixteenth-century New Castilians, including rural commoners, see Christian, *Local Religion in Sixteenth-Century Spain,* pp. 126–141.

227. [Allen], *Briefe Historie,* sig. [c7v].

228. Barret to Agazzari, May 3, 1583, in *Douay Diaries,* ed. Knox, no. 23, pp. 327–328 (English trans. in CRS, vol. 58, pp. 50–51). Barret praised Hart's martyrdom and the way it inspired the crowd's holy zeal, despite the risks entailed by their enthusiasm. Ibid., p. 328.

229. Southwell to Aquaviva, August 31, 1588, in CRS, vol. 5, p. 324.

230. John Geninges briefly recounted this story in a draft of his *Life and Death of Edmund Geninges.* He mentioned Lucy Ridley by name and reported that she "soon after became a nun of St. Benet's order in Louvain, and now liveth Anno 1600." CRS, vol. 5, p. 207. The published story was considerably fuller, yet (probably to preserve anonymity) it omitted Ridley's name and stated only that she "not long after crossed over to the Continent, bringing her precious relic with her; she devoted herself to St. Augustine and became a nun of that Order." [Geninges], *Life and Death of Edmund Geninges,* pp. 91–94, quotation on 94. Geninges apparently learned that Ridley had become an Augustinian, not a Benedictine, nun.

231. *REPSJ,* vol. 4 (1878), p. 130.

232. Pollen, ed., *Acts of English Martyrs,* p. 203.

233. Cornelius Thielmans, *Cort Verhael, van het Leven der Heijlighen van S[.] Franciscus Oirden met haer Levende Figvren wt Diuersche historie scryuers genomen* . . . ('s Hertogenbosch: Jan Scheffer, 1606), p. 220. Thielmans is ambiguous about the location of Linthers's book, but presumably he meant the Franciscan house in 's Hertogenbosch, of which he was then the guardian: "The book is still in the convent, all bloodied [*seer gebloet*] from when they cut off his ears and nose and fingers when he was praying there." Ibid. For Pieck's hair shirt, see the enlarged edition of the same work, published after Thielmans had become the guardian of the Aachen house. Idem, *Cort Verhael* . . . ('s Hertogenbosch: Jan Scheffer, 1620), p. 238.

234. Several sources record this translation of their relics. See [Jan Boener], *Waer-achtighe ende levende Figvren van de H. Martelaers van Gorcum. Met een cort verhael van hen leven ende sterven* . . . ('s Hertogenbosch: Antonius Scheffer, 1623), p. 19; Thielmans, *Cort Verhael* (1620), p. 252; and Antoine Gambier, a Franciscan from Mons, who dedicated the 1618 French edition of Hessels van Est's history of the Gorcum martyrs to the city's magistrates. Gambier, in Hessels van Est, *Martyrs de Gorcum,* sigs. +2v-+3.

235. In *REPSJ,* vol. 4, pp. 127, 130, 199–200.

236. [Robert Parsons], *The Copie of a Double Letter Sent by an Englishe Gentilman from beyond the seas, to his frende in London* . . . [Rheims: Jean Foigny, 1581], pp. 3–5, quotations on 3, 4. For the author, printer, and date of publication, see A & R, no. 623.5. The "outer" letter of the two is dated October 20, 1581. *Copie,* p. 23. Hanse was a seminarian in the English College at Rheims beginning in June 1580, was ordained in March 1581, and was sent to England one month later. Godfrey Anstruther, *The Seminary Priests: A Dictionary of the Secular Clergy of England and Wales 1558–1850,* vol. 1 (Ware and Durham: Northumberland Press, 1968), pp. 145–146. The two contemporary printed accounts about Hanse were probably [Anthony Munday], *The Arraignement and Execution of a wilfull and obstinate Traitour named Eueralde Ducket, alias Hauns* . . . (London: John Charlewood and Edward White, 1581); and [Robert Crowley], *A True Report of the Araignment and Execution of the late Popishe Traitor, Everard Haunce* . . . (London: Henrie Bynneman, 1581). Hanse was executed in London on July 31, 1581.

237. Allen to Agazzari, February 7, 1582, in *Letters and Memorials,* ed. Knox, no. 52, p. 111.

238. Allen to [Gilbert], May 12, 1582, in ibid., no. 63, p. 135.

239. Allen to Agazzari, March 2, 1583, in ibid., no. 89, p. 176. Allen's comments imply success in obtaining the relics of additional martyrs for which Agazzari, and perhaps others as well, were making requests. His words make clear his concern with authenticity and an apparent unwillingness to perpetrate pious frauds to please Agazzari: "I sent along various relics of the recent martyrs with the students. Only some from [Ralph] Sherwin have I been able to obtain as you wished, although I tried very hard" [*multum laboraverim*]. Ibid. For Hart's clothes and letters, see Allen to Agazzari, June 10, 1583, in ibid., no. 102, pp. 196–197.

240. For Ignatius Loyola, see his *Personal Writings,* ed. Munitiz and Endean, p. 357. For Trent, see "De invocatione, veneratione et reliquiis sanctorum, et sacris imaginibus," in *Canons and Decrees of Trent,* ed. Schroeder, p. 483.

241. Douai-Rheims *New Testament,* pp. 710, 711.

242. For the relics, see Gregory Martin, *Roma sancta* [1581], ed. George Bruner Parks (Rome: Edizioni di storia e letteratura, 1969), pp. 26–44; for the people's devotion, see ibid., pp. 47–53. Financial pressures on the English College at Douai-Rheims obstructed the publication of Martin's work, although parts were excerpted and incorporated into his posthumously published *Treatise of Christian Peregrination* (1583). Parks, "The Life and Works of Gregory Martin," in Martin, *Roma sancta,* p. xviii. Anthony Munday, an English Protestant

who feigned Catholic sympathies and was given hospitality for a time in Rome's English College, largely corroborated Martin's picture, while disparaging what Martin had praised. See Anthony Munday, *The English Romayne Lyfe* . . . (London: John Charlewoode for Nicholas Ling, 1582), pp. 38–42, 45, 48.

243. Thielmans, *Cort Verhael* (1620), pp. 247-[251]. This paragraph is based on Thielmans's account. He received the description of the procession, held on St. Nicholas's feast day, from Balduinus van Cranendonck, the guardian of the Franciscan house in Brussels. Ibid., p. 247.

244. Thielmans, *Cort Verhael* (1620), pp. 249–250.

245. Ibid., pp. 250, [251].

246. For examples of this Augustinian maxim quoted in the late sixteenth century, see [Allen], *Briefe Historie,* sig. [c7]; [Parsons], *Copie of a Double Letter,* p. 5.

247. Stapleton, *Tres Thomae* (1612), pp. 354–355.

248. The Counter-Reformation papacy could not have been entirely opposed to this unofficial recognition. Gregory XIII and his successor, Sixtus V, were well aware of the goings-on at the English College in Rome and of the veneration of the English martyrs. Indeed, evidence of a popular cult played a role in canonization proceedings in general. Yet with the papacy still smarting from the miscalculation of Pius V's bull *Regnans in excelsis* and the failed Northern Rebellion of 1569, to have opened official proceedings for someone like Campion would have been an act of provocative bridge-burning, tantamount to giving up on England's reconciliation to the Church. Popes between Gregory XIII and Urban VIII seem to have permitted veneration of the martyrs as saints without drawing attention to the fact. In so doing, they avoided the politically sensitive issue of canonization without contesting the faithful's response to their new heavenly advocates.

249. Mush, "Life and Martyrdom of Margaret Clitherow," in *Troubles,* ed. Morris, 3rd ser., p. 440. See also ibid., pp. 384, 392.

250. Ibid., pp. 395–396, quotation on 395. Longley dates these nocturnal sojourns to likely between August and November 1582, considering the heightened danger after William Hart's arrest in December 1582 and the events that led to Clitherow's third imprisonment, in March 1583, for offenses related to her Catholicism. Longley, *Saint Margaret Clitherow,* pp. 79, 82. Missionary priests William Lacey and Richard Kirkman were executed outside York on August 22, 1582; the death of their colleague, James Thompson, followed on November 28.

251. Hessels van Est, *Martyrs de Gorcum,* p. 388.

252. CRS, vol. 5, p. 196. Pollen dates this anonymous poem to ca. March 1591. Ibid., p. 194. Flower (also known as Richard Lloyd) was executed at Tyburn on August 30, 1588.

253. In [Alfield], *True reporte,* sigs. [F2v–F3].

254. Agazzari to Aquaviva, October 14, 1583, in *REPSJ,* vol. 3, p. 700.

255. [Geninges], *Life and Death of Edmund Geninges,* p. 102.

256. Gambier, in Hessels van Est, *Martyrs de Gorcum,* sig. +4v. Louis Richeome, *La peinture spirituelle, ov L'art aimer et lover Dieu en toutes ses oeuures* . . . (Paris: Pierre Rigaud, 1611), pp. 207–208.

257. See, for example, [Richard Whitford], *The Martiloge in englysshe after the vse of the chirche of salisbury, and as it is redde in Syon, with addicyons* (London: Wynkyn de Worde, 1526), fol. 1v; *The Roman Martyrologe, according to the reformed Calendar . . .*, trans. G[eorge] K[eynes the Elder] ([St. Omers: English College], 1627), sig. A2.

258. Molanus, *Vsvardi Martyrologivm*, fols. 246v–247, quotation on 247.

259. Thielmans, *Cort Verhael* (1606), p. 223. See also Solier, in *Martyrologe Romain* (1600), sig. *2v.

260. This view is presupposed by the explicit distinction between *either* the demonstration of heroic virtue *or* the reality of martyrdom as a prerequisite for canonization in the revised guidelines. It is also evident in the less rigorous scrutiny of purported posthumous miracles for martyrs, as opposed to other saints, in the process of beatification and canonization specified under Urban VIII. See R. Naz, "Causes de béatification et de canonisation," in *Dictionnaire de Droit Canonique*, ed. R. Naz, vol. 3 (Paris: Letouzey et Ane, 1942), cols. 29–34. On Urban VIII's definitive declaration of the papacy's monopoly on canonization, see Giuseppe Löw, "Canonizzazione," in *Enciclopedia cattolica*, vol. 3 (Vatican City: Enciclopedia cattolica and Libro cattolico, 1949), cols. 591–594.

261. Other artists and clerical authors scrupulously avoided applying the title "saint" to uncanonized sixteenth-century martyrs. See, for example, Circignani, who pictured "S. Thomas" of Dover, but depicted Fisher, More, and Margaret Pole without any honorific title; Biverus, who did not attribute the title to any of the few sixteenth- and early seventeenth-century martyrs in his work on devotion to the cross; and Jacques Sévert, who contrasted the caution of Catholic canonization procedures with the hasty publicization of alleged Calvinist martyrs and approved the lack of any large collection of recent Roman Catholic martyrs, "since they have not yet been visited with or accompanied by miraculous occurrences as a proof in the visible Church of their being in a state of grace in God's presence." *Ecclesiae Anglicanae trophaea*, engravings 26, 27; Biverus, *Sacrvm sanctvarivm crvcis*, pp. 436–472; Sévert, *L'Anti-Martyrologe, ov Verite Manifestee contre les Histoires des Svpposes Martyrs de la Religion pretendue reformée . . .* (Lyons: Simon Rigaud, 1622), p. 441.

262. Herz, "Imitators of Christ"; Richeome, *Peinture spirituelle*, pp. 190–211 (on the painting of the forty martyrs killed at sea in the Jesuit refectory at San Andrea al Quirinale, an engraving of which appears on p. 190). For paintings of the Jesuit martyrs of Salsette (1583) and Nagasaki (1597) in the same room, see Mâle, *L'art religieux*, pp. 118–120.

263. These figures are derived from Pamela M. Jones's reconstruction of Borromeo's collection in *Federico Borromeo and the Ambrosiana: Art Patronage and Reform in Seventeenth-Century Milan* (Cambridge: Cambridge University Press, 1993), pp. 285–336. Borromeo also possessed paintings of Saints Catherine and John the Baptist that were not in the portrait collection. Ibid., pp. 251, 254.

264. David Freedberg, "The Representation of Martyrdoms During the Early Counter-Reformation in Antwerp," *Burlington Magazine*, 118 (1976), 128–138. Freedberg argues that the taste for large, explicit martyrdom paintings particularly characterized the years between the reestablishment of Catholicism

in 1585 and the truce between Spain and the Netherlands in 1609. Ibid., p. 138. Yet the seventeenth-century martyrdom paintings in other Belgian churches, such as the cathedrals of both Mechelen and Ghent, demonstrate that the earlier works were part of a longer-lived predilection. In 1633, for example, the Jesuits of Ghent commissioned Rubens to paint his *Martyrdom of Saint Livinus* for their church in the city (the scene was rendered complete with the martyr's freshly cut tongue being fed to a dog in the middle foreground). See *Corpus Rubenianum Ludwig Burchard*, pt. 8, *Saints*, vol. 2, ed. Hans Vlieghe (London and New York: Phaidon, 1973), no. 127, pp. 111–112, plate 74.

265. William H. McCabe, *An Introduction to the Jesuit Theater*, ed. Louis J. Oldani (St. Louis: Institute of Jesuit Sources, 1983), pp. 37–46, 171. See also Jean-Marie Valentin, *Le théâtre des Jésuites dans les pays de langue allemande (1554–1680)*, vol. 1 (Berne: Peter Lang, 1978), pp. 373–379, 421–427; ibid., vol. 2, pp. 558–559, 602–611.

266. For the "local Baronios," see Ditchfield, *Liturgy, Sanctity, and History*, esp. 273–360.

267. Heribert Rosweyde, *Generale Legende der Heylighen . . .* , 4th ed., vol. 1 (Antwerp: Hierome Verdussen, 1649), pp. 322–329. Sometimes, but not consistently, a given day's saints were arranged chronologically: all days, however, were subordinated to the collection's overarching calendrical organization. Rosweyde's work first appeared in 1619 and went through seven editions by 1711. Carlos Sommervogel, ed., *Bibliothèque de la Compagnie de Jésus*, vol. 7 (Brussels: O. Schepens, 1896), col. 202. Rosweyde based his work on Ribadeneira's *Flos sanctorum*, which was first published in Spanish in 1599 and went through dozens of editions, translations (Latin, German, English, Dutch, French, Italian), and abridgments in the seventeenth and eighteenth centuries. Ibid., vol. 6 (Brussels: O. Schepens, 1895), cols. 1737–1754.

268. Cornelius Thielmans, *Seraphische Historie van het Leven des Alderheylichste Vader S. Francisci van Assysien . . .* (Louvain: Cornelius Coenensteyn and Ioan Oliviers, 1628), pp. 84–123, 125–130.

269. Thielmans, *Cort Verhael* (1620), pp. [251]-252.

270. Hessels van Est, *Martyrs de Gorcum*, pp. 392–394, 401–405. For his gradual recovery from a deadly illness after making a vow to the Gorcum martyrs, see ibid., pp. 444–448.

271. Indeed, purported miracles of this sort are notably absent from all the early modern Catholic martyrological accounts I have studied. Closest to them are reports about publicly displayed martyrs' heads retaining or acquiring a lifelike appearance, as was the case with Fisher and Henry Garnet. For Fisher, see [Dumont and Erasmus?] *Expositio fidelis*, sig. [A7v]; "Vie du Jean Fisher," *AB*, 12 (1893), pp. 201–202. For Garnet, see *REPSJ*, vol. 4, pp. 123–124, 129–130. That authorities removed Fisher's head and repositioned Garnet's due to the swarming crowds suggests that there was *something* unexpected about their appearances. Similarly, John Gerard reported a story told to him by more than one source that after Edward Oldcorne's execution on April 7, 1607, his intestines burned for sixteen days, bursting out in flame even during heavy rain before the fire was eventually smothered. Gerard, *The Autobiography of a*

Hunted Priest, trans. Philip Caraman (New York: Pellegrini and Cudahy, 1952), p. 202. The anonymous account mostly about Garnet's miraculous kernel of wheat (see below, n. 279) also mentioned Oldcorne's intestines, saying that the fire continued for fourteen days. In *REPSJ,* ed. Foley, vol. 4, p. 131. Again, *something* unusual must have happened with the fire to inspire the story in the first place.

272. For some Catholic examples, see "Vie du Jean Fisher," in *AB,* 12 (1893), pp. 232–246, on the fates of several people responsible for Fisher's death; Hessels van Est, *Martyrs de Gorcum,* pp. 440–444, on the sickness and death of the Count of Lummen for his persecution of the Gorcum martyrs; and "Warford's Recollections," in Pollen, ed., *Acts of English Martyrs,* pp. 264, 266, on the demise of those involved in Thomas Pilchard's execution in Dorchester on March 21, 1587, and on the storms in and around the city that persisted until his limbs were removed from display.

273. [Southwell], *Epistle of Comfort,* fols. 200–202v, quotation on 202v.

274. Allen to Agazzari, March 2, 1583, in *Letters and Memorials,* ed. Knox, no. 89, p. 177.

275. [Geninges], *Life and Death of Edmund Geninges,* pp. 98–100, quotation on 100.

276. Hessels van Est, *Historiae Martyrvm Gorcomiensvm,* pp. 251–254.

277. Ibid., pp. 255–256.

278. [Geninges], *Life and Death of Edmund Geninges,* pp. 90–94, quotation on 93.

279. The story in this paragraph is based on Bancroft's examinations of Hugh Griffin, November 27, 1606, and of Peter Wilkinson (John's brother) on December 1–2, 1606; an anonymous, contemporary Catholic document (now in BL Additional MS 21,203), which contains a detailed account of the incident; John Wilkinson's own account of the episode, written shortly before he died at St. Omers in 1607; and an account by Garnet's fellow Jesuit, John Gerard. All are reprinted in *REPSJ,* vol. 4, pp. 121–124, 127–131, 198–200.

280. In *REPSJ,* vol. 4, p. 128.

281. Thielmans, *Cort Verhael* (1620), pp. 246–247, quotation on 247.

282. Surius, *De probatis sanctorum historiis,* vol. 6 (Cologne: Gervinus Calenius, 1575), p. 5.

283. In Martin, *Roma sancta,* p. 227.

284. [Boener], *Martelaers van Gorcum,* sig. A3.

285. For Musius, see Hessels van Est, *Historiae martyrvm Gorcomiensivm,* p. 270. For Warford and the English missionary martyrs, see "Warford's Recollections," in Pollen, ed., *Acts of English Martyrs,* pp. 250–278.

286. [Boener], *Martelaers van Gorcum,* sig. [A6v]. For the same practice with lives of the saints in Italy, see Ditchfield, *Liturgy, Sanctity and History,* pp. 130–131.

287. See, for example, Surius on St. Justus in *De probatis sanctorum historiis,* vol. 5, p. 6. Teresa of Avila, *Way of Perfection,* in *Collected Works,* ed. and trans. Kavanaugh and Rodriguez, vol. 2, 12.2, p. 82.

288. Jacques Le Brun, "Mutations de la notion de martyre au XVIIe siècle d'après les biographies spirituelles feminines," in *Sainteté et martyre dans les religions du livre,* ed. Jacques Marx, vol. 19 of *Problèmes d'Histoire du Christianisme* (Brus-

sels: Editions de l'Université de Bruxelles, 1989), pp. 77–90. Similarly, the Benedictine nuns of Santa Radegonda in *seicento* Milan incorporated a precise, graphic Latin vocabulary of martyrdom into certain of their motets. See Robert Kendrick, *Celestial Sirens: Nuns and Their Music in Early Modern Milan* (Oxford: Clarendon Press, 1996), pp. 383–388.

289. Solier, in *Martyrologe Romain* (1600), sigs. ā3v–*4 [*sic*]. See also Hide, *Consolatorie Epistle*, sig. F4, F4v.

290. John Gee, *The Foot out of the Snare . . .* , 2nd ed. (London: H. L[ownes] for Robert Milbourne, 1624), p. 90. I thank Alastair Bellany for this reference.

8. The Conflict of Interpretations

1. David Bagchi, "Luther and the Problem of Martyrdom," in *Martyrs and Martyrologies,* ed. Diana Wood, vol. 30 of *Studies in Church History* (Oxford: Blackwell, 1993), pp. 213–215.

2. Pontien Polman, *L'Élément Historique dans la Controverse religieuse du XVIe Siècle* (Gembloux: J. Cuculot, 1932), pp. 498–499.

3. Johannes Faber, *Ursach warumb der widerteuffer patron vnd erster Anfenger Doctor Balthasar Hübmayer zum Wienn . . . verbrennet sey* [Vienna: n.p., 1528], sigs. [A1v]-A2, quotations on sig. A2.

4. Thomas More, *A Dialogue Concerning Heresies* [1529], in *CWTM,* vol. 6, pt. 1, ed. Thomas M. C. Lawler, Germain Marc'hadour, and Richard Marius (New Haven: Yale University Press, 1981), pp. 31/7–32/2, 423/3–18 (quotation at 423/11–13). In 1532, More called the executed Thomas Hitton, whom Tyndale had exalted, "the devil's stinking martyr." More, *The Confutation of Tyndale's Answer,* in *CWTM,* vol. 8, pt. 1, ed. Louis A. Schuster et al. (New Haven: Yale University Press, 1973), p. 17/1. For Tyndale's remark about Hitton, who was executed at Maidstone on February 23, 1530, see Tyndale, *An answere vnto Sir Thomas Mores dialoge* [Antwerp: Symon Cock or Martinus de Keyser? 1531], fol. 69.

5. Jean Meyhoffer, *Le Martyrologe protestant des Pays-Bas 1523–1597: Étude critique* ([Brussels?] Nessonvaux, 1907), pp. 75–76; Léon-H. Halkin, "Les martyrologes et la critique: Contribution à l'étude du Martyrologe protestant des Pays-Bas," in *Mélanges historiques offerts à Monsieur Jean Meyhoffer* (Lausanne: L'Imprimerie La Concorde, 1952), pp. 58–59; A. G. Dickens and John Tonkin, "Weapons of Propaganda: The Martyrologies," in *The Reformation in Historical Perspective* (Cambridge, Mass.: Harvard University Press, 1985), p. 48; Victor Houliston, "St. Thomas Becket in the Propaganda of the English Counter-Reformation," *Renaissance Studies,* 7 (1993), 63–64; Bagchi, "Luther and Martyrdom," pp. 214–215. For a concise treatment of the phenomenon, see Henri Meylan, "'Martyrs du Diable'," *Revue de théologie et de philosophie,* 9 (1959), 114–130. For an extended treatment of several of Crespin's most important seventeenth-century Catholic critics (Raemond, Garasse, Sévert, Maimbourg), see Jean Piaget and Gabrielle Berthoud, *Notes sur le Livre des Martyrs de Jean Crespin* (Neuchâtel: Secretariat de L'Université, 1930), pp. 75–147. Meylan as well as Piaget and Berthoud tend to dismiss the antimartyrological writers as abusive or misguided and fail to take them as seriously as the martyrologists.

6. For example, Elizabeth Hanson dwells on the bodies of those executed without attempting to understand religion or doctrinal controversy, and thus claims that "the religious conflicts of the sixteenth century have made true martyrs hard to distinguish from heretics" for Robert Southwell in his *Epistle of Comfort*. Hanson, "Torture and Truth in Renaissance England," *Representations,* 34 (1991), 69. This is completely mistaken. It would have been so only if Southwell—a Jesuit who was himself later executed for his Catholic convictions—had been uncertain about the difference between Catholic truth and heresy. Southwell did not look to endurance of torments in order to resolve any "anxiety about the ambiguity of martyrdom." Ibid., p. 83 n. 61. Rather, he depended on the clear distinction between truth and heresy to resolve an otherwise ambiguous steadfastness in death that Catholics shared with Protestants and Anabaptists, as well as with ancient heretics, Jews, and pagans. Chapter 13 of Southwell's *Epistle* is a lucid manifesto *against* the idea that heroic death as such makes a martyr or, in Hanson's words, that martyrdom could be simply a matter of "visible signs" or a "fleshly act." Ibid., p. 69; [Southwell], *An Epistle of Comfort* . . . [London: Arundel house, 1587 or 1588], fols. 182–188. Lionello Puppi is similarly mistaken when he calls the difference between the execution of Catholic martyrs and criminals (including heretics) "only one of concept, not of substance." Puppi, *Torment in Art: Pain, Violence and Martyrdom* (New York: Rizzoli, 1991), p. 56. On a related point, Victor Houliston has recently alleged that John Wilson's *English Martyrologe* (1608) "aims not at an emotional effect but at demonstrating, by the number of her martyrs, the identity of the true Church." Houliston, "Becket," p. 61. Not only did Wilson not state this, but he explicitly noted that the English Catholic martyrs for the period 1535–1608 were listed because they had resisted the royal supremacy. I[ohn] W[ilson], *The English Martyrologe conteyning a svmmary of the lives of the glorious and renowned Saintes of the three Kingdomes, England, Scotland, and Ireland* . . . [St. Omer: English College], 1608), sig. Aa1r-v. Not their number, but rather the reason for their death, made them martyrs. Controversialists expressly rejected the view that the plenitude or scarcity of execution victims affected their status as martyrs.

7. More, *A Dialogue of Comfort against Tribulation* [1534–1535], in *CWTM,* vol. 12, ed. Louis L. Martz and Frank Manley (New Haven: Yale University Press, 1976), p. 314/12–14.

8. "Cardinal Pole's speech to the citizens of London, in behalf of religious houses," in John Strype, ed., *Ecclesiastical Memorials* . . . , vol. 3, pt. 2 (Oxford: Clarendon Press, 1822), p. 499.

9. See, for example, the section entitled "De haereticorum pseudomartyrologijs" in Johannes Molanus, ed., *Vsvardi Martyrologivm, qvo Romana Ecclesia, ac permvltae aliae vtuntur* . . . (Louvain: Hieronymus Wellaeus, 1573), fols. 239–240v. The longest of the ten chapters in Baronius's prefatory treatise to the *Martyrologium Romanum* is entitled "De falsis haereticorvm Martyribus, eorundemque Pseudomartyrologiis." Caesar Baronius, ed., *Martyrologium Romanum* . . . (Venice: Petrus Dusinellus, 1587), pp. xi–xiv. The engraving reproduced in Figure 35 faces p. 1 in this edition. See also Heribert Rosweyde, "Van de valsche Martelaers der ketteren, ende hun Martelaers-boeck," in his *Generale*

Legende der Heylighen met het leven Iesv Christi ende Marie . . . , 4th ed., vol. 1 (Antwerp: Hierome Verdussen, 1649), sig. [+5r-v].

10. John Bale, *A brefe Chronycle concernynge the Examynacyon and death of the blessed martyr of Christ syr Johan Oldecastell the lorde Cobham* . . . ([Antwerp: A. Goinus], 1544), fol. 2v. Bale concluded the work by comparing *in extenso* the false, popish martyr, Thomas Becket, and the true martyr for Christ, John Oldcastle, six years after the destruction of Becket's shrine at Canterbury. Ibid., fols. 52v–55v. Three years later, in his second installment about Anne Askewe, he distinguished Christ's "true martyrs, from the pope's and Mohammed's counterfeit martyrs." Bale, *The lattre examinacyon of Anne Askewe, latelye martyred in Smythfelde, by the wycked Synagoge of Antichrist* . . . ([Wesel: Dirik van der Straten], 1547), fols. 3–9v, quotation on fol. 3v.

11. [Joris Wybo?] *Historie ende ghesciedenisse van de verradelicke gheuangenisse der vromer ende godsaligher mannen, Christophori Fabritij* . . . (n.p., 1565), repr. in *BRN*, vol. 8, ed. Frederik Pijper (The Hague: Martinus Nijhoff, 1911), pp. 283–301 at 284–290. For Wybo as the likely author, see ibid., pp. 272–274. Guy de Brès published a French translation of the same work, also in 1565. For the section on true and false martyrs, see [Wybo?] *Histoire notable de la trahison et emprisonnement de deux bons et fideles personnages en la ville d'Anuers* . . . , trans. Guy de Brès (n.p., 1565), sigs. A3-[A8].

12. Crespin 1570, sig. α4.

13. Christoph Rab in [Crespin and Goulart], *Märtyrbuch: Darinnen merckliche, denckwürdige Reden vnd Thaten viler heiligen Märtyrer beschriben werden* . . . , ed. and trans. Rab (Herborn: [Christoph Rab], 1590), p. 4.

14. [Hans de Ries et al., eds.], *Martelaers Spiegel der Werelose Christenen t'zedert A°. 1524* (Haarlem: Hans Passchiers van Wesbusch, 1631[-1632]), pp. 9–16, quotations on 9, 10. Earlier, in his *History of the Martyrs* (1615), de Ries acknowledged that Protestants and Catholics celebrated their respective martyrs, yet he denounced both groups for their policies and practices of persecution. [Hans de Ries, Jacques Outerman, et al., eds.], *Historie der Martelaren ofte waerachtighe Getuygen Jesu Christi* . . . (Haarlem: Jacob Pauwels Hauwert for Daniel Keyser, 1615), sigs. +3-+5, [+6v], ++1v-++4.

15. Implicitly, Anabaptists agreed with Augustine's dictum as well, insofar as the delineation of martyrological communities, including their own, simultaneously involved exclusion. In the seventeenth century, for example, Thieleman Jans van Braght was concerned to leave out of his *Martyrs' Mirror* those guilty of "gross errors, much less bloodshedding" [*groove dwalingen (veel min bloedvergieten)*]. Van Braght 1685, vol. 1, p. 122.

16. *Opus epistolarum Des. Erasmi Roterodami,* ed. P. S. Allen and H. M. Allen, vol. 5 (1522–1524) (Oxford: Clarendon Press, 1924), no. 1384, p. 327/3–9.

17. [Nicolas Meynderts van Blesdijk], *Christelijcke Verantwoordinghe* . . . [n.p., 1607], fols. 32v–33. According to a concluding note, the work "came out [*wtgegaen*] in 1546." Ibid., fol. 46v.

18. John Mush, "A True Report of the Life and Martyrdom of Mrs. Margaret Clitherow," in *The Troubles of Our Catholic Forefathers Related by Themselves,* ed. John Morris, 3rd ser. (London: Burns and Oates, 1877), p. 422. On Giles

Wigginton, see *DNB*, vol. 21, pp. 193–194; Patrick Collinson, *The Elizabethan Puritan Movement* (1967; reprint, Oxford: Clarendon Press, 1990), p. 130. For his relations with Clitherow, see Katharine M. Longley, *Saint Margaret Clitherow* (Wheathampstead, England: Anthony Clarke, 1986), pp. 131, 133–134, 145–150.

19. Bale, *Lattre examinacyon of Anne Askewe*, sig. 46v.

20. Reginald Pole, *Reginaldi Poli Cardinalis Britanni, ad Henricum Octauum Britanniae Regem, pro ecclesiasticae unitatis defensione, libri quatuor* (Rome: Antonius Bladius, ca. 1538), fols. 93–94, 99–100, 116v.

21. Justus Menius, *Der Widdertauffer lere vnd geheimnis, aus heiliger schrifft widderlegt, mit einer schönen Vorrede, Martini Luther* (Wittenberg: Nickel Schirlentz, 1530), sigs. [G4v]–H1.

22. John Calvin, "Le second sermon, contenant exhortation a souffrir persecution pour suyvre Iesus Christ et son evangile," in *Quatre sermons de M. Iehan Calvin, traictans des matieres fort utiles pour nostre temps . . .* (Geneva: Robert Estienne, 1552), in *CO* 8, col. 393.

23. Ibid., col. 407 (my emphasis).

24. Luther, *Von Bruder Henrico in Ditmar verbrannt samt dem zehnten Psalmen ausgelegt* [1525], in *WA* 18, 225/18–20.

25. Hugh Latimer, "The Fourth Sermon Preached before King Edward," in *The Seven Sermons of the Reverend Father M. Hugh Latimer . . .*, repr. in *Sermons by Hugh Latimer*, ed. George Elwes Corrie (Cambridge: Cambridge University Press, 1844), p. 160.

26. Guy de Brès, *La racine, sovrce et fondement des Anabaptistes ov rebaptisez de nostre temps . . .* ([Rouen]: A. Clemence, 1565), sig. [a7].

27. Miles Huggarde, *The displaying of the Protestantes, and sondry their practises, with a description of diuers their abuses of late frequented . . .* (London: Robert Caly, 1556), fols. 46v–47v, quotation on 46v. Huggarde distinguished behavior from belief just as Latimer had done, then quoted from the latter's sermon, turning Latimer's criticism of Anabaptists against Protestants as well. Ibid., fols. 43v, 45r–v. On Huggarde (or Hogarde), see J. W. Martin, "Miles Hogarde: Artisan and Aspiring Author in Sixteenth-Century England," in *Religious Radicals in Tudor England* (London: The Hambledon Press, 1989), pp. 83–105.

28. Molanus, ed., *Vsvardi martyrologium*, fol. 240.

29. [Robert Parsons], *The Third Part of a Treatise, Intituled: Of three Conuersions of England . . .*, vol. 2 ([St. Omers: F. Bellet], 1604), sig. g4v. For Harpsfield, see his *Dialogi sex contra Svmmi Pontificatvs, Monasticae vitae, Sanctorvm, Sacrarvm imaginvm oppugnatores, et Pseudomartyres . . .* (Antwerp: Christopher Plantin, 1566), pp. 751–766.

30. Johannes Anastasius Veluanus [Jan Gerrits Verstege], *Kort Bericht in allen principalen punten des Christen geloues . . . genant der Leken Wechwyser* (Strasbourg: Balthasar von Klarenback, 1554), repr. in *BRN*, vol. 4, ed. Frederik Pijper (The Hague: Martinus Nijhoff, 1906), p. 343.

31. Stanislaus Hosius, *A Most Excellent Treatise of the begynnyng of heresyes in oure tyme . . .*, trans. Richard Shacklock (Antwerp: Aeg̈ Diest, 1565), fols. 44v–46v, quotation on 46v. The Latin original of this work appeared in 1559.

32. In fact Calvin wrote that Anabaptist martyrs ought to be denounced in proportion as true martyrs were praised. See his *Brieve instruction pour armer tous les bons fideles contre les erreurs de la secte commune des anabaptistes* (Geneva: Jean Girard, 1544), in *CO* 7, cols. 141–142. In the early seventeenth century, the French lay Catholic controversialist Florimond de Raemond also implied that the number of people executed was irrelevant to their status as martyrs. See his *L'histoire de la naissance, progrez et decadence de l'heresie de ce siecle* (Rouen: Estienne Vereul, 1622) [p. 868]. This work was first published, posthumously, in 1605.

33. In a published address to Albrecht of Brandenburg the year after Zwingli's death, Luther classed Zwingli and his followers with the Müntzerites. Luther, *An den durch leuchtigen Hochgeboren Fürsten vnd Herrn, Herrn Albrechten, Marggraffen zu Brandenburg* . . . [1532], in *WA* 30.III, p. 550/25–31. According to More, Zwingli was "by the hand of God this year [1531] slain in plain battle against the Catholics with many a thousand of his wretched sect." More, *Confutation of Tyndale's Answer*, pp. 29/36–30/11, quotation at 30/6–8. See also ibid., p. 10/29–33.

34. Luther, *Sendbrieff an Albrechten*, in *WA* 30.III, p. 551/4–7.

35. More said of Bilney's death that God "would not suffer such obstinate untruth at length to pass unpunished, but of his endless mercy brought his body to death, and gave him yet the grace to turn and save his soul." More, *Confutation of Tyndale's Answer*, p. 23/7–9. Controversially, More alleged that Bilney recanted before his execution.

36. G[eorge] J[oye], *A present consolation for the sufferers of persecucion for rughtwysenes* ([Antwerp: Steven Mierdman], 1544), sigs. [F8v]-G1. Joye here anglicized and supplemented Urbanus Rhegius's original, which mentioned only persecutors of ancient Christians (whom Joye also appropriated). See Rhegius, *Trostbrieff an alle Christen zum Hildeshaim, die vmbs Euangeliums willen yetzt schmach vnd verfolgung leyden* . . . ([Magdeburg: Hans Walther], 1531), sigs. c2v–c3.

37. [Antoine de la Roche Chandieu], *Histoire des persecvtions, et martyrs de l'Église de Paris depuis l'An 1557. iusques au tepms* [sic] *du Roy Charles neufuiesme* . . . (Lyons: [Claude Senneton], 1563), pp. 54–56.

38. Antoine Du Val, *Mirover des Calvinistes et armvre des Chrestiens, pour rembarrer les Lutheriens et nouueaux Euangelistes de Genéue: Renouuellé et augmenté* . . . (Paris: Nicolas Chesneau, 1562), fols. 15–59. This treatise was first published in 1559.

39. [Parsons], *Third Part of a Treatise*, vol. 2, pp. 172, 177. Edmund Campion implied that in number and social range, Catholic martyrs overshadowed English Protestant martyrs. See [William Allen], *Briefe Historie of the Gloriovs Martyrdom of XII. Reverend Priests* . . . ([Rheims: Jean Foigny], 1582), sig. [e7].

40. De Brès, *Racine, sovrce et fondement des Anabaptistes*, sig. [a7].

41. *The New Testament of Iesvs Christ, Translated Faithfvlly into English, out of the authentical Latin* . . . [ed. Gregory Martin et al.], (Rheims: Jean Foigny, 1582), p. 457. See also ibid., p. 13, on Matt. 5:10, which explained that heretics and

evildoers cannot be blessed even if they "sometime suffer willingly and stoutly" because "they suffer not for justice."

42. Huggarde, *Displaying of the Protestantes,* fols. 46v–48; Hosius, *Treatise of the begynnyng of heresyes,* fols. 43v–44; Du Val, *Mirover des Calvinistes,* fols. 47v–48; Molanus, ed., *Vsvardi martyrologium,* fol. 239r-v; [Southwell], *Epistle of Comfort,* fol. 187r-v, quotation on 187 (my emphasis).

43. Du Val, *Mirover des Calvinistes,* fols. 53–54v; Jacques Sévert, *L'Anti-Martyrologe, ov Verite Manifestee contre les Histoires des Svpposes Martyrs de la Religion pretendue reformée . . .* (Lyons: Simon Rigaud, 1622), pp. xxix, lxx.

44. Thomas Harding, *A Reioindre to M. Iewels Replie against the Sacrifice of the Masse . . .* (Louvain: John Fowler, 1567), fol. 181; [Parsons], *Third Part of a Treatise,* vol. 2, sigs. ++1v–++2.

45. [William Cecil], *The Execution of Iustice in England . . . against certeine stirrers of sedition . . . without any persecution of them for questions of Religion, as is false reported and published by the fautors and fosterers of their treasons* (London: [C. Barker], 1583), sig. [A4].

46. Baronius, ed., *Martyrologium Romanum* (Antwerp: Christopher Plantin, 1589), pp. xxiv–xxv; Rosweyde, ed., *Generale Legende der Heylighen,* vol. 1, sig. [+5v].

47. [Harpsfield], *Dialogi sex,* pp. 919–922; Du Val, *Mirover des Calvinistes,* fols. 45r-v, 55v–56.

48. John Bale, *The first examinacyon of Anne Askewe, latelye martyred in Smythfelde . . .* [Wesel: Dirik van der Straten], 1546), sigs. +4v, +5.

49. Huggarde, *Displaying of the Protestantes,* fol. 64r-v, quotations on 64v.

50. More, *Dialogue Concerning Heresies,* pp. 201/30–32, 422/7–19; Tyndale, *Answere vnto Mores dialoge,* fol. 69v.

51. The latter point is also noted by Halkin, "Martyrologes et la critique," pp. 58–59.

52. See Meylan, "'Martyrs du diable,'" pp. 114–119, which surveys the patristic foundations of the early modern debate. On antimartyrology and the conflicting martyrological communities in the early Church, see Hans Freiherr von Campenhausen, *Die Idee des Martyriums in der alten Kirche,* 2nd ed. (Göttingen: Vandenhoeck and Ruprecht, 1964), pp. 166–175; W. H. C. Frend, *Martyrdom and Persecution in the Early Church: A Study of a Conflict from the Maccabees to Donatus* (Oxford: Blackwell, 1965).

53. For explicit Catholic quotation or paraphrase of Cyprian's dictum in this context, see John Christoferson, *An exhortation to all menne to take hede and beware of rebellion . . .* (London: John Cawood, 1554), sigs. I4v–I5; Hosius, *Treatise of the begynnyng of heresyes,* fol. 44; Du Val, *Mirover des Calvinistes,* fols. 46v–47; [Harpsfield], *Dialogi sex,* p. 764; Molanus, ed., *Vsvardi Martyrologivm,* fol. 239r-v; Douai-Rheims *New Testament,* p. 457 (comment on 1 Cor. 13:3); Baronius, ed., *Martyrologium Romanum* (Antwerp, 1589), pp. [xxiii]–xxiv; [Southwell], *Epistle of Comfort,* fol. 183r-v; [Parsons], *Third Part of a Treatise,* vol. 2, sig. [g5v]; Raemond, *L'histoire de l'heresie,* p. 866; Sévert, *L'Anti-Martyrologe,* pp. xxix–xxx.

54. More, *Confutation of Tyndale's Answer*, pp. 14–16, quotations at pp. 14/4, 16/33–34.

55. Pole, "Speech to the citizens of London," in Strype, ed., *Ecclesiastical Memorials*, vol. 3, pt. 2, pp. 499–501; Huggarde, *Displaying of the Protestantes*, fols. 43v–48, 51v–52; Christoferson, *Exhortation*, sig. [H7r-v].

56. Harding, *Reioindre to Iewels Replie*, fol. 186.

57. [Southwell], *Epistle of Comfort*, fol. 182v.

58. Du Val, *Mirover des Calvinistes*, fols. 4–15, 31v–59, respectively. In between (fols. 15–31v) Du Val defended the practice of punishing and burning heretics.

59. For the articles of faith, see Sévert, *L'Anti-Martyrologe*, pp. 165–350. The most extensive treatment of Sévert's work misses entirely the nature and purpose of his critique. Piaget and Berthoud, *Notes sur le Livre des Martyrs*, pp. 100–137. The authors write: "In his *Antimartyrology* Sévert discusses not facts but doctrines. His task is that of a theologian, not a historian. He claims to show that the Protestant heretics are 'misbelievers,' 'most unworthy of the holy name of martyrs' and that their 'infidelity' prevents them from being qualified with such a title." Ibid., pp. 101–102. This was precisely Sévert's aim; he knew full well that only doctrines, not actions, could distinguish true from false martyrs. It was also the objective of virtually every other Catholic and Protestant controversialist in a context of competing martyr claims. Sévert was simply more explicit and extensive than most.

60. Christoph Andreas Fischer, *Antwortt auff die Widerlegung so Clauß Breütel . . .* (Bruck an der Teya: Praemonstrarian cloister, 1604), sig. [K4r-v], quotation on [K4v].

61. Arnoudt van Geluwe, *Eerste deel over de Ontledinghe van dry verscheyden Nieuw-Ghereformeerde Martelaers Boecken, ofte Reden-Kamp-Strydt Tusschen de Lutheriaenen, Calvinisten, ende Weder-doopers . . .* (Antwerp: widow of Jan Cnobbaert, 1656), sig. [****4v]. The "three books of martyrs" to which the title alluded were the 1608 and 1634 editions of van Haemstede, plus the unfinished martyrology by Abraham Melinus published at Dordrecht in 1619. Geluwe was also familiar with and critical of Mennonite martyrologies. See, for example, his references to the 1599 edition of *Het Offer des Heeren* and to (presumably) the *Martelaers Spiegel* of 1631–1632. Ibid., pp. 28, 274.

62. *QGT*, vol. 7, *Elsaß I: Stadt Straßburg, 1522–1532*, ed. Manfred Krebs and Hans Georg Rott (Gütersloh: Gerd Mohn, 1959), pp. 88/20–89/2.

63. *QGT*, vol. 8, *Elsaß II: Stadt Straßburg, 1533–1535*, ed. Manfred Krebs and Hans Georg Rott (Gütersloh: Gerd Mohn, 1959), p. 463/21–25. The fact that the same letter, with this passage verbatim, was sent to Philipp of Hesse in the summer of 1536 suggests a general attitudinal change by the Strasbourgers. *QGT*, vol. 15, *Elsaß III: Stadt Straßburg, 1536–1542*, ed. Marc Lienhard et al. (Gütersloh: Gerd Mohn, 1986), pp. 33–38, this passage at 37/6–10.

64. Luther, *An die Pfarrherrn wider den Wucher zu predigen, Vermahnung*, in *WA* 51, pp. 401/26–402/19, 402/24–403/20, quotations at 401/28, 402/25–27.

65. De Brès, *Racine, sovrce et fondement des Anabaptistes*, sig. [a6r-v]. See also [Wybo?] *Historie van Christophori Fabritij*, in *BRN*, vol. 8, p. 287.

66. Crespin 1570, sig. α4v. Aldo Stella notes Crespin's inclusion of Italian Hutterites in this edition, men who were active in Venetian conventicles in the 1550s and 1560s, and concludes that "it was surely after due reflection that Crespin judged these Italian Hutterites 'true martyrs' . . . for he had gathered firsthand evidence regarding them in Venice." Again, Crespin "admired them not so much as Anabaptists but rather—in spite of their membership in the Hutterite communities—on account of the religious illuminism which caused them to be missionaries of a new universal, progressive and rational Christian church." Stella, "Hutterian Influences on Italian Nonconformist Conventicles, and Subsequent Developments," *MQR,* 64 (1990), p. 203. I find this an inexplicable characterization of a doctrinaire, Genevan Calvinist's ecclesiology. Moreover, it misrepresents Crespin's view of these martyrs. Although he indeed included several Venetian Italians executed in the 1560s, Crespin nowhere suggested that they were anything but good Reformed Protestants, who after 1560 even had the services of a Calvinist minister for a time ("a minister of the Word of God, so as to introduce some proper ecclesiastical order, having already begun to administer the holy Lord's Supper"). Crespin claimed that they were "put to death for the Reformed religion"; they were the "faithful . . . chased from their land for the Gospel"; Giulio Gherlandi was executed after having "purely confessed Jesus Christ and his doctrine"; Antonio Rizzetto and Francesco Sega persevered "steadfastly in the confession of the pure doctrine of the Gospel." Crespin 1570, fols. 698–699v, quotations on 698, 698v. Even if Crespin had known that they were Hutterites, he would not have acknowledged it; had he done so, they never would have appeared in his martyrology.

67. Philipp Melanchthon, draft for his *Verlegung etlicher vnchristliche Artickel, welcher die Wiedertäufer fürgeben,* in *CR,* vol. 3, p. 34.

68. For Erbe's story, see John S. Oyer, *Lutheran Reformers against Anabaptists: Luther, Melanchthon and Menius and the Anabaptists of Central Germany* (The Hague: Martinus Nijhoff, 1964), pp. 68–70, quotation on 70 (Oyer's trans., from Paul Wappler, *Die Stellung Kursachsens und des Landgrafen Philipp von Hessen zur Täuferbewegung* [Münster: Aschendorff, 1910], p. 208).

69. [Wybo?] *Historie van Christophori Fabritij,* in *BRN,* vol. 8, p. 286 (my emphasis).

70. *OH,* in *BRN,* vol. 2, ed. Samuel Cramer (The Hague: Martinus Nijhoff, 1904), pp. 245–246. The impact of these martyrs on de Praet is noted in A. L. E. Verheyden, *Anabaptism in Flanders, 1530–1650: A Century of Struggle* (Scottdale, Pa.: Herald Press, 1961), pp. 40–41, 41 n. 24. De Praet was executed in Ghent between May 10, 1556, and the early months of 1557. For the costs of his execution, see SAG, Stadsrekeningen, vol. 64 (1556–1557), fol. 177; Verheyden, *Het Gentsche martyrologium (1530–1595)* (Bruges: "De Tempel," 1945), p. 23. The four whose deaths impressed him were Margriete van den Berghe, Jooris Cooman, Wouter van der Weyden, and Naentgen Bornaige, burned on the Sint Veerleplein on April 11, 1551. For their execution sentence, see RAG, Raad van Vlaanderen, secrete camere, vol. 7613 (1549–1554), fols. 137v–138; Verheyden, *Gentsche martyrologium,* pp. 13–14.

71. Raemond, *L'histoire de l'heresie,* p. 864.

72. Pole, *De unitate,* fols. 96, 103, 103v, 104v.

73. Pole, "Speech to the citizens of London," in Strype, ed., *Ecclesiastical Memorials,* vol. 3, pt. 2, pp. 498, 499.

74. *Historia de duobus Augustinensibus, ob Euangelij doctrinam exustis Bruxellae . . .* [n.p., 1523], in *BRN,* vol. 8, p. 38.

75. Renard to Charles V, March 27, 1555, in *Calendar of Letters, Despatches and State Papers Relating to the Negotiations between England and Spain,* vol. 13, ed. Royall Tyler (1954; reprint, Nendeln: Kraus, 1978), no. 161, p. 148 (Tyler's trans.).

76. [Parsons], *Third Part of a Treatise,* vol. 2, pp. 153–154, quotation on 154.

77. Ibid., pp. 155–157, quotations on 155, 155–156, 156.

78. Ibid., p. 171.

79. Ibid.

80. Ibid., pp. 175–178, quotation on 178.

81. Luther, *Wider den Wucher,* in *WA* 51, p. 401/18–24.

82. For Taylor, see David Loades, *The Oxford Martyrs* (1970; reprint, Bangor: Headstart History, 1992), p. 155. Christoferson, *Exhortation,* sig. I3. For another Marian Catholic example, see Huggarde, *Displaying of the Protestantes,* fol. 48.

83. See, for example, Veluanus, *Leken Wechwyser,* in *BRN,* vol. 4, p. 343; Du Val, *Mirover des Calvinistes,* fol. 41; [Wybo?] *Historie van Christophori Fabritij,* in *BRN,* vol. 8, p. 290; van Geluwe, *Ontledinghe van dry verscheyden Martelaers Boecken,* pp. 273–274.

84. For references to Bernard's sixty-sixth sermon on the Song of Songs on this point, see Johannes Fabri von Heilbronn, *Von dem Ayd Schwören: Auch von der Widertauffer Marter, vnd wo her entspring, das sie frölich vnnd getröst die peyn des tods leyden* ([Ingolstadt? n.p.], 1550), sig. F1; Hosius, *Treatise of the begynnyng of heresyes,* fol. 45r–v; Du Val, *Mirover des Calvinistes,* fol. 33v; [Harpsfield], *Dialogi sex,* p. 752; [Parsons], *Third Part of a Treatise,* vol. 2, pp. 160–161. For the passage most often quoted, see Sancti Bernardi, *Opera,* vol. 2, ed. J. Leclerc, C. H. Talbot, and H. M. Rochais (Rome: Editiones Cistercienses, 1958), pp. 186–187. Van Geluwe made the point without referring to Bernard, instead citing Jer. 7:31, while de Brès used scriptural examples (Saul, Judas) to argue likewise. Van Geluwe, *Ontledinghe van dry verscheyden Martelaers Boecken,* sigs. [****4v]–*****1; de Brès, *Racine, sovrce et fondement des Anabaptistes,* sig. [a7].

85. For example, Raemond wrote that Protestant martyrologists "make Wyclif their St. Stephen," even though Luther and Melanchthon conceded that he held many heresies. Raemond, *L'histoire de l'heresie,* p. 866. Rosweyde noted that Hus regarded the Mass as a sacrifice and assented to transubstantiation, invocation of the saints, purgatory, and prayers for the dead. Rosweyde, ed., *Generale Legende der Heylighen,* vol. 1, sig. [+5v]. On the Catholic critique of the Protestantization of medieval heretical martyrs, see also Euan Cameron, "Medieval Heretics as Protestant Martyrs," in *Martyrs and Martyrologies,* ed. Wood, pp. 203–205.

86. [Parsons], *Third Part of a Treatise,* vol. 2, sigs. ++1v–++2.

87. Sévert, *L'Anti-Martyrologe,* pp. 417–437, where he carefully considers virtually every early evangelical martyr in Crespin and excludes them on this basis.

88. Reported by Rab, in [Crespin and Goulart], *Märtyrbuch,* trans. and ed. Rab (1590), sig. [7r-v].

89. Pole, "Speech to the citizens of London," in Strype, ed., *Ecclesiastical Memorials,* vol. 3, pt. 2, p. 501.

90. Latimer, "Fourth Sermon preached before King Edward VI," in *Sermons,* p. 160.

91. [Robert Parsons], *An Epistle of Persecution of Catholickes in Englande . . .* ([Rouen: Parsons's press], 1582), pp. 97–98.

92. [Allen], *Briefe Historie,* sig. [A7]. [John Geninges], *The Life and Death of Mr Edmund Geninges Priest, Crowned with Martyrdome at London, the 10. day of Nouember, in the yeare M.D.XCI* (St. Omers: Charles Boscard, 1614), p. 86.

93. Felician Gess, ed., *Akten und Briefe zur Kirchenpolitik Herzog Georgs von Sachsen,* vol. 2, 1525–1527 (Leipzig: B. G. Teubner, 1917), pp. 317–319. Robert Scribner notes this conversation in "Oral Culture and the Transmission of Reformation Ideas," in *The Transmission of Ideas in the Lutheran Reformation,* ed. Helga Robinson-Hammerstein (Dublin: Irish Academic Press, 1989), p. 89.

94. Charles de Croy to Charles V, 1555, quoted in Gérard Moreau, "La corrélation entre le milieu social et professionel et le choix de religion à Tournai," in *Sources d'histoire religieuse de la Belgique* (Louvain: Publications universitaires de Louvain, 1968), p. 293.

95. Du Val, *Mirover des Calvinistes,* fol. 31v. See also ibid., fols. 3, 33v, 38, where Du Val repeated his observation, which suggests the extent of his concern.

96. For further examples of the impact of false martyrs' deaths, see More, *Dialogue Concerning Heresies,* pp. 31/21–32/2; Christoferson, *Exhortation,* sigs. [H6], [H7r-v]; Huggarde, *Displaying of the Protestantes,* fol. 125v; Pole, "Speech to the citizens of London," in Strype, ed., *Ecclesiastical Memorials,* vol. 3, pt. 2, p. 498; de Brès, *Racine, sovrce et fondement des Anabaptistes,* sig. [a6]; Molanus, ed., *Vsvardi martyrologium,* fol. 240; Raemond, *L'histoire de l'heresie,* pp. 864-[865].

97. Mush, "Life and Martyrdom of Margaret Clitherow," in *Troubles,* ed. Morris, 3rd ser., p. 418.

98. *CDN,* vol. 5, p. 225.

99. David Nicholls, "The Theatre of Martyrdom in the French Reformation," *P&P,* 121 (1988), 49–73.

100. For the case of Elizabethan and Jacobean Catholic religious traitors, see Peter Lake and Michael Questier, "Agency, Appropriation and Rhetoric under the Gallows: Puritans, Romanists and the State in Early Modern England," *P&P,* 153 (1996), 64–107.

101. For examples of this sentiment, see Puppi, *Torment in Art;* Piaget and Berthoud, *Notes sur le Livre des Martyrs;* Meylan, "'Martyrs du diable.'"

102. [Parsons], *Third Part of a Treatise,* vol. 2, p. 177.

Index

Abel, as unjustly persecuted, 119, 146, 177, 222, 223, 224, 240, 404n90
Abjuration. *See* Recantation of beliefs
Abraham, 130, 159, 230
Act of Succession, 256
Act of Supremacy, 255
Acts and Monuments, 186, 191, 336; editions, 3, 168, 193, 194, 439n304; martyrs' writings in, 23; as reverential object, 174–175; influence of, 193–194, 439n303; adaptations of, 193, 194, 439–440n305; and controversy among English Protestants, 194–195; appeal to puritans and dissenters, 195. *See also* Foxe, John; Martyrologies, Protestant
Acts of the Apostles, 108, 206
Adiaphora, 240, 344
Aerts, Lijsken, 115
Affair of the Placards (1534), 90, 91, 164
Aken, Gillis van, 226, 233
Alban, Saint, 270, 271
Alenson, Hans, 242–243
Aleworth, John, 186
Alfield, Thomas, 19–20, 287–288, 291–292; on Elizabethan martyrs as paradigmatic, 282–283; on cause of martyrs' deaths, 294
Allen, William, 11, 104, 198, 279, 313; exhortations to persecuted Catholics, 123; on ancient martyrs as paradigmatic, 123, 405n92; on martyred priests as Maccabees, 123; on Protestant persecution, 274, 295, 393–394n77; political activities, 275; and English College at Douai-Rheims, 275; on impact of martyrdom, 283–284, 303, 485n160; correspondence about martyrs, 288, 289, 292, 299–300; *Brief History*, 288, 292, 295; and Elizabethan martyrs' relics, 299–300, 493n239; on dying

behavior and martyrdom, 337; regret for not meriting martyrdom, 482n140
Alva, Duke of, 91, 274
Amish, Old Order, 249
Anabaptists: diversity of groups within, 199, 243; persecution of, as reinforcer of separatism, 201, 212, 249; disputes among, 205, 206, 207, 218, 228, 231, 232–235, 237, 239, 241–243; clandestine meetings, 209, 237, 244; singing by, 209–211, 447n59; missionary activity, 211; on baptism by blood, 211; martyrological exclusion of Protestants and Catholics, 213; internationalization of martyrology, 228, 464n219; as false martyrs, 315–316, 318, 324, 325, 331, 332, 333; and disputes about true vs. false martyrs, 318–319; indifference to Catholic and Protestant criticisms, 325; and Augustine's dictum, 464n222, 500n15. *See also* Anabaptists, South German/Austrian; Davidites; Hutterites; Melchiorites; Mennonites; Münsterites; Philipites; Swiss Brethren
Anabaptists, South German and/or Austrian, 199, 200, 203, 204–206, 211
Andrew, Saint, 123, 281
Andries, Laurens, 233
Anne, Saint (*Anna Selbdritt*), 37
Anselm of Canterbury, 55
Anshelm, Thomas, 37
Anticlericalism, in early Reformation, 152
Antimartyrology. *See* Sources, antimartyrological
Anti-Nicodemism: among Protestants, 114, 150–151, 153–162, 188, 193, 280, 419n94; broad conception of, 150, 155, 443n16; linked to martyrdom, 150–151,

509